A C

HERODOTUS

A COMMENTARY ON
HERODOTUS

WITH INTRODUCTION AND APPENDIXES

BY

W. W. HOW

FELLOW AND TUTOR OF MERTON COLLEGE

AND

J. WELLS

WARDEN OF WADHAM COLLEGE, 1913-1927

IN TWO VOLUMES

VOLUME I (BOOKS I–IV)

OXFORD · NEW YORK
OXFORD UNIVERSITY PRESS

Oxford University Press, Walton Street, Oxford OX2 6DP

Oxford New York
Athens Auckland Bangkok Bombay
Calcutta Cape Town Dar es Salaam Delhi
Florence Hong Kong Istanbul Karachi
Kuala Lumpur Madras Madrid Melbourne
Mexico City Nairobi Paris Singapore
Taipei Tokyo Toronto

and associated companies in
Berlin Ibadan

Oxford is a trade mark of Oxford University Press

Published in the United States by
Oxford University Press Inc., New York

First published 1912
First issued in paperback 1989

British Library Cataloguing in Publication Data
Data available

Library of Congress Cataloging in Publication Data

How, W. W. (Walter Wybergh), 1861–1932.
A commentary on Herodotus with introduction and appendices.
Reprint. Originally published: 1912.
1. Herodotus History. 2. Ancient history.
I. Wells, J. (Joseph), 1855–1929. II. Title.
PA4004.H6 1988 930 88–28960

ISBN 0–19–814384–2

5 7 9 10 8 6 4

Printed in Great Britain on acid-free paper by
Ipswich Book Co. Ltd., Suffolk

HENRICI DEVENISH LEIGH

AMICI FIDELISSIMI

VERITATIS INDAGATORIS ACERRIMI

LIBRUM AB IPSO INCEPTUM

MEMORIAE DEDICAVERUNT

QUIBUS PERFICERE CONTIGIT

PREFACE

THIS commentary on Herodotus was planned and begun by Mr. H. D. Leigh, of Corpus Christi, in conjunction with Mr. How, more than ten years ago. At the time of his too early death, Mr. Leigh had written notes and excursuses on the first book; but unfortunately they were found to be on too large a scale for the present work, although the material collected in them was most valuable, and was largely used. Thus for the book as it now is we are entirely responsible. We have been frequently interrupted by more pressing duties, and we fear that in a work the composition of which has thus been spread over many years, some inconsistencies may have crept in undetected. The readers of the Clarendon Press have earned our sincere gratitude by their zeal and care in removing blemishes of form, but for any graver faults that remain we can only ask indulgence.

The commentary on Books I–IV, with the corresponding appendixes, has been written by Mr. Wells, that on Books V–IX, also with the appendixes, by Mr. How. We have each read and re-read the other's work, but the ultimate responsibility for the views expressed rests in the first volume with Mr. Wells, in the second with Mr. How.

Since the book is intended principally for the use of undergraduates, we have prefixed short summaries of the subject-matter to the various sections of the notes, and for the same reason we have, where possible, quoted English translations of foreign works, and have referred to antiquities readily accessible in museums at Oxford and in London. But we have not hesitated to add many references to foreign works and periodicals, in the hope that they may be of use to more advanced students and to teachers.

A commentary is of necessity to a large extent a selection from the work of others, and on every page our debt to our predecessors is manifest. Here we can only acknowledge our principal obligations. Of commentators, Stein and, in the later books, Macan have been of the greatest assistance to us; Rawlinson has also been of use in a less degree.

In the Oriental history we owe very much to Maspero, and in the history of the Persian War to Grundy and to Munro. Throughout we have derived much benefit from the learned labours of Busolt, and still more from the masterly and comprehensive history of E. Meyer. Nor must we forget our large debt in anthropology and antiquities to the untiring industry of Frazer.

The plans of Thermopylae and Plataea are based on those in *The Great Persian War*, by the kind permission of Dr. Grundy and Mr. John Murray.

So many friends in Oxford have given us help on particular points that to give a catalogue of such obligations might be tedious, but special mention must be made of the kindness of Mr. H. R. Hall, of the British Museum, who read through the whole of the notes on Book II and Appendixes IX, X, and made many valuable suggestions and corrections. He cannot, however, be held responsible for any of the views finally expressed.

It will be seen that our notes are almost entirely on the subject-matter of Herodotus. We have accepted Hude's text, only discussing critical problems where they seriously affected the sense. As to points of grammar and translation, such notes only have been given as seemed necessary to help an ordinary scholar to understand the text.

In the spelling of names we have adopted definitely the old system. It is less correct, at least in appearance; but so many names, such as 'Croesus', 'Cyrus', and 'Lycurgus', have by their use in literature become English that consistency is impossible, or at any rate would be too dearly bought.

The index is not an index to the text, a want already supplied by Stein and by Hude, but to the commentary. As it is supplemented by many cross-references, only the more important notes have been indexed.

1912.

Owing to the high cost of making changes on stereotyped plates we have only been able in this second impression to correct a few obvious errors and to append some additional notes (to which references are given) dealing with work done since 1912, and one longer essay on 'Arms, Tactics, and Strategy'. For permission to reprint this from the *Journal of Hellenic Studies* (1923) we have to thank the Council of the Society.

1928.

CONTENTS OF VOLUME I

LIST OF PRINCIPAL AUTHORITIES WITH ABBREVIATED TITLES

[N.B.—The works most frequently used have been quoted simply by their authors' names; in other cases the titles have been abbreviated, as given in this list.]

ABBOTT, E. Herodotus V, VI. 1893.

BÄHR, I. C. F. Herodotus. 4 vols. 2nd edit., 1856–61.

BALL, C. J. Light from the East.

BARTH, H. Wanderungen durch die Küstenländer des Mittelmeeres. 1849. W.

BELOCH, J. Griechische Geschichte, vol. i. 1893.
Die Bevölkerung der griechisch-römischen Welt. Bevölkerung or B.

BERGER, H. Erdkunde der Griechen. 2nd edit., 1903.

BERGK. Poetae Lyrici Graeci. 3rd edit. or 4th. P. L. G.

BLAKESLEY, J. W. Herodotus. 2 vols.

BOECKH, A. Kleine Schriften. Kl. Sch.
Die Staatshaushaltung der Athener. 3rd edit., 1886.

BURY, J. B. Greek History. 2 vols. (the smaller edition in one vol. is quoted by page only).
Ancient Greek Historians. A. G. H.

BUSOLT, G. Griechische Geschichte. 2nd edit., 1893 and later.

DITTENBERGER. Sylloge Inscriptionum Graecarum. 2nd edit.

DUNCKER, M. History of Antiquity, translated by E. Abbott. 6 vols. (vol. vii in the German original).

FARNELL, L. R. Cults of Greek States. 5 vols., 1907, 1909. G. C.

FRAZER, J. G. Pausanias. 6 vols., 1898. (Sometimes 'P.' or 'Paus.')
Golden Bough (usually 2nd edit.). G. B.

FREEMAN. History of Sicily. S. or Sicily.

GARDNER, E. A. Ancient Athens. Athens.
Handbook of Greek Sculpture. G. S.

GARDNER, P. New Chapters on Greek History. 1892. N. C. G. H.

GILBERT. Greek Constitutional Antiquities. 1895 (vol. ii in the German original). G. C. A. or Gr. St.

LIST OF PRINCIPAL AUTHORITIES

GOODWIN. Greek Moods and Tenses. 2nd edit.
GROTE, G. A History of Greece. 12 vols., 1869.
GRUNDY, G. B. Great Persian War.
Thucydides. 1911. — Thuc.
HAMILTON, W. J. Asia Minor.
HARRISON, Miss J. Mythology and Monuments of Ancient Athens. — Athens, or Myth. and Mon.
Prolegomena to the Study of Greek Religion. — Prolegomena.
HASTINGS, J. Dictionary of the Bible. 4 vols. — Dict. Bib. or D. B.
HAUVETTE, A. Hérodote historien des guerres médiques.
HEAD, B. V. Historia Numorum. 2nd edit. 1911. — H. N.
HICKS, E. L. A Manual of Greek Inscriptions, by E. L. Hicks and G. F. Hill. 2nd edit.[1] — Hicks.
HILL, G. F. Historical Greek Coins. 1906. — G. C. or H. G. C.
Handbook of Greek and Roman Coins. 1899. — G. and R. C.
HERMANN. Handbuch der griechischen Antiquitäten.
HOGARTH, D. G. Accidents of an Antiquary's Life. 1910. — A. A. L.
Authority and Archaeology. 1899. — A. and A.
Excavations at Ephesus. 1908. — Ephesus or E.
Ionia and the East. 1909. — I. and E.
HOLM. History of Greece, vols. i and ii. 1895.
Geschichte Siciliens. — G. S.
KIEPERT, H. Formae Orbis Antiqui. (New edition.)
KING and HALL. Egypt and Western Asia in the Light of Recent Discoveries. 1907.
KRÜGER, K. W. Herodotus.
LASSEN, C. Indische Alterthumskunde. 1847 seq. — I. A.
LEAKE, W. M. Asia Minor. — A. M.
Northern Greece. — N. G.
MACAN, R. W. Herodotus IV–VI. 1895.
Herodotus VII–IX. 1908.
MAHAFFY, J. P. Greek Literature. 2 vols. — Gk. Lit.
Social Life in Greece. — S. L.
MARCO POLO. Yule's edition, edited by Cordier. 2 vols., 1903.
MASPERO, G. Histoire ancienne de l'Orient. 3 vols., 1895. (The abridged form of this book in one volume (6th edit., 1904) is quoted by page only.)
Causeries. — Caus. or C.
MEYER, E. Geschichte des Alterthums (vol. i, 2nd edit.[1]). 4 vols.
Forschungen zur alten Geschichte. — F.
MÜLLENHOFF. Deutsche Alterthumskunde. 3 vols. — D. A.
MURE, W. History of Greek Literature. 5 vols., 1859.

[1] Unless otherwise stated.

MURRAY, A. S. History of Greek Sculpture. 1880. G. S.
MYRES, J. L. Anthropology and the Classics. A. and C.
NISSEN. Italische Landeskunde.
PERROT ET CHIPIEZ. Histoire de l'Art dans l'Antiquité.
PRÁŞEK, J. Geschichte der Meder und Perser. 1906.
PRELLER. Griechische Mythologie. 4th edit.
RAMSAY, W. M. Cities and Bishoprics of Phrygia. C. and B.
Historical Geography of Asia Minor. 1890. H. G. or A. M.
RAWLINSON, G. Herodotus. 4 vols. 3rd edit. 1875.
RECLUS. Géographie Universelle.
ROBERTS, E. S. Greek Epigraphy, vol. i. Gk. Epig.
ROHLFS, G. Kufra. 1881. K.
ST. MARTIN, V. Le Nord de l'Afrique dans l'Antiquité.
SMITH, W. ROBERTSON. Religion of the Semites. 2nd edit. Rel. Sel.
Kinship in Ancient Arabia. 2nd edit. Kinship.
STEIN, H. Herodotus.
TORR, C. Ancient Ships. A. S.
TOZER, H. F. History of Ancient Geography. 1897. A. G.
Islands of the Aegean. I. Aeg.
TYLOR, E. B. Primitive Culture. 2 vols. 4th edit. P. C.
Early History of Mankind. E. H. M.
WESTERMARCK. History of Human Marriage. 3rd edit. 1901.
WILAMOWITZ-MOELLENDORFF. Aristoteles und Athen. A. und A.
Philologische Untersuchungen. Phil. U.
WINCKLER, H. Altorientalische Forschungen. 2 vols. A. F.

(Where a book has been used only once or twice, the title has been usually given either in full or at least with sufficient fullness for the reference to be traced. Cf. also i. 155, 302, and the first or last paragraphs of the Appendixes, for books used on special parts of H.'s work.)

Additional Authorities

BUSOLT, G. Griechische Staatskunde. 2 vols. and index, 1920–6. Griech.Staats.
CAMBRIDGE ANCIENT HISTORY. C. A. H.
GARDNER, P. A History of Ancient Coinage, 700–300 B.C. 1918. Hist. Coin.
JACOBY, F. Pauly-Wissowa, VIII. Supplemt.-Bd., 379 f. Jacoby.

LIST OF PRINCIPAL ABBREVIATIONS

Cf. also i. 155 and 302.

A. E. G. Annuaire des Études Grecques.
B. C. H. Bulletin de Correspondance Hellénique.
B. I. Behistun Inscription.
B. M. G. British Museum Guide.
  Assyrian Antiquities. 1908.
  Egyptian Collections. 1909.
B. P. W. Berliner Philologische Wochenschrift.
B. S. A. British School of Athens, Annual of.
C. C. Cyrus Cylinder.
C. I. A. Corpus Inscriptionum Atticarum.
C. I. G. Corpus Inscriptionum Graecarum, ed. Boeckh, &c. 4 vols.
C. R. (or Cl. R.). Classical Review.
D. of A. Smith's Dictionary of Greek and Roman Antiquities. 3rd edit.
E. B. Encyclopaedia Britannica. 11th edit. (unless otherwise indicated, e. g. thus, E. B.[9]).
Enc. Bib. Encyclopaedia Biblica.
E. H. R. English Historical Review.
F. H. G. Fragmenta Historicorum Graecorum. 4 vols., ed. C. Muller. 1885.
G. G. M. Geographici Graeci Minores. 2 vols., ed. C. Muller. 1853.
G. J. Geographical Journal.
I. G. A. Inscriptiones Graecae Antiquissimae. ed. Röhl, 1882.
J. H. S. Journal of Hellenic Studies.
J. of P. Journal of Philology.
J. R. A. S. Journal of Royal Asiatic Society.
J. R. G. S. (or R. G. S.) Journal of Royal Geographical Society (*v. s.* for Geographical Journal).
L. and S. Liddell and Scott, Greek Lexicon. 8th edit.
M. A. I. Mittheilungen des Deutschen Archaeologischen Instituts (Athenische Abtheilung).
P. G. Paroemiographi Graeci. 2 vols., ed. Leutsch and Schneidewin. 1839.
P. L. G. Poetae Lyrici Graeci. 3 vols., ed. Bergk, 3rd or 4th edit. 1878.
P. W. Pauly-Wissowa, Real-Encyclopaedie (new edit. now appearing).
Q. R. Quarterly Review.
R. E. Revue Égyptologique.
R. E. G. Revue des Études Grecques.
R. M. (or Rhein. Mus.) Rheinisches Museum.
R. P.[1] Records of the Past (First Series).
R. P.[2] " " " (Second Series).
S. B. E. Sacred Books of the East.
T. S. B. A. Transactions of the Society for Biblical Archaeology.
W. K. P. Wochenschrift für klassische Philologie.

INTRODUCTION

The Life by Rawlinson (vol. i), or the De vita et scriptis Hdt. of Bähr (vol. iv), is still worth looking at, as giving the evidence and the older views. A good criticism of modern theories will be found in Hauvette, Hérodote (Paris, 1894). The best general estimate is perhaps that of A. Croiset, Hist. de Litt. Grecque, vol. ii (2nd ed.).

§ 1. **The life of Herodotus in tradition.** The main source of our information as to H., apart from his works, is the notice in Suidas[1] (*s.v.*): 'H., the son of Lyxes and Dryo, a man of Halicarnassus, was born of parents in good position, and had a brother, Theodorus; he migrated and took up his abode in Samos, because of Lygdamis, who was tyrant of Halicarnassus next but one after Artemisia; for Pisendelis was the son of Artemisia, and Lygdamis of Pisendelis. At Samos then he both became familiar with the Ionic dialect and wrote a history in nine books, beginning with Cyrus the Persian and Candaules king of the Lydians. He returned to Halicarnassus and expelled the tyrant, but when later he saw himself disliked by his countrymen, he went as a volunteer to Thurium, when it was being colonized by the Athenians. There he died and lies buried in the market-place. But some say that he died at Pella. His books bear the title of the Muses.'

To this notice must be added the statements in Suidas (*s.v.* Panyasis) that he was the nephew or the cousin of Panyasis, the epic poet and 'marvel-seer' (τερατοσκόπος), and that Panyasis was also of Halicarnassus, and was put to death

[1] Suidas' Lexicon contains notices of events as late as the eleventh cent. A.D., but no doubt much of it is far earlier in date.

by Lygdamis (see also § 3). Finally there is the familiar date of his birth, 484 B.C., given by A. Gellius.[1]

Some of these statements are demonstrably incorrect, e.g. that H. wrote his history in Samos, and that he learned the Ionic dialect there,[2] and it has been maintained that all the account of Suidas is based on mere inference, not on definite evidence, and was made up by the Alexandrine scholars of the third century B.C., out of combinations from H.'s own book. It is unlikely, however, that there was no genuine tradition as to an author whose work at once became so widely famous (p. 36).

We may then assume as accurate the following traditional facts, confirmed as they are by the indications of his work.

§ 2. Facts that are fairly certain.

(1) That H. was well born and a native of Halicarnassus.[3]

(2) That he was connected with Panyasis, who was the poet of Hercules and of the story of Ionian colonization; his

[1] Noct. Att. 15. 23, on the authority of Pamphila, a learned lady of the time of Nero. Diels (R. M. 1876, xxxi. 1 seq.) argues that this and other literary dates probably depend on the calculations of Apollodorus, who reckoned a man's birth forty years before some famous event in his life. So H.'s birth (p. 49) is calculated from the foundation of Thurii (444–3); Thucydides' (471 B.C.) from the beginning of the Peloponnesian War; that of Thales (624 B.C.) from the eclipse of 585. The argument is ingenious, but mainly important as emphasizing the fact that Greek chronology, especially so far as it concerns private persons, has always been a matter of calculation, not of definite record.

[2] The two contemporary inscriptions of Halicarnassus (cf. Hicks, No. 27) are Ionic, not Doric (cf. i. 144. 3 n.). H., moreover, wrote his history in Ionic, because it was the established literary prose medium of his time; his contemporary, Hippocrates of Cos, also a Dorian, did the same. Hence his language is called by Hermogenes (De Gen. Dic. ii. 12) Ἰὰς ποικίλη i.e. it was a literary blend of the various Ionic dialects (for which cf. i. 142 3, 4); it became, owing to the success of his work, Ἰάδος ἄριστος κανών (Dion. Hal. ad Cn. Pomp. c. 3, vii. 775).

[3] But cf. i. 1 n. Some have conjectured a relative of H. in 'Herodotus the son of Basilides' (viii. 132. 2). But the name is a common one; Bähr (iv. 401–3) makes a list of about twenty.

influence may be traced in H.'s history (cf. especially ii. 43–5, iv. 8–10, and i. 142–150 respectively).

(3) That he lived for part of his early life in Samos, a fact which is borne out by his special familiarity with, and favour for, that island (cf. iii. 60 *et pass.*).

(4) That he took part in the colonization of Thurii, and that he died there. This latter point is disputed, e.g. by Meyer (F. i. 199), but may be accepted for the following reasons:

(*a*) The famous epitaph in Steph. Byz. (*s. v.* Θούριοι) on his tomb in the market-place

Ἡρόδοτον Λύξεω κρύπτει κόνις ἥδε θανόντα
Ἰάδος ἀρχαίης ἱστορίης πρύτανιν,
Δωριέων βλαστόντα πάτρης ἄπο, τῶν γὰρ ἄτλητον
μῶμον ὑπεκπροφυγὼν Θούριον ἔσχε πάτρην.

is itself later, but raises a presumption that he died at Thurii.

(*b*) It is difficult to understand the prevalence of the name, 'the Thurian' (cf. i. 1. 1 n.) unless H. died and was buried there.

(5) The most important fact of all recorded by tradition is the date of H.'s birth; this may be accepted, as being entirely in agreement with his own testimony; he never speaks as a contemporary of the events he describes, but he always implies that he knew personally those who were contemporary. He stood to the men of Salamis and Plataea exactly as Thackeray (born in 1811) stood to the heroes of Waterloo, when he wrote 'Vanity Fair' in 1848.

§ 3. **Herodotus and the tyrant of Halicarnassus.** One important point in the traditions has so far not been dealt with, that H. was expelled by Lygdamis and that in turn he took part in the expulsion of the tyrant. These statements might well be mere inferences from the dislike of tyrants shown throughout his work (App. XVI), but it is more natural to accept them as facts and to connect them with the state of things indicated in the contemporary inscription from Halicarnassus (*u. s.*). There we find recorded an agreement between Lygdamis and his subjects, in which, apparently after political troubles, a compromise[1] is arrived at whereby the tyrant is continued in authority alongside of the popular assembly.

The name of Panyasis occurs in this inscription (l. 16). Its exact date is uncertain; but the compromise did not last, as we find Halicarnassus free (with no despot mentioned, C. I. A. i. 226; Hicks 33) in the first Athenian quota-list of 454 B. C.

Various combinations are made of the traditional facts and of inferences from the inscription; perhaps the easiest is to suppose that H. was banished in the troubles[2] which preceded the reconciliation thus recorded, and that he had his revenge in expelling the tyrant later.

§ 4. **The evidence for Herodotus' life from his history.** There are two other pieces of traditional evidence which are important, but they must be discussed in connexion with the two great problems as to H.'s life which are raised by his work. These problems are:

(1) The dates of his travels;

(2) The date of the composition of his work.

To some extent these problems are themselves connected, but not entirely. In discussing them, the assumption will be made that H. speaks the truth, and that his indications as to his own movements may be trusted.[3]

[1] Cf. the similar compromise at Cyrene, iv. 161–3.

[2] Stein (pp. iii, ix) dates these 468–7, because the seventy-eighth Olympiad is mentioned in Suidas as important in the life of Panyasis, and Euseb. Chron. writes *s. a.* 468 Ἡρόδοτος Ἁλικαρνησσεὺς ἱστοριογράφος ἐγνωρίζετο.

[3] For the discussion of crucial instances as to H.'s veracity cf. his statements about Chaldea (i. 178 seq. nn.), and about Elephantine (ii. 29 nn.); it may be added at once that a belief in it does not imply a belief in his accuracy. The chief modern assailant of H. is Professor Sayce (H. i–iii.

His travels in (*a*) Egypt. What information then does H. give us as to his movements? The first group of inferences is as to his Egyptian visit.[1] This may be dated almost certainly after 449 B.C., how much later must be discussed presently. It may also be inferred with some confidence that H. had been in the Euphrates valley before he was in Egypt, for (ii. 150. 1 n.) he uses a story as to Nineveh to confirm his information as to Lake Moeris.

(*b*) **Scythia.** The next inference that we can form as to H.'s travels concerns Scythia. He speaks (iv. 76. 6) of conversing with Tymnes, the 'agent of king Ariapeithes'. As Ariapeithes succeeded Idanthyrsus, the enemy of Darius (*circ.* 512 B.C.), and as his own life ended by violence (iv. 78. 2), his reign is not likely to have lasted after 460. Probably, therefore, the Scythian voyage is the earliest distant one of H.,[2] a conjecture which is the more probable since there was a close commercial connexion between the Aegean and the Pontus. If we might trust the restored text of Suidas (*s. v.* Ἑλλάνικος) that Hellanicus *διέτριψε σὺν Ἡροδότῳ παρὰ Ἀλεξάνδρῳ τῷ Μακεδόνων βασιλεῖ*, we should have a confirmation of this early date[3]; for Alexander died circ. 454 B.C. H. might then have visited Macedonia on his way to or from Scythia.

(*c*) **Cyrene.** The commercial connexions of Samos especially extended to Cyrene (cf. iv. 163 n.), and so we should naturally connect H.'s visit to Cyrene with his Samian period. A slight indication of the date of this visit has been seen in

1883). For answers to this attack cf. Edinburgh Review, April 1884 (Sir R. Jebb), and A. Croiset in R. E. G. vol. i (1888).

[1] For the evidence cf. App. IX. 1.

[2] Duncker connects the visit to Scythia with the expedition of Pericles to the Pontus, perhaps in 444 B.C. (cf. Busolt, iii. 585). As H. makes not the shadow of an allusion to Athenians in the Pontus, the suggestion can hardly be called happy.

[3] The MSS. read Ἀμύντᾳ, and this seems to agree better with the following words, 'in the times of Euripides and Sophocles.'

the oracle which limits the number of the Battiad kings to eight (iv. 163. 2 n.). This must have been forged after the death of Arcesilaus IV, i. e. not earlier than about 460 B. C. But H. may well have heard the oracle later, and no certain inference is possible.

§ 5. **Herodotus at Athens.** (1) **His recitations.** So far there has been no trace of H. *in Greece proper*, or Athens. But that he was familiar with this city and must have lived some time there, is evident both from constant allusions in his works and from traditional evidence. This, so far as it bears on his migration to Thurii, has been already noticed; the other two points in it omitted above must now be discussed.

The first of these is as to his recitations at Athens. Syncellus, the chronologer, definitely states that H. *ἐτιμήθη παρὰ τῆς Ἀθηναίων βουλῆς ἐπαναγνοὺς αὐτοῖς τὰς βίβλους.* This event is dated by Jerome in 445 B. C., by the Armenian version 446. There is no reason to doubt this fact, which is partly confirmed by the statement of the fourth-century Athenian historian, Diyllus, that H. *δέκα τάλαντα δωρεὰν ἔλαβεν ἐξ Ἀθηνῶν Ἀνύτου τὸ ψήφισμα γράψαντος.*[1] Such recitations would be the natural method for H. to publish the results of his labours, and they seem to be clearly referred to

[1] F. H. G. ii. 360, quoted by Plut. de mal. H. c. 26. This is obviously the origin of the fiction of Dio Chrys. Or. 37 (p. 456) that H. 'rewrote' his history of the behaviour of the Corinthians at Salamis (cf. viii. 94 nn.) because the Corinthians would not 'buy reputation' by paying him. A similar fiction is the legend that H. was offended by not being allowed to open a school at Thebes (Plut. ibid. c. 31). H.'s recitations have also given rise to the famous legend of his triumph at Olympia, when (Lucian, H. 1–2) he recited his works to assembled Greece, became 'better known than the Olympic winners', and won the title of the Nine Muses for his books. Suidas (*s. v.* Θουκυδίδης) improves on this by making the boy Thucydides moved to tears, and complimented by H. because *ὀργᾷ ἡ ψυχὴ πρὸς τὰ μαθήματα.* There is an amusing confutation of the whole story in Mure, Gk. Lit. iv. 258 seq.

in the words of Thucydides (i. 22. 4); he contemptuously says that his own history is not composed as an ἀγώνισμα ἐς τὸ παραχρῆμα ἀκούειν and may lack charm ἐς ἀκρόασιν, owing to 'the absence of the mythical elements'. The date 446–5 [1] is fully consistent with all we know of H.'s life. We may therefore accept the fact of H.'s Athenian recitations at this period.

§ 6. (2) **His friendship with Sophocles.** The second traditional fact which has been so far omitted is the supposed intimacy of H. with Sophocles. The evidence for this is partly the poem [2] addressed to H. by the poet about 445 B.C., partly the correspondences [3] in the works of the historian and the tragedian. Certainly these are much more than accidental in two passages at least, if the texts in their present form are original, and the friendship of the two great writers may well be a fact.

§ 7. **His visit to Thurii.** H., however, whatever his relations with leading Athenians, was not in sympathy with the dominant tendencies of the Athens of his day. His interest was in the wide world of the East; the Athenians were devoting themselves to the politics of Greece proper; his enemy was the barbarian, theirs the Lacedaemonian and the Corinthian; his sympathies were for ἰσηγορίη in the old sense, theirs for democracy in the new sense, his belief was in the

[1] Meyer (F. i. 200) rejects it as a false combination, and puts the date of the grant to H. about 430. His reason for this is that it was proposed by Anytus, whom he identifies with the accuser of Socrates; 'his admiration for H. corresponds to his persecution of Socrates.' This is ingenious though not convincing; but Meyer's further conjecture that 'H. may have served Athens diplomatically, perhaps in negotiation with Persia', is mere guessing of a most unlikely kind. The extravagant figure of 'ten talents' weakens the value of the evidence of Diyllus.

[2] Plut. Mor. 785, An seni sit Resp. gerenda, c. 3.

[3] The most important are between iii. 119. 6 and Antig. 904 seq.; and ii. 35. 2 and O. C. 337–41; cf. also i. 32. 5 and O. T. 1530; iv. 95. 4 and Elec. 62–4; i. 31. 4, vii. 46. 3–4 and O. C. 1225 seq.

religion of the past, theirs in the philosophy of the present; his very style was different in dialect and structure. Hence it is not surprising that H. did not remain permanently in Athens; if for no other reason, so great a traveller was not likely to be willing to remain quiet. But we can fix with some definiteness the date of his leaving Athens, and at the same time suggest a plausible reason for his departure for the West. In iii. 160. 2[1] he mentions the desertion of the Persian prince of the royal blood, Zopyrus, to Athens; his arrival seems to have happened early in 440. He died in the following year, but H. never mentions this, though it is his habit to complete the story of his incidental characters in this way. The omission is most naturally to be explained by his own departure for the West, where he never heard of the Persian's death. And the quarrel between Athens and Samos, the two cities to which H. was most attached, may well have been the deciding motive which made him start on his travels once more. How long H. was in the West is one of the uncertain points of his history, as is also the question whether part of his Eastern travels, and especially his Egyptian visit, fall after 440 B.C. These points will be touched on in answering the question, 'Where did H. write his history?' But there is one more point as to his life which is important.

§ 8. **His probable return to Greece proper.** Did Herodotus return to Greece proper and to Athens after his departure for Thurii? The usual view is that he did so return,[2] and the following reasons may be given for it:

(1) He refers, evidently as an eye-witness (v. 77. 4), to a brazen quadriga which stood at the entrance to the Athenian Propylaea; if this could be identified with the famous building

[1] For the dates and for the importance of Zopyrus cf. iii. 160. 2 nn. and J. H. S. xxvii, 'The Persian friends of H.'

[2] Hauvette ingeniously maintains the contrary (pp. 47 seq.) but he is not convincing.

of Mnesicles, we should infer with certainty that his return was after 432 (but cf. v. 77. 4 nn.).

(2) There are in his later books a number of references to comparatively unimportant facts,[1] which would hardly have been known to him had he not returned to Athens.

Hence we may fairly assume that H. was in Athens in 431–430 B.C., even if we believe him to have returned to Thurii later.

§ 9. **The date of his death.** The date of his death must remain uncertain, but in view of the fact that he mentions no event which can certainly be dated after 430, and that he seems not to have heard of the destruction of the Aeginetans in Thyrea (424 B.C.),[2] it is natural to place his death in the first five years of the Peloponnesian War. Certainly that war was a death-blow to the ideals that H. embodied in, and sought to commend by, his History.[3]

§ 10. **Where did Herodotus write his history?** To turn now to the question, Where did Herodotus write his history? The traditional accounts, that he wrote it at Samos

[1] These are, chronologically arranged,

(1) The attack of the Thebans on Plataea under Eurymachus in 431 (vii. 233. 2).

(2) The expulsion of the Aeginetans at the end of 431 (vi. 91. 1).

(3) The sparing of Decelea in the wasting of Attica (431 or 430) (ix. 73. 3).

(4) The execution of Aristeas and the Lacedaemonian envoys in 430 (vii. 137. 3).

The general reference to the evils due to the rivalry of the leading Greek states (vi. 98. 2) might have been written before the Peace of 445 and in any place.

[2] Thuc. iv. 57. H. must surely have mentioned this in vi. 91 had he heard of it. It has been inferred from his language in vii. 235. 2 that he knew of Nicias' occupation of Cythera in 424 B.C. But this passage has also been taken to prove the exact contrary—and this is the more probable view.

[3] The view that H. lived till the last decade of the fifth century is now generally given up. The best statement of it is in Mure, iv. 538–47. It is based on the facts referred to in i. 130. 2 and iii. 15. 3 (cf. ii. 140. 2) and on the wording of vi. 98. 2, vii. 137. 3, ix. 73. 3 (*vid.* nn.).

(Suidas, *u. s.*) or at Thurii,[1] have long been given up. A new method of investigation was employed in Kirchhoff's famous paper read before the Berlin Academy in 1868. This laid stress on two principles: (1) that H.'s work was not composed at one time, a point which had been already recognized (e.g. Rawlinson, i. 24 seq.); (2) that the indications of H.'s own work are the best evidence for settling the question.

(*a*) **Kirchhoff's theory.** It will be well therefore to summarize Kirchhoff's argument, since it marks a new departure, although it must be added that his results have been accepted by many with a confidence which they are very far from deserving. His main points were (pp. 26–7)[2]: (1) H.'s history was written in the order in which it at present stands. (2) The first two books, and Bk. III as far as c. 118, were written in Athens. (3) The next section, to some point in Bk. V before c. 77, was written in Italy. (4) H. finished his work, as we have it, after his return to Athens late in 431, and was interrupted, perhaps by death, while he was still writing it, about 428 B.C.

Kirchhoff lays stress on the fact that there are no allusions to the West in the first part of H.; but he overlooks the important passage i. 163 seq. (this of course might be a later addition). The most that can be said is that there is a presumption that the present order of the History was original.

In support of his second point, the break in Bk. III, he argues:

(1) H., in i. 106. 2, 184, makes promises which are never fulfilled; these would naturally have been fulfilled after iii. 160. Again, in i. 130. 2, H. refers to a Median revolt which would naturally have been described in the latter part of Bk. III, but is not. The inconsistencies need explanation, and Kirchhoff (pp. 6, 13) maintains that this may be found in H.'s migration

[1] Plin. N. H. xii. 4. 18 'urbis nostrae CCCXmo anno auctor ille eam condidit Thuriis'; the exact date is amusing.

[2] References are to 2nd ed., published 1878.

to Thurii, which made him forget his promises and previous intentions.

(2) The frequent references to Athens in the first two books point to that city as their place of composition (e.g. i. 29. 1, 98. 5; ii. 7. 1 seq),[1] and H. is proved by i. 51. 4 (*vid.* nn.), and by tradition (*u. s.*), to have been in Greece proper between 450 and 440.

(3) The gap in the history must be placed after iii. 119, because of the correspondence between that chapter and the Antigone of Sophocles, which was produced in the spring of 441 (pp. 8–9), while the chapters which follow, with the story of Democedes (iii. 125, 129 seq.), are clearly full of Western elements.

As to all these arguments it will be sufficient to point out that unfulfilled promises[2] are found in many writers, and that there is no need to postulate a change of abode to explain them.

The references to Athens are far from proving residence there, and the passage of the Antigone is gravely suspected of being a later interpolation (cf. iii. 119 nn.).

With regard to Kirchhoff's third point, the Western origin of the middle part of H.'s work, there is no doubt that iv. 99 was (in part at any rate) written in the West, while other passages, e.g. iv. 15, imply residence in the West at some time; but all these might be later additions, and the bulk of Bks. IV and V might have been written anywhere.

Kirchhoff's fourth point, the return to Athens, is supposed to be proved by v. 77. 4 (*u. s.*), and to be exactly dated (p. 18–19) by the fact that H. never heard of the earthquake of Delos which happened in the spring of 431 (Thuc. ii. 8. 3; cf. H.

[1] Other instances are i. 192. 3; ii. 156. 6, 177. 2.

[2] As H. in iv. 159 does fulfil (though not very satisfactorily, *vid.* nn.) a promise given in ii. 161. 3, Kirchhoff's supposed lapses of memory on his part are only partial.

vi. 98). This date is confirmed by the quotation from Pericles in vii. 162 (but see nn.).[1]

Finally, Kirchhoff thinks that we can see H. at work in 428, for he refers to the sparing of Decelea when Attica was ravaged, in ix. 73. 3, though he had previously failed to mention this in connexion with Decelea in ix. 15 (pp. 20–2). This ravaging Kirchhoff identifies with that of 428 B.C., and dates the two chapters by reference to it.

Kirchhoff's theory is ingenious in method, but it assumes the most important point it sets out to prove, viz., the present order of the work, and it is far too absolute in details; its further argument that H.'s work is unfinished will be discussed later.

(*b*) **Bauer's theory.** The theory of A. Bauer[2] is the opposite of Kirchhoff's. He holds (p. 171) that H.'s work was originally composed in parts, of which the account of the campaign of Xerxes (Bks. VII–IX), though not necessarily the earliest, was composed at Athens about 445 B.C. From Athens he travelled to Scythia and then composed his Scythian history; finally (about 440) he went to Egypt, and published Bk. II on his return, which made him so unpopular,[3] owing to its frank criticism of Greek ideas (*v. i.*), that he had to leave Athens for Thurii. Here he conceived the plan of uniting the existing λόγοι into one general work (p. 173); at Thurii he carried out this as far as the middle of Bk. V, and then returned to Athens and completed the revision.

The minute proofs by which this order is established, it is impossible to follow in detail, nor are they very convincing. Broadly speaking, they are of two kinds:

(1) H. in his later books mentions persons and places already mentioned in the earlier books as if they were un-

[1] vi. 121–31 is also brought by Kirchhoff (somewhat arbitrarily) into connexion with Pericles' condemnation in 430 B.C. (p. 46).

[2] Die Entstehung des Herodotischen Geschichtswerkes, Vienna, 1878.

[3] For this unpopularity cf. Suidas and H.'s epitaph (*u. s.*).

familiar; e. g. in Bk. VII, Darius, Mardonius, Demaratus are formally introduced to the reader (p. 129 seq.).[1]

(2) In the earlier books, topics dealt with in the later books are described with the fulness of additional and sometimes inconsistent knowledge: e. g. the Aethiopians in vii. 70 are simply the Aethiopians of Homer: in ii. 29, iii. 17 seq. H. has much fuller information about them (p. 44).

It must be said, however, that a large part of the inconsistencies which Bauer notes[2] are trifling and such as could easily be paralleled in many long books, even in the present day, or that they are not inconsistencies at all, but simply differences of treatment, due to difference of context.

Against all definite theories such as those of Kirchhoff and Bauer, it cannot be too strongly urged that they are based on the quite misleading analogy of modern book production. An ancient prose work was never published in our sense; an author might leave off writing it and allow his friends to have copies made: if he chose to rehandle or expand any part of his work, he could at any time do so without the formality of a new edition. This is an obvious truism, but it is neglected in such arguments as those summarized above.[3] (See Note A, p. 447.)

§ 11. **Peculiar tone of Bk. II.** There is, however, one

[1] It is not only that they are described by the addition of their patronymic; this might be done for emphasis, e. g. Pausanias gets this distinction as late as ix. 64. 1; but, to take one instance out of many, Demaratus' past is summarized (vii. 3. 1) in a way which seems needless if Bk. VI had been already written.

[2] e.g. ii. 148. 2 and iii. 60. 4 (as to Heraeum), i. 105. 1 and ii. 157 (as to Psammetichus), i. 3–4 and ii. 118 (as to Helen), ii. 164 and ix. 32. 1 (as to warrior castes of Egypt).

[3] Hence it is impossible to conclude anything from cross references, e.g. in iii. 80. 1 and vi. 43. 3. That H. was referring to criticisms on his own work seems certain (though Bauer (p. 11) has the improbable theory that H. is censuring the incredulity of other writers as to a source common to himself and to them); but the criticism may well have been evoked by his own recitations.

part of Bauer's argument which seems fairly convincing; he lays great stress (pp. 46–54) on the anti-Hellenic attitude which H. takes up in Bk. II.[1] In that book the ordinary story of the Iliad is set aside as a μάταιος λόγος (118. 1); the dependence of Greek religion on Egypt is emphasized (50. 1), even the management of the Olympic games is treated with scarcely veiled irony (160. 1). This list might be extended almost indefinitely. But if the tone of Bk. II is really different from that of the rest of H.'s work, this fact may well be connected with another obvious difficulty as to it. It is hard to conceive an author possessed of the literary skill and sense of form which H. undoubtedly had, deliberately composing it in its present place on its present scale. If, on the other hand, we suppose that it was written by itself when the rest of the history was practically finished,[2] and then introduced into its present place later, both the difference of tone and the difference of scale explain themselves. It seems not unlikely, therefore, that Bk. II is the latest part of the work of H.

§ 12. **Priority of Books VII–IX.** One more view of Bauer's may be accepted with some confidence, viz. that the last three books were the earliest composed. This point has been elaborately re-argued by Macan.[3] Apart from the consideration of the separate passages, he points out a striking peculiarity in the references to events later than the battles of Plataea and Mycale; of these, in the last three books, the great majority refer to events before 456 B.C., three or four to the years 431–430, while only one (vii. 151) falls in the interval.[4]

[1] A similar attitude may be traced elsewhere, e.g. iv. 36. 2; 95–6; but it is not nearly so marked as in Bk. II; in this book, however, the contrast between Greece and Egypt (cc. 35–6) gave especial reason for it.

[2] The repetitions in ii. 1 and iii. 1 look very like an attempt to piece together independent works.

[3] Pp. xlv–lxvii (1908).

[4] Ibid. pp. lii–iii. A list of them is given in note 1 at the end of this Introduction.

The most natural explanation of this curious distribution is that H. was composing the story of the invasion of Xerxes before 445 B.C., and probably before 450, that he came to Greece, and gave recitations from this part of his history at Athens, and then laid his work aside.

§ 13. **Conclusions as to order of composition.** If this theory is adopted, we have three fixed points for the composition of H.'s history: (1) The priority of VII–IX, written before 445, and perhaps a little earlier. (2) The lateness of Bk. II; (3) A revision—at any rate of the later books—at Athens during the early years of the Peloponnesian War. Beyond this it is impossible to go, though it is tempting to connect Bk. IV especially with the stay in the West (*u. s.*). North Africa concerned the inhabitants of Italy and Sicily more than it did those of Greece proper; and it might even be suggested that it was the Pythagoreanism of Croton[1] which sent H. back to the East to study these doctrines at their source.

§ 14. **Is Herodotus' work finished?** Part of Kirchhoff's theory which he has since re-stated[2] was the adoption of the old view that the work of H. was unfinished. This has been maintained on two grounds: (1) There are in H.'s work three unfulfilled promises[3]: i. 106. 2, 184, and vii. 213. 3. (2) The capture of Sestos is no real end to the Persian Wars; this must be found in the battle of the Eurymedon, if not in the 'Peace of Callias'.

But these arguments really prove nothing. Two of the unfulfilled promises refer to the Ἀσσύριοι λόγοι; perhaps these were actually written as an independent work and have perished (cf. App. II. 6); but even if this is not the case, the fuller

[1] Cf. ii. 81. 123 and iv. 95–6 nn.

[2] Sitz. Berl. Acad. 1885, p. 301 seq.

[3] It must be admitted, too, that viii. 137 is a very meagre fulfilment of v. 22. 1; contrast i. 75. 1, carried out in 107 seq., and other instances.

accounts would certainly have been introduced somewhere in the first three books; they could have had nothing to do with events after 479 B.C. The third instance—the promised story as to Ephialtes—might have been introduced in many places in the history, and its omission is a mere oversight.[1] Whether 479 B.C. is a good ending to H.'s history is an arguable question. It might fairly be said that as the year of the last campaign of united Greece, and of the last defensive campaign,[2] it is the natural point at which to stop. But such *a priori* arguments are unnecessary. There is no doubt that both H. and Thucydides looked on the events of 480–479 (τὰ Μηδικά) as distinct from the following struggle.[3] To ignore this recognized distinction, and to suggest that H. breaks off in 479 merely by accident, is simply to encumber a subject, already difficult enough, with an unnecessary hypothesis.

§ 15. **The travels of Herodotus.** Few points in the narrative of H. are more interesting than his travels, which have made him in some ways the father of Geography, as well as of History. He may with good reason be called the Marco Polo of Antiquity. It is unnecessary here to describe in detail the journeys of H.[4] Certain points as to their date have already been indicated. Here, then, it will be sufficient to discuss briefly their probable motive, the indications in H. by which we can determine their extent, their main outlines, and their characteristics.

[1] Kirchhoff thinks it would have formed part of the story of Leotychides in Thessaly *circ.* 476 B.C.; but H. actually tells this in vi. 72, without a hint that he intends to tell it more fully later.

[2] This seems to be H.'s own point of view. The campaign of 478 is περὶ τῆς ἐκείνου (Πέρσου) viii. 3. 2.

[3] For H. cf. ix. 64. 2, the Messenian rebellion of 464 B.C. is μετὰ τὰ Μηδικά; for Thuc. cf. i. 18. 3; 23. 1. Meyer, F. i. 189 seq., argues convincingly for H.'s work being finished.

[4] Cf. shortly Rawlinson, i. 8–11, or more fully Bähr, iv. 423–33; for Asia cf. the special study by Matzat (Herm. vi. 392 seq.).

Motive. As to their motive, it is plausible to suggest that H. travelled as a merchant, at any rate in the North and the East. The following points may be noticed :

(1) He is careful to mention articles of commerce, not only the more exciting cassia and cinnamon (iii. 110–111), but ordinary wares, e. g. different kinds of linen (ii. 105), hempen garments and horns in Thrace (iv. 74 ; vii. 126), salt fish in South Russia (iv. 53. 3), sweetmeats at Callatebus (vii. 31).

(2) He is fond of describing methods of transport, e. g. the boats on the Euphrates and on the Nile (i. 194, ii. 96), and specially mentions their freight capacity. So too he is familiar with all the apparatus of a seaman's life, e. g. the plummet (ii. 5, 2), the pitch of Pieria (iv. 195. 3).

(3) He notes how far a river is navigable, e. g. Euphrates, i. 194. 5 ; Nile, ii. 96, 3 (cf. also c. 29) ; Dnieper, iv. 53. 4.

(4) He mentions curious forms of trade, e. g. iv. 24, the 'seven interpreters' of the Trans-steppe caravan route ; iv. 196, the 'dumb commerce' of West Africa.

(5) He uses what seem to be trade terms, e. g. the 'Lesbian bowls' (iv. 61. 1), the 'Argolic bowl' (iv. 152. 4)

Such indications may be merely accidental ; whether H. like Solon (Plut. Sol. 2) began life as an *ἔμπορος* it is impossible to decide ; what is certain and important is that his attitude to trade and commerce is that of older Greece, not that of the Periclean circle. 'The Greeks have learned to despise handicraft' (ii. 167. 2) he notes ; but this is not his own point of view.

§ 16. **Criteria of extent.** The evidence by which the extent of H.'s travels will be determined will be differently estimated by different interpreters :

(1) The places which he tells us definitely he has visited are few, and the mention of them is largely accidental, just as is the mention of personal informants ; the most important are Elephantine (ii. 29), Tyre (ii. 44), the Arabian frontier of Egypt (ii. 75).

(2) To these must be added the places where he implies that he speaks as an eyewitness, e. g. the Euphrates valley (i. 183. 3, 193. 4), Exampaeus on the Dnieper (iv. 81. 1).

So far there can be no doubt for those who believe in H.'s veracity; but—

(3) the third class of evidence for H.'s presence will be interpreted variously, i. e. the vividness and accuracy of his descriptions. To take two instances: a visit to Cyrene may be inferred with fair certainty from the account of the threefold harvest (iv. 199 n.) and from the minuteness of the account of the statute of Ladice (ii. 181. 5); so too the evidence for a visit to Susa is (apart from H.'s vivid description of Persian customs and dress, cf. i. 131–140 and especially vii. 61 nn.) the minute account of the Eretrians at Ardericca (vi. 119. 2, 3).

(4) Of Cyrene and of Ardericca H. uses the phrases (frequent also elsewhere) ἐς ἐμέ and μέχρι ἐμεῦ[1]; but these do not always imply the eyewitness; no one would now conclude that he had been in Bactria, though he speaks of the Barcaean exiles there *ἔτι καὶ ἐς ἐμέ*.

§ 17. **The most important journeys.** Assuming then the accuracy of these criteria, we find that the most important journeys of H. are the following (H.'s journeys in Greece and the Aegean islands are assumed):

(1) In Asia Minor his visit or visits to Sardis. He had travelled from Ephesus to Sardis (as we can judge from his elaborate account of the tomb of Alyattes (*u. s.*)), and back to

[1] It is interesting to note, however, that in the majority of passages where H. uses these or similar phrases he admittedly speaks as an eyewitness; such are i. 52, 66. 4, 92. 1, 93. 2 (?) Thebes, Tegea, Delphi, the tomb of Alyattes; ii. 154. 5, the docks at Bubastis; v. 77. 3, Athens. In two other cases this would be admitted by the majority of critics, i. 181. 2, Babylon; ii. 181. 5, Cyrene. In two cases the phrase ἔτι ἐς ἐμέ refers to what H. can hardly have seen, iv. 124. 1, the forts on the Oarus, iv. 204. 1 as to Bactria.

Smyrna. He had also perhaps been as far east as Celaenae (but see vii. 26. 3 n.), and had reached the Royal Road by another route from the Maeander valley by Cydrara (vii. 30–1).

(2) He had travelled by ship from the west to the east of the Black Sea (iv. 86) and had been in Colchis (ii. 104. 1); this voyage would have been along the south coast. Probably it would have been a different coasting voyage which gave him his familiarity with the south-east and east of Thrace shown in iv. 89–93, and brought him to Olbia. Whether it was on the same voyage that he visited Thasos (vi. 47. 2) and took the opportunity of a journey inland to the dwellings on Lake Prasias (v. 16), it is impossible to say. From Olbia he saw Exampaeus (iv. 81. 2) and a Scythian royal tomb (ib. 71–2 nn.), though probably not among the Gerrhi.

(3) It is probable that H. had not himself traversed the Royal Road (v. 53); the measurements he gives are Persian, and he speaks from hearsay (viii. 98. 1) of the Persian post. Nor is there any proof that H. was ever north of Mount Taurus. On the other hand we can conjecture his starting-point for his overland journey to the Euphrates; the importance he gives to the Mariandynian Gulf (iv. 38. 2), and his details as to Poseideum (iii. 91. 1, vii. 91) point to this town as being familiar to him. Once the Euphrates was reached, he was again on a definite trade route (i. 194), and his course to Babylon was easy; his descriptions, however, are, to speak mildly, confused (i. 185 nn.).

(4) It is natural to suppose that from Babylon H. continued his journey to Susa (cf. vi. 119. 2, 3); that he went thence north to Ecbatana is not likely, though some see the αὐτόπτης in i. 98. 5, 6.

(5) H. had entered Egypt both by sea and by land; this at least is the natural inference from ii. 5. 2 and iii. 5, 6. As he himself tells us that he went to Tyre to inquire about the Egyptian Hercules (ii. 44. 1), it is probable that he returned

to Egypt by the land-route along the coast of Syria. Here we can trace him in the neighbourhood of Beyrout (ii. 106. 1 n.), at Cadytis (iii. 5. 2 n.), and at Papremis (iii. 12. 4). For his travels in Egypt itself cf. App. IX.[1]

(6) That H. had been to Cyrene is almost certain from the fullness and accuracy of his knowledge of North Africa. He seems to have sailed along the coast from Tripoli at any rate to the Cinyps (iv. 192.) But his description of an oasis (iv. 181. 2) does not show the eyewitness, and there is no evidence that he had seen Carthage.

(7) H.'s personal familiarity with the West was probably limited to South Italy and Sicily; no doubt it was on his way there that he saw the pitch-wells of Zacynthus (iv. 195. 2). The chief places where we seem to trace the traveller are (besides Thurii), Croton (v. 45), Metapontum (iv. 15, 18–20), Tarentum (iv. 99. 5), and in Sicily, Syracuse, Gela (vii. 153), and Egesta (v. 47. 2).

The travels of H. are those of a true Greek; he goes as a rule by water, and does not under ordinary circumstances quit the coast. He travels, too, under the protection of the order[2] established by the Persian Empire, and draws his information from his own countrymen, settled in the dominions of the Great King.

§ 18. **Written evidence.** The evidence used by Herodotus may be classified under three heads, Written, Oral, and

[1] It would be very interesting if it could be assumed with safety that the vase bearing the name 'Herodotus', found at Naucratis in 1903, was dedicated by the historian (J. H. S. xxv. 116).

[2] Some have seen a difficulty in H.'s travels through the Persian Empire, because he had attacked his native prince, who was a dependent of the Great King. They postpone his oriental travels, therefore, till after 450 B.C., in order that the traveller may at any rate have the advantage of the 'Peace of Callias'. But there were far too many Greeks in the Persian service all through, for any Greek to have difficulty in Asia Minor, in Syria, or even at Susa itself.

Archaeological: each of these kinds must be considered separately. The travels of H. are specially interesting as having enabled him to collect the materials of his history from the most various oral sources, and to some extent to use his eyes in seeing the scenes of the events he desciibes. But it is certain also that he had some written evidence; poetry is continually quoted by him; he knew his Homer as an Englishman used to know his Bible[1]; he not only quotes most of the poets,[2] but says confidently[3] that the Lacedaemonians in their account of their royal house (vi. 52. 1) are ὁμολογέοντες οὐδενὶ ποιητῇ.

In one case the obligations of H. to a poet are really important. Whether he used the Μιλήτου ἅλωσις of Phrynichus cannot be proved, as no fragment of it survives, but he certainly used the Persae of Aeschylus.[4] Unfortunately the historian borrows from the tragedian not the description of the battle, in which Aeschylus was a combatant, but the scenes in the Persian court, where his story is imaginary. One mistake of the poet, however, is avoided by the historian; the counsels of moderation put by Aeschylus inappropriately in the mouth of Darius, are more suitably given by H. to Artabanus and Artemisia.

When H. so continually uses poetic evidence, it is certainly

[1] Cf. Mure, iv. 558 seq., for a list of parallels. Perhaps even more striking is the use of the Epic machinery; cf. Macan (1908) xlviii. Longinus (de Subl. 13. 3) well calls H. 'Ὁμηρικώτατος' along with Archilochus and Plato.

[2] He denies the Homeric authorship of the Cypria confidently (ii. 117), of the Epigoni doubtfully (iv. 32). He quotes Hesiod (ibid.), Olen (iv. 35. 3), Archilochus (i. 12. 2) Alcaeus (v. 95. 2), Sappho (ii. 135. 6), Solon (v. 113. 2), Aristeas (iv. 13), Simonides (v. 102. 5), Pindar (iii. 38. 4), Phrynichus (vi. 21.2), Aeschylus (ii. 156. 6), not to mention oracle-writers like Musaeus, Bacis, and Lysistratus (all in viii. 96). He also mentions Aesop (ii. 134. 3), Anacreon (iii. 121. 1) and Lasus (vii. 6. 3).

[3] For a similar confident verdict cf. ii. 156. 6.

[4] For H.'s obligations to the Persae cf. Hauvette, pp. 125-6.

curious that he quotes only one prose-writer by name, Hecataeus (vi. 137. 1). This solitary mention does not prove that H. used no other prose-writer; it might as well be argued that H. had only six (?) personal informants, because he mentions no others (*v. i.*). It is natural to suppose that the discussion and refutation of various views as to the Nile flood (ii. 20 seq.) are directed against written errors. But at any rate the silence of H. as to prose-writers raises a presumption that he was largely independent of their help, and this is confirmed by general probability; without adopting the ultra-sceptical views of Paley,[1] who holds that 'Thucydides did not know of any written history,' it may be affirmed that the generation to which H. belonged itself marked the transition from a public educated on poetry to one in which prose began to assume almost an equal share in culture.

§ 19. **Herodotus and previous prose-writers.** This, however, is hardly the prevalent view; H.'s debt to literary sources, not only poetical but in prose, is now thought to be considerable.[2] It is worth while therefore to consider the testimony of ancient writers, and to test their evidence, so far as is possible, by the surviving fragments of the works of H.'s predecessors.

There are four main testimonies as to H.'s obligation to other prose-writers:

(1) Ephorus (fr. 102, F. H. G. i. 262) *μνημονεύει (Ξάνθου) ὡς παλαιοτέρου ὄντος καὶ Ἡροδότῳ τὰς ἀφορμὰς δεδωκότος.*

(2) Dionysius of Halicarnassus (de praec. Hist. vi. 769) writes: Ἡ. *τῶν πρὸ αὐτοῦ συγγραφέων γενομένων, Ἑλλανίκου τε καὶ Χάρωνος, τὴν αὐτὴν ὑπόθεσιν προεκδεδωκότων, οὐκ ἀπετράπετο, ἀλλ' ἐπίστευσεν αὐτῶν κρεῖσσόν τι ἐξοίσειν.*

(3) Porphyry (apud Euseb. Praep. Evang. x. 3; F. H. G. i. 21) says that H. in his second book *πολλὰ Ἑκαταίου τοῦ*

[1] J. of P. v. 224; P. even denies that Thucydides had seen the work of H.
[2] Cf. Macan (1908) pp. lxxiii seq.

Μιλησίου κατὰ λέξιν μετήνεγκεν ἐκ τῆς περιηγήσεως βραχέα παραποιήσας, and goes on to quote H.'s accounts of the phoenix, the hippopotamus, and the crocodile-hunting (ii. 73, 71, 70).

(4) Suidas (*s. v.* Ἑκαταῖος) says that H. 'profited by' Hecataeus, a statement also found in Hermogenes (de Gen. Dicendi, ii. 12).

It will be noticed that all these statements, except that of Ephorus, are very late,[1] and belong to a period when forgers had been busy with the older names of Greek literature.[2] We are therefore confronted with the double difficulty: (i.) The works of the predecessors of H. have survived, if at all, only in the scantiest fragments, and (ii.) we have no guarantee that these really come from sixth-century authors, and are not late forgeries.

Bearing these difficulties in mind, we may proceed to compare the work of H. with the authors from whom he is said to have borrowed.

(*a*) **Xanthus.** So far as Xanthus is concerned, there is clear evidence that H. was largely independent of him; Dionysius (Antiq. Rom. i. 28) distinctly says that Xanthus made no mention of the Tyrrhenian migration to Italy (H. i. 94 n.). and that he called the son of Atys, 'Torrhebus' not 'Tyrrhenus'. It is probable too that the story of Gyges in Xanthus was different (cf. App. I. 8). So, though there may have been resemblances between him and H., we quite fail to trace them.

(*b*) **Charon.** The same is true as to Charon of Lampsacus. He is quoted twice by Plutarch (?) (de mal. Hdti.

[1] Dionysius belongs to the first century B.C., Hermogenes to the second century A.D., Porphyry to the third.

[2] So Galen twice over says (e.g. in Hippoc. de Nat. Hom. xv, p. 109) that under the Alexandrine and Pergamene dynasties (i.e. the third and second centuries B.C.) forgeries of works bearing famous names became profitable and common. The Letters of Phalaris is an instance which should be familiar to every Englishman, from Macaulay's essay on Temple.

cc. 20. 24) to refute the stories of H. as to Pactyas (i. 160. 3 n.) and as to the capture of Sardis (v. 102 n.). Tertullian also quotes him as telling the same story as H. about Astyages (i. 107).[1]

On the other hand, H. was obviously unfamiliar with his work on Lampsacus (cf. vi. 37 n.). Possibly there is a reference to him in vi. 55, where H. says that he will not speak of the way in which the Heraclidae obtained kingship at Sparta; but even so the passage would only prove that H. had not used him there.

(*c*) **Hellanicus.** Of the other writers mentioned in the quotations above, Hellanicus may be dismissed as being probably junior to H.; at any rate he was still writing in 406 B.C.[2] The most obvious resemblance between him and H. is fr. 173 as to Salmoxis (cf. H. iv. 93); but there it is clear that either Hellanicus, or more probably a forger, has stolen a Herodotean story wholesale.

§ 20. **Hecataeus.** There remains, however, the crucial instance, Hecataeus, in whose case the charge of plagiarism against H. is definitely made.[3] It is worth while, therefore, to collect the passages which bear on the relations of H. and Hecataeus.

These fall into three classes:

(1) Passages where Hecataeus is mentioned by name, vi. 137. 1 (as a writer from whom H. differs); ii. 143. 1 (as a somewhat vain and ignorant traveller); v. 36. 2; 125 (as a prudent statesman).

[1] Fr. 4, F. H. G. i. 32. Charon also (fr. 3) mentioned the disaster of Mardonius at Mount Athos, but the 'white doves', which were a feature of his story, are unknown to H. (vi. 44; cf. i. 138. 2 n.).

[2] Fr. 80 (F. H. G. i. 56) refers to the enfranchisement of the slaves after Arginusae. Fr. 74, as to Theseus and Helen, is clearly a different tradition from ix. 73. 2.

[3] This charge is elaborated by Sayce (xxi seq.), who tries to prove that H. 'drew without scruple on the work of the writer he desired to supersede'.

(2) Passages where views attributed by ancient writers to Hecataeus are mentioned for censure: ii. 21 (the circumambient Ocean (fr. 278); iv. 36 (the same point, and the Hyperboreans); probably ii. 15–16 (the opinion of the Ionians that the Delta only is Egypt.[1] In ii. 5. 1 ('Egypt, the gift of the river'), and ii. 156. 2 (fr. 284, the floating island of Chemmis), there is a tone of self-assertion on the part of H., but not of censure.

(3) Finally, there are the passages quoted above as 'transferred' by H.

Diels' theory. The view now usually held as to these is probably that of Diels (Hermes, xxii), which may be summarized as follows:

(1) Hecataeus as a traveller and geographer had a wider range than H.

(2) H. on his travels used the Περίοδος Γῆς of Hecataeus freely as a guide-book, testing his sources wherever possible.

(3) When H. read parts of his work at Athens, he introduced quotations from his guide-book; some of these were afterwards rewritten, but some (e.g. those quoted by Porphyry) remained in the original form.

(4) There is no question of plagiarism. Aristotle quotes verbally these very passages from H., without mentioning his name, and only correcting a few of the mistakes (see ii. 70. 71 nn.). (It may be remarked, however, that the quotations of Aristotle are not a parallel case, for he was writing a book of a completely different kind from that of H.)

Diels points out that H.'s own words, especially ii. 5. 1, imply that he was following some previous source. He adds that the forms of the Egyptian words in Hecataeus are more correct (e.g. Χέμβις, ii. 156. 1; *v. n.*) than those in H.

'Hecataeus' probably a forgery. The whole point is

[1] Perhaps we may add i. 146. 1, as to the purity of Ionian blood.

of some importance, for, if H. borrowed freely without acknowledgement in Bk. II, he may well have borrowed elsewhere, and it is easy to conjecture obligations of H. to Hecataeus, though impossible to prove them.[1]

Many scholars, however, including the great Cobet, have held the view that the genuine Περίοδος Γῆς of Hecataeus perished early, and that the 'borrowings' are borrowings not by H. but from H., on the part of a forger in the third century B.C. The following points may be urged:

(1) Diels' arguments quoted above prove nothing. A clever forger would introduce into his work any phrases or views which H. attacks or seems to attack, and, as he may well have been an Alexandrine, he would naturally correct, if he could, H.'s Egyptian transliteration (which sorely needed such correction).

(2) It is difficult to conceive how passages such as are supposed to have been 'borrowed' could have found place in a universal geography of two (or at most three) books. The Περίοδος of Hecataeus probably was a bald list of names like the work of the pseudo-Scylax.

(3) If Hecataeus really wrote an important book of foreign travel, it is curious that Aristotle never refers to it, though that master of Greek knowledge refers to H. and to the earlier Ionians frequently.

(4) We know that Callimachus considered the geographical work that passed under the name of Hecataeus, in the third century, to be a forgery, wholly or in part, although Eratosthenes, his successor in the Alexandrine library, believed in its genuineness.

The matter must be left uncertain,[2] but the *a priori* improbability remains that Herodotus, who had certainly travelled in Egypt, should have troubled to borrow from another a

[1] e.g. cf. i. 193. 3, 198 nn. for such a supposed borrowing.

[2] For a full discussion cf. J. H. S. xxix. 41 seq.

description of what he could as easily have seen for himself. Whatever we may think of the diffusion of prose literature in the fifth century, Diels' theory of Hecataeus as a 'traveller's handbook' requires much more proof than can be given for it. The rolls, whether of papyrus or of parchment, would have been a bulky addition to the luggage of H.

§ 21. **Herodotus and written sources: summing up.** To sum up the whole question. If there were an easily accessible prose literature in fifth-century Athens or Samos, H. ought certainly to have studied it; perhaps he did so. But in view of his own silence, and of the uncertainty of the connexions traced between him and his predecessors, it is more natural to conclude that he collected the mass of his information, apart from poetry, by word of mouth, when he could not use his own eyes. Had his sources been largely literary, we should have had clearer evidence of the fact. H. was too successful a writer to be popular; many would have been eager to point out his obligations.

Foreign official documents. There is, however, one kind of written evidence which H. certainly used. In some way that we cannot explain, he had obtained access to Persian official documents, which he incorporates in his history; of this character are the accounts of the Persian satrapies (iii. 89–97), of the Royal Road (v. 52–3), and of the Persian army list in Bk. VII. This evidence is of the highest importance. It must, however, have come to H. through a Greek source, for he knew no language but his own[1]; there were many Greeks in the service of Persia, and we have one instance at least of a a Persian grandee Hellenizing himself, Zopyrus (cf. iii. 160. 2 n.).

§ 22. **Oral tradition.** The dependence of H. on oral

[1] For his ignorance of Persian cf. i. 139; of Egyptian, ii. 125. 6, 143. 4; and for the whole subject Meyer, F. i. 192 seq.

tradition for most of his evidence is usually accepted[1]; but the point is so important that his language on the subject must be carefully examined. He himself always uses the phraseology of 'speaking' and 'hearing', but this in itself is not decisive; for (1) he refers to his work as a λόγος and to different parts of it as λόγοι.[2] (2) He uses φημί and λέγω of evidence drawn from written works (e.g. vi. 137. 1 Hecataeus; iv. 13. 1 Aristeas). (3) He makes not only inscriptions (iv. 91) and oracles (v. 60) 'speak', but even a letter (i. 124. 1). (4) Hearsay (ἀκοή) is used for any report, written or verbal, as opposed to the author's own sight (ὄψις, ii. 29. 1).

The use of λέγω, ἀκούω and such words, however, raises a presumption that the sources of evidence were generally oral, and this presumption becomes stronger when these verbs are used in past tenses, which imply actual conversations. Moreover, H.'s narrative, though it rarely gives the names of his informants, continually implies that he is repeating a tradition heard on the spot (e. g. at Tyre, ii. 44. 2). It may be noticed, too, that the phraseology of 'speaking' and 'hearing' occurs most frequently in those portions of the history where H. is least likely to have had written evidence (cf. especially Bks. II and IV, on Egypt and Scythia).

Effect on his history. The fact that his evidence was largely oral has a very important bearing on the character of the narrative; this represents the popular traditions of the past, whether the remote past of Egypt, as told in the streets of Memphis or in connexion with the shrines of Ptah (cf. App. X. 10), or the recent story of the Persian wars, as narrated by the Greek combatants to their children.

Informants named by him. H. himself on three occasions

[1] For the contrary view cf. H. Panofsky, de Historiae Herodoteae fontibus (1885), criticized by Hauvette, pp. 170–6.

[2] e.g. vi. 19. 3 ἑτέρωθι τοῦ λόγου, *et pass.* For a collection of instances cf. Macan (1895) lxxv, and (1908) lxxi.

certainly gives us the names of his informants ; these are Archias the Spartan (iii. 55. 2), Tymnes at Olbia (iv. 76. 6), and Thersander of Orchomenus (ix. 16. 1). It can hardly be fanciful to see in these, representatives of three different kinds of evidence—as to sixth-century Greece, as to foreign lands, and as to Τὰ Μηδικά proper ; but beyond this we cannot go, or even suggest why H. names these three especially.[1]

§ 23. **Archaeological evidence.** H. is much more free in mentioning the works of art or other objects from which he derived, or in connexion with which he heard, the stories that make up his work, than in naming his actual informants. There is hardly a country within the wide range of his travels to whose monuments he does not refer. At Cyrene were statues sent by Amasis and Ladice (ii. 182. 1, 181. 5), at Metapontum one to Aristeas (iv. 15. 4). In Scythia tombs of the kings (iv. 71. 1), a great bowl at Exampaeus (iv. 81. 3), at Byzantium the bowl of Pausanias (ibid.) and inscriptions of Darius (iv. 87. 1), in Thrace another such inscription (iv. 91. 1) and lake dwellings (v. 16). In Lydia, the tomb of Alyattes (i. 93), an inscribed boundary stone of Croesus (vii. 30. 2), and the supposed memorial of Sesostris at Kara-Bel (ii. 106). In Palestine, a similar monument (ibid.) and the temple of Melcarth at Tyre (ii. 44. 2). In Babylon the tomb of Nitocris (i. 187) and the temple of Bel (i. 181, 183). In Egypt we may mention—at Sais, the supposed memorials of Mycerinus' family (ii. 129 f.), the genuine monuments of Amasis (ii. 175), and the tombs of Osiris and of the Saite kings (ii. 169, 170) ; near Memphis, the Pyramids (ii. 101. 2, 125–7, 134, 136, 149), and the

[1] H. seems also to have spoken to the 'three priestesses' (ii. 55. 3) he names at Dodona ; but they only told him a legend of more than doubtful truth. Dicaeus the Athenian (viii. 65. 1) does not seem to have told his vision to H. personally. The attempt to make him a written source for the story of the Persian War (Trautwein, in Hermes, 1890) is ingenious, but quite unconvincing.

Labyrinth and lake of Moeris (ii. 148–9). It must, however, be noted that H. could not read inscriptions in any foreign language, and was at the mercy of his guides (cf. ii. 125. 6 n.).

For Hellenic lands it is impossible to give a complete catalogue, but beside the long list of offerings at Delphi, Samos, and elsewhere noted below, we may add the following: At Tegea, Spartan fetters and the manger of Mardonius (i. 66. 4, ix. 70); at Aegina, prows of Samian ships (iii. 59. 3); at Thebes, offerings of Croesus (i. 52, 92) and three tripods inscribed with Cadmean letters (v. 59, 61); at Delos, tombs of Hyperborean maidens (iv. 34. 2, 35. 4); and in the temple of Ephesian Artemis, pillars offered by Croesus (i. 92. 1). These last, like the offerings of Micythus at Olympia (vii. 170. 4 n.), and the trophies set up at Athens for a victory over Thebes and Chalcis (v. 77. 4 n.), have a special interest because fragments of them have been discovered by modern excavators.

It is worth while to notice three or four points as to this class of evidence.

War monuments. (1) The historian of the Persian War would naturally examine the monuments which commemorated the fallen (cf. vii. 225. 2, 228 for Thermopylae; ix. 85 for Plataea); it is therefore all the more strange that he does not mention the *Σωρός* at Marathon in vi. 117. Under this head come the trophies dedicated, e.g. three Phoenician triremes at the Isthmus, at Sunium, and at Salamis (viii. 121.1), the statues of Poseidon at the Isthmus and of Zeus at Olympia (ibid.), and above all the famous tripod at Delphi (ix. 81. 1 n.).

§ 24. **Temples.** (2) It is a commonplace to say that the temples were the museums of the old world, but this fact has an important bearing on the sources of H.'s history; e.g. many facts were derived by him from the Samian Heraeum[1] and

[1] It was clearly at Samos that H. heard the story of the discovery of the West (iv. 152), the details as to Darius on the Bosphorus (iv. 88), and part at least of the fate of Polycrates (iii. 123. 1), and learned something of the

from the temple of Ptah at Memphis (cf. ii. 101. 2; 110. 1 nn.). Delphi especially furnished H. with many stories. He was familiar with the past history and the present arrangements of the oracle (cf. especially i. 50–51). His Lydian history is only the first of a series of narratives derived largely from this source.[1]

Temples as record offices. (3) It is difficult not to think that temples, especially oracular temples, were record offices as well as museums. Obviously the responses so eagerly sought would be carefully kept by those who gave them, if only in their own interest; and a collection of oracles would be a source from which the inquirer could write the history of the past, partly as it had been, still more as the keepers of the oracle wished men to think it had been.[2]

The following responses may have been taken from a Delphic collection, since they are quoted in full: those given to Croesus (i. 47, 55, 85), to the Spartans (i. 65. 2), to Miletus and Argos (vi. 18, 77. 2; vii. 148. 3), the warnings to Siphnos (iii. 57. 4), to Corinth (v. 92), and to Athens (vii. 140–1), and the series concerned with the colonization of Libya (iv. 150 f.). The Pisistratidae left at Athens a collection of oracles (v. 90. 2); in their collection were some ascribed to Musaeus (vii. 6. 3). H. may have used some such work of Musaeus or Bacis; cf. viii. 77. 2, 96. 2 (Salamis), ix. 43. 2 (Plataea), viii. 20. 2 (Euboea).

Lists of officials. (4) Perhaps under this head may be put the lists of kings and priests which were the beginning of Greek secular official records. H. shows a knowledge of the list of

foreign relations of Samos in the sixth century (i. 70. 3; ii. 182. 1). In the market-place there he read the names of the patriotic Samian leaders at Lade (vi. 14. 3).

[1] We may mention especially beside the offerings made after Salamis and Plataea (*u. s.*), the Corinthian and the Siphnian (i. 14. 2 n.; iv. 162. 3) treasuries at Delphi (iii. 57. 2 n.), and the Argive, the Lacedaemonian and the Phocian offerings there (i. 31. 5, 51. 4; viii. 27. 4).

[2] Cf. i. 13. 2 for a clear prediction *post eventum*.

the Spartan kings twice over (vii. 204; viii. 131. 2), but he only once (viii. 51. 1) uses these lists for the purpose of dating his events as Thucydides sometimes does (ii. 2, v. 25) those of archons and priestesses.

§ 25. **Herodotus' use of his evidence.** The manner in which H. uses his evidence varies greatly. With regard to the mythical period of Greek history, it is interesting to see that he has it all mapped out in his mind as the background of subsequent events. The traditions current later were already definitely formed; Greek history is represented as beginning with a period of great migrations (cf. viii. 73, and vii. 161. 3 for Athens as the exception); Greek civilization is due to foreign influences (ii. 52, Greek religion, and v. 58, the alphabet). The whole tradition of the 'Return of the Heraclidae' is implicit in i. 56, viii. 43, 73 (cf. also vi. 52), while the ulterior results of this Dorian migration are given in i. 145–7, v. 76. Finally, to give one more instance, the history of mythical Athens is told in viii. 44.

All this H. accepts without question. Homer is to him a witness who does not 'contradict himself' under ordinary circumstances.[1] Moreover the mythical history has already been spaced out chronologically in generations (cf. v. 59; ii. 44. 4; and App. XIV. 2).

At the same time H. is conscious that there is a difference between historic and prehistoric periods; in iii. 122. 2 (*v. n.*) he contrasts Minos and Polycrates as belonging to different categories; in this respect Thucydides is less scientific than H., for he, without any reserve, turns Minos into a prehistoric Pericles (i. 4).

§ 26. **Rationalization of myths.** In spite of his acceptance of the myths, however, even H. cannot escape the tendency to rationalize them, by changing the elements of the marvellous

[1] ii. 116. 2. Contrast Thuc. i. 9. 4 for depreciation of Homer's testimony.

which they contain into commonplace matter of fact. This tendency was to be fully established in the next generation. A good example is ii. 57. 2, as to the priestesses of Dodona, who 'chattered like doves'. H. presents a curious instance of the mixture of the theological and the positive attitude when (in vii. 129. 4) he blends Poseidon and earthquakes in one geological theory.

Two or three other points as to H.'s treatment of the myths deserve notice:

(1) He confuses the mythology of Greece and of the East; he is ever ready to find an Oriental source for Greek beliefs and worships; e.g. ii. 43, the Egyptian origin of Hercules. This is characteristic of his whole attitude; he is one of those of whom it might be said, 'If you 've 'eard the East a callin', you won't ever 'eed naught else.'

(2) He objects to his countrymen's habit of introducing themselves everywhere (iv. 96. 1, the story of Salmoxis); but he himself does this in his derivation of the names of the Persians and the Medes from Perseus and Medea respectively (vii. 61. 1).

(3) The clear division in his mind between the mythical and the historical period makes it easier for him to overlook the inconsistency of his Pelasgian views (see App. XV. 3), and to hold that peoples, barbarians in his own day, were survivals of the general stock of the prehistoric Greeks (i. 57. 1).

§ 27. **The historical period.** Outside the mythical period, the procedure of H. is different. He sees that history is a matter of evidence; hence his anxiety to record accepted traditions, and where possible, the origin[1] of divergent accounts, and the reasons or proofs urged on either side (v. 45. 1). Above all, he at times distinguishes clearly the different kinds of evidence on which different parts of his narrative rest.

[1] Thus in the account of the foundation of Cyrene he distinguishes the part resting on the evidence of Theraeans only (iv. 150. 1) from those where this is supported by Cyrenaean evidence (cf. also iv. 5, 12; vi. 75, 84).

Thus, in speaking of Egypt, he distinguishes the description of the land and people, where he relies mainly on his own observation (ὄψις) and inquiry, from the past history, drawn principally from Egyptian report (ii. 99. 1). Further, he shows a perception of the nature of evidence in discriminating between that part of Egyptian history which rests on the witness of the priests (ii. 142. 1) and the story of the Saite Kings, for which there is independent confirmatory testimony (ii. 147. 1), doubtless that of the Greek settlers. Finally, considerations of probability (cf. iii. 9. 2, 45. 3; viii. 8. 3) or the actual evidence adduced occasionally lead to a decision, express (iv. 12) or implied (cf. viii. 94), between two conflicting stories, though more often H. leaves the matter doubtful, refusing to judge between opposing authorities (cf. iv. 154; v. 85 f.; vi. 14, 32 f., 134, 137). These attempts at balancing evidence give him some title to be called the 'first critical historian', for he has grasped the principles that 'eyewitnesses' are all-important (iii. 115), and that it is necessary to test and examine all evidence. However defective to us seem his criteria, the fact remains that he had criteria, and that his narrative was a critical one, as judged by the standard of his own day. It is necessary to emphasize this general point because it is often overlooked, while of necessity H.'s weaknesses must be set forth in detail. The most important of these weaknesses may be classified as follows:—

§ 28. **Weaknesses of Herodotus as a critic of evidence.** (1) H. is more prepared to accept marvels in the accounts of remote ages and remote places. His principle of being guided by the evidence of eyewitnesses was obviously impossible for remote times, and for remote places H. seems unconsciously to relax his standard. So of the floating gold dust in West Africa (iv. 195. 2) he says, τὰ δὲ λέγεται γράφω· εἴη δ' ἂν πᾶν; and not unnaturally he is prepared to believe that the 'ends of the world' have the most remarkable products (iii. 106 seq.). But even in describing these, he has still an indefinable instinct which makes him reject monstrosities (iv. 25. 1; 191. 4 n.); he is 'the broker of traveller's winnings, insatiate after some new thing, unerring by instinct rather than by experience to detect false coin'.[1]

(2) He is full, especially as to the periods that precede the fifth century, of stories which are amusing and instructive as to the ideas of his contemporaries, but of no historical value, at any rate in the strict sense of 'historical'. Gyges and Periander, Psammetichus and Amasis are real persons; but they had become to the Greeks the centre of a cloud of fable, in which the real facts were obscured, if not lost.

The tendency to throw character into a story was an innate part of Greek dramatic genius.[2] It has been well said that the beginnings of the Greek novel are to be found in H., but interesting as this is from the literary point of view, the fact impairs the historical value of H.

(3) H.'s lack of a chronological framework involves him in inconsistencies, especially as to the sixth century. Owing to the absence of this, the historical perspective of his story is frequently distorted. The most famous instance is the story of Solon and Croesus (i. 29 seq.); for others cf. App. XIV. 6.

(4) Finally, H. was himself conscious that his criteria of truth were deficient. Hence the principle so definitely laid down by him in vii. 152. 3 *ἐγὼ δὲ ὀφείλω λέγειν τὰ λεγόμενα, πείθεσθαί γε μὲν οὐ παντάπασιν ὀφείλω*; this is repeated in ii. 123. 1 in different words. He himself gives this maxim a general application to his whole history, and emphasizes it by a curious antithetical style, very unlike his usual phraseology. The failure to remember this principle has often led to H. being charged with credulity, where he himself was incredulous (e. g. by Sayce, p. 28, as to ii. 29). But the meaning of the maxim has

[1] Myres, A. and C. p. 124.

[2] For a similar tendency elsewhere cf. Freeman's Essay (vol. i) on The Mythical Element in Early English History.

been entirely distorted in Nitzsch's[1] famous article, where it is maintained that H. did not venture to modify or blend different λόγοι, but set them down side by side regardless of their inconsistency. This theory makes H. a mere scissors-and-paste historian; but it is clear that he did his best to compare and combine, though naturally he was not always successful in uniting divergent traditions.

§ 29. **Success of the history of Herodotus.** The history of H. seems to have taken at once a leading place in Greek literature. Apart from the parodies of Aristophanes (cf. i. 4. 2 n.), which are good proof how familiar it was to an Athenian audience, the attitude of Thucydides is sufficient evidence. That the historian of the Peloponnesian War did not like his predecessor is clear;[2] it is also pretty clear that he underestimated him; but he wrote his own history to continue that of H., taking up the story at the capture of Sestos. Perhaps it was a literary fashion to write down predecessors; Hecataeus certainly did it, and H. in his turn depreciated Hecataeus. We have evidence of the same fact in the next generation; Ctesias, the Cnidian physician at the court of Persia,[3] wrote his Περσικά, professedly from native records, to contradict H., whom he calls ψεύστης καὶ λογοποιός. There may well have been some personal motive (they both came from Greek towns in Caria) to explain

[1] Rhein. Mus. xxvii, p. 226 (1872). For criticism cf. Hauvette, pp. 133 seq.

[2] For a full account of Thucydides' criticisms of H. cf. Hauvette, pp. 65–76. The most important points of divergence are Thuc. i. 20. 3 and H. vi. 57. 5; ix. 53. 2, as to Spartan kings and the Pitanate λόχος; Thuc. i. 126. 8 and H. v. 71. 2, as to Cylon; Thuc. ii. 8. 3 and H. vi. 98, the earthquake at Delos; Thuc. ii. 97. 6 and H. v. 3. 1, as to extent of Scythia. We may perhaps add Thuc. i. 14. 3 and H. vii. 144. 2, the purpose of the fleet of 482 B.C.; and Thuc. i. 138. 3 and H. viii. 58, the story of Mnesiphilus, where some see in Thucydides a vindication of Themistocles (οὔτε προμαθὼν οὔτε ἐπιμαθών) against the depreciation of H.

[3] For the reckless inventions of Ctesias cf. nn. *passim*, and Xenophon's refutation of his claims to diplomatic activity after Cunaxa (Plut. Artax. 13).

the virulence of Ctesias' mendacious attack. On the other hand, Xenophon pays H. the compliment of imitating his phrases.[1]

It is not necessary to illustrate the use of H. by Ephorus, Aeneas Tacticus, and others in the fourth century. It is sufficient to quote the great authority of Aristotle, who not only quotes H. seven times by name, but refers to him frequently without naming him, both in his works on natural history (cf. p. 25), and in his account of Athenian history in the Ἀθηναίων Πολιτεία.

The fame of H. has continued to be a battle-ground ever since, wherever classical literature has been studied. Manetho,[2] the Egyptian priest, in the third century B.C., accused him of having πολλὰ τῶν Αἰγυπτιακῶν ὑπ' ἀγνοίας ἐψευσμένον; Lucian, in his Vera Historia, puts him, with Ctesias and many others, among those who suffer the severest punishments in the Isle of the Wicked, because they did not write the truth. (Ver. Hist. ii. c. 31; ii. p. 127.)

The reputation of H. has survived all these attacks; but his greatest admirers would admit that certain points have been fully established against him; these must now be stated. It is natural to speak first of the attacks on his impartiality.

§ 30. **The impartiality of Herodotus: (*a*) the Persians.** His general equity and candour should never have been questioned, though some critics have attributed to him the 'malignity' exhibited in their own censure. A striking proof may be found in his fairness to foreigners and to enemies; he is free from the ordinary Greek contempt for barbarians; he extols the maritime and engineering skill of the Phoenicians (vii. 23. 3, 44, 99. 3), the monuments of Egypt and Babylon (i. 93. 2), the natural products of the ends of the earth (iii. 106–114). He derives the Greek alphabet from Phoenicia

[1] Cf. Hauvette, p. 4.

[2] F.H.G. ii. 566, fr. 42. The justice of the charge is obvious, but Manetho himself fares little better with some modern Egyptologists.

(v. 58), and coinage from Lydia (i. 94), measurement of time from Babylon (ii. 109. 3), and exaggerates the debt of Greece to Egypt (p. 33) and to Africa (iv. 180, 189). This freedom from national prejudice shows itself in his generous estimate of the Persians; he emphasizes their truth (i. 136. 2, 138. 1) and devoted loyalty (iii. 128. 4, 154 f.; viii. 118. 3) and ascribes their defeat to inferiority in arms and discipline, not to lack of valour (ix. 62. 3). Even the Greek retainers of the great king, Demaratus and Artemisia, are depicted as counsellors whose foresight is justified by events (vii. 101 f., 234 f.; viii. 68 f., 101 f.).

(*b*) **The Greeks generally.** If Herodotus recognizes the merits of the enemy, he is equally clear-sighted in refusing to see a hero in every professed patriot. For this he has been bitterly attacked by Plutarch,[1] whose main thesis is that any stain on the fame of those who saved Hellas from the barbarian must be due to the 'malignity' of the historian. No doubt Plutarch detects certain errors in Herodotus, and adds from his reading facts of value, but this unsound principle vitiates his whole method. He rejects any hint that the policy of Sparta was selfish or calculating (cf. cc. 22, 25 with H. iii. 47; vi. 108), or that Argos was open to censure (c. 28; cf. H. vii. 139 and *inf.*). Although Plutarch makes one or two good points against the treatment of Thebes and Corinth in H. (*v. i.*), yet the absurd accusation that he is too modest in his praise of Athens, diminishing the glory of Marathon by underestimating the number of the slain, and of Artemisium by representing it as a drawn battle, shows us the worthlessness of the critic's

[1] The De Malignitate Herodoti may be ascribed provisionally to Plutarch (cf. Hauvette, p. 98 f.). Its extreme bitterness of tone, which seems inconsistent with his free use of H. elsewhere, may be due to misplaced Boeotian patriotism. There are many minute correspondences both of language and of fact between it and the Lives, and the tendency to hero-worship pervades both alike. It is interesting as the first instance in literature of the slashing review; of its author, as of Croker, it might be said, 'He meant murder but only committed suicide.'

judgement. H. exercised discretion in recognizing the dissensions by which Greece was torn, and in rejecting the extravagant claims of local patriotism; the De Malignitate, in fact, is valuable if indirect testimony to H.'s good sense and fairness.

(*c*) **The Corinthians.** But if H. is not blinded by the glamour of patriotism, he does not wholly escape the influence of the political sympathies of his own day.[1] He felt warm gratitude to the cities which gave him a home, Samos and Athens, and at these he learned many of the traditions embodied in his work. His very simplicity predisposed him to place a ready confidence in his authorities and to accept as trustworthy the stories and beliefs current among the men with whom he lived. This leads him to palliate the treachery of the Samians at Lade (vi. 13), and, more frequently, to become the mirror of Athenian prejudice. Among the states that fought at Salamis Corinth played no inglorious part, as was admitted on all hands (cf. viii. 94 nn.), and H. records this; yet he represents the Corinthian admiral, Adimantus, as having to be bribed by Themistocles to fight at Artemisium (viii. 5. 2), and also as his chief opponent in the Greek councils of war. But these dramatic scenes seem to owe their origin to a misinterpretation of the purpose of Themistocles' message to Xerxes, which was not to compel the Greek, but to induce the Persian, to give battle in the Straits of Salamis (cf. App. XXI. 2). It would seem that Adimantus, whose pride in the part he played in the war is proved by the names of his children, as well as by his epitaph and other incriptions (Plut. de Mal. 39), has had to suffer in the Attic tradition for the sins against Athens of his son Aristeas, who took a leading part in stirring up the Peloponnesian war (cf. vii. 137. 3 n.).

(*d*) **Thebes.** Yet more striking are the differences in the measure meted out to states that favoured the Mede. Thebes

[1] On this whole subject cf. Meyer, F. ii. 196–229.

is assailed with peculiar bitterness. If she sends four hundred men to Thermopylae, they go and stay only under compulsion (vii. 222); though they surrender at the first opportunity, they are by Xerxes' orders branded as slaves (cf. 233. 2 n.). This curious method of encouraging partisans of Persia must surely be an invention of Attic spite (Plut. de Mal. 31, 33), sharpened by the (probably mistaken) tradition that the Theban leader at Thermopylae was Leontiades, father of the man who opened the Peloponnesian war by attacking Plataea. Nor will H. accept the plea, later urged by the Thebans, that their Medism was the work of a narrow clique (Thuc. iii. 62), not of the whole people; he makes the oligarchic leader (ix. 87) Timagenidas declare that the whole state Medized, and insists on the zeal of the Thebans for the Persians (ix. 40, 67).

(*e*) **Argos and Thessaly.** But with the faults of Thessaly and Argos H. deals tenderly; they had joined hands with Athens in 461 B.C., and might do so again.[1] Unquestionably the Thessalian princes had been foremost in inviting Persian intervention (vii. 6. 2, 130. 3; ix. 1), and the whole people had gone over when Xerxes reached their borders. Yet in their case H. admits a plea not allowed the Thebans; the betrayal of Greece is ascribed to the nobles alone, the people do but submit to necessity when the Greeks, by refusing to defend Tempe, surrender Thessaly to the Persian (vii. 172. 1, ix. 1). Yet more remarkable is the case of Argos. The Argives warned Mardonius of Pausanias' march against him (ix. 12. 2), indeed, their neutrality was, under the circumstances, a proof of Medism (viii. 73. 3). Yet H. inclines to accept the Argive apology, with its insistence on gloomy oracles and on the unjust claims of Sparta to hegemony (vii. 148. 4), though the

[1] It may be noted, however, that H. in one case is severe on Phocis (viii. 30), in spite of its Athenian leanings, and still more so on the Athenian ally, Corcyra. For a different estimate of the attitude of Argos cf. Grundy Q. R. 418 (1909), p. 128.

common report spread through Hellas, that Argos was in alliance with Xerxes, was confirmed by the reception accorded later by Artaxerxes to the Argive embassy at Susa (vii. 150. 1).

Yet though H. according to his principle (p. 35) records the pleas for Argos current at Athens, he does not conceal his opinion that the dealings of Argos with the Mede were a stain on the city's honour, only palliated by the misdoings of others (vii. 152, viii. 73). Nor does he paint the Thebans wholly black; he praises the valour of their horsemen at Plataea (ix. 67–9), and records a striking instance of self-sacrificing patriotism in their leader Timagenidas (ix. 87. 2). To the Corinthians moreover, except Adimantus, he is in general favourable; twice they foil unjust Spartan projects for the enslavement of Athens (v. 75, 92), once they reconcile Athens and Thebes (vi. 108. 6); in the Persian war they contribute large contingents both to the fleet (viii. 1. 1; 43) and army (ix. 28. 3), and at Mycale behave with distinguished gallantry (ix. 105).

(*f*) **Athens.** Herodotus does not wholly surrender his judgement to Athenian prejudices. He surely does right in extolling the 'freedom' which encouraged her citizens to devote their whole energies to her service (v. 78), and in defending their claim to be considered the saviours of Hellas (vii. 139. 2 n.) Some exaggeration of their valour at Marathon (vi. 112. 3), heightened by contrast with the slowness of Sparta (viii. 40. 2; ix. 7), is easily pardoned. The most elaborate lauds of Athens (vii. 161. 3, ix. 27) would seem to be a reminiscence of the funeral orations in the Ceramicus,[1] and are suitably put into the mouth of Attic orators. But H. does not hesitate to censure as well as to praise; he represents the Athenian people as suffering tyranny gladly, and as gulled by the childish fraud of Pisistratus (i. 60. 3), or the glib tongue of Aristagoras (v. 97. 2); he condemns their cruelty to the Persian heralds (vii. 133. 2), and implicitly their retention of the Aeginetan hostages (vi. 86); he

[1] Cf. Meyer, F. ii. 219 f.

tells us that Athens set the example of appealing to Persia (v. 73), and admits that up to the day of Marathon there were waverers in her army and traitor within her walls (vi. 109. 5; 115 nn.).

§ 31. **Alcmaeonid tradition in Herodotus.** This recognition of Athenian shortcomings may be due in part to divergent traditions drawn by H. from the records of the two great rival houses, the Alcmaeonidae and the Philaidae. The triumph of democracy and the ascendancy of Pericles had favoured the prevalence of the Alcmaeonid tradition, which is in the main followed. In two points, at least, it would seem to have led him into error; the attempt to clear the house of the guilt incurred by Megacles in the slaughter of Cylon's partisans, leads to a falsification of the early history of the Athenian constitution (cf. v. 71. 2 n.), and the supposed disproof of Alcmaeonid treachery at the time of Marathon will not bear examination (vi. 121 f. n., App. XVIII. 6). Yet H. does not always accept the Alcmaeonid tradition; the victories of Cimon over the Mede had kept the memory of the Philaid Miltiades green, so that the stories [1] of his attempt to rid Hellas of the Persian king at the bridge (iv. 137), of the taking of Lemnos (vi. 136), and above all of the crowning glory at Marathon, have their place in the history of H.

The character of Themistocles. Both of these noble houses, Whig and Tory, united against the upstart democrat Themistocles (vii. 143. 1), and unless the almost unanimous verdict of antiquity is rejected, he was his own worst enemy by his vanity (Plut. Them. 22) and his greed (ib. 25 *ad fin.*). Accordingly we find H. somewhat unfavourable to the most brilliant of Athenian statesmen. The creation of the great navy, and the plan of fighting at sea, could not be denied him, but the final resolve to fight at Salamis is ascribed (in part) to the advice of Mnesiphilus (viii. 57 n.), and the glory of the victory

[1] Possibly these were pleas used at his trials; cf. Macan (1895) p. lxxxvi.; and in general, Nitzsch, Rhein. Mus. 1872.

is dimmed by the victor's attempt to secure himself a refuge at the Persian court (viii. 109. 5). In fine, the ambition of a great leader is represented as mere self-seeking, his cleverness as cunning (viii. 110), while his greed for gain is exaggerated (viii. 4, 5, 112) and emphasized by contrast with the uprightness of Aristides. Thucydides does not deny the moral failings of Themistocles, but he has a juster appreciation of his originality as a statesman (i. 138).

We may sum up that, if now and then there are traces of malice and calumny in the work of H., they come from an over-faithful reproduction of the stories told him, and not from any native malignity; his own judgements are just and even generous; the bent of his mind is towards excess rather than defect of charity.

The question of the impartiality of H. is largely a moral one; the criticisms on his intellectual failings may be more briefly stated; four of these must be emphasized:—

§ 32. **Intellectual defects in Herodotus.** (1) **His history is too theological.** It is written, at any rate in part, to point a moral, and is a sermon on the text, 'pride goeth before a fall.' His general views on religion will be discussed later; here it may be said that in his case the religious machinery is not, as with Livy's[1] 'prodigies', a mere ornament introduced when any striking point is to be emphasized; it is essential to the narrative. And it is necessary to point out that H. is a man of his time, a contemporary of the pious Nicias and of the men who went mad at the mutilation of the Hermae. Moreover, the very nature of his sources (*vid.* p. 31) made emphasis of immediate divine action inevitable. When his evidence is good, H. is not afraid to suggest an alternative explanation for the accredited miracles of his day (cf. vii. 189. 3, 191. 2); but the fact remains that with H. the philosophy of history is wholly theological.

[1] But cf. Fowler, Religious Experience of the Roman People, p. 316, and Lect. XIV generally, for a different view of Livy.

(2) **Fondness for the marvellous.** The second charge against H. is that he has a foolish fondness for the marvellous; even in his own day this was obviously a joke against him,[1] and it has always been so; he was certainly in Juvenal's mind when he wrote 'Quidquid Graecia mendax Audet in historia' (Sat. x. 174). This charge is of course true, especially in the matter of numbers; H.'s estimate of the Persian army (vii. 185–6) is hopeless.[2] It is true that nothing is so difficult to estimate as the numbers of a crowd or an army, and figures to the ordinary man have little meaning or importance; but H.'s mistake is a deliberate one; though it does not invalidate his testimony as to the facts of the Persian war, it must always remain a serious count against him as a historian. And, indeed, it must be frankly stated that H.'s attitude to the world of history and of nature is like that of the Elizabethan navigators. He and they had seen so many marvels which were real that they were quite prepared to accept other marvels on hearsay, which the superior knowledge of later times has shown not to be real. But modern science is much kinder to H. in this matter than was the 'critical' attitude of the early Victorian scholars; Mure spends many pages (iv. 382–92) in enumerating the marvels of H., and concludes: 'it could hardly fail that a man who believed such stories, would become the butt of humorous or malicious persons'; yet some of the very stories that he quotes with contempt are now used by anthropologists like Tylor and Westermarck as most valuable materials for reconstructing the primitive history of mankind.

(2) **Contradictions in the history.** Little need be said as to the contradictions in the work of H., of which some critics make much. They are bound to exist in a work drawn

[1] Cf. Aristoph. Birds 1130 with ii. 127. 1, and i. 4. 2 n.

[2] 5,283,220! It should be noticed, however, that the Greek contemporary estimate of the fighting men (3,000,000, vii. 228) exceeded considerably that of H. Cf. App. XIX. 3 for whole subject.

from many sources and written at many times and in many places; but their importance has been much exaggerated. The best known instance is perhaps vi. 112. 3. H. here is writing dramatically; he means just what Creasy[1] means when he writes: '(Marathon) broke the spell of Persian invincibility, which had paralysed men's minds'; neither statement is literally true; both give a correct impression. (Cf. also viii. 132. 3 n. and i. 71, contrasted with i. 126. 3–5.)

(4) **Failure to appreciate real causes of events.** The last and most serious charge that is brought against the work of H. is his weakness in tracing the real relation of events; he continually confuses the mere occasion and the cause[2]; he has nothing of the greatness of Aristotle, who knows that (Pol. v. 4. 1, 1303 B) *γίγνονται αἱ στάσεις οὐ περὶ μικρῶν ἀλλ' ἐκ μικρῶν, στασιάζουσι δὲ περὶ μεγάλων.* Hence H. is always laying stress on personal activity and motive, and understands little of the great movements of which persons are only the expression. The best instance perhaps is his treatment of Cleisthenes, the Athenian legislator (cf. v. 69 nn.); the measures which founded the first true democracy are put down to imitation of a maternal grandfather! It is only necessary to compare Aristotle's penetrating analysis of the same facts (Pol. vi. 4. 19, 1319 B), an analysis as illuminating for modern Reform Bills as for ancient, to see the difference between the insight of the real historian and the uncertain vision of the childhood of history. Similarly the chief battles of the Persian war dissolve away into a series of isolated combats and romantic incidents, because H. has little grasp of tactics or strategy, though he appreciates two great causes of the Persians' defeat—the inferior arms of the land troops (vii. 211. 2; ix. 62. 3) and the overcrowding and consequent confusion in the fleet (viii. 16. 2; 86).

[1] Decisive Battles, p. 47.

[2] Plut. de Mal. H. 21 makes this point well against the explanation of Lacedaemonian policy in iii. 47; but see App. XVI. 10.

In fact, with H. everything is personal ; this is illustrated by the dramatic way in which he tells his story. To him is first due the custom which prevailed so long in history, both ancient and modern, of putting imaginary speeches in the mouths of real persons. Such a method was natural to a Greek trained on poetry ; it says much for the conservatism of mankind that it prevailed so long after the conditions of its origin had disappeared.

§ 33. **Merits of Herodotus' history.** But to recognize H.'s weakness on this point is only to say that history with him was not born complete and at once. It may be claimed with confidence that his merits far outweigh his defects. Three points must be insisted on :—

(1) As has been said, he really does attempt to test various kinds of evidence and to estimate their degrees of value. This is the foundation of history. Perhaps Hecataeus had done this before him ; he certainly seems to adopt a critical attitude in the well-known opening of his history : *τάδε γράφω ὥς μοι ἀληθέα δοκέει εἶναι· οἱ γὰρ Ἑλλήνων λόγοι πολλοί τε καὶ γελοῖοι* (fr. 332) ; but how far this claim was justified, we do not know. All we do know is that H. is the first writer who has survived to give us real history.

(2) Even if in this he were anticipated by Hecataeus, his second merit is all his own ; he is the first to construct a long and elaborate narrative, in which many parts are combined in due subordination and arrangement to make one great whole. This is well brought out by Dionysius of Halicarnassus in his contrast between H. and Thucydides (Epist. ad Cn. Pomp. c. 3 ; vi. 774): *συμβέβηκε τῷ μὲν* (Thucydides) *μίαν ὑπόθεσιν λαβόντι, πολλὰ ποιῆσαι μέρη τὸ ἓν σῶμα· τῷ δὲ* (H.) *τὰς πολλὰς καὶ οὐδὲν ἐοικυίας ὑποθέσεις προελομένῳ σύμφωνον ἓν σῶμα πεποιηκέναι* ; the whole comparison is worth reading, whatever we may think of the critic's preference for the elder historian. The elaborate structure of H.'s work and the skilful parallelism between its

various parts have never been better shown than in Macan's analyses.

(3) So far we have dealt with H.'s claims on the student of history in the strict sense. But it is for another reason that the world generally values him most highly; he is one of the great story-tellers of mankind; to him, as to Tacitus or to Macaulay, all can be forgiven, for they are never dull. This gift looks the easiest of all for a historian; it is in reality the rarest. And in his case the merit is all the greater because he was a pioneer; to quote Dionysius again (Thuc. c. 23; vi. 865), H. first gave prose the attractiveness of poetry, *παρεσκεύασε τῇ κρατίστῃ ποιήσει τὴν πεζὴν φράσιν ὁμοίαν γενέσθαι.*

§ 34. **Herodotus as a portrayer of character.** It is needless to illustrate the charm of his narrative. In his character sketches, however, the success is rather artistic than scientific. Often he shows inconsistency in his judgements; for instance, he never determines whether Cambyses and Cleomenes were insane by nature and throughout their lives, or were visited with madness as a punishment for impiety. Even of Xerxes H. does not give us a comprehensive judgement: he brings out individual traits, but does not combine them into a character. Xerxes shows a royal liberality to those who have done him service (vii. 29. 2), a royal mercy to captured spies (vii. 146. 3), and surrendered heralds (vii. 136. 2). He recognizes the loyalty of those who give him frank (e. g. Artemisia, viii. 69; Demaratus, vii. 237), if unpalatable, advice; and though unable to brook opposition (vii. 11. 1), will after reflection apologize for his anger (vii. 13. 2) and acknowledge his error. But there is a dark side to the character of this typical sultan; his pretended courage (vii. 50. 1) fails him under defeat (viii. 103. 1); if he listens to the advice of counsellors, he never follows it unless it agrees with his own inclination. In spite of a fear of the supernatural (vii. 191. 2, 197. 4), which drives him even to human sacrifice (vii. 114. 1), he cannot refrain from insults to the gods (vii. 35. 2). Oriental barbarities are sparingly recorded (vii. 35, 38. 9), but there is no reason to doubt that incest and murder stained the Persian, like other Eastern courts (ix. 107). Rather it is to be feared that the noble traits in the character are fictitious ; certainly the scenes where H. carries pyschological portraiture furthest, the interviews with Artabanus and with Demaratus, are most open to suspicion ; here if anywhere we have to do with dramatic invention, not tradition.[1]

Characters more remote from the historian's day are painted with a yet freer hand. In the case of Croesus, a certain epic unity had been given the tradition before it reached H. ; he, in his interview with Solon, shows the overweening pride of a barbarian, but his sorrows teach him wisdom. Yet the change of character does not involve inconsistency ; there is a trace of the old pride in his longing to taunt Apollo with perfidy, just as the later nobler Croesus is revealed in his forgiveness of Adrastus for his son's death. But this unity is not the result of adherence to historic fact, but rather the work of creative imagination.

§ 35. **Herodotus' theological attitude.** But it may well be said that literary art with H. is largely a means of religious teaching. The history of nations is but the grand stage on which may be seen the workings of Divine Providence. That H. was not unaffected by the questioning spirit of his age has been noticed above ; he says that the whole scheme of the Greek Pantheon is the work of the poets (ii. 53. 2) ; he also seems to contrast Greek anthropomorphism unfavourably with Persian nature-worship (i. 131. 1), and he sees its impure elements, e. g. the rites of Dionysus (ii. 49, 1; iv. 79). But all this rationalistic criticism does not lead him to deny either the existence of the gods or their intervention in human affairs. Their appearance on earth is rare (vi. 105. 1), but the indication of their will by dreams, omens, and oracles is frequent and

[1] Cf. further Bruns, Das literarische Porträt der Griechen, pp. 71–114.

incontestable (viii. 77). The historian frankly craves pardon for anything that may seem to detract from the honour of the gods (ii. 45. 3).

§ 36. **His religious pessimism.** But while the manifestations of divine power are almost as frequent in H. as in Homer, the gods are further removed from men; there is more unity, less personal caprice, in their action. H. does not find it easy to trace the principles of divine rule; in this he differs from the thinkers of the preceding generation, who had boldly 'justified the ways of God to men'; every play of Aeschylus is a complete theodicy; but H. shares the half-conscious pessimism of the masses, who could not rise to the ethical conceptions of Aeschylus and Pindar, and who were oppressed by the apparent injustice of the world, by the riddles of life. H. then resigns himself to accept facts which are beyond mortal comprehension. In Nature, indeed, God appears as a principle of order (ii. 52. 1), and Providence is kindly in the balance it maintains (iii. 108. 2), but this very principle of balance presses hard on the individual man. The doctrine of Nemesis is set forth in the story of Croesus in its crudest form; God will have none exalted but himself.[1]

It may seem strange that the piety of H. did not revolt from such a view of the Deity. But we must remember that while mere prosperity did in itself provoke divine jealousy, yet as a rule it was accompanied by pride and presumption (cf. i. 32. 1 nn., i. 34. 1), and frequently by guilt, personal or inherited (i. 91. 1). And in the most striking cases, those of Croesus and Xerxes, the application of the doctrine had been already accepted by his countrymen as a historic fact. In these parts of his narrative (Bks. I and VII–IX), H. uses the stronger and more human words *φθόνος* and *νέμεσις*, but vaguer and more abstract expres-

[1] Cf. *τὸ θεῖον πᾶν φθονερόν τε καὶ ταραχῶδες*, i. 32. 1 nn.; also iii. 40. 2; and vii. 10. 1; vii. 46. 4.

sions, such as τίσις and δίκη in the story of the Scythian expedition or of the Ionic revolt.[1]

H., like Sophocles, saw that in this world the innocent suffer as well as the guilty, and refused to explain away what was inexplicable. Hence in both writers there is a profound sadness,[2] due not to weariness of life, but to a sense of the limitations of man's lot. In Periclean Athens there was still that religious faith which alone can produce great art, but it had lost the triumphant certainty of Aeschylus, and had not yet been re-established by Socrates and Plato.

The doctrine of Nemesis. The doctrine of Nemesis profoundly affected the history of H., it supplied a theological solution for moral and political problems, and so often prevented him from seeing the real springs of events. Thus he cannot be accounted a scientific or philosophical historian. His credulous piety, his love of anecdote and romance, his inaccuracy in statistics and chronology, above all, his lack of military knowledge and of political insight, made it impossible for him to forestall Thucydides. Yet if H. is something less than a historian he is also far more. He is the prince of biographers and story-tellers. he is a great geographer, and a still greater anthropologist. In spite of many mistakes in details, his panorama of the ancient civilization (Bk. I–III), and of the more primitive barbarism Bk. IV) of the world, remains among the most instructive as well as the most delightful of histories. If his account of the Persian wars is permeated with patriotic and religious feeling, yet we gain from its warmth and colour a deeper insight into the heart and mind of Hellas than if we had only the cold dry light of criticism to guide us. And throughout, the broad sympathies and the sterling honesty of an indefatigable seeker after truth more than compensate for defects in critical acumen. To none of his many successors does History in the largest sense owe more than to its founder and father, Herodotus.

[1] Macan (1895) cxiv. seq. [2] Cf. Meyer, F ii. 254 f.; Soph. O. C. 1226 f.

NOTE I.

Events subsequent to the Capture of Sestos mentioned in Books VII–IX (cf. p. 14) with Dates.

1. Transfer of naval hegemony to Athens. 478. viii. 3.
2. Story of Masistes. 478 (?). ix. 108 seq.
3. Capture of Eion. 476. vii. 107.
4. Expulsion of Persians from Thrace. vii. 106.
   (Doriscus is not taken till after, at earliest, 465.)
5. Defeat of Tarentines by Iapygians. 473. vii. 170.

6 and 7. Battles of Tegea and Dipaeeis (between 473 and 470). ix. 35.

8. Death of Hermolycus in the war of Carystus. *Circ.* 470. ix. 105.
9. Flight of Themistocles to Persia. 466. viii. 109.
10. Expulsion of Micythus from Rhegium. 466. vii. 170.
11. Death of Sophanes at Datum. 465. ix. 75.
12. Third Messenian War. 464. ix. 35, 64.
13. Death of Achaemenes in Egypt. 460. vii. 7.
14. Capture of Halieis. (Between 460 and 455.) vii. 137.
15. Battle of Tanagra. 457. ix. 35.
16. Peace of Callias. *Circ.* 448. vii. 151.
17. Death of Amestris. *Circ.* 430. vii. 114.
18. Theban attack on Plataea. 431. vii. 233.
19. Sparing of Decelea. 431. ix. 73.
20. Execution of Lacedaemonian ambassadors. 430. vii. 137.

It will be obvious that many of these dates are only approximate.

This note has been based on Macan (1908) p. li., but neither his exact dates nor his order has been altogether followed. He collects some fifteen other passages in these books, in which reference is made to rewards or punishments on the Greek or the Persian side, and to monuments commemorating those who fell in the war. But it is obvious that these prove nothing as to the date of writing Books VII–IX ; they could only have been mentioned in these books, whether written first or last.

NOTE II.

The present division of the books of H. dates from Alexandrian times : it is first used by Lucian (Herodotus c. 1, i. 833). For H.'s own divisions of his work cf. v. 36. 2 n. ; also i. 75 and 107 f., and vii. 93. The whole subject is well discussed by Mure IV. 474 f. and V. 623 f.

BOOK I

THE opening sentence embodies the title in the work. Cf. the opening words of Hecataeus (fr. 332) Ἑ. Μιλήσιος ὧδε μυθεῖται and Thuc. i. 1. Θουρίου (*vid.* app. crit.) seems to have been the usual reading at the end of the fourth century (cf. Duris of Samos, fr. 57, F. H. G. ii. 482). Plutarch (Mor. 605) writes Ἡ. Ἁλικαρνασσέως ἱστορίης ἀπόδειξις ἥδε· πολλοὶ μεταγράφουσιν Ἡροδότου Θουρίου, μετῴκησε γὰρ εἰς Θουρίους, which seems to be intended to reconcile the two traditions. The Alexandrine librarians, however, must have had good reasons for restoring Ἁλικ. in the text. (For H.'s birth, &c., cf. Introd. §§ 1–2.)

ἱστορίης: properly 'inquiry', and so the 'result of inquiry' (ii. 99. 1); only once in H. = 'history' (vii. 96. 1) in the modern sense. Croiset (Litt. Grec. ii. 589) well says that the word 'marks a literary revolution'; the λογογράφοι had written down the current stories, the historian sets out to 'find' the truth.

The reason given for writing is characteristic of H.; he is the born chronicler, and his interest is in the past: Thucydides (i. 22. 4) is the scientific historian, and his eye is on the future—τῶν γενομένων τὸ σαφὲς σκοπεῖν καὶ τῶν μελλόντων ποτὲ αὖθις κατὰ τὸ ἀνθρώπινον τοιούτων καὶ παραπλησίων ἔσεσθαι.

The **ἔργα** are the permanent results, 'monuments', &c.

τά τε ἄλλα is in loose apposition to τὰ γενόμενα and ἔργα.

1 1 **οἱ λόγιοι** (= 'skilled in history') cf. ii. 3. 1. H.'s story is decidedly Greek, and not Persian, in colouring: cf. vi. 54; vii. 150. 2 for a like (supposed) Persian acquaintance with Greek myths; a similar knowledge is attributed to the Egyptians ii. 91. 5. Such combinations certainly come from Greek sources, not native ones.

Φοίνικας. The name (whence Lat. 'Poenus') seems to be pure Greek; it certainly occurs in places where there is no trace of foreign influence; e. g. the harbour Φοινικοῦς, near Erythrae (Thuc. viii. 34), a stream near Thermopylae, &c. (Meyer, ii. 92). As applied to a race, it may well be a colour name, 'Red men'; cf. Αἰθίοψ and 'White Syrians' (6. 1 n.). This derivation, however, is not inconsistent with it being also a foreign name. The old connexion with 'Fenchu', supposed to occur at Karnak in the inscriptions of Thothmes III, is now given up; others see in the name the Egyptian 'Punt', the land of South Arabia and East Africa. This last is the view of E. Gläser, Punt und die Südarabischen Reiche

(1899), who holds that from this 'original home' (p. 62) the Phoenicians spread both north (*v. i.*) and south to Mashonaland and Socotra; he says (p. 65) the gods of Phoenicia can be almost all easily recognized as South Arabian. This derivation would agree with the legend of their migration from the shores of the Indian Ocean (vii. 89. 2), which first occurs here; for a later version cf. Strabo, 766 (based on Androsthenes, a seaman of Alexander), who says that the islands of Tyros (*v. l.* Tylos) and Arados (*hod.* Bahrein) in the Persian Gulf claimed to be the mother cities of the Phoenician towns; he elsewhere (35) rejects the story. Justin (xviii. 3) actually professes to give their route when migrating: for a discussion of these passages cf. Maspero, ii. 63 seq., who accepts the general fact of the migration from the south-east, and dates it soon after 3000 B.C., on the evidence of ii. 44. 3. General probability confirms this north-west movement of the Semitic peoples, though Meyer (i. 356) rejects the whole story. The position of the Phoenicians, wedged in on the narrow strip of coast, shows they were the earliest among the Semitic migrants (cf. the position of the Celtic peoples in Wales, Brittany, &c.). But beyond this all is uncertain.

Ἐρυθρῆς θαλάσσης (cf. ii. 8. 1 *et pass.*). H. means by this all the water south-east and south of Asia; our 'Red Sea' was its western limit, and has the special name of Ἀράβιος κόλπος (ii. 102. 2 *et pass.*); beyond it to the south-west lay ἡ νοτίη θάλασσα (iv. 42. 3); the Persian Gulf proper has no special name in H. (cf. i. 180. 1, where the Euphrates runs into the Ἐρυθρὴ θάλασσα). The name 'Red Sea' is Egyptian, and is derived perhaps from the colour of the sand.

2 The pre-eminence of Argos in early times is an inference from Homer, and even more from the Cyclic poems, e.g. the Thebais and the Epigoni (cf. v. 67 n.). Hellas did not obtain its name till after the Dorian invasion (cf. i. 58 nn.).

φόρτον. For the scene here described cf. Od. xv. 416 (**Φοίνικες**) μυρί' ἄγοντες ἀθύρματα νηὶ μελαίνῃ.

3 That Io was the daughter of Inachus was the usual form of the legend (cf. Apollod. ii. 1. 3; F. H. G. i. 125; who gives two other forms). The cow-headed Io of Argos is another form of Hera (cf. Homeric epithet βοῶπις; but see Farnell G. C. i. 16), and represents the cow-goddess of an early race; this animal-worship was not understood, and so was explained by a myth. Io, whose descendant, Danaus, migrates from Egypt to Argos, was identified with Isis; the identification was probably due in part to similarity of name, in part to the resemblance of the horned maiden, Io, to Hathor-Isis (see ii. 41. 1 n.). This identification may be subsequent to the foundation of Naucratis, but more probably belongs to Mycenaean times. H. rationalizes the old myths into plain matter of fact (cf. ii. 56–7 for the similar treatment of the myth of Dodona and Intr. § 26).

2 1 The usual Greek myth (not in H.) was that Io was turned into a heifer, and wandered till she came to Egypt, where she bore Epaphus (Apis; cf. ii. 38. 1 n.).

βασιλέος. Homer calls him 'Phoenix' (Il. xiv. 321), but H. gives the usual form 'Agenor' (iv. 147. 4; in vi. 47. 1 we must translate *Θάσου τοῦ Φοίνικος* 'Thasus the Phoenician').

Κρῆτες. This is H.'s own suggestion; the usual form of the legend was that Europa bore Minos and Rhadamanthus to Zeus in Crete; he means that, if this were properly interpreted, it would agree with the Persian version here told; 'these would then be Cretans.' The words *ταῦτα μὲν κτλ.* imply that the balance of criminality now was equal; hence the Greeks were really to blame for the next act of aggression.

2 **μακρῇ.** 'A ship of war' is emphatic; it was an organized raid.

τἆλλα: i. e. the winning of the Golden Fleece.

3 1 **δευτέρῃ**: translate 'the next generation'; the children of the Argonauts took part in the Trojan War. H. counts inclusively.

4 2 **νομίζειν**, 'they (i. e. the Persians) thought.'

ἀνοήτων. H. probably saw the humour of this argument; but this part of his history gave offence. It was parodied by Aristophanes (Achar. 524 seq. *ἐκ τριῶν λαικαστριῶν*), as to the origin of the Peloponnesian War; and 'Plutarch' (de Malig. 11) is very angry at the 'passive resistance' imputed to the much-respected Io, and that 'the fairest and greatest exploit of Greece, the Trojan War, should be put down as *ἀβελτερία*' ('fatuity'). For other parodies of H. cf. Achar. 82–6 with 133. 1 and 192. 1; Av. 552 and 1124 seq. with 179. 1 (Babylon), Av. 1130 with ii. 127. 1 (measurement of pyramid), Av. 1142 seq. with ii. 136. 4, Nub. 273 with ii. 25 and (perhaps) Av. 488 with vii. 14. These references prove how soon the work of H. became well known. (See Note B, p. 448.)

Ἀσίην. For the Persian claim to Asia cf. ix. 116. 3.

5 2 **ἐθελοντήν.** For this form of the story cf. Od. xv. 420 seq.

3 **ἐπεξιών**: translate 'dealing with'. The phrase used (with which cf. *oratione obire*), and the reference to Od. i. 3 *πολλῶν ἀνθρώπων ἴδεν ἄστεα*, suggest the author's wide travels.

H.'s religious feeling shows itself at once; he desires not only to record men's 'great deeds', but to show the instability of human fortune (cf. c. 32 nn.). The idea was a commonplace with the Ionian philosophers, e.g. Xenophanes *ἀεὶ δ' ἐν ταὐτῷ μίμνει κινούμενον οὐδέν* (R. and P. p. 84), and with the Greeks generally, e. g. Soph. Trach. 132 seq.

6–94 *The Lydian history* (of course, with digressions, especially cc. 56–68).

6 1 H. ignores the upper course of the Halys, where it flows from north-east to south-west; it was its lower course which formed the boundary of the Lydian Empire; cf. c. 72 for a fuller account of it.

By 'Syrians' H. means the North Cappadocians (i. 72. 1), called by Strabo (542, 737) also 'the White Syrians', in contrast to the darker Syrians of the Levant. Some have distinguished Σύριοι (= 'Cappadocians') from Σύροι (= 'the inhabitants of Palestine'), but the variety of spelling seems due merely to copyists. The name is probably a corruption of 'Assyrian'; H. (vii. 63) actually uses it of the Assyrians, and says 'Syrian' is the Greek, 'Assyrian' the barbarous form. When the Greeks came in contact with the empire of Assyria in the eighth century, e. g. from Sinope, they began to use the term of all its subjects; the name first occurs in Pindar, fr. 173 (in Strabo, 544), the Amazons Σύριον εὐρυαίχμαν δίεπον στρατόν, which Strabo says refers to the settlement at Themiscyra near Amisus.

2 **πρῶτος.** H. shows real insight in seeing that, though the complete conquest of the Asiatic Greeks by Lydia was brief, it was an event of first-rate importance, as the 'beginning' of the subjection of Greeks to barbarians.

3 For the Cimmerians cf. 15 nn.

7 2 Nicolaus Damascenus (F. H. G. iii. 383) calls Candaules 'Sadyattes'. Hesychius (*s. v.* Κυνάγχη) says that Κανδαύλας = Hermes or Heracles (cf. Hipponax, fr. 1, Ἑρμῆ κυνάγχα, Μῃονιστὶ κανδαῦλα); in this case 'C.' may be a cult-name, assumed by the king in addition to his own (cf. the new names taken by Popes).

Hall (J. H. S. xxix. 19) points out that the name Μυρσίλος ('Mursil') has been found by Winckler at Boghaz Keui as that of a Hittite king. He suggests that the name, which is that of Pelops' charioteer, tends to confirm the old tradition that Pelops was an immigrant into Greece, and to show that perhaps in the fourteenth century B. C., Greece was subject to a Hittite dynasty.

Σαρδίων. H. almost always follows (cf. iii. 120. 1 n.) the Persian usage in calling the Lydian satrapy by the name of its capital.

Ἀλκαίου. H. is the only writer who mentions Alcaeus as the son of Heracles, though both the grandfather of Heracles and Heracles himself (Diod. i. 24) are sometimes called Alcaeus.

The Greeks identified the Asiatic Bel, in Cilicia (Meyer, i. 484) and perhaps in Lydia called 'Sandon' (cf. i. 71. 2), with Heracles, because he was a lion-tamer and a bow-bearer; he was probably a sun-god, though Meyer (*v. s.*) makes him a vegetation-god.

H.'s list, then, may be a piece of genuine native tradition with Graecized names; at the head of it appear two great deities, Heracles and Omphale, representing the sun-god and Ashtoreth. But H. is inconsistent in vii. 61, where he makes Perseus, an ancestor of Heracles, rescue Andromeda, the granddaughter of Belus. It is more probable, however, that Heracles has no proper place in the genealogy, and is brought in by a piece of Greek syncretism, because the δούλη (§ 4) was supposed to be Omphale. The genealogy itself seems hopelessly confused; the (otherwise unknown, *v. s.*) son of a Greek hero is father of a Babylonian god and grandfather of the eponymous hero of Nineveh.

While, however, the form in which the genealogy is presented is Greek, it may represent a real tradition of early connexion with the East. This can hardly have been with the great kingdoms of the Euphrates valley, for Assurbanipal states that when the ambassadors of 'Gugu of Luddi' arrived at Nineveh (R. P. i.[1] 68), 'the king's very fathers had not heard speak of its name'; but it may have been with the Hittite empire in Asia Minor, as was suggested by Sayce (ad loc.) as long ago as 1883. Hogarth says (I. and E., p. 75): 'it may well be that the rock monuments near Smyrna are memorials of a definite political occupation by the power of the Hatti.' Garstang too (p. 63) is disposed to accept H.'s traditions as having elements of truth in them.

Ninus was, according to the Greeks (Ctes. Ass. ii, p. 390), the founder of Nineveh; but his name does not appear on the monuments.

Belus is properly a common name, 'lord,' but became identified with the chief god of Babylonia (cf. Hastings' D. of B., *s.v.* Baal).

3 This dynasty traced back its descent to the god Μήν (J. H. S. xix. 80); it has a more genuine sound than that of the Heracleids above. The dynasty was

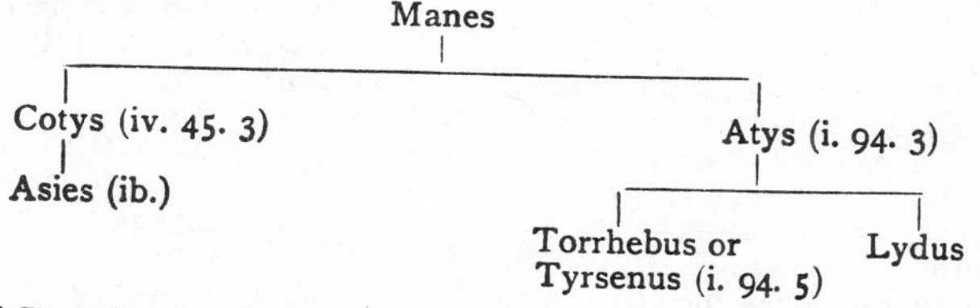

If Cotys be rightly connected with the Thracian goddess Cotytto, whose rites (Strabo, 470) were like those of the Phrygian Cybele, then the genealogy may represent the combination of the European (Cotys) and the Asiatic (Atys) elements (App. I. 4); but all this is most uncertain.

Μηίων. For 'Maeonians' cf. App. I. 8. Homer only knows this name (Il. ii. 864; x. 431, &c.); the earliest occurrence of 'Lydian' in a Greek author is in Xanthus, fr. 1. The identification of Maeonians with Lydians was not always accepted (Strabo, 572). Assuming its truth, however, it may be conjectured that the Lydians represent rather the European element in the people, the Maeonian the Asiatic. Radet (p. 59) thinks that the statement on the monuments of Assurbanipal (*u. s.*) means only that the Luddi were unknown *by that name*; he therefore connects 'Lydian' with the rise of Gyges; but this is very doubtful. 'Maeonian' survived as a tribal name

(vii. 77), and as the name of a city (Plin. N. H. v. 111) and a district on the upper Hermus (Strabo, 576, 628), including the Κατακεκαυμένη.

4 **δούλης.** The usual story (Apollod. ii. 6. 3) is unknown to H.; it called Omphale a daughter of Iardanus (whose name may be Semitic, cf. 'Jordan'), and made Hercules her bought slave. Later writers, especially the Roman poets, make him assume women's dress and do women's work. Meyer (i. 487) considers that this story is based upon the special Anatolian rites of the great nature-goddess, in which her worshippers cut themselves in sympathy with her sorrows, and even unsexed themselves (cf. story of Attis); so, too, maidens sacrificed their chastity to her (cf. 93. 4; 199 nn.). But if this is the origin of the myth, it is curious that its special feature, the woman's dress, &c., appears only in late versions. It seems better, therefore, to compare the story of Hercules serving Omphale with that of Apollo serving Admetus, and to explain both as a sort of atonement by service; the price of blood shed is worked off in this way.

Whence H. derived the figure 505 is a puzzle. According to some it is a calculation based on the average length of a reign; if a generation was taken at $33\frac{1}{3}$ years (ii. 142. 2), a reign might average $22\frac{1}{2}$. R. Schubert (Kön. von Lyd., p. 8) adds the five generations of the Mermnadae (c. 13) to the 22 here, and allows an average of 25 years per generation, thus getting ($27 \times 25 =$) 675 for the total. Deductig the 170 years of the Mermnadae, he gets the 505 given to the Heraclidae (cf. App. XIV. 5). This is plausible, but only one thing is certain, that the figures have no historic value.

8 1 Gyges is called son of 'Dascylus' (Nic. Dam., fr. 49; F. H. G. iii. 383), a name which suggests 'Dascyleum', a town on the south-east of the Propontis, which gave its name to a Persian satrapy. This connexion agrees with the Northern origin suggested for the Mermnadae (App. I. 8), and would explain why a town, otherwise unimportant, was made a centre of Persian government, as being the origin of an earlier royal house.

ὑπερετίθετο, 'communicated' (cf. 107. 1); it governs also τὸ εἶδος, ὑπερεπαινέων being added epexegetically.

It is curious that the only other story of Candaules also implies aesthetic enthusiasm; he bought a picture by Bularchus of the 'proelium Magnetum' for its weight in gold (Plin. N. H. xxxv. 55). Radet (p. 131) accepts both stories. It is safer to reject both; but if the 'battle of the Magnesia' be a reality and be that against the Cimmerians, their raids must be antedated.

Some suppose H. to be imitating Heraclitus (fr. 15) ὀφθαλμοὶ τῶν 2 ὤτων ἀκριβέστεροι μάρτυρες; but the sentiment is a common one (cf. 'seeing is believing') and the verbal resemblance nil. The gnomic character of the story is obvious; cf. σκοπέειν τινὰ τὰ ἑαυτοῦ.

9 1 **ἀρχήν,** 'at all,' put first for the sake of emphasis (cf. iii. 39. 4);

but in ix. 60. 2 ἀρχήν = 'to begin with', and this may be the sense everywhere in H.

2 The door 'stood open' for light and air; the present participle (for the past) is common in H.

10 3 'Even for a man', much more for a woman. For the contrast of barbarian and Greek feeling cf. Thuc. i. 6. 5 and Pl. Rep. v. 452 C, who points out that it was only recently the Greek ideas of propriety had changed.

11 1 **φοιτᾶν.** These visits to the queen are purely Greek; a Lydian queen would be secluded in the harem.

3 **ἐνδέειν.** Cf. Il. ii. 111 *Ζεύς με μέγα Κρονίδης ἄτῃ ἐνέδησε βαρείῃ.*

4 **αἱρέεται**: asyndeton used for colloquial effect; cf. *τέῳ καί*, 'just in what way,' for another vivid colloquialism.

12 2 It is quite in accordance with Eastern usage that the usurper should take the wife of his predecessor. Cf. 2 Sam. xvi. 21–2 (Absalom and David), and iii. 68. 3.

τοῦ καὶ. The editors bracket these lines, which disturb the connexion, and the technical *ἰάμβῳ τριμέτρῳ* is suspicious; H. (47. 2 *et al.*) uses *τόνῳ.* But Crusius, P. W. (*s. v.* Archilochus), accepts them as genuine. The line of Archil. (fr. 25) is *οὔ μοι τὰ Γύγεω τοῦ πολυχρύσου μέλει* (cf. Arist. Rhet. iii. 17, 1418 b).

13 The decision of the Pythia may perhaps be historic; Gyges' gifts were probably given for a good reason (cf. *ἀπέπεμψε*, 'he duly sent,' 14. 1); but the prophecy of future vengeance is clearly *post eventum.* H.'s simple faith (*λόγον οὐδένα κτλ.*) might almost be irony. Cf. viii. 96. 2 for a similar instance of an oracle, if not conveniently remembered, at least only understood, after fulfilment.

14 This chapter, and still more cc. 50–1, are important as illustrating the sources of H. (cf. Intr. § 24). It may be noted, however, that, while he repeats the stories of the Delphic sacristans, he tries, here as elsewhere, to exercise his critical faculty (14. 2; 51. 3, 4); he did not reproduce his information mechanically (as Nitzsch maintains, R. M. 1872, Intr. § 28), but blended one story with another.

2 Important states had their own treasuries, where the dedicated objects were under the national charge. The importance of Corinth is seen in the fact that foreign kings put their offerings under its care (so Midas *inf.*; Croesus, 50. 3; Euelthon of (Cypriot) Salamis, iv. 162. 3). For this treasury cf. Frazer, P. v. 295; its remains were discovered by the French in 1893. For the treasuries at Olympia and elsewhere cf. Dyer, J. H. S. xxv. 294 seq.; no foreign treasury is known but the *οἶκος Λυδῶν* at Delos (ib. 309). For Cypselus cf. v. 92 n. This passage illustrates the constant endeavour of tyrants to conciliate important shrines; so the mediaeval tyrants in Italy sought confirmation of their usurpations from the Holy See or the Holy Roman Empire. After the overthrow of the Cypselids Delphi permitted this change in the dedications, but the Eleans refused to allow it at Olympia (Plut. De Pyth. Orac. 13).

3 The kings were alternately 'Midas' and 'Gordias' (cf. the place-names Mideum and Gordium. For Phrygia and Midas cf. App. I. 7).

προκατίζων. *προ* is emphatic, 'sat for judgement and gave justice.' Cf. 97. 1.

ἐπωνυμίην: cogn. accus. with *καλέεται*. For *Γυγάδας* cf. 94. 1 n.; the Doric form is retained.

καί: as well as his successors. The attack on Miletus was un-4 successful, and Gyges seems to have entered into friendly relations with the city; he 'allowed' it to plant Abydos on the Hellespont (Strabo, 590). No doubt the common danger from the Cimmerians led to this attempt to guard the north-west entrance into Asia. Gyges was also repulsed at Smyrna (Paus. iv. 21. 5, and Mimnermus, frs. 13, 14). Stein takes *τὸ ἄστυ* as emphatic, the 'lower town' as opposed to the citadel. For the history generally cf. Theognis, 1103–4 *ὕβρις καὶ Μάγνητας ἀπώλεσε καὶ Κολοφῶνα καὶ Σμύρνην*.

Gyges attacked the Greeks at the mouths of the great river-valleys, i. e. Maeander (Miletus), Cayster (Colophon), Hermus (Smyrna); the Lydian kings naturally wished to obtain the trade-outlets to the Aegean. H.'s account of Gyges' campaigns is very insufficient; he also conquered the Troad (Strabo, 590), and Caria seems to have been subject to him; perhaps also he took Magnesia (on the Hermus: Nic. Dam. fr. 62). (See Note C, p. 448.)

The Cimmerians of fable (cf. Hom. Od. xi. 15 seq. *οὐδέ ποτ᾽ αὐτοὺς | 15 Ἠέλιος φαέθων καταδέρκεται ἀκτίνεσσιν*) lived in perpetual darkness; cf. our 'Cimmerian', a use as old as Milton's L'Allegro, 'In dark Cimmerian desert ever dwell.'

For the Cimmerian invasion in H. cf. also cc. 103, 105–6, and (especially) iv. 11–12. It is an event of the greatest importance; the main points as to it may be summarized under four heads.

1. **Its course**. The Cimmerians seem to have lived originally in South Russia (cf. iv. 12. 1 and 'Crimea'): they were expelled thence by the Scythians, who were fleeing 'across the Araxes' (probably the Volga) from the Massagetae (iv. 11. 1). This 'common tradition of Greeks and barbarians' (iv. 12. 3) may well be true; it is in accordance with all analogy. As to the route, however, which the Cimmerians took, opinion is much divided. H. is clearly wrong in his details: (1) he brings the horde along the east coast of the Black Sea, which is impossible, owing to its precipitous nature; (2) he combines the original expulsion of the Cimmerians from Europe (end of eighth century) with the Scythian raids of the last quarter of the seventh century (c. 103 nn.).

As to the accuracy of his general view, there is much uncertainty. It used to be maintained (e.g. Meyer, i[1]. 452, 463; but he has now altered his opinion so far as to bring the Cimmerians from the East, i. 473) that the Cimmerian and the Scythian raids were quite independent movements, different in direction and different in date, which H. or his informants wrongly combined. Some of the most modern orientalists, however (Maspero, iii. 342 n.; Prášek, Gesch. der Med. et Pers., 1906, pp. 113–14), accept H.'s chief point, that both Cimmerians and Scythians entered Asia Minor from the north-east. The Cimmerians settle round L. Van, the Scyths round L. Urumiah; then, under Esarhaddon, the Scyths drive the Cimmerians west into Asia Minor (Prášek, p. 120). This view may well be right in the main; it explains the importance of Sinope as a seat of the Cimmerians (cf. iv. 12. 2). But it is extremely probable that another body of Cimmerians was at the same time entering Asia Minor from the north-west (cf. iv. 11. 4 n.); they held Antandrus for a century (Arist. in Steph. Byz. *s. v.*), and they were accompanied (Strabo, 61, 647) by the Treres, a Thracian tribe (Thuc. ii. 96. 4). This invasion from the north-west may be compared to that of the Gauls in 278 B.C. (See Note I, p. 454.)

2. **Its date.** In the time of Sargon (722–705) we hear of the Gimirrai and Iškuza ('Cimmerians and Scyths', Prášek, p. 115) north of the kingdom of Ararat; both Esarhaddon (681–668) and Assurbanipal (668–626) speak of victories over the Cimmerians. It is in connexion with them that the Assyrian monuments mention Gyges, who was on the throne of Lydia when they appeared, and who, warned by the god Assur in a dream, sought Assyrian aid against them (R. P. i[1], p. 68). Revolting from Assyria later (cf. ii. 152. 3 n.), he was killed by them. Sardis was taken about 657; Strabo (627), quoting Callisthenes, makes it taken twice, which is doubtful. H. wrongly makes the Cimmerian invasions begin under Ardys; the reason is that his earlier Lydian kings are antedated. The date for the Cimmerians in Eusebius—1078 B.C.—is explained by the confusion of them with the Amazons (cf. Diod. ii. 44; perhaps we have a trace of this confusion in H. iv. 110).

3. **Its relation to the Greeks.** Magnesia was captured (Archil. fr. 20), but Ephesus, encouraged by Callinus (fr. 3), successfully resisted the hordes (Strabo, 647–8) *νῦν δ' ἐπὶ Κιμμερίων στρατὸς ἔρχεται ὀβριμοεργῶν*. H. rightly says it was 'a plundering raid', not a conquest (i. 6. 3). In fact, it may be said to have benefited the Greeks by breaking for a time the Lydian power; so the Mongols of Timour, by their victory over the Turks at Angora (A. D. 1402), postponed for half a century the fall of Constantinople.

4. **General effects.** Asia as a whole suffered more than the Greeks. The Bithynians, formerly a European tribe (vii. 75. 2), now settled in Bithynia; the Phrygian kingdom received a blow from which it never recovered; the old kingdom of Urartu disappears, and the Armenians (and perhaps also the Cappadocians, Prášek) come on the stage of history. It was an early 'wandering of the nations'.

Perhaps even more important was the blow to the great Assyrian Empire. Although its diplomacy made use of the Scyths (c. 103 n.), yet the raids of these northern barbarians in the seventh century were one of the causes of its overthrow.

Of the effect produced by these early 'Vandals and Huns' we have a clear trace in the contemporary Isaiah (v. 26 seq.) and in Ezekiel's picture (c. 39), drawn early in the sixth century, of the army of destruction from the north; by a curious confusion, Gyges, the victim of the Cimmerians, has become 'Gog', the 'prince of Meshech and Tubal', i. e. of the Moschi and Tibareni, part of the invading hordes. The best short account of the Cimmerian invasion is Busolt, ii. 461–4, who does not accept H.'s combination.

16 2 For the Median war and the general policy of Alyattes cf. cc. 73–4 nn. He was the founder of Lydian greatness, extending his power to the Halys.

κτισθεῖσαν, 'colonized from'; it was previously an Aeolian city. Smyrna was destroyed as a city, and only inhabited *κωμηδόν* (Strabo, 646); it does not occur in the Athenian tribute-lists, but its coins begin again in the fourth century, at least fifty years before its re-founding by Antigonus and Lysimachus, circ. 300 B.C. (Head, H. N. 591). The Lydian conquest was generally merciful; but Smyrna, commanding as it did the outlet of the Hermus valley, was too formidable to be spared. Clazomenae also was attacked in order to secure this valley. The defeat of Alyattes at Clazomenae must have been after his capture of Smyrna; it lay further west on the gulf of Smyrna. All these later campaigns are after the Median war (cf. c. 73 and Busolt, ii. 469).

17 1 For the 'flutes, lyres, and oboe of high and of deep note' see D. of A., *s. v.* tibia and lyra (for *πηκτίς*). The *αὐλός* differed from the flute (*σῦριγξ*), in having 'a mouthpiece in which a vibrating reed was fitted'; it seems always to have been played in pairs. Varro (in Serv. ad Aen. ix. 618) says the Phrygian 'tibia sinistra duo (foramina habet) quorum unum acutum sonum habet, alterum gravem', i. e. it had the two octaves in the same instrument.

The *πηκτίς* is condemned by Plato (Rep. 399) as being *πολύχορδος*; it was akin to the Lydian *μάγαδις*, which had twenty strings.

Aul. Gellius (i. 11), mistranslating H., speaks of the musicians, male and female, as 'lascivientium delicias conviviorum'; Meyer (ii. 390) thinks the reference is to organized movements of cavalry, controlled by music (cf. Thuc. v. 70 for military music). But the point is simply that the Lydian raids were easy and unresisted.

2 **ὁ δὲ τά τ.'** In antithetical sentences, especially when the first is negative, H. often puts the subject in the second before the *δέ*, even though (as here) both sentences have the same subject (cf. 66. 3).

18 1 The Limeneion seems to be the coast district in which lay the four (Strabo, 635) 'harbours' of Miletus.

2 The words *τὰ μέν νυν . . . ἐντεταμένως* interrupt the narrative, and Stein sees in them one of the later additions of H. to his

work; but the passage reads more like a first draft than an afterthought.

3 Chios, commanding the sea approach to Erythrae, was its natural enemy; it was also a rival to Samos, which was the perpetual trade competitor of Miletus. Hence the alliance of Miletus and Chios is natural; cf. Thuc. viii. 17.

19 1 **Ἀσσησίης.** Athena Assesia is probably a local deity adopted by the Greek settlers; this seems indicated by her cult epithet, for which cf. the place-ending '-assus' (App. I. 4).

3 It would be usual in prose to have *πρὶν ἄν* after the negative, but H. usually, like Homer, writes *ἤ*. Cf. L. and S. *s. v.* B. II. 2 a.

20 The mention of Delphi confirms the inference, probable on other grounds, that H. is writing from Delphian sources. As usual, at any rate in his early history, H. prefers a religious motive; probably it was the pressure of Median aggression on the east (cf. 16 n.) which compelled Alyattes to leave the Milesians alone.

The asyndeton emphasizes the confident reliance (*οἶδα*) of the historian on his oracular source; to the 'further' statement of the Milesians he does not commit himself, though they might be supposed to be well-informed about their own country. Cf. Macan (1895) civ. for the use of *οἶδα* in H., which is used alike for what he has seen himself, for what he has been told, and for mere inferences.

Περίανδρον. For P. and Thrasybulus cf. v. 92; the mediation of P. is probable, for he had friendly relations with both parties (cf. the scandalous story of iii. 48, and the Lydian offerings in the Corinthian treasury at Delphi, cc. 14, 50), and Corinthian trade suffered from the war.

21 2 The ostentation of plenty in a besieged city is common in picturesque history (cf. a similar story of Bias at Priene, Diog. Laert. i. 5. 83, and the deliverance of Perugia from Totila the Goth by this means, at the suggestion of St. Herculanus); but Miletus, having command of the sea (17. 3), probably had really suffered little.

22 4 **ξείνους** implies only friendly relations; **συμμάχους** is stronger, an offensive and defensive alliance (cf. 69. 3).

23 The Lesbians are quoted as the countrymen of Arion (of Methymna); there was a variant of the story (Lucian, Dial. Mar. 8) placing it in the Aegean, when Arion was returning to Methymna. For tyrants as patrons of art cf. App. XVI, § 3.

5 Arion's date is the end of the seventh century. Meyer (ii. 373) makes him as mythical as Orpheus or Marsyas, and Crusius (in P. W. *s. v.* 840) suggests that his name simply = 'prizewinner,' but his reality may be admitted, although the only poem attributed to him (Ael. H. A. xii. 45; Bergk, P. L. iii. 80, describing the miracle) is a forgery. H. is wrong in attributing the *διθύραμβος* to him; the word occurs in Archilochus (circ. 680–640, Crusius in P. W. *s. v.* p. 490), fr. 77 *ἐξάρξαι μέλος Οἶδα διθύραμβον, οἴνῳ συγκεραυνωθεὶς φρένας.*

Perhaps Arion elaborated the dithyramb and arranged it antistrophically for a chorus (cf. διδάξαντα); the invention of κύκλιοι χοροί is ascribed to him by the older authorities, e.g. Hellanicus (fr. 85; F. H. G. i. 57; but others assigned them to Lasus (ib.)). If this be so, the fact underlying H.'s view as to the origin of the dithyramb at Corinth would be that the choric Dionysus song developed in north Peloponnese (Crusius in P. W. ii. 841; cf. v. 67 n. for such choruses at Sicyon). So Pindar (Olym. xiii. 19) attributes the dithyramb to Corinth, although the scholiast to this passage says he attributed it elsewhere to Naxos and to Thebes; all these places were connected with Dionysus. Its proper subject was Διονύσου γένεσις (Pl. Leg. 700 B), but it was extended.

Arist. (Poet. 4, 1449 *a*) says tragedy begins ἀπὸ τῶν ἐξαρχόντων τὸν διθύραμβον ('ἐξάρχειν δ. is practically a synonym for διδάσκειν δ.' Bywater). Solon in 'his elegies' is quoted as saying τῆς τραγῳδίας πρῶτον δρᾶμα 'Αρίων εἰσήγαγεν (R. M. 1908, p. 150).

24 4 The ἑδώλια were seats in the vessel's stern, for the steerer and others in command, on a raised deck, though Torr (Anc. Ships, p. 57 and n.) says this was not always the case.

5 τοῖσι is subject of ἀναχωρῆσαι, attracted into the dependent clause. For ὄρθιος νόμος cf. Bergk, P. L. G. iii. 7, and for its familiarity Aristoph. Eq. 1279. It was attributed to Terpander and especially used in the worship of Apollo. Arion's song was an act of worship; it is this religious element in the story that commends it to H. The ὄρθιος νόμος was in solemn and measured rhythm; cf. the fragments of Terpander (*u. s.*) for its spondaic character.

6 The story of the dolphin is probably connected with a familiar coin type—a hero riding on a dolphin—e.g. Taras at Tarentum (Hill, G. & R. C. 175, Pl. 11); so too Arion on the later coins of Methymna (Head, H. N. 561). At Corinth also Melicertes was represented on a dolphin. It cannot be accidental that all these places, Tarentum, Lesbos, and Corinth, come in H.'s tale. The story is told at length in Plut. Sept. Sap. Con. 18 seq., where other dolphin stories are told, of Hesiod's murdered body, and of Enalus of Lesbos (cf. Frazer, P. iii. 398, for these stories). H. no doubt heard it at Taenarum, in connexion with the Arion monument (§ 8), which may have been dedicated by the poet; Pausanias (iii. 25. 5) saw it, and supports H.'s account by the story of the dolphin of Poroselene. The Taenarum monument bore the inscription ἀθανάτων πομπαῖσι 'Αρίονα Κυκλέος υἱὸν 'Εκ Σικελοῦ πελάγους σῶσεν ὄχημα τόδε, Ael. H. A. xii. 45. A small figure of this kind was actually found at Taenarum (Frazer, *u. s.*).

An early inscription found at Thera was restored by Boeckh thus [Κυκλείδας Κ]υκλῆος ἀδελ[φ]ε[ιῶι 'Αρίων]ι τὸν δελφὶς [σῶσε μνημόσυνον τέλεσεν]. Kaibel (Epig. Graec. 1086) says 'ingeniose haec Boeckh mihi lusisse videbatur'; cf. Roehl, I. G. A. 453, for a different restoration. Even were B.'s restoration accepted, the inscription would only be parallel to H.'s Καδμήια γράμματα (v. 59). It will be noticed that H. does not commit himself (§§ 1, 8) to the story.

2 The bowl-stand was the only Lydian dedication remaining at Delphi when Pausanias (x. 16. 1–2) visited the shrine; he describes it as 'in shape like a tower, broader at the base . . . the sides are not each in a single piece, but the iron crossbands are arranged like the rungs in a ladder'. Athenaeus (210 c) quotes Hegesander, a Delphian, as saying that on it were figures of animals in relief.

Glaucus was a contemporary of Gyges (Eusebius); this work therefore was made some time before its presentation (cf. vii. 27 n., the golden plane-tree). For Glaucus cf. Overbeck, Schriftquellen, 263–72. Frazer (P. v. 313–14), who has a good note on 'welding' and 'soldering', explains κόλλησις as 'welding', i. e. the beating of two pieces of white-hot iron into one, without any uniting substance. Murray (Gk. Sculpt. i. 81–2) translates 'soldering', i. e. uniting two pieces of metal by interposition of a third of different metal; but no method of soldering iron was known till quite recently. The art of welding was known in Egypt very early.

26 1 Alyattes had tried to gain Ephesus by marrying his daughter to its tyrant Melas; there was always a strong Asiatic element there (cf. the character of its temple worship, 92 n., and the exclusion of its citizens from the Apaturia, 147. 2). Pindarus, however, the next tyrant, though nephew of Croesus, was head of the patriotic party; his exile was made a condition of the terms granted to Ephesus on its submission (Ael. V. H. iii. 26).

2 For symbolic dedication cf. Thuc. iii. 104 (Polycrates and the island of Rheneia) and Plut. Sol. 12 (the supporters of Cylon).

ἔστι: in singular, though the subject is plural, a σχῆμα Πινδαρικόν. For the site of Ephesus cf. v. 100 n.

3 Grote points out (iii. 260 n.) that the 'two generations' of στάσις (v. 28 n.) before the Ionic Revolt explain the failure of Miletus to resist further.

27 2 For Pittacus, the αἰσυμνήτης of Mitylene, cf. Arist. Pol. iii. 14. 9, 1285 A (with Newman's notes, iii. 267 seq.), and his life in Diog. Laert. i. c. 4. He really belonged to the generation before Croesus, i. e. 600–570 B. C., as he was a contemporary of Alcaeus; Diog. Laert. i. 4. 79 says that he died in 570, having been tyrant ten years and having survived his tyranny ten years more. For the chronological weakness of H. on the sixth century cf. App. XIV. 6.

Winckler (A. F. i. 511 f.) finds the name of Pittacus on an inscription of Nebuchadnezzar, as an ally of Amasis, and thinks that P. anticipated the Eastern policy of Polycrates (cf. iii. 39 nn.). This would agree with the fact that one of the Lesbian exiles, brother of Alcaeus, Antimenides, an enemy of Pittacus, is found serving as a mercenary at Babylon (Strabo, 617).

Pittacus and Bias were both reckoned among 'the Seven Sages' whose sayings form one of the 'sources' of H. Cf. cc. 29, 74 nn.; for them cf. Holm, i. 344–6, and Meyer, ii. 441. For Bias cf. Diog. Laert. i. 5. 82–8; his wisdom was proverbial, Hipponax, fr. 79. He is said to have composed a poem of 2,000 verses, showing how Ionia 'could prosper' (cf. 170. 2 n., where H. tells us he advised the Ionians to emigrate in a body to Sardinia). He was of Priene, and arbitrated between his city and Samos in the quarrel which was constantly renewed from the sixth to the second century (cf. Hicks[1], 152, l. 22 for his name in the famous inscription as to this quarrel, now in the Ashmolean). H.'s story here is unhistorical; it is a piece of Gk. proverbial philosophy, which was fathered on any sage, just as Oxford stories are attributed to successive holders of an office. Croesus had good reason for inaction in the west, when affairs on his east frontier were so threatening (cf. i. 75. 1).

3 **αἲ γάρ** (only here in H.) is Homeric. 'Sons of the Lydians' is also poetic (cf. iii. 21. 3).

4 **ἀρώμενοι** is unnecessary, but added epexegetically after the parenthesis *ἐπείτε . . . νέας*: it is made (by an anacoluthon) to agree with the subject of this parenthesis.

28 The Cilicians are not 'within the Halys' at all. The larger part of these conquests were the work of Alyattes; but H. uses the aorist participle with *ἔχω*, a construction which implies not only the act, but also the state resulting from the act.

The last four lines are probably a gloss that has crept into the text (Stein), for

(1) The mention of the Lydians as 'subdued' is absurd.

(2) H. omits here tribes he knows elsewhere, e.g. the Caunii (c. 171), and inserts the Θυνοί, whom he knows nothing of in vii. 75.

(3) The list includes the *Χάλυβες*, who were always placed east of the Halys till Ephorus, probably identifying them with the *Ἀλίζωνοι* of the Catalogue (Il. ii. 856–7), brought them to the west of it. Strabo 678 (cf. also 552) refutes this error, but makes no mention of a similar mistake in H.

29 1 The order of the words *ἄλλοι τε οἱ* (not *οἵ τε ἄλλοι*) shows H. did not consider Solon a *σοφιστής*; he uses the word (ii. 49. 1) of the followers of Melampus and (iv. 95. 2) of Pythagoras. The word here has, of course, no bad sense, though the causal participle (*ἀκμαζούσας πλούτῳ*) reminds us of the reproach of venality made against the sophists.

ὡς ἕκαστος, 'on whatever grounds each might come,' opposed to Solon's *θεωρίῃ*; the optative is distributive. Ephorus (Diog. Laert. i. 1. 40) said that all the Seven Sages except Thales met at the court of Croesus. H. knows nothing of this fiction.

The truth of his story as to Solon and Croesus was early doubted, and it is now universally given up, on chronological grounds, though Plutarch (Sol. 27) declined to surrender a story 'so famous and so becoming to the character of Solon', because of *χρονικοί* τινες λεγόμενοι κανόνες. Solon's legislation is put in 594 B.C. (or perhaps in 591, 'Αθ. Πολ. 14. 1), while Croesus came to the throne in 560 (or later); hence the Athenian's travels belong to the generation before Croesus. Of the travels there is no reason to doubt; they probably were mentioned in Solon's poems (cf. v. 113. 2, the praise of Philocyprus at Soli). A similar chronological mistake occurs when H. makes Solon borrow a law from Amasis of Egypt (cf. 30. 1; ii. 177. 2 n.). Early attempts (e.g. by Clinton) to save the credit of H. are refuted by Grote (iii. 150–1).

Were the general chronology of H. for the sixth century less weak (cf. App. XIV. 6), the story of this meeting might be defended by adopting the later form of the tradition (Diog. Laert. i. 2. 50–1), that Solon's travels were after the usurpation of Pisistratus, i.e. after 560; D. L. improves on H. by making Solon say that Croesus in all his glory was not arrayed like a pheasant and a peacock. This date is given in a fourth century (?) philosophical dialogue (Oxyrhynchus Papyri, iv. 72 seq.), which also synchronizes the tyrannies of Pisistratus and Periander (cf. v. 95 nn.); but this only proves that H.'s mistakes had gained wide acceptance. It is best to look upon the tale as a piece of popular philosophy, in which Croesus and Solon are introduced as illustrations, on ethical and not on historical grounds.

The fact that H. tells us nothing of the laws of Solon is a good instance of the danger of the 'argumentum ex silentio'; it is over-subtle to suppose, as some have done, that H.'s informants suppressed the constitutional work of Solon, in order to exalt the credit of the Alcmaeonid Cleisthenes as the founder of Athenian democracy. The explanation of the omission is probably that H. has no interest in constitutional history.

πρόφασις includes the real as well as the ostensible cause. Translate 'having set forth, as he said, to see the world'.

2 Plutarch (Sol. 25) says the laws were to be valid one hundred years; the exaggeration is characteristic of later Greek historians.

30 1 Αἴγυπτον. It is probably true that S. visited Egypt. The story is embellished by Plato (Tim. p. 24); he says that Solon learned from the Egyptians about the lost continent of Atlantis. Cf. 29 n. and ii. 177 n. for Solon and Amasis.

4 εὖ ἡκούσῃς for the more usual εὖ ἔχω (cf. our 'farewell'). Elsewhere (as just below and 102. 2) it has a genitive with it. βίου = 'in substance', but the Gk. standard of wealth was not the Lydian (ὡς τὰ παρ' ἡμῖν). Cf. Ps. cxxviii. 5-6 for a similar idea of happiness.

5 Grote (iii. 71) by a mistranslation assumes that the battle was against the men of Eleusis, and uses this passage to prove the lateness of the union of Attica. This latter fact is probable on other grounds (cf. Thuc. ii. 15. 1), but the battle here mentioned was almost certainly against the Megarians at the border-town of Eleusis (for this war cf. 59. 4 n.).

ἔθαψαν, ἐτίμησαν. The two clauses go together; Tellus was honoured, as were the dead of Marathon, by burial on the spot (cf. Thuc. ii. 34. 1 for the usual custom of burial at Athens). Paus. i. 32. 4 says οἱ Μαραθώνιοι σέβονται τούτους οἱ παρὰ τὴν μάχην ἀπέθανον, ἥρωας ὀνομάζοντες, which may imply that the Athenians did *not* so worship them. It is not necessary here to think that Tellus received a ἡρῷον (cf. i. 67 n.; v. 47); this would be inconsistent with the simplicity of the story, which lays stress on the happiness of an ordinary man who did his duty.

31 1 **προετρέψατο,** 'had moved' (to inquire further). τὰ κατὰ τὸν Τέλλον, 'as to the matter of Tellus,' is an ordinary accusative of respect.

2 The element common to this story and that of Tellus is 'the glorious end', but there is a note of pessimism in this one; this may be characteristic, not of Solon, but of H. himself (cf. Intr. p. 49 and L. Campbell, Religion in Gk. Literature, p. 183). But cf. Solon, fr. 17 πάντῃ δ' ἀθανάτων ἀφανὴς νόος ἀνθρώποισι, and also fr. 14 οὐδὲ μάκαρς οὐδεὶς πέλεται βροτός, ἀλλὰ πονηροὶ | πάντες ὅσους θνητοὺς ἠέλιος καθορᾷ.

For Greek pessimism in general cf. ib. pp. 113, 115, 275–6.

For Cleobis and Bito cf. Paus. ii. 20. 3, and Frazer iii. 193 for other references.

For the Heraeum cf. Paus. ii. 17. The site has been explored by the American School since 1892 (cf. Waldstein's The Argive Heraeum, and a summary in Frazer, P. iii. 165 seq.). It stood on the road from Argos to Mycenae, about three miles south of the latter. The temple was burned in 423 (Thuc. iv. 133). As the site is a rocky terrace above the plain, the feat of strength was considerable; but H. avoids the absurdity of making Bito on another occasion carry a bull on his shoulders (Paus. ii. 19. 5).

3 **ὁ θεός** here = 'Hera'. But it is often used in an abstract sense (cf. vii. 10 ε). H., though a polytheist, is, like Sophocles, not uninfluenced by the philosophic tendencies which were affecting Greek religion in the sixth and fifth centuries; he is, perhaps, also influenced by Persian religion (c. 131 n.). For the monotheistic tendency of Pindar cf. Campbell, *u. s.* pp. 171, 183 f. For a good note on H.'s use of ὁ θεός κτλ. cf. Macan (1895), cxi. n. 3.

ἄμεινον . . . τεθνάναι. The sentiment is common in Gk. literature (cf. Butcher, Some Aspects of Gk. Genius, p. 134); perhaps the best-known example is Soph. O. C. 1225 seq., with its parallel in Theog. 425 seq.; cf. too Bacchyl. iii. 47 θανεῖν γλύκιστον, said by Croesus himself, and Il. xxiv. 525–6.

ὡς γὰρ ἐπεκλώσαντο θεοὶ δειλοῖσι βροτοῖσι,
ζώειν ἀχνυμένοις, αὐτοὶ δέ τ' ἀκηδέες εἰσί.

Death is welcomed as an escape from troubles. This is different from the doctrine of the Pythagoreans, who taught that death was a good, as delivering the soul from the prison of the body. The Thracian Trausi (v. 4. 2 n.) are credited with the same idea as Solon.

A similar story to that of Cleobis and Bito is told of Trophonius and Agamedes (who received death as a reward from Apollo for building his temple at Delphi) and of the poet Pindar (Plut. Consol. ad Apoll. c. 14, pp. 108–9).

5 Homolle discovered these statues at Delphi (cf. Frazer, v. 563). The identification was disputed, but the actual inscription has now been found, and 'confirms most strikingly the accuracy of H.' (B. P. W. 1911, pp. 789-90); cf. also Philologus lxx, pp. 312–13, for the conjecture Ἡραῖόνδε), and J. H. S. xxxi. 300 for a brief summary.

32 1 **φθονερόν.** The thought is as old as Homer; cf. Od. v. 118 σχέτλιοί ἐστε, θεοί, ζηλήμονες ἔξοχον ἄλλων.

Other instances in H. beside the story of Croesus are that of Polycrates and the whole account of Xerxes (iii. 39 seq.). It is one of the main motives of his history (cf. Intr. pp. 49–50), as being the cause of the changes of fortune (i. 207. 2) which he has to record. Since the Greeks conceived their gods in their own likeness, it was natural that they should make them tyrants; cf. φιλέει ὁ θεὸς τὰ ὑπερέχοντα κολούειν (vii. 10 ε) with the τοὺς ὑπερόχους τῶν ἀστῶν φονεύειν of the tyrant (v. 92 η).

For other parallels cf. Hesiod, W. and D. 6 ῥεῖα δ' ἀρίζηλον μινύθει καὶ ἄδηλον ἀέξει, and Aesop's answer to Chilon (Diog. Laert. i. 3. 69) that Zeus was τὰ μὲν ὑψηλὰ ταπεινῶν τὰ δὲ ταπεινὰ ὑψῶν; also S. Luke i. 52, and Hor. Odes, i. 35. 2–4.

The idea gradually became purified and moralized, so that it is no longer mere prosperity, but the pride bred of it, which the god hates. This form of the belief is found in H. (34. 1), but it occurs even earlier in the tragedians; cf. the magnificent lines of Aeschylus (Pers. 821–2)

ὕβρις γὰρ ἐξανθοῦσ' ἐκάρπωσε στάχυν
ἄτης ὅθεν πάγκλαυτον ἐξαμᾷ θέρος.

In this form it may be compared to the teaching of the Hebrew prophets, e. g. Isa. x. 12 'I will punish the glory of his high looks'.

Plato, Phaedr. 247 A excludes φθόνος from the θεῖος χορός; so too Arist. Metaph. i. 2 οὔτε τὸ θεῖον φθονερὸν ἐνδέχεται εἶναι, ἀλλὰ κατὰ τὴν παροιμίαν πολλὰ ψεύδονται ἀοιδοί.

φθόνος originally included all the πάθη λυπηρά excited by prosperity in others; Aristotle (Eth. ii. 7. 14) distinguished them into φθόνος, νέμεσις, and ἐπιχαιρεκακία, cf. Intr. p. 49 and Rhet. ii. cc. 9 and 10 (with Cope's notes).

2 **τῷ μακρῷ χρόνῳ,** 'the whole duration of human life' (cf. v. 9. 3 for a different sense).

The Greek 'limit', like that of Psalm xc. 10, varied from seventy to eighty years (cf. iii. 22 for the latter, and Solon frag. 27 (l. 17) and 20 ὀγδωκονταέτη μοῖρα κίχοι θανάτου for the two limits respectively).

3 **ἐνιαυτός** (v. L. & S. *s. v.*) is any season of time (cf. Od. i. 16 ἔτος ἦλθε περιπλομένων ἐνιαυτῶν); here it is made 360 days, a rough average between the solar and the lunar year (for the length of these and for the Calendar generally cf. ii. 4 nn.).

H. makes a mistake as to 'intercalary months'; if they were ever inserted every other year, then the ordinary months were strictly lunar (i.e. 29½ days), and made up only 354 days (not 360, *v.s.*): it is more probable, however, that there were only three intercalary months in eight years. H.'s calculation would give an average of 375 days a year.

4 **συμφορή.** Tr. 'man is altogether a thing of chance'; cf. vii. 49. 3 for the sentiment, and Heraclitus' famous *πάντα ρεῖ, οὐδὲν μένει*.

5 This Solonian paradox is discussed by Aristotle (Eth. i. 11). Cf. Soph. O. T. 1528 seq. for an almost verbal repetition and Intr. p. 7; but the idea is a commonplace of Greek thought.

Join **μετρίως ἔχοντες βίου** (partitive genitive): the contrast between the 'wealthy unhappy men' and 'the lucky men of moderate means' is forced and not consistent with the omnipotence of chance; if H. meant that wealth is not *εὐδαιμονία* (as Aristotle, in Eth. x. 8. 9–11, where he refers to this passage), he certainly fails to say so; if he means that a man may be unlucky (*ἀτυχής*) though wealthy, he is elaborately stating the obvious.

ἄπηρος κτλ.: for some of these conditions (*ὧν οὐκ ἄνευ*) necessary to happiness cf. Arist. Eth. i. 8. 16; *τὸ εὖ ζῆν* combined for a Greek the two ideas of 'good life' and 'good living' (i.e. prosperity).

8 The insufficiency of man causes the formation of the *πόλις* (Plat. Rep. ii. 369 seq.); the *πόλις* is to be *αὐτάρκης*, Arist. Pol. vii. 4. 14 seq., 1326 B; but Plato (Rep. 370 E) sees (as Solon here) that no *πόλις* can supply all it needs.

9 **προρρίζους.** Cf. vii. 46. 4 for the sentiment, and iii. 40. 3, where *πρόρριζος* is again used.

33 The change of subject from Solon (*ἐχαρίζετο*) to Croesus (*ἀποπέμπεται*) is harsh (though not without parallel; cf. 31. 1), and so is the non-correspondence of *οὔτε, οὔτε*.

34 1 **ὀλβιώτατον.** For the thought cf. 32. 1 n.

2 **ἐπέστη.** For the phrase and idea cf. Il. ii. 20, the dream of Agamemnon.

The name Atys is that of the Phrygio-Lydian deity, Attes or Attis, clearly connected with the Syrian Ate (whose female double is Atargatis; cf. Meyer, i. 487): the cult itself is probably of Hittite origin and is closely connected with that of Adonis (Thammuz; cf. ii. 79. 2 n.). Frazer (G. B.[2] ii. 130–7) describes the cult, and says that Attis is 'a deity of vegetation whose divine life manifested itself in the pine tree and the spring violets' (used in his ritual). According to one form of the legend Attes was killed by a boar, according to the other form (current in Pessinus) by self-mutilation (Paus. vii. 17. 10–12); this latter story is immortalized in the Attis of Catullus. Attes is both son and lover of the great mother-goddess, Cybele. For the worship of the mother and the son in Asia Minor cf. Ramsay, C. and B. pp. 87, 264. The swine, originally 'the sacred victim', typical of the god himself, has become by false interpretation the enemy of the God (Farnell, G. C. ii, p. 646). The interest of the story, from the historical point of view, is that H. (or his informants) has introduced a cult-myth into history; it has received a Greek colouring, for the steps taken to avert calamity are the means of bringing it to pass. (Cf. the myth of Oedipus.) The fact underlying the story seems to be that Croesus had a son, Atys, who died young. For Atys' son, Pythius, cf. vii. 27. 1.

3 **οἱ**: an Ethic dative; but it is used by H. also as a sort of possessive pronoun, e.g. iii. 14. 7 *τῶν συμποτέων οἱ*.

35 Phrygia had probably been conquered by Alyattes (cf. App. I. 7); but Winckler (A. F. ii. 141) thinks the story here implies that it was still independent: Aeschylus (Pers. 770) speaks of its conquest by Cyrus as distinct from that of Lydia.

2 The rite of purification (as performed by Circe for Jason and Medea) is described in Apol. Rhod. iv. 693 seq.; among other ceremonies a sucking pig was slain, and the blood poured on the guilty hands. The rite never occurs in Homer; it first appears in Gk. literature in the fragment of the Aethiopis of Arctinus, where Achilles is purified for the murder of Thersites. The old view was (Grote, i. 25) that the idea of purification was not Greek and was introduced from abroad; the usual modern view (Harrison, Prol. to Study of Gk. Rel.) is that the chthonian worships, with which rites of purification were connected, were pre-Homeric, i.e. pre-Achaean, and deliberately ignored by Homer in the interests of the Olympian deities. Cf. Frazer, P. iii. 53 seq. for rites of purification generally.

For the similarity between Greeks and Lydians cf. App. I. 5.

3 The name Adrastus seems to refer to the goddess Adrasteia (= 'Necessity'; cf. Aesch. P. V. 936); for her connexion with Nemesis cf. Farnell, G. C. ii. 499–500; he shows that she was a form of Cybele, who, 'through a misunderstanding of the name', acquired the character, really foreign to her, of 'a stern goddess of justice'. The Phrygian and the Argive Adrastus (cf. v. 67 n.) are both the victims of 'inevitable fate'.

36 **χρῆμα** with gen. is a colloquialism common in H. and Aristoph. Cf. *χειμῶνος χρ. ἀφόρητον* vii. 188, and Nub. 2 *τὸ χρ. τῶν νυκτῶν ὅσον*.

2 H., like a true Greek, gives the Lydians an *ἀγορά* and calls them 'citizens'.

1 **τό** goes with *λέληθε*, as well as with *μανθάνεις*, as an accus. of respect (tr. 'wherein').

2 **ὀφείλω . . . χρηστοῖσι.** A striking instance of tragic irony.

2 H. lays stress on the significant name; cf. 35. 3 n.

2 Zeus is invoked in a triple character, as the god who enjoined purification from unintentional guilt, and as the protector both of the hearth and of the rights of friendship; this (i.e. three attributes

of one god) is a sort of intermediate stage to the idea of three gods with different attributes.

ἐπίστιον. The suppliant actually took refuge in the hearth when appealing to Zeus *ἐπίστιος*. For cult titles cf. Farnell, G. C. i. 35.

Croesus not only asks for vengeance, but himself has a grievance against heaven; this he gives up (45. 2), just as he accepts Apollo's explanation in c. 91. 'The ways of god to men' are 'justified' in the wisdom which Croesus learns by experience.

45 3 **φονεὺς μέν.** The rhetorical turn is to be noted, and the contrast between Adrastus' royal birth and the disasters which had befallen him. **φονεύς** is of course not literally true, but the exaggeration is natural. So Euripides makes Hecuba (882) call the murderer of her son *τὸν ἐμὸν φονέα.*

46 Croesus was the brother-in-law of Astyages (74. 4); but he had other than personal motives. The power of Persia was a menace to all the secondary powers (cf. 77. 2 for their union), just as that of Media had been under Cyaxares (cf. 73. 3 n. for diplomatic interference with Media). Moreover, Lydian trade was in danger from the uncivilized Persians (cf. 71. 2).

2 For wholesale consultation of oracles cf. viii. 133–4.

For Greek oracles in general cf. Myers' brilliant essay in Hellenica, and Boucher-Leclercq, Divination dans l'Antiquité, vol. iii.

For the locality and oracle of Dodona cf. Frazer, P. ii. 159–60, for Zeus of Ammon ii. 42 n.

Abae in E. Phocis; for its oracle cf. viii. 27, 33 n., 134, and Paus. x. 35 (with Frazer, v. 436 seq., who describes the present state of the ruins).

For Amphiaraus and Trophonius cf. viii. 134 nn. The temple of Apollo at Didyma (cf. 157. 3 for description of it, 158 for its Medism (?), and vi. 19. 3 for its destruction in 494 B. C.; also 92. 2 nn.) was 22½ miles from Miletus; it was often called 'of Branchidae', from the priestly family (cf. *τοὺς Βραγχίδας* 158. 1), in whose charge it was; the name of the mythical founder, Branchus, has been connected etymologically with the Sans. *Brahman*, Lat. *flamen*. Some see in Apollo of B. a pre-Greek god (Meyer, i. 483; Paus. vii. 2. 6). Its site was explored by Newton (Essays, 75 seq.), who brought (1858) from its Sacred Way to the B. M. ten great seated figures of priests, which are interesting as showing Egyptian influence on Greek art in the sixth century (cf. Frazer, P. iv. 126). One of them, that of Chares (No. 14), is probably the oldest extant Greek portrait. The explorations were resumed by the Germans in 1899.

47 **συγγραψαμένους,** 'causing them to be written down for them,' i. e. by the *προφήτης*, who put the answer of the *πρόμαντις* (vii. 111. 2) into proper shape, usually into hexameters (cf. c. 174 for iambics); here, however, the Pythia or *πρόμαντις* seems to have given her answer in verse directly, without intermediary. In later times, from third century onwards, prose was the usual medium. As the answers were given all together, once a year originally, and once a month later (Plut. Q. G. 9, Mor. 292), it is obvious that the προφήτης was all-important. Cf. Frazer, P. v. 235 for the inspiration of the πρόμαντις.

2 **μέγαρον** is always used by H. in a religious sense, though in Homer it means simply 'chamber' or (mostly in plural) 'house' (cf. *aedes*). Perhaps the Herodotean sense is the original one; the word may be connected with Semitic *maghar* ('cave,' Robertson-Smith, Relig. of Sem. p. 200). This use survives in the μέγαρα or 'caves' into which pigs were thrown at the Thesmophoria (Paus. ix. 8. 1 and Frazer, v. 29). For an underground shrine (of Palaemon) cf. Paus. ii. 2. 1.

μέγαρον is the temple itself as opposed to the τέμενος (cf. vi. 134. 2), and especially the shrine proper, where stood the image of the god (ii. 141. 3); it sometimes seems to be used interchangeably with ἄδυτον (cf. vii. 140. 1 and 3). It is, however, used for the whole building (not merely the shrine), ii. 143. 2. The 'shrine' at Delphi was at the west end of the *cella*, and beneath was the chasm into which it is said the priestess went down to divine (Frazer, v. 352–3; but cf. Oppé, J. H. S. xxiv, for good reasons against believing in 'the chasm').

3 The **δέ** is common in oracles (cf. 174. 5 *et pass.*); it marks off an answer from a preceding one given to other inquirers (*u. s.*).

For a like claim to omniscience cf. Pind. Pyth. 9. 44 seq.

χαλκόν, cogn. acc. Cf. Il. iii. 57 λάινον ἕσσο χιτῶνα, 'with brass is it (the tortoise) clad above'; cf. 48. 2 for explanation.

48 1 **προσίετο.** This verb is more often used by H. with a personal subject, e. g. 135. 1 ξεινικὰ νόμαια Πέρσαι προσίενται, but here of the thing, tr. 'none took him' (cf. our 'I take it' and 'it takes me'). This second use is found in Aristoph., e. g. Eq. 359, Vesp. 741. Some see in the remark as to Amphiaraus (c. 49) a tradition inconsistent with the statement here. But the story—no doubt a Delphic one—is consistent; Apollo alone gave a complete answer, but the neighbouring shrine of Amphiaraus did well enough to save its credit.

προσεύχετο: he 'worshipped', recognizing in the oracle the power of the god. If the whole story is not simply a Delphic invention, we must suppose that Croesus was 'working the oracle' for the benefit of his Greek allies.

2 **αὐτός** is emphatic; Croesus carried out his own plan, so as to keep his secret to the last.

50 1 **πάντα**: 3000 of every kind (cf. the idiomatic πάντα δέκα, iv. 88. 1). The account of this holocaust is like that given by Lucian (de dea Syria 49, p. 485) of the spring sacrifice at Hierapolis; the offering of Croesus, however, is the provision of a feast for the god on a great scale, with all the furniture of the costliest, while that in Lucian leads up to self-mutilation in ecstatic frenzy.

2 The πλίνθος or 'ingot' was square; they were 'beaten out' with the hammer (cf. 68. 1 for ἐξήλαυνε); these ἡμιπλίνθια were about 18 by 9 by 3 inches. H. no doubt takes all these measurements from the inventory of Delphic treasures, and therefore is calculating by the Greek πῆχυς, not the Persian (cf. 178. 3 n.).

τρίτον ἡ., '2½ talents'; for this colloquial commercialism cf. Latin *sestertius*, German *drittehalb*, &c.

λευκοῦ χρυσοῦ: ἤλεκτρον, a natural alloy of gold and silver, obtained from the washings of the Pactolus; it was also made artificially later. It consisted of at least 20 per cent. of silver to 80 of gold (cf. Plin. N. H. xxxiii. 80 'ubicumque quinta argenti portio est, electrum vocatur'); the usual proportion of silver was 27 per cent. Its value was to that of silver as 10 to 1 (that of gold to silver was reckoned at 13·3 to 1, cf. iii. 95. 1 n.), and so it was the first metal used in coins (cf. 94. 1 n.), for convenience of calculation as well as for its greater durability (Head, H. N.[1] xxxiv). Stein thinks that, as electron ingots of this size, if solid, would weigh more than two talents, these were hollow. The number he explains by the arrangement of the pedestal; the lion stood on the 'four ingots of pure gold', under which were three stages of electrum ones, 15 (5 by 3), 35 (7 by 5), and 63 (9 by 7) respectively (i. e. 4 + 15 + 35 + 63 = 117). The 'ingots' were melted down by Phayllus in the Sacred War (Diod. 16. 56, who makes them 120, and mentions statues of a lion (cf. 50. 3) and of a woman (51. 5) as meeting the same fate).

3 The lion was the beast of Cybele and Sandon, and appears as a type on early Lydian coins (cf. Hill, G. C. Pl. I. 7); nearly half the coins found at Ephesus (1904–5) show it (Hogarth, E. p. 90). For its place in Lydian mythology cf. 84. 3 (the story of Meles' lion cub), and in Anatolian art J. H. S. xix. 46–7 (with fig.); a stone lion from Branchidae of this date is in the B. M. (No. 17).

The temple at Delphi was burned down in 548 B.C. [Paus. x. 5. 13; cf. ii. 180. 1 n.; for the restoration and the general history of the temple cf. v. 62 n., and Frazer, P. v. 328 seq.]

51 This chapter is most interesting as showing the familiarity of H. with Delphi.

2 For the Croesus bowl in its 'angle' cf. viii. 122. 1. Stein thinks the reference is to the projecting 'angle', formed by one of the two antae, with which the walls of the cella ended in front towards the πρόναος.

γάρ. H. knows its size, because it was filled at the Theophania, a spring festival, which commemorated at Delphi the reappearance of the Sun-god.

3 For Theodorus cf. Murray, G. S. i. 74 seq., where his works are enumerated and his originality discussed. He and Rhoecus (iii. 60. 4 n.) διέχεαν χαλκὸν πρῶτοι καὶ ἀγάλματα ἐχωνεύσαντο (Paus. viii. 14. 8); cf. also Plin. N. H. xxxiv. 83. For an early instance of bronze casting at Samos cf. iv. 152. 4. Theodorus was the maker of Poly-

crates' ring (iii. 41. 1 n.), and also of the golden plane-tree (vii. 27. 2, though H. does not give his name in this case); he probably was a contemporary of Alyattes. Overbeck (Schriftq. 274–93) distinguishes an elder and a younger Theodorus.

For ceremonial sprinklings cf. Tylor, P. C. ii. 434; the vessels stood, like modern holy-water stoups, by the entrance.

φαμένων . . . λέγοντες: the anacoluthon is very harsh. Kirchhoff argues (1) that the falsification was official, (2) that a motive for such complaisance towards Lacedaemonians is found in 448 B.C. (Thuc. i. 112. 5); therefore H.'s visit must have been about 447. The gaps in this argument are obvious. It is interesting to see H. exercising his critical faculty on the Temple records.

5 **οὐκ ἐπίσημα**: L. & S. 'without an inscription' (as opposed to *ἐπιγέγραπται* § 3), not, as Stein, 'indistinguishable'; this implies that most of the articles bore the name of Croesus as giver.

ἀρτοκόπου. The step-mother of Croesus attempted to poison him, and his life was saved by his 'baker' (cf. Plut. Mor. 401 E, de Pyth. Orac. c. 16, and c. 92 for the conspiracy of Croesus' step-brother, Pantaleon).

τὸ ξυστόν should be a genitive absolute, but as it is a part of the *αἰχμή* it is attracted into the same case (cf. ii. 41. 4).

53 1 For the temple of the Ismenian Apollo cf. 92. 1 n.

The Parian marble (App. XIV. 6) dates this embassy 555 B.C., which Busolt (ii. 460 n.) makes the year of Croesus' accession.

There seems to be no difference in sense between the subjunctive and the optative here; they are both deliberative; cf. i. 185. 6, where the optative precedes, for a similar change.

2 We may suppose that the liberality of Croesus was intended to secure the Lacedaemonian alliance through Delphic influence.

3 The oracle ran *Κροῖσος Ἅλυν διαβὰς μεγάλην ἀρχὴν καταλύσει* (Arist. Rhet. iii. 5).

54 1 The staters were rather more than 25 per cent. heavier than darics, and therefore worth about £1 8*s*. each. Plutarch, however (de Sera Num. Vind. 12, p. 556), makes Croesus propose to give a larger sum—'four minae' = about £16.

2 The *προμαντεία* was the right of either consulting the oracle on behalf of others (Homolle) or of consulting the oracle before ordinary visitors, whose positions were determined by lot; the analogy of *προεδρία* makes the second explanation preferable. The whole question is discussed in R. E. G. xiii., p. 281 seq., which sums up on the whole against Homolle's view. *ἀτέλεια* was freedom from taxes for Lydians consulting the shrine; the *προεδρία* was the right to front places at the Pythian and other festivals (cf. ix. 73. 3 for such rights). These honours and similar ones (e.g. *προδικία* and *ἔγκτησις καὶ γῆς καὶ οἰκίας*, which corresponds to the *γίνεσθαι Δελφόν* of this passage) are found in inscriptions at Delphi (e.g. Dittenberger, 484, 662; the former of these is in favour of Sardes—'as

an ancient friend'). Radet (p. 217) compares the decree in honour of Croesus with the rights given by the Amphictyons to Philip in 346 B.C.; it made him a member of the Hellenic world (cf. Jebb, Essays, p. 223, for similar grants at Delos).

55 1 **ἐνεφορέετο**, 'filled himself full of,' i.e. 'used to the full'; cf. Plut. Cic. 19 *μὴ δοκοίη τῆς ἐξουσίας ἄγαν ἐμφορεῖσθαι*, (Cic. feared) 'lest he should be thought to abuse his authority' (against the Catilinarians).

2 For explanation of this oracle cf. c. 91. 5.

ποδαβρέ. The effeminacy of the Lydians was later (cf. App. I. 4 and 79. 3; 155); but they had already developed a luxurious civilization (cf. 71. 2, the story of Sandanis).

56–8 *A digression on the races of Greece.* With this generally cf. App. XV.

56 2 A Dorian himself, H. identifies the Dorians with the Hellenes. Hellas was originally a district in Thessaly, closely connected with Phthia and ruled by Achilles (Il. ix. 395), whose followers are 'Myrmidons and Hellenes' (Il. ii. 684). But in the Catalogue (ii. 530) it is also used as a general name, Πανέλληνες (cf. *καθ' Ἑλλάδα καὶ μέσον Ἄργος*, Od. i. 344 *et pass.*—a verse condemned by Aristarchus as an interpolation). 'Hellas' was already used in a general sense by Archilochus and Hesiod (Strabo, 370), i.e. in the seventh century, and had become established in this sense before 580 B.C., when two 'Hellanodicae' (cf. I. G. A. 112) were appointed for the Olympic games; but the date depends on the reading in Paus. v. 9. 4, 5, which is a little uncertain (cf. Frazer, P. i. 584; iii. 489). Thucydides (i. 3) describes the transition from the special to the general sense; this was probably due to the influence of the myth of Achilles; as the Greeks, by contrast with the barbarians, became conscious of their own similarity, it was natural they should assume the name of the people whose chief was the hero of the national epic and the type of heroic manhood. The adoption of the name may be connected with the spread of Dorian influence (cf. Ζεὺς Ἑλλάνιος and Ἀθανὰ Ἑλλανία in the *ῥήτρα* of Lycurgus, Plut. Lyc. 6).

The origin of 'Hellenes' is uncertain; it may be connected with the Σελλοί, the priests of Zeus at Dodona (Il. xvi. 234, where Achilles prays to this god). This is partially confirmed by Aristotle (Meteor. i. 14, 352 A), who says that 'ancient Hellas' was *περὶ Δωδώνην*. For the whole subject cf. Busolt, i. 196 seq. Bury has an ingenious theory that the name received its first great extension in connexion with the Achaean colonies in Magna Graecia (J. H. S. xv. 236); but his proof is by no means complete.

This chapter (with c. 145, and viii. 43 and 73) is interesting as showing that the story of the Dorian Invasion was fully developed in H.'s time: he assumes its main points and even refers to details, e.g. vi. 52, ix. 26. 3. The questions as to it may be summed up under two heads:—

I. Evidence for reality of Dorian Invasion.

The oldest evidence for it is Tyrtaeus, fr. 2 (in Str. 362)—

Ζεὺς Ἡρακλείδαις τήνδε δέδωκε πόλιν·
οἷσιν ἅμα προλιπόντες Ἐρινεὸν ἠνεμόεντα,
εὐρεῖαν Πέλοπος νῆσον ἀφικόμεθα.

(Cf. Pind. Pyth. i. 63 seq.) Beloch (R. M. xlv) argues that the story is an invention, based on mistaken etymologies (e.g. of 'Naupactus') and unhistorical combinations, to explain the difference between Homeric Greece and Historic Greece. His arguments are briefly these: (1) The evidence is late; there is nothing as to the migration in Homer (but Homer is equally silent as to Greek migrations to Asia Minor which are pretty generally accepted). (2) Race names are very late (Thuc. i. 3; but this argument confuses name and fact: races exist as distinct, though their general names may be late). (3) There was no real gap between 'Mycenaean' and historic times, e.g. a Dorian column is found in the Lion Gate at Mycenae. The transition was gradual, but the Greeks, not understanding such a process, invented a catastrophe. (This argument is not admitted by archaeologists generally; it makes the Mycenaean culture too late; cf. Busolt, i. 116 n.)

Arguments for the historic reality of the invasion are (cf. generally Meyer, ii. 47): (1) Modern archaeological research tends to vindicate the accuracy of Greek myths in their general outlines. (2) If tradition is ever good evidence, it would be so for an event of such importance. (3) Tradition is confirmed by the existence of subject classes (probably subject races) in many parts of the Peloponnese. (4) The Dorians always looked on themselves as being new-comers in the Peloponnese. (5) The tradition explains such facts as resemblance of Dorian and Aeolian dialects (Busolt, i. 195) and the connexion of the Lacedaemonians with Doris, which is of great importance in historic times (Thuc. i. 107. 2).

It must be frankly admitted, however, that we know nothing of the details of the Invasion.

II. Main points as to Dorian Invasion.

(1) *As to its origin.* It was part of a general movement from the North, connected with the Phrygian migration (vii. 73), and perhaps (but remotely) with the invasions of Egypt under the Nineteenth Dynasty (cf. App. X. 8).

(2) *As to its course.* (*a*) The invaders were of mixed race; all probability (cf. the invasion of the Cimbri and Teutones) confirms tradition on this.

(*b*) Doris was a stage in the progress of part of the invaders.

(*c*) Some of the conquerors came by sea (cf. the local tradition as to Solygeius (Thuc. iv. 42. 2) and the Temeneion near Argos (Strabo, 368)).

(*d*) The conquest was gradual, and may have been assisted by the discontented elements in the population of the Peloponnese.

(3) *As to its ultimate results.* It was part of a series of movements. Thucydides (i. 2. 3) connects it, though not causally, with the conquest of Boeotia; and it may have led to the migration to Asia Minor (c. 145).

3 **τὸ μέν**: obviously the Pelasgic race, although this sense is inconsistent with what H. says of Pelasgians in Asia Minor (146. 1) or of those in Attica (vi. 137); he writes too absolutely, having in view only the contrast between the mass of the Athenians, who were *οὐ μετανάσται* (vii. 161. 3), and the much-wandering Dorians. These are placed first in Phthiotis, because this was the traditional home of Deucalion, the Greek Noah, the grandfather of Aeolus, Xuthus, and Dorus. H. may be following the post-Homeric epic, 'Aegimius.'

Histiaeotis was in north-west Thessaly; H. transfers it to the north-east (the district really of Thessaliotis (57. 1)), probably in accordance with Cretan tradition (for Dorians in Crete cf. Od. xix. 177). The invaders of Crete must have originally lived on the sea coast.

Καδμείων. For the Cadmeans cf. v. 61. 2 n.; as there it is said that the Cadmeans fled to the Illyrian Encheleis, their migration must have been to north-west; hence it is obvious that the legend placed the Dorians in north-west Thessaly (not north-east).

Πίνδῳ. P. is one of the towns of the Dorian Tetrapolis, the others being Erineus (cf. viii. 43 and Tyrtaeus, *u. s.*), Boeum, and Cytinium (Strabo, 427); it lay on a river of the same name on the south-east of Mount Oeta; for it cf. Pind. Pyth. i. 65 *ἔσχον δ' Ἀμύκλας ὄλβιοι Πινδόθεν ὀρνύμενοι.* Others (less probably) take Pindus to be the mountain chain, i.e. H. would bring his Dorians from north-east to north-west Thessaly and then later (*ἐνθεῦτεν αὖθις*) to their home in Doris.

Μακεδνόν. Stein doubts whether H. means to connect the Dorians with the Macedonians (cf. viii. 43), arguing that H., if he had believed this, would have explained the unusual form (Μακεδνόν) by the common one (Μακεδών). It seems, however, as if H. must have been thinking of the claim of the Macedonian kings to be Argives (cf. v. 22. 2; viii. 137); but this would prove nothing as to connexion of the races. He may be referring to some unknown tradition, connecting the Dorians in north-west Thessaly with their Macedonian neighbours to the north; e.g. Myres (J. H. S. xxvii. 178) shows that in the Homeric Catalogue the strip of coast between Mount Olympus and the Axius is unaccounted for; he argues that the Dorians (unknown to Homer except in Od. xix. 177) had already reached this.

Δρυοπίδα. D. was the original name of the lower part of the

Pindus valley, which in historic times was Doris (viii. 31; cf. Strabo, 434). The Dryopians originally dwelt on both sides of Mount Oeta, and south as far as Parnassus; they are said to have been expelled from the coast by the Malians, and by Heracles from the Pindus valley (Apollod. ii. 7. 7). Heracles was especially honoured by the Malians (vii. 176. 3), and in the east of Central Greece generally (Meyer, ii. 166). Here the Dorians learned his worship, and made his son Hyllus to be adopted by king Aegimius, and so to be the ancestor of the Spartan kings. The expelled Dryopes settled at Hermione and Asine in the Peloponnese (viii. 73. 2), at Styra (viii. 46. 4), and Carystus in Euboea (Thuc. vii. 57. 4); also in Cythnus (viii. 46. 4) and in Ionia (146. 1). For an account of the Dryopes, based in part on cult usage, cf. Paus. iv. 34. 6.

οὕτως: i. e. they get their Dorian name when they conquer the Peloponnese. This is probably wrong; 'it is native in the upper Cephissus valley' (Meyer, ii. 47).

57 For H.'s Pelasgian theories and for the relation of Pelasgi to Hellenes cf. App. XV. He here tries to infer the original language of the whole people from survivals in his own day; his method is scientific, whatever may be thought of his results.

1 **Κρηστῶνα.** If this is read, Creston is a town in Thrace, north of Chalcidice, on the high ground between the Axius and the Strymon; this district is called Κρηστωνική (vii. 124. 1; cf. Thuc. ii. 99. 6 Γρηστωνία). This reading is open to objections: (1) Creston is not definitely mentioned *as a town* elsewhere except in St. Byz., who is quoting H. (2) H. calls the inhabitants of the district Κρηστωναῖοι (v. 3. 2), not Κρηστωνιῆται as here. (3) The only Pelasgians in this district are in the Athos peninsula (Thuc. iv. 109. 4), and these are definitely called 'the Tyrsenians who formerly settled in Lemnos and Athens'; but H. distinguishes the people here from the Tyrsenians and from the Pelasgians 'who lived with the Athenians'.

Hence Niebuhr conjectured Κροτῶνα and Κροτωνιῆται in § 3, i. e. Cortona in Etruria, originally an Umbrian town, which H. distinguishes from the famous Croton in South Italy by the words ὑπὲρ T. This conjecture has been widely accepted (e.g. by Meyer, F. i. 23–4); the reasons are:

(1) Τυρσηνοί everywhere in H. means 'the Etruscans'.

(2) Dion. Halic. i. 29, quoting this passage, *καὶ γὰρ δὴ . . . ἐν φυλακῇ* (3), reads Κροτωνιῆται, and (i. 18 seq.) describes the migration of the Pelasgians to Umbria, where they made Cortona their chief town (cf. Hell. Fr. 1 for the same tradition; but Hell. identifies the Pelasgians and the Etruscans).

(3) The reading Κρηστῶνα, it is suggested, is a later correction, based on an inaccurate remembrance of Thuc. iv. 109.

For the objections to this conjecture cf. Myres, J. H. S. xxvii. 195 seq.; he argues 1) H. is unfamiliar with Italy, and would not compare an Italian town with Aegean peoples; 2) he knows this part of the Aegean coast-line well; 3) the passage of Thucydides really confirms H. It may be added that the MSS. agree in giving Κρηστῶνα. For H.'s familiarity with North Italy cf. 196. 1.

Thessaliotis lay west of Olympus and Ossa (cf. 56. 3 for Dorians there); it was more often called 'Pelasgiotis'.

2 Placie and Scylace lay east of Cyzicus on the Propontis (here called 'Hellespont'; cf. iv. 38. 2 n.). For the expulsion of 'Pelasgians' from Attica cf. vi. 137 n., from Lemnos, vi. 140, and App. XV, § 5.

3 **χαρακτῆρα.** H. uses this word of the four Ionian dialects (142. 4); from this parallel Thirlwall (i. 53) argued that H. meant here that 'the Pelasgian language . . . sounded to him a strange jargon, as did the dialect of Ephesus to a Milesian, and as the Bolognese does to a Florentine'. This is ingenious, but the Pelasgian question cannot be settled so easily.

58 **ἀποσχισθέν.** The sense of this word is shown in iv. 56. 1, where H. uses it of a river separating from another; so in 143. 2, of the 'separation' of the Ionians of Asia Minor from the rest of the Ionians. Obviously, therefore, H. thought his 'barbarian' Pelasgi closely akin to the Hellenes. In 60. 3 H. says *τὸ Ἑλληνικὸν ἀπεκρίθη τοῦ βαρβάρου ἔθνεος*, i.e. marked itself off as somewhat superior. Thucydides (i. 3. 2) carries the process a stage further; the development is not 'spontaneous', but the result of 'contact with the *φύσις* of the genuine Hellene'; T. s' 'explanation of the transmissibility of culture is to be sought not in physiology but in psychology' (Myres, A. and C. p. 152). Whether **ἀποσχισθέν** here implies local or ethnical separation, it is impossible to decide, but probably the latter.

μέντοι: contrasted with *μέν*, growth as compared to language.

προσκεχωρηκότων. Thucydides (i. 3) also speaks of the 'Hellenes' absorbing Pelasgic and other peoples; among these 'others' are the Minyans of Orchomenus, the Abantes, the Dryopes (146. 1), &c.

59-64 The account of the tyranny of Pisistratus, one of the most valuable of H.'s contributions to sixth century history; for it cf. App. XVI, §§ 5–8. It should be read with Arist. Ἀθ. Πολ. c. xiii. 3–17, an account based in part on H., but with many additions (cf. Busolt, ii. 302 n. 2). For H.'s general judgement of the Pisistratidae cf. v. 78 n.

59 1 **κατεχόμενον καὶ δ.** These words have been attacked as unfair; but it must be remembered that they are a description of Athens, as Croesus would hear of it circ. 550 B.C.; as such they are too compressed, but in the main accurate; Athens was 'held down' by P., and the fact that it was 'torn asunder' gave him his opportunity.

2 Chilon was ephor at Sparta about 560; Sosicrates said of him *πρῶτος εἰσηγήσατο ἐφόρους τοῖς βασιλεῦσι παραζευγνύναι* (Diog. Laert. i. 68); this is taken by scme (e. g. Niese in P. W. s. v. Chilon) to

mean that he established the ephorate; but more probably it only implies that he greatly increased its power. A fragment of a second century author (Rylands Papyri, No. 18) says of him with King Anaxandridas that τυραννίδας κατέλυσαν; it goes on to mention Hippias of Athens and Aeschines of Sicyon, apparently as put down by these two (cf. Plut. de Mal. H. 21, and App. XVI, § 10); but the fragment breaks off suddenly. This tradition may well be true in the main, though the chronology is inaccurate. For his connexion with the Lycurgean discipline cf. c. 65 n. He was reckoned as one of the Seven Sages (cf. 27. 2 n.), and Plut. (Mor. 35 F) says a collection of his pithy sayings was extant. Cf. vii. 235. 2 for his practical wisdom.

3 **τῷ λόγῳ**, 'making himself the champion of the cause of'; λόγος is partly the 'account' to be taken of his partisans, partly what could be urged in their favour. Stein thinks there is an implied opposition to ἔργῳ, 'nominally' he was for others, really for himself; but this is forced. Myres (A. and C. p. 165) says: 'the phrase suggests that it was not a district, but a region that was in question—a region above the corn level.' He adds that any one from the Acropolis in spring can 'recognize the abrupt change from emerald green to purple and brown, which tells where πεδίον and cornland end, and the goats of the ὑπεράκρια begin'.

The rise of these factions was the natural result of the Solonian changes, which had broken down the traditional rule of the Eupatridae. The local divisions, on which the factions were largely based, are reflected in the myth of the four sons of Pandion (Strabo, 392); but no doubt the main struggle was between the old landed aristocracy and the rising mercantile class.

The παραλία is the southern half of Attica, the triangle terminating in Sunium, the πεδίον is the south-west of Attica, the basin of the Cephissus and the Thriasian plain. Cf. Thuc. ii. 55. 1 οἱ Πελοποννήσιοι, ἐπειδὴ ἔτεμον τὸ πεδίον, παρῆλθον ἐς τὴν Πάραλον γῆν καλουμένην μέχρι Λαυρείου, where the Athenians have their silver mines'. Ure (Origin of the Tyrannis, J. H. S. xxvi. 136) suggests that the Διάκριοι are not local, but are 'the mining population of Attica' supporting 'the great mine-owner, Pisistratus'. But, not to speak of the evidence of Thucydides (*u. s.*), there is no reason to think that any large section of the Athenian population was employed in the mines at this time, even if free men ever worked there, which is very doubtful; Solon, fr. 13. 49–50, quoted by Ure, refers to manufactures not to mines.

H. differs from A. P. 13. 4 in making the third faction later than the rest (it certainly would be organized later); he also gives its name differently, ὑπεράκριοι, not διάκριοι (cf. Plut. Sol. 29 for the latter form).

For Megacles cf. the story of Agariste's wooing, vi 126 seq.; for the Alcmaeonid family cf. 60. 2 n.; his great-niece was the mother of Pericles, whose second son was called 'Paralus'. Lycurgus was an Eteobutad; to this aristocratic faction belonged the Philaidae; cf. vi. 35 seq. for the story of their chief, Miltiades.

The faction of Pisistratus was in east and north-east Attica; his own deme, *Φιλαῖδαι* (Plut. Sol. 10), lay near Brauron some twenty miles south of Marathon; cf. c. 62 for his strength in this region. Near Brauron was discovered the *στήλη* of an Aristion, who may well be (Bury, pp. 192–3) the man of that name who proposed (A. P. 14. 1) the tyrant's bodyguard.

4 **δῆθεν** shows the statement is false; cf. 73. 5. The *πολυθρύλητον αἴτημα* (Plat. Rep. 566 B) for a bodyguard was the first step to tyranny.

στρατηγίῃ. H. probably uses this word in a non-technical sense, but even if he meant it to be technical, it would prove nothing; he is often anachronistic in his constitutional details; cf. vi. 109 n. There is no evidence for the existence of the *στρατηγοί* before Cleisthenes, except in the more than suspicious 'Constitution of Draco' (A. P. 4); if they existed, they were mere subordinates of the Polemarch. For the tyrant owing his rise to distinction in war cf. Ar. Pol. v. 5. 6–8 (1305 A) with Newman's note. For the chronology of the wars with Megara cf. Busolt, ii. 217 seq. Some (e. g. Sayce) have supposed that H. makes here a mistake similar to that as to Croesus and Solon (cf. c. 29 nn.), introducing Pisistratus into a war that really belongs to the previous generation. Others (e. g. Beloch, i. 327) make Pisistratus the conqueror of Salamis, not Solon; but apart from Solon's own poems (frags. 2 and 3) all tradition gives the conquest to the older man. It is more natural therefore to suppose that the Megarian war, victoriously ended by Solon (Plut. Sol. 10), had been renewed during the confusion at Athens that followed his legislation (cf. A. P. 13), or perhaps even before his legislation, as Plutarch (c. 12) definitely states, and that the struggle with Megara was finally ended by Pisistratus; Justin, ii. 8, describes the capture of Nisaea by him, though without naming the town.

The inscription discovered in 1884 may perhaps refer to the settlement of Salamis after the conquest by Pisistratus; but others date it at the end of the sixth century (cf. Hicks, pp. 6–7; Busolt, ii. 444 n. 2).

5 These 'clubmen' (*κορυνηφόροι*), fifty in number (Plut. Sol. 30), were not called by the usual name of a tyrant's guard, *δορυφόροι*.

6 **ἀκρόπολιν.** Cf. Mayor, Juv. x. 307 n., for this first step to tyranny. Pisistratus was unlike the usual tyrant (iii. 80. 5), cf. App. XVI. 5. H. forms a just estimate of the home, but not of the foreign (App. XVI. 8) policy of Pisistratus.

The *τιμαί* are the members of the two Councils and the archons; the Pisistratidae *αἰεί τινα ἐπεμέλοντο σφῶν αὐτῶν ἐν ταῖς ἀρχαῖς εἶναι* (Thuc. vi. 54. 6).

60 2 **τῇ στάσι:** Stein translates 'harassed by the attacks of his own

party', and cf. 61. 2; but 'troubled by the party strife' is simpler. The willingness of the Alcmaeonid family to marry with, and to restore, a tyrant is very inconsistent with their character as 'tyrant-haters' in vi. 121, 123; cf. App. XVIII. 6.

3 ἐπεί is to be taken closely with τότε γε, 'at that time when the Greek race had long been separated.' It is noticeable that here, as elsewhere, H. holds inconsistent views as to the Pelasgi; they are 'barbarians', but they become Hellenes without difficulty.

4 The story of the sham Athene is one of the most curious in H.; he is shocked by it, and introduces sarcastic touches (e. g. σχῆμα οἷόν τι ἔμελλε) into it; but he completely believes it. Grote has an excellent note (iv. 32) on the contrast between the views of the sixth and of the fifth century, implied in H.'s criticism here; he compares the contrast of views as to a combat of champions in H. i. 82 and Thuc. v. 41. As H. had met possibly the sons and certainly the grandsons of men who had seen the restoration, and as he carefully sifted his traditions as to the Pisistratidae (cf. v. 55. 1 n.), it is safer to accept the story, as e. g. Grote, Curtius, Busolt (ii. 321), and others do. Cf. vi. 105. 3 for Athenian acceptance of the supernatural (Pan and Philippides). Somewhat similar acts are that of Telines (vii. 153) and the share of St. Catherine in the return of Gregory XI to Rome in 1376. Beloch, however (Rh. Mus. 45, 1890, whom Meyer, F. ii. 248, follows), rejects the whole story as a 'poetic variation of the historic tradition of the victory at Pallene'. The argument is as follows: the victory was gained at the temple of Athene Pallenis (c. 62. 3); hence Athene was metaphorically said to have restored Pisistratus. The metaphorical version grew into a myth, perhaps with the assistance of a commemorative monument—this suggestion had been made by Stein before Beloch—and then the fiction found a place in history, side by side with the real fact. Beloch concludes that Pisistratus was only restored *once* and expelled *once*, and that the intrigue with Megacles belongs to the first usurpation.

It argues almost greater credulity to suppose that history and myth could become thus inextricably mixed in the course of two generations than to accept the story of Phya. It may be noted that there is independent fourth-century evidence for the story in A. P. 14. 4 and in Cleidemus (Athen. 609 C; F. H. G. i. 364), who makes Phya wife of Hipparchus.

This passage is very significant for Greek stature: this 'daughter of the gods divinely tall and most divinely fair', was only about 5 feet 10 inches.

πανοπλίῃ: i. e. with helmet, breastplate, spear, and shield, as in the familiar Athene statues; cf. iv. 180. 3 for the investing of a mortal with these attributes of Athene.

5 The demes were pre-Cleisthenean, though he gave them political importance (v. 69. 2 n.); here and in 62. 1 they = 'the country dis-

tricts' as opposed to τὸ ἄστυ; they were the strongholds of Pisistratus, who had the peasants on his side, as opposed to the landowners and the trading class; cf. 59. 3 n.

61 3 **προαιδέατο**, 'were under obligations to'; cf. iii. 140. 2. The friendship of the Thebans for the Athenian tyrant is very noticeable; the continuous rivalry of the two great cities in middle Greece through the fifth century was the result of the diplomacy of Cleomenes; cf. vi. 108 nn.

4 For Lygdamis cf. Ar. Pol. v. 6. 1, 1305 a 41, with Newman's note; he had become tyrant as leader of the people in avenging an aristocratic outrage (Athen. 348). Apparently he lost his tyranny (this is implied here) and was restored by Pisistratus (64. 2). If we may trust Polyaenus (i. 23) he had assisted Polycrates to obtain the tyranny of Samos, thus forming a link between the two great Ionian tyrants. He seems to combine the two characters of democratic champion and well-born condottiere. For his fall cf. 'Plut.' de Mal. Hdt. c. 21.

For the curse cf. v. 71 n.

62 1 H. gives two notes of time as to the Pisistratid rule, in this passage and in v. 65. 3 (that it lasted thirty-six years): Aristotle (Pol. v. 12. 5, 1315 b 32) gives it thirty-five years, and to Pisistratus himself seventeen; A. P. 17. 1 gives him nineteen years. There are numerous other data in A. P. cc. 14–17, but they are hopelessly confused; see Sandys on A. P. 14. 3 for a discussion of the subject.

The ultra-sceptical view is that of Beloch (i. 328), that the traditional dates are merely based on calculations of generations, one for Pisistratus himself and a half for his sons, i. e. 33 + 17 = 50 years in all, and that one-half of his rule is given to exile. Rejecting this argument as a not very probable guess, we may take the following dates as approximate: First tyranny, 560–559, archonship of Comeas (this traditional date is accepted even by Beloch). First exile, 555. Second tyranny, 550. Second exile, 549. Third tyranny, 539. Death, 527. Expulsion of Hippias, 510 (Thuc. vi. 59. 4). But certainty is impossible.

Μαραθῶνος. In the Diacria where his party was strong. Cf. 59. 3 n.

3 **ἐς τὠυτὸ συνιόντες**, 'intending to join battle.' Pallene lay south of Mount Pentelicus, commanding the pass between it and Hymettus; here the road from Marathon on the north-east joins that from Brauron on the south-east of Athens. The place was the scene of the mythical battles between the Athenians and Eurystheus (Strabo, 377) and between Theseus and Pallas (Plut. Thes. 13); this latter battle, like the one here (cf. the oracle), was decided by a surprise.

4 For **θείῃ πομπῇ χρεώμενος** cf. iii. 77. 1; iv. 152. 2; H. obviously looks on P. as favoured of heaven.

Ἀμφίλυτος ὁ Ἀκαρνάν. Some propose to read ὁ Ἀχαρνεύς, because Plato (Theag. 124 D) calls him ἡμεδαπός, i. e. an Athenian; but the

Acarnanian mountaineers were famous seers (cf. vii. 221, Megistias, and the prevalence of second-sight among the Scotch Highlanders). Stein suggests that Pisistratus may have given him citizenship, and compares for this ix. 33 seq.

χρησμολόγος (cf. vii. 6. 3) may mean either the seer himself or the collector of oracles (cf. Thuc. ii. 8. 2). The Pisistratidae were closely connected with oracles (cf. ἐκ τῶν λογίων 64. 2) and seers; they had a collection of oracles (v. 90. 2), and were friendly with Onomacritus the Orphic teacher (vii. 6. 3 n.). Pisistratus himself was nicknamed Bacis (Schol. Aristoph. Peace 1071). This connexion, like their temple-building and encouragement of cult, was a convenient support of their rule (cf. App. XVI, § 7).

63 1 **ἄριστον**: here the midday meal; the 'siesta' or games follow it.

2 **ἀναβιβάσας.** Helbig (Les Ἱππεῖς Athéniens, p. 191) thinks the phrase indicates that the young men were serving as mounted hoplites, not as cavalry; he thinks (p. 231 seq.) Athens had no real cavalry till the period 478–457 B.C.

64 1 A. P. 15. 3 mentions a general disarmament. This seems hardly consistent with Thuc. vi. 56, 58. The passage here gives two of the distinguishing marks of a tyranny, direct taxation of citizens and a mercenary force.

συνόδοισι is rare for προσόδοισι. **αὐτόθεν**: the reference is to the mines of Laurium and to the land-tax of 10 per cent. (A. P. 16. 4), reduced by P.'s sons to 5 per cent. (Thuc. vi. 54. 5).

Στρυμόνος. A. P. 15. 2 tells us that Pisistratus during his second exile made money from the regions round Mount Pangaeus', i. e. near Amphipolis, where Philippi was founded later. The mines here are to be distinguished from those of Σκαπτὴ Ὕλη opposite Thasos, and owned by that island (vi. 46. 3). The mention of the Thraceward 'revenues' agrees with the conjecture, probable on other grounds, that Thucydides the historian, who had possessions in that region (iv. 105. 1), was connected with the Pisistratidae; but cf. Grundy, Thucydides, p. 16.

For a tyrant's hostages cf. iii. 45. 4.

2 For Delos cf. vi. 97 n., and App. XVI, § 8 for general foreign policy of Pisistratus.

3 **μετ' Ἀλκμεωνιδέων.** As Alcmaeon was agent of Croesus (vi. 125), there were other reasons than those given by H. (59. 1, 65. 1) for Croesus not seeking Athenian alliance.

65–8 *A digression on Lacedaemonian history, containing accounts of* (1) *Lycurgus* (c. 65), (2) *the foundation of the Lacedaemonian hegemony, especially the war with Tegea.* (For the questions as to Lycurgus cf. especially Meyer, F. i. 213–86.)

I. Lycurgus a 'heroized god'.

The historical reality of Lycurgus is often denied (e.g. by Meyer (*u. s.*); Busolt, i. 578; Gilbert, G. C. A. p. 15; Bury, p. 135) because:

1. The evidence for him is late; apart from Simonides (Plut.

Lyc. 1) H. is our oldest witness; the fragments of Tyrtaeus never mention him; yet it is equally hard to believe either that Tyrtaeus would have said nothing of Lycurgus, had he ever existed, or that any mention of him by Tyrtaeus, had there been one, would have failed to be quoted when the subject was so much discussed.

2. The statements as to Lycurgus are contradictory (cf. 65. 4 for variations of date); and his work was attributed by Hellanicus to Eurysthenes and Procles (Fr. 91; F. H. G. i. 57).

3. His name (i. e. 'Wolfheart', Meyer, *u. s.* 281, or 'Light-Worker', Gilbert) is suspicious, as are also those of his father (Eunomus or Prytanis, Plut. 1), and of his son (Eucosmus, Paus. iii. 16. 5).

4. He was worshipped as a god at Sparta (*v. i.*), and Meyer (ii. 277) denies that we find mortals deified in Greece before Alexander; but this is doubtful.

5. Greek legends tended to ascribe all institutions to some law-giver; cf. Solon, Zaleucus, &c. 'The omnipotence of law' is a 'strange Greek superstition'; 'they have no sufficient conception of the way in which things are stronger than men, and the passive resistance of circumstances stronger than the insight and will of an individual' (Oncken, Arist. Staats.-Lehre, i. 244–5).

Meyer (F. i. 279) goes so far as to suggest that the legend of Lycurgus as founder grew up 'gradually after the Persian wars, when the Spartans became conscious of the peculiar character of their native institutions'. He is 'borrowed from the original population, like the cults of Helen, the Dioscuri, and Agamemnon' (ib. p. 282). Hence Lyc. is a 'heroized divinity'; Gilbert makes him a form of Apollo Λύκειος, Meyer (ib. 282, following Wilamowitz) and Busolt of Zeus Λυκαῖος (the 'Wolf-Zeus'), an Arcadian god. Grote, Curtius, Holm, and others, however, make

II. Lycurgus a real man.

1. Because of the analogy of similar legends; Charlemagne, Roland, and Archbishop Turpin are historical persons, however much their story was embellished in the Chansons de Geste (cf. the discussion as to the historical existence of King Arthur, E. B. ii[9]. 651).

2. The peculiar character of Spartan institutions is best explained by the dominating personality of some individual, who did not invent them, but who systematized them and rendered them permanent. Holm (i. 188) well compares the part played by the Doge Gradenigo in settling the Venetian constitution, Reich the foundation by great personalities of the religious orders in the Roman Church.

III. Lycurgus a historical fiction.

A further difficulty arises from the archaeological discoveries of the British School at Sparta since 1906: these show that the city was a centre of art down to after 600 B.C., and then almost suddenly ceases to be so. It is possible that the Lycurgean ἀγωγή actually dates from this period, and was the work of a reformer (perhaps of Chilon, cf. 59. 2 n.), who attributed his drastic innovations to a supposed ancient founder, or that at any rate an old and weakly enforced discipline was reintroduced in a stricter form. (For this latter view cf. Dickins in Class. Quart. v. 241.) Such a view would account for the absence of genuine tradition as to Lycurgus, while it satisfies the main argument for his existence, viz. that a strong personality is needed to explain so peculiar a development.

If, however, we accept the personality of Lycurgus (Frazer, v. 606, goes so far as to say 'It should never have been called in question'), it must be admitted that we know nothing of him; H.'s account is not real history; it is only valuable as the fifth century official Lacedaemonian account of history. (See Note D, p. 449.)

65 Leon, father of Anaxandridas and grandfather of Cleomenes, and Agasicles, father of Ariston and grandfather of Demaratus, ruled between 600 and 560 B.C. 'The other wars' are probably (1) those connected with the overthrow of the Cypselidae after 585 and of other tyrants (cf. Thuc. i. 18. 1), (2) those against Argos and (in alliance with Elis) those against Pisa (cf. Busolt, i. 705–6).

2 **καί** introduces the second cause of Lacedaemonian hegemony, i. e. they had overcome their difficulties; they had recently defeated Tegea, and they had 'also' before this got a good constitution. Thuc. (*u. s.*) seems to refer to this passage; he dates the change 'a little more than four hundred years before' 404 B. C.; but he pointedly omits Lycurgus.

ἀπρόσμεικτοι. The exclusiveness of Sparta is made pre-Lycurgean; this is doubtful; H. makes the Minyae to be received (iv. 145) as citizens in the earliest days; in the seventh century the Ionic Epos and Aeolic music came in (cf. the stories of Terpander and Alcman). It was only in the sixth century that exclusiveness was intensified or more probably introduced.

3 The oracle as quoted in Diodorus (vii. 12) ends with the lines

ἥκεις δ' εὐνομίαν αἰτεύμενος· αὐτὰρ ἔγωγε
δώσω τὴν οὐκ ἄλλη ἐπιχθονίη πόλις ἕξει.

These are probably a later addition.

θεόν. For his *ἱερόν* cf. 66. 1 n.; Plutarch (Lyc. 31 *θύουσιν ὡς θεῷ*) speaks of his divine honours; he is mentioned as a god in inscriptions, e. g. C. I. G. 1256. But all this does not disprove his original humanity.

4 It is worth while to tabulate the more important differences between the Herodotean and the other accounts of Lycurgus:

1. H. denies that he derived his institutions from Delphi; but this was the usual fourth century account, e. g. Xen. Rep. Lac. viii. 5 and Plat. Leg. 624; cf. 691 E. Meyer (F. i. 231 seq.) ingeniously ascribes this later view to King Pausanias (408–395 B. C.), and maintains that the verses of Tyrtaeus (Plut. Lyc. 6) which assert it are a later forgery.

2. H. makes Lycurgus guardian of Leobotes, his nephew, i. e.

he is an Agiad and his date is about 1000 B.C. But Simonides (Plut. Lyc. 1) makes him a Eurypontid and uncle of Charilaus (king 884 B.C.); so too Ar. Pol. ii. 10. 2, 1271 B. Plut. (ib.) also quotes Aristotle for a third date, i.e. Lycurgus is put in the eighth century, and made to organize 'the Olympic Truce' (on the strength of the inscription on 'the quoit at Olympia'). No wonder Timaeus thought there were two Lycurgi.

3. H. makes him legislate as regent, Ephorus (Strabo, 482) at a time when Charilaus was actually king.

4. H. gives him the whole Spartan constitution; but *v.i.* for other dates for the Ephorate and Gerousia.

It may be added that the one point on which traditions agree, viz. that he legislated as uncle of the king, was an obvious guess; for his name was not on the royal list, and yet men felt he must have been a Heracleid.

κόσμον. The well-known Spartan *ἀγωγή* is implied; H. gives this to Lycurgus as a matter of course.

For a comparison of the institutions of Sparta and of Crete cf. Ar. Pol. ii. 10 (1271 B seq.). Ephorus (Strabo, 481–2) argued elaborately for the priority of Crete; but his view as to the similarity of the two constitutions is criticized by Polybius (vi. 45–6); there is not sufficient evidence to decide the question. The institutions are in each case the expression of 'the warrior life of a conquering primitive people' (Oncken) surrounded by enemies and hostile subjects.

5 **ἐφύλαξε.** The 'security' was an oath to observe the laws till his return (Plut. Lyc. 29); this is probably borrowed from the story as to Solon (c. 29. 2). So, too, the statement that he travelled is considered by some to be an invention copied from the genuine travels of the Athenian.

The **ἐνωμοτίη**, i.e. 'sworn brotherhood', was the smallest tactical unit of the army, containing in 418 B.C. about thirty-two men (Thuc. v. 68. 3), at Leuctra 'not more than thirty-six' (Xen. Hell. vi. 4. 12); but the number no doubt varied.

τριηκάδας, 'companies of thirty.' For conjectures as to their nature cf. Hermann, Staats-A. i. 197. n. 4; perhaps the word is a gloss to explain *ἐνωμοτία* (a case of 'obscurum per obscurius'). The number 'thirty' occurs again in Sparta in the Senate, and perhaps in the number of the *ὠβαί* (Plut. Lyc. 6 *ad init.*; *sed incerta lectio*).

The **συσσίτια** were originally military organizations, the band of warriors united by the common meal.

ἐφόρους. Three views are taken as to H.'s statements about the Ephors and the Gerousia:

(1) That both statements are right; Ephors and Gerousia were part of the primitive constitution, and so associated with Lycurgus. Cf. Xen. Rep. Lac. c. 8 for Ephors, c. 10 for Gerousia; Isocrates, Panath. 165–6. Meyer (F. i. 246) accepts this view; holding that

Lycurgus has no historical reality, he identifies his supposed institutions with the primitive constitution.

(2) That the first is right and the second wrong. Clearly the γέροντες are the old council of chiefs and pre-Lycurgean; but the Ephors may be definite officers, created by Lycurgus to superintend the ἀγωγή.

(3) That both statements are wrong. The Ephorate is assigned to a date later than Lycurgus, i. e. the reign of Theopompus: for (*a*) Aristotle (Pol. v. 11. 2, 1313 A) tells the story of his answer that he left the kingship ἐλάττων but πολυχρονιωτέρα (cf. Plat. Leg. 692; Plut. Lyc. 7, Cleom. 10). (*b*) The list of ephors begins 755–754 B.C., i. e. in the reign of Theopompus (but this date, if it be historical at all, might refer to an alteration in the power of an old office). Meyer (F. i. 250) argues that the post-Lycurgean date for the Ephorate is due to King Pausanias (cf. 65. 4 n.) and the constitutional struggles at Sparta early in the fourth century. Owing to the authority of Aristotle (*u. s.*), it displaced the earlier view and was generally adopted.

All we can say for certain is that (1) the Ephorate is found in the colonies of Thera, Cyrene, and the Tarentine Heraclea, and so may have been an early institution in Sparta, their reputed μητρόπολις (but cf. iv. 145 nn.); (2) that the office was closely connected with the ἀγωγή. For the whole subject of the Ephorate cf. Busolt, i. 555 seq.

66 1 **ἱρὸν εἰσάμενοι.** Pausanias (iii. 16. 5) adds οἷα δὴ θεῷ; this is implied in ἱρόν; a hero had only a τέμενος or a ἡρῷον; Frazer (P. ii. 153–4) gives the differences; the ἡρῷον faced west not east, and ἐναγίζειν (not θύειν) is used for the sacrifices in it, i. e. the worship was chthonian, not celestial.

Ἀρκάδων. The earlier Arcadian war is important as a turning-point in the policy of the Lacedaemonians; the stubborn resistance of the highlanders of Central Peloponnese made them give up attempting complete conquest (which they had carried out in Messenia), and be content with a hegemony over dependent allies. Pausanias (iii. 7. 3 *et al.*) puts this war in the time of Charilaus (884–824); but it really belongs to the beginning of the sixth century (65. 1).

2 The Arcadians were considered (probably rightly, cf. the survival of the Iberian Basques in the Pyrenees) as of the race of the aboriginal Pelasgians (viii. 73. 1 n.); hence the epithet 'acorn-eating', which implies a primitive civilization (cf. Lucr. v. 939) before the days of agriculture. Cf. the epithet προσέληνοι, Plut. Mor. 282; Quaes. Rom. 76; Schol. ad Arist. Nub. 398.

Tegea lay in the southern part of the great eastern plain of Arcadia. Being surrounded with hills (Frazer, P. iv. 422), it is compared to an ὀρχήστρα: so Epaminondas called the Boeotian plain ὀρχήστρα πολέμου (Plut. Mor. 193 E; Apoph. Imper. 18).

σχοίνῳ. The reference to allotments is proof of land assignment as an early Spartan institution. The later story that the land was divided *equally* by Lycurgus (cf. Plut. Lyc. 8) is a manifest fiction; but the poem of Tyrtaeus, quoted by Aristotle (Pol. v. 7. 4, 1307 A 2), refers to the fact that ἠξίουν ἀνάδαστον ποιεῖν τὴν χώραν. Early Sparta, like early Rome, had agrarian troubles, and solved them in the same way—at the expense of its neighbours.

3 **κίβδηλος**: properly of false coin; used by H. especially of oracles (cf. 75. 2; v. 91. 2). There is a double meaning in the 'juggling' oracle (cf. Macbeth, v. 8. 19–20: 'And be these juggling fiends no more believed That palter with us in a double sense'); ὀρχήσασθαι might be referred either to the 'dance' of triumph or to ὄρχος, a 'row of vines', and so to slave labour. Again the land might be 'measured' (διαμετρήσασθαι) by the Lacedaemonians as conquerors or as captives.

4 **πέδας.** No doubt the 'temple of Athena Alea' was the source of the story; Pausanias (viii. 47. 2) saw the fetters there in the second century A.D. For the 'fetters' as evidence of Lacedaemonian overconfidence cf. similar story of Armada (but see Froude, xii. 380). For this temple cf. H. ix. 70. 3; it was burned in 395 B.C. (Paus. viii. 45), but restored on a magnificent scale with sculptures by Scopas, Frazer, P. iv. 425–6. For the name 'Alea' cf. Farnell, C. G. S. i. 274.

67 1 The traditional dates for Anaxandridas and Ariston are 560–520; 560–510. This second Arcadian war (circ. 550 B.C.) is historical; but it is interesting to see that H.'s account is made up of oracles and legendary details (cf. the similar account of the first Aeginetan war, v. 82–7, which is a little earlier in date).

2 Perhaps there is a confusion between the famous Orestes and an Arcadian hero Oresthes (cf. ix. 11. 2 n. 'Ορέσθειον). Pausanias (viii. 5. 3) makes the former migrate from Mycenae to Tegea, but this is probably a late invention. The discovery of supposed relics is no doubt a fact; we may compare the legend as to Alexander's body (Ael. V. H. xii. 64), and the removal of the bones of Theseus to Athens (circ. 470 B.C.; Plut. Cim. 8). The present translation is the consecration of the Lacedaemonian hegemony in Peloponnese, as the later one is that of Athenian hegemony in the Aegean.

For the work of Delphi in unifying local cults cf. Paus. viii. 9. 2 (the translation of the bones of Arcas from Maenalus).

Two ideas underlie the Lacedaemonian policy:

(1) They were consciously aiming at identification with Achaean traditions (cf. v. 72. 3, vii. 159).

(2) The local hero's remains were the talisman that secured the land's security (cf. Soph. O. C. 1522 for their concealment, and Tylor, P. C.[4] ii. 150).

The discovery of gigantic fossil bones (Frazer, P. ii. 483) probably is the origin of this and similar stories; the almost mediaeval character of the tradition (cf. the translation of St. Mark's relics to Venice in the ninth century) reminds us how far removed from their predecessors and from the mass of their countrymen were the rationalist Athenians of the fifth century and later.

4 **καὶ τύπος κτλ.**: here the 'sound' is 'the echo of the sense'.

πῆμα: a reference in part to the idea that the iron age was the last and worst; but also (cf. 68. 4) to the fact that iron is the material of deadly weapons.

ἐπιτάρροθος. The finder of the hero's bones would by their aid become the helper, i. e. 'patron' of Tegea.

5 The Spartan royal bodyguard were called Ἱππεῖς, although we only hear of them serving on foot; we are expressly told (Strabo, 481) that they differed from the Cretan ἱππεῖς in having no horses; the name is a survival from early times (cf. ἡνίοχοι and παραβάται in Theban Sacred Band (Diod. xii. 70) for a like survival). This is more probable than that they were mounted infantry, like the early Athenian ἱππεῖς (cf. 63. 2 n.), who used horses as a means of transport, but fought on foot. There was no genuine cavalry in Laconia till 424 B.C., when παρὰ τὸ εἰωθός (Thuc. iv. 55. 2) a corps of 400 horsemen was set up.

The Spartan 'horsemen' were three hundred in number, cf. vii. 205. 2 (though this corps at Thermopylae was perhaps specially selected), viii. 124. 3; Thuc. v. 72. 4. In vi. 56 the king's bodyguard is only one hundred. H. seems to imply that they served by rotation; perhaps thirty were enrolled each year, one from each ὠβή. Some see in this the explanation of τριηκάς (65. 5); if this be so, perhaps the five seniors among those serving their last year were ἀγαθοεργοί and had civil functions. Xenophon (Rep. Lac. iv. 3) speaks of a special body of three hundred, chosen each year by three ἱππαγρέται, nominated by the ephors; if these three hundred are the 'knights', the change in method of election may be a mark of the increased power of the ephors in later times.

68 1 **ἐπιμειξίης.** The detail of a 'truce for intercourse' comes in to explain how Lichas could be in Tegea.

ἐξελαυνόμενον (cf. 50. 2); the surprise at the working of iron is a very primitive feature that has become incorporated in a sixth-century myth.

2 **χαλκεύς** is used even of an iron-worker; cf. Lucr. v. 1287 'Prior aeris erat quam ferri cognitus usus'.

3 Cf. Il. i. 272 and H. ii. 91. 3 for the great stature of early heroes; a tall mortal might be six feet; cf. Arist. Ran. 1014.

5 **ἐκ λόγου πλαστοῦ**, 'banished him on a fictitious charge'; the prosecution was a pretence to secure Lichas admittance to Tegea. As an alien he had no ἔγκτησις γῆς there, and so was compelled to 'hire' the court.

6 **ἤδη δέ σφι**: an exaggeration, although Lacedaemonian hegemony was established over Arcadia by 550 B.C.

69 2 This is the earliest instance of the recognition of Lacedaemonian

headship in Greece. Later instances, chronologically arranged, are: i. 152 (Ionians, c. 546 B.C. In the same cap. the Lacedaemonians themselves also claim it); vi. 108 (the Plataeans, 519 B.C., but vid. n. *ad loc.*); iii. 148 (Maeandrius, c. 514 B.C.); vi. 84 (the Scythians); v. 49 (Athens against Aegina, 491 B.C.). All these lead up to the recognized hegemony against Xerxes, vii. 161. 2; viii. 2. 2.

4 Thornax lay to north of Sparta (Frazer, P. iii. 322). Pausanias (iii. 10. 8) says the gold was used to decorate the statue of Apollo Pythaeus at Amyclae, which was similar to that at Thornax but more important; he describes (iii. 19. 2) it as a brazen pillar about 45 ft. high, with head, feet, and hands, i.e. it was a primitive cult-statue, marking transition from the aniconic age.

70 **ζῴδια** = ζῷα, 'figures', not of animals alone, in relief round the rim: H. had seen it in the Heraeum (cf. iii. 47. 1 n.).

71–92 *Story of Croesus resumed* (after digressions of cc. 56–70).

71 2 By the story of Sandanis H. illustrates dramatically, after his manner, the contrast between the simplicity of the early Persians (Strabo, 734) and the luxury of the older kingdoms; in his own day (cf. § 4 Πέρσῃσι γάρ κτλ.) the Persians had become notorious for luxury (cf. c. 135). Such contrasts are characteristic of Oriental history (cf. the Moguls in India).

σκυτίνας. For Persian dress cf. c. 135 nn.

3 **οὐ σῦκα δέ**, 'not even figs,' the commonest fruit in the East.

72 1 For Καππαδόκαι cf. 6. 3 n.

2 H. rightly recognizes the importance of the Halys, which is the ethnic frontier in Asia Minor (cf. App. I, § 1); its change in direction from south-west to north-west is implied in ἄνω; it rises in 'Little Armenia'. The Armenians, who were Φρυγῶν ἄποικοι (vii. 73), had already spread beyond the Halys.

For H.'s Cilicia cf. iii. 90. 3 n.

Ματιηνούς. The passages as to the Matieni may be summarized as follows (cf. T. Reinach, R. E. G. vii. (1894) 313 seq.):

(1) They are placed on the south-west of the Caspian, though not touching it (Strabo, 514; in 509 S. puts them in Media), but had originally a greater extension to the south-west; so Xanthus, fr. 3 (F. H. G. i. 36) places L. Urmiah (L. Matianus) among them.

(2) This wider sense is the usual one in H.; the Matieni (iii. 94. 1), are grouped with the Saspeires (south-east of Trapezus) and the Alarodii (in valley of Araxes) in the eighteenth satrapy; so the Araxes rises ἐκ Ματιηνῶν (202. 3).

(3) But their name extends even more widely, e.g. Mount Zagros = 'Matienian Mountains' (189. 1), and in v. 49. 6, 52. 4–5 Matiene fills the whole space between Armenia and Susiana, and is crossed by the Royal Road in thirty-four stages; i.e. it includes what H. elsewhere calls 'Assyria', and = modern Turkish and Persian Kurdistan. But H. is inconsistent: for in v. 52. 4 he makes the

Greater Zab rise in Armenia, though its source, being south-east of that of the Araxes, should be in Matiene.

(4) Quite different is the meaning in the passage here and in vii. 72. 2, which put the Matieni on the bend of the Halys, near the Paphlagonians.

Reinach conjectures they were once a widespread race, reaching from the Halys to near the Caspian; but they were cut in two by Armenian immigration, and so survived at two ends of their former home; perhaps they may = the 'Mitani' of Tell-El-Amarna tablets. Of the four uses of Ματιηνοί (2) is the official name, while (3) is the older geographical name of the whole region.

Συρίους Καππαδόκας. H. sometimes puts the general name first (as here and in vi. 20), sometimes the special name (Ἀρκάδες Πελασγοί 146. 1).

3 **πέντε**: this estimate is repeated ii. 34. 2, where Sinope is given as the northern limit; but the distance from Sinope to the Mediterranean is about 350 miles, while Asia Minor is 300 miles across where narrowest. Moreover, the route across Asia Minor is through difficult country. Similarly Pliny (N. H. vi. 7) gives the distance as '200 miles'. Some suppose that H. has confused with the ordinary time for the journey the 'record' of Persian couriers (cf. viii. 98. 2 for their relays). Pheidippides (vi. 106. 1) is credited with about 140 miles in two days, and Rawlinson (*ad hunc loc.*) says a modern Persian courier covers 50 miles a day. But H. is speaking simply of an εὔζωνος, i.e. *expeditus*, and he elsewhere calculates a day's journey at 200 stadia, i.e. about 23 miles (iv. 101. 3). We can explain the mistake easily if we suppose that H. misunderstood his informant; it was 'about five days' journey' from Sinope to the northern boundary of the Persian Cilicia (iii. 90. 3); H. took the distance as referring to the southern boundary. Meyer (ii. 287) thinks the mistake proves that there was a direct road across Asia Minor here. H. is followed in the mistake by the pseudo-Scylax (Per. 102).

73 2 **γαμβρός** is any connexion by marriage, here a 'brother-in-law' (74. 4); H. as usual gives a personal motive; for other reasons cf. 46. 1 n.

3 The story may be true in outline (cf. Morier, J. R. G. S. vii. 242, for wars in the East caused by nomad migrations). No doubt many Scyths remained in Media, when the main body had been expelled or annihilated (106. 1 n.). The story of the Thyestean banquet (§ 5), however, is suspiciously reminiscent of the story of Harpagus (c. 119) and of the myth of Tantalus.

For the Scythian bow cf. iv. 9. 5 n.; cf. Plat. Leg. 795 A, who says the S. were ambidextrous in its use, and Jer. v. 16 'their quiver is an open sepulchre'.

74 1 Night battles were rare in ancient warfare (cf. Thuc. vii. 44, the attack on Epipolae); this one is not the 'eclipse battle' (*v. i.*).

2 This date is one of the few definite points in the history of the period; it is fixed as May 28, 585, by the astronomers; the other eclipse of the period, that on Sept. 30, 610, was only partial in Asia

Minor. The later date (585) is given by Plin. (N. H. ii. 53) and (approximately) by the ancient chronologers, Eusebius and Jerome. It suits also the circumstances:

(1) The fall of Nineveh c. 606 had enabled Cyaxares to extend his power north-west, and so brought him into contact with Lydia.

(2) Labynetus (i.e. Nebuchadnezzar) did not begin his reign till 604.

It used to be argued (e.g. by Stein) that H., because Cyaxares was conqueror of the Scyths, had wrongly introduced him here, and that Astyages began to reign in 594 B.C. But the revised Median chronology (App. III, § 6) makes all the dates nine years later, and so the account in H. becomes possible.

Thales is the Merlin or Michael Scott of Greek sixth-century tradition. It has been maintained that this prediction is impossible, in view of what we know of his scientific theories; Stein thinks that he can only have explained the phenomenon afterwards. But H., who rejects the story as to his engineering (75. 6), accepts this one. Thales' prediction may have been based on Chaldean calculations (cf. Burnet, Early Gk. Phil. 35). (See Note E, p. 450.)

3 **συμβιβάσαντες.** No doubt the mediating princes were glad to limit the dangerous growth of Cyaxares' power.

Syennesis (like 'Pharaoh') is a title (probably Semitic) borne by the native rulers of Cilicia (v. 118. 2; vii. 98); they seem to have submitted voluntarily to Cyrus, and so were allowed to retain their kingdom (cf. App. VI, § 7); they were dependent or independent as the central power was strong or weak (ix. 107 n.). The dynasty disappears at the beginning of the fourth century. For Labynetus cf. App. II, § 5.

4 **ἐπαλλαγήν.** We know of no Median queen in Lydia; the 'mutual' element may have been furnished by Nebuchadnezzar's marriage with a Median princess (c. 185 n.).

ἀναγκαίης = *necessitudo*; ancient diplomacy believed as firmly as modern in marriage alliances, and with as little reason.

6 For the resemblance cf. 35. 2 (purification) and App. I, § 5.

ὁμοχροίη, 'the outer skin'; cf. the proverb for superficiality, *οὐδὲ ἅπτεται τῆς ὁμοχροίας* (Plat. (?) Axio. 369 D). For the blood covenant cf. iii. 8. 1 n.

75 1 **ἐν τοῖσι ὀπίσω.** For this promise fulfilled cf. cc. 107 seq.

3 **τὰς ἐούσας**, 'the (then) existing bridges': for a bridge on the Great Road cf. v. 52. 2. Garstang (Hitt. p. 28) places the bridge near Cheshme Keupru, where the road from Caesarea to Angora recrosses the river.

5 For final use of optative with *ἄν* (Homeric) cf. Goodwin, M. and T. p. 117 (ed. 1889).

76 1 **κατά**: not 'near' but 'on the line of'. For H.'s rough attempt to construct geographical 'parallels' cf. ii. 34. 1 and App. XIII, § 4. Pteria is probably Boghaz Keui, within the bend of the Halys (lat. 40°), about 60 miles north-east of the bridge; the exploration of the ruins began by Winckler in 1906 has brought to light a mass of tablets in cuneiform script, partly in Babylonian, partly in a language as yet untranslated (cf. King and Hall, pp. 468 seq.); they include fragments of diplomatic correspondence with Egypt and the East, of the thirteenth and fourteenth centuries B.C. The 'Royal Road' (cf. v. 52 nn.) crossed at Pteria the road running north and south from Sinope, *via* Mazaca and the Cilician gates, to Tarsus (Ramsay, A. M. p. 33). The early importance of Pteria probably determined the direction of both these roads, neither of which follows the easiest line for a through route. It seems to have been the capital of an Anatolian kingdom which we may call 'Hittite'; for the history of this cf. Garstang, Hitt. pp. 315 seq.; for a description of the ruins of Pteria, ib. p. 197 seq., well illustrated with photographs.

2 H. emphasizes the guilt of Croesus as aggressor, to justify his later overthrow (cf. 130. 3). Garstang (pp. 33, 199) seems to think that the Hittite power survived till the capture of Pteria by Croesus, but this is very doubtful.

1 Later writers (Just. i. 7; Polyae. vii. 8) say that Croesus was defeated. H.'s story may be due to Lydian vanity, but is probable in itself. Croesus found he had advanced too far; perhaps he had expected Egyptian co-operation at Pteria; at any rate he may well have thought that Cyrus would not attack him, with Babylon and Egypt hostile in flank and rear.

2 **Λαβύνητος.** Not the Labynetus of 74. 3, but Nabonidus, the last Babylonian king (cf. 188. 1 n.).

3 **ἐς χρόνον ῥητόν.** No doubt he had summoned his allies before, though H., dwelling on the personal element, omits to mention it.

4 **ξεινικός,** 'so far as it was mercenary.' The Lydian kings depended for infantry on Greeks and Carians; the Lydians were horsemen (77. 3). This disbanding may be an invention; but Croesus, not expecting to be attacked, may have wished to save the expense of an army through the winter; H. is at least consistent.

2 For the genitive after *ἐς* cf. Plat. Prot. 325 D *εἰς διδασκάλων πέμποντες*; but the *τῶν* before *ἐξηγητέων* is unusual.

There were three places called Telmessus—in Pisidia, in Caria, (about seven miles from Halicarnassus), and in Lycia; probably the last is here meant (cf. 84. 3). Arrian (Anab. ii. 3. 3) says the gift of prophecy was hereditary there. Cf. Head, H. N. 698, for Apollo on the (late) coins of Telmessus.

3 **ἀλλόθροον.** For the interpretation of the well-known struggle in Attica between Poseidon, whose symbol is the horse, and Athene, whose fosterling, Erechtheus, is 'earth-born' and snake-like in form, cf. viii. 41. 2 and J. H. S. xix. 215.

3 **τοῦτον τὸν χρόνον.** H. adds this, because the Lydians of his own day were a proverb for effeminacy. Cf. App. I, § 4 (and Bacchylides iii. 23 *δαμάσιππος Λυδία*).

80 For the topography of Sardis cf. Perrot et Chipiez, v. 249-50, and

84. 3 n. Its citadel (τεῖχος, § 6) stood on a spur projecting north from Mount Tmolus, with which it was connected by a low ridge; this rises very sharply to the height of about 600 feet, fully justifying H.'s account of its inaccessibility (c. 84). Round it flow two rivers, the gold-bearing Pactolus on the west, and on the east a perennial stream, H.'s Hyllus. The ἄστυ lay on these (84. 5) between the πόλις (84. 3, i.e. the 'citadel') and the rivers. συρρηγνῦσι gives the personal touch of one who has seen these mountain streams.

One branch of the Hermus flows from the Murad Dagh, a ridge west of Pessinus, from which town Cybele's aniconic image was brought to Rome in 204 B.C. On this ridge she was worshipped as 'Dindymene' (Hor. Odes, i. 16. 5); for other local names cf. Strabo, 469, and for another cult-statue of her in high places cf. the 'Niobe' of Mount Sipylus. She had a temple in Sardis (v. 102. 1). For her worship generally cf. App. I, § 2.

2 For Harpagus cf. 109. 3 n. and App. IV, § 4.

82–3 *The Lacedaemonian Conquest of Thyrea.*

The narrative of H. (§ 3 βοηθησάντων) seems to imply that Thyrea was now conquered by the Lacedaemonians for the first time; they had, however, begun their aggressions on Argive territory before this, for H. (vii. 235. 2) implies that Cythera was theirs soon after 600 B.C. The conquest of the east coast may well have been gradual. The chronologers speak of a Lacedaemonian victory in Thyrea under Polydorus in 718 B.C., and Pausanias (iii. 2. 2) puts the conquest of Cynuria down to Echestratus (1059–1025); but these are probably inventions. The Argive chronology seems to have been artificially constructed in periods of fifty years, reckoning back from the Battle of Mantinea in 418; we have 718 as here, and 668, their victory at Hysiae. For a short epitome of Busolt's excellent notes (i. 595–7) on these dates cf. Bury, ii. 468.

The Thyreatis remained a bone of contention in the fifth century; for the negotiations of 420 B.C. cf. Thuc. v. 41, with its implied reference to this passage.

82 2 H. is Elizabethan in his impartial spelling. Cf. Μαλέων here with Μαλέην of iv. 179. 2. Thyrea was the northern part of Cynuria, which certainly once belonged to Argos (viii. 73. 3 n.).

ἑσπέρην. The east coast of Laconia does lie west of Argolis; but H. ignores the fact that it also lies south (for his weakness in orientation cf. vii. 176. 3 n.; ix. 14.

αἱ λοιπαί. Several small islands lie off Cythera (Strabo, 363); hence there is no need to see an echo of the well-known line, Il. ii. 108.

3 For the combat of picked warriors cf. ix. 26. 3 and the legend of the Horatii (Liv. i. 25). An historical instance is the conflict on the North Inch of Perth in 1396, so well described in Scott's 'Fair Maid of Perth'. The Spartan three hundred may be the Hippeis (67. 5 n.), but this is very doubtful.

5 Pausanias (x. 9. 12) says the Argives dedicated an offering at Delphi for the victory; but his narrative is inconsistent (Frazer, P. v. 265, 637).

7 κατακειράμενοι. The story is suspicious, as it looks like an attempt to explain a difference of custom between kindred peoples; the Greeks originally all wore long hair (*κάρη κομόωντες Ἀχαιοί*), and the conservative Spartans may have retained the custom, which died out elsewhere merely from motives of convenience. Certainly in fifth-century Athens *κομᾶν* was a sign of Laconizing (Arist. Av. 1281–2).

The custom of cutting the hair as a sign of grief (ii. 36. 1; Il. 23. 141), and of wearing it long as a sign of pride (cf. Absalom), is a well-authenticated one. Cutting the hair and the flesh for mourning (for the combination cf. iv. 71. 2) was forbidden to the Jews (Deut. xiv. 1). The hair was regarded as the symbol of the man; so a priest's tonsure is a sign of dedication. For the whole subject of hair cf. Tylor, P. C. ii. 400 f.; Robertson-Smith, Rel. Sem. p. 323; and Hastings' D. B., s. v. 'Hair'.

8 Pausanias (ii. 20. 7) makes Othryades killed by an Argive. Chrysermus, a Corinthian writer of unknown date, said that he, left on the field seriously wounded, set up a trophy with an inscription in his own blood (F. H. G. iv. 361); this is a mere embellishment on H.'s narrative.

84 2 For a like capture of Sardis (by Antiochus in 215 B.C.), owing to over-confidence, cf. Polyb. vii. 15 seq.

3 ἐστι. H. as an eyewitness uses the present. There were two kings called 'Meles' (Nic. Dam. frags. 24, 49; F. H. G. iii. 371, 382). For the defence of a fortress by magic cf. the burial of King Lud's head at Ludgate (Geoffrey of Monmouth, iii. 20), the removal of which by the over-confidence of a later king enabled Caesar to take London.

American explorers have been digging at Sardis since the beginning of 1910. They have discovered a great temple of Artemis, with a dedicatory inscription in Lydian of some length, but so far nothing that throws light on the earlier history of the city. Cf. J. H. S. xxx. 361, xxxi. 301.

τὸν λέοντα. The germ of the story may be a genuine native myth for the lion was the sacred beast of Sandon, the Lydian sun-god (cf. 50. 3 n.).

ἔστι δὲ πρός, κτλ. Translate, 'It is the part of the citadel (*πόλιος*, cf. 80 n.) facing Tmolus.'

4 For a similar clue given by the besieged cf. Liv. v. 47. 2.

85 1 ἐπιφραζόμενος: H. unites a finite verb with a participle frequently, perhaps for emphasis (cf. 129. 1).

The son of Croesus became a proverb for silence, just as Croesus himself did for self-inflicted misfortunes (P. G. ii. 686).

2 ἀμφὶς ἔμμεναι = *abesse*.

86 The chronologers give Croesus fifteen years, but H. does not reckon the last year (as unfinished), perhaps because he wished to

bring out the coincidence of the 'fourteen days' and the 'fourteen years'.

For the date of the capture of Sardis cf. Busolt, ii. 459–60. The usual date, 546 B.C., is that of Eusebius and most of the chronologers; the Parian marble, however, made it 541, and this date seems to have been that given by Xanthus: between these two dates it is impossible to decide. Duncker (iv. 326) put it in 549, as he thought it must have preceded (cf. 90. 4) the burning of the Delphic temple (548, 50. 3 n.), but this conjecture has not been generally accepted.

As to the fate of Croesus we have two contradictory traditions:

I. *That he perished.* Bacchyl. iii. 23–63 (Ode to Hiero, 468 B.C.; Jebb, pp. 195–7, 256–61) makes the pyre voluntary; Apollo carries Croesus off to the land of the Hyperboreans. This is confirmed, as to the voluntary nature of the act, by the Louvre amphora (No. 194, figured J. H. S. xviii. 268, where it is dated circ. 500, and in Bury, p. 228). The authority for this tradition is therefore slightly the older.

II. *That he was spared.* We have this in three main forms: (*a*) That of H., supported by Ephorus (Diod. ix. 34; cf. also Nic. Dam. fr. 68 (F. H. G. iii. 407), who adds embellishments of his own). (*b*) Xen. Cyr. vii. 2 makes Croesus spared to be the adviser of Cyrus, but omits all marvels. (*c*) Ctesias (c. 4, p. 64) says nothing of the pyre, but makes Croesus saved by other marvels, and adds that Cyrus gave him the town of Barene (near Ecbatana).

There is, apart from the miraculous elements, the further objection to the story that Cyrus, as a fire-worshipper, would not have polluted the sacred element (cf. iii. 16. 2). It may be argued that, not to speak of the possibility of mad freaks like those of Cambyses, Cyrus' beliefs sat lightly on him (cf. the Cylinder Inscription, R. P.[2] v. 166–8, for his behaviour to the Babylonian gods, and Tac. Ann. iii. 62). But the objection, though not itself decisive, is serious.

To return to the main difficulty: it is hard to believe that Croesus perished (as Maspero holds, p. 656), in defiance of the independent evidence of Ctesias and of H. The latter also tells stories of Croesus later (cc. 155, 207, iii. 14, 36) which could hardly have gained currency as to a dead man; they seem, moreover, to come from sources different from those of the Lydian history. The explanation then of Bacchylides' story may be that he gives, as Jebb shows, a Delian version of the facts. Croesus was, so to speak, canonized as a model of piety (this is implied in his being represented on a vase at all, C. R. 1898, p. 85), and so a myth had grown up around him; cf. for his religious character Pind. Pyth. i. 94, his *φιλόφρων ἀρετά.*

We may then reject the evidence of Bacchylides, and assume that Croesus survived; but it is difficult to decide the further points:

(1) Meyer, i[1]. 503, thinks his pyre was a solemn act of self-devotion; cf. for instances of voluntary burnings vii. 107 (Boges), vii. 167 (Hamilcar), 1 Kings 16. 18 (Zimri), and the legend of

Sardanapallus, the last king of Nineveh (F. H. G. ii. 505). This is the most probable view; it is supported by the oldest evidence, and consistent with Cyrus' religious beliefs.

(2) Nöldeke (E. B.[9] xviii. 566) accepts the pyre as the act of Cyrus, of course discarding the miraculous embellishments.

(3) A less probable view is that the whole pyre story is an invention, due to the confusion of myth with history. This view makes Croesus to be confused with the sun-god, Sandon, who perishes in fire (cf. Hercules on Mount Oeta), just as his son was confused with Atys (34. 2 n.).

2 **δὶς ἑπτά.** The 'twice seven' (the sacred number) boys are a religious touch.

3 **ἀνενεικάμενον,** 'fetching a deep sigh.' Cf. Il. xix. 314 of Achilles; the meaning is defined by the synonym *ἀναστενάξας*.

5 **οἷα δή,** 'with such and such words.' H. spares his readers the repetition of what they have read in c. 32.

οὐδέν τι μᾶλλον, 'referring to all mankind just as much as to himself.' The *οὐκ* (not in MSS.) must be restored, or the sense would be 'just as little' (cf. iv. 118. 3 and Thuc. vi. 82. 3 for omission of negative).

περιέσχατα. H. adds this touch to explain how Croesus could talk at such length on a burning pyre.

7 1 **εἴ τί οἱ.** An echo of the prayer in Il. i. 37 seq.; for similar echoes cf. *φίλον ἦν* (§ 4) and Il. ii. 116, 88. 1 and Il. xxiv. 631.

2 Bacchylides (iii. 55) makes Zeus send the rain.

4 The aversion to war is characteristic of H. Cf. v. 97. 3 and viii. 3. 1.

9 1 **οἱ ἐνορῴη**: i. e. to the prejudice of Cyrus.

3 For dedication of a tithe of spoils cf. vii. 132. 2 n. and Liv. v. 21. 2, 25. 5 (Camillus at Veii).

0 1 **ἀναρτημένου,** 'ready.' For the Persian belief in royal blood cf. iii. 15. 2 n.

2 **οἱ**: i. e. **τῷ θεῷ**: dat. after *ἐπηγορέων* (which is a *ἅπ. λεγ.*).

1 1 **τὴν πεπρωμένην**: the answer is significant for the theology of H. Not only men (cf. iii. 43. 1; ix. 16. 4) are bound by Fate, but gods also (vii. 141. 3), in so far as they cannot save their worshippers (cf. Apollo in Euripides' Alcestis). If this be H.'s meaning, it is an advance on the early idea that the gods themselves were ruled by destiny, which survives in the Prometheus of Aeschylus. But there was a growing tendency from the beginning of the fifth century to identify Fate and the will of Zeus, who is thus exalted above all subordinate deities (cf. vii. 141. 3).

πέμπτου. The reckoning ('fifth' from Gyges) is inclusive; for the bearing of this and of the 'three years of grace' (§ 3) on Lydian chronology cf. App. I, § 9.

2 **Λοξίας** is Apollo's title at Delphi; cf. Aesch. Eum. 19 **Διὸς** *προφήτης ἐστὶ Λοξίας πατρός*. The old derivation from **λοξός**,

'crooked,' referring to his 'dark' oracles, is unlikely in an official title. Some derive from the root ΛΥΚ, i. e. 'light-giver'; others connect with ἀλεξιτήριος, i. e. 'averter'.

5 For the birth of Cyrus cf. c. 107 seq.

6 ὑπό, with dative, as the Persians were not so much directly ruled by the Medes as 'in bondage under' them.

92 1 H. here winds up his Lydian history. This chapter shows Croesus in a new light, as a cruel Oriental prince (§ 4), and also gives a non-Delphian account of his oracular success (contrast c. 49). It clearly comes from another source. As it is not likely to be a later addition, it is probably a fragment of H.'s original material, which he has not worked into harmony with his narrative.

The temple of Ismenian Apollo (cf. viii. 134. 1; v. 59) was just outside the city of Thebes, on the hill of St. Luke (Paus. ix. 10. 2 and Frazer, v. 40). Tripods were especially dedicated at it (Pind. Pyth. xi. 4 τριπόδων θησαυρόν). Divination at it was by inspection of fire and ashes (cf. Soph. Ant. 1005–11). Every eight years it was the scene of the Daphnephoria, familiar from Leighton's great picture. Golden 'cows' were perhaps dedicated (as a symbol of fertility) to Artemis, as representing the great 'Mother Goddess' (cf. App. I, § 2).

For the Artemision cf. Hogarth, Excavations at Ephesus, 1908, especially pp. 5–8, 245–6. The earliest shrine was probably at Ortygia, under Mount Solmissus, to the south of Ephesus; this was no doubt earlier than the Greek settlement (cf. Paus. vii. 2. 6, who rejects the statement of Pindar that it was founded by the Amazons; but παρθένοι were always associated with the cult); the earliest, near the city itself, dated from about 700; this was destroyed by the Cimmerians circ. 660 B.C. The next two temples followed rapidly, and then the famous one, which owed so much to Croesus, was begun about 550. It seems not to have been finished till about 430, and was destroyed by the arson of Herostratus in 356. Pliny (N. H. xxxvii. 98) states that the Hellenistic temple which followed had 127 columns, 'a singulis regibus factae' (obviously in contrast to αἱ πολλαί here). Hogarth (pp. 327 seq.) points out that the 'many-breasted' Artemis as a coin type seems to belong to Roman times, not to be archaic.

Croesus' name can still be read on an Ephesian column-base in the B. M. (Cat. i. 29; Hicks, p. 7).

Athena's temple at Delphi stood near the entrance to Apollo's; hence the epithet 'of the fore-shrine', which is confirmed by inscriptions (Ditt. i. 186). The same epithet is used of Athena and Hermes, in reference to the shrine of the Ismenian Apollo (Paus. ix. 10. 2).

For A. Προναία at Delphi cf. viii. 37. 2 n., Aesch. Eum. 21, and Paus. x. 8. 6 (Frazer, v. 251). The epithet later was made Πρόνοια with an ethical significance (Farnell, G. C. i. 306).

2 H. had not seen the offerings at Branchidae; they no doubt

perished when the temple was destroyed in 494 B.C. (cf. vi. 21 n.); the story that they were treacherously handed over to Xerxes by the people of Branchidae (Strabo, 634), who for this were massacred later by Alexander (Curtius, vii. 23; Strabo, 518), is to be rejected. On the similarity of weight and form, and on the supposed lack of Croesus-inscriptions (but cf. 51. 5 n.) at Delphi, C. Niebuhr founds the wild theory that Croesus never gave gifts to Delphi at all, but that the Branchidae offerings were feloniously transferred thither, about the time of the Ionic Revolt (Mitt. der Vorder-As. Gesell. 1899, pp. 27–8). The whole article is a tissue of guesses and uncritical assumptions.

ἀνδρός. His name was Sadyattes; cf. Nic. Dam. fr. 65, F. H. G. iii. 397, who says that he offended Croesus when crown prince by refusing a loan; Croesus then vowed to devote his property to Artemis, if he ever became king (cf. *ἔτι πρότερον* § 4).

3 Pantaleon may have been the elder, as Croesus was born in the twenty-third year of his father's reign (cf. 25. 1 and 26. 1). For the conspiracy cf. 51. 5 n.; Pantaleon perhaps had some Greek support, as being *ἐξ Ἰάδος*.

4 The *κνάφος* was an instrument of torture, like a fuller's comb; probably it resembled the mediaeval wheel for breaking criminals. Cf. Plat. Resp. 616 A *ἐπ' ἀσπαλάθων κνάμπτοντες*.

1 **θώματα.** H. says nothing of the volcanic region, *ἡ κατακεκαυμένη* (Strabo, 628), in NE. Lydia, though it had been described in the work of Xanthus (cf. Introd. § 19).

καταφερομένου: i. e. by the Pactolus (v. 101. 2).

2 **σῆμα.** The 'Tomb of Alyattes' lies on the north edge of the Hermus plain. It is one of more than sixty mounds (called Bin Tepeh), of which three are conspicuously larger than the rest. Perrot et Chipiez (v. 265 seq.) make the largest rather more than 1,200 yards round, and not quite 400 in diameter; this falls a little short of H.'s measurements (§ 5), viz. about 1,280 and 440 yards respectively. The base (*κρηπίς*) is hewn in part out of the native limestone, above which comes a wall of large blocks; H. does not notice this difference of construction. This base holds together a truncated cone of earth, of which the upper part is faced with bricks. A rectangular chamber inside contained bones of men and animals which had been burned. The *σῆμα* is referred to by Hipponax. fr. 15 *Ἀττάλεω* (v. l. *Ἀλυάττεω*) *τύμβον καὶ σῆμα Γύγεω*, and briefly described by Strabo (627).

3 **οὖροι,** 'record-pillars.' These were phallic in shape, set up on the flat top; two of them have been found, one *in situ*; but they bear no trace of an inscription.

4 **πορνεύονται.** Many see in this custom a religious significance, e. g. Ramsay, C. and B. pp. 94–5, 115; Radet compares the worship of Mylitta (c. 199 nn.), a view which is supported by Aelian, V. H. iv. 1, and Strabo, 532, who definitely compares the Lydian custom to that in the temple of Anaitis in Armenian Acilisene—noble maidens *κατα-*

πορνευθεισας πολὺν χρόνον παρὰ τῇ θεῷ, μετὰ ταῦτα δίδοσθαι πρὸς γάμον, οὐκ ἀπαξιοῦντος οὐδενός. Ramsay quotes an inscription of the second century A.D., as to a woman of considerable position, παλλακεύσασα καὶ κατὰ χρησμόν, and no doubt such religious prostitution had been more common in early times. But there is no good evidence that it was ever universal in Lydia; and the custom itself may be paralleled in countries of quite different religions, e.g. in Japan. L. Oliphant (Lord Elgin's Mission (1857–9) ii. 496 says: 'No disgrace attaches to women who have been brought up in this manner (i.e. as courtesans), and they generally make good marriages.' No doubt the custom in Lydia was mainly confined to the lower classes, who may have been of a different race (cf. App. I, § 4). For freedom of choice in marriage cf. Westermarck, c. 10.

5 **Γυγαίη**: now L. Colve; for the name cf. App. I, § 8.

94 1 **παραπλησίοισι.** For the similarity cf. App. I, § 5. The statement as to the invention of coinage is usually accepted as in the main accurate (G. F. Hill, G. and R. C. p. 7, Hist. Gk. Coins, 1–2, 18–20; Head, H. N. 643). Pollux ix. 83 quotes Xenophanes (fl. circ. 540) for the same statement, but he quotes also four divergent views. Bars and rings of metal of uniform weight had been used in Egypt and Babylon, but these needed frequent reweighing; coinage begins when some authority issuing coins guarantees the value by a stamp. The invention was natural for the Lydians, who, as 'the Phoenicians of the land', held the outlets of the great Eastern trade-routes. So the Aeginetans, the 'pedlars of Greece Proper', were the earliest coiners there. P. Gardner, however (B. A. P. iii. 110 seq.), thinks the earliest coins were probably of Asiatic Greek origin, perhaps struck privately by temples or bankers.

The earliest Lydian coins date from the reign of Gyges; cf. Γυγάδας χρυσός, Poll. iii. 87, vii. 98; both passages imply that Gyges struck coins of gold of peculiar purity; but the earliest coins were really of electrum (cf. 50. 2 n.); they were oval in shape, with a type on one side and punch-mark on the other. B. V. Head (in Hogarth, E. E.) considers that eleven of the seventy-eight Lydian coins found at Ephesus in the temple deposit are at latest of the time of Gyges; but he thinks they were issued privately and not by the king; the earliest royal Lydian coins were those of Alyattes, whose name perhaps can be read on some of them (H. N. 645).

Croesus introduced a gold and silver coinage, stamped with the confronting heads of a lion and a bull. The Aeginetans had anticipated him in silver (Hill, G. C. p. 20 and Pl. 1); but the statements of Ephorus, that Pheidon first coined silver in Aegina (Strabo, 376) and that he invented gold and silver coinage (Strabo, 358), are probably merely embellishments of H.'s statement as to his measures (vi. 127. 3 n.).

H. then may well be right as to the priority of the Lydians, but he omits the early electron coins, in view of the more famous issues of Croesus, and he is wrong in saying the Lydians were the first to coin 'silver'. For the standards cf. Hill, G. C. p. 18.

κάπηλοι. This statement as to 'retail trade' is, taken literally, false; such trade was familiar in Egypt and Babylon much earlier; but the Lydians were proverbially a nation of shopkeepers; cf. the proverb *Λυδὸς καπηλεύει* (P. G. ii. 510). Radet, pp. 295 f., gives a brilliant picture of the wealth and vice of Sardis.

3 For this ethnic genealogy cf. c. 7. 3 n.

For **Tyrsenus** Xanthus (fr. 1; F. H. G. i. 36) read Torrhebus. Cf. Introd. p. 23.

4 The same story was told of Palamedes at Troy (Soph. Fr. 380). For Greek games cf. W. Richter, Die Spiele der G. u. R.

κύβοι differed from *ἀστράγαλοι* (marked on four sides only) in having pips on all six sides. Athenaeus i. 19 rightly corrects H.'s tale as to the Lydian invention of games; Nausicaa's ball play is familiar.

5 For a similar migration to relieve over-population, and determined by lot, cf. Livy v. 34 (the Gauls); it is a usual motive in primitive history.

6 The Umbrians are vaguely extended by H. iv. 49. 2 to the 'river Alpis', i. e. to the Alps. The story, here first given (cf. App. XV, § 6), of the Lydian origin of the Etruscans is familiar, especially from Horace (Odes, iii. 29. 1 *et pass.*). It was rejected with contempt in the early days of criticism (cf. Mommsen, R. H. i. 128 seq.), and the Etruscans were brought into Italy by land from the north. Modern archaeology is now accumulating evidence which confirms Greek tradition; it tends to show that native Italian civilization in the north developed without interruption from abroad, while Etruscan civilization in Central Italy was introduced by sea (like that of Carthage), and resembles that of the later Aegean periods, e. g. in its Cyclopean walls. (Cf. A. and A. pp. 304 seq. and (for a fuller statement of the evidence) App. I. 13.)

-140 *Median and Persian History.*

This is one of the most interesting divisions of the history of H. He describes (1) the unification of Media (95–101) and its history till Cyaxares (101–6). (2) The early history of Cyrus and the fall of Media (107–30). (3) The customs of the Persians (131–40). For the sources of (1) and (2) cf. App. IV, § 4; for (3) H. uses his own observation as a visitor to Susa (cf. Intr. § 17). The important facts are given in the Appendixes on Assyria, Media, and Cyrus (II–IV), with especial reference to the narrative of H.

5 1 **σεμνοῦν.** For the anti-Achaemenid prejudice of H.'s source cf. J. H. S. xxvii. 40.

2 The pres. part. *ἀρχόντων* shows that the Median kingdom arose before Nineveh fell; but H. is wrong in implying that the Medes took the lead in revolt because of their bravery; it was to their

remoteness from Nineveh they owed their comparative freedom. The κως (καί κως οὗτοι) indicates that he knows no details.

96 For Deioces cf. App. III, § 3. The story here is historical only in three points:

(1) H. rightly conceives the Medes as previously without unity.

(2) The foundation of Ecbatana was at once the symbol and the cause of union; but H.'s contrast of κατὰ κώμας (§ 2) and ἐν πόλισμα (98. 3) is Greek.

(3) He gives the true Oriental colour in laying stress on the importance of Deioces as judge; but the other details, e.g. the tyrant's 'friends' (97. 2), the body-guard (98. 2), the spies (100. 2) are parts of the ordinary Greek 'Tyrant's progress'.

97 1 **προκατίζων**: an Oriental touch, cf. v. 12. 2 n.; justice was administered 'in the gate' (cf. Ruth iv).

2 **κατηκόντων**, present circumstances.' The word is frequent in H., cf. iv. 136. 1; viii. 19. 2 ἐπὶ τοῖσι κατήκουσι πρήγμασι.

98 3 **περιστέλλοντας**, 'attending to this (town), &c.'; Deioces is described as carrying out a kind of συνοίκισις.

'Αγβάτανα is usually identified with Hamadan, 'where the passes of Mount Zagros emerge, uniting Iran to the basins of the Euphrates and Tigris' (Maspero, iii. 326); this was certainly the later Ecbatana. Sir H. Rawlinson's view that the Ecbatana of H. lay to the north-east in Media Atropatene (Rawlinson *ad loc.*) has not been generally adopted. The name (Pers. Hangmatána) means 'place of gathering'.

4 This description of the citadel is partly fact (Perrot et Chipiez v. 769). It was usual to have concentric lines of fortification; M. Dieulafoy has traced two only at Susa, but these were each very complex (ib. p. 767). H.'s 'sevenfold' defence, however, is an embellishment, due in part to a confusion with the Mesopotamian terrace-temples or Ziggourats, e.g. the great temple of Nebo at Borsippa (181 n.), in part to the desire to bring in the sacred number 'seven'. The colours of the seven circles are no doubt connected with the planets (Rawlinson quotes a parallel from the Persian poet Nizami, J. R. G. S. x. 127), but the order in H. is wrong. The effect was mainly produced by glazed bricks (cf. the frescoes in the Louvre from Susa), but also by a lavish use of the precious metals (cf. Polyb. x. 27. 10 for the riches of this very town, Ecbatana).

5 The circuit of Athens was about 60 stades (Thuc. ii. 13. 7); it is the *citadel* (99. 1) which is compared to this. Diodorus (xvii. 110. 7) gives that of the *town* of Ecbatana as 250 stades. Some have seen in this passage a proof that H. had himself been at Ecbatana; Kirchhoff argues from the comparison with Athens that the early books were written there (Introd. § 10 *a*); but neither of these inferences is probable.

99 1 The ceremonial of an Eastern Court is, of course, far older than Deioces. Stein takes τοῦτό γε as limiting καὶ ἅπασι to πτύειν, i.e.

none might spit in the king's presence, but those nearly connected with him might smile; it is impossible, however, to get this sense out of the words; καί adds emphasis to ἅπασι; cf. 133. 3 n. for the wickedness of spitting.

101 For the position of the Magi cf. App. VIII, § 3. The Median tribes seem to have been originally local; H. uses the same word, γένεα, of the Persian tribes (125. 3) which certainly were so (cf. for the situation of the Παρητακηνοί iii. 92. 1 n.). Ammianus (xxiii. 6. 32 seq.), in the fourth century A.D., gives a full account of the Magi, and speaks of them (§ 35) as 'inhabiting towns without walls' in Media, where they live 'protected by religious awe'. But the local tribe had an especially religious development (cf. the tribe of Levi in Palestine), and the priesthood was confined to its members; so among the Parsees to this day only the son of a Dastur can be a Dastur (Darmstetter, S. B. E. iv. p. xlvii). Perhaps some of the tribes were non-Aryan.

1 The conquest of Persia by the Medes is disputed, because it is inferred from the B. I. that the title 'king' was borne by the Achaemenids as far back as Teispes I (perhaps circ. 675), and Cyrus calls his three immediate ancestors 'great king' (App. IV, § 1); but this does not disprove H.'s statement, for apart from the possibility of filial flattery, in any case Persia must have been dependent on Media in the time of the next king, Cyaxares; and the reference in Ez. 38. 5 to Persia as an ally of Gog (circ. 580 B.C.) is too late and too vague to prove anything. All we can say is that H.'s statement may be true; but it quite lacks confirmation, and may be an invention of Median vanity (Prášek, i. 137; cf. App. IV, § 4).

2 **κατεστρέφετο**; it is important to notice the inceptive imperfect; H. knows the real founder of the Median Empire (103. 1, 2) was Cyaxares.

τότε: H. antedates the break up of the Assyrian Empire; Phraortes died circ. 625 B.C., and Assurbanipal's reign (circ. 668–626) seemed to leave Assyria as strong as ever; Babylon had been humbled (648), and Elam wiped out (circ. 640). But the mistake is venial, for the strength of Assyria was exhausted (App. II, § 4). The conquests of Phraortes may have been really aided by the Assyrian victory over Elam.

1 **διέταξε**. H. does not mean that horse and foot were previously mixed up with each other (cf. App. III, § 4), but that Cyaxares first organized his tribal contingents as a regular army.

2 For the eclipse battle cf. 74. 2 n.

3 For the Cimmerian-Scythian invasions in general cf. c. 15 nn. H.'s chief mistakes here are that—

(1) He confuses the *original* migration with the later raids. The Scyths were already in the earlier part of the seventh century settled south of the Caucasus round Lake Urmiah. It is probable, however, there were new bands of invaders from the north-east (cf. 104 nn.).

(2) It is probable the Scythian attack on the Medes was not accidental (*v. i.*).

(3) He makes too definite the 'rule of the Scyths'; as he himself says, the '28 years' (106. 1; iv. 1. 3) included the whole time of their wanderings.

For these later Scythian raids cf. Zeph. i (circ. 630–620 B.C.); Jer. i. 13–14, 'I see a seething pot and its face is towards the north'; and Maspero, iii. 472 seq. Rawlinson (i. 399) quite underestimates their importance.

Protothyes is probably the Bartatua of the monuments, to whom Esarhaddon gave his daughter in marriage. If the Assyrians really called in the northern barbarians as allies, they paid in the end dearly for the temporary relief, while the Medes suffered little, as they were protected by their mountains; it was like the inviting of Germans by the Sequani (Caes. B. G. i. 31). The name of Madyes, too, is confirmed by the monuments; Strabo (61) couples him with Sesostris and others as a leader of *οἱ ἐπὶ πολὺ ἐκτοπισμοί*.

104 1 **τριήκοντα.** The distance (about 300 miles) is a little more than that across Asia Minor (about 250 miles), to which H. assigns only five days (72. 3 n.), while here he allows thirty days, a far more probable estimate. H.'s distances are not actual measurements, but are only estimates based on the usual time taken for the journeys. Here, on the Black Sea coast, a great detour would be necessary.

For the Saspeires north-west of Media and south of the modern Georgia, cf. iii. 94 n. H.'s words here and in iv. 37 seem to point to the fact that one of the great roads of the Persian Empire ran from Ecbatana, past Lake Urmiah, into the upper valley of the Araxes, where the Saspeires lived, and thence over the mountains, to the Phasis valley and the Black Sea.

2 **Καυκάσιον ὄρος.** There are only two roads across the Caucasus:

(1) The 'Caucasian Gates', nearly in the centre, where the modern road past Vladikavkas runs.

(2) The road on the west of the Caspian, past Derbend, where the railway runs; probably H. means this second road. Stein, however, thinks neither of these can be called 'much longer', and so brings the Scyths east of the Caspian. This was probably the actual route of part of the invaders, but H. clearly did not know it.

105 1 For **Παλαιστίνῃ Συρίῃ** cf. iii. 5. 1 n.

2 For **οὐρανίῃ 'Α.** cf. c. 131 n; at Ascalon she was called Derceto, and her image was half woman, half fish.

3 **πυνθανόμενος.** For H.'s question cf. ii. 44. 1, where he says that he had travelled to Tyre to ask a similar question. For the temple at Paphos cf. J. H. S. ix. 193 seq., and for that of Cythera, Paus. iii. 23. 1; the statue in the latter was a *ξόανον ὡπλισμένον* (Frazer, iii. 338) which recalls the martial side of the goddess Ishtar. The temple was the oldest in Greece to the goddess. For the Phoenicians in Greece cf. iv. 147 n.

4 **θήλεαν νοῦσον.** The disease, described by Hippocrates (περὶ ἀέρων 22), is said by Ar. (Ethics vii. 7.6) to be hereditary in the Scythian royal families. Littré (Hippoc. ii, p. xl seq.) is inclined to follow Rosenbaum, Gesch. der Lustseuche, vol. i. (1839), that the θήλεα νοῦσος is παιδεραστία; this is the usual meaning of the words among the ancients, and the vice was thought hereditary. He admits, however, that this explanation does not correspond to the description of the disease in Hippocrates, and it is not a natural explanation of H. here. In iv, p. x, moreover, Littré quotes some curious cases of impotence described by the great French surgeon, Larrey, in the army of Syria (1799 A.D.), which seem to fit the words of H. much better than Rosenbaum's explanation.

ἅμα τε ought properly to follow the λέγουσι οἱ Σ.

For the ἐνάρεες cf. iv. 67. 2.

106 1 The 'twenty-eight years' are a piece of unexplained tradition; the old explanation that they are the interval between Cyaxares' accession and the fall of Nineveh breaks down, because we now know Cyaxares came to the throne in 625 not in 634 B.C.

The first χωρίς is an adverb, the second a preposition.

The Scyths were mere destroyers, and have been compared to the Huns of the fifth century A.D. (cf. Jer. vi. 22–3 for the description of them).

2 **καταμεθύσαντες.** The story is doubted by some (Meyer, i[1]. 465, who compares the legend of the Nibelungen-Lied); others accept, e.g. Nöldeke (E. B.[9] xviii. 563, s.v. Persia), who quotes parallels from Oriental history; there is nothing unlikely in it.

The capture of Nineveh took place c. 606. The strength of its fortifications is well described by Maspero, iii. 468–9.

ἐν ἑτέροισι. For the unfulfilled promise cf. Introd. § 14; for the Ἀσσύριοι λόγοι cf. App. II, § 6.

3 **τῆς Βαβυλωνίης μοίρης.** This is the only hint in H. that Babylon had a share in the overthrow of Nineveh; his informant knew this, though he himself did not.

For Astyages cf. App. III, § 5.

107–30 *The story of Cyrus*; 107–22 *his birth and upbringing*; 123–30 *his overthrow of Astyages.*

107 1 **αὐτὰ ἕκαστα,** 'the truth in detail,' as opposed to the dream; cf. Gen. c. 41 and Daniel *pass.* for 'interpreters of dreams', a genuine Oriental feature. This dream is by Ctesias (Nic. Dam. fr. 65; F.H.G. iii. 399) transferred to Cyrus' mother. The name of Mandane is otherwise unknown. H. is wrong in making Cyrus the grandson of Astyages, and Ctesias equally wrong in saying (c. 2, p. 64) that he married Astyages' daughter, Amytis. H. is right as to the name of Cyrus' father (III. 5), though he does not know that he was a king.

108 Justin (i. 4) tells the same story of Astyages' dream.

4 **παραχρήσῃ**, 'disregard'; cf. viii. 20. 1 *παραχρησάμενοι τὸν χρησμόν*; vii. 223. 3 (used absolutely of the Spartans at Thermopylae).

παραβάλῃ, 'strike aside,' and so 'deceive'; cf. the more common *παρακρούεσθαι*.

5 **φυλασσόμεθα δέ**, not *τε*, to show that the second clause is the more important.

109 1 **κόσμησιν** must be supplied to *τήν*; cf. vii. 62. 1.

3 **συγγενής.** Harpagus is of royal blood himself (*οἰκήιον* 108. 3).

ἄπαις. Xenophon (Cyr. i. 4. 20) gives Astyages a son, but H. is confirmed by the silence of the monuments.

110 1 The name Mitradates is clearly connected with the god Mithra (131. 3 n.); so in the Romulus legend, the herdsman Faustulus with the god Faunus.

Κυνώ. The dog was a sacred animal among the Iranians (140. 3 n.), and no doubt in the original legend the hero is suckled by a bitch as was Sargon of Accad; Justin (i. 4) gives both stories, the 'canis femina', and the nurse 'cui Spaco postea nomen fuit'. For the rescue by the sacred animal cf. App. IV, § 5. For the rationalization (122. 3) cf. Livy, i. 4. 7 (the she-wolf (*lupa*) becomes Acca Laurentia, a *lupa* by profession). This version of the story is Greek, but whether H. or his informants be responsible for it, it is impossible to say. For *Σπακώ*, which H. seems to be right in calling 'Median', cf. L. & S. s. v. *κύων*.

2 H. means the north part of Media, Atropatene, which is mountainous and wooded; but the statement that the rest is flat (*ἄπεδος*), even by comparison, is an exaggeration. Hecataeus (fr. 172; F. H. G. i. 12) says *περὶ τὴν Ὑρκανίην θάλασσαν οὔρεα ὑψηλὰ καὶ δασέα ὕλησι*; on this resemblance among others Prášek (Klio, iv. 205) bases his theory that H. borrowed this part of his story from Hecataeus, but the borrowing is probably the other way; cf. Introd. § 20.

111 1 **τόκου** is loosely dependent on *ἐν φροντίδι*.

5 The names, Cambyses and Cyrus, are correct (cf. 107 n. and App. IV, § 3).

112 1 For the beauty of the babe cf. the story of Moses (Ex. ii. 2; Heb. xi. 23).

μηδεμιῇ τέχνῃ, 'in no way'; cf. ix. 57. 1 *ἰθέῃ τέχνῃ*.

113 2 **προβοσκῶν.** A *ἅπ. λεγ.*; 'under-herdsmen,' because they feed the flock away from (lit. 'in front of') the homestead.

3 **ὕστερον.** Strabo (729) says Cyrus was first called 'Agradates'.

114 2 **ὀφθαλμόν.** The 'eyes and ears' of the Great King (cf. Xen. Cyr. viii. 2. 10) were thought by the Greeks to be a sort of spy system (cf. 100. 2), but this is an exaggeration. The 'eye of the king', however, was a real officer, in constant attendance on him (cf. Aesch. Pers. 980, and 'Pseudartabas' in Arist. Ach. 92).

ἀγγελίας: cf. iii. 84. 2 for *ἐσαγγελεύς*, a chamberlain admitting to audience with the king.

3 Artembares, in the other version of the story, is the eunuch cup-bearer of Astyages, who adopts Cyrus (Nic. Dam. fr. 66; F. H. G. iii. 398).

6 3 If reading **μοῦνος μ.** is right, it is modelled on Homeric *οἰόθεν οἶος* (Il. vii. 39).

5 **κατέβαινε** is used with a sort of zeugma here. Tr. 'he had recourse to prayers and (ended by) urging him'. For the use of the part. *κελεύων* cf. 90. 3.

7 3 **θυγατρί.** 'A murderer in the sight of your daughter.'

4 Harpagus (110. 3) had threatened the herdsman in the name of the king. As this was an invention, he softens it down, and proceeds to justify it. The whole speech is very dramatic.

5 In 113. 3 he sent 'spearmen'; some see in the 'eunuchs' here a trace of another version (cf. 95. 1) and even profess to find the character of Harpagus different (e.g. in c. 119). This is over-subtle.

8 2 **διαβεβλημένος,** 'being set at variance with'; cf. v. 35. 1.

9 3 **εὔτυκα,** 'ready,' a rare word except in Aeschylus; cf. Supp. 959.

0 1 **εἰ ἐπέζωσε.** The aorist with *εἰ* implies that the child's destiny could not now be realized, as they believe that he had been put to death.

3 **παρὰ σμικρά.** Translate: 'For in small things indeed have some of our oracles issued, and that which concerns visions altogether ends in weakness.' This utterance is dramatic, but, even so, it is curious in so strong a believer in oracles as H.

3 3 The Persian control of the roads is transferred back to the time of the Medes. Cf. v. 35. 3 n., vii. 239. 3, for similar secret messages. **μηχανησάμενος** ('having prepared') is explained by *ἀνασχίσας* and *ἀποτίλας*.

4 1 **φονέα.** For a parallel to this idea that the murderer in intention is a murderer in reality cf. Soph. O. T. 534.

5 3 Xenophon (Cyr. i. 2. 5) makes the Persian tribes twelve, a number to which he is partial in the Cyropaedia; but the authority of H. is preferable. Meyer (iii. 10) lays stress on the 'fundamental importance' of H.'s account here. Spiegel (Eran. Alt. ii. 238) says, 'The inscriptions as well as the Avesta show us that H. was right as to the tribal divisions of the Iranians.' It is interesting to contrast H.'s contemporary list with the artificial one in Strabo (727), in which the Achaemenidae and the Magi are inserted. The distinction of rank and privilege (cf. iii. 93. 2 n.; the Sagartians pay tribute) among tribes has parallels in H. (iv. 20. 1, the Royal Scyths as opposed to the 'Husbandmen' and the 'Nomads'), and elsewhere (cf. the 'Golden Horde' among the Tartans). Stein suggests that §§ 3, 4 are a later addition by H.

The Pasargadae (cf. iv. 167. 1) gave their name to the capital under Cyrus and Cambyses. It is identified with Murghâb, in the mountains to the north-east of Persepolis. That city was founded by Darius, as Pasargadae was too out-of-the-way for a capital.

The name, 'Persepolis,' however, does not occur till Macedonian times.

For the identification of Pasargadae and Murghâb cf. Perrot et Chipiez, v. 443–5. The view of Oppert, that Pasargadae is to be placed south-east of Shiraz, is impossible, as it removes the site too far from Persepolis.

At Murghâb is a building known as 'the tomb of the Mother of Solomon', which is usually identified with the tomb of Cyrus (for a defence of this traditional view cf. Curzon, Persia, ii. 74 seq.; for the tomb itself, P. et C. v. 597-607, with picture). The tomb is in seven tiers, with a chamber on the top, and answers to the description of Cyrus' tomb in Arrian (Anab. vi. 29. 4-8). On one of the pillars of the palace at Murghâb is a figure which once bore an inscription, 'I am Cyrus the king, the Achaemenian.' Difficulties have been raised as to this figure, because the head-dress is Egyptian, and the four wings and the fringed garment are usually called Assyrian (cf. 135. 1 n. for Persian borrowing). But E. Herzfeld (Klio, viii. 63-4) says the dress is Elamite, and so suitable to Cyrus; and Curzon (*u. s.*) ingeniously shows that the description of Arrian implies that the body of Cyrus was buried in Egyptian fashion, i. e. like a mummy; he refers doubtfully to iii. 2, the story of Nitetis, as explaining how this could be. The identification, therefore, of the figure with that of the great Cyrus may be accepted.

Μαράφιοι. We have a Maraphian in command against Cyrene iv. 167. 1. The Achaemenidae were a 'clan' (*φρήτρη*) of the royal tribe.

4 The nomad 'Sagartians' are Persian 'in speech' vii. 85. 1 and partly in dress, and yet, as (iii. 93. 2) part of the fourteenth satrapy, they paid tribute. It may be suggested that the nomad Persian tribes took no part in the national rising under Cyrus, and hence forfeited their privileges.

The name of the **Γερμάνιοι** (cf. for the change *Ἀγβάτανα* and *Ἐκβάτανα*) seems to be found in Carmania (*hod.* Kerman), the district to the east of Persia, where H. (iii. 93. 2) places the **Οὔτιοι**, who also form part of the fourteenth satrapy. The Mardi (Strabo, 508 *Ἄμαρδοι*) were mountaineers to the south-west of Persepolis; the cragsman Hyroeades (84. 2) was a Mardian. The other tribes are only doubtfully identified; some connect the Dai with the Dadicae (iii. 91. 4), and the Dropici with the Derbicae (Strabo, 514), but these tribes are much too remote. Aesch. Pers. 774 seq. inserts *Μάρδος* and *Μάραφις* in his list of Persian kings.

H. is only repeating what he has heard; but he is right in laying stress on the nomadic tribes; large parts of modern Persia are desert, or habitable only at certain seasons (for its shape cf. Réclus, Geog. Univ. ix. 144), and the Ilyâts or nomads are a considerable part of the population.

126 The promises of Cyrus (e.g. § 5) have been thought by micro-

scopic critics to be inconsistent with the account of Persian simplicity in c. 71, but each is true in its place.

127 The account of H., that the victory of Cyrus was rendered easy by treachery, is far more like the real facts as told in the Annalistic Tablet (cf. App. IV, § 1) than the long and picturesque version of Nicolas Damascenus (fr. 66; F. H. G. iii. 405-6, probably from Ctesias); cf. App. IV, § 4.

2 **θεοβλαβής.** H., as a pious Greek, believes 'Quem deus vult perdere prius dementat'.

2 **ἄστεϊ**: i.e. in Ecbatana.

4 The 'slavery' is only that of contrast; the Medes to some extent shared the Persian rule (App. VI, § 3).

1 **παρὲξ ἢ κτλ.** For the chronology of this passage cf. App. III, § 6. H.'s usage, as well as the general sense, seems to require that the 128 years should be inclusive of 'the Scythian rule'; he puts a deduction, which has still to be made, *after* the words limited (cf. vi. 5. 3), a deduction already made, *before* them (ii. 77. 5); but he is not quite consistent.

2 The Median revolt here referred to was long supposed to be that against Darius Nothus in 408 B.C. (Mure, 1859, iv. 540-2, argues ingeniously for this), and so to prove that H. lived on till nearly 400 B.C. But it is now generally thought that the revolt is that of 520 B.C. (cf. B. I. col. 2), for the following reasons:

(1) Darius in H. always means D. Hystaspes (except in ix. 108. 2, where it is the name of a son of Xerxes).

(2) There is some point in Median 'repentance' after 30 years; after nearly 150 their repentance is impossibly tardy.

(3) It is usually thought that H. was dead before 420 B.C. (Intr. § 9).

3 **πάσης τῆς Ἀσίης.** H. resumes his connexion before going on to his excursus on the Persians. He means that the victory over Croesus was the beginning of a career of conquest which made Cyrus 'lord of all Asia'; but he writes very loosely, for Babylon and Bactria were subdued later, and it is not certain that Cyrus ever conquered Phoenicia at all (cf. iii. 19. 3 n.).

-40 *The manners and institutions of the Persians.* This section is one of the most valuable in H.; for a summing up as to his account of the Persian religion cf. App. VIII. [The Zendavesta is quoted from Sacred Books of the East, vols. IV (part I), XXIII, XXXI; the references are to pages in the introductions unless otherwise stated].

1 **ἀγάλματα κτλ.** This passage is accurate in the general sense; there were no cult-statues in Persia (but *v. i.*), and the Persians worshipped in the open air; Dinon, a fourth-century writer (fr. 9, F. H. G. ii. 91), affirms this, adding *θεῶν ἀγάλματα μόνα τὸ πῦρ καὶ τὸ ὕδωρ νομίζοντες.* They had, however, huge altars on the hill-tops (cf. Maspero, iii. 591, for picture of those at Nakhsh-I-Roustem), and there were

others in temples (cf. further in App. VIII, § 4), on which the ever-burning fire was maintained. H. here gives the strict theory of the religion, but there were inconsistencies in practice. For a similar belief and a similar inconsistency in Germany cf. Tac. Germ. c. 9 contrasted with cc. 7, 40; we might add that there is a similar reasonable inconsistency in Christianity. H. is on the whole confirmed by the usage of the Parsees, among whom the word for fire-temple (Dâdgâh) seems to mean also the place for any object (e.g. for the dead or the dog). Spiegel, Avesta, vol. ii, p. lxiv (1859).

ἀνθρωποφυέας. Ormazd (cf. figs. in Maspero, iii. 577, 681) is represented e.g. on B. I. as a form, human to the waist, proceeding from the winged disk, the symbol of eternity and omnipresence; this was borrowed from Assyria (cf. 135. 1), which perhaps had in turn borrowed it from the winged sun-orb of Egypt.

2 **Διί.** H. naturally speaks of the supreme as 'Zeus'; he is quite right as to the worship on the mountain-tops (*v. s.*), but writes loosely in identifying him with the sky; 'Ormazd clothes upon himself the firm stones of the heavens (as his robe)' (Yasna, 30. 5; xxxi. 31); 'the sun and the star are his eyes' (ib. 68. 22, p. 324); but the strict creed had spiritualized him, and distinguished him from his attributes, cf. Yast 13. 1, 2; xxiii. 180; Ahuramazda speaks, 'I maintain that sky, there above, shining and seen afar, and encompassing this earth all round.' But 'many features, though ever dimmer and dimmer, betray his former bodily, or rather sky, nature' (iv. 58).

For invocations addressed to the sun and the moon, along with the waters, cf. Vendîdâd, Farg. 21, iv. 231–4. H. is quite right in laying stress on the sacredness of the four elements.

3 **τῇ Οὐρανίῃ.** This passage is important in three ways:

(1) It illustrates Persian borrowing from foreigners (135. 1); they had mixed with their dualistic creed many alien elements. The worship of the Oriental love-goddess Anaitis was combined with the old Iranian worship of Ardvî Sûra by Artaxerxes Longimanus (465–425) (Berosus, fr. 16, F. H. G. ii. 508; he calls him *τοῦ Δαρείου τοῦ Ὤχου*, but this must be a mistake). The king set up her statues for worship in Ecbatana and Susa, though previously the Persians *ἀγάλματα θεῶν οὐ ξύλα καὶ λίθους ὑπειλήφασιν ὥσπερ Ἕλληνες, οὐδὲ μὴν ἴβιδας καὶ ἰχνεύμονας, καθάπερ Αἰγύπτιοι, ἀλλὰ πῦρ τε καὶ ὕδωρ ὡς φιλόσοφοι.* For the worship of Anaitis, which was especially established in Armenia, cf. Strabo, 532. For the quaint story of her worship in Skye cf. Boswell's Johnson, v. 218 (B. Hill's edition). For Ardvî Sûra, originally 'the holy water spring', cf. Yast 5; xxiii. 52 seq.

(2) H. makes a strange mistake in confusing this worship with that of Mithra, the god of heavenly light, 'who foremost in golden array takes hold of the beautiful summits' (Yast 10. 4; xxiii. 123). Mithra, at first only closely connected with the sun, was later

identified with him (cf. the frequent inscription 'Deo invicto Soli Mithrae'). His worship became most important in the later developments of the Persian religion; Artaxerxes II is the first to invoke him and Anaitis, along with Ormazd. His feast was a solemn festival, at which the Persian king was expected to get drunk (Duris, fr. 13, F. H. G. ii. 473). For Mithraism in Roman times, when it was a formidable rival to Christianity, cf. Dill, Roman Society from Nero, pp. 585 seq.; it was the special religion of the legions (cf. R. Kipling's fine poem in Puck of Pook's Hill). H. seems to have been misled by the likeness of the names 'Mylitta' and 'Mithra', and perhaps by the fact that they were both heavenly divinities (*v. i.* for Mylitta).

(3) The passage shows the close connexion of Aphrodite with the Babylonian Mylitta, the Assyrian Ishtar, the Phoenician Astarte; whether there was actual borrowing, or whether independent cults were assimilated, it is impossible to say; probably both were the case (*v. i.*). Ishtar was the queen of the gods, at once warrior goddess and goddess of generation, the destroyer of life and its renewer. From Assyria her worship spread to Phoenicia (cf. 105. 2 n. for her temple at Ashkelon), and thence to Cyprus (for her temple at Paphos cf. Tac. Hist. ii. 2–3; 105. 3 n.). Her shrine at Cythera was founded by Phoenicians (105. 2 n.), and was the oldest in Greece (cf. her epithet Κυθέρεια in Od. viii. 288). For the rites at her temple in Babylon cf. c. 199 n.; for impure ritual in Greece (at Corinth only) Strabo, 378, and Athen. 573. She was identified at once with the evening star, 'the star of love,' and with the moon (cf. Milton, P. L. i. 439, 'Astarte, queen of heaven, with crescent horns'); this later identification was probably due to a confusion with Isis and Hathor, who are represented as supporting on their horned heads the solar disk; these symbols were mistakenly interpreted as the crescent and the full moon. That the Greeks were conscious of the partially foreign origin of Aphrodite is shown by her epithets Κύπρις (Il. v. 330), Κυπρογενής (Hesiod), &c.; for these cf. Od. viii. 362.

There may have been an original native goddess in Greece who was identified with the Oriental goddess; so at Mycenae are found naked female figures with hands on breasts, and in some cases with a dove (cf. Schuchhardt's Schliemann, figs. 180–2), which may well be independent of direct Oriental influence. The Greeks took over from the East her title of Οὐρανία without understanding it: hence they attempted to distinguish Aphrodite O., the goddess of pure love, from A. πάνδημος (Paus. ix. 16. 4; cf. Xen. Symp. 8. 9–10 for the supposed contrast in their worships); but this is a later and artificial explanation. (For the evidence cf. Driver, Hastings' Dict., s. v. Ashtoreth, and more fully Farnell, C. G. S. ii. 618 seq.)

The name Mylitta is probably the 'bilit' or 'belit' of the Assyrian inscriptions = 'lady', i. e. the feminine of Baal or Bel = 'lord'.

Alilat (cf. iii. 8. 3) = Al Ilât, 'the goddess.' What was originally a common noun became a proper name; so 'Astarte', properly an epithet signifying fruitfulness (Deut. vii. 13), became the name of a goddess.

132 1 **θυσίη.** For the resemblances of the 'manner of sacrifice to the rites of the Ali Allahis in modern Persia' cf. Rawlinson, *ad loc.*; the open air sacrifice, the 'myrtle', the 'hymn' (*ἐπαοιδήν*), the 'boiling of the flesh', and its distribution to the worshippers all occur in the modern rite. There can be no doubt that H. had watched a Persian sacrifice. Strabo (733) gives a fuller description, based partly on H., and partly on what he had seen in Armenia.

H.'s object throughout is to contrast Persian and Greek customs; this will explain his verbal inaccuracies. The victim is not burned as in Greece, but H. writes loosely (cf. 131. 1 n.) in saying 'no fire is kindled'; there was fire in the Persian sacrifices, but it was fed with wood; there were no 'libations' of wine; but the sacred water ('zasthra', S. B. E. iv, p. 69) was sometimes poured (cf. vii. 54. 2 (Xerxes at the Hellespont), 188. 2 n.); the fillet (*ἐστεφανωμένος*) was not a Greek *στέμμα*, which was always intertwined with woollen threads.

οὐλῇσι. For the sacred 'barley' and its *πρόχυσις* cf. 160. 5, and Gardner and Jevons, G. A. p. 250. The meal offering of barley went with the burnt offering, as bread goes with meats in a meal (cf. Lev. ix. 17 R.V.). Another contrast is that the Greeks sacrificed bare-headed but for a garland, the Persian wore his 'tiara'.

καθαρόν. The idea is double, partly a place free from pollution, partly one where there is no obstacle to sacrifice; cf. vii. 183. 2 *τὸ ἐμποδὼν ἐγεγόνεε καθαρόν.*

2 **ἁπαλός,** 'fresh'; cf. ii. 92. 4 *ἁπαλὰ καὶ αὖα.* **ὦν** marks the apodosis.

3 For the Magians cf. 101 n. and App. VIII, § 3.

οἵην δή. Translate 'for such they say the invocation is'; H. does not profess himself to have understood the incantation. Darmstetter (iv. 53) says, 'H. may have heard the Magi sing the very same Gathas which are now sung by the Mobeds in Bombay.' The hymns invoke Ormazd and his ministering spirits and dwell upon their attributes; they are not a 'Theogony' in the Hesiodic sense (ii. 53. 2 n.).

ὁ θύσας. Greek usage left a portion for the priests. Strabo (732) says the Persian god's share was the life (*ψυχή*) of the victim.

λόγος αἱρέει. More often without an object (cf. vi. 124. 3); 'as reason takes him,' i. e. as he pleases.

133 1 **ὅλους κτλ.** Aristophanes (Ach. 85–7) parodies this passage; cf. 3. 2 n.

Cf. ix. 110. 2 for the royal birthday.

τὰ λεπτά: i. e. sheep and goats; *πρόβατον* includes, especially in Ionic Greek, all beasts of the herd that 'go before' the shepherd.

2 The Greeks, like the moderns, had their 'dessert dishes' (*ἐπι-*

φορήματα) served up after the solid food (σῖτα, cf. ἀπὸ δείπνου); the Persians had them, not 'as one course' (ἁλέσι), but at intervals during the meal. H. Rawlinson (*ad loc.*) compares the fondness of the modern Persians for sweetmeats (but these are now served before the meal).

3 Anything that left the body became separated from life and so unclean. For the strange rules of the Avesta on these subjects cf. Fargard, xvii, as to paring the nails; ib. xviii. 40–9, as to the urine (iv. 185, 197).

4 The first part of this custom is ascribed by Tacitus (Germ. 22) to the Germans; he gives the reason 'Deliberant dum fingere nesciunt, constituunt dum errare non possunt' (cf. Mrs. Nickleby, 'Wine in, truth out'). Lack of humour in historians has erected into a system what was merely due to excess.

For Persian drinking cf. Curzon, ii. 506, (The Persian) 'is not a tippler but a toper, not a drinker, but a drunkard', quoting other authorities for the same view.

4 1 H. Rawlinson compares the devotion to etiquette among the modern Persians, 'the Frenchmen of the East'; the salute, however, now is never on the lips.

The prostration of an inferior is familiar in the East (iii. 86. 2); it was as repulsive to the Greeks as the Chinese 'kotow' to Doyle's 'Private of the Buffs'. Cf. vii. 136. 1, and the refusal of Callisthenes to prostrate himself before Alexander (Arr. Anab. iv. 10. 5 seq.).

2 **ἀρίστους.** The Persian Shah, till he was deposed, was called 'the centre of the Universe'. H., however, makes too systematic the conceit common to all nations, civilized as well as uncivilized.

Two points must be distinguished:

(1) The Persian system of graduated respect.

(2) The Median system of graduated rule, which H. compares to it (§ 3 *ad fin.* 'in the same way as the Persian show degrees of honour').

As to (2) H. is again too systematic, but he represents accurately the broad facts of the contrast between Persian and Median rule; under the Medes, the subject kingdoms paid tribute or sent gifts, while they still ruled their own dependents; under Persia, all districts alike were under the satraps, and in direct relation to the great king (iii. 87 seq.).

3 The sentence is carefully balanced; καὶ τῶν ὁμούρων answers to μάλα (= μαλ' αὖτις, 'in their turn') τῶν ἐχομένων.

προέβαινε γὰρ κτλ. is variously explained:

(1) Rawlinson refers τὸ ἔθνος to the Persians; but this is incorrect in fact and spoils the antithesis.

(2) Stein takes it of the Medes; translate 'The race went forward thus ever from government by themselves (ἆρχον) to government through others' (ἐπιτροπεῦον); but it is hard to get this sense out of ἐπιτροπεῦον, which = 'administering' (iii. 36. 3) or 'being regent

for' (655); the above sense would require ἐπιτρέπον, i. e. 'deputing' (τὴν ἀρχήν), and the ellipse would be harsh.

(3) It is simplest therefore to make τὸ ἔθνος distributive, 'each nation took its place in order as ruler and administrator.' This sentence then simply repeats generally what H. has already said more definitely above; it may be a gloss, and Krüger brackets it.

135 Hellanicus (fr. 169; F. H. G. i. 68) says the Persians learned the practice of castration from the Babylonians; cf. H. iii. 92. 1.

ἐσθῆτα. H. describes the 'Median' armament (σκευή) of the Persian 'Immortals' in vii. 61 (*v. n.*); the real Persian dress was of leather (σκυτίνη), and its main feature the trousers (71. 2); such a dress, fitting closely, is worn by the common soldiers on the monuments, while the king and his attendants have a long flowing dress. (Rawlinson, *ad loc.*, gives pictures.) Cf. Strabo, 525, for the borrowing. Curzon, ii. 633, speaks of '(Persian) imitativeness long notorious in the East'. He also agrees with c. 134 as to Persian conceit (p. 628).

παισί: the vice was older and is denounced in the Vendidad (Farg. 8. 5; iv. 102); Greek influence may have helped to spread it.

136 1 **πολλοὺς παῖδας.** Cf. Vend. Farg. 4. 47; iv. 46, 'He who has children is far above the childless man.' Large families were both commended for religious motives (Ormazd is the Lord of Life), and politically were all-important to a small ruling caste.

2 **ἱππεύειν.** Xenophon (Cyr. i. 3. 3) says that Cyrus made the Persians a nation of horsemen; this is thought by some (e. g. Meyer, iii. 9) to be a pure invention; it is argued that Xenophon, as a cavalry officer, wished his countrymen to develop that arm of their forces; hence Cyrus' supposed development is merely an object-lesson to the Greeks. But as the Persians were largely a race of mountaineers, cavalry can hardly have played much part among them till Cyrus began a career of conquest. Hence Xenophon may be right on this point.

ἀληθίζεσθαι. The importance of 'Truth' is brought out in the B. I. i. 10, 'The lie became abounding in the land'; iv. 13, (Ormazd helps Darius) 'because I was not wicked nor was I a liar' (cf. also col. iv. 4, 5, 6, 8). The liar is a 'Mithra-drug'; he offends against the all-seeing sun-god, who is the guardian of contracts (cf. 138. 1). For a transgression of the rule as to Truth cf. iii. 72 n. H. is right in crediting the Persians with the virtues of chivalry.

137 **μηδένα** is both subject and object; this double use of a word is frequent in H. (e. g. viii. 142. 3).

For compensation in mitigation of punishment cf. Sandoces, vii. 194. 2. The principle was extended to religion; in modern Parseeism every offence and every good deed has a price, and so a balance is struck (S. B. E. iv. 99 n.).

138 Aristotle (Hist. Anim. iii. 11, p. 518) describes the λεύκη, which seems to have been a mild form of leprosy. Leper isolation was general in the East; cf. Lev. xiii. 46 for the Jews, who (like the Persians) looked upon the disease as the symbol and the result of moral evil. The Vendidad is a Persian Leviticus, and is mainly comprised of laws of purification (cf. Farg. 5. 21; iv. 55); 'Purity is for man, next to life, the greatest good.' Savage analogies are numerous; cf. Tylor, Prim. Cult. ii[4]. 429 for 'Lustration'.

2 Charon (fr. 3, F. H. G. i. 32) spoke of 'white doves' in connexion with Mardonius' expedition in 493 B.C. (described in vi. 44–5) (cf. Introd. § 19); perhaps these doves belonged to the Phoenician sailors. H. here seems to connect them with leprosy.

ἐς ποταμόν. The prohibition is due to respect to the element, water (cf. c. 140 for respect to the earth, and vii. 113. 2 for worship of rivers). So in later developments of the religion, the Magi are said to have deposed a king for building bath-houses; bathing smacked of heresy (S. B. E. iv. 90 n.).

139 1 H. is at his weakest as a linguist (cf. explanation of royal names, vi. 98. 3 n.); yet he seems to have valued himself on this score. He makes two remarks on Persian names, which are both inaccurate:

(1) That they all have a certain meaning. σῶμα is variously taken (*a*) by Stein, in a general sense, 'individuals (32. 8) and their honourable nature'; (*b*) by Macaulay, 'their bodily shape' (which is simpler). Whichever sense be given, H. is too absolute; nor is he consistent; cf. vi. 98. Some Persian names referred to deities (cf. Mithradates, 'given by Mithra'); others to personal appearance (Otanes, 'fair of body'); others (e.g. Darius, 'possessor') to position, &c.

(2) That all names end in S. This, in the first place, ignores all feminine names. Even of men's names, it is only true of the Greek forms; in Persian, *s* (sh) was retained after *i* or *u*, e.g. Darayavaush = Darius, but not otherwise, e.g. Vistâçha (Hystaspes), where, however, the final *a* was not written.

For the interesting statement as to the Greek alphabet cf. Roberts, Gk. Epig. p. 8 seq. The Phoenicians had four signs for sibilants, each of which was borrowed in part by Greece:

(1) The hard Samech (No. 15 in the Phoenician alphabet; sign Ξ), probably = 'Sigma'. Others, however, make 'σίγμα' ('the hissing letter') a genuine Greek word (from σίζω).

(2) The lingual Tsade (No. 18; sign ⊬).

(3) The palatal Shin (No. 21; sign W).

(4) There was also the soft Zazin (No. 7; sign I).

Of these the name Tsade survives in Zeta, while 'Samech' was transferred to the place of 'Shin'. The sign of Samech and its place in the alphabet after 'N', were left to the later Xi.

For 'San' cf. Pind. fr. 79. H. probably means by 'San' the M of the old Dorian inscriptions, while his 'Sigma' is the ϟ Σ of the older Ionic ones.

140 1 The dead body had passed under the control of the evil spirit

Ahriman; hence it had to be kept from the elements fire, water, earth. This custom of burial still prevails among the Parsees. For the precepts of the strict Mazdean creed cf. Vend. Farg. 6. 44 seq. (iv. 73); the corpse was fastened down to prevent polluting fragments being carried away. Heraclitus, who seems to have been acquainted with Mazdeism, left his dead body to be torn by dogs. Meyer, who quotes other instances (i. 12), thinks that Zoroaster has simply embodied in his creed the original usage as to the dead among the primitive Iranians (ib. 579). Cf. S. B. E. iv. 91 for a description of the Parsee 'Dakhmas', first called 'Towers of Silence' by an Irish journalist in Bombay (cf. letter in *Times*, Aug. 8, 1905).

H. is quite right, however, in saying that these rules of burial were not observed by the ordinary Persian.

2 **δὲ ὦν**, 'at any rate'; this concession was made by the Persians to the strictness of their creed; for 'covering with wax' cf. iv. 71. 1.

3 The dog was sacred to Ormazd (cf. its part in the Cyrus legend c. 107 n.); there are rules for the care of bitches in pup in Farg. 15, iv. 176 seq. On the other hand, it was a meritorious act to kill the creatures of Ahriman (ib. 166). Other creatures also were sacred to Ormazd, e. g. the 'water dog' (otter), and the 'prickly dog' (hedgehog), because it killed so many of the creeping things of Ahriman.

141–76 *The Persian conquest of the Asiatic Greeks.* This continues the general narrative from c. 94.

141 1 **τοῖσι αὐτοῖσι.** The Ionians had paid tribute to the Lydians (27. 1), and had had their walls dismantled (*v. i. τείχεα π.*); this is more probable than Stein's view that previously the citadels only had been fortified; the fact that a citadel could still resist when a town was taken (c. 15 bis) does not prove the town itself was unfortified (cf. 163. 4 n.). The Ionians now have to serve in war also (171. 1).

αὐλητήν. The fable is part of a collection bearing Aesop's name. For it cf. St. Matt. xi. 17. For Cyrus' invitation to rebel cf. 76. 3.

4 The long resistance of Miletus to Alyattes (c. 17 seq.) must have been known to Cyrus, who therefore allowed it favourable terms. Perhaps it obtained trade privileges; the southern route, down the Maeander and past Miletus, would be more used, if Sardis on the Hermus, and Phocaea, just north of the Hermus mouth, had suffered.

142 1 'Ionians' was the general name of the Greeks in the East (for the whole question of the Ionians cf. especially Busolt, i. 277 seq., and Meyer, F. i. 127 seq.); cf. Persian 'Yauna' in the B. I., and 'Javan' Gen. x. 2; also vii. 9. 1, and Aesch. Pers. 178 *Ἰαόνων γῆν οἴχεται πέρσαι θέλων.* It was this stock that first came in contact with Orientals. So 'Frank' was used in the East of all Crusaders. As to the origin of the name 'Ionian', two views are held:

(1) That it developed in Asia Minor, and was gradually extended

to the islands and Attica. 'The central part of the Aegean formed in language, commerce, and civilization a closely connected whole, whose unity found its clearest expression in the great fair at Delos' (Meyer, *u. s.* 133), though its original home was the Asiatic mainland.

(2) That it was brought to Asia from Europe by the most important tribe among the immigrants, which was connected with part of the population of Attica.

This latter in the main is H.'s view (c. 147), and may be accepted for the following reasons (see Note F, p. 450):

(*a*) The four Ionian tribes are found in Attica (v. 66. 2 n.), and are proved by inscriptions to have existed in Delos and in Teos; as we have inscriptions also as to them in Cyzicus and in Perinthus, we may infer their existence in Miletus and in Samos (Busolt, i. 279).

(*b*) The festival of the Apaturia is found in Athens and in the Ionic cities of Asia Minor (not in the Orientalized Ephesus and Colophon (147. 2)). But the Athenian cult of Apollo *πατρῷος* (in spite of Plato, Euthyd. 302 C) is not found in Ionia (Farnell, G. C. iv. 161).

(*c*) Attica is Ionic very early. Cf. Il. xiii. 685, and Solon ('Αθ. Πολ. 5) calls it *πρεσβυτάτην γαῖαν Ἰαονίας*. It was as head of the Ionians that Athens took part in the Amphictyonic Council.

At the same time it is possible that there was a survival of pre-Ionic population in Attica. Ion in the legend comes from abroad (cf. viii. 44. 2), from the later Achaia, originally called Aegialus (Paus. vii. 1. 1; H. vii. 94); Euripides (in the Ion) gives him a native mother, Creusa. For the strife of races in Attic myth cf. 78. 3 n. The peculiar feature in Attica, however, is that the two races amalgamated before history begins.

As to the first view, viz. that 'Ionian' rose in Asia Minor, three theories may be briefly mentioned:

(1) Curtius' famous paradox (Die Ionier vor der Ion. Wanderung, 1855) was that the Ionians came into Greece from Asia Minor. This is accepted by Holm (i. c. 7), but it contradicts all tradition; and the fact that the Ionians always were confined to the coast points clearly to their having reached it by sea.

(2) Meyer maintained (*u. s.* p. 150) that the settlement of Ionia took place in Mycenaean times. But the almost complete absence in Ionia of the 'stirrup vases' and of the gems, so characteristic of Mycenaean civilization, is against this (Busolt, i. 277 n.).

(3) Bury (E. H. R. 1900, p. 288 seq.) thinks the name 'Ionian' was borrowed by immigrants from a pre-Greek population in Asia Minor; cf. the possible identification of the 'Yaunna', allies of the Hittites against Rameses II in the thirteenth century B.C. (App. x. 8), with 'Ionians'. But there is no sufficient evidence for this view.

καλλίστῳ. Cf. the view in Arist. Pol. vii. 7. 2–3, 1327 b that the Greek race owed to equable climate the fact that it was at once ἔνθυμον and διανοητικόν, a mean between the reckless Northerners and the cowardly Easterns. Hippocrates (de Aer. 12) claims for Asia παντὸς ἰσομοιρίη in natural advantages. The κρῆσις τῶν ὡρέων gives μετριότης; but he goes on to admit that courage and endurance cannot be expected in a region so favoured.

3 **τρόπους τέσσερας.** H. is probably more trustworthy in his linguistic remarks here than as to non-Greek tongues; but there are too few early inscriptions for us to be able to refute or to confirm him.

Miletus, with Myus and Priene, lay on or near the Latmian bay.

4 **οὐδέν.** Stein thinks H. is exaggerating here, and is preparing the way for his attack on the purity of Ionic blood (cc. 146–7). But the words only mean that the dialectic peculiarities of each group were different; that all spoke Ionic is assumed.

Erythrae lies opposite Chios.

143 2 The antithesis to κατ' ἄλλο μέν is never directly given; but is implied in § 3, i.e. 'these twelve cities formed the Pan-Ionium'. H., in explaining the reason for this separate policy, loses his construction.

ἀσθενέστατον. H. is accused of anti-Ionian bias (cf. v. 69. 1; vi. 13. 1 n.), as a Dorian and as an admirer of Periclean Athens. But he especially limits his statement here to the second half of the sixth century (τότε), of which it is true, if we except Samos; the greatness of Miletus in trade and in politics was already largely a thing of the past.

Meyer (F. i. 129 seq.) denies that in the fifth century there was any inferiority attached to the name 'Ionian'; he says (p. 131) that H. is simply trying to explain why the Athenians, who are the representatives of the Ionian *race* (cf. Solon in 'Αθ. Πολ. quoted on c. 142), are never called so as a *people*. It is clear, however, that there was some contempt in 'Ionians' in the fifth century [cf. iv. 142; Thuc. v. 9. 1 (Brasidas), vi. 77. 1 (Hermocrates), viii. 25. 5, with Hauvette, R. E. G. 1888, 257 seq.], no doubt because, as Hermocrates says, they had been subject to barbarians, and because of their increasing Oriental admixture; so the Ionian dress is imposed on the Athenian ladies as a punishment (v. 87. 3). The name too was being specialized for the inhabitants of the Lydian and north Carian seaboard [cf. the 'Ionian' circle in the Athenian Empire, and the inscription as to Tanagra (Paus. v. 10. 4), which distinguishes Athenians from Ionians.

Athens was playing a double and inconsistent part; on the one hand she was championing Ionism (ix. 106. 3; Thuc. iii. 86. 3–4, vi. 82); on the other she was enslaving her Ionian kinsmen; but it must be remembered that the Ionic Apaturia was always celebrated at Athens (c. 147. 2 n.), and that the Athenians retained the 'Ionic' tribes, at least for religious purposes.

144 1 **προσοίκων.** Among these may be mentioned Carpathos, Syme (174. 3), Calydna, and Nisyros (vii. 99. 2). Melos, Thera, and Phaselis (ii. 178. 2 n.) were too remote to join in the festival.

The Triopian peninsula (cf. 174. 3) lay just north of Cnidus (Thuc. viii. 35. 2); its temple was the centre of the Dorian Amphictyony.

3 **διὰ ταύτην τὴν αἰτίην.** H. no doubt tells the Halicarnassian story. At best it was an occasion, not the cause of exclusion, which was no doubt due to the Carian and Ionian admixture at Halicarnassus. (Cf. Hicks, p. 41, and Introd. p. 2.) That town was the furthest point to the north of Dorian colonization, which crossed the Aegean by way of Crete, probably in the tenth century, and spread up the coast till it met the tide of Ionic migration.

Lindus, Ialysus, and Camirus were the three cities in Rhodes, synoecized about 408 B.C.

145 Here as elsewhere (cf. 56. 3 n.) H. accepts the usual tradition of the Dorian migration and its results. That the colonization of Ionia was connected with that early 'wandering of the nations' is probable; that it took place all at once, as H. implies, is most unlikely. Whether any great mass of the colonists came from the north of Peloponnese, as is stated here and also by Strabo (383, though with variations), is very uncertain.

The arguments for this last point are (1) the common number, twelve states; (2) the supposed connexion of Poseidon of Helice (Il. viii. 203) with P. Heliconius (but see 148 n.); (3) the fact that Attica is a very natural pier of embarcation for dispossessed tribes. On the other hand, (1) and (2) may well have led to the invention of the tradition; and the noble genealogies of Ionia were traced back to Pylos (Strabo, 634, quoting Mimnermus) and not to Athens. This last point, however, is consistent with the tradition, which made Melanthus of Pylos king at Athens. On the whole, the balance of probability is for the traditional view, but it is possible that there was direct emigration from Argolis to Ionia: cf. the prominence of Hera-worship at Samos and at Argos.

Κρᾶθις. This Crathis did not dry up in summer (*ἀένναος*); H. is interested in it from its namesake at Sybaris (v. 45. 1), which was not so permanent.

Βοῦρα. The tribe *Βωρεῖς*, found at Cyzicus, Perinthus, and elsewhere, may possibly be connected with this town.

1 **μωρίη.** H.'s argument is that the number 'twelve' is determined by history only, not by exclusive and superior purity in the Dodecapolis. He is obviously attacking some one (Intr. p. 25); cf. for a like acerbity of tone ii. 16. 1. Paus. vii. 2. 3–9 gives additional details as to this migration.

Ἄβαντες. Aristotle (in Strabo, 445) said this tribe were Thracians, who passed from Abae in Phocis to Euboea.

Μινύαι. The Minyans settled in Teos (Paus. vii. 3. 6), the Cadmeans (but cf. v. 61. 2 n.) in Priene (ib. vii. 2. 10) and in Colophon (ib. vii. 3. 1–3, where the oracle was connected with the daughter of Tiresias), the Dryopes in Styra (ib. iv. 34. 11), the

Phocians in Phocaea (Paus. vii. 3. 10). These statements it is impossible to test; they may rest on genealogical evidence.

No other tradition connects the Molossi (Thuc. i. 136. 2) who lived in the east of Epirus, north of Ambracia, with Asia Minor. Probably the reference is to some forgotten story, connecting Dodona (cf. Aesch. P. V. 829) with the migration to the East. Pausanias (vii. 4. 2) makes Ionians from Epidaurus (not Dorians) settle in Samos. The *ἄλλα ἔθνεα* are probably not Lydians and Carians (as Stein), but other Greek tribes from Hellas proper; H. mentions the admixture of native races below.

ἀποδάσμιοι. Cf. ii. 103. 2 *ἀποδασάμενος*. H. lays stress on the fact that Phocaea was founded by a part of the Phocians, who left their home by a voluntary migration, not from external compulsion; in this it resembled the later colonies, and not its contemporary foundations. The Arcadians are called 'Pelasgi', because they were *αὐτόχθονες* (cf. viii. 73. 1) and not immigrants, cf. 66. 2 n.

2 **πρυτανηίου.** For connexion with Athens as a test of Ionism cf. 147. 2. H. writes as if prehistoric migrations had been carried out with the ceremonies of colony-founding in his own day; for the 'common hearth' cf. Frazer, iv. 441–2. The argument is again directed against Ionian pride of birth; even the purest-blooded of them had foreign wives and foreign rulers (147. 1); but the claims of Athens as *μητρόπολις* are asserted.

3 Pausanias (vii. 2. 6) tells the same tale shortly. H. here seems to be incorporating in his argument a piece of very early custom. Among some savage tribes, e. g. the Caribs in North America, the wife neither eats with the husband nor calls him by his name (cf. Frazer, iv. 116). The myth of Cupid and Psyche preserves in a curious form this primitive separation of husband and wife. There may have been some strange survival of this at Miletus, but it can hardly have been as absolute as H. states.

147 1 For Glaucus cf. Il. vi. 119 seq.; for his *ξενία* with Diomede, ib. 215 seq.; the story may well reflect some early connexion of Greek settlers and native princes.

For the Pylian families at Athens cf. Busolt, i. 287, n. 3, who thinks (following Töppfer, Att. Geneal. 225 seq.) that the story of their migration to Asia *via* Attica is an Athenian invention; he argues that Peloponnesian wanderers would have gone directly by sea to Asia, which is most unlikely. It is true there never was a *γένος* of Nelidae at Athens; but then tradition was unanimous that the family had again migrated. For Pylians at Athens cf. v. 65. 3, Hell. fr. 10 (F. H. G. i. 47), Paus. ii. 18. 9.

For the *Καύκωνες* cf. iv. 148. 4 n. Homer (Od. iii. 357 seq., speech of Athena as Mentor) distinguishes the Caucones from Pylos, but puts them near at hand.

Κόδρου. The rulers of Miletus were traditionally Nelidae, descended from Nileus the son of Codrus (ix. 97; Paus. vii. 2. 1).

συναμφοτέρους seems to imply a double kingship, the arrangement so familiar at Sparta (cf. vi. 51 n.). Kingship disappeared as a form of government in the eighth century or even later (cf. Busolt, ii. 455, n. 6, for its disappearance), and authority passed into the hands of an oligarchy claiming descent from the founder. Strabo (633) says that even in his own day the Codridae at Ephesus were called 'kings' and had honorary privileges.

2 The Apaturia (see Töppfer in P.-W. *s. v.*) was the festival (in the month Pyanepsion) of the Phratries at Athens, at which new members were enrolled; cf. Schol. Aristoph. Ach. 146, where its three days are described, and Xen. Hell. i. 7. 8 (its fatal influence on the trial of the generals in 406 B.C.). Various deities were connected with it, especially Zeus Phratrios and Athena Phratria. The derivation from the ἀπάτη of Melanthus is an etymological legend; it really = ὁμοπατόρια, the gathering of 'fathers' (cf. ἄκοιτις). We can trace the festival widely, e.g. in the Aegean, at Cyzicus, and at Olbia; but the only inscription found as to it comes from the Crimea (? Phanagoria), I. G. A. 350.

No doubt the cause of the absence of the Apaturia at Ephesus was the Orientalized character of that city; it was divided into five tribes, which are independent of the four Ionic tribes (c. 142 n.), except that one of its five had a sub-division 'Argadis'. Its worship of Artemis too was full of Eastern elements (cf. Strabo, 641). So Ephesus takes little part in Ionic revolt (vi. 8 n.; 16. 2).

For an Oriental party in Colophon cf. Thuc. iii. 34. 1.

1 The Panionium was in the territory of Priene (Strabo, 384, 639), three stades from the sea. It is identified at Tshangli, between Ephesus and Cape Trogilium (Leake, A. M. p. 260), at the north-east corner of the promontory; here the name has been found on an inscription (cf. Dittenberger, 189).

Ἑλικώνιος would naturally mean 'of Helicon', and Farnell (C. G. S. iv. 29 seq.) argues that the neighbourhood of Mount Helicon must have been 'long the abiding home' of the Ionians, where they came in contact with the Minyae. There was a Ἵππου κρήνη, a fountain of the Poseidon horse, Pegasus, near its top (Paus. ix. 31. 3). If Farnell's view is right, the worship of Poseidon at Helice in Achaia (c. 145 n.) would have been only an isolated local cult.

Πανιώνια. This religious amphictyony (cf. Freeman, Federal Government, p. 185 seq.) is as old as Homer (Il. xx. 404). It never developed into a complete political union, though it tended to do so (c. 170 n.). We have instances of united action in 141. 1, v. 108. 2, vi. 7. Thucydides (iii. 104) pointedly ignores this festival when he speaks of the gathering of the Ionians at Delos; but Strabo (*u. s.*) says it was still celebrated in the time of Augustus. Thucydides' festival was for the περικτίονες νησιῶται, not for Ionians only.

2 τοῦτο: i.e. that the names end in *a*. Cf. c. 139 n. for Persian names.

1 For the Aeolian migration cf. Busolt, i. 272 seq. It was tradition-

ally four generations earlier than the Ionian (Strabo, 582), and like it was connected with the Dorian invasion. It was, however, an even more gradual movement, and neither in conduct nor in results had it the unity which is attributed (no doubt in exaggeration) to the Ionian migration. There is no reason to doubt the tradition that connects the Aeolians especially with Thessaly and Boeotia (Thuc. iii. 2. 3; vii. 57. 5; viii. 5. 2, 100. 3); this is supported by the likeness of the Lesbian and the Boeotian dialects (e.g. broad vowels *πώνω* for *πίνω*, feminine endings in *ις* and *ω*; Busolt, i. 195, n. 2). The name Aeolis is used in four senses:

(1) A district in south-west Thessaly (Apoll. i. 7. 3; F. H. G. i, p. 111; H. in vii. 95. 1 alludes to this sense).

(2) The district of Calydon in Aetolia (Thuc. iii. 102. 5).

(3) The twelve old Aeolic towns given here by H.

(4) All the settlements in the northern half of the west coast of Asia Minor, about thirty in number. Cyme and Lesbos were the *μητροπόλεις* (Strabo, 622).

The name 'Aeolian' (first used in Hes. W. and D. 636—of Cyme) perhaps arose in Asia Minor, and was transferred back to Greece proper; it seems to be used of all 'colonies' which were neither Dorian nor Ionian. The name may be connected with *αἰόλος*, 'glancing, changeful.'

For the identification of the 'old' Aeolic towns cf. Bähr, *ad loc.*, and Ramsay, J. H. S. ii. 271 seq. Except Cyme, they were unimportant; only this town (Head, H. N. 552) and Pitane (ib. 537) issued coinage before the fourth century. They lay on or near the coast from south of the Hermus to the Caicus.

Φρικωνίς: so called to distinguish this Cyme from other towns of the same name; Φ. is said to be derived from Mount Phricius over Thermopylae (Strabo, 621), but this is probably a mere invention; the epithet was shared by Larisa.

Λήρισαι: a form of the oft-recurring 'Pelasgic' **Λάρισσα**.

2 For **ἥκειν** cf. 30. 4 n.

150 1 Smyrna was Ionian before the twenty-third Olympiad (Paus. v. 8. 7), i.e. about the end of the eighth century. H. is confirmed by a poem of Mimnermus, who says (we Ionians) *κεῖθεν δ' ἀκτήεντος ἀπορνύμενοι ποταμοῖο | θεῶν βουλῇ Σμύρνην εἵλομεν Αἰολίδα* (Strabo, 634). Strabo, however, himself represents the town as a colony of Ephesus; this is obviously an Ionian invention to justify their aggression. The town, however, lying more than ten miles south of the Hermus, and having Phocaea on the coast between it and Cyme, belonged naturally to the Ionian sphere.

151 1 The Ida region stretched from the Gulf of Adramyttium to the Propontis.

2 The 'Hundred Isles' lay between Lesbos and the mainland. Strabo (618) says their number was estimated at from twenty to forty, and that the name means 'Islands of Apollo', from his epithet **Ἕκατος**; Strabo quotes 'Peloponnesus' for a similar nasalization of *σ*.

3 The words δεινὸν οὐδέν take up 143. 1.

152 The appeal is neither to king (as in iii. 148. 1) nor to 'the authorities' (ἄρχοντες, iii. 46. 1 n.), but to the whole people; this detail alone proves the story unhistorical; it is an invention to show the contrast between Ionic luxury and Spartan simplicity.

Xenophanes (Fr. 3) attacks the παναλουργέα φάρεα of his countrymen, the Colophonians, ἁβροσύνας δὲ μαθόντες ἀνωφελέας παρὰ Λυδῶν. For the Spartan constitution and policy in the sixth century cf. App. XVII. For Lacedaemonian headship cf. 69. 2 n.

Φωκαιέα: for this leadership cf. 141. 4 n., and position of Dionysius at Lade (vi. 11).

153 1 **τίνες ἐόντες.** For the contemptuous question cf. v. 73. 2 (Artaphrenes), v. 105 (Darius after the burning of Sardis); it is most appropriate here.

The words put into Cyrus' mouth bring out dramatically the contrast between the town life of the Greeks and the village life, feudal in its arrangements, of Persia; the rich Persians lived on presents or the produce of their land. Cf. Xen. Cyr. i. 2. 3–4 for a fancy picture of the ἐλευθέρα ἀγορά (i.e. 'free' from trade) in Persia. Aristotle (Pol. i. 9, p. 1257) analyses the prejudice against τὸ καπηλικόν in his day, when the Greek attitude to trade had changed greatly from that of H.

3 This passage is the best instance of the division of power among the officers of the Persian Empire (cf. Xen. Cyr. viii. 6. 1 and App. VI, § 7). Tabalus commands the garrison (cf. Mithrines at Sardis in Arr. Anab. i. 17. 3), Mazares (cc. 156–7) the field forces, while Pactyas has civil authority. If κομίζειν = 'manage', this sense is common in Homer, e.g. Il. vi. 490 τὰ σ' αὐτῆς ἔργα κόμιζε, but rare later; Pactyas would then be a satrap with limited powers. But κομίζειν may have its ordinary sense, 'bring,' i.e. to Ecbatana. In any case the position and behaviour of Pactyas resemble those of Harpalus under Alexander.

4 Justin (i. 7) makes the Babylonian War, Ctesias (2. 3, p. 64), the wars with the Bactrians and Sacae, precede the attack on Sardis; the order of events in H. (73. 1 n.) is more probable. Justin (ib.) has an absurd story that all Greece was coming to attack Cyrus, had he not spared Croesus. For the subsequent conquests of Cyrus cf. c. 177 n.

155 1 Cyrus quotes a proverb of Stasinus νήπιος ὃς πατέρα κτείνας παῖδας καταλείπει (Arist. Rhet. i. 15; 1376 A 6).

3 **ἀναμάξας.** Cf. Od. xix. 92 κεφαλῇ ἀναμάξεις, usually translated 'you will wipe off' (tr. ἀναμάσσω), i.e. 'suffer for in your own person'; but Stein derives from ἀν-αμάγω, i.e. 'heap up', which he thinks is supported by φέρω here.

4 Cf. App. I, § 4 for the aetiological legend.

156 2 **ἄνδρα Μῆδον.** It is noticeable that Medes already were being employed in high office (cf. App. VI, § 3).

158 2 A kinsman of Aristodicus was tyrant in the next generation (v. 37. 1).

159 3 τοὺς στρουθούς. Cf. Ps. lxxxiv. 3 for birds in a temple. Ael. V. H. v. 17 records that the Athenians put a man to death for killing a temple sparrow.

4 For the oracular teaching that sin of intention is equal to sin of act cf. vi. 86 (story of Glaucus).

160 3 πολιούχου. Cf. 'Α. Πολιάς (v. 82. 3)—a more common form. For other references to her as guardian deity cf. Farnell, G. C. i. 298, 398 seq. 'Plutarch' (de Mal. H. 20, F. H. G. i. 32) quotes 'verbally' the account of Charon of Lampsacus: Πακτύης ὡς ἐπύθετο προσελαύνοντα τὸν στρατὸν τὸν Περσικόν, ᾤχετο φεύγων ἄρτι μὲν εἰς Μιτυλήνην, ἔπειτα δὲ εἰς Χίον· καὶ αὐτοῦ ἐκράτησε Κῦρος. In this account, as 'Plutarch' says, οὐδὲν ἄγος προστέτριπται; but Charon's silence is not inconsistent with the account here (cf. Intr. § 19).

4 Atarneus, a fertile district (vi. 28. 2), had belonged to the Mysians (viii. 106. 1). The dense population of Chios (Thuc. viii. 40. 2; Beloch, Bevölk., pp. 233–4) made it important for the island to secure a food-supply on the mainland. The Chians still had Atarneus in 398 B.C. (Xen. Hell. iii. 2. 11).

χῶρος must be taken twice over, with Ἀταρνέος and with Μυσίης (cf. 137. 1 for another double construction; but the one here is very harsh). For the position of Atarneus cf. vii. 42. 1 n.

5 For the οὐλαί cf. 132. 1 n. The price of blood might not be used for sacred things (cf. St. Matt. xxvii. 6).

161 1 Magnesia above the Maeander valley (cf. iii. 122. 1), not the northern Magnesia by Mount Sipylus in the Hermus valley.

162 1 ἀνόμῳ τραπέζῃ. For the Thyestean meal cf. c. 119.

2 The Persians had learned Assyrian methods of attack, and so were more formidable than the Lydian cavalry; for mounds against the wall cf. pictures in Maspero, iii. 241, 250, and Thuc. ii. 75–6.

163–7 *The story of the Phocaeans.* This digression is invaluable, as giving us our earliest evidence of the 'Barbarian Reaction' in the West, which kept the Greeks out of Corsica and west Sicily, and prevented the west Mediterranean from becoming a Greek lake. It was checked for more than half a century by the Deinomenidae, at Himera in 480 B.C. (vii. 166) and at Cumae in 474. For the whole subject cf. Bury, pp. 296 seq. These chapters are well discussed by Clerc in the R. E. G. xviii. 143 seq.; he proves that the later traditions (Antiochus, fr. 9; F. H. G. i. 183; Timagenes, ib. iii. 323) are mistaken, which attribute the foundation of Massilia, in whole or in part, to the exiles fleeing from Persia. This later date has been supported by Thuc. i. 13. 6; but the order of events in that chapter need not be chronological.

163 1 πρώτῃ. Phocaea as leader is attacked first; cf. 152. 1 for a Phocaean spokesman. Harpagus changed the plan of campaign;

Mazares had attacked the Ionian towns of the south (c. 161). The Thalassocracy of Phocaea is variously dated 602–560 and 577–533 B.C. (Myres, J. H. S. xxvi, pp. 102–3). Cf. Thuc. i. 13. 6 for their foundation of Massilia (which H. does not mention, though he knows the town: v. 9. 3), and for their 'repeated victories' over the Carthaginians; by this colony they secured the 'tin-route' across Gaul. For their coinage cf. Hill, G. C. pp. 8–11; Head, H. N. 587–9; it was both early and widespread. The coins of Phocaea, with those of Mytilene and Cyzicus, formed the chief currency for the coast towns of west Asia till the time of Alexander.

οἱ καταδέξαντες. H. rightly lays stress on the Phocaeans being 'openers-up' (not the discoverers; cf. iv. 153. 2 for Samians at Tartessus) of the West. Their activity gave the name to the 'Ionian' sea, south of Italy. Myres (*u. s.*, p. 102) refers these voyages to the last half of the eighth century, but Tartessus was a 'virgin' market in 630 B.C. when Colaeus discovered it.

Ἀδρίην. The Adriatic Sea (cf. iv. 33. 1), named from the Etruscan town of Adria, near the mouth of the Po (Liv. v. 33. 8).

Ἰβηρίην: only mentioned here by H. (but Iberians among other western peoples: vii. 165. 1); probably he means north-east Spain near the Ebro. The Greeks had a colony here, Rhodae (*hod.* Rosas) near Emporiae; Strabo (654) ascribes it to the Rhodians before the first Olympiad, an impossible date; he adds that it was afterwards colonized by the Massiliots. Probably his statement is a mere etymological guess, and Rhodae was connected from the first with Massilia (and so with Phocaea), which certainly owned it later.

Ταρτησσόν: the region at the mouth of the Baetis, probably the Tarshish of the Old Testament (but cf. Hastings, D. B. *s. v.*, where the evidence is fully given, for a different view). It was the Eldorado of the ancients (cf. Strabo, 146, for its gold, silver, brass, and iron); Stesichorus (Strabo, 148) sang of the *ἀργυρόριζοι παγαί* of the Tartessus river. Cf. Meyer, ii. 428–9, for the whole subject.

2 The Phocaeans, like the Elizabethan navigators, were buccaneers (cf. 166. 1 and Dionysius of P., vi. 17 n.) as well as traders; hence the character of their ships. The penteconter was the main Greek ship-of-war in the sixth century, although Thucydides (i. 13. 2–3) says that the Corinthians were building triremes by 700 B.C. (this is his meaning, in spite of Torr, A. S. p. 4, n. 8). The Samian and the Phocaean navies were mainly composed of penteconters; they had, however, a few triremes (Thuc. i. 14. 1). H.'s details as to Samos (contrast iii. 39. 3 and 44. 2) confirm this view, that the navies of the period were mixed. Thucydides further seems to suggest that large fleets of triremes were first formed in Sicily and at Corcyra. The lighter penteconter would be used in preference for a long voyage or for a piratical raid. In the penteconter there were twenty-five oars a side; but the principle of superimposed banks may

be as old as the Homeric Catalogue (Il. ii. 510—the Boeotian ships have 120 men each; cf. Thuc. i. 10. 4). For its use in Phoenician warships as early as 700 B.C. cf. Torr, p. 4, and figs. 10 and 11.

3 The longevity of Arganthonius was proverbial (cf. Anacreon, fr. 8, in Strabo, 151); that he reigned eighty years is accepted as *prope certum* by Pliny (N. H. vii. 156), who gives (154–5) an amusing string of instances, ending in 'Tyriorum regem DC. atque, ut parce mentitus, filium eius DCCC'.

⟨τὰ⟩ **πάντα**, 'in all,' as opposed to *πάντα*, 'quite.'

4 **λίθων μεγάλων**. The wall obviously had been seen by H. (cf. 141. 1 n.).

164 1 **κατιρῶσαι**, 'consecrate,' as a sign of submission, which was to be at once material and symbolical.

2 **βουλεύσασθαι**. Probably Phocaea was actually besieged, and these negociations took place during an interval in the siege. Harpagus' offer can hardly have been genuine, for Cyrus had refused to accept submission on terms less favourable to the Greeks (c. 141). The Phocaeans on their part were probably seeking to gain time, so as to be able to escape by sea.

165 1 The Chians were friendly with the Milesians (18. 3 n.) and the league trading East, the Phocaeans with the league trading West (cf. iii. 59. 4 n.). The Oenussian Islands lie between Chios and the mainland.

ἐκ θεοπροπίου. This passage throws interesting light on the policy and methods of the Delphic oracle. The Pythia not unnaturally wished to secure for Hellenism one of the keys of the west Mediterranean (cf. v. 43 for a similar attempt in west Sicily). For this Delphic policy cf. Curtius ii. 37–42 (though he exaggerates it); Holm (i. 232) thinks the oracle simply sanctioned projects suggested to it by would-be colonists. But probably it also originated projects itself (cf. v. 42. 2 n.).

3 **μύδρον**. Cf. Hor. Epod. xvi. 17–26, and for a similar sanction to the Delian league Ath. Pol. 23 *ad fin*.

166 1 **Κύρνον**. Antiochus (fr. 9, F. H. G. i. 183) says that some of them also went to Massilia; but (see 163 n.) Ἀλαλίαν should be read in that passage for Μασσαλίαν.

περίοικοι: probably the native Corsicans, who appealed to Carthage and Etruria for help.

Τυρσηνοί. The Etruscans were at this time at the height of their power; not improbably they ruled Rome in the sixth century; the Romans, on becoming free, made a treaty with Carthage in 509 B.C. (Polyb. 3. 22). The occupation of Alalia was a direct challenge to the Etruscans, and no doubt it was the common danger from the Greeks which led them to form the commercial treaty with Carthage spoken of by Aristotle (Pol. iii. 9. 6; 1280 a).

2 A Cadmean victory was a proverb, derived from the mutual slaughter of the two sons of Oedipus, Eteocles and Polynices, in the war of 'the Seven against Thebes'.

ἐμβόλους: acc. of respect; lit. 'they were bent back as to their beaks'. Cf. 180. 2 ἐλήλαται τοὺς ἀγκῶνας; the great danger to the ancient warship was that, in ramming another, it often disabled itself; cf. especially Thuc. vii. 34. 5, 36. 2–3.

1 Agylla, the later Caere in south Etruria.

2 For the oracle teaching mercy and atonement for blood guilt cf. Myers, Hellenica, p. 455; for the curse on offspring cf. vi. 139. 1 n.

σφι: the dead Phocaeans. The atonement consisted in setting up Greek games in their honour as heroes; the connexion of funeral games with the dead is as old as Il. xxiii; for other examples cf. Frazer, ii. 549–50. For ἐναγίζω ('hero-worship') cf. ii. 44. 5; v. 47 n.

3 Oenotria (Strabo, 209) is the toe of Italy 'from the Sicilian strait to the Tarentine Gulf'.

Ὑέλη: i.e. Elia or Velia, so famous in the history of philosophy. For 'paltering in a double sense' on the part of Oracles cf. iii. 64. 4 n.

4 Κύρνον: a son of Heracles (Serv. ad Verg. Ec. ix. 30). Heracles is the pioneer of Greek enterprise, cf. v. 43; there is no need to conjecture ἕλος ἐόντα, in reference to the fact that Velia was founded in a marsh (Dion. Halic. i. 20).

1 The name 'Abdera' is perhaps Phoenician (Strabo, 157). Abdera coined with the griffin of Teos as type, but it followed the Phoenician heavy standard (Head, H. N. 253 seq.). The town was famous as the birthplace of Democritus and Protagoras, yet its people were proverbially stupid (for their idea of wit cf. vii. 120). For the site cf. vii. 126 n.

Timesias had founded it about 653 B.C., driven from Clazomenae by his undeserved unpopularity (cf. Ael. V. H. xii. 9); for the formula οὐκ ἀπόνητο cf. Od. xi. 324; for hero-worship of a founder cf. Thuc. v. 11. 1 (at Amphipolis).

1 ἕκαστος, ἕκαστοι. H. emphasizes the weakness of Ionia, i.e. the absence of union.

2 νήσους. H. is thinking of the bigger islands, Chios (iv. 138. 2), Samos (iii. 44. 1, but Samos was really independent iii. 120. 3); he himself says that of the Cyclades οὐδεμία ἦν ὑπὸ Δαρείῳ (v. 30. 6); and in 174. 3 he implies that the Persian power 'stopped on the shore'. Chios had territory on mainland (160. 3 n.), so too had Lesbos, but H. here is speaking of 'Ionians' only.

As the Ionians had command of the sea they could still meet at Mycale.

1 For Bias cf. 27. 2 n.; Mahaffy (G. L. i. 198) thinks a fragment of his poem urging migration is preserved in Theognis, 757–68.

2 Sardinia was barred to the Greeks by Carthage; hence, on the principle of *omne ignotum pro magnifico*, they exaggerated its size; the Italian official figures are for Sicily 9860 square miles, for Sardinia 9187 (E. B.[11] xxv. 20, xxiv. 210). Cf. v. 106. 6, 'Scylax' Perip. 114, and Timaeus (in Strabo, 654) for the mistake, which has been revived by Freeman (Sicily, i. 2, 241). Strabo (123) was

the first writer to give the real proportion. Cf. v. 124. 2 for another proposal to conquer Sardinia. Corsica was already (c. 165) partially held by Phocaeans.

3 **Φοίνικος.** 'Plutarch' (de Mal. Herod. 15) attacks this statement, as 'making Thales barbarian'; H. only means that he was descended from the Thelidae, original settlers of Miletus, who were descended from Cadmus. As the father of Thales bore a Carian name (Examius, Diog. Laer. i. 1. 22), he probably had non-Hellenic blood in him. Thales' proposal shows the practical wisdom for which he was ranked among the Seven Sages (27. 2 n.); he alone of these was also a philosopher. His proposal was to secure united action by a genuine federal government (cf. Freeman, F. G. pp. 187–90). Thucydides (ii. 15. 2) uses almost the same phrases of the supposed work of Theseus in Attica, and H. seems to think the proposal of Thales was for complete political unification, as he says the cities were to be mere 'demes'; but Thales can only have meant that the *ἓν βουλευτήριον* was to control foreign relations.

Teos was not chosen only for its central position; its insignificance would prevent it being dangerous to the independence of the federated states. So Washington (not New York) was made capital of the United States.

171 1 Of the Carians and Leleges may well be quoted the words of Strabo (322), when, after describing the wide diffusion of the Leleges, he says (speaking of north-west Greece): 'Now that most of the land has become desolate, and the settlements and especially the cities have disappeared, even if a man could give a definite account, he would do nothing useful, owing to the uncertainty (*ἀδοξία*) and to the fact that the peoples have disappeared, a movement which began long since.' The best English accounts are those of Myres and Paton, J. H. S. xvi. 264 seq., and (of the Leleges) of Holm, i. 63–4, 72. The following are the most important points as to the two races:

I. In Asia Minor.

(1) In Homer (Il. x. 428–9) Dolon places them both with the Lycians, Mysians, and Phrygians among the allies of Troy. In the Catalogue (ii. 867) the Carians are *βαρβαρόφωνοι*, and inhabit Miletus.

(2) Leleges are placed by Homer at Pedasus in the Troad (Il. xxi. 86–7), but do not occur in 'the Catalogue'.

(3) Strabo (321, 611) tells us that ancient 'tombs and forts' in Caria were called 'Lelegian'.

(4) Philippus, a Carian writer of the third century B.C., makes the Leleges serfs of the Carians; Plutarch (Qu. Gr. 46; Mor. 302) says that the survivors of the Leleges were serfs at Tralles.

We may conclude they were genuine tribes on the Anatolian coast, of whom the Carians were the later comers and the conquerors. The two races were often identified, especially as the

Carians seem to have adopted the speech of their subjects; for two races in Caria cf. 171. 6.

II. **In Greece proper.**

(1) Carians are traced at Megara (citadel called 'Caria', Paus. i. 40. 6), in the Argolid at Epidaurus and Hermione (Strabo, 374, quoting Aristotle), at Athens (Isagoras, H. v. 66. 1). But the last instance proves nothing, and the first may be connected with the later military importance of the Carians.

(2) Leleges are mentioned continually as early inhabitants, e.g. by Strabo, 321–2 (quoting Arist.), in Acarnania, Aetolia, Boeotia, &c. This is probably invention based (*a*) on the fact that the Leleges, like the Pelasgians, are merely a prehistoric stop-gap; where nothing was known they were put in; (*b*) on resemblances of place-names in Caria and in central Greece (Busolt, i. 185. 4 n.), e.g. Abae in Caria and in Phocis.

We may conclude that there is no sufficient evidence for the presence of Carians and Leleges in Greece proper.

III. But it is not unlikely that the primitive population of Greece and of Anatolia was really akin; we find place-names ending in -νθος, -*nda* (and perhaps -ασσος, -ασα) common to both regions, and a number of words 'earthy of the soil', e.g. βόλινθος, with a similar termination (cf. Conway's list, B.S.A. viii. 155). We may also compare the primitive cist-graves of Assarlik in Caria with the pre-Mycenaean graves in the Cyclades. So the double axe was a symbol of the Carians, but perhaps they and the Cretans borrowed it equally from some earlier people. (For this view generally cf. Mackenzie, B.S.A. xii, p. 217 seq.) The double axe seems to be the symbol also of the Hittite god, Tesub.

IV. **The races in the islands.**

Greek theory made the Carians native in the islands (171. 2; Thuc. i. 4. 1, 8. 1, though with differing details). Thucydides seeks to confirm this by archaeological evidence; but the weapons found in the island-graves do not resemble the Carian weapons of c. 171. Probably, therefore, the native tradition is right (171. 5), that they were originally a mainland people, and the Greek tradition is a mere inference from the Thalassocracy of Minos. There were Carians in the islands, however, in the ninth and eighth centuries (*v. i.*).

V. The theory once maintained that the Carians were the authors of the Mycenaean culture (e.g. by Köhler and Dümmler) must be abandoned, in view of the facts that hardly any Mycenaean remains are found in Caria, and those found show the culture in its decadence (J.H.S. xvi. 265).

VI. For the affinities of the Carians with the Indo-European races cf. App. I, § 4. The Carians seem to have been the advanced guard of the tribes that invaded Anatolia from the north at the end of the second millennium B.C. Conway (*u. s.* 156) thinks the Carian names may belong to the Indo-European family of speech. If this be denied (with Kretschmer), we may suppose the conquerors adopted the language of the conquered earlier population.

It is to this later conquering element we must attribute: (1) The Carian Thalassocracy (Myres, J. H. S. xxvi. 107–9). There were Carians in the islands at the time of the Greek settlement (171. 5). (2) The characteristic Carian weapons (171. 4 n.). (3) The Carian mercenaries of the seventh century (ii. 152. 5).

4 **τριξὰ ἐξευρήματα.** This passage is of great importance for our knowledge of Greek armour. The difference between the weapons of Homeric and those of later times is well known; H. here attributes three changes to the Carians, who were prominent as mercenaries in the seventh and sixth centuries (cf. Helbig, Hom. Ep., p. 344; Archil. fr. 24; and ii. 152, 154, v. 111. 1). The statement is repeated by Strabo (661), who says (662) the Carians *καθ' ὅλην ἐπλανήθησαν τὴν Ἑλλάδα, μισθοῦ στρατεύοντες.* Pliny (N. H. vii. 200) also credits the Carians with greaves. H. has grasped the difference between the huge body-covering shield (*ἠύτε πύργος*) [Lang, Homer and his Age, 110 f. compares the shields in the Bayeux Tapestry and refutes the theory that they were only used in a chariot] and the round shield of manageable size, borne on the left arm. Some (e. g. Tsountas, p. 193) think he is wrong as to the 'badges', and refer to the 'stars' on Mycenaean shields and the well-known shield of Achilles of Il. 18. Curtius, however (Ges. Abh. ii. 89), accepts the statement of H., who is probably referring to some particular form of badge, which was specially Carian.

With regard to *λόφος* and *ὄχανον* Strabo (661) quotes from Alcaeus *λόφον σείων Καρικόν*, and from Anacreon, *Καρικοεργὲς ὄχανον.*

The *λόφος* is frequent in Homer (Il. vi. 469, Hector's boy *ἐκλίνθη . . . ταρβήσας χαλκόν τε ἰδὲ λόφον ἱππιοχαίτην*), as H. must have known. Hence he may be referring to the later form of crest which fits right on the helmet, as opposed to the earlier form which was raised on a *κύμβαχος* (Il. xv. 536); the two forms of crests are seen in the Euphorbus plate (Brunn, Griech. Kunstg. (1893), fig. 114). With the later form comes in the more frequent use of cheek-pieces to the helmet, which, by hiding the face, would make 'badges' more necessary.

The *ὄχανον* (or *ὀχάνη*) is used by the Schardana on the Egyptian monuments of the thirteenth century (Helbig, Hom. Ep., fig. 124, at Ipsambul); the 'shield-band', therefore, may have been borrowed by the Carians from an earlier Anatolian race. The 'band' (of metal, wood, or leather) was placed across the diameter of the shield from rim to rim (cf. picture in D. of A., s. v. 'Clipeus'); the shield also had a grip (*πόρπαξ*) of leather running round inside the rim. Hence *πόρπαξ* and *ὄχανον* are used as convertible (Schol. to Arist. Eq. 849). They were, however, properly distinct; the conservative Spartans used only the *πόρπαξ* till the third century (Plut. Cleom. 11).

The ὄχανα may be the Homeric κανόνες (Il. xiii. 407; Helb., pp. 324–57), but it is more probable these latter are the ῥάβδοι of Hesych. (s. v.), the stiffening rods in the centre of the leather shield. Cf. Leaf, Iliad, vol. i, App. B, for this and other points as to Homeric armour.

περικείμενοι. We have a shield hung from the left shoulder (cf. Il. xvi. 106 ὁ δ' ἀριστερὸν ὦμον ἔκαμνεν | ἔμπεδον αἰὲν ἔχων σάκος) represented in the famous hunting scene on the dagger-blade from the fourth grave at Mycenae (Helbig, fig. 125); Reichel (Hom. Waff., p. 10) elaborately explains the working of the shield. In Il. v. 795–7 (cf. Il. v. 98), however, Diomede has his shield τελαμών on his right shoulder.

This early shield also had a 'grip', which H. takes for granted; this omission hardly justifies Helbig's criticism, 'H. either did not understand the old use or has expressed himself obscurely' (p. 323).

To περικείμενοι supply τελαμῶνας. The reason for placing the 'shield belt' on the left shoulder was that the sword belt had to be on the right one (Il. xiv. 404-5), as the sword itself was on the left side, so as to be drawn more easily.

5 **ὕστερον:** i. e. at the time of the Greek colonization, about 1000 B. C.

τῷ αὐτῷ. The Greek story made them Leleges originally (§ 2).

For Ζεὺς Κάριος cf. v. 119. 2 n.; it is curious that while he is worshipped by Mysians and Lydians also (§ 6), Z. Στράτιος is Carian only.

172 1 Caunus lay in south Caria: it was in the Rhodian περαία. Thucydides (i. 116. 3) also distinguishes it from Caria.

κατ' ἡλικίην, 'according to age and affection.' H. puts this in to show the drinking bouts were not tribal.

2 **ἡβηδόν,** 'in full force' (vi. 21. 1).

Calynda lay to the south-east on the Lycian frontier.

ἐκβάλλειν. For this expulsion cf. Tylor (P. C. ii. 199) who says the Australians 'annually drive from their midst the accumulated ghosts of the last year's dead'. So too the modern Greek will discharge firearms to drive away an earthquake.

173 The Lycians are as great a racial and linguistic puzzle as the Carians. Their language is usually thought to be Indo-European, on account of the resemblance of its inflexions to those of Greek; but it has not yet been satisfactorily explained, and its connexion with Greek is very doubtful, Meyer i. 476.

The name 'Lycian' may be explained: (1) As that of a conquered Anatolian tribe. Cf. the Luka of the great Egyptian invasions (App. X. 8), and the sea-roving Lukki of the Tell El-Amarna Tablets. (2) Or, more probably, as a Greek name derived from a confusion of Apollo Λύκειος (the wolf god) with the deity of Patara (Farnell, G. C. iv. 113). The geographical position of the Lycians on the sea-coasts seems to confirm the tradition of their origin as immigrants ἐκ Κρήτης. They borrowed much from Greece, including partially their alphabet, but retained their nationality and political individuality (for the Lycian League cf. Freeman, F. G. p. 208 seq.). Their abundant coinage is evidence of great prosperity in fifth and fourth centuries (Head, H. N. 688 seq.).

2 This Sarpedon is grandfather (Diod. v. 79) of the Homeric hero, the leader of the Lycians (Il. *pass.*).

Milyas (iii. 90. 1) is in historic times the high ground north-east of Lycia, as far as Pisidia (Strabo, 631). As no Lycian remains are found here, it was inhabited probably by a distinct people (cf. Arr. Anab. i. 24. 5 ἔστι μὲν τῆς μεγάλης Φρυγίας, συνετέλει δὲ ἐς τὴν Λυκίαν, οὕτως ἐκ βασιλέως μεγάλου τεταγμένον).

'Solymi' seems to be the name of the original inhabitants, who were driven into the mountains; so in Il. vi. 184, 204, they are enemies of the Lycians. Strabo (631) says the neighbouring tribe, the Kabaleis (iii. 90 n.), were thought to be 'Solymi', and Steph. Byz. (s. v. Πισιδία) says the same of the Pisidians.

3 The name Τερμίλαι is confirmed by quotations from Hecataeus and Panyasis (fr. 364, F. H. G. i. 30; iii. 236), and by the TRXMΛI of the Harpagus obelisk in the British Museum.

The aetiological myth as to the name 'Lycians' is part of the expansion of the Theseus story (Aegeus was the human father of Theseus), which accompanied the rise of Athenian power under and after the Pisistratidae (Bury, i. 213).

4 For explanations of, and parallels to (e. g. Tacitus, Germania, c. 20), this interesting survival of primitive usage cf. Westermarck, cap. v; he argues that it does not prove (as McLennan thought) a time when promiscuity was the rule and paternity uncertain. In many most primitive tribes (W. gives a list, pp. 98 seq.) kinship through males was the rule. Kinship through females may be based on various ideas, e. g. the fact that 'paternity is a matter of inference, maternity of observation' (Maine), on the closer connexion between mothers and their children, or on primitive polygamy. It is confirmed for Lycia by Il. vi. 196-206; Sarpedon, the sister's son, is chief, and the male heir, Glaucus, subordinate.

Probably the usage belongs to the primitive Anatolian stock; cf. App. I. 3.

174 2 **Λακεδαιμονίων.** Strabo (653) brings the Cnidians from Megara. Tr. 'As their territory lies towards the sea, being called Triopion, beginning from the Chersonese of Bybassia'; τό is neuter from attraction of the predicate Τριόπιον. Properly Τριόπιον is the name only of the extreme point.

3 **οἱ Κνίδιοι** takes up οἵ of § 2; but the whole section is a model of confusion. It is to be noticed that H., as a Halicarnassian, knows the Cnidian territory minutely.

5 The oracle, for which H. does not vouch (cf. ὡς αὐτοὶ κτλ.), looks like an *ex post facto* excuse for non-resistance. The isthmus still shows traces of the unfinished cutting.

175 1 For Pedasus cf. v. 121 n. This part of Caria was again the only one that resisted at the time of the Ionic revolt (v. 119-21); this may be connected with the fact that the Leleges were especially at home here.

τρίς. This portent is mentioned again (viii. 104 n.) in almost the same words, but as having only happened 'twice'; if both passages be genuine, they clearly prove that Bk. I was written later, but the words in Bk. VIII are probably a gloss.

176 1 συνήλισαν. A like desperation was shown against Brutus in 42 B.C. (App. B. C. iv. 80, who says it had been shown also against Alexander in 334: this is obviously wrong; cf. Arr. Anab. i. 24. 4).

3 ἐκδημέουσαι. For a parallel in the Fabius who survived the Cremera (477 B.C.) cf. Liv. ii. 50. Some explain their absence by their having gone up into the hills in the summer.

Harpagus seems to have become hereditary satrap of Lycia (though there were also native rulers; cf. vii. 98 n.). A descendant of his, Karmis (?), was ruler there about 430 B.C., and is commemorated on the Xanthian Stele in the British Museum (l. 5, Hicks, No. 56, pp. 96-7; Meyer, iv. 683, refers it to 413 B.C.): it is suggested that the 'triquetra' of the Lycian coins may be a pun on the family name (ἁρπάγη = a hook); but Head (H. N. 688) makes it a solar symbol connected with the Apollo cult.

7-216 Resumption of story of Cyrus.

177-83 *Description of Babylon.* 184-7 *Works of Semiramis and Nitocris.* 188-91 *Capture of Babylon by Cyrus.* 192-200 *Description of Babylonia.* 201-3, 215-16 *Geographical position and customs of Massagetae.* 204-14 *Cyrus' expedition against Massagetae and his death.*

177 Prášek (i. 224-5) interprets H. as placing the wars in the east against the Bactrians, Sacae, &c., before the attack on Babylon. This is against the order of names in 153. 4, and also against probability (cf. also 190. 1 n.); the passage here obviously gives no chronological evidence. That Cyrus, however, extended his rule to the Jaxartes is likely in itself, and is confirmed by the list of satrapies in the B. I. (App. VII, § 1). It is confirmed too by the position of Kyra, which claimed to be his foundation, on the river Jaxartes (Strabo 517), and by the story of the Arimaspi as εὐεργέται of Cyrus (cf. viii. 85. 3 n.); they saved his army on the north borders of the Gedrosian desert.

-183 For ancient Babylon the main authority is the East India House inscription of Nebuchadnezzar, 619 lines long (quoted as E. I. H. from R. P.[2] iii. 104 seq.). The best English account is that of Pinches, in the Enc. Bib. (s. v. Babylon). H. is our oldest Greek witness; Sayce (Introd. p. 28 seq.) denies that he ever visited

Babylonia, but this view has not been generally accepted. Cf. Baumstark in P. W. (about 1896) s. v. Babylon, 'that [H.'s statements] really rest on his own observation, should never have been disputed. But it is also indisputable that in them what the writer has himself seen and what he was told by his oriental guides, is mixed up in a suspicious way' (ii. 2689). F. H. Weissbach, however, Das Stadtbild von Babylon (1904, Der Alte Orient V), produces a plan of Babylon based on recent German excavations (still going on), which differs entirely from the account of H. or of any other Greek writer; Weissbach (p. 15) indeed claims the support of Berosus, who says (F. H. G. ii. 507) that Nebuchadnezzar ὑπερεβάλετο τρεῖς μὲν τῆς ἔνδον πόλεως περιβόλους, τρεῖς δὲ τῆς ἔξω, but there is no trace of περίβολοι on W.'s plan. This plan, not to mention other difficulties, represents Babylon as having no defence on the west except the river Euphrates, which is absurd. It is therefore ignored here. (See Note G, p. 451.)

178 1 H. includes (cf. iv. 39. 1) under 'Assyria' the whole region between the Iranian plateau, Armenia, and the desert; this province (for its history cf. iii. 92. 1) is called 'Assyria' also in the Minaean inscriptions (from South Arabia, which go back to ninth century B.C.). Hence in his Ἀσσύριοι λόγοι (cf. App. II, § 6) H. includes both the Assyrian and the Babylonian Empire (cc. 106, 184). The confusion was natural, owing to (1) H.'s ignorance, especially of Assyria. (2) The identity of their religion and culture. (3) The fact that Babylon was often a vassal of Nineveh. But the two empires were historically and ethnographically distinct. We may compare the similar identification of Medes and Persians by the Greeks.

ἄλλα πολίσματα: this is correct; the land is full of ruins. Cf. a striking passage in Layard, Nineveh and Babylon (1853), p. 245, beginning 'On all sides, as far as eye could see, rose the grass-covered heaps, marking the site of ancient habitations. The great tide of civilization had long since ebbed, leaving the wrecks on the solitary shore'. This refers to the district west of Mosul, i. e. near the site of Nineveh.

2 μέγαθος and μέτωπον (= 'side'; elsewhere κῶλον) are both accusatives of respect. ἐούσης τετραγώνου: a bold anacoluthon.

εἴκοσι καὶ ἑκατόν. There are four main questions as to the walls of Babylon:

I. Are the two walls, outer and inner, mentioned by H., the Imgur Bel and Nimitti Bel of E. I. H. viii. 43–6? Their identity is accepted by Baumstark (*u. s.*), Maspero (iii. 563), and others, but denied by the recent excavators, e. g. Weissbach (p. 12). This point does not affect H.'s narrative.

II. Had H. seen either or both walls?

(1) Berosus (F. H. G. ii. 508) says that Cyrus 'arranged to destroy the outer walls', because Babylon was 'troublesome and

hard to take'. But this statement seems inconsistent with the fact that he entered the city peaceably as a deliverer (App. IV, § 1).

(2) H. himself says (iii. 159. 1) that Darius τὸ τεῖχος περιεῖλε καὶ τὰς πύλας πάσας ἀπέσπασε. This is usually explained as referring to the outer wall, and meaning that this had ceased to exist before H.'s visit. H. then either would be describing the outer wall from hearsay (Baumstark), or (as Lehmann, Klio, i. 274; cf. H. iii. 150. 1 n.) incorporating whole passages from Hecataeus (cf. the tenses of ἐνεστᾶσι 179. 3, and κεῖται 181. 5). But there is no good evidence that Hecataeus had ever been in Babylon, or that H. copied him (Introd. § 20), and either alternative seriously prejudices the credit of H.

(3) It is more natural to suppose, as the words πύλας . . . ἀπέσπασε in fact imply, that Darius simply dismantled the outer wall. He left Babylon in the state which Scott (in Quentin Durward) describes at Liége. To remove such enormous masses of brick-work entirely would have been at once difficult and needless. H. throws in touches which rest mainly on hearsay (e.g. 179. 3, the presence of the 'brazen' gates), but he had seen enough of the wall to warrant him describing it as existing.

III. The extent of the walls.

(1) H.'s figure of 480 stades is supported by the statement of Philostratus, supposed to be derived from Hellanicus (see P. W. ii. 2693).

Oppert's attempt to trace the line of this great square on the modern site is now given up; Weissbach (p. 30) says it is fifty times too big; but Nikel [Herodot und die Keilschriftforschung (1896), pp. 25–7] points out that the extent of the ruins (roughly fifteen miles by twelve) corresponds to H.'s figures, which are accepted by Baumstark and Lehmann (*u. s.*). If this is right, the outer wall included the neighbouring town of Borsippa (cf. 181. 2 n.), which had also a wall of its own. Many, however, maintain Borsippa was quite separate from Babylon, following Berosus (F. H. G. ii. 508). The recent excavations render somewhat doubtful the enormous size of Babylon; but as Lehmann points out (*u. s.*), even if their results were more certain than they are, the literary tradition is very strong, and walls of brick might disappear, leaving little or no trace (cf. 179. 1 n.).

(2) The figures of other Greek writers are smaller, e. g. Ctesias (Ass. fr. 5, p. 397) gives 360 stades, Strabo (738) 365 stades, Cleitarchus (in Diod. ii. 7; he was one of the historians of Alexander) the same; Bähr (Ctesias, pp. 401–4) collects all the evidence. These are taken as being the extent of the inner wall, which (Abydenus, F. H. G. iv. 284) lasted down to the time of Alexander.

Of course all this vast area was not inhabited. At any rate H. is only giving the estimate he had received; he could not have measured even one side (contrast ii. 127. 1). For the size of Babylon cf. Arist. Pol. iii. 3. 5 (1276 A) ἥτις ἔχει περιγραφὴν μᾶλλον ἔθνους ἢ πόλεως· ἧς γέ φασιν ἑαλωκυίας τρίτην ἡμέραν οὐκ αἰσθέσθαι τι μέρος τῆς πόλεως.

IV. The height of the walls.

H.'s estimate, about 335 feet by 85, to some extent agrees with that of Ctesias, who gives 50 fathoms (i.e. 300 feet, Diod. ii. 7). Nebuchadnezzar describes his wall as 'mountains high' (E. I. H. viii. 51; cf. Jer. li. 53), and Xenophon makes the ruined wall of Nineveh (with its base, κρηπίς) 150 feet high and 50 feet wide (Anab. iii. 4. 10–11; perhaps he is including the mound on which it stood). Strabo (738, with whom Diod. ii. 7 and Q. Curt. v. 1 agree), however, makes the wall of Babylon only 32 feet thick and 75 high (90 in the towers). H. probably follows the exaggerated figures of his guide. Maspero (iii. 563), who gives a picture of a conjectural restoration, makes the height of Nimitti Bel, the main wall, 30 metres, i.e. not quite 100 feet), and says it 'resembled rather a chain of mountains with battlements and towers than a boulevard of man's handiwork'. H.'s wall is not broad enough for stability in proportion to its height, and it is possible that he even underestimated its thickness; that of Khorsabad, which is much lower, is nearly 80 feet thick.

He is quite right in saying that there was a walled ditch (178. 3; 179. 2) in front of the outer wall, and that inside there was a second wall 'of less extent' (181. 1 στεινότερον). For the walls generally cf. E. I. H. col. 8. To sum up, it may be said that H. gives a striking impressionist picture of this great scheme of fortification, but that it is incorrect in details.

ἐκεκόσμητο. Babylon was undoubtedly the most splendid city in the East, when the great works of Nebuchadnezzar were complete. Cf. E. I. H. *pass.* and Dan. iv. 30.

3 For the 'royal' and the 'ordinary cubit' cf. F. Hultsch, Metrologie (1882), especially pp. 46, 388. H. illustrates the Oriental measures from the Greek; but to us the process is reversed, as we know the Oriental measures, from measurements of Babylonian bricks and buildings, better than the Greek. The 'royal cubit' (which was practically the same as the Egyptian royal cubit, though a fraction longer, ib. p. 552) is calculated at from 532 (or 533) to 525 millimetres; the Greek cubit, therefore, being in the relation of 8 to 9 (the 'finger' is $\frac{7}{10}$ of an inch), was from 473 to 466·6 millimetres. Stein, however, says the relation is 7 to 8, not 8 to 9, basing this on the length of the Attic ell, i.e. 462 millimetres. The Samian cubit was the same as the Egyptian ell (ii. 168. 1); of this there were two kinds, the 'royal', about 527 millimetres (Hultsch, p. 355), the smaller about 450. That the Samian corresponded to the former, i.e. the longer ell, has been finally proved by the measurements at the Samian Heraeum (ib. p. 551).

1 **ἑλκύσαντες πλίνθους.** Translate 'having moulded enough bricks'; it corresponds to ἐπλίνθευον above. The passage is parodied in Aristophanes' Aves, 552; cf. i. 3 n.

Babylonia, owing to the absence of building stone, was the special home of brick-work. Crude bricks were used inside the walls, and even the baked bricks, from their larger size, were inferior in hardness to Roman, and to good modern, brick. Hence the wall was liable to be destroyed by water (cf. the tradition as to the fall of Nineveh (Ctes. Ass. fr. 16, p. 437; Diod. ii. 27), and to become in ruins a shapeless mass (cf. Lehmann, *u. s.*). It was to hinder destruction by water that the 'mats of reed' (ταρσοὺς κ.) were 'stuffed in' (διαστοιβάζοντες), but really at much more frequent 'intervals' (διά) than H. gives.

2 **ἀσφάλτῳ.** On 'bitumen' for 'mortar' (τέλμα) cf. E. B. s. v., and Gen. xi. 3 (A. V. 'slime'); it was used mixed with clay. The inscriptions (E. I. H. cols. 7 and 8) confirm H. as to this.

δόμων, 'layers.' Cf. ii. 127. 3 τὸν πρῶτον δόμον (in the pyramid of Chephren).

3 **ἔσχατα:** absolute; 'the edges' of the wall.

οἰκήματα. These 'one-storied chambers' (called πύργοι in iii. 156. 1 and Strabo, 738, and προμαχεῶνες in iii. 151. 1) served as guard-houses; no doubt they were machicolated.

περιέλασιν, 'to drive round' (not 'to turn'). This, too, Aristophanes parodies (Aves, 1125–9).

ἐνεστᾶσι. For the tense *v. s.* The gates were probably 'plated with brass'; hence πᾶσαι is distributive 'all of them'.

4 H. reckons a day's journey on the flat at 200 stadia (iv. 101. 2), i. e. about 23 miles; but Hit lies only about 125 miles north of Babylon. Matzat (Hermes, vi. 445) suggests that the explanation of H.'s larger figures lies in the river windings at Ardericca (185. 2 n.); the road, he thinks, would follow the river. Hit is still the chief source of bitumen for Babylonia; there are two springs, one cold and one hot; 'the whole place is redolent of sulphuretted hydrogen' (Peters, in E. B.[11] s. v. Hit).

2 **ἀγκῶνας.** Literally 'is carried down as to its angles', i. e. 'is carried down at an angle'. The river rampart (αἱμασιή, i. e. a rougher kind of wall) and the city wall made a salient angle, excellent for purposes of defence.

ἐπικαμπαί. 'From this point the return-walls stretch in the form of a rampart along each quay' (χεῖλος): παρατείνει is attracted into the singular to agree with αἱμασιή. The quays (Diod. ii. 8) were 160 stades long; parts of them were discovered by the French explorers in 1853; the bricks bear the name of Nabonidus. H. (186. 2) attributes them to Nitocris, the mother of the last king, Labynetus (188. 1 n.), who in part corresponds to the historic Nabonidus.

The Euphrates was navigable by sea-going ships up to Babylon (Strabo, 739).

3 The streets were some of them (ἄλλαι) parallel to the river, others were cross-roads (ἐπικάρσιαι, cf. iv. 101. 3) leading to it; the latter were merely 'alleys' or 'wynds' (λαῦραι). Streets which ran parallel to the river could hardly be 'straight', but H. exaggerates this feature, from their contrast to the winding streets of a Greek town.

4 **πυλίδες.** H. carefully distinguishes these 'little gates' from the main *πύλαι* of 179. 3.

181 2 **τὰ βασιλήια.** The question of the palaces and temples of Babylon is one of the most disputed in H. The following facts may be taken as fairly certain:

(1) That there were three palaces: (*a*) That on the right bank built by Nebuchadnezzar, in which Alexander died. (*τὰ πέραν βασίλεια*, Plut. Alex. 76; Arr. Anab. vii. 25. These authorities are specially important as quoting *αἱ βασίλειοι ἐφημερίδες* as to Alexander's last days.) (*b*) That on the left bank, close to the temple of Merodach (cf. E. I. H. viii. 31 seq.). (*c*) Another built by Nebuchadnezzar to the north. As this was built in fifteen days (E. I. H. cols. 8 and 9, and Berosus, F. H. G. ii. 507) it was less important.

(2) That there were two pre-eminent temples, that of Bel Merodach or Marduk in Babylon proper, on the left bank of the river (the 'Esagila'), and that of Bel Nebo in Borsippa, on the right bank of the river (the 'Ezida').

(3) That one palace (viz. 1*b* above) has been proved to be identical with the mound of El Qasr, and the 'Esagila' temple (less certainly) with Tell Amran.

(4) That Xerxes destroyed the great temple of Bel-Marduk in the centre of Babylon (Arr. Anab. vii. 17. 2); Strabo (738) calls it *ὁ τοῦ Βήλου τάφος*, but this is obviously the terraced tower, the ziggurat, the most important part of the Esagila.

There are, then, two main difficulties in the account of H.:

(1) He mentions only *one* palace and *one* temple, although in this there is a lower shrine *κάτω νηός* (183. 1), distinct from the great ziggurat of c. 181.

(2) He claims to have seen the temple; but if, as is probable, Xerxes had destroyed the Esagila, he could not have seen it.

Three explanations may be given (disregarding that of Sayce, that H. had never been in Babylon):

(1) Baumstark in P. W. thinks the 'palace' of H. is that on the right bank, and that he does not mention the palace on the left bank, because he considers it part of the Esagila temple; it actually was close to it (*v. s.*). How H. could describe a temple which had probably ceased to exist, Baumstark does not explain; presumably this is one of the 'suspicious confusions' of which he speaks.

(2) Hommel (in Hastings, D. B. s. v. Babel) says that Arrian and Strabo were mistaken. Because Xerxes removed the statue from Esagila (cf. 183. 3), they thought he had destroyed the temple.

This explanation is possible; a brick building dismantled about 480 B.C. would speedily fall into decay, and though H. might have seen it in fair repair circ. 450 B.C., it might well need rebuilding, as Alexander proposed, in 323 (Strabo, Arrian, *u. s.*).

(3) The most probable explanation, however, is that of Lehmann (Klio, i. 273–5), that by the 'temple of Belus' H. means the Nebo temple in Borsippa. H. distinctly says his temple was on the other side of the river (ἐν τῷ ἑτέρῳ) from the palace; and as both Marduk and Nebo were called Bel ('Lord'), H. may well have confused them, and transferred the story of the statue to the Nebo temple. In fact it is not unlikely that the priests told him falsely that the perished statue had been in their temple, though it had never belonged to them. It will be seen (184 n.) that H. had special knowledge of the Nebo temple, and that he carefully avoids saying where the statue had stood; he leaves it ἐν τῷ τεμένεϊ (183. 2).

The Borsippa temple is the best preserved of the ruins of Babylon, because of the imperishable material, blue slag, of which its uppermost story was formed. The present mound, Birs-Nimrud, is 153 feet high; its circumference is given variously, by Rich, 762 yards; by Rawlinson, 694 (ii. 582); H. gives 811 (four stades, § 3) for the lowest story, or rather for the brick platform on which it was raised. It may be noted that H. does not give the absurd height (606 feet) which Strabo (738) gives to the τάφος Βήλου. The ἱρόν, which is eight stades round (δύο σταδίων πάντῃ), is the sacred τέμενος in which the tower stood.

It will be noticed that H. says nothing (in this agreeing with E. I. H.) of the famous hanging gardens attributed to Nebuchadnezzar by Berosus (F. H. G. ii. 507); cf. 185. 1 n.

3 **πύργος.** For the eight stories cf. the Cyrus tomb at Murghab (125. 3 n.). H. is undoubtedly describing a tower with one story set upon another, each decreasing in size, and thus the ziggurat is usually restored (cf. Rawlinson, ii. 583–4, for picture). But Meyer, i. 380 n., says it was a rounded cone, with a sloping way winding about it to the top; he follows E. Herzfeld (Samarra, 1907), who gives a beautiful picture of the still-existing minaret of the Samarra mosque, which, he claims, embodies the idea of the old ziggurat. The form is certainly very primitive, and Herzfeld maintains that the sun-burned bricks were not strong enough for such a tower as H. describes. The Babylonians had, however, kiln-baked bricks as well, and there is no sufficient reason for describing H.'s view as mistaken.

5 For the table of Bel cf. the story of Bel and the Dragon in the Apocrypha; for the deity consuming his offerings cf. viii. 41. 2 n. and Tylor, P. C. ii. 380 seq., who quotes parallels among modern savages. For divine amours cf. Josephus, Antiq. xviii. 3. 4 (of Anubis at Rome); and Strabo 816 (at Thebes). The carvings at Luxor and Deir el Bahari support the story (cf. ii. 143. 4 n.). It is possible,

however, that H. may be misled by Egyptian titles; connected with the temple of Amon were his 'singing women', chief among whom was 'the wife of the god'. These are to be distinguished from the ἱερόδουλοι, and were often women of good position, e.g. Psammetichus I made his daughter 'wife of the god'; cf. Erman, Egypt, 295–6. If these are referred to, H. is wrong in saying (182. 2) they were unmarried. Frazer (Kingship, p. 170) considers H.'s evidence very important, as bearing on the supposed 'divine' origin of kings; he thinks the human bride was one of the 'brides of Marduk' referred to in the code of Hammurabi.

Χαλδαῖοι. The original home of this people was on the Persian Gulf (the 'Chaldeans' of Xen. Anab. v. 5. 17 are a different tribe near Armenia, though Rawlinson, *ad loc.*, thinks them the same); thence they pushed north, amalgamating with the earlier inhabitants. Their prince, Merodach Baladan II, ascended the throne of Babylon in 721 B.C.; the rivalry between his house and race and the priests of the older races was one of the great causes of the weakness of Babylonia (cf. 185. 1 and App. II, § 5). By a curious change of meaning, the Greeks later called the wise priestly class 'Chaldeans', and so a tribal name became a caste name (cf. 'Magi' 101 n.). For this use, which is not native, cf. Daniel (*pass.*), Strabo 739, &c., and for Roman times Mayor, ad Juv. x. 94.

182 2 Patara lay on the coast just east of Xanthus; Apollo was at home there for the six winter months, at Delos for the rest (cf. Hor. Odes iii. 4. 64 'Delius et Patareus Apollo'). So he was supposed to be away from Delphi for the three winter months. For the periodical migrations of the gods cf. Frazer, P. iii. 58. When the god was away, he naturally could not divine (cf. the irony of Elijah, 1 Kings xviii. 27).

183 1 **ἄγαλμα μέγα.** H. does not make it clear whether this statue is the same as the one destroyed (§ 2); probably it was not. Lehmann (B. W. für K. P. 1900, 964 n. 6) considers that H. is here borrowing from Hecataeus (cf. 178. 2 n.); he quotes *χρόνον ἐκεῖνον* (§ 2) in proof (but ***v. i.***). H. here records an important fact (as Lehmann points out), though he does not understand it. The god's statue was the symbol of the independent existence of Babylon, and the king at the beginning of the year (in the month Nisan) solemnly grasped the hand of Bel-Marduk, thus acknowledging his supremacy. A conqueror by doing this conciliated the prejudices of the Babylonians, owning himself a native king. So in our earliest important Cassite inscription (before 1000 B.C.) a Cassite king records that he brought the statue of Marduk back to Babylon, and becomes 'king of Babylon' (Winckler, Der Alte O. vi, 1904, pp. 23–4). So too Cyrus, in the Cyrus Cylinder (App. IV, § 1 and R. P.[2] v. 167), professes that he rules by the grace of Marduk. Xerxes, giving up this policy of conciliation, removed the statue, and so 'destroyed the personal union between Babylon and Persia'; Sennacherib had done the same, but his successors had restored the temple and statue of the god. It is to be noted that Xerxes' title changes at the same time; in 485 B.C. he is 'King of Babylon and the lands', afterwards he is 'King of Persia and Media' (Meyer, iii. 80). Apparently the change of policy was provoked by Babylonian rebellions which began at the end of the reign of Darius (so Darius is said 'to have intended' (ἐπιβουλεύσας) to take the statue; cf. Klio, vii. 447–8, for new inscriptions as to these rebellions).

2 **ἐκεῖνον**, 'at that time,' i.e. when Cyrus conquered Babylon.

184 1 H. undoubtedly confused the kings of Babylon and Assyria (cf. 178. 1 n.). For his Ἀσσύριοι λόγοι cf. App. II, § 6.

Σεμίραμις. For this queen cf. inscriptions of 'Kalach' (B. M. G. p. 31) now in B. M. She was a Babylonian princess, the wife of the Assyrian Rammânnirari III (812–783 B.C.), and seems to have introduced the worship of Nebo into Nineveh; hence H. no doubt heard of her name at the Nebo temple. Her real date almost corresponds to the 'five generations' of H., i.e. 167 years before Nebuchadnezzar's accession, 605 B.C. (*v.i.*) = 772. It is noticeable that H. gives none of the wild Greek fables as to the mythical Semiramis (cf. Diod. ii. 5 seq., following Ctesias), which make her a sort of Assyrian Catherine II, distinguished equally in war and for sensuality. No doubt in these stories is reflected the double character of the goddess Ishtar (cf. 105. 2 n.). Berosus censures the Greeks (F. H. G. ii. 507) for saying that she founded Nineveh. For Semiramis cf. Lehmann in Klio, i. 256 seq.

The **χώματα** and the accompanying canals were a well-known feature of Babylonia from the time of Hammurabi (cf. App. II, § 1) onwards; they were needed at once to control the floods of the river (Strabo, 740 seq., a very interesting passage), and for the irrigation which was essential to the life of the country; it was the filling up of these canals which has turned one of the most thickly populated regions of the Old World into the waste of to-day. Their defensive use (cf. 185. 1 n.) was only secondary. The remains of thirty or forty canals are still passed in a day's journey (Nikel, p. 9). For Alexander's care of the canals cf. Strabo, 740–1. For canals in Babylonia generally cf. Winckler, Hist. of Bab. (tr. by Craig, 1907), pp. 135–9.

No such queen as Nitocris is found either in the Babylonian inscriptions or in Berosus; H. perhaps misheard the name, and assimilated it, when he wrote, to the Egyptian name with which he was more familiar; Lehmann (*u. s.*) sees in it the consonants of the Persian form of Nebuchadnezzar, i.e. 'Nabukadracara', sounded 'tracara'. Others, however, think that it was not the ignorance of H., but his informants' prejudice (cf. 181. 5 n.) which is responsible for the suppression of all mention of this great king; they consider that in the priestly tradition the works of Nebuchadnezzar were attributed to his wife, who was a Median princess, Amuita, the daughter of

Astyages (Berosus, F. H. G. ii. 505); this marriage is probably referred to i. 74. 4 n. She is said to have suggested the famous 'hanging gardens', from a longing for her Median mountain home (cf. 181. 4 n.). H. confuses her with the mother of the last king, Nabonidus ('Labynetus,' 188. 1); this lady seems from the 'annalistic tablet' to have been an important person (R. P.[2] v. 160). Hence in H. the works of the great Chaldaean king are given to one composite queen.

προεφυλάξατο. This motive is probable in itself (but *v. i.*), and is confirmed by E. I. H. (vi. 39–56); Nebuchadnezzar knew the value of loyal alliances. He also made the great 'Median Wall', 100 feet high (Xen. Anab. i. 7. 15), from the Euphrates to the Tigris, at the point where the two rivers approached each other most nearly. H. does not mention this, probably because it did not quite reach the Euphrates (Grote, iv. 137 n.); his knowledge is mainly confined to Babylon and what he could see from the river.

2 **ἐς τὸν Εὐφρήτην**, the reading of all MSS., must mean that travellers from the north became involved in a labyrinth of canals at Ardericca, from which it took them three days to get clear into the Euphrates. It is usual, however, to omit ἐς, in which case H. means that a traveller on the Euphrates passed the same village three times in three days; in this land of marvels he accepted this statement from some waggish fellow-traveller, who hoaxed him. H. probably travelled straight by boat from Thapsacus to Babylon (cf. Grote, *u. s.*), and the villages he passed were no doubt as much alike as castles on the Rhine to-day. Matzat (p. 445), however, very ingeniously tries to prove that H.'s statement is possible. The river runs thus 1 + 2 3, each bend being fourteen to eighteen miles long (+ = site of Ardericca; 1, 2, 3 = the position of the boat on three following days). He finds a confirmation of these windings in 179. 4 (q. v.), the distance of Is from Babylon.

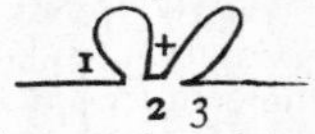

If Ardericca be a real place, it may be Idikara (cf. Ptol. v. 17. 19), about fifty miles above Sippara, where the course of the Euphrates was much diverted on account of rapids. The 'Ardericca' of vi. 119 (near Susa) is a different place.

4 **ἔλυτρον.** The 'reservoir' (cf. iv. 173. 1) at Sippara, also the work of Nebuchadnezzar, is meant; it lay 'along, a little distance from the river'. But really it was not 'far above' Babylon; H. is either making a mistake, or he is calculating by the time spent on his journey down stream; he writes as if his boat had made the circuit of the reservoir (*περίοδος*, § 6), which can hardly have been the fact. Abydenus (fr. 9, F. H. G. iv. 283) makes it 40 parasangs, i.e. 1,200 stades, in circumference and 20 fathoms deep. There is no trace of this reservoir now, but an inscription of Hammurabi says, 'I set a marsh around and dug a canal and made a protecting quay' (at

Sippara).' This work was renewed by the father of Nebuchadnezzar (V. Scheil, Sippara, 1902, pp. 23, 65). It was intended for irrigation (cf. the reservoir at Assuan), but no doubt could also be used to flood the country against an invader. This must be the meaning of *ὄρυγμα πᾶν ἕλος* (§ 6), but H. has quite failed to understand his informant, and so his own account is most obscure. He seems to confuse the canals, along which his boat may well have travelled, with the great 'basin' which he only saw, and the uses of which were described to him.

ἐς τὸ ὕδωρ, 'to the water level'; the phrase is Chaldaean (E. I. H. vii. 60).

5 **κρηπῖδα.** Abydenus (*u. s.*) speaks of 'great sluice-gates' (*ἐχετογνώμονες*).

H.'s account bears all the marks of an eyewitness; but possessed as he is by the Median terror, he pays no regard to the pacific use of the reservoir; hence he contradicts himself; he thinks of it as a marsh (*v. s.* and cf. 191. 3), but also as navigable.

7 **κατὰ τοῦτο.** Translate 'In this way she wrought (in that part of) her country where were the entrances, and the shortest way from Media'; cf. iv. 136. 2 for *τὰ σύντομα*. The territory of Assyria was now in the Median hands (cf. for its being called 'Media' Xen. Anab. ii. 4. 27), and so the natural line of attack (*ἐσβολαί*) would be down the right bank of the Tigris.

1 **ταῦτα μέν.** Translate 'These were the defences with which she surrounded (her city) by digging (*ἐκ βάθεος*), but she took advantage of them to add such a supplementary work (*παρενθήκην*) as' (the river wall and bridge).

2 Sayce (*ad loc.* and p. xxix) is very angry with H. for his mistake in speaking of 'huge stones' in Babylonia; but Nebuchadnezzar makes the same mistake (!) (E. I. H. ix. 24). Of course the stones were brought down the Euphrates from the north. Xenophon (Anab. i. 5. 5) speaks of a village on the Euphrates, where millstones were made for sale. Diodorus (ii. 8), who gives the bridge to Semiramis, makes it 5 stades long and 30 feet wide.

3 These *ξύλα* were no doubt a sort of drawbridge in the middle, pulled up on both sides; this feud (*κλέπτοιεν*) between the two river banks may be an unconscious echo of the rivalry between Babylon and her suburb, Borsippa.

2 Lehmann (Klio, i. 259) says the inscription uses the phraseology of the royal monuments; the *οὐ γὰρ ἄμεινον*, however, is quite Greek.

3 The presence of a dead body made the gate impassable for a Persian. Some see in the mention of 'gates' a contradiction to iii. 159. 1, but it is purely verbal (cf. 178. 2 n.). The story is a curious one; for treasures buried with the dead cf. Josephus, Ant. Jud. vii. 15. 3, pp. 392–4, who says that Solomon buried David with great treasures, and that when the tomb was robbed by Hyrcanus and by

Herod, they took away great wealth, but failed to find the real royal treasure. Lehmann (W. für K. P. 1900, p. 962) sees in H.'s story a confusion of Darius and Xerxes (cf. iii. 150 n.); he follows Aelian (V. H. xiii. 3), who tells a similar story, with additional marvels, of Xerxes violating the tomb of Belus. But A.'s version has every mark of being an explanation of οὐ γὰρ ἄμεινον, and Lehmann's theory is at best only possible. Stein thinks the tale may have arisen from a misunderstood inscription. All we can say for certain is that we see in it the Babylonian hatred of their conquerors.

188 1 The last king of Babylon was called Nabonidus (556 B.C.); he was no relation of Nebuchadnezzar (d. 562); between them were three kings, of whom H. knows nothing.

The Choaspes is the 'river Ulai' of Daniel viii. 2. H. here gives an interesting point; the water of other lands was impure for the worshipper of Ormazd; hence the Choaspes water was taken both for drinking ('boiled') and for preparing the Haoma (cf. Indian Soma) libation (cf. vii. 54. 2 n.); for the earthly plant used for this, which corresponded to the white immortality-giving Haoma, cf. S. B. E. iv. 69.

189 1 The Gyndes is the Diyâla, which runs into the Tigris from the north-east about fifty miles from Babylon; this identification is clear from v. 52. 5, where it is the next river to South.

For the Matieni cf. i. 72. 2 n. and iii. 94. 1. The Dardanians are otherwise unknown.

Ὦπιν. H. mentions Opis because it is the highest point of navigation from the sea up the Tigris (Strabo, 739). Opis, which lay nearly fifty miles north of the Diyâla, at the junction of the Physcus and the Tigris (Xen. Anab. ii. 4. 25), was the scene of the Macedonian mutiny in 324 B.C.

συμψήσας: literally 'rub together', and so 'obliterate'. Here = 'sucking down'.

3 **κατέτεινε**: i. e. his army. 'He extended it.' Maspero (iii. 635) accepts the story as partly true; Cyrus, he thinks, with the main army turned the defensive works on the north of Babylon, by lowering the water in the Tigris and the Gyndes. (Cf. Caes. B.C. i. 61 for a similar operation on the Sicoris in 49 B.C.) There was one battle (R. P. v². 162) near Opis, as H. says (190. 1), and it was immediately followed by a revolt in Akkad (i. e. N. Babylonia). Meantime Gobryas, marching down the left bank of the Gyndes with a portion of the army, took Babylon by treachery, while the main defensive force was resisting Cyrus. In the same way Prášek (i. 229) accepts the story of c. 191 as describing the preparations to intimidate the capital, and force a capitulation.

Even if these views be correct, the story told to H. was completely misleading; the city was taken by treachery (App. IV, § 6). But it is more likely that H. is partly right (as thus suggested) than that the whole narrative is an invention borrowed from the irrigation works on the Gyndes (as Sir H. Rawlinson, *ad loc.*). The form it takes is religious in colouring; 'white horses' were sacred to the sun (iii. 90. 3 n.; cf. vii. 40. 4); hence the offending river is divided into as many channels (360) as there are days in the year.

0 1 The war lasted longer than H. thinks; it perhaps began in 546 B.C., as the annals of Nabonidus seem to speak of an attack on Akkad (i.e. N. Babylonia) from Elam in that year (R. P. v^2. 161); but the record is much mutilated.

2 **προεσάξαντο.** The use of this word in viii. 20. 1 seems to show that it is from *προσάττω*, 'they packed up beforehand,' not from *προεσάγω* (as Schweighäuser); cf. v. 34. 1 n.

1 2 **ἅπασαν.** Used loosely for 'the main army', as two other contingents are at once mentioned.

3 **ἕλος.** Cf. 185. 4, 5 nn.

ὑπονοστήσαντος, 'when the river had sunk' (cf. iv. 62. 2).

6 For Aristotle's account of the capture of Babylon, which even exaggerates the one here, cf. 178. 2 n.

ὁρτήν. The 'feast' agrees with the well-known story in Dan. v.

πρῶτον. H. calls it 'the first' capture, in contrast to that by Darius (iii. 158). No doubt, however, he heard in Babylon nothing of Assyrian captures, e.g. by Assurbanipal in 648 B.C.

-200 *The account of the Babylonian land and people.*

2 1 **τροφήν.** This general payment in kind is not mentioned in iii. 90–5; the only corn contribution there (91. 3) is that of Egypt. The omission of the corn-tax in Bk. III goes to show (what is antecedently probable) that H. is there quoting an official document, drawn up for one special purpose, not giving an account of the whole revenue system. The corn contribution here mentioned corresponds to the Roman (1) *frumentum in cellam* (for the governor and his suite); but this was paid for; (2) *annona militaris* (for the soldiers in the province); (3) *annona civica*, i.e. for Rome, from Egypt and Africa (Marquardt, Staats-V. ii. 189, 232–3). For contributions in kind in Persia cf. Theop. frs. 124–5 (F. H. G. i. 298) and Meyer, iii. 51.

2 For the use of **Ἀσσυρίη** cf. 178. 1 n. For **σατραπηίην** cf. iii. 89. 1 n.

This Tritantaechmes, who was clearly satrap of Babylon when H. was there, is to be distinguished from the nephew of Darius (vii. 82); for his father Artabazus cf. viii. 126 and ix. *pass.*

3 As the *μέδιμνος* held 48 *χοίνικες*, the 'artaba' held 51, i.e. about 13 gallons. A *χοῖνιξ* of wheat was a man's daily allowance, vii. 187. 2. For its size cf. vi. 57 n.

4 For the hunting dogs see Rawlinson, *ad loc.* (with illustration).

Ctesias (Ind. 5, p. 248) says they were able to cope with a lion, a characteristic exaggeration. M. Polo (ii. 19; i. 400) says the Great Khan had about 10,000 hunting dogs.

3 1 H. is describing the Babylonian plain proper, i.e. the southern

part of Mesopotamia; at the present time the Euphrates and the Tigris unite in the Shat-El-Arab, but originally they reached the sea separately.

ὕεται. Rain, which is abundant in Assyria proper, falls in Babylonia chiefly in the winter and spring, and then as a rule not in large quantities. Willcocks' table (Irrigation of Mesopotamia, 1910, p. 68) shows that from May to October the land is practically rainless, in the other six months the rainfall is about eight inches, fairly evenly distributed. So far as rain is concerned the country is not a desert like Egypt, but rather a 'steppe region capable of sustaining millions of sheep' (p. 10). Grote (iii. 295) lays stress on the accuracy of H. in contrasting the light rains here with practically rainless Upper Egypt (iii. 10 n.). H. is quite right in saying that while the scanty spring rain (τοῦτο) 'causes the corn to sprout, the crop ripens from irrigation'. His description of this is accurate, if we remember that he is contrasting the natural (αὐτοῦ τοῦ ποταμοῦ) Nile flood with the artificial Babylonian system. The present Euphrates, however, now that the canals are gone, floods its banks from March to July, when the Armenian snows melt.

κηλωνηίοισι, 'by swipes worked by hand' (cf. vi. 119. 3), i.e. the shadoufs which are still used in Mesopotamia and Egypt (cf. Maspero, i. 764, and 340 for illustrations). Colonel Chesney (Survey of Tig. and Euph. 1850, ii. 653) describes it as a wooden lever, 13–15 feet long, revolving on a post 3–4 feet high with a bucket at the end, balanced when full by a weight at the other end. From the top of the bank the water was distributed over the fields in artificial channels.

2 For the canals cf. c. 184 n. The canal here is the 'royal canal' restored by Nebuchadnezzar, which ran south-east from above Babylon to the Tigris, near the later Seleucia.

πρὸς ἥλιον τὸν χειμερινόν. The ancients divided the sky into

ἀνατολή and δυσμὴ ἰσημερινή = E. and W.
ἀνατολή and δυσμὴ θερινή = NE. and NW.
ἀνατολή and δυσμὴ χειμερινή = SE. and SW.

(cf. Arist. Meteor. ii. 6 *ad init.*, where a diagram is given). Here ἥλιος = ἀνατολή (cf. vii. 70. 1 οἱ ἀπὸ ἡλίου Αἰθίοπες).

3 H. is contrasting broadly and rightly the treeless cornland of Babylonia with Greece.

Strabo (742 *ad fin.*) says 'three hundredfold', without H.'s careful limitation. Lehmann (Fest. für Kiepert, 1898, pp. 305 seq.) argues that the accounts of H. and of Strabo are borrowed independently from Hecataeus (cf. c. 199 n.). His arrangement of the two accounts in parallel columns is useful, though his argument quite breaks down.

φύλλα, 'blades.' Ancient (e.g. Theophrastus, viii. 7. 4) and modern writers confirm H. as to the fertility of Babylonia; so Chesney (ii. 602) says 'those portions which are still cultivated, as round Hillah, show that the region has all the fertility ascribed to it by H.' An inscription of Assurbanipal claims, with perhaps pardonable exaggeration, that grain grew five cubits high, and that the heads were five-sixths of a cubit (Winckler, Hist. of Babylonia (E. T.), p. 138).

4 **τὰ . . . ἐχόμενα,** 'the various kinds of corn already mentioned'; the perfect *ἀπῖκται* has been thought to refer to a previous description by Hecataeus (*v. s.*). It is, however, only a picturesque anticipation of criticism; cf. Matzat, pp. 438–9.

σησάμων. Layard (Nineveh, ii. 423) confirms this; cf. Xen. Anab. iv. 4. 13 for this and other substitutes for olive oil (in Armenia). It was made from the 'sesame' seed.

φοίνικες. H. is quite right as to their abundance.

καρποφόροι marks the contrast to those in the Aegean regions, which do not ripen their fruits. Cf. Theop. Hist. Plant. iii. 3. 5.

Dates were a main article of food in Babylonia; for the manifold uses of the palm-tree cf. Strabo 742, who says they were 360 in number, and E. B.[11] xx. 642 s. v.

5 H. here rightly describes the process of fertilization of figs, *ἐρινασμός* (Theop. H. P. ii. 8. 1; cf. also Arist. H. A. v. 32). The *caprificus* or wild fig produces inedible figs which are inhabited by the fig-wasp; the female wasps, hatched in these figs, make their way from them, laden with pollen, to the young figs of the *ficus* or fig proper, in order to lay their eggs in them; they pollinate their flowers, and thus fertilization is effected. H. wrongly thinks the purpose of the process was to prevent the fig falling off. He is wrong, too, in transferring the process to palm-trees; fertilization in these is rightly described by Theop. (*u. s.* ii. 8. 4) *ὅταν ἀνθῇ τὸ ἄρρεν ἀποτέμνουσι τὴν σπάθην ἐφ' ἧς τὸ ἄνθος εὐθὺς ὥσπερ ἔχει, τόν τε νοῦν καὶ τὸ ἄνθος καὶ τὸν κονιορτὸν κατασείουσι κατὰ τοῦ καρποῦ τῆς θηλείας.* He too, however, gives the object wrongly, i. e. to prevent the falling off of the fruit.

The process is represented on the monuments (cf. B. M. G. 36, and Maspero, i. 555, for picture).

H. obscures his meaning by using different words *βάλανος* and *καρπός* for the same thing, and wrongly substituting *ὄλυνθοι*, 'the untimely figs,' for *ἐρινεοί*, i. e. *fici caprifici*.

194 1 H. is always interested in means of navigation (cf. ii. 96).

These round skin-covered boats (kúfah) are still used on the Lower Euphrates, but not of the size described here; the largest, however, can still carry a camel (cf. for their construction the British coracles, for a full description, Chesney, ii. 639 seq., and for a picture, Maspero, i. 542). H. does not mention the rafts on skin-bladders, which are now more used on the Upper Euphrates. Both kinds are alike in sailing down stream only, and in being broken up and sold (all but the skins, *v. i.*) when the voyage is over. The rafts are always, the kúfahs only usually, broken up.

2 H. omits to mention that the boats are usually smeared with bitumen.

οὔτε πρύμνην: the usual processes in shipbuilding, 'distinguishing (ἀποκρίνοντες) the stern and narrowing the prow,' are not used.

καλάμης, 'straw,' not for packing, but for stuffing in the interstices of the ribs (νομέας).

φοινικηίους. It is the casks that are of palm-wood; grape wine was imported (cf. 193. 3), but Babylonia had plenty of palm-wine (193. 4).

3 The two men stood facing each other; but in the picture (*u. s.*) there are four men, sitting in pairs opposite each other. We may cf. with H.'s account, the lightermen on the Thames, one of whom pulls (ἔσω) while the other backs (ἔξω); the object was to guide the boat, which was carried by the current. For other explanations cf. Macaulay, *ad loc.*

καί, 'quite five thousand.' This would give a burden (γόμος) of about 125 or 175 tons, according as the Attic or Aeginetan talent is taken.

4 **ἀπ' ὧν ἐκήρυξαν.** This form of tmesis is common in H. (but always with aorist) in describing customs, &c. Cf. ii. 39. 2 *et pass.*

195 H. gives five pieces of Babylonian dress: (1) The tunic reaching to the feet; this was frequently flounced and fringed (cf. picture in Maspero, iii. 546). The warlike Assyrians wore it shorter. (2) The upper woollen tunic; this is often concealed by (3). (3) The white cloak thrown round the shoulders. (4) The open shoes. For the 'Boeotian shoes' cf. Dicaearchus, Perieg. 19 (G. G. M. i. 103), who says they were ὑσκλωτός ('with an edge laced over the foot', L. & S.), 'so as to leave the feet almost bare.' The Babylonians, however, generally went barefoot. (5) The high cap; *v. s.* or Rawlinson, *ad loc.*, for pictures.

H. is right as to their long hair and their fondness for cosmetics.

2 **σφρηγῖδα.** The 'seals' are the well-known Babylonian cylinders which were so used (cf. B. M. G. 156 seq. with pictures). The Babylonians frequently (but not always) are shown carrying staves; the heads of these are often elaborately wrought.

196 1 Information as to the Veneti (distinguished as οἱ ἐν τῷ Ἀδρίῃ, v. 9. 2) must have reached H. in Italy.

ἐποιέετο. H. uses the past tense, as the custom was discontinued (*v. i.*). Strabo (745), however [so too Nic. Dam. fr. 131, F. H. G. iii. 462; and Ael. V. H. iv. 1], uses the present, copying H. loosely. The Babylonian contracts speak of the sale of brides, but no trace is found of this fixed custom. For marriage by purchase cf. Westermarck, pp. 391–5.

2 **συνοικήσει.** They were sold 'for marriage', not for slavery.

4 **ἀποφέρειν**: i. e. the poorer classes of buyers might 'return' bride and dowry together.

5 The decay of prosperity in Babylon may well be partially the cause of the fact that the collection of 2,500 private contracts in the B. M. does not extend beyond the reign of Darius I (Meyer, iii. 81). For its supposed result here cf. the Lydian custom, 94. 1.

198 The connexion of ideas in H.'s mind seems to be that sickness suggests death, and death suggests the beginnings of life. Lehmann, however (cf. 193. 3 n.), says Strabo preserves the order of the original ('Hecataeus'), putting together the various kinds of impurity (from the dead and from sexual intercourse, 745). But S. is even more confused than H., for he interpolates (746) his account of 'dress' between his accounts of sickness and of death.

For the ideas of the Babylonians as to death and for their burial rites cf. Maspero, i. 683 seq. For the use of honey as a preservative against corruption cf. 140. 2 (the use of wax in Persia); Lehmann says (*u. s.*, p. 314) that in the same way the bodies of dead Shiite Mahometans are sent to Kerbela, covered with saffron. For a similar use of honey in prehistoric Greece cf. Busolt, i. 66 seq.; cf. also vi. 58. 3 n. For the Egyptian *θρῆνοι* cf. ii. 79 n.

199 1 H. is obviously writing as an eyewitness, and his account is of great value anthropologically; but he is mistaken in making universal one single set of rites, those of the goddess Nana at Erech. He may also be confusing the *ἱερόδουλοι* attached to the temple (*v. i.* *ἱρὸν τὸ ἀργύριον*) with the ordinary worshippers. For the custom cf. Strabo (745), who inaccurately condenses H. and adds *κατά τι λόγιον*, and Baruch vi. 43. Lucian describes the same custom from personal inquiry, but as an exception, in speaking of the Adonis worship (De Dea Syria, p. 454, c. 6); women there could escape the rite by cutting off their hair. For other instances cf. 94 n.; W. Robertson Smith, Kinship [2] &c. p. 297; Westermarck, p. 72 (who thinks the custom *not* a survival of communal marriage but connected with phallic worship as a late development); and especially E. S. Hartland (Essays presented to E. B. Tylor, 1907, pp. 187–202), who considers the custom a 'puberty rite', belonging to a primitive stage of ideas, and only connected later with the worship of Mylitta; he quotes many parallels among modern savages.

Women as a rule in Babylon had a position which, for a Semitic people, was high; the system of dowry, paid to the parents and secured to the wife (cf. 196. 4), gradually emancipated her; she could hold property and make contracts.

2 **θώμιγγος.** The 'cord' is a symbol of their service due to the goddess.

3 For Mylitta cf. 131. 3 n.

4 **ἀποσιωσαμένη,** 'having discharged her sacred duty to the goddess' (cf. iv. 154. 4).

5 For Aphrodite in Cyprus cf. 105. 2 and Hor. Odes i. 3. 1. Justin (xviii. 5) speaks of this custom there, when telling the story of Dido.

200 1 **πατριαί**, 'clans.' H. refers to the dwellers in the marshy regions along the lower course of the rivers and on the Persian Gulf. Diodorus (iii. 22) gives an interesting account of the methods of fish-catching there. H. exaggerates their fish diet.

For the pounding of dried fish 'with pestles' (ὑπέροισι) in a mortar (ὅλμον) cf. iv. 172. 1. The μᾶζα is a soft cake, softened with water, the ἄρτος (a superior form) was baked.

201 For the Araxes, i.e. the Jaxartes or Syr-Daria, *v. i.*

ἀντίον: a primitive attempt to express longitude; the expression Ἰσσηδόνες ἄνδρες is poetic; H. is perhaps borrowing from the Ἀριμάσπεα of Aristeas (iv. 13 n.). For Σκυθικόν cf. App. XI; for the Issedones, iv. 26.

202 H.'s account of the Araxes is a characteristic specimen of his geographical knowledge (and ignorance). He mentions it (1) here, where it rises among the Matieni (cf. 72. 2 n.) and (*a*) falls with one mouth into the Caspian, (β) loses thirty-nine others in marshes; (2) in iv. 40. 1, flowing east, it forms with the Caspian the north boundary of his Asia; (3) iv. 11. 1 the Scythians are driven across it by the Massagetae into Cimmeria.

He is combining four rivers: No. 1 (*a*) is the Aras, which unites with the Kur and flows into the S.W. Caspian; in H.'s day the Aras flowed into the Caspian direct (Hermes, 1884, p. 169); No. 2, and perhaps No. 1 (β), are a confused account of the two great rivers of Central Asia, the Oxus and the Jaxartes, which flow north-west into the Aral Sea; probably at this period the Oxus also flowed into the Caspian. H. has inverted their direction and combined them, misled by his information (right in itself) that some of the rivers of Central Asia lose themselves in swamps (cf. E. B.[11] ii. 735). The East of the world was to H. unknown sandy desert (iii. 98. 2). No. 3 is the Volga. It is quite possible that the 'marshes and shoals' may be a confused account of the great Volga delta, and not of the Central Asian rivers, as suggested above.

The name Araxes probably survives in 'Aroxolani' (Jornandes, c. 74), i.e. 'the Alani of the Araxes'. 'Rha,' Ptolemy's name for the Volga (v. 9), is probably a different word. H.'s confusion may be pardoned when we find Aristotle (350 A, Meteor. i. 13. 15) making the Tanais a branch of the Araxes (which he rightly makes to rise in Mount Paropamisus). So Alexander and his army thought the Jaxartes to be the Tanais (Plin. N. H. vi. 16. 49); Arrian (iii. 30. 7, 8) corrects this mistake, but makes the Jaxartes rise in the Caucasus. Even in our own day the head-waters of the Congo were thought by Livingstone to be the source of the Nile (cf. ii. 33. 1. n.).

2 **τῇ ὀδμῇ**. For this primitive form of smoking cf. iv. 75, the vapour baths of the Scythians. Probably some kind of hemp is meant; the *Cannabis sativa* is indigenous in Central Asia; hashish is still prepared from *Cannabis indica*.

3 H., in making the Araxes rise in the same region as the Gyndes,

is (quite needlessly) supposed to be misled by a forced analogy between the many mouths of the Araxes and the canalization of the Gyndes; these rivers, though at their nearest point 250 miles apart, and at their sources much more, both do rise in the watershed between Mesopotamia and the Caspian basin.

The number 'forty' probably is a round number meaning 'very many'; so 'Kyrk' (= forty) is used in Turkish. We may compare without irreverence the 'forty' of the O. T. (Gen. viii. 6 *et pass.*).

4 H.'s knowledge of the Caspian is one of his geographical triumphs; subsequent writers, except Aristotle, to the time of Ptolemy (second century A.D.) thought that it was a gulf of the Northern Sea, as the Persian Gulf is of the Southern; Alexander (Arr. Anab. vii. 16. 2) was preparing to test this theory when he died. Even after Ptolemy mediaeval cartographers returned to the old blunder (Tozer, A. G. p. 367).

μία ἐοῦσα. This was known since Necho's circumnavigation of Africa (iv. 42). The name 'Atlantic' occurs first here, but was obviously already familiar. For the 'pillars of Hercules' cf. ii. 33. 3 n.

1 In ii. 11. 2 the Red Sea is forty days by 'rowing'; if we assume that H. knew the real length of that sea, i.e. 1,200 miles, we have an average of thirty miles a day. Hence his figures here are too small, at any rate for length; for the Caspian is about 750 miles long and 280 wide.

ὑψηλότατον. Aristotle (350 A, Meteor. i. 13. 15) limits this by saying the Caucasus is the highest of the mountains of the East; both he and H. were ignorant of Mount Demavend, which rises to the south of the Caspian, 3,000 feet higher than the Caucasus (to over 20,000 feet).

2 **ἐμφανέα.** Cf. Xenophon (Anab. v. 4. 33, an eyewitness), who records this lowest stage of degradation among the Mossynoeci (cf. iii. 94. 2), at the south-east corner of the Caspian (cf. Apoll. Rhod. ii. 1025); Theopompus (fr. 222; F. H. G. i. 315) relates it also of the Etruscans. But among modern savages it is, to say the least, very rare (Crawley, Mystic Rose, p. 180).

1 **ἄπειρον.** H. well describes the great plains of N.W. Asia.

2 For towers at a bridge-head as a protection cf. Caes. B. G. vi. 29.

1 **παθήματα.** For the antithesis cf. Aesch. Agam. 177. Croesus, by a dramatic irony, gives fatal advice to his patron, just as Adrastus (c. 35 seq.) unwillingly had returned evil for good to himself.

2 The possibility of disaster is euphemistically expressed, to avoid words of evil omen.

4 **ἐκείνῳ**, 'the course above,' i.e. the advance of the Massagetae, if victorious. *τὠυτό* is explained by *ὅτι νικήσας . . . Τομύριος*, i.e. both Cyrus and his enemies would use their victory to the full.

6 The stratagem is related by Polyaenus (Strat. viii. 28) of Tomyris,

queen of 'the Amazons,' against Cyrus; this version is equally appropriate and equally unhistorical with that of H.

208 **ἐδίδου**, imperfect, 'he proposed to give.' Cf. for the Persian custom vii. 2. 1, the appointment of Xerxes as successor.

209 1 For the genealogy of Darius cf. App. IV. 3.

For the wings cf. the figure on the tomb at Murghab (125. 3 n.).

3 For the primitive belief that a man was responsible for acts done in dreamland cf. Tylor, P. C. i. 438 seq.; the soul was supposed to go abroad in sleep or trance; cf. the old belief that it was unlucky to turn a sleeper over for fear the soul should not find its way back. Here it is combined with the later and more general belief that dreams foretell the future. For a somewhat similar combination cf. 'the dreams' of Joseph (Gen. xxxvii. 5 seq.).

211 3 **Spargapises** recurs (iv. 76. 6) as Spargapithes, the name of a Scythian king; it is perhaps of Aryan derivation.

214 3 Other authorities give Cyrus thirty years, e.g. Ctesias (8, p. 66), Justin (i. 8), Dinon (fr. 10, F. H. G. ii. 91). H.'s exact figure is more probable; Cyrus therefore began to reign in 558 B.C.

4 For a similar outrage on the dead cf. the treatment of Crassus' head after Carrhae (Dio Cass. xl. 27 the pouring in of molten gold).

215 Sir H. Rawlinson thinks the *σάγαρις* = the khanjar of modern Persia, a short curved double-edged dagger; but in vii. 64. 2 it is explained by *ἀξίνη*; it must therefore be a weapon for hacking, not thrusting, probably like the Gurkha 'kukri'. Gold is abundant both in the Ural and the Altai Mountains (cf. iv. 27 n.). The Massagetae were still in the Bronze Age.

216 1 **γυναῖκα.** Strabo (513) simply repeats H.; for a similar custom among the Agathyrsi cf. iv. 104; among the Nasamones, iv. 172. 2 n.; M. Polo (ii. 47; ii. 54, 56) found it in Caindu (i.e. Yunnan), where 'a hat' was hung up as a sign that a stranger was in possession. For its bearing on the theory of communal marriage cf. Westermarck, p. 72 seq. There is clear evidence for a system of marriage among the Massagetae, but they were polyandrous, ib. 454 seq. Myres (A. and C. p. 155) says: 'It can hardly be accident that every one of the strange marriage customs which H. mentions happens to be typical of a widespread type.'

2 **τῆς γὰρ ἐπιθυμήσῃ.** For the omission of *ἄν* cf. iv. 46, and Goodwin, p. 208 (§ 540).

οὖρος ἄλλος is explained by the following; for the same custom among the Indians cf. iii. 99. 1; among the Issedones, iv. 26. 1 (where see n.).

BOOK II

The following have been used especially for the notes on this book and on iii. 1. 38; references are made by the titles in brackets.

Baedeker. Guide-book to Egypt. (Baedeker.)
Breasted, J. H. History of Egypt. 1906. (Breasted, E.)
— Ancient Records of Egypt. 5 vols. 1906–7. (Breasted, R.)
British Museum Guide. 1909. (B. M. G.)
Brugsch. History of Egypt under the Pharaohs. 2 vols. (English translation). 1881. (Brugsch.)
Budge. The Egyptian Sûdân. 1907. (Budge, S.)
— The Mummy. (Budge, M.)
Egypt Exploration Fund Reports. (E. E. F.)
Erman, A. Life in Ancient Egypt (English translation). 1894. (Erman, E.)
— Handbook of Egyptian Religion (English translation). 1907. (Erman, R.)
Lepsius. Denkmäler aus Ägypten. 12 vols. 1848–50. (L. D.)
Maspero. Contes Populaires. (Maspero, C. P.)
— Études de Mythologie Égyptienne. 2 vols. 1893. (Maspero, E. M.)
Murray. Handbook for Egypt and the Sûdân. (11th edit. by H. R. Hall.) 1907.
Petrie, Flinders. History of Egypt. Vols. I–III. (Petrie.)
Sourdille, C. Hérodote et la Religion d'Égypte. 1910. (Sourdille, R.)
— La Duration et l'Étendue du Voyage d'Hérodote en Égypte. 1910. (Sourdille, H. E.)
Wiedemann, A. Herodots Zweites Buch. 1890. (Wiedemann.)
Wilkinson, Sir J. G. Manners of the Ancient Egyptians. New ed. 1878. (Wilkinson.)
Zeitschrift für Ägyptische Sprache. (Z. A. S.)

1 1 **Pharnaspes** was an Achaemenid, though not of the direct royal line; it was usual for Persian kings to marry members of their own family (e. g. Darius and Atossa, daughter of Cyrus). H. lays stress on the name and lineage of the mother of Cambyses, because the Egyptians made him the son of an Egyptian princess (iii. 1 n.).

2 The mention of **Ionians** connects this book with i. 141–76; cf. the mention of Amasis (iii. 1), which links together Bks. II and III.

H.'s custom is to give some account of the manners and the past history of each new people, as he brings it on the stage of his history; but this account of Egypt, even more than that of Scythia in Bk. IV, is out of all proportion to the rest of his history. Hence the idea that it was composed separately, probably after the rest, and only later incorporated in his general scheme (cf. Introd. § 11).

2 1 That the Egyptians were the oldest race in the world was a general

belief; cf. Arist. Pol. vii. 10. 8, 1329 b, and Diod. i. 101, who says the Nile, πολύγονος ὤν, was a special cause of the priority of the Egyptians. Antiquity and nobility of race were supposed to go together.

2 **ἐπιτεχνᾶται.** Frederick II of Germany and James IV of Scotland are said to have repeated the experiment of Psammetichus, and to have proved by it that Hebrew was the speech of Paradise.

ἐς τὰ ποίμνια: a *constructio praegnans*, 'to take to the flocks and rear.' τροφὴν τοιήνδε (cogn. acc.) is explained by the following participle, ἐντειλάμενος.

τὴν ὥρην, 'at the proper time.' The dative with ἐν would be more usual; but cf. ἀκμήν, καιρόν.

3 **βεκός**: in the Ionian dialect = 'bread'; cf. Hipponax, fr. 82 **Κυπρίων** βεκὸς φαγοῦσι κἀμαθουσίων πυρόν. This story is frequently referred to, e. g. in Aristoph. Nub. 398 βεκκεσέληνε (cf. i. 4. 2 n.). Even in ancient times the word βεκός was explained as onomatopoetic, from the cries of the goats. Ramsay has recently found it on a Phrygian inscription (Jahreshefte des Öst. Arch. Inst. in Wien, 1905, Beibl. p. 95 seq.).

4 The Phrygians were generally considered a recent people; cf. vii. 73 for their immigration from Europe.

5 The Egyptians certainly attached great importance to the cries of children; but H.'s story sounds like a Greek invention, a protest against the Egyptian claim to priority, which he elsewhere accepts. The Egyptians could have claimed βεκός as evidence for their own antiquity, for it resembles one of their words for 'oil'.

Ἡφαίστου: i. e. Ptah; cf. iii. 37. 2 n. One of the sacred names for Memphis was *Het-Ka-Ptah*, i. e. 'temple of the Ka (i. e. the "double") of Ptah', from which name some have derived Αἴγυπτος. 'Memphis' (= *Mennefert*, the good place) was only the profane name of the city.

For the temple's importance as a source of H.'s information cf. App. X, § 10, and Introd. § 24.

μάταια: this is perhaps a hit at Hecataeus; for H.'s critical attitude to his countrymen cf. c. 45 nn. Bury (A. G. H. p. 51) thinks H. would have written Ἴωνες, had he meant to criticize Hecataeus, and that he really is here borrowing a point from that writer. But there is no evidence for the borrowing, and it is not likely in itself. It has been argued that this second version is the original form of the story, which H., as a philo-Egyptian, has softened down; on the other hand, the more brutal story may well be only an attempt to rationalize the older legend.

3 1 Memphis, Heliopolis, and Thebes represent the three chief forms of the older Egyptian worship, i. e. of *Ptah* at Memphis, of *Atum* or *Tumu* (the Sun) at Heliopolis, and *Amen-Ra* at Thebes.

Memphis perhaps was founded by Merpeba, the sixth king of the First Dynasty, who was combined with Mena the first king (King and Hall, pp. 91–3). Its age was proverbial in Egypt. Even when, under the 'new Kingdom', Thebes became the capital, M. was a second capital. Its ruins were largely used for building Cairo, about fourteen miles to the south of which town it lies, on the left bank of the Nile, under the rubbish heaps of Bedrashēn.

Thebes. The usual Egyptian name of the town was *Nu*, 'the town' i.e. of Amen-Ra (cf. Hebrew *No*, Jer. xlvi. 25, and *No-Amon*, Nahum iii. 8); the Greek name is from the less common Apet. Thebes first became a royal residence under the eleventh Dynasty. It remained important till the seventh century B.C., when it was sacked by the Assyrians; from this it never recovered. Its most important temple was that of Amen-Ra at Karnak; H. (c. 143 nn.) calls it a temple of Zeus.

Heliopolis. Its sacred name was House of Ra, i.e. the Sun-God; it is the Hebrew *On*. Its ruins are near Matarieh, which is six miles NNE. of Cairo, and about four miles E. of the Nile; when H. speaks (9. 1) of the ἀνάπλοος from Heliopolis to Thebes, he is writing loosely. Heliopolis was important as a religious, and not as a political, centre. H. rightly speaks of its inhabitants as 'most skilled in tradition' (λογιώτατοι); from it were said to have come the teachers of Pythagoras, Solon, and Plato. Strabo (806) describes it as a seat of learning, though in his day it was only a show-place.

2 **θεῖα** are contrasted with ἀνθρωπήια (4. 1); for similar scruples cf. c. 86—the account of the embalming—and *pass.*

ἶσον . . . ἐπίστασθαι. The meaning of these words has been much disputed.

(1) It is clear that αὐτῶν refers to divine *things*, not merely to the divine *names* (as Bähr); H. did not think all men knew equally the names of the gods.

(2) Wiedemann's explanation, too, must be rejected. He argues that H. means that, since all men agree as to the gods, it is only necessary to mention their names (which differ in different races), and then men will understand each other. But this statement again is not true; H. does not think all men's knowledge of divine things is equal; on the contrary, he thinks Greek knowledge much inferior to that in Egypt (cf. e. g. 43. 2 as to Heracles). (3) The usual explanation (e. g. Stein's) is that ἶσον = just as much, i. e. 'just as little'; since men really know nothing of divine things (cf. ix. 65) they should not laugh at each other's beliefs. This pessimistic view would be quite in accordance with H.'s general attitude (cf. Introd. § 36), and may be compared to Xenophanes' sentiment (fr. 14, R. and P. p. 80) οὐδέ τις ἔσται εἰδὼς ἀμφὶ θεῶν. (4) But this explanation does not take account of the character of the passages where H. lays stress on his silence (*v. i.*); in view of these Sourdille (R. pp. 2–26), who discusses the whole subject at length, maintains that the reference is to the 'mysteries'. Since these, H. thinks, are virtually the same in all countries (cf. 81. 2, 123. 2, 3), to describe the Egyptian mysteries would be to reveal the secrets of the Greek ones. Hence H. is careful only to

touch on them (cf. 65. 2 αὐτῶν ἐπιψαύσας, ἀναγκαίῃ καταλαμβανόμενος); he will describe details, but not relate the ἱρὸς λόγος which explained them. The following are the passages in Bk. II where H. is religiously silent: 46. 2 (the goat-footed Pan), 47. 2 (the sacrifice of swine), 61. 1, 132. 2 (the sacred mourning at Busiris), 65. 2 (animal worship, the most important passage), 86. 2 (embalming), 170. 1 (the tomb of Osiris at Sais), 171. 1 τὰ δείκηλα τῶν παθέων (of Osiris) τὰ καλέουσι μυστήρια Αἰγύπτιοι. In 48. 3 (the phallic ceremonies for Dionysus), 51. 4 (the Samothracian Hermes), 62. 2 (the feasts of lights at Sais), 81. 2 (wearing wool), though he refuses to tell a ἱρὸς λόγος, he does not especially refer to his silence. It will be noticed (*vid.* nn.) that most of these passages refer to Osiris.

4 1 τὸν ἐνιαυτόν. **I. The Problem of the Calendar.** The difficulty of all calendars is to reconcile a lunar and a solar system of reckoning; by the former the year consists of 354 days, by the latter of about 365¼.

(The exact figures are:	days	hours	min.	sec.
a lunation	29	12	44	3
a lunar year	354	8	48	36
a solar year	365	5	48	48.)

The calendar had to be regulated (1) in order to secure the proper recurrence of feasts (hence month-names are often taken from festivals; cf. Curtius, G. H. ii. 23 f. for the connexion of Delphi and the calendar). (2) To regulate civil procedure. Two problems arise: (*a*) to adjust the civil month to the motions of the moon; (*b*) to adjust the lunar month and the solar year.

II. Greek Solutions. The Greeks adopted a lunar reckoning, making the months alternately of 30 and 29 days; this was arranged by Solon (cf. Plut. Sol. 25, and L. and S. *s. v.* ἕνος). It is said that he tried further to rectify the error thus arising from the shortness of his year (which was only 30 × 6 + 29 × 6 = 354 days), by inserting an intercalary month every other year (διὰ τρίτου ἔτεος, for which phrase cf. 37. 2 διὰ τρίτης ἡμέρης, and iii. 97. 3). H. here and in i. 32. 3 definitely asserts that this was the Greek system in his day.

Others, however (e.g. Stein), argue that H. has misunderstood the system; an intercalary month every other year would give 738 days in two years, instead of 730½. Hence they argue that the real system in H.'s time was to introduce three (not four, as H.) intercalary months in every period of eight years; this would give a fairly accurate result, i.e. 354 × 8 + 90 = 2922 = 8 × 365¼. This seems really to have been the arrangement in H.'s own day; but the date of its introduction is uncertain. Unger argues (I. Müller, Handb. der klass. Alt.-Wiss. i. 569–70) that the eight-year period existed from quite early times, at any rate from the eighth century, as is shown by myths and customs (Plut. Mor. 418), and (presumably) that the three intercalary months in each period are also early; Solon may have used this system. The calendar was further adjusted by

Meton in Periclean times, who introduced a nineteen-years' cycle. For a brief account of the whole subject cf. Abbott, Outlines of Gk. Hist. pp. 10 seq.

III. Egyptian Solutions. The Egyptians were the first people who definitely adopted a solar year of twelve months with thirty days in each; this began July 19 (according to the Julian calendar), i.e. 1st of Thoth according to the Egyptian, which was about a month in advance of the real solar year. On this day Sirius (Sothis) is first visible in the morning, in the latitude of Memphis (cf. *ἄστρων*). This coincides with the beginning of the rise of the Nile (19. 2 n.). Five days were added (*ἐπαγόμεναι*) at the end of the year. So far H. is right; but he quite fails to grasp the methods by which the Egyptians tried to reconcile this year of 365 days with the real solar year of 365¼ days (roughly) (cf. *ὁ κύκλος . . . ἐς τὠυτὸ παραγίνεται*). This is not surprising, as scholars are not agreed even now as to their methods.

Brugsch says they had anticipated the Julian calendar, and to every fourth year added an extra day, i.e. making it a leap year. Certainly J. Caesar was said to have derived his calendar from Egypt (Dio Cass. xliii. 26). This view seems to be a mistake. Ptolemy Euergetes (238 B.C.), by the decree of Canopus, tried to introduce this (i.e. the Julian) system, but in vain. The Egyptians, however, recognized that their common year and the real year (the 'Sothic year') did not agree, and that the 'common year' grew later and later; hence the calculation of the 'Sothic period' (*κυνικὸς κύκλος*) of 1,460 years (= 1,461 'common years'), at the expiration of which the mistake had rectified itself (¼ day per year for 1,460 years = a year of 365 days). The first 'Sothic period' is said to begin 4241 B.C. (but cf. App. X, § 2). Hence the date of the arrangement of the calendar is fixed for this year, 'the first certain date in the world's history' (Meyer, i, §§ 159, 195–7). Cf. also B. M. G. pp. 182 seq. for a short but clear account of the Egyptian calendar.

The five 'extra days' can be traced on the monuments as far back as the 6th Dynasty.

2 **δυώδεκα θεῶν.** For the Egyptian Pantheon in H. cf. c. 145 nn. Here he only means that the names of the twelve chief gods of the Greek Pantheon were Egyptian (c. 52). For the pictures of the Egyptian gods cf. B. M. G. pp. 123 seq.

ζῷα (cf. i. 70. 1 n.); not the hieroglyphs (which the Greeks did *not* borrow), but 'figures' of animals, men, plants, &c., e.g. on the scarab, worn as amulets; these were largely exported to Greece.

Μῖνα: cf. c. 99 n.

3 **Θηβαϊκοῦ νομοῦ** = the southern part of Upper Egypt, the later Thebais. H. is not consistent here with his own statement (c. 99) that Menes founded Memphis; that town lies some way 'below' (*ἔνερθε*), i.e. north of, L. Moeris (for which cf. c. 149 n.). The legend also is exaggerated; but 'it contains the truth that Lower Egypt

remained a land of swamps far later than Upper Egypt' (Erman, E. p. 16). For νομοῦ cf. 164 n.

5–18 *The origin* (5, 10–14), *dimensions* (6–9), *and boundaries of Egypt* (15–18).

5 1 **δῆλα γὰρ δή.** This passage naturally means 'I should have seen this for myself, even if I had not been told'. The phrase δῶρον τ. π., however, is attributed by Arrian (Anab. v. 6—doubtfully) to Hecataeus; hence some see in it a proof that H. used the work of his predecessor as a guide-book; but cf. Introd. § 20.

The Greeks were quick to observe the action of rivers in forming deltas; cf. c. 10 and Thuc. ii. 102. H. is quite right that Egypt is alluvial deposit; this is true of the whole country up to the first cataract; but the process of silting up had taken far longer than he supposes (e.g. some place it at 74,000 years). The elevation of the ground is now very slow—only four inches in one hundred years.

ἐς τήν. The words mark off one part of Egypt, i.e. the Delta.

τὰ κατύπερθε . . . πλόου. This clause also refers to Αἴγυπτος, being roughly parallel to ἐς τὴν Ἕλληνες ν.; it marks off a second part of the country which is also 'a gift of the river'. The construction is adverbial. Translate, '(this is true) with regard to the parts,' &c.

τριῶν ἡμερέων: see 8. 3 n. for this limit.

ἔστι δὲ ἕτερον. This refers to the following sentence.

2 **ἔτι καὶ ἡμέρης.** H. calls a day's πλοῦς 540 (9. 1) or 700 stades (iv. 86); either of these figures is far too much here; a depth of eleven fathoms is reached some twelve or fifteen miles from the coast near Aboukir.

Both facts in § 2 are quoted to show the effect of the Nile on the coast, viz. the presence of alluvial mud and the small depth of water.

6 1 **μῆκος.** H. (in c. 7. 1 and c. 10) continues his proof that Egypt is alluvial, but digresses here to give its dimensions.

σχοῖνοι. Properly a 'rope', cp. Eng. 'cord' and 'chain' as measures. The extent of a σχοῖνος was uncertain, probably because it was a practical measure, not strictly a measure of length (cp. Germ. 'Stunde'). Strabo (804) says that it varied from 30 to 120 stades. H. gives it a uniform value of 60 stades, and so is inaccurate in his results; here he exaggerates, and makes Egypt, which has really only about 2200 stades of sea-coast, to have '3600'. It is noticeable that '60 stades' was the estimate of a σχοῖνος from Thebes to Syene (Artemidorus in Strabo, 804), which confirms H.'s statement that he had been south of Thebes (29 nn.).

Lehmann (W. K. P. 1895, pp. 180–2), however, explains more elaborately H.'s errors here and in cc. 9, 149. He argues (1) that the σχοῖνος = the parasang = 30 stades; (2) that H. has taken the figures from his source—probably Hecataeus—and has wrongly doubled the size of the σχοῖνος; (3) that perhaps this mistake is due to the confusion of the smaller and the larger 'kaspu'—Babylonian measures of one and of two parasangs respectively. His proof may be given in the following table:

	H.	H. corrected.	Reality as crow flies.
Breadth of Egypt	3,600 st.	1,800 st. = 357·1 km.	355–360 km.
From Thebes to Elephantine ...	1,800 ,,	900 ,, = 178·2 ,,	182 km.
Heliopolis to Thebes ...	4,860 ,,	2,430 ,, = 482·09 ,,	490·4 km.
Lake Moeris (c. 149)	3,600 ,,	1,800 ,,	Pliny v. 50, 2,000 st.

It is not certain, however, that measurements 'as the crow flies' were made before Eratosthenes (circ. 230 B.C.), and the fact that in Egyptian land measurement 'all angles were treated as though they were right angles' (Lyons, Survey, p. 48) does not inspire confidence; there is no evidence that Hecataeus or any other Greek before H. had attempted to give measures for Egypt. H. certainly seems to speak in c. 9 as if he were measuring along the river.

τοῦ Πλινθινήτεω. Plinthine lay near the later Alexandria, on the Mareotic Lake; H. (18. 2) mentions Marea as one of the border towns towards Libya.

Σερβωνίδος. This lake (now dry) lay parallel to the sea on the east side of Egypt (cf. iii. 5. 3 n.). It was much feared for its swampy shores, which were said to be covered with drifted sand, and so to engulf the unwary (cf. Diod. i. 30; Milton, Paradise Lost, ii. 592–4):

> A gulf profound as that Serbonian bog
> Betwixt Damiata and Mount Casius old,
> Where armies whole have sunk.

The army of Darius Ochus in 350 B.C. was said to have perished thus. It lay under Mount Casius, the real boundary of Egypt and Syria (158. 4); this was a sand dune of no great height, the modern Râs el Kasrûn, crowned with a temple to Baal (cf. the Baal-Zephon of Exodus xiv. 2, 9); Pompey was killed at its foot.

2 Parasang (cf. v. 53 n.) in H. and Xenophon = 30 stades = 4 Roman miles; thus it corresponds to modern Persian 'farsang' = $3\frac{1}{2}$ to 4 English miles. Other writers estimated it variously from 30 to 60 stades (cf. Strabo, 518), while Agathias (sixth century A.D.) made it as small as 21 stades.

1 **ὁδὸς ἐς Ἡλίου πόλιν**: i.e. sailing up the Pelusiac arm, which is the natural approach to Heliopolis; like a true Greek, H. went everywhere he could by water; by this route his measurement of 1,500 stades is roughly right. In c. 9 he is found to give the distance from the sea to Heliopolis as 1,260 stades

(i.e. from the sea to Thebes	... ...	6,120
less from Heliopolis to Thebes	... ...	4,860
		1,260);

but in that passage he is reckoning directly north and south, in estimating the size of Egypt.

The reference to Athens (cf. 156. 6; 177. 2) is one of the passages on which Kirchhoff bases his theory that Bk. II was written at Athens, but of course it proves nothing. (Cf. Introd. § 10.) For the altar and its use as a starting-point for measurements cf. vi. 108. 4 n.

The town of Pisa had been destroyed in 572 B.C.; the distance here given by H. is very exact.

2 The negative μή is due to idea of prevention in διάφορον (*quominus pares sint*).

8 1 **ὄρος παρατέταται.** H. is quite right in remarking that the mountains begin at Heliopolis, but his conception of them is very vague; he gives them an extension (μακρότατον) from east to west of 'two months' journey'.

ταύτῃ: 'the mountains cease at the quarries, and bend back to the sea.' This is the most natural translation of the passage; but others translate 'ceasing at the parts mentioned (i. e. at the Red Sea), bend back', i. e. are double. The quarries are still a conspicuous feature in this region.

ἀπὸ ἠοῦς. Stein thinks H. says 'from east to west', because he is reproducing Phoenician information; cf. ἐπυνθανόμην (but *v. i.*).

2 **τὸ πρὸς Λιβύης.** H. does not accept the name of 'the Libyan mountain' (cf. § 3 *ad fin.* Λ. καλεόμενον); to him it is 'the Egyptian mountain on the side of Libya', as opposed to τὸ τῆς Ἀραβίης ὄρος.

ψάμμῳ. This drifting of the sand is well seen at the Sphinx, of which only the head is left exposed.

τρόπον, 'direction' (cf. i. 189. 3).

3 **ὡς εἶναι Αἰγύπτου**, 'so long as it is Egypt' (cf. A. ἐοῦσα *inf.* in same sense); i. e. H. thinks that the land becomes wide again when Egypt ceases and Nubia begins. Others refer these phrases to the *breadth*, not the length of the land, meaning that beyond the Nile Valley on east and west lie Arabia and Libya, *not Egypt*.

καὶ δέκα: these words are inserted without MS. authority to make H. consistent. It is calculated that he gives the whole distance from Heliopolis to the frontier as $13\frac{2}{3}$ days; for from Heliopolis to Thebes, reckoning 540 stades a day, is 9 days (9. 2); from Thebes to Elephantine is $3\frac{1}{3}$ days more ['1,800 stades', 9. 2]; from Elephantine to the frontier is 12 σχοῖνοι, which, according to his usual method of calculation (6. 1 n., i. e. 9 σχοῖνοι to the day's journey), make $1\frac{1}{3}$ days; i. e. $9 + 3\frac{1}{3} + 1\frac{1}{3} = 13\frac{2}{3}$ in all. This change of reading also would explain H.'s strange statement (below) that Egypt becomes 'broad again'; he would mean the same as in 29. 3, i. e. that where Egypt and Aethiopia join, at the island of Tachompso, there is a 'smooth plain'. Of course this is not accurate geographically, but H. does not pretend to have seen the country beyond Elephantine (29. 2).

It is usual to alter the reading; but the mistake (of omitting δέκα) is as old as Aristides (ii. 343), i. e. as the second century A. D.

If the reading be not altered, three explanations of H.'s mistake are possible, not to mention the drastic measure of arguing that he had never been up the Nile beyond the Fayûm at all (c. 29 nn.):

I. That H. never left his boat, and hence was misled by a merely temporary widening of the Nile valley; of these there are several; we may compare for such a mistake his strange statement as to Ardericca on the Euphrates (i. 185 n.). Measurements were always difficult to ancient travellers; so Strabo (789), a trained geographer, says that the maximum width of ἡ ποταμία Αἴγυπτος is 300 stades, which is nearly three times too much.

II. Wiedemann argues that H. is misled by a theory of Hecataeus (?), that Egypt was like a double axe in shape ▷—◁ (cf. Scylax, p. 106, G. G. M. i. 81). This theory was based on symmetry, and there is supposed to be another fragment of it in 28. 3 (see n.), the statement that the Nile flowed north as well as south. But (*a*) Hecataeus could not have held this theory, for to him only the Delta was Egypt (16. 1 n.); (*b*) if Hecataeus had held it, surely H. would have been eager to refute a view so absurd (cf. c. 45 n.).

III. A new and very ingenious explanation of H.'s geography of the Nile Valley has been given by Sourdille (H. E. pp. 112 seq.).

He maintains three points:

A. That the 'Arabian mountain' is conceived of as running in *two directions, practically at right angles to each other*, starting from the 'quarries'. He translates 8. 2 ταύτῃ λῆγον κτλ. 'The mountain ceases on this side and makes a bend towards what I have said' (he means the Ἐρυθρὴ θάλασσα in its northern extension, i. e. the Red Sea proper); 'in its most extended part (i. e. that from east to west) it would take, as I learned, two months' journey from east to west, and its eastern end would produce incense.'

He argues:

(1) That as the 'Arabian mountain' is described at first as running north and south, its course after its 'bend' (ἀνακάμπτει) must be different, i. e. east and west.

(2) μακρότατον must refer to the 'length' east and west of the chain, not (as Stein) to its 'broadening' out in the south.

(3) H. clearly distinguishes two parts of the 'Arabian mountain' in § 2; he mentions one part of the τὸ πρὸς Λιβύης ὄρος as running south, τεταμένον τὸν αὐτὸν τρόπον καὶ τοῦ Ἀραβίου τὰ πρὸς μεσαμβρίην φέροντα; this implies that there was another part of the Arabian mountain that did not 'run south'. Sourdille points out that H. always gives a direction as from east to west, even though (as here) the starting-point is in the west; also that the mention of the 'spice-bearing regions' (8. 1) at once suggests Arabia (iii. 107. 1).

For the geography generally of this part of the mountain chain, cf. 73. 1 n. and 158. 2–3, where he mentions the 'gap' in the mountains, *running east and west*, through which the canal of Necho passed. This explanation is almost certainly right.

B. That the reading τεσσέρων is right. Sourdille points out that the Ethiopians (29. 4) hold τὰ ἀπὸ Ἐλεφαντίνης; hence the conjecture 'fourteen' carries H. *outside Egypt* (cf. 8. 3 n.). Retaining 'four', he thinks that τὸ ἐνθεῦτεν αὖτις εὐρέα refers to the Fayûm. This really is only one day south of Heliopolis; but H. clearly thought it much further south; for

(1) He obviously conceives it as bordering on the 'Thebaic nome' and as 'seven days' voyage from the sea' (4. 3).

(2) The branch of the Nile, the Bahr Yûsûf, which waters the Fayûm, finally leaves the Nile almost exactly 'four days' journey' above Heliopolis, near the modern Siût. If H. conceived this as running west, instead of north and south, we can understand how 'Egypt' appeared to him to broaden out 'four days' above Heliopolis (cf. 150. 1 n.). He certainly did not realize that it ran parallel to the Nile, as a branch of it, for he says (17. 3) the Nile above the Delta flows εἰς ἑών.

(3) This seems confirmed by what H. says as to Egypt being 'the gift of the Nile' (5. 1). The priests told him this was so as far as L. Moeris, i. e. as far as the source of the Bahr Yûsûf mentioned above. H., however, tacitly corrects this by adding 'the land above the lake for three days' journey' as ἕτερον τοιοῦτον, i. e. he thinks the Nile deposit begins, *not* 'seven days from the sea', but further up still where the Bahr Yûsûf *first* leaves the Nile, near Farshût, 'three days' journey' above Siût. This explanation is possible; it saves the veracity of H., but at the expense of his geographical intelligence.

C. *That in this misunderstanding lies the explanation of H.'s statement that the Nile overflows 'for two days' journey*, more or less, on each side' (19. 1).

What the canals of the Nile do, that it does itself. The Bahr Yûsûf on the west and the canal of Necho on the east have the extension here mentioned, which is obviously wrong if attributed to the Nile itself.

Αἴγυπτος ἐοῦσα: this word has a double construction—it is the subject of the sentence, and yet goes especially with ἐοῦσα.

διηκοσίων. This breadth, about twenty-three miles, is too great. In the four days' journey above Heliopolis, the widest place is only about fifteen. The mistake is natural, as H. kept mainly to the river and had to judge distances by the eye.

9 1 **ἐννέα.** H. here allows 540 stades (4860÷9) for a day's journey; at this rate the whole distance from the sea to Elephantine *up stream* would be done in 6120+1800÷540, i. e. 14⅔ days. But in c. 175 the voyage *down stream* only to Sais takes twenty days.

Two explanations may be given of the discrepancy: (1) Wiedemann's (doubtfully) that H. went up stream by an unusually fast boat, a fact which would partly explain his scanty knowledge of Upper Egypt; the figure in c. 175 is that of a heavy-laden cargo boat. (2) (More probably) the figure here is a mere calculation, based on the supposed rate of 'nine schoenes a day'; the figure in c. 175 is that of an actual voyage. Sourdille (H. E. p. 109) thinks the 'nine days' the official estimate for a fast government boat (cf. viii. 98 for the post system); H. has taken this as if it were the normal speed. The journey from Heliopolis to Thebes by boat usually now takes over twelve days (Stein).

2 **συντιθέμενοι κτλ.**, 'if we put together the number of stades in Egypt.' The words have no construction. In any case H.'s figures are too big, owing to his over-estimate of the *σχοῖνος* (cp. 6. 1 n.); from Thebes to Heliopolis is really 421 miles, not 552 (as H.).

1 At Iliun the rivers are the Simois and the Scamander, in Teuthrania the Caicus, at Ephesus the Cayster and (to the south) the Maeander. At Ephesus the sea has receded about three miles (Leake). The whole subject is dealt with in Strabo (691), who calls the plains *ποταμῶν γεννήματα*, quoting H. (cp. Thuc. ii. 102; but his prophecy, that all the Echinades would become mainland, has not been fulfilled).

2 H. gives the five mouths in c. 17; he omits here the Bolbitic and the Bucolic mouths as artificial.

1 For the *Ἐρυθρὴ θαλάσση* and the *Ἀράβιος κόλπος* cf. i. 1. 1 n.

2 **εἰρεσίῃ.** H. uses this measurement of the Caspian (i. 203. 1 n.); for a 'day's sail' cf. vii. 183. 3 n. His calculation seems to suit the length of the Red Sea (which is about 1,200 miles), but his breadth is much too small; he seems to have confused the north-west arm, the Gulf of Suez, and the main sea. The former averages 30 miles in breadth, but the sea itself varies from 130 miles in the north to 250 in the south (E. B. xxii. 970).

3 **τὸν μέν**: in loose apposition to *ἕτερον κόλπον*: H. then forgets his construction, and goes on to mention again the other gulf, i. e. the 'Arabian Gulf'. The two gulfs, the Red Sea and that which is now Egypt, are conceived as 'boring together', so as to make their 'ends' (*μυχούς*) nearly meet, but 'missing' each other by 'a little strip of land'.

4 **τί μιν κωλύει.** H. seems, from his rhetorical tone, to be answering some criticisms on his geological views. Probably he allows '20,000' years, because this was roughly his conception of the duration of Egyptian history.

12 H.'s geological remarks in this chapter are mainly right (cf. 5. 1 n.), and show his excellence as an observer. The coast of Egypt does 'project' (*προκειμένην*), 'shells' are frequent, the 'salt efflorescence' on the monuments is well known, and the soil is black and 'friable'

(*καταρρηγνυμένην*). The sand, however, extends much more widely than he says.

2 The Egyptians called their land Qemt or 'Qem', 'the black' (cp. Bible 'Ham'), hence *alchemy* = (properly) 'the Egyptian art'.

13 1 For Moeris cp. c. 101 n., and for his date App. XIV.

ὅτε τῶν . . . ἤκουον. These words seem to imply that some interval had elapsed between the time when H. heard the statement and when he wrote this passage; Meyer (F. i. 156) concludes that H. was in Egypt about 440 B.C., and wrote Bk. II about 430.

The height of the Nile flood was measured at Memphis, just above Rodah near Cairo, where the Nilometer now stands. A scanty Nile rises 20 feet or less, a good one from 24 to 27. The sixteen child figures on the well-known Nile statue in the Vatican symbolize a rise of 16 cubits (24 feet), i. e. a good Nile.

πήχεας: H. seems to take the cubit as $18\frac{1}{2}$ inches (as in Greece), not as 21 (the royal cubit, cf. i. 178. 3 n.).

H. is wrong in saying the height of the inundations had altered so much in historic times; perhaps he has confused geographical variations (i. e. at different parts of the Nile) with historical ones (i. e. at different periods).

εἰ μὴ . . . ἀναβῇ: for omission of *ἄν* cf. iv. 172. 2, and Goodwin, § 468.

2 **ἢν οὕτω ἡ χώρη.** Translate 'If this land rises in height proportionately (to its rise in the past) and duly makes (*ἀποδιδοῖ*) a like increase in extent', then it will be reached by the flood water with more difficulty. H. ignores the fact that the river-bed rises proportionately to the river-banks.

3 **ἀποστροφή**: properly an 'escape from', so a 'resource' (viii. 109. 5). Here used oddly with gen. = 'a resource for getting water'.

For the contrast between artificial irrigation and rainfall cf. Deuteronomy xi. 10–12. For rain in Egypt cf. iii. 10. 3 n.

14 In this chapter H. exaggerates the contrast between Egypt and Greece (cp. c. 35 nn.). It was only in parts of the Delta that the plough could be dispensed with.

2 Sheep are represented on the monuments of the 'Old Kingdom' as treading in the seed (cf. Breasted, p. 92), and swine also on one tomb at Thebes (B. M. G. p. 95) tread out the corn. Quite recently a monument has been discovered at Dra abu'l Naga which absolutely confirms H. (Ann. du Serv. des Antiq. xi. 162 seq.). Cf. also Eudoxus (in Ael. H. A. x. 16), and Pliny, N. H. xviii. 168, who says the custom had been given up in his time.

ἀποδινήσας, 'completely treading it out' (lit. winnowing). Other animals were also used. Cf. Deut. xxv. 4, 1 Cor. ix. 9 for oxen among the Jews.

15 1 H. is here probably attacking Hecataeus (F. H. G. i 22, fr. 295), who seems to have thought that the Delta only was Egypt.

ἀπὸ Περσέος. The usual identification of the 'watch-tower of Perseus' is with C. Aboukir, in which case it would lie *outside* the

Delta. Strabo (801) places it near the Bolbitic mouth, which is probably right. In that case H. is wrong in making it the extreme west limit of the Delta (Sourdille, H. E. 58–9).

τῶν Πηλουσιακῶν. Pelusium was the east gate of Egypt (cp. 141. 4 and 154 n., where H. describes the planting of the Greek mercenaries of Psammetichus there. The estimate of '40 schoenes' is nearer right than H.'s 60 (6. 1 n.).

Cercasorus is about four miles north of Cairo; the Nile now divides a little lower down.

λεγόντων: agrees with Ἰώνων, but is parallel to λέγοντες, which goes with *οἵ φασι*.

Canobus lies about fifteen miles north-east of Alexandria, at the north-east end of Aboukir Bay, the scene of Nelson's great victory in 1798. It was said to have been founded by Menelaus, in memory of his pilot, who died there of snake-bite (Tac. Ann. ii. 60); at any rate, it was a comparatively recent town. It was famous for its temple of Serapis, and still more for its vice (cf. Juv. vi. 84; Sen. Ep. 51). It is to be noticed that Greek myths in Egypt were especially connected with the north-west corner of the Delta (cf. 178 nn.): so we have the watch-tower of Perseus (15. 1), Archandrus (98. 2), and Helen (113. 1) in these parts.

3 H. adopts the view that Egyptian culture began up the Nile and came down stream 'gradually' (ὑπο-); this was inevitable, as he thought the Delta so comparatively recent; it was also supported by the fact that 'Thebes' only was mentioned by Homer. He is confirmed by the First Dynasty tombs at Abydos (King and Hall, pp. 59 f.), though the buildings of Thebes belong to the 'Middle' and the 'New Kingdom'.

περίμετρον. This figure, 6,120 stades, for the 'circumference' of the Thebaic nome, was given to H.; it is not the result of his own measurements. But its exact recurrence here and in 9. 2 is suspicious.

16. 1 H. has refuted the Ionian view, that Egypt was only the Delta (15. 1) in the preceding chapter; he now proceeds to argue that it is inconsistent with the accepted doctrine that there were three continents (*οἵ φασι τρία μόρια κτλ.*: cf. iv. 45. 5). He seems to think that if Egypt were the Delta, it was in neither Asia nor Libya (*v. i.*), but a 'fourth' part. His argument, however, is very obscure.

λογίζεσθαι, 'they cannot count,' as they ignore the Delta.

2 **τοῦτον τὸν λόγον.** The argument seems to be; Egypt is enclosed by the Nile, therefore the Nile cannot be the boundary of Asia and Libya, as this would leave Egypt unaccounted for.

τῇ Λιβύῃ: the dative is curious. Cf. a similar use of *χωρίζω* in iv. 28. 2.

17 H. states two geographical positions in this chapter: (1) that Egypt is one and indivisible (*not*, as the view of the Greeks would imply, half in Asia and half in Africa); (2) that the boundaries of Asia and Africa are (*not* the Nile, but) the boundaries of Egypt. To which continent H. would assign Egypt he leaves uncertain (cf. iv. 39 2 n.).

Καταδούπων: the first cataract, i.e. the furthest to the north; for it cf. 29. 2 n.

4 For the Nile branches (*στόματα*) cf. 10. 2 n.

The number of 'branches' (*στόματα*) is usually given as seven. Of these the 'Tanitic', i.e. the second from the east, between the Pelusiac and the Mendesian, is not named by H., who calls it 'Saitic'. Cf. Strabo (802) *τὸ Τανιτικὸν ὅ τινες Σαϊτικὸν λέγουσι.*

Three explanations are given: (1) the simplest is that of Stein, that beside the well-known 'Sais', there was a second town of that name in the eastern Delta. But there is no monumental evidence for a second 'Sais'.

(2) Wiedemann seems to suppose that the Saites claimed the Canopic arm, on which their town stood, as their own, and that H., misled by them, counts it twice over, under its real name 'Canopic', and under its supposed name 'Saitic'.

(3) Sourdille (H. E. 53) thinks that the Tanitic arm was called 'Sanitic', and that H., not recognizing its connexion with the *Τανίτης νομός* of c. 166, confused the unfamiliar name with the familiar *Σαιτικόν.* We may compare the probable confusion in 'Nitocris' (cf. i. 185. 1 n.).

The order from east to west is: (1) Pelusiac (or Bubastic), (2) Tanitic (or ? Saitic), (3) Mendesian, (4) Bucolic, (5) Sebennytic, (6) Bolbitinic (or Rosetta), (7) Canopic (or Naucratic).

18 1 **τῆς ἐμεωυτοῦ**: cf. 104. 1 for a similar touch of complacency as to Colchis. If the modern theory (cf. Introd. § 11) is held that Bk. II is the last composed by H., this 'oracle of Ammon' must be one of his latest pieces of information.

2 **Μαρέης**: the frontier garrison of Egypt (cf. 30. 2 n.) on the west under the Saite dynasty, on the well-known Mareotic Lake.

Ἄπιος: a place called 'Apis' lay (Strabo, 799) twelve miles west of Paraetonium and five days' journey from the oracle of Ammon; it was over 150 miles due west of Alexandria. But this place is obviously too remote to be the 'Apis' mentioned here, which probably lay a little south of Naucratis.

As Isis (to whom the cow was sacred) was especially worshipped in this region, Wiedemann thinks the reason given here improbable, and that the real question was—should they join Inaros in revolt or remain loyal to the Great King? This is a probable date for the oracle, but the two explanations are consistent; Inaros belonged to the Egyptian party among the Libyans, who abstained from cow-flesh (cf. iv. 186); but these Libyans wished to be free from Egyptian restrictions, and hence were unwilling to join in the revolt.

19 1 **δύο ἡμερέων.** Sayce says (J. of P. xiv. 260) that it is only in the

region of the Fayûm that the Nile rises so much; 'H. (wrongly) assumed that what was true of one part of its course might be true of other parts.' However, H. may still be speaking of the region of the Delta, and mean that not only the Delta, but the adjoining country, was flooded. For a more elaborate explanation cf. 8. 3 n.

2 The date of the rise of the Nile varies with the place; it begins at Khartoum early in April, but at Cairo about the end of June; H. therefore is fairly right in his 'summer solstice'; so, too, is he in his statement that it rises for 'one hundred days'. As he does not notice its changes of colour, first green, then blood-red, it is inferred with some reason that he did not himself see the beginning of a Nile flood.

3 The statement that no winds 'blow from' the Nile has been much attacked (e.g. by Sayce), because it has been understood to mean that no breeze is felt *on* the river; but H. himself tells us of the Etesian winds (20. 2) and of the 'fresh wind' (96. 3) up the Nile. He means (cf. c. 27) that there are no breezes down the Nile, i. e. *from* the south, whence the Nile flows; this is practically right. In five months (from June to October) scientific observation shows that the wind blows from this direction only about one day in twelve (Sourdille, H. E. 111), and from the south (speaking strictly) less than one day in thirty.

1 **εἰ μὴ ὅσον**: sc. *μνησθήσομαι*, 'except in so far'; the views (cc. 20, 21) of Thales and Hecataeus, H. thinks, need no refutation, although he proceeds to refute them. H., as usual, is contemptuous of his countrymen.

2 Thales of Miletus (Athen. ii. 87) attributed the rise of the Nile to its being held back by the Etesian winds. H.'s refutation is sensible; the winds blow from the north-west, and so would have affected equally the rivers of Africa and of Syria. But it must be admitted that neither land has 'many rivers', and of the Syrian ones, the Orontes flows south-west, and so would not have been affected. In Africa H. knew of the Cinyps and the Triton (iv. 175, 178 nn.).

21 The theory that the Nile flowed from the circumambient Ocean (cf. c. 23 n.) was widely held. H. is probably refuting Hecataeus (cf. F. H. G. i. 19, fr. 278 for his view); but the Egyptian priests gave the same explanation of the Nile flood (Diod. i. 37).

λόγῳ εἰπεῖν: not 'so to speak', but 'more marvellous to state'.

22 The view that the Nile rose because of melting snow is called by H. by far the 'most attractive', but also 'especially inaccurate'. It was held by Anaxagoras (Diod. i. 38) and his pupil, Euripides (fr. 230), but can be traced further back, in Aeschylus (fr. 304)

ἐν δ' ἥλιος πυρωπὸς ἐκλάμψας χθονι
τήκει πετραίαν χιόνα· πᾶσα δ' εὐθαλὴς
Αἴγυπτος ἁγνοῦ νάματος πληρουμένη.

It is very near the truth. The Nile rises partly because of the heavy rains on the Abyssinian plateau, partly from the melting snow on the mountains round the Great Lakes; the former are brought down by the Blue Nile, the latter by the White Nile, which meet at Khartoum. H. rejects the theory because: (1) 'It flows from the hottest lands to those of which most are colder', as is shown by the warmth of the winds. (2) Upper Egypt was rainless (cf. iii. 10. 3 n.), and Aethiopia must also be so; but snow is always followed by rain within five days (§ 3). (3) The inhabitants are black from the heat (§ 3). (4) The birds do not migrate from Aethiopia, as they would do were there winter there (§ 4). H. tries to apply critical tests to a fact which seems to him insufficiently supported by evidence, and so arrives at a wrong conclusion (cf. iii. 115. 1 n. for similar criticism).

4 **καὶ ὅσον ὦν**, 'ever so little.'

23 **ἀφανές.** The reference is clearly to a definite person, i. e. Hecataeus. H. means that the theory of the circumambient ocean is, as we should say, outside the region of science. It was based on various kinds of evidence:

(1) Homer, Il. xviii. 607–8, speaks of Ocean as encircling the shield of Achilles. The theory may have been Phoenician in origin (Tozer, A. G. p. 21), but (2) it suited the Greek notion of symmetry; Delphi was the centre of the earth, and the Ocean supplied a natural circumference. (3) Facts were supposed to confirm it; the Greeks knew of water in the furthest west and south, and the Caspian was supposed to be an arm on the North Ocean; cf. i. 202. 4 n. for H.'s rejection of this view. Berger, pp. 36, 41, asserts that H. is wrong in deriving the theory of the Ionian physicists from Homer; but his assertion is neither proved nor probable. H. rightly rejects the theory of the circumambient ocean as unsupported by evidence. For a similar rejection of *a priori* geography cf. iv. 36. 2 n.

24 1 **ἀρχαίης**: i.e. the sun's 'usual course', direct east and west. To H. the earth is a flat surface, over which the sun moves in an arc (cf. iii. 104 n. and App. XIII. 3).

χειμώνων. The theory that the sun's course was affected by storms was adopted by Democritus, who applied it also to the moon and stars. Cp. Lucr., R. N. v. 639 seq.

Qui (*sc.* aer) queat aestivis solem detrudere signis
Brumales usque ad flexus gelidumque rigorem.

25 H. now states 'more fully' the theory sketched in c. 24 (*ἐν ἐλαχίστῳ δηλῶσαι*). The sun 'in the winter is blown out of his course by the storms' (24. 1) from the north, and so 'crosses over the upper parts of Libya'. Hence evaporation there is abundant (§§ 1–2) and so the Nile loses its water; the south and south-west winds blowing from this quarter are wet, but part of the moisture 'remains with' the sun (§ 3, *v. i.*). When 'the winter storms begin to be less severe' (§ 3), the sun returns to his normal course, and then 'draws water from all rivers equally'. Hence in the summer the Nile is like all other rivers in the amount of evaporation from it; but in the winter 'it alone suffers from the sun', and so its course is 'lower than in the summer' (§ 5). In fact, H. thinks the normal height of the Nile is its summer flood, and the low Nile of the winter is the exception.

This theory is referred to in Aristoph. Nub. 273, and is attacked by Diodorus, i. 38, and Aristides, ii. 341, who rightly say that if it were true, other African rivers ought to show the same phenomenon.

αἰθρίου κτλ. Evaporation is assisted 'as the air is clear and the soil dry, even without cool winds'.

2 **τήκουσι**, 'waste,' i.e. the water drawn up from the Nile. The 'south and south-west winds' are wet in Greece, but are not really so in Egypt.

3 **ὑπολείπεσθαι**, 'to let some remain behind with himself,' i.e. as nourishment. This is the theory of Thales that the sun and the stars were fed by water; later, the Stoics adopted it in the form that the sun was nourished by the sea (Cic. de Nat. Deo. ii. 15 'cum sol igneus sit Oceanique alatur humoribus'); cf. for it Milton, P. L. v. 423-5:

> The sun, that light imparts to all, receives
> From all his alimental recompense
> In humid exhalations.

4 **τέως**: i.e. in the winter = *τοῦτον τὸν χρόνον* below (§ 5); the land 'being soaked with rains and furrowed with channels', lets the rain flow into the rivers, unlike the *ἀλεεινὴ χώρη* (§ 1) in Libya.

οἱ μέν: the rivers of the north as opposed to the Nile.

26 **τὸν ταύτῃ**: i.e. in Aethiopia.

27 H. applies his theory to answer his other question why there is no wind from the river (19. 3 n.); he thinks no wind from the south could be expected, as it was too hot. It is needless to add that H. knew nothing of the causes of winds.

ὡς κάρτα is emphatic from its separate position.

28 The name 'Nile' is probably Semitic = 'river', the native name was Hāpi; for an image of the river-god cf. B. M. G. p. 12. The source of the Nile was an insoluble problem till the latter half of the nineteenth century. H. wisely gives it up, but narrates a story which he heard on good authority, but thinks was meant 'as a joke' (*παίζειν*). His narrative is attacked in two ways.

(1) He is accused of believing the story which he definitely rejects, e.g. by Strabo (819 *Ἡρόδ. φλυαρεῖ ἥδυσμά τι τῷ λόγῳ τὴν τερατείαν προσφέρων.* Cf. Mure, iv. 387). This charge simply proves the carelessness of his critics.

(2) The second charge is more serious, and is as old as Aristides (ii. 344-5): If H. had been on the spot, how could he repeat a story so obviously false? Three answers may be given: (*a*) Stein thinks H. simply refers to the narrow bed of the river at Syene; but this explanation cannot be got out of the text. (*b*) Perhaps Sourdille (H. E. 227 seq.) is right in saying that H. thought

the town on the island 'Elephantine' and Syene opposite to be only *one town*; this he called 'Elephantine' and frequently mentions; Syene, on the other hand, he never mentions except here. He may well therefore have thought Syene to be some place, *unvisited by him*, away to the south; *hence the Saite's story might be right*, and he gives it and criticizes it. (*c*) Hauvette's (pp. 16, 17) view, however, is preferable, that H. means παίζειν to indicate definite rejection of the story, which he still goes on to criticize. It may be noted that H.'s account made so great an impression that Tacitus (Ann. ii. 61) puts 'angustiae et profunda altitudo nullis inquirentium spatiis penetrabilis' among the wonders of Egypt, to which Germanicus 'gave his attention'.

A further point arises—what did the Saite really mean? Probably 'he was speaking what (he meant to be) true' (§ 5 γινόμενα). Three views may be mentioned: (1) Maspero thinks (E. M. iii. 382 seq.) that H. has taken as geography what was really mythology. In the Ritual of Embalmment the dead is addressed, 'He (the Nile) gives thee the water which has come from Elephantine, the Nile which has come from the two gulfs, the Nou which has come from the two rocks.' A bas-relief has been found at Philae representing the Nile god in a cavern under a rock, pouring out two Niles (cf. B. M. G. p. 8 for picture). Maspero further explains 'Krophi' and 'Mophi' to be 'Qer Hāpi' (cavern of the Nile god) and 'Mu-Hāpi' (water of the Nile god). He thinks that the priest also said that there were two Niles, one of Egypt, and one of Ethiopia; of these the former flowed along the right bank, the latter along the left. H. misunderstood his informant, and supposed the 'Nile of Ethiopia' meant the Nile flowing towards Ethiopia, as opposed to the Nile of Egypt. (2) The B. M. G. makes the two Niles the rivers of Upper and of Lower Egypt respectively. (3) Breasted (pp. 55-6) says there was supposed to be an underground Nile, by which the sun returned at night to the east; some thought it came up again as the Indus; this was connected with the real Nile at Elephantine, which was originally the limit of Egyptian knowledge to the south.

Maspero's view is probably nearest to what the Saite said. It is quite needless to see the influence of Hecataeus (cf. 8. 3 n.) in the story.

1 **γραμματιστής**: the temple treasurer; this Saite was probably the only high official whom H. met. For Athena cf. 62. 1 n.

2 **Syene**: *hod.* Assûan; its name 'Suan' is as old as the Sixth Dynasty. Under the Ptolemies it succeeded Elephantine as the capital of Upper Egypt; it was the Roman frontier garrison-town; cf. Tac. Ann. ii. 61 'claustra Romani imperii'.

4 For the inquiring turn of Psammetienus I cf. c. 2.

29 1 **αὐτόπτης.** This statement is especially attacked as untrue by Sayce (*ad loc.* and Introd. p. 27; also in J. of P. xiv). His arguments are (answers are added in brackets):

(1) Elephantine is an island—not a town (it is both, cf. Artace iv. 14. 2, and in Egyptian records is frequently called 'a town').

(2) H. makes Amasis bring stones from Elephantine (175. 3 n.); the red granite quarries were really at Syene (cf. 'Syenite'). (But Egyptian sources also call granite 'stone from Elephantine'.)

(3) H. could never have been at Thebes, or he would describe the great buildings there. (The argument *ex silentio* is always most untrustworthy; cf. also 143. 2 n.)

(4) Had H. been at Elephantine he would have known more of the Nile's course above it. (But cf. notes on following chapters, which show that his knowledge was really considerable.)

Sayce's attack is usually held to fail completely.

Elephantine = 'Elephant town', because here the Nubians brought their ivory for tribute (iii. 97. 3) or to exchange it for Egyptian products.

2 H. is quite right in his description of the way in which a boat is towed up the first cataract—'from both sides' (δια-; ἀμφοτέρωθεν is really superfluous); he does not give the exaggerated difficulties which later writers ascribe to the cataracts, e.g. that the dwellers around were permanently deaf from the noise (Cicero, Som. Scip. 5). 'The foaming rapids of the Great Cataract are now things of the past' (Baedeker, p. 335), owing to the Nile Dam built just above.

3 For the rest of this chapter cf. E. Sparig, Herodot's Angaben über die Nilländer oberhalb Syene's, Halle, 1889. He seems clearly right in identifying Tachompso with Djerar, an island south of Dakkeh, some 78 (Murray, p. 519 and map) miles from Syene; H. here, as usual, reckons the σχοῖνος at 60 stades (cf. Strabo, 804, and 6. 1 n.), which gives about 80 miles for the distance. This was the natural boundary of the two nations (§ 4); just below Djerar was Hierasykaminos, the southern limit of Egypt under the Ptolemies. H. makes no distinction between the first cataract, which begins just below Philae, and the Nile above it.

Others, however (e.g. Wiedemann), wrongly identify Tachompso with Philae; Strabo (818) calls Philae κοινὴ κατοικία Αἰθιόπων καὶ Αἰγυπτίων. σχοῖνος is then explained as the space a man could tow before being relieved, i.e. about 500 yards; cf. Jerome (on Joel iii. 18) 'In Nilo solent naves funibus trahere, certa habentes spatia, quae appellant funiculos'. But this identification of Tachompso with Philae is not what H. says, and it leaves his 'four days' quite unexplained. The distance from Syene to Philae could really be done in rather more than five hours, but perhaps the boatmen demanded such a fee of H. that he imagined it must mean a four days' journey. At all events he never went up the cataract.

There is no lake either at Philae or at Djerar; but the Nile widens out above Philae, and at various places south of that island.

4 H. does not give the time spent on 'the lake', i.e. between Philae and the second cataract at Wadi Halfa (where the boat was left

ἀποβάς). If this be reckoned at four days, H.'s account gives 60 days from Syene to Meroe, i.e. 4 days for the rapids, 4 days for the lake, 40 days' land journey, and 12 more by boat again. This corresponds to the estimate of Timosthenes, admiral of Ptolemy Philadelphus (60 days from Syene to Meroe, Pliny, N. H. vi. 183); 'this is a very fair approximation to the truth' (Bunbury, i. 302).

5 **σκόπελοι κτλ.**: the obstructions on the river, beginning with the second cataract just above Halfa. The river in modern times is usually left here by travellers; the railway from Halfa runs to Abu Hammed, where the Nile turns south-west; the caravan route went straight across the desert from Korosko, 90 miles below Halfa.

6 The 'island' of Meroe later was formed by the Nile and the Atbara (Astaboras), just south of Berber, and ruins of pyramids have been found in this region at Bakarawiya, south of the junction of the two rivers. H., however, probably means the town of Napata, the northern capital of the Aethiopian kingdom, which lay (near the modern Merawi, which preserves the name) some thirty miles south-west of the fourth cataract, under the 'holy mountain', Gebel Barkal. (So Sparig, and Hall in Murray, p. 552.)

H. had certainly never heard of the River Atbara (cf. iv. 50. 1), and the southern site for Meroe seems inconsistent with (30. 1) the statement that Meroe is only half way to the 'Deserters'.

If, however, Meroe be Napata, then the 'twelve days' voyage' must be explained as *not continuous*, as H. had been told, but made up of two parts, one from just below Djerar (*u. s.*) to Halfa, and one from El Debba (south of Dongola) to Merawi.

Δία. There is a temple of Amon (i.e. Zeus) at Napata, where he was worshipped in a ram-headed shape. H. is quite right in speaking of the theocratic character of the Ethiopian kingdom; the oracle at Napata chose the king (cf. Diod. iii. 5. 6 of the later Meroe). As Ethiopia had been conquered by kings from Thebes, the Theban deities naturally were more prominent there, and the high priests of Amon, expelled by the 22nd dynasty from Thebes, had retired to Ethiopia (Maspero, Annuaire des E. G. 1877, p. 126 seq., gives interesting details as to the working of the oracle).

30 1 **ἴσῳ**: i.e. in 60 days; this estimate may well be exaggerated. As usual H. becomes less accurate as he gets further away from his own observations.

The Deserters. Some moderns (e.g. Wiedemann) have doubted the whole story, but it is now generally accepted. Maspero (iii. 498) points out that in the seventh century the military Mashauasha disappear from the monuments; he considers the divisions of ii. 164 seq. to be the new army arrangements of Psammetichus. For an interesting parallel under Apries to the desertion cf. statue of Nesuhor, in Louvre, with its inscription (Klio, iv. 152 seq.; Breasted, R. iv. 989 seq.).

Eratosthenes (in Strabo 786) calls these deserters Σεμβρῖται, i.e. ἐπήλυδες. They are variously placed in Abyssinia, on the Blue Nile, or in Sennaar (Bunbury), about 150 miles south of Khartoum, or where the Sobat joins the White Nile, about 400 miles south of Khartoum. It is in the last region that the Nile ceases to flow west and north-west and turns north (cf. 31 n.).

Ἀσμάχ. The translation 'left' is a popular explanation, perhaps given by an interpreter; the real meaning of the word was 'forgetting', i.e. it = 'runaways'. But the word for 'left' in Egyptian is very similar in sound (Spiegelberg, Z. Ä. S. xliii. 95).

2 The number 240,000 is doubtless much exaggerated.

Elephantine, Marea, Daphnae are the three gates of Egypt towards Ethiopia, Syria, and Libya. For Marea cf. 18. 2 n. and *inf.* Daphnae has been identified as Tell Defenneh, near L. Menzaleh, between the Delta and the Suez Canal; it lies on the Pelusiac arm of the Nile (now a canal). (Petrie, E. E. F. iv. (1888) 47.) Here the earliest remains belong to the Ramesside age; but the fort was founded by Psammetichus I, and the oldest finds in it were mainly Greek (ib. p. 48); then from the sixth century Greek remains disappear (p. 52). All this agrees with H.; cf. 107. 1 for Sesostris (i. e. Rameses II; but cf. App. X. 5, 7) at Daphnae, and 154. 3 for the planting the Greeks on the Pelusiac arm, and their subsequent removal by Amasis. H., however, distinguishes Daphnae and 'the Camps', whereas Petrie makes them the same; probably both are right; one of the military 'camps' lay outside the native town, but continuous with it. Daphnae guarded 'the great highway into Syria' (Petrie *u. s.*); cf. 141. 4 ταύτῃ εἰσὶν αἱ ἐσβολαί.

3 ἔτι ἐπ' ἐμεῦ: this reference to the Persian garrisons seems to show that H. was in Egypt after 454 B.C. (cf. App. IX, § 1). The garrison at Marea was given up, because the Libyans to the west were completely reduced (Stein, cf. iii. 91; iv. 167 seq.); this reason is more probable than that of Krall, viz. that the defence of the west was entrusted to native princes, e.g. Inaros and Thannyras (iii. 15). Sourdille (H. E. p. 3) thinks that H. had been told generally that 'the Persian garrison system was the same' as the Egyptian, but says nothing special as to Marea, because he had not verified the statement as to the garrison there personally, as he had done at Elephantine and at Daphnae. This explanation seems over-subtle.

ἐς Αἰθιοπίην. One of the points attacked in the story is the implication that the fugitives traversed the whole of Egypt. The story is at least consistent; it would not be easy to stop '240,000' armed and organized runaways.

4 δέξαντα. The grossness here (cf. 162. 3, the reply of Amasis) belongs to the story of a guide, catering for Greek taste; the native Egyptian had far too much respect for royalty to answer thus.

5 Wiedemann denies that Egyptian influence on Ethiopia is so late; he considers that the story was invented to explain Egyptian

influence in that country, and points out that Ethiopia had been conquered, as far as the second cataract, under the 12th Dynasty, not to mention later relations (cf. App. X, § 9).

31 1 **τεσσέρων.** Cf. 29. 4, 30. 1 nn. for the figure.

ῥέει δὲ ἀπὸ κτλ. These words are taken two ways:

(1) The usual view, e.g. Rawlinson's, is that H. means the Nile was flowing from east to west at the furthest point at which he knew of it, i.e. in the land of the Deserters.

(2) But this is not the natural sense of the passage, and it is better to suppose that H. conceives the Nile as flowing from the west in *all its course* above Elephantine (Bunbury, i. 266, 303), because

(*a*) He compares it with the Danube, c. 33;

(*b*) Europe is 'beyond comparison' the broadest of his continents (iv. 42. 1 n.); but this could hardly be the case, if Africa were more than four mountains 'broad' from north to south, as explanation (1) would make it.

(*c*) When Cambyses attacks the Ethiopians, at 'the end of the world', 'on the sea to the south of Africa' (iii. 17. 5), he does not march up the Nile, but plunges into the deserts just south of Thebes. Obviously, then, the Nile is here conceived as coming not from the south but from the west. Some have tried to identify the Ethiopians with the Deserters, but this is flatly contradictory to H.

H. is at any rate consistent in this mistake. Its origin is no doubt the fact that the Nile from 21° to 23° S. Lat. flows north-west, and almost down to Philae (which is about 24°) is a little west in direction.

32 The story of the Nasamones (cf. Bunbury, i. 306) is a good instance how valuable at times is a traveller's tale; it reaches H. third-hand, and hence is naturally untrustworthy in detail; but in its main point it seems to be true. There is nothing impossible in a 'well-equipped' native expedition crossing the Sahara and reaching the Niger, which at its nearest point comes within about 1000 miles of the oasis of Fezzan. That Negro land was really reached seems probable from the following points: the natives were entirely strange in speech (§ 6), black (§ 7), very small (§§ 6, 7), 'all wizards' (33. 1). The story is accepted by R. Neumann (pp. 78 seq.) and by St. Martin (pp. 17–18), who, however, brings the explorers north-west to the oasis of Wargla in the Algerian Sahara.

Κυρηναῖοι. That H. had been in Cyrene is almost certain (cf. Introd. § 16).

Etearchus is probably a Greek form of the Nubian Taharka.

Ἄμμωνος. The oracle of the ram-headed (cf. c. 42 for the origin of the figure) Zeus was one of the most famous of antiquity. Croesus consulted it (i. 46), Lysander (Plut. Lys. 20), and above all, Alexander the Great; for it cf. 18. 2; iii. 25 It was in the oasis of Siwah, a great caravan centre. H. is always careful to distinguish it from its parent oracle, that of the Theban Amon, who was also ram-headed. For the connexion of Cyrene and Zeus Ammon cf. the ram-headed god on the coins of Cyrene, Head, H. N. 865, 868.

2 For the Nasamones cf. iv. 172, 182. They had most of the trade with the interior in their hands, and were also well known as free-booters; hence they were a likely people to turn explorers.

Σύρτιν: the greater Syrtis, as always in H.; he does not know the lesser one.

4 **τὰ μέν** (*sc.* *οἰκέουσι*): the construction changes to *παρήκουσι παρά*.

βορηίην: the Mediterranean Sea.

Σολόεντος (cf. iv. 43. 4); Cape Spartel on the coast of Morocco (near Tangier); others make it Cape Cantin (in latitude of Madeira).

τὰ δὲ ὑπέρ: adverbial, as is *τὰ κατύπερθε*; for the threefold belt of North Africa cf. iv. 181 n.; for the Libyans iv. 168 seq.

5 **ζέφυρον**: properly 'westward'; but if it be translated strictly, the travellers would have had nothing but deserts and ultimately the Atlantic before them (*v. s.*). The word, however, is decisive against the theory of the journey, which makes the explorers only reach some river running into Lake Tchad; this would be *due south* of the Fezzan.

6 The story of the 'little men' (cf. iv. 43. 5), the Pygmies, is as old as Homer (Il. iii. 3–7), and recurs repeatedly in ancient writers. It was much doubted by modern writers till the explorations of Du Chaillu, Schweinfurth, and others proved completely the existence of these dwarfs, both north and south of the Equator (cf. Rev. Hist. 47 for a collection of the evidence on the subject by Monceaux). This is one of the best-known of the many instances in which H.'s 'credulity' has been shown to be scientific. H. does not exaggerate their smallness as other writers do; their average height is said to be about 4½ feet. Dwarfs from the south were favourites at the Egyptian court as early as the Old Kingdom (cf. Breasted, A. R. i. 351, of the 6th Dynasty).

7 The 'swamps' (*ἑλέων*) are characteristic of all Central African rivers, and are abundant on the Niger. The town has been supposed to be Timbuctoo, but this was only founded about 1000 A. D.

Crocodiles were supposed to be peculiar to the Nile. So Alexander (Arr. Anab. vi. 1. 2), seeing crocodiles in the Indus, thought that he had found the source of the Nile.

33 H.'s theory that the Nile rose in West Africa never had much popularity till Roman times; it was held by the learned Juba of Mauretania (Plin. v. 51). We may compare it with the theories of forty years ago, which identified the Lualuba, when discovered by Livingstone, with the Nile, till Stanley proved it to be the upper waters of the Congo. H.'s view is based (cf. also 31 n.) on (1) the supposed analogy of the Danube; cf. cc. 33, 34, and especially *ἐκ τῶν ἴσων μέτρων*; as the Danube flows across Europe from the

west, so the Nile is supposed to flow across Libya; (2) the story of the Nasamones.

2 **τοῖσι ἐμφανέσι**: this is one of the maxims of Solon—*τὰ ἀφανῆ τοῖς φανεροῖς τεκμαίρου*; *τε* has no corresponding *καί*; c. 34 continues the account.

3 **Ἴστρος.** H. is much interested in this river, which he describes again in iv. 48–50 (where 'it is the greatest of all rivers that we know'; cf. also iv. 99). Here he supposes it to rise in the extreme west of Europe. This view was held also by Aristotle [Meteor. i. 13 *ἐκ δὲ τῆς Πυρήνης (τοῦτο δ' ἐστὶν ὄρος) ῥέουσιν ὅ τε Ἴστρος καὶ ὁ Ταρτησσός*: the Ister then 'flows through the whole of Europe']. It is difficult to see how the Greeks reconciled it with their knowledge of the Rhone, but it is suggested that this was looked on as a southern offshoot of the Danube. Older geographers had made the Ister rise in the Rhipaean mountains, among the Hyperboreans; H. rightly ignored this mythical explanation, but his information was insufficient for an accurate account.

Πυρήνη: an old town at the foot of the Pyrenees (*hod.* Port Vendres); its trade passed to Massilia, and its name was transferred to the neighbouring mountains (cf. iv. 49. 2 n. for a similar transference of *Ἄλπις* and *Κάρπις*).

Κελτοί. H. derives his information, indirectly at any rate, from he Phoenicians, and therefore speaks of the Celts as being 'outside the Pillars of Hercules', where the Phoenicians found them.

The 'Pillars of Hercules' are not found in Homer, but in Pindar (Olym. iii. 44) they occur, as the limit of the world; by H.'s time they had been definitely fixed. For the legends connecting Heracles with the W. cf. iv. 8 seq. The name was partly due to the identification of Heracles with the Tyrian Melcarth, partly to the tendency (Tac. Germ. 34) to give him 'quidquid ubique magnificum'. Strabo (169–72) discusses the legends as to them; but Pomponius Mela (i. 5. 27), as befits a Spaniard, is the first to give an accurate account of them. So far as they are a reality, they correspond to Calpe and Abila (i.e. Gibraltar and the African Ceuta).

The Kynesioi (*Κύνητες*, iv. 49. 3) are placed by Avienus (201 seq.) on the Guadiana. Their name disappears early from geography.

4 **Ἰστρίην**: near the modern Kustendji: it lies some sixty miles south of the St. George's mouth of the Danube.

34 1 **ἀντίη κεῖται.** H. seems to be trying to construct a rough parallel of longitude (cf. App. XIII, § 4). If he meant that the Ister mouth is about opposite the west mouth of the Nile he is right (they are each about 28° E. Lat.); but his arguments are wrong, for Cilicia Trachea is east of all the Nile mouths and Sinope further east still.

2 **πέντε.** Cf. i. 72. 3 n.

ἐξισοῦσθαι. H. ends with the statement with which he began The comparison is based on the love of symmetry which he tries in vain to banish from his geography (cf. App. XIII, §§ 2, 7); but this does not lead him to distort the facts he knows, e.g. he rightly says that the Ister (iv. 99. 1) runs into the sea πρὸς εὖρον, though obviously this direction does not suit his theory here.

35 *H.'s account of Egypt*, cc. 35–98. This is the most valuable part of Bk. II (cf. App. IX, § 4). It opens with the famous paradox that everything in Egypt is the reverse of what it is elsewhere (§ 2). This point is borrowed by Sophocles (O. C. 337 seq.), who makes Oedipus contrast his daughters and his sons.

ὢ πάντ' ἐκείνω τοῖς ἐν Αἰγύπτῳ νόμοις
φύσιν κατεικασθέντε καὶ βίου τροφάς.

[For the relations between H. and Soph. cf. Introd. p. 7]. But it must be added that there are no verbal similarities in the two passages. The point is made by other Greek writers, e.g. Anaxandrides (Athen. 299), a comic poet circ. 370 B.C., draws an elaborate contrast between Greece and Egypt; his illustrations are from the treatment of animals, e.g. βοῦν προσκυνεῖς, ἐγὼ δὲ θύω τοῖς θεοῖς. It is even more exaggerated later, e.g. by Diod. i. 27 (as to incestuous marriages). Nymphodorus (a third-century writer, F. H. G. ii. 380) absurdly puts the topsyturvydom down to Sesostris, who wished to make his subjects effeminate and so prevent their demanding liberty.

As so large a part of the details furnished by H. are on religious matters, it may be worth while to sum up here the main points in which his account of Egyptian religion is defective or erroneous (cf. Sourdille, R. pp. 367–401):

(1) It quite fails to bring out the importance of certain cults, e.g. of Ptah, of Râ (the Sun), of Hâpi (the Nile), of Thoth (Hermes, who is only mentioned c. 67, Ἑρμέω πόλις), of Hâthor (Aphrodite).

(2) It has far too much uniformity. H. speaks as if all Egypt had the same beliefs; 'but no people is so destitute of the systematic spirit as the Egyptians.' But cf. 43. 2 n.

(3) The religion is made too Greek:

(*a*) It is distinctly anthropomorphic; τὤγαλμα is made everywhere the centre of the temple worship, and H. seems to have conceived of this as usually in human form (46. 2); correspondingly the theriomorphic character of Egyptian religion is underestimated.

(*b*) Greek ideas, e.g. of mysteries and oracles, are wrongly introduced. (Some, however, maintain that the Egyptians really had mysteries in the Greek sense of the word; cf. 171. 1 n.)

(4) The magic, which is so marked a feature of all Egyptian religion, is ignored.

On the other hand, H.'s merits as an observer are now recognized. Erman, the leading German Egyptologist, writes (R. p. 175):

'Where our Egyptian sources fail us, we receive for the first time help from outside; about 450 B.C. H., an indefatigable and careful observer, travelled in Egypt. He observed exactly those things which are of special interest to us.' He proceeds to sketch later Egyptian religion, mainly from the data given by H. (pp. 176–81).

2 **τὰ πολλὰ πάντα**, 'in almost all cases.'

αἱ γυναῖκες: the monuments certainly show women marketing and men weaving, but these are the exceptions: H., struck by the contrasts to Greece, forgets to notice they are only occasional in Egypt.

κρόκην: the 'woof' pushed home to its place in the warp (*στήμων*) by the *κερκίς*. This was done from below by the Greeks and Romans, and from above by the Jews (cf. John xix. 23, the seamless coat of Christ, 'woven from the top'); the Egyptians used both methods, more usually the latter; H. is so far right, but they also used horizontal looms as well as perpendicular ones. For pictures of weaving see Wilkinson, i. 317; ii. 170 (horizontal), 171.

3 **τὰ ἄχθεα κτλ.**: this contrast is wrong; all that can be said is that some loads were carried by men 'on their heads', e. g. the baker in Gen. xl. 16, while the women probably carried their babies 'on their shoulders', like the modern Fellahîn (cf. B. M. G. p. 78).

ἐσθίουσι: the Egyptian upper classes certainly did not eat out of doors; H. only saw the Egyptians of the streets.

4 H. is struck by the fact that he heard of no women in Egypt in positions like that of Hera's priestess at Argos, and he (as often) generalizes from a single point. But he himself knew that there were women in the temples, cf. i. 182. 5 n.; ii. 54. 1. He is quite wrong in his statement; two contrary instances may be quoted; women under the Old Empire especially devoted themselves to Neith and Hathor, while under the Saites, the 'consort of Amon' was the nominal ruler of Thebes.

Wiedemann has a more elaborate explanation. As the Egyptians called all the dead, men and women alike, 'Osiris', and made them male, he thinks that H. was told this, but misunderstood it, and, transferring it from the other world to the present one, supposed that no woman could appear before the gods as priestess. Wiedemann is very fond of charging H. with confusion; he seems to estimate the historian's capacity by his own.

τρέφειν κτλ. Sons at Athens were, as usually in Greece, required to care for their parents; a law of Solon fixed *ἀτιμία* as a penalty for neglecting this duty (Diog. Laert. i. 55). In Egypt the duty of seeing to a parent's grave was certainly imposed on sons; the law in c. 136 implies this. H. is supposed to be referring to the comparative independence of Egyptian women (B. M. G. p. 77), who were able to incur obligations on their own account; struck by this contrast to their dependent position in Greece, he states, in an exaggerated way, that daughters alone had duties to their parents. But this explanation seems very far-fetched.

36 1 **ξυρῶνται.** H. says (37. 2) the priests shaved their whole body every third day; of this there is no evidence on the monuments, but other authorities confirm it (e.g. Diod. iii. 3 (vaguely) and Plut. Mor. 352; de I. et O. 4), and it is probable, in view of the extreme cleanliness of the Egyptians. He is too absolute in saying that all Egyptians shaved (*τέως ἐξυρημένοι*); in fact he himself says (iii. 12. 3) that in few countries are bald men so rare as in Egypt. Probably some classes, e.g. the priests of the New Empire, completely shaved (Erman, E. pp. 218–19), and most had their hair very short. But soldiers wore their natural hair, and so did artists, if we may trust the curious self portrait of Hui (of the time of Amenophis III, eighteenth dynasty, Z. A. S. xlii. 130).

κεκάρθαι. So Achilles (Il. xxiii. 141) cuts off his hair on the death of Patroclus.

ἱκνέεται: *sc.* *κῆδος*, 'whom the grief concerns.'

2 Only the lower classes in Egypt live with animals, and this is true of other countries as well; H.'s generalization is quite wrong.

ὄλυρα. L. & S., s.v., suggest 'rye', but leave the question of its identity with 'spelt', *ζειά* (s.v.), open. Wiedemann thinks it = 'durra', which is often represented in the monuments, while 'spelt' is absent from them. H. here (cf. c. 77) again generalizes wrongly from his guide; the lower classes in Egypt eat bread made of 'durra'; wheat and barley were both also used by the upper classes, but (B. M. G. p. 82) wheat only 'rarely' by the lower.

3 **φυρῶσι.** The monuments (e.g. the bakery of Rameses III, Erman, E. p. 191; but the work was also done by hand) show us dough being kneaded with the feet, as is still done in the south; Strabo, 823, also confirms the statement as to clay and dough. Dung is still collected for burning in Egypt, and in other eastern countries where wood is scarce.

τὰ αἰδοῖα. H. says (with Strabo, 824, and Diodorus), probably rightly (cf. App. IX. 4), that *all* Egyptians were circumcised, Josephus (c. Ap. ii. 13) says only the priests. H. (104. 2, 3 nn.) is certainly wrong in saying that only the Egyptians with the Ethiopians and Colchians, who had learned it from them, practised the rite *ἀπ' ἀρχῆς*; it was widespread among both Semitic and non-Semitic tribes. Its primitive nature is shown by the use of 'flint knives' (Exod. iv. 25; Josh. v. 2, R. V.). Some scholars hold (with H.) that it was introduced on sanitary grounds (*καθαρειότητος εἵνεκα*); but no doubt originally it was a religious rite, by which a male was initiated as a full member of the nation or clan (cf. Encyc. Biblica, s.v.). The Egyptian evidence, which is comparatively scanty, is well summarized in Hastings (Enc. Rel. iii. 670–6); the majority of scholars seem to interpret it as showing that the rite was general in Egypt; some, however, think it refers only to the priests. It is curious that only once do the monuments lay any stress on circumcision, i.e. in describing the repulse of the uncircumcised 'peoples of the sea' by Merenptah; even here the interpretation is disputed.

ἔχει = φορέει; in 81. 1 the two garments worn by men are described as a linen *κιθών* round the legs, and a woollen over-cloak. Roughly speaking, this is confirmed by the monuments, but only for members of the lower classes. H. is much too absolute. So far as men are concerned, he omits the cape introduced under the New Empire, and he quite fails to notice that the *κιθών* round the legs was often worn double (Erman, E. pp. 205–7). As to the Egyptian women, it is true that they, down to the eighteenth dynasty, wore only one close-fitting dress; but in H.'s day two, and sometimes three, garments were worn. The servants and the women in the fields, however, wore only one (Erman, E. pp. 212–16). It is from these that H. generalizes.

4 **κάλους**: H. is right that the Egyptians fastened the 'sheet' of their vessels (for these cf. c. 96) inside. Torr (p. 80), however, says the *κάλος* (Att. *κάλως*) is a 'brailing rope'; these ran across the sail from the yard.

γράμματα. Egyptian writing is generally from right to left; but in drawing the individual signs they usually began on the left (cf. *αὐτοί φασι ἐπὶ δεξιά*). H. is speaking of the direction of the writing as a whole, the natives of the formation of each special letter. He does not mention the older forms of Greek inscriptions, which are from right to left, or *βουστροφηδόν*, though he must have seen them.

There were really three kinds of Egyptian writing: (1) The hieroglyphic, in which the symbols are still recognizable pictures; this was sometimes from left to right, and sometimes up and down (like Chinese). (2) The hieratic, a shortened form of this; a few symbols remain as before, most become purely conventional. (3) The demotic, which developed still further out of the hieratic, and was known by the Egyptians as 'the book script', while the two first were 'the Gods' script'. The enigmatic, which was invented under the eighteenth dynasty, is only a way of writing hieroglyphs in cipher. H. fails to distinguish between (1) and (2), as he well might.

For Egyptian writing cf. B. M. G. p. 36 seq., where an interesting account of the decipherment (pp. 41 f.) is given, with a picture of the famous Rosetta Stone.

37 1 **θεοσεβέες**: the religion (or superstition) of Egypt was proverbial. H. rightly lays stress on their cleanliness and their elaborate ritual.

χαλκέων. The Egyptians did use vessels of bronze, but also of gold, silver, glass, &c. H. again generalizes from insufficient data.

2 **περιτάμνονται.** For shaving and circumcision cf. 36. 1, 3 nn.

3 **λινέην.** It was forbidden to enter a temple wearing a woollen garment (81. 1); H. is right as to the priests wearing linen and sandals of papyrus. Cf. Exod. xxxix. 27–9 for the linen garments of the Jewish priests.

λοῦνται. Chaeremon (fr. 4, F. H. G. iii. 498; Chaeremon was an Egyptian priest(?) of Strabo's time, Strabo, 806) says they washed thrice daily; the difference between him and H. may well be due to variety of rituals. The symbol for a priest in the hieroglyphs is a man washing.

4 **ἀγαθά.** The priestly colleges possessed lands of their own, to the extent (Diod. i. 21) of one-third of all Egypt; from these they and the sacrifices were maintained. H. means by *οὔτε ... δαπανῶνται* that no individual priest had to keep himself. For the priests' property and privileges cf. App. X, § 9, and Erman, E. pp. 298 f.

κρεῶν. Plut. I. et O. 5 says the priests did not eat sheep or swine flesh.

οἶνος. H. says (77. 4) there are no 'vines' in Egypt; here and elsewhere (e. g. cc. 60, 121) he speaks of wine as common. As he mentions the importation of wine (iii. 6. 1) there need be no inconsistency. But certainly the monuments (cf. Erman, E. pp. 198–9) show an extensive cultivation of vines in Egypt, and certain kinds of its wines were famous, e. g. the Mareotic (Hor. Odes, i. 37. 14). Cf., too, Gen. xl. 11; Ps. lxxviii. 47. Probably, therefore, H. is mistaken in c. 77. Others, however (e. g. Brugsch), accept his statement, and argue that the monuments belong to a period before H., and that in his day Greek competition had killed vine-growing in Egypt. This may be partially confirmed by the present state of things there; grapes are still grown, but wine is not made, as 'Egypt is already amply supplied with cheap wines from every part of the Mediterranean' (Baedeker, p. lix).

ἰχθύων. H. is right that the priests were forbidden to eat fish. This food might not be offered in sacrifice; hence the Pythagorean refusal to eat fish may have come from Egypt; for it cf. Plut. Quaes. Conv. viii. 8; Mor. 728 F. But fish was a frequent article of diet among the Egyptians generally, as H. rightly says (77. 4).

5 **κυάμους.** H. is right that the priests did not eat beans; cf. the Pythagoreans again, and Juv. xv. 174 (Pythagoras) 'ventri indulsit non omne legumen', with Mayor's notes for parallels. Diogenes Laertius (viii. 24, 34), in speaking of this Pythagorean abstinence, quotes Aristotle as giving various reasons, the most probable of which is that beans *αἰδοίοις εἰσὶν ὅμοιοι*. The aversion to beans is supposed by some to have been derived by Pythagoras from Egypt (cf. 123 nn.); but it is common in many primitive civilizations, e. g. in India and in early Rome, where beans were supposed to tend to unchastity, while on the other hand they were especially used in funeral banquets; cf. Plut. Rom. Quaes. 95, the introduction to which

(Carabbas Library, by F. B. Jevons, pp. 86–94) has an interesting discussion of the meaning of the superstition; he connects it with 'sympathetic magic'. The Flamen Dialis might neither touch nor name beans; cf. Fowler, Rom. Fest. p. 110. For recent discussions, cf. Gruppe, Myth. Liter. (1908), pp. 370–1.

τρώγουσι: cf. i. 71. 3, 'munch' (like animals), i. e. things uncooked.

ἀρχιερεύς. H. is right here; there were grades of rank among the priests; the highest were in later (i. e. Ptolemaic) times the high-priest or prophet, the overseer of the ritual, and the scribe (28. 1).

τούτου ὁ παῖς. Stein takes this to mean that the son was admitted 'into the college', but 'in the lowest position'. This, however, is not what H. says, and there seem to be clear cases on the monuments of son definitely succeeding father (as other Greeks, e. g. Diod. i. 88, besides H. state). But this was not the rule, and H. as usual generalizes too much.

38 1 **Ἐπάφου**: i. e. Apis (cf. c. 153), the holy calf of Memphis, by which the god, Ptah-Socharis-Osiris, was represented on earth. H. gives in iii. 28. 2, 3 (cf. *ἄλλῳ λόγῳ*, § 2) an account of his origin and marks. It was from the time of the twenty-sixth dynasty that the Apis-cult became especially important; under the Ptolemies, as Serapis, he was the chief god in Egypt. The Greeks identified him with Epaphus, son of Zeus and Io (cf. Aesch. P. V. 850–1); but, apart from Aelian's contradiction (Hist. An. xi. 10), this is obviously mistaken. An account of the Apis is given in Maspero, pp. 37–9. They were buried in the Serapeum at Memphis, rediscovered by Mariette in 1851–2.

Any beast that bore the same marks, e.g. the 'black hair' (Plut. I. et O. 31; Mor. p. 363, says 'white or black'), was holy and could not be sacrificed. So red cattle were properly used as offerings (cf. Numb. xix. 2, the 'red heifer'); but great freedom was allowed, as the monuments show. H.'s account is confused; he seems to mean that no beast could be sacrificed that had black hairs or that had the marks of an Apis; if it had *neither* of these sacred features it was marked as *θύσιμον*.

καθαρόν here = 'fit to be sacrificed', but below (§ 3) 'without the marks of an Apis'.

2 **τεταγμένος.** The title of these priests was 'web' (i. e. pure). The *σφραγιστής* was appointed for the work of inspecting beasts.

The tongue of Apis was marked beneath with a 'beetle' (*scarabaeus*).

κατὰ φύσιν: i. e. not 'double', as in an Apis.

3 The 'seal' used to mark the beast was a kneeling man with hands bound and a knife at his throat. (Plut. *u. s.* p. 363.)

σημαντρίδα: cf. Cic. Verr. Act. ii. 4. 26, 58 for 'cretula' used for seals.

ἀσήμαντον: because the 'unmarked' beast might have been sacred, death was the penalty for killing it.

1 **αὐτοῦ**: i.e. on the altar; but the Egyptians had no altars in the Greek sense.

2 **κείνῃ** = *τῇ ἐκείνου*. Cf. 40. 2 *κοιλίην κείνην* for construction.

φέρουσι is superfluous, as it is repeated (*φέροντες*) in one of the two parts into which the sentence is resolved. The usage of transferring 'curses' to the head of a sacrificed beast may be illustrated from the Jewish scapegoat (Lev. xvi. 21). Plut. I. et O. 31 mentions it of red oxen, but H. is wrong in supposing it to be part of all Egyptian sacrifices, for in early times the head and the haunch were especially chosen to be placed on the tables of offerings. Hence Erman (R. p. 180) thinks the curse was an innovation, due to foreign (i.e. Semitic) influence, as was also the burning described in 40. 3.

4 **ἄλλου οὐδενός.** H. is wrong in making the refusal to eat the head universal; but it was sometimes given away (Wilkinson, pl. xi), and it certainly appears less often than other joints (ib. ii. 28).

1 H., in c. 39, has described the libation and the killing which are common (he thinks) to all sacrifices; he now goes on to the 'cleaning out' (*ἐξαίρεσις*) and the 'burning' which vary; he describes them in the case of a sacrifice to Isis, for to her worship obviously the chapter refers (cf. 61. 1 n.); her festival is the 'greatest' though that of Bast (c. 59. 1) is 'most popular' (*προθυμότατα*).

ταύτην really refers to *ὁρτήν*, but grammatically to *δαίμονα*. *οἱ* in place of the relative *τῇ*: cf. i. 146. 1 (*τῶν* and *σφι*); H. avoids repeating the relative when used in a different case.

2 **κατευξάμενοι**: cf. 39. 2 for imprecations; but *κατεύχομαι* may be used of prayer for blessings.

κοιλίην: translate 'clean out its belly'; for this sense of *ἐξαιρέω* cf. 86. 4; iii. 6. 2.

κείνην = *τὴν κείνου*.

ἐξ ὧν εἷλον. H. (cf. i. 194. 4) often uses this tmesis of the empiric aorist, in describing customs, &c.

ὀσφύν. The Greeks offered the 'rump', the Egyptians reserved it.

4 **ἀποτύψωνται**: 'when they have done mourning,' not 'beating themselves', as Macaulay. Cf. 73. 4 *ἀποπειρηθῇ* for force of *ἀπό*, and 42. 6, 61. 1 for *τύπτονται*, but in these places it has an accusative.

τά: i.e. the parts not burned, i.e. legs, rump, &c.

1 The cow was the living symbol of Isis-Hathor, represented sometimes as a cow, at others as a woman with a cow's head, at others as a horned woman. She was worshipped all over Egypt (cf. the emphatic *πάντες ὁμοίως*). The Greeks usually identified her with Demeter, but also with other goddesses. Isis is important in the Egyptian pantheon as the sister and wife of Osiris, and mother of Horus. H. is quite right that in Egypt (as among the Hindoos) cows were not sacrificed.

2 Cf. i. 1 for Io's story; H. avoids the usual Greek mistake of

confusing her with Isis. Some make 'Io' to be Egyptian = 'the moon goddess', but 'the moon' is masculine in Egyptian.

3 **οὔτ' ἀνήρ.** For the separateness of the Egyptians cf. Gen. xliii. 32, the feast to Joseph's brethren.

4 **θάπτουσι.** It is wrong to say that dead cows were thrown into the river; this was only done when they were given to crocodiles. On the other hand the heads of oxen are found buried as H. describes. He is wrong in saying they were *all* removed to Prosopitis (cf. c. 67 for a similar mistake); but his account of the composite burial is clearly confirmed by the mummies, which often contain the remains of several beasts, e. g. one found at Abûsir was made up of seven (Maspero, Caus. p. 247). Erman (R. 177) says generally in reference to animal burial 'H. is certainly correct in these facts'.

τὸ κέρας . . . ἀμφότερα : in apposition to *ἔρσενας*.

5 **Prosopitis.** This island lay between the Canopic and the Sebennytic Niles and a canal, in the south of the Delta. The Greeks made their last stand there, after the suppression of the revolt of Inaros (Thuc. i. 109. 4).

Aphrodite corresponds to the Egyptian Hathor; her symbol also was a cow; her chief temple was at Denderah. Her name is probably found in 'Atarbechis', which may well be the *Ἀφροδίτης πόλις* of Strabo (802), in the Prosopitic nome.

42 1 **Διός.** Originally a local god, Amon became, with the rise of Thebes, the great god of Egypt, and was identified with the sun, as Amon RA. The Greeks therefore naturally called him 'Zeus', and this was the more easy as the ram was sacred to Zeus (cf. Farnell, G. C. i. 94–5). From his oracle at Thebes, which was itself of little importance, was derived that of Zeus Ammon in the oasis of Siwah (cc. 32 n., 55).

For Amon's temple at Thebes cf. 143 n. He is occasionally represented as *κριοπρόσωπος* (cf. Perrot et Chipiez, i. 395), but it is not his usual form.

2 **ὁμοίως.** Various as were the cults of Egypt, Osiris and Isis were worshipped everywhere, at any rate in later times, i.e. in the days of H. This was partly due to political influences, i.e. the decline of Thebes which worshipped Amon, and the rise of Sais, partly to the confusion of Osiris with the sun-god (cf. Sourdille, R. 58–62). Osiris was usually identified by the Greeks with Dionysus, but also with Zeus, Hades, Eros, and other gods. The main points of resemblance to Dionysus are: (1) Osiris is originally a corn god (cf. Frazer, Attis, &c. pp. 268 f.; but Egyptologists doubt this); (2) his mutilation by Set is parallel to that of Dionysus by the Titans; (3) his resurrection cf. Plut. I. et O. c. 35, p. 364 *ὁμολογεῖ τὰ Τιτανικὰ* (in the story of Dionysus) *τοῖς λεγομένοις Ὀσίριδος διασπασμοῖς καὶ ταῖς ἀναβιώσεσι.*

There is a marked similarity between the Dionysiac *Ἀνθεστήρια* and the rites of Osiris; both were a combination of joy and of mourning, of Shrove Tuesday and of All Souls' Day (cf. Maspero, Caus. pp. 276–9, who discusses Foucart's theory that the rites of Dionysus were Egyptian in origin; but against this see Farnell, G. C. v. 174 seq.). For the Osiris myth cf. 62 nn.

Mendes lay in the north-east Delta, near the Mendesian arm of the Nile; it was an important seat of the cult of Osiris; for his worship there cf. 46 n.

3 **Ἡρακλέα.** The Egyptian Heracles is variously identified with Shu, the burning sun, or with Chunsu, a moon-god, the god-son of the Theban triad.

κριὸν ἐκδείραντα. No native authority confirms H.'s story, which seems to be an attempt to explain the ram-headed figure of Amon. Wiedemann thinks it borrowed from Hecataeus, but there is no reason to believe this. It is not unlikely that the story may be connected with the meaning of the name 'Amon', which = 'the concealed one' (Manetho in Plut. de Is. 9; Mor. 354). At any rate the idea is Greek; so Pythagoras, when initiated in Crete, put on a black fleece (Porphyry V. Pyth.).

4 **φωνήν**: 'using a speech between that of the two nations.' Cf. Th. vi. 5. 1 for the full construction.

5 **τὴν ἐπωνυμίην ἐποιήσαντο** forms one idea, 'called themselves,' and so takes cogn. acc., *τοὔνομα*, cf. *καλέεται ἐπωνυμίην* (i. 14. 3 n.).

6 Brugsch says this feast is part of the great festival of the Theban Amon, which lasted five days; but there is no evidence on the monuments that the ceremony described by H. took place then. The ceremony seems to rest on the Egyptian idea that a god must die when he has begotten a son; Amon therefore, in the form of his ram, is killed when he has seen his son Heracles. Legrain (R. de T. E. xxviii. 1. 46) found many sheep bones at Karnak, so far confirming H.'s statement.

For **τύπτονται τὸν κριόν** cf. 40. 4 n.

1 For the '**twelve gods**' and the '**eight gods**' (§ 4) cf. c. 145 n. To H. the Greek Heracles is a mortal, the son of Amphitryon; he neglects the story that he is son of Zeus, according to his usual practice (cf. vi. 53. 2 n.). He makes the name Egyptian; the usual derivation was 'he to whom Hera gives glory'. H. here does what later was usual among mythologers, i.e. multiplies personalities to explain variant legends; so Varro actually counted forty-three bearers of the name 'Hercules'.

2 **οἱ θέμενοι** for *οἳ ἔθεντο*, i.e. the poets, Homer and Hesiod (c. 53).

οἱ γονέες. Heracles' parents were both descended from Aegyptus, brother of Danaus, who came from Egypt (c. 171). For the genealogy and its importance in H.'s chronology cf. App. XIV. 2.

3 The argument is: had the Egyptians learned any divine names from the Greeks, they would have been those of the sea gods, Poseidon and the Dioscuri, but these are unknown to the Egyptian pantheon; *a fortiori* then it is unlikely that they learned that of

'Heracles'. The words ὥστε τούτων . . . Ἡρακλέος restate more strongly the preceding argument.

4 The reign of Amasis, 570–526 B.C., is mentioned, as marking the end of Egyptian independence.

44 1 This passage is interesting as one of the few in which H. tells us as to himself; we infer from it with some certainty (1) that he was in Egypt before he went to Tyre; (2) that he was a man of wealth, able to travel in pursuit of special knowledge.

The Heracles of Tyre is Melcart, the Baal of the O.T., a sun-god.

2 **στῆλαι.** The importance of columns in early worship is well known; cf. Evans, Mycenaean Tree and Pillar Cult, J. H. S. 1901, and 1 Kings vii. 21 (Jachin and Boaz).

σμαράγδου. This 'emerald' was famous as the largest on record (Theoph. de lapid. 25), who adds εἰ μὴ ψευδὴς σμάραγδος. It is impossible to believe in so large a stone; perhaps it was a piece of green jasper or malachite. What is certain is that Wiedemann is wrong, who supposes it to have been a forgery of glass, and this in one of the richest temples of the East! Whether the light was really that of the emerald (as Stein) or due to reflection (as Larcher), can hardly be decided.

λάμποντος μέγαθος Stein explains = μέγαθος (*acc. resp.*) τοσούτου ὥστε λάμπειν τὰς νύκτας; but some conjecture seems necessary.

3 **ἄλλο.** This second temple was probably founded by Thasian merchants; for Thasos as a Phoenician colony cf. vi. 47 n.

καί emphasizes πέντε: 'at least five'; cf. v. 59 for a similar reckoning of five generations from Cadmus to the period before the Trojan War, and App. XIV. 2.

5 At Sicyon Heracles was worshipped (Paus. ii. 10. 1) both as a god and as a hero, with variant ritual. The Athenians claimed to have first worshipped him as a god (Diod. iv. 39). H. carefully distinguishes between θύειν (for gods) and ἐναγίζειν ('inferias offerre', for heroes, cf. i. 167. 2).

45 1 **καὶ ἄλλα** answers to καὶ ὅδε ὁ μῦθος in next line. H.'s scornful attitude to his countrymen is characteristic; in this book we may compare cc. 2 (rationalization of story of Psammetichus), 16 (as to the boundaries of Egypt), 20–2 (as to the rise of the Nile), 134 (as to Rhodopis), 143 (as to the genealogy of Hecataeus). There is no need to suppose that he is borrowing here from Hecataeus, who expresses a similar view in his genealogies, cf. frag. 332 (F. H. G. i. 25) οἱ γὰρ Ἑλλήνων λόγοι πολλοί τε καὶ γελοῖοι. H. would be especially glad to reject a story attributing human sacrifices to Egypt.

ὁ μῦθος. The story of Busiris, to which H. here refers, occurs first in Pherecydes (Fr. 33, F. H. G. i. 79), and was made by Euripides the subject of a satyric drama; it occurs frequently in classical writers. Busiris is really the name of a town ('house of Osiris'), 59. 1, 61. 1.

κατάρχοντο: i.e. by cutting the lock of hair.

2 H. seems right in denying that human sacrifices were performed in Egypt in his day; no exact representations of them have been found on the monuments, and the massacre of captives before a god after a victory is only a partial parallel. There are, however, traditions as to them in the past; cf. Diod. i. 88 (there were human sacrifices *τὸ παλαιόν* at the tomb of Osiris) and Porph. De Abstin. ii. 55 (Amosis put down the custom at Heliopolis). Manetho (in Plut. Is. et Os. 73) speaks of human sacrifices 'in the dog-days', but uses the past tense; cf. Frazer, G. B. ii. 255, for their meaning. More valuable evidence still is given by the figures of slaves (Ushabti 'answerers') found in the tombs of the wealthy. (For a fine collection of these in the Ashmolean cf. Guide, p. 87.) No doubt originally the slaves themselves were killed with their masters.

Probably the 'Nile bride', a noble maiden, who is said to have been thrown into the Nile annually before the canals were opened (Maspero, i. 24 and n.), was a similar symbolic representation of an old custom.

3 **εὐμένεια.** H. fears that he may be thought to be depreciating the divine Heracles.

1 **δή** refers back to 42. 2; for the 'eight gods' cf. 145 n.

2 **αἰγοπρόσωπον**: translate 'with goat's head and a he-goat's legs'; *τράγος* is used because *αἴξ* is common in gender, *v. i.* *σέβονται πάντας τοὺς αἶγας κτλ.*

ἥδιον: a weakened comparative; cf. Latin 'non erit melius'; the meiosis is characteristic of Greek courtesy; cf. 47. 2; i. 187. 2 for similar uses.

αἶγας. H. and other Greeks (e.g. Diod. i. 84; Pindar *v. i.*) say the beast was a goat, and they are confirmed by the nome coins (cf. B. M. Cat. Alexandria, p. 347); the monuments, however, show the beast as a ram. Perhaps the monuments are wrong (Sourdille, R. p. 166); cf. the mistake of representing both wolf and dog by a jackal.

The beast was the incarnation (*not* the symbol as H. thinks; cf. *οὔτι τοιοῦτον*) of Osiris, considered as the giver of fruitfulness; so it is called 'the lord of maidens, the begetting ox'. H. is wrong in connecting it with Pan; the confusion is due to the fact that Min of Chemmis (c. 91 n.), whom the Greeks usually identified with Pan, is goat-headed.

τούτων: i.e. *τῶν αἰγῶν*; the sentence repeats *σέβονται κτλ.*

ἐκ δὲ τούτων εἷς, *si vera lectio*, translate 'Of the he-goats there is one especially honoured, and when he dies, great mourning', &c.; but this is very harsh.

4 **ἀναφανδόν.** The 'marvel' was in the openness of the act; the Greeks believed that unnatural intercourse with animals regularly took place in secret at Mendes. The story is as old as Pindar (fr. 215; Strabo, 802). The fact is probably true, and was due to the belief that the ram was the god incarnate (cf. the Jewish prohibitions against such abominations, Lev. xx. 15-16).

47 1 **ἀπ' ὧν ἔβαψε**: cf. 40. 2 n., and *κατ' ὧν ἐκάλυψε* (§ 3).

μιαρόν. H. is quite right as to the dislike of swine; they are very little represented on the monuments (but *v. i.*).

ἐόντες: concessive, 'although they are.' Cf. c. 164 for caste of swineherds.

2 Manetho confirms the fact of this swine offering at a lunar festival. **Selene** (= 'Nekhebet') was the deity of El Kab, and on a tomb there large herds of swine are mentioned. (Ann. du Service des Antiq. xi. 163). Others suppose that *Σελήνη* here = Isis; cf. 41. 1 n. for her horns. H. is obscure here; he says that swine's flesh was eaten in honour of Dionysus, but in c. 48 he seems to imply it was sent away uneaten; perhaps then the flesh was eaten in honour of Dionysus and Selene *together*, but not of Dionysus alone.

εὐπρεπέστερος. For the comparative cf. 46. 2 n.; for the sentiment, i.e. reverential silence, cf. 3. 2 n. Plutarch gives the story (I. et O. c. 8, p. 354) that Typhon was pursuing a pig when he found the coffin of Osiris, and scattered its contents; he says, however, this story was rejected by many, and it is obviously a later invention.

καταγίζει (cf. 44. 5 n.) implies that it was a funeral sacrifice, i.e. connected with the dead Osiris.

3 **σταιτίνας.** This offering of symbolic 'dough' cakes is a genuine native custom, and is found elsewhere, e.g. among the Chinese the poor make paper votive offerings (cf. too Plut. Luc. 10 for it at Cyzicus). For such symbolism cf. Tylor, P. C. ii. 405.

48 1 **δορπίῃ**: the evening meal; hence Schweighäuser translates 'the eve of the feast'. This was the name of the first day of the Apaturia, which began with a meal at 6 p.m. The Egyptian day began at midnight, not 6 p.m., and Stein translates 'the closing feast' (i.e. the *δόρπον* here ended, *not* began, the festival). But H.'s words 'they keep the *rest of* the feast' imply that he at least thought that the *δόρπον* came first.

2 For phalli at the Greek Dionysia cf. Farnell, G. C. v. 125, and Aristoph. Ach. 260–1. For their meaning, as assisting the powers of nature by sympathetic magic, cf. E. B.[11] s. v. Phallicism.

νεῦον strictly should be a gen. absolute; but as *τὸ αἰδοῖον* is a part of the *ἀγάλματα*, it stands in loose apposition; cf. i. 52 n.

3 For the *ἱρὸς λόγος* cf. Plut. Mor. 365; I. et O. 18 *μόνον τῶν μερῶν τοῦ 'Οσίριδος* (cf. 62 n.) *τὴν Ἶσιν οὐχ εὑρεῖν τὸ αἰδοῖον . . . ἀντ' ἐκείνου μίμημα ποιησαμένην καθιερῶσαι τὸν φαλλόν, ᾧ καὶ νῦν ἑορτάζειν τοὺς Αἰγυπτίους.*

49 1 **ἐξηγησάμενος**, 'taught'; cf. *κατηγησάμενος inf.*

ἀτρεκέως refers to whole clause, not to any special word; translate 'to speak accurately'.

σοφισταί: his descendants, e.g. Amphiaraus, and still more the Orphic teachers (cf. 81 n.) of Greece, e.g. Onomacritus.

Melampus was placed in the fourth generation after Hellen.

According to later writers he was an Egyptian or had travelled in Egypt; H. does not carry his rationalization of the myth so far.

ποιεῦσι τὰ ποιεῦσι: an euphemism for the obscenities of the Dionysia, which Heraclitus (fr. 127) had called *ἀναιδέστατα*.

2 **συστῆσαι.** H. excludes the miraculous elements of the story (e.g. in Apollodorus i. 9. 11), which make Melampus learn his lore from young snakes and from meeting Apollo. H.'s argument is as follows: the similarity of Dionysiac worship in Greece and Egypt might be explained by three hypotheses (cf. *ἂν ἦν* below for one apodosis): (*a*) the Greeks might have borrowed from the Egyptians; (*b*) the resemblance might be accidental (cf. *συμπεσεῖν*, 'agree by mere chance'); (*c*) the Egyptians might have borrowed from Greece. Having accepted (*a*), H. proceeds to refute (*b*) and (*c*); (*b*) is rendered impossible by the facts that Dionysiac rites were not 'like any other Greek rites, *ὁμότροπα*, and were known to have been 'introduced lately' (*νεωστί*); (*c*) he rejects without argument (*οὐ μὲν οὐδὲ φήσω*).

τοῖς Ἕλλησι = *τοῖς τῶν Ἑλλήνων τρόποις*.

νεωστί. The recent origin of the rites was shown by legends like those of Lycurgus and of Pentheus; that Dionysus was a later element in the Greek pantheon is usually accepted by scholars; cf. Farnell, G. C. v. 87-92.

3 **Cadmus** was usually placed three generations earlier than Melampus; he was the grandfather of Dionysus. Perhaps it was this which determined H.'s choice of legend; he wished to make the introduction of the new rite into Greece coincide in time with the birth of the god. Cadmus, as Stein says, was said to be (iv. 147 nn.) a Phoenician, not an Egyptian; but H. obviously thinks Cadmus must have known the rites of Egypt, as it was a neighbour of Tyre; so (c. 116. 1, 2) he proves that Homer knew Paris had been in Egypt, because he mentions his visit to Sidon.

καλεομένην: cf. Thuc. i. 12. 3 for the Greek tradition that Boeotia did not receive its name till sixty years after the fall of Troy, i.e. long after the time of Cadmus.

1 **οὐνόματα.** H. does not mean that the actual name came from Egypt; he himself continually mentions the difference of name, e.g. Amon and Zeus (c. 42). But the name of a deity involved his personality, and so H.'s position is that the Greek deities were defined, and their attributes and cult settled, by Egypt; for nameless gods cf. Fowler, Rel. Exp. of Rom. p. 119. H. is merely giving the inferences of himself and others, not genuine tradition; deeply impressed with the antiquity of Egypt, he was prepared to derive everything from it.

πυνθανόμενος: e.g. at Dodona (c. 53. 3). H. contrasts his 'inferences' (*δοκέω*) with the results of inquiry.

2 Broadly speaking, H. is right that there are no Egyptian equivalents for these Greek divinities. For Poseidon and the Dioscuri cf. 43. 2; the Egyptians hated the sea, and had no sea deities. H.'s

statement is quite inaccurate on one point only; the Egyptian Maa, the goddess of justice, corresponds to Themis. It is true that an inscription at Philae (C. I. G. 4893) equates Hera with Satis and Hestia with Anukis; but Satis is really quite unimportant in the Egyptian pantheon, and Anukis is only important in Upper Egypt.

For the Libyan origin of Poseidon cf. iv. 188.

3 νομίζω is here used with dative on analogy of χράομαι. H.'s statement as to the absence of hero worship is accurate only in the sense that there was no subordinate order of demigods in the Egyptian pantheon corresponding to the Greek ἥρωες. But for the birth of mortals from gods cf. c. 143 n., and the god, Imhotep, whom the Greeks identified with their Asclepius, had been actually a physician under the third dynasty.

51 1 Ἑρμέω. The ithyphallic Hermes, as a god of fruitfulness, was represented at the street corners in Athens (Thuc. vi. 27. 1); Pausanias (iv. 33. 4) says the rest of Greece learned this form of statue from the Athenians. It is true that there were no such statues in Egypt.

For H.'s views on the Pelasgians cf. App. XV; he uses the name here of the later Pelasgian settlement in Attica (as in i. 57. 2), not of the original Pelasgian inhabitants of Greece.

2 These later Pelasgians began to be considered Greek after their settlement in Attica; the Athenians 'already ranked as Greeks' (for τελεῖν ἐς cf. vi. 53. 1).

The Cabiri (cf. Daremberg and Saglio, s. v.) are one of the most difficult subjects in mythology. The name is probably connected with καίω = 'the burners'; so Aeschylus' tragedy on the subject seems to have borne the name of Κάειροι. Others connect the name with a Semitic root = 'mighty', and derive the Greek Cabiri from those of Phoenicia, which became familiar to the Greeks as the figure-heads of galleys. (So Bloch in Rosch. ii. 2540.) But the Phoenician Cabiri were eight in number, those of Greece vary from two to four. Probably then the Cabiri belong to the early stages of Greek religion and are in this sense rightly called 'Pelasgic'. They were worshipped in many places. e.g. Lemnos, Thebes (cf. Frazer, v. 136 seq., for their temple there), as local genii, subordinate to the Olympian gods; so H. makes them (iii. 37) the 'sons of Hephaestus'. But in Samothrace they had remained 'cosmic deities of the first rank', and were identified with Hermes and Hephaestus. As the symbol of the ithyphallic Hermes shows, they were connected with fruitfulness. Some have identified the Cabiri with the Phoenician Παταῖκοι (iii. 37. 2 n.), also used as figure-heads, but H. expressly distinguishes them, in spite of their likeness. He had obviously been himself initiated in their mysteries (cf. Aristoph. Pax 277–8).

3 πρότερον: i. e. before they were driven out by the Samians (Strabo, 457).

τά in loose apposition to λόγον. The obscene story is referred to Cic. de Nat. Deor. iii. 22.

1 The Pelasgi worshipped divine powers, without having definite names for them (cf. 50. 1 n.), e.g. the sun, but not Apollo. So Preller (Rom. Myth. i. 48, 3rd ed.) says of early Roman religion, 'most of the names of the oldest Roman gods have such a shifting indefinite meaning that they can hardly be regarded as proper names'; he quotes this passage in illustration.

ἔθυον δὲ πάντα: translate 'in all their offerings called on gods'.

θεούς. H. forgets that he himself had proved (i. 57. 2) that the Pelasgi were βάρβαρον γλῶσσαν ἱέντες; his derivation from the root of τίθημι is as worthless as that of Plato (Crat. 397 D) from the root of θέω (I run).

2 For the oracle of Zeus at Dodona cf. Il. xvi. 233 Ζεῦ ἄνα, Δωδωναῖε, Πελασγικέ (cf. App. XV. 2). It was admittedly the oldest in Greece; this fact is one of the arguments for the view that the Greeks entered their country from the north-west, not from the east. For the oracle cf. P. Gardner (N. C. Gk. H. c. 14), Frazer (ii. 159–60), and Farnell (G. C. i. 38 seq.). Zeus, who is prominently an oracular god nowhere else in Greece proper, had the titles of Νάιος (i.e. a rain spirit) and Εὔδενδρος, i.e. he lives in the tree and speaks in its rustling. (For tree-worship cf. Tylor, P. C. ii[3], p. 218; and Evans, J. H. S. 1901.)

53 This chapter is most interesting for estimating H.'s own views. It is clear that: (1) he has definite opinions as to chronology; Homer and Hesiod are contemporaries and four hundred years before his own day. (2) He recognizes the importance of Homer and Hesiod as fixing the canon of Greek mythology. Cf. his predecessor Xenophanes πάντα θεοῖς ἀνέθηκαν Ὅμηρός θ' Ἡσίοδός τε | οἷ πλεῖστ' ἐφθέγξαντο θεῶν ἀθεμίστια ἔργα. It is not fair to blame H. (as Strabo does, 43) for not distinguishing the systematic theogony of Hesiod from the poetic treatment of Homer; this distinction is irrelevant to his point of view here. (3) He clearly distinguishes them from the other epic poets (cf. c. 117). But on the other hand it is equally clear that: (1) his date is his own, not based on tradition nor universally accepted; (2) he does not realize that Homer and Hesiod simply gave form to ideas which had been gradually taking shape before their time, and that they embodied former lays in their works; (3) still less has he any doubts of the historic reality of the events described by the poets.

To sum up, his opinions have no objective value for the solution of the Homeric question, interesting though they are as showing the ideas of an educated Greek in the fifth century.

2 ἐπωνυμίας: i.e. patronymics, e.g. Κρονίδης, local names, &c. Others make a contrast between θεογονίην (Hesiod) and ἐπωνυμίας κτλ. (Homer), explaining ἐπωνυμίας as = such epithets as γλαυκῶπις; but

this seems forced. For the whole point cf. Hes. Theog. 73 (Ζεὺς) εὖ δὲ ἕκαστα Ἀθανάτοις διέταξεν ὁμῶς καὶ ἐπέφραδε τιμάς.

3 **πρότερον**: i.e. Linus, Orpheus, Musaeus.

τὰ πρῶτα: i.e. c. 52, as opposed to his own special views in this chapter (53). H. is careful to distinguish tradition from his private inference (cf. emphatic ἐγώ).

54 Sourdille (H. E. 184) well summarizes the differences between Greek and Egyptian oracles, of which H. is quite unconscious. (1) All Egyptian gods, not seven (cf. c. 83) only, could prophesy; (2) but their responses were for king or priest, as representing the people, not for all, as in Greece; (3) nor had they a special μαντεῖον, apart from their ordinary temple. The oracles H. speaks of in Egypt were those of Greek settlers.

χρηστηρίων. H. proceeds from the Greek gods to the Greek oracles; some of these also in Greece he thinks of Egyptian origin. The story which he gives of the founding of Dodona is a rationalization of the myth (given in c. 55). Sayce maintains (J. of P. xiv. 275) that the 'priests in Thebes' that H. talked with were 'ciceroni' connected with some temple of the Theban Amun in the north of Egypt, and that H. never was in Thebes itself. Though there is no reason to doubt H.'s veracity, the story is clearly of Greek origin; H. may have heard it in Greece, and his guides would answer in the affirmative all his 'leading questions'; the mention of 'Phoenician robbers' is certainly more suited to Greeks than to natives of Upper Egypt. But Sourdille (E. pp. 175–89) thinks that there was probably a Greek community at Thebes, which had set up an oracle professing to be that of the Theban god (cf. 57. 3 n.); to this H. applied, thinking in all good faith that it was native (cf. the repeated emphasis laid on his informants, 54. 1, 55. 1), though it was really Greek.

The story as to the 'priestesses' is an attempt to turn myth into history; it substitutes natural causes for the supernatural ones, which were, to those among whom the myths grew up, the real essence of the narrative. For a criticism of such rationalizing in H. and in Thucydides cf. Grote, i. 381 seq.

55 1 **προμάντιες.** In Homer (Il. xvi. 235) those in charge of the oracle are men, ὑποφῆται; Strabo (329) says women were appointed later.

2 **φηγόν**: cf. 57. 3 n.

3 H. seems to have met these priestesses himself. Cf. Intr. p. 22.

56 1 **τῆς Ἑλλάδος** depends on ἐς Θεσπρωτούς.

τῆς αὐτῆς ταύτης emphasizes the fact that the country was the same though the name changed; cf. i. 144. 1.

2 **πεφυκυίῃ**: the 'natural' oak is a feature in all the stories.

3 **κατηγήσατο.** The change to *oratio recta* is odd.

57 1 **πελειάδα.** 'To speak like a bird' was a Greek expression for speaking unintelligibly. Cf. Aes. Ag. 1050 δίκην χελιδόνος ἀγνῶτα φωνὴν βάρβαρον κεκτημένη, (contemptuously) of Cassandra, and

Aristoph. Ran. 681 Θρηκία χελιδών, of Cleophon. Various suggestions are made to explain H.'s unusual rationalism; there is supposed to be a reference to the fact that the aged were called in Epirus πέλειοι (Hesych.); others suggest that the priestesses were called 'doves' metaphorically (cf. the title μέλισσαι for the priestesses of Ephesian Artemis), and that the myth grew up to explain the title. Such suggestions are ingenious but unnecessary. H.'s conjectures are quite in accordance with Hellenic ideas, and also quite valueless.

3 At Dodona the voice of Zeus was heard in the leaves of the oak; cf. Od. xiv. 327–8 ὄφρα θεοῖο | ἐκ δρυὸς ὑψικόμοιο Διὸς βουλὴν ἐπακούσαι. So at Thebes the wind blew always in a prophetic grotto except for one day in each month (Hellan. fr. 152; F. H. G. i. 66).

ἱρῶν. There were two kinds of divination from sacrifices, viz. δι' ἐμπύρων and ἱεροσκοπία (watching the fire and examining the entrails); no trace of either has been found in Egypt.

58 H. proceeds to another borrowing, that of processions, &c.

There are many points of resemblance between the religious festivals of Greece and of Egypt. An important part of these in the latter country were the processions (πομπαί) in which the image of the deity was taken to visit (προσαγωγαί) another deity; others explain προσαγωγή=πρόσοδος, i. e. the procession to the temple with sacrifices, &c. For the whole cf. Claudian (de Quar. Hon. Cons. 570 seq.):

> Sic numina Memphis
> In vulgus proferre solet: penetralibus exit
> Effigies, . . .
> . . . Nilotica sistris
> Ripa sonat.

δὲ ἄρα=the more usual δ' ὦν, i.e. whether the divination be like or not, 'at all events' the festivals have much in common.

59 H. now proceeds (cc. 59–63) to describe six famous festivals: these were celebrated throughout all Egypt on the same day (62. 2); but every district in Egypt had its special festivals. The fact that H. says nothing of the festival of the rising of the Nile is urged (Sourdille, E. p. 7) with good reason as showing that he arrived in Egypt after the inundation had begun; cf. 19. 2 n.

1 **οὐκ ἅπαξ.** H. shows the inferiority of Greece; there, of the four great festivals, the Olympian and the Pythian came once in four years, and the Isthmian and Nemean twice in the same period, i. e. only six festivals in four years.

Bubastis, *hod.* Tell Basta (¼ mile south of Zagazig), was a town in the East Delta on the Pelusiac Nile. It was the capital of the twenty-second dynasty. H. obviously had a weakness for it (cf. 40. 1 n.); he calls its temple 'the most attractive' that he knew (137. 5); cf. also 154. 3 for the planting of the Greek mercenaries near. The goddess worshipped here was Bast; H. and other classical writers give her tne name of her town, instead of her own.

He wrongly identifies her with Artemis; she had more in common with Aphrodite, e.g. in the licentious nature of her festival (60. 2). She was represented with the head of a cat, like Pacht in Middle Egypt, and Sechemt at Thebes and Memphis.

60 1 No confirmation is found on the monuments for this feast at Bubastis; but there was a similar one for five days, in the month Thoth, at Denderah, the details of which correspond closely to the description here.

The **κρόταλα** and flutes are genuine Egyptian instruments; *κρόταλα*='rattles'; others translate 'cymbals'; H. does not mention the *σεῖστρον*, which is the most common of all. Clapping of hands, to mark time, was as common in ancient as it is in modern Egypt.

3 **καί** makes the figure more emphatic (cf. 44. 4). The number is exaggerated; Wiedemann well compares the 70,000 pilgrims who, according to Mohammedan belief, go to Mecca every year, and whose number is made up by angels, if it would otherwise fall short.

61 1 **Busiris.** There were several places of this name, i.e. 'town of Osiris'. H. (59. 2) says this one was 'in the midst of the Delta', i.e. he probably means the capital of the Busiris nome, on the left bank of the Sebennytic Nile.

πρότερον. Cf. c. 40; for *τύπτονται* cf. 40. 4; it takes an accus. ad sensum here as in 42. 6.

τόν: Osiris, whom (as usual, cf. 86. 2; 132. 2) H. does not name.

2 The Carians were the mercenaries of Psammetichus (152. 5). They may have brought the usage of self-mutilation into the Egyptian rite; cf. for it the 'prophets of Baal' at Mount Carmel (1 Kings xviii. 28); it was expressly forbidden to the Jews (Lev. xix. 28).

62 1 The ruins of Sais lie near Sâ el Hagar, about half a mile east of the Rosetta Nile. Neith, 'the mother of the sun,' who was especially worshipped at Sais, was identified with Athena; like her, she has for emblems (on the coins of the Saitic nome) an owl on her right hand and a lance in her left. Her worship spread widely under the twenty-sixth dynasty, when Sais was the capital of Egypt. In her attributes and her representation on the monuments she is another form of Isis; hence her feast, here described by H., is a part of the mourning for Osiris (like that at Busiris, c. 61).

2 **τὰ λύχνα.** For this 'feast of lamps' cf. Plut. I. et O. 39 *βοῦν διάχρυσον* (cf. 132. 1) *ἱματίῳ μέλανι περιβάλλοντες ἐπὶ πένθει τῆς θεοῦ* (Isis) *δεικνύουσι* for four days; then on the 19th of Athyr (November) the body of Osiris is found with loud shouts. Cf. Juv. viii. 29 'Exclamare libet populus quod clamat Osiri Invento' (cf. Mayor's notes for references). The lights, then, are to assist the goddess in her search; the story is splendidly used by Milton in the Areopagitica, where he compares the search for Truth to the search of Isis for Osiris. Others, however, see in the 'lights' simply a reference to Osiris as 'lord of the Sun' (Bähr). Brugsch and Sourdille (R

85–7) identify the 'feast of lights' with another Osiris feast, that in the month Choiak, at the time of the winter solstice. Cf. Inscrip. of Denderah, R. T. E. et A. iii. 49, iv. 27 for the '34 boats' and their '365 lights'. As the feast described by H. is clearly connected with Osiris, either of these views is more probable than that of Maspero (p. 794), that it is the Egyptian 'All Souls Day' (the 17th of Thoth) that is here referred to. The festivals of cc. 61 and 62, though both Osiris feasts, are probably distinct from each other.

ἐμβάφιον: a 'vessel' full of salt steeped with oil; hence the wick burned slowly. It seems better to explain it thus than to suppose a reference to the oil of the *σιλλικύπρια* (c. 94), which is separated from the moisture it contains by the use of salt (cf. Plin. xv. 25 'sine igni et aqua sale aspersum exprimitur').

For the story of Osiris cf. Plut. I. et O. cc. 13–19 and Erman, R. p. 32 seq. (mainly from Egyptian sources). It is, briefly, as follows (the references in H. ii are inserted after each point): Osiris, the beneficent ruler and civilizer, was killed by his brother Set (Typhon). (For Osiris' *πάθεα* cf. c. 171.) His wife, Isis, set out to search for his body, leaving her son, Horus (Apollo), at Buto to be protected from Set (c. 156). The body of Osiris was found, but Set again obtained possession of it, and cut it into fourteen pieces, which were only rediscovered by Isis after long and patient search (cf. cc. 47, 48, 62 nn.). Wherever she found a part she erected a tomb; but the various members were reunited, and restored magically to life by the jackal god Anubis. As Osiris, however, could not rule a second time on earth, he became lord of the other world, Amenti, 'the hidden place' (cf. cc. 86 n., 123). His son, Horus, after a long struggle, defeated Set (iii. 5) and reigned in his stead (c. 144)

Almost all these points are referred to by H., but always with reserve (cf. c. 3 n.). It is noticeable that H. thinks of Osiris as buried at Sais (c. 171), and never even mentions Abydos in Upper Egypt, which was especially considered his tomb, and where, accordingly, wealthy Egyptians had themselves buried, *φιλοτιμουμένους ὁμοτάφους εἶναι τοῦ σώματος Ὀσίριδος* (Plut. *u. s.* c. 20). For the whole Osiris myth in H. cf. Sourdille (R. c. 3, especially pp. 87–9).

1 **Buto**, a town in the north-west Delta on the Sebennytic Nile, was probably near the village of Ibtu; cf. Petrie (E. E. F. xxvi. (1904–5) pp. 36–8); it was famous for its oracle (cf. cc. 152, 155). Leto is the Egyptian Uat, the patron deity of the Lower Delta.

Papremis (cf. cc. 71, 165 for the 'nome' of Papremis) was the site of the battle in 460 B.C., when Inaros defeated Achaemenes (iii. 12. 4); its exact position is uncertain, but Sourdille (E. p. 90 seq.) shows that probably it was the original native town which was absorbed later by the Greek Pelusium (so Rhakoti was absorbed by Alexandria). His arguments, briefly, are: (1) identity of position; Papremis was on the Egyptian frontier, on or near the Nile (Diod. xi. 74); H. says Pelusium is 'the entrance' into Egypt from the east (141. 4, the story of Sethos); (2) the Coptic name of Pelusium is 'Peremoun', which may well be derived from Papremis; (3) πηλούσιον is a Greek adjective, and was probably the name of the settlement of the mercenaries in the territory of Papremis (cf. 165 n.). It is noticeable that H. never calls Pelusium a 'town'.

H. says the god worshipped here was Ares (59. 3); whom he means is uncertain. Some explain 'Ares' as the Egyptian Anhur (Greek Ὄνουρις), the son of Ra; he stands in Ra's boat, and clears his course of snakes and hippopotami; his title was 'foe-smiter'. More probably, however, Ares = a form of Set, i.e. Typhon (Sourdille, R. p. 188 seq.); for (1) they have a common character of violence. (2) The hippopotamus, sacred in Papremis only (c. 71), was the symbol of Typhon (Plut. I. et O. 50); of it the Greeks said τῇ μητρὶ βίᾳ μίγνυσθαι, which explains the story told by H. below. (3) Papremis was somewhere in the north-east Delta, near the Serbonian Lake (cf. iii. 5 n.).

ἐπὶ τὰ ἕτερα: i. e. opposite those in the entrance.

2 Transference of 'shrines' of this kind is represented on the monuments, both on men's shoulders and (as H. says) on 'four-wheeled wagons'. Erman (E. pp. 278–9) quotes a picture from a grave at Thebes, commemorating the return to life of Osiris, in which the ceremony is followed by a battle (πληγήν) as here; cf., for similar car-battles in north-west India, J. R. A. S., 1884, p. 29.

3 **οὐδένα.** For a similar miraculous escape from wounds in a religious ceremony cf. iv. 180. 2.

4 **ἀπότροφον**: i. e. brought up apart from his mother. The story may be an explanation of the Egyptian title 'ka-mutf', i.e. husband of his mother, applied to Amon and other gods; but probably it is a Greek invention (*v. s.*).

συμμεῖξαι, *coitum habere*; cf. iv. 114. 1; the sense elsewhere in H. is *colloqui* (e.g. iv. 151. 2). He probably uses an ambiguous word designedly, though the *sensus obscenus* is clear.

64 H. fears that the story which he has just told may lead to depreciation of Egyptian morals; he therefore hastens to point out that they do not practise such rites as those of Mylitta (i. 199; though even there ἔξω τοῦ ἱροῦ, § 3). He is right in his general statement, but there were exceptions; cf. i. 182 n. (at Thebes). The reason he gives for the licence of other countries is a Greek speculation; he does not understand the real meaning of the impure Semitic rites (for which cf. i. 7. 4 n.; ii. 48. 2 n.).

2 Animals were supposed to act on direct impulse from the gods, and to show their will (Tac. Germ. 10). This mention of animals skilfully forms the transition to the next division of H.'s work (cc. 65–76), the account of the 'Sacred Beasts'.

65 2 **ἐοῦσα**: concessive; for the beasts of Libya cf. iv. 191. Egypt is comparatively free from beasts, owing to the extent of cultivated land and the small amount of waste.

ἐόντα agrees with θήρια understood from θηριώδης. Strictly taken the words mean that *all* beasts were sacred everywhere in Egypt; but this is absurd, and inconsistent with H.'s own details. The respect paid varied from nome to nome; cf. Juv. xv. 36 'numina vicinorum odit uterque locus'. H. quite fails to distinguish the various kinds of animal worship (Sourdille, R. p. 235 seq.): (1) animals worshipped by individuals as fetiches. Of this class there is little evidence, though no doubt such worship was widely spread among the lower classes; (2) individual animals supposed to be gods incarnate. Cf. c. 46 (the goat at Mendes); iii. 27–8 (Apis at Memphis; (3) whole classes of animals sacred to a god. Strabo, 803, distinguishes these clearly, θεοὶ μὲν οὐ νομίζονται ἱεροὶ δέ. Most of H.'s details refer to (3). For animal worship in general cf. 75. 3 n.

ἀνεῖται: properly 'are let go'; hence ἀνίημι is used either with ἱρός (as here) or without (cf. Plato, Leg. 761 C ἄλσος ἀνειμένον = 'consecrated').

φεύγω: cf. for this reserve 3. 2 n.

3 The office of 'caretaker' of the beasts was certainly not always hereditary: H. is too absolute.

4 **εὐχάς**. The 'vows' are obviously for the restoration of children's health; so Diodorus (i. 83) understood this passage; he mentions the various kinds (*not* 'fish' only) of food given to the beasts, and that land was set apart for their maintenance. Rob. Smith (Kinship[2], p. 179; Rel. Sem. p. 330) compares the Arabian sacrifice ('acica') at birth of a child, when its head was shaved and a sheep sacrificed for it; by devoting its hair it was admitted into the family.

5 **τὸ δ'**. The antecedent for this is **τούτου** understood with ἡ ζημίη.

ἶβιν. Cic. Tusc. v. 27, 78 implies that it was a capital offence to kill an ibis, a snake, a cat, a dog, or a crocodile. Diodorus (i. 83 *ad fin.*), who was himself present, relates that Ptolemy Auletes was unable to save from death a Roman who had unintentionally killed a cat, although he and his people alike were at the time most anxious for Roman friendship.

1 H.'s good sense suggests the difficulty that animals protected so strictly would multiply unduly, and to meet this he accepts an explanation which, though fictitious in itself, is based on two rightly observed natural facts; these are that it might be thought, from the noise she makes, that the process of impregnation is painful to a she-cat, and that tom-cats do in some cases kill their young, if they seem to attract the mother's attention too much.

3 It is quite true that cats will run into a burning house.

4 **ἐσάλλονται . . . ταῦτα δὲ γινόμενα**. This should either be a genitive absolute or the sentence should end τοῖς Αἰγυπτίοις ἐστι; but the events described in the participle γινόμενα and in the verb καταλαμβάνει are looked on as identical (cf. vii. 157. 2 ἁλὴς μὲν κτλ.).

5 **ξυρῶνται**: H. forgets his own generalization (36. 1) that the Egyptians, unlike other men, let their hair grow in bereavement.

67 1 For **Bubastis** cf. 59. 1. A great cemetery has been excavated there, with many bronze figures representing cats, and also cats' skeletons; but they were very rarely mummified there (Naville, Bubastis, p. 54); H. is right that dead cats were transferred, but it is not true that all cats were brought to Bubastis, for similar cemeteries have been found at Sakkara, at Beni Hasan, and elsewhere; the mummied cats at Beni Hasan were brought to Europe a few years ago and sold as manure. Cats were honoured all over Egypt in ancient times as they are to this day.

H. makes a like exaggeration as to 'sparrow-hawks' (ἴρηκας) and 'ibises', the mummies of which have been found in many places besides Buto and Hermopolis; he himself (c. 65 *ad fin.*) implies that these were sacred birds everywhere.

κύνας. Dogs, wolves, and jackals were sacred to Anubis, the dog-headed god, who was (like Hermes) ψυχοπομπός; hence a jackal is often represented as guarding the door of Hades. Mummied dogs have been found at various places, but at Cynopolis, the chief centre of their worship, the great majority of the mummies are of jackals; H. puts the three kinds together.

For the worship of 'ichneumons' and 'field-mice' (μυγαλᾶς) cf. Strabo, 812, 813; it is confirmed by the monuments.

ἴρηκας. The 'sparrow-hawk' was specially honoured in Egypt; it was sacred to the sun; Osiris also is represented by a sparrow-hawk. So, later, its picture stood for 'god' in the hieroglyphs.

Ἑρμέω = Egyptian Thoth; his chief city, Hermopolis, was near the modern Ashmunên, some 180 miles south of Cairo; there were others of the same name. Many ibis mummies have been found there.

2 **ἄρκτους.** The bear only appears on the monuments as a present from foreign nations. As, however, it certainly was found in North Africa, Sayce is not justified in saying 'it did not exist in Egypt', still less in gratuitously suspecting H. of confusing it with the hyena. A 'bear' of the archaic period is figured in B. M. G. (p. 86).

H. is right that the Egyptian wolf is much smaller than the European variety.

68 For the supposed borrowing by H. in this chapter and in cc. 70, 71, 73 from Hecataeus cf. Introd. pp. 22–6. It has been thought that the style in cc. 68, 69 resembles that of c. 73, and 'shows the epitomator' (C. Müller, ad Hecat. Fr. 294; F. H. G. i. 22). But, if Porphyry's statement be worth anything, it implies that the *description* of the crocodile is not borrowed, since only 'the capture' of it is mentioned by him. Full of marvels as H.'s account is, he is moderate compared to his successors, e. g. Seneca (Nat. Quaes. iv. 2. 13) tells a marvellous story, on the authority of an eyewitness, the Roman prefect Balbillus (Tac. Ann. xiii. 22), of a battle between crocodiles and dolphins at the Heracleot mouth of the Nile.

1 **μῆνας.** The crocodile does not hibernate; but it is much less seen in the winter, when apparently it lives for long periods without food.

2 **τὸ πολλόν.** H. is quite right here; the crocodile sleeps on shore by day in the summer.

Aristotle's description (H.A. v. 33, 558 a 17–24) is worth comparing with that of H.: *ὁ δὲ ποτάμιος κροκόδειλος τίκτει μὲν ᾠὰ πολλά, τὰ πλεῖστα περὶ ἑξήκοντα, λευκὰ τὴν χρόαν, καὶ ἐπικάθηται δ' ἡμέρας ἑξήκοντα (καὶ γὰρ καὶ βιοῖ χρόνον πολύν), ἐξ ἐλαχίστων δ' ᾠῶν ζῷον μέγιστον γίνεται ἐκ τούτων· τὸ μὲν γὰρ ᾠὸν οὐ μεῖζόν ἐστι χηνείου, καὶ ὁ νεοττὸς τούτου κατὰ λόγον, αὐξανόμενος δὲ γίνεται καὶ ἑπτακαίδεκα πήχεων. λέγουσι δέ τινες ὅτι καὶ αὐξάνεται ἕως ἂν ζῇ.* The whole of the latter part of the passage is borrowed, in several cases verbally, from H. Aristotle (ib. i. 11) also repeats the statement as to the crocodile 'not moving its under-jaw', and (ib. 9. 6) the account of the *τροχίλος*; the verbal similarities are not so marked in these passages. In ii. 10 Aristotle inserts most of H.'s other particulars, i. e. as to the crocodile's habits by day and night, as to its eyes and teeth, and as to its claws and skin. In this last passage the resemblance is again most marked. For the relations of H. and Aristotle on this subject cf. Diels, Hermes, xxii. 430–2, where the passages are given in full.

ἑπτακαίδεκα. Some ancient writers give even larger estimates, e.g. Phylarchus (fr. 26, F. H. G. i. 340) speaks of one just over forty feet. The Nile crocodile only reaches fifteen feet in length, but further east another species is often over twenty feet long, while one monster of thirty-three feet is on record; E. B.[11] vii. 479.

γλῶσσαν. The tongue of a crocodile is very small; it is more accurate to say with Pliny (N. H. viii. 89) 'linguae usu caret'.

οὐδὲ κινέει. This statement, like that as to 'no tongue', was often made in antiquity, but is of course wrong; the crocodile raises its head to bite, and so presents the deceptive appearance of moving its upper jaw.

4 **τυφλόν.** Aristotle (*u. s.*) corrects to *φαύλως*; both statements are wrong, for the crocodile sees excellently in water.

τροχίλος. The service rendered by the *τροχίλος* seems to be a genuine piece of native information. There are no leeches in the Nile, but eyewitnesses say that the 'Spurwing' actually does pick flies and other morsels out of the crocodile's mouth. Curzon (Monasteries of Levant, p. 150) says he has seen a crocodile warned of danger by a kind of plover ('ziczac'). For the whole subject cf. letters in *Spectator*, Feb. 13 and 20, 1909. The *τροχίλος* became a proverb for those who serve the great through fear, P. G. ii. 691.

69 1 The crocodile was sacred to Sebak or Sobk, who was represented with a crocodile head. As the calf Apis was the incarnation of Ptah, so was the sacred crocodile, *Σοῦχος*, at Arsinoe (called by the Greeks 'Crocodilopolis') in the Fayûm, an incarnation of Sebak. (Cf. Strabo, 811–12, for an account of a visit to this creature and how it was fed.) The crocodile was worshipped at many other

places, but H. is right in mentioning specially 'those that dwell round Thebes and L. Moeris', and in making the people of Elephantine especially hostile (but see Sayce, J. of P. xiv. 268–9).

2 **ἀρτήματα.** The holes bored for these 'pendants' can still be seen in the skulls of mummied crocodiles. *λίθος χυτή* was a kind of glass, an older name for *ὕαλος*.

θήκῃσι. The labyrinth (ii. 148. 5) was built partly for the burial of the sacred crocodiles. The most extensive finds of mummied crocodiles have been near Monfalût, some 220 miles south of Cairo.

3 The Egyptians called the crocodiles 'em-suh' ('that which is born of the egg'); hence the name *χάμψα*, in which the aspirate has become prefixed. For the Ionic name, *κροκόδειλοι*, cf. alligator, i.e. the Spanish *al lagarto* ('the lizard').

70 For the bearing of cc. 70, 71 on the relations of H. and Hecataeus cf. 68. 1 n., and Intr. pp. 22–6.

δελεάσῃ: sc. *ὁ θηρευτής*; supplied from *ἄγραι*.

κατ' ὧν ἔπλασε: cf. 40. 2 n. In spite of its sacredness the crocodile was hunted in some places, e.g. at Tentyra (Ael. N. H. x. 21). Crocodiles are now seen only occasionally, even as high up as Abu Hammed, i.e. above the Third Cataract (Baedeker, p. 322).

71 The hippopotamus now is not seen north of the Third Cataract, but the monuments show that it was once found even in the Delta; Hogarth (A. A. L. p. 100) says there is good evidence for one having been killed there in 1818, and traditions of it still survive in the marshes. H. is wrong in his negative statement, for it was a sacred animal in some places, e.g. Thebes, though hated in others as the symbol of Set (Typhon); there seems no other trace of its connexion with Paprensis. Of H.'s description it can at best be said that it is highly impressionist. The hippopotamus has not a 'cloven hoof', nor has it a 'horse's mane' and 'tail' (it really is almost hairless); and it is much bigger than an ox. But its teeth are prominent, the lower ones are often over five feet long, and it is certainly *σιμός*. The resemblance to a horse can be well seen in Dugmore's photographs (p. 90, Camera Adventures, 1910). H., or his informant, however, must have had a very flying glimpse of behemoth. Aristotle (502 a, 9–15), H. A. ii. 7, copies H.'s account almost verbally without naming him; he corrects him by substituting *κέρκον ὑός* for the 'horse's tail', and by *half*-concealing the tusks (*ὑποφαινομένους*); on the other hand he says that the hippopotamus is only 'as big as an ass', which is a change for the worse.

ξυστόν is the part, 'the shaft,' *ἀκόντιον* the whole. The hide was more frequently used for whips, the well-known 'Kurbash', and for shields.

72 1 **ἐνύδριες**: perhaps = a kind of ichneumon; 'otters' are not found in the Nile.

Strabo (812) says that the 'Lepidotus' was honoured by 'all the Egyptians alike', with cows, dogs, cats, sparrow-hawks, and ibises.

It was also called *κυπρῖνος*='carp'. Wilkinson thinks it=the 'dog-fish' of the Nile.

ἔγχελυν: there is no trace on the monuments of the 'eel' being considered holy; but the Greeks certainly jested at the Egyptians' respect for it, e.g. Anaxandrides (in Athen. 299; cf. 35 n.).

χηναλώπεκας. The 'vulpanser' was sacred to Keb (who was compared to the Greek Κρόνος), the god of the earth. Mummies of it have been found at Thebes.

1 The account of the phoenix is one of the passages which Porphyry says was stolen by H. from Hecataeus (cf. c. 68 n.). The phoenix is usually said to correspond to the 'bŏin' (or 'bennu') of Egyptian theology. It was represented on the monuments as a 'heron', and was the symbol of the rising sun, and also of the resurrection. It was especially reverenced at Heliopolis. Round this symbolic bird grew up a great mass of myth (cf. e.g. Plin. N. H. x. 2; Tac. Ann. vi. 28). H. reproduces one specimen of this, but expressly says that he does not believe it. The later and more familiar form of the story is that the phoenix came to Heliopolis and burned itself on the altar, and that from the ashes the new phoenix arose; it was this myth which was used by the Fathers to illustrate the Resurrection (cf. Clemens Rom. ad Cor. i. 25-6). Manilius (in Plin. *u. s.*) connected the life of the phoenix with the 'great year' (of 540 years), after which 'significationes tempestatum et siderum easdem reverti'.

δι' ἐτέων. Pliny (*u. s.*) gives 540 years' 'interval', Tacitus (*u. s.*) 500, but says some gave 1,461 years, i.e. a 'Sothic period' (cf. c. 4 nn.); there is no trace of these huge figures on the monuments. It need hardly be said that the phoenix became a proverb for age (P. G. ii. 712).

2 The bennu of the monuments has not these gorgeous colours, which Pliny (*u. s.*) repeats; some suppose that H. is confusing it with a golden pheasant. Sayce says this passage proves that H. had never seen the monuments; it only proves that H., like other men, made mistakes.

περιήγησιν, 'outline.' It is impossible to say where H. got his idea of the likeness to the eagle.

3 **'Αραβίης**: i. e. the region of the rising sun, where myrrh is found (iii. 107).

74 H. here speaks of the cerastes, a snake about two feet long; it has been found mummied at Thebes. Maspero (M. A. E. ii. 405) says a serpent was looked on by the lower classes at Thebes as the embodiment of Miritskro (Merseker), goddess of healing; H. may have been misled by this into calling it not venomous, which is quite wrong.

1 **Βουτοῦν**: this is not the Buto mentioned in cc. 59, 63 (which was in the North-west Delta). It is doubtfully identified with Amt, near Tanis, in the North-east Delta (E. E. F. v. 37, for 1888);

here Uto (Uat) was certainly worshipped. But Sourdille (E. p. 76 seq.) argues ingeniously that the words here show Buto was outside the Delta (in 'Arabia') and *off* H.'s main route. He thinks that H. conceives the serpents as coming from the south, and turning west, through 'a pass' (ἐσβολή), along the line of the canal described in 158. 2–3. Hence he places Buto somewhere near the Bitter Lakes. The 'great plain' of § 2 then is that north of the Wadi Tumîlât (158. 2 n.).

πτερωτῶν. The 'winged snakes' are mentioned again in iii. 107 as guarding the frankincense trees; cf. for the belief in them, Isaiah xxx. 6, where 'the viper and the fiery flying serpent' are mentioned among the terrors of the 'land of trouble and anguish' to the south. Probably the snakes are a reality; Strabo says the region near the Bitter Lakes was full of serpents, which lay hid in the sand; but their 'wings' are a mere traveller's tale. Sayce supposes that H. is trying 'to give probability and local colouring by telling the tale in the first person; he compares the valley of the roc in the Arabian Nights. But H. simply says that he *saw* a number of snake bones piled up, the rest of the story is what he was *told*.

Other explanations are (1) that of Brugsch, that 'locusts' are meant. The ibis certainly kills locusts; but in no other point does the explanation fit H.'s statements.

(2) The story is supposed to have a mythological origin. The goddess of Buto was represented as a snake with hood inflated and with wings; but the representation is certainly not that of a 'water-snake' nor are its wings 'like those of bats' (76. 3).

(3) Sourdille (E. p. 75) suggests that the tree-lizard of the East, which has a collar which it expands, was once found in the region east of Egypt, and may be the 'winged snake'.

3 Whether the sacred ibis really kills snakes or not is disputed; at all events the Greeks thought that it did. Cf. Diod. i. 87 (also 86) for this and other explanations of animal worship; he gives a list of creatures worshipped by the Egyptians because they were useful; cats and ibises are both mentioned as killing snakes. It need hardly be said that this explanation of animal worship is an afterthought; its origin is to be sought in the superstitions of primitive peoples (cf. 65. 1 n).

Sourdille (R. p. 251) sums up (with regard to H.'s account of the worship of animals): 'the striking point is not the inaccuracy of the points related; a great number of them agree with what appears to have been the case; but they are too generalized, too systematized' (cf. 67. 1 nn.).

76 H. is singularly accurate in his description of the two kinds of ibis (cf. E. B.[9] *s.v.*), but is wrong in saying that the black kind was the sacred one: the *Ibis religiosa* is not all black, but white with a black head, neck, &c., as H. describes the common ibis. The black ibis only appears to be black at a distance; seen close, it is dark chestnut in colour, with a brilliant gloss in parts. Strabo says the sacred ibis was in his day a perfect nuisance in the streets of Alexandria.

κρέξ: the 'corncrake' is really smaller than the ibis.

77–98 *An account (with digressions) of the manners of the Egyptians* (*αὐτῶν*, c. 77. 1), *as contrasted with the animals already described.*

77 1 **σπειρομένην.** H. contrasts 'cultivated' Egypt (i. e. Upper Egypt and the south parts of the Delta) with the marshes of the Delta (c. 92).

μνήμην: not 'practising the memory', but 'caring for the records of the past'. For *λογιώτατοι* cf. i. 1. 1; 'most skilled in history.'

2 **συρμαΐζουσι.** The medical papyri fully confirm this prominence of 'purging' in Egyptian treatment.

3 **Λίβυας.** For the healthiness of the Libyans and its alleged cause cf. iv. 187.

οὐ μεταλλάσσουσι. H.'s view is that of his contemporary, Hippocrates; cf. Aph. iii. 1 *αἱ μεταβολαὶ τῶν ὡρέων μάλιστα τίκτουσι νοσήματα.* For the accuracy of his statement cf. E. B.[9] vii. 302 (*s. v.* Egypt): 'The climate of Egypt, being remarkably equable, is healthy to those who can bear great heat': the daily range of temperature in the Libyan desert is 35°, but in Egypt the range is less (Baedeker, p. lx). Even in classical times, consumptive patients were sent to Egypt (cf. Pliny (the younger) Epis. v. 19, who sends his freedman Zosimus).

4 **ἀρτοφαγέουσι**: cf. 36. 2 n. and Hecat. fr. 290 (F. H. G. i. 20) *Αἰγυπτίους ἀρτοφάγους φησὶν εἶναι, κυλλήστιας ἐσθίοντας, τὰς δὲ κριθὰς εἰς ποτὸν καταλέοντας.*

ἄμπελοι. For absence of vines cf. 37. 4 n. Diodorus (i. 34) says the Egyptian beer was called *ζῦθος*; it was considered to be as necessary for the dead in the other world as for the living in this. Aristotle (Athen. x. 418) noted that a man drunk with wine lay on his face, while beer laid him on his back.

5 **τὰ δὲ ἄλλα**: translate 'which they consider to belong to the class of birds or fishes'. For salting birds cf. Wilkinson, fig. 99, i. 290.

78 **νεκρόν.** Plutarch (Mor. 357; I. et O. c. 17) and Lucian also mention this custom. It has not been confirmed by the monuments, but Maspero (A. E. G., 1876, p. 186) points out that the little wooden figures, so common in museums, of a mummy on a bier 'exactly correspond to the description of H.' The lesson which it was intended to teach (*ἐς τοῦτον ὁρέων κτλ.*) is found in native poems; cf. the two versions (time of the New Empire) quoted by Erman, E. 386–7, e. g. 'cast behind thee all cares and mind thee of the joy, Till there cometh that day when we journey to the land that loveth Silence'.

For the same lesson elsewhere cf. 1 Cor. xv. 32, and Petron. Satyricon 34, where a 'larva argentea' is shown to the guests.

γραφῇ: i. e. by painting, ἔργῳ by the shape of the wooden figure. Stein says the figure was that of Osiris, the lord of the dead; for every righteous man became 'an Osiris' on death; cf. 86. 2 n. for H.'s silent reference to Osiris in his account of embalming: Plutarch, however (*u. s.*), says 'it was not a memorial of the passion of Osiris', but rather 'a reminder χρῆσθαι τοῖς παροῦσι καὶ ἀπολαύειν ὡς πάντας αὐτίκα μάλα τοιούτους ἐσομένους'.

πάντῃ cannot here = 'in all directions' as usually; translate 'quite, altogether'.

79 1 **πατρίοισι**: the conservatism of the Egyptians was as marked as that of the Chinese; for an even stronger assertion of this cf. 91. 1. Here H. proceeds (cc. 79, 80) to add two apparent exceptions.

ἐπάξια here and in vii. 96. 2 must = 'worthy of mention'; but in vii. 96 παραμέμνημαι immediately precedes.

2 The Greek Linus corresponds to Adonis, the Syrian Tammuz (cf. Ezek. viii. 14 'the women weeping for Tammuz'), the Lydian Atys, the Mysian Hylas; cf. H.'s remark 'his name varies from tribe to tribe'. All these were conceived of as beautiful young men, beloved of the goddess, and perishing untimely. The story is said to be a sun-myth (Sayce, *s.v.* 'Tammuz' in Hastings's Dictionary). Frazer, however (G. B. ii. 115 seq.), with more probability, says it represents 'the death and resurrection of vegetation'. For the connexion of the reaper's song with the myth cf. ib. pp. 253-8. If Frazer is right in explaining the story of Osiris (ii. 137 seq.) in the same way, it is only natural that Linus-Maneros should have been introduced into the Osiris myth (cf. Plut. I. et O. c. 17). For Adonis worship, which was especially a female cult, cf. Theocr. Id. 15 and Milton, P. L. i. 446 seq., of Tammuz

Whose annual wound in Lebanon allured
The Syrian damsels to lament his fate
In amorous ditties all a summer's day.

Linus, who was worshipped in Argos, was said to be the son of Urania, killed by Apollo from jealousy of his voice (Paus. ix. 29. 6–7); but there are other versions of the story. The name is as old as Homer (Il. xviii. 570), who makes it a reaper's song. In Hesiod (fr. 132) it has a wider extension; he says of ἀοιδοί

πάντες μὲν θρηνοῦσιν ἐν εἰλαπίναις τε χοροῖς τε,
ἀρχόμενοι δὲ Λίνον καὶ λήγοντες καλέουσι.

It is said to be the Eastern cry, 'woe unto us,' raised at the festival; the Greeks first borrowed this as αἴλινον (cf. Soph. Aj. 627), and then, by a mistaken etymology, interpreted it as 'alas for Linus'.

ὡυτός. As the context shows, H. means the 'same person', not name.

3 H. (c. 99) calls the 'first' king Menes, and perhaps he is meant here; others suppose a reference to some earlier god-king. The name 'Maneros' does not occur on the monuments; perhaps it means 'come thou back' (*maa-ne-hra*, a formula which occurs in the Book of the Dead).

μούνην. There were certainly other 'hymns' in Egypt; probably H. refers to the 'tune'; the monotony and uniformity of all oriental popular songs is well known; from their sad character they reminded the Greeks of the Linus song.

1 For the Lacedaemonian custom cf. the story in Cic. de Sen. 18, of the Lacedaemonian envoys setting the Athenians an example of respect for old age. Respect to parents is a frequent subject in the papyri; it is so common, however, among all nations (cf., e. g., Levit. xix. 32 'Thou shalt rise up before the hoary head'), that it seems strange H. should deem it worthy of notice.

2 In early Egypt complete prostration had been usual, but under the New Kingdom only the lower classes practised this, while the higher made a deep reverence, as here described. H. had seen this in the streets, though he did not mix with the upper classes (cf. 36. 2, 3 nn.).

1 κιθῶνας: for dress cf. 36. 3 n.; for the Καλασίριες 164. 2 n.

2 The Orphic rites spread widely in sixth century Greece; their popular character, as opposed to the exclusiveness of the old worships, led to them being patronized by the tyrants; Onomacritus, 'the Orphic apostle' (Busolt, ii. 364), was a friend of the Pisistratidae (vii. 6. 3 n.); so too Cleisthenes, tyrant of Sicyon, encouraged the worship of Dionysus (v. 67. 5), with which the Orphic rites were closely connected. (Cf. Gomperz, Gk. Thinkers, ii, p. 137.) For the Orphic doctrines and their relation to those of Pythagoras cf. Gomperz (ib. caps. 2 and 5; Busolt, ii. 362 seq.): a shorter account is given by Bury (pp. 311–18). The teaching was at once cosmological and religious; the latter is the more important. The Orphic sect taught the doctrine of metempsychosis (cf. 123. 2 n.); they laid stress on the worship of Chthonian deities, and on initiation into mysteries, and on other methods of purifying the soul from sin. Gruppe, however, in Roscher, Lexicon, iii. 1105, *s. v.* 'Orpheus', denies that an 'Orphic sect' can be proved; there were, he thinks, numerous associations, the members of which looked on Orpheus as their founder, and followed similar practices, but these were disconnected and were no 'more united as a sect than modern vegetarians or wearers of Jäger clothing' (pp. 1107-8).

Ὀρφικοῖσι: neuter here, 'Orphic Rites'; there is an antithesis between *καλεομένοισι* and *ἐοῦσι*, they were 'called Orphic' but 'were really Egyptian, brought by Pythagoras from Egypt' (cf. 53. 3 for disbelief in a primitive Orpheus). There is no contradiction between this passage and the statement as to *τὰ περὶ τὸν Διόνυσον* in 49. 2; H. means that Melampus brought Dionysiac mysteries from Egypt, Pythagoras copied rules of life.

1 μείς. Each month in Egypt was consecrated to a god, from whom sometimes its name was derived. The days of the month too were assigned, the first to Thoth, the second to Horus, the third to Osiris, &c.

H. is right that horoscopes were much cast in Egypt. The day on which a man was born determined his fate, e.g. a man born on the 9th Phaophi would live to be old, on the 23rd would be killed by a crocodile; no child born on the 23rd of Thoth could live, &c. Cf. Papyrus Sallier IV, now in the B. M., for a calendar of this kind.

οἱ ἐν ποιήσι, 'those who have employed themselves in poetry'; the contemptuous reference is to books like Hesiod's Works and Days, and also to the oracular poems attributed to Orpheus and Musaeus.

2 **τέρατα**, 'prodigies,' i.e. for forecasting the future, as the context shows; although no collection of prodigies has been found in Egypt, there is abundant evidence that they were observed and explained; but such collections were more frequent in Chaldaea.

83 1 H. is right in saying that in Egypt there was no official prophet like the Pythia at Delphi; the gods themselves communicated their will through dreams (cf. Gen. xli for those of Pharaoh), but cf. 54. 1 n.

For Heracles cf. 42. 3 n.; for Athena 62. 1 n.; for Ares 63. 1 n.; for Apollo c. 156; for Artemis 59. 1 n.; for Zeus 42. 1 n.; for Leto c. 156.

84 The Egyptians are already famous as physicians in the Odyssey; cf. iv. 227–32 Helen has drugs from Egypt where *πλεῖστα φέρει ζείδωρος ἄρουρα | φάρμακα*. Maspero (p. 89) doubts whether H. does not exaggerate; there were general practitioners as well as 'specialists'; for an Egyptian oculist cf. iii. 1. 1.

For Darius' Egyptian physicians and their drastic methods of treatment cf. iii. 129, 132.

Egyptian medical science goes back to the Old Kingdom, e.g. in the B. M. Papyrus 10059 some prescriptions date from the time of Cheops; it was a curious mixture of sense and magic, e.g. it was believed that a decoction of a black calf's hair kept off grey hair. A specimen of it is the famous papyrus edited (1875) by Ebers. It greatly affected European medicine; Erman (E. 364) quotes a curious instance of an old Egyptian prescription for determining the sex of an unborn babe, which survived down to late in the eighteenth century.

85 1 **κατ' ὧν ἐπλάσατο**: cf. 39. 2 n. The practice of mourners smearing themselves with mud is still found in Egypt; that of uncovering the upper part of the body, and 'girding themselves up' below the breasts, is seen on the monuments. Cf. for it Homer, Il. xxii. 80 *κόλπον ἀνιεμένη, ἑτέρηφι δὲ μαζὸν ἀνέσχεν* of Hecuba. Diodorus (i. 72) gives a similar account of the mourning for the Egyptian king. There are resemblances also in the burial ceremonies of the Spartan kings, which H. (vi. 58. 2) compares to those of barbarians in Asia.

2 **οὕτω.** The funeral procession is represented on the monuments much as H. describes it.

86 Embalming was connected with the Egyptian idea as to the

soul, the Ka; the continued existence of this depended on the survival of the body; if the body perished, the soul perished. No doubt the means of preventing this were originally suggested by the dry air and sand of the desert, which parched the flesh and prevented decay; then artificial means were invented; Anubis was said to be their author (cf. Maspero, i. 112, 178 seq.). H.'s account of embalming is on the whole very accurate; it should be compared with that of Diodorus (i. 91), which is somewhat fuller, and with Budge, The Mummy, 1893, pp. 173-84. It may be noted: (1) Mummied bodies are found exactly as described, some preserved by bitumen and some by saltpetre. (2) They have a hole bored from the 'nostrils' (*μυξωτήρων*) to the brain and an opening in the 'flank' (*λαπάρην*). (3) Obsidian or flint knives (*λίθῳ*) are frequently found in graves with mummies; for the use of these primitive implements in religious ceremonies cf. Josh. v. 2 (R. V.), 'knives of flint' for circumcision. (4) The linen wrappings and the 'wooden figure (*ξύλινον τύπον*) in form of a man' are familiar in all museums. (5) H. is often too absolute in his statements; he makes invariable what was only usual. (6) It is curious that he makes no reference to the Book of the Dead, the formulae of which were at first inscribed on the coffin, while later the whole collection was bound up inside the bandages. For the various forms of this and other funeral literature cf. B. M. G. pp. 58 seq.

κατέαται, 'set themselves to this very thing'; cf. *κατίζω* in 126. 1, but there the local sense is more clearly present.

τέχνην. Diodorus (*u. s.*) says the calling was hereditary, and H. implies the same; this was usual, but not an absolute rule.

2 **οὐκ ὅσιον**: the reference is to Osiris; the mummy was made like him, in order that the dead man might obtain access to the realm where he ruled (cf. Maspero, i. 182 seq.); the dead man in fact became an Osiris. H. declines to mention the name 'in regard to such a matter', cf. c. 3 nn. for parallels to, and explanation of, this religious reserve; Wiedemann thinks H. omits the name 'because he had no clear conception of Egyptian mysteries'. This is incredible; H. was familiar with hundreds of names in Egypt, and yet we are to suppose that he did not recognize that of Osiris, the most familiar of all.

δευτέρην: Diodorus says that the best embalming cost a talent of silver, the second twenty minae, the third very little; there were more varieties than he and H. describe.

3 **οὕτω**: i.e. 'by a crooked iron', corresponds to the *ἐγχέοντες φάρμακα*. 'The skulls of mummies are found to contain absolutely nothing' (Budge), which confirms H.

4 **ἐξεῖλον**: translate 'they clean out the belly completely', cf. 40. 1 n. *ἐξεῖλον* is taken up by *ἐκκαθήραντες*. The viscera extracted were placed in four jars, popularly but wrongly called 'Canopic jars',

each covered with the head of a genius, a son of Osiris (cf. Erman, E. p. 306, for picture).

5 **νηδύν** = *κοιλίην* above. For the spices cf. iii. 107 seq. It is curious that H. does not mention the 'asphalt' employed; perhaps he thought it merely a foundation for the more expensive materials. 'Frankincense' was not used, because it was sacred to the gods.

ὀπίσω: they 'sew up the back passage', i. e. to prevent the entrance of air.

λίτρῳ is either 'saltpetre' (Stein) or 'soda' (Wiedemann); the object of this pickling was to remove the moisture and fat, and to harden the skin. The Papyrus Rhind agrees with H. as to the length of time for embalming, 'seventy' days; it seems, however, to have varied; cf. Gen. l. 3 for 'forty' days (in the case of Jacob).

6 **σινδόνος** is the general word, *βυσσίνη* gives the special material, 'linen'; H. is right, as the bandages were universally made of linen (Budge, p. 190).

κόμμι. 'Gum' exuding from the acacia is mentioned, 96. 1. No doubt the finer sorts for embalming were imported.

7 The mummy was kept 'upright' for a time, till the death sacrifices, &c., ceased; then it was transferred to a lower 'vault', where it was laid down. The vaults of the rich were often hewn out of the hills, because of the dryness of the air there. It seems probable, however, that in the Fayûm the mummies were kept above ground, owing to the dampness of the soil.

87 1 **σκευάζουσι.** The Greek is much compressed; H. means *σκευάζουσι (νεκροὺς) τοὺς τὰ πολυτελέστατα σκευάζουσι*, while the second sentence really = *τῶν τὰ μέσα βουλομένων . . . φευγόντων (τοὺς νεκροὺς) σκευάζουσι.*

2 **κέδρου.** A sort of turpentine seems meant; H. has, however, misunderstood the object of its use; this was to check corruption till the *λίτρον* had done its work. The discharge (*ἐξιεῖσι*) was that of humours generated before the 'pickling' was complete. H. was misled by the fact that in a mummy only skin and bones are left, and inferred the cause wrongly.

ἕδρην is used instead of *ὀπίσω ὁδός* (cf. 86. 5), for variety.

ἐσηθήσαντες: i. e. by means of *κλυστῆρες*.

ἐπιλαβόντες, 'checking.'

88 1 **συρμαίῃ**: oil made of radishes; cf. 77. 2 for its purpose. Here, too, the work of preservation was done by the *λίτρον*.

89 **οὐ παραυτίκα**: this delay in embalming women is confirmed by archaeology; cf. report of E. E. F., 1908, p. 19.

90 1 **τούτους.** *Constructio ad sensum* with *ὃς δ' ἂν κτλ.*

2 For the sacredness of the dead drowned or destroyed by a crocodile cf. Griffith, Z. A. S. xlvi. 132, and Nat. Home Reading Mag., June, 1904; the evidence is later than H., but the belief may well be earlier than the surviving evidence. Ael. N. H. x. 21 says mothers even rejoiced when their children were killed by crocodiles.

91 The visit to Chemmis, which H. here implies, is denied by Sayce *ad loc.*, and (more in detail) J. of P. xiv. 267–8. He argues (1) Chemmis is not near Neapolis (Kenneh), but eighty-four miles away; (2) the description of the temple and its statues is quite un-Egyptian. He is answered by D. D. Heath (ib. xv. 227 seq.), who points out that H. is describing a non-Egyptian building; it may be noted that he uses *πρόπυλα*, not the usual *προπύλαια*. Heath conjectures that H., writing from memory, has put 'Chemmis' for 'Coptos', which latter town is close to Neapolis. It is probable, however, that Neapolis is wrongly identified (*v. i.*).

1 **Χέμμις**: *hod.* Akhmîm (*not* the island of Chemmis in the Delta; cf. c. 156), used to be called by the Greeks 'Panopolis', as being the shrine of 'Chem' or 'Min' (the hieroglyph is variously read), who was usually identified with Pan, as being ithyphallic and 'on account of his Priapic nature'.

Νέης πόλιος: this is usually thought to be Neapolis (*hod.* Kenneh), which lies opposite Tentyris on the right bank of the Nile; but it may well have been quite a different town, on the site of the later Ptolemais; this last was only about six miles from Chemmis.

ἱρόν here = *τέμενος*, the whole sacred enclosure (so Heath, who well compares, i. 181. 2, that of Belus at Babylon); it is called below *τῷ περιβεβλημένῳ*.

Περσέος. The identification of Perseus with 'Chem' it is impossible to explain for certain; perhaps it was connected with Chem's title 'Peh'resu', which sounded like 'Perseus'. At all events it is as baseless as the story that (vii. 61) the Persians derived their name from this hero. The whole story is Greek in (1) the idea of an anthropomorphic god, who leaves his temple and can be traced by his footsteps; (2) the organized games; (3) the character of the prizes. There must have been a Greek settlement at Chemmis; but Maspero's (iii. 649 n.) suggestion that it may really have belonged to the time of the 'Philhellene' Amasis (cf. Hecat. fr. 286, F. H. G. i. 20 for possible similar Greek settlements on islands in the Nile, called 'Ephesus, Chios, Samos', &c.) must be rejected, as quite inconsistent with ii. 178.

For games in the worship of Chem at Edfu cf. Lepsius, D. iv. 42 b (vol. ix); but they are quite un-Greek in character.

The footstep of Heracles stamped in rock by the Tyras (iv. 82) was also 'two cubits'; cf. that of Buddha in Ceylon, which measures about 5½ by 2½ feet, or that of St. Peter in the Domine Quo Vadis Chapel at Rome.

4 **ἔχοντα**, 'extending over every kind of contest,' i. e. the 'meeting' embraced running, jumping, wrestling, javelin, and discus.

5 **Δαναόν.** According to Greek story Lynceus was the nephew and son-in-law of Danaus (cf. Hor. Odes, iii. 11. 37 f.), and four generations removed from Perseus. The connexion of the Perseidae with Egypt is a genuine Argive legend, not like the late invention

(Diod. i. 29) which makes the γηγενής Erechtheus come from Egypt to Athens. Perrot and Chipiez suggest (L'Art Mycénéen, pp. 77–8) that perhaps soldiers of fortune belonging to northern tribes, who, after having served in Egypt, were expelled and settled in Argolis, were considered to be Egyptians; but this is the merest conjecture. Genuine Egyptians certainly never settled in Greece. No historical conclusions can be drawn from the legends, though for other reasons early intercourse between Egypt and the Aegean, especially Crete, is certain. Cf. J. H. S. xii. 199 seq. (1891) and E. Meyer i. 172, 228, 291, 510, 520–3.

H. (vi. 53. 2) lays stress on the Egyptian ancestry of the Spartan kings, as descendants of Perseus; this all Greeks affirmed. He is supposed by Panoffsky (p. 55) to be here (ii. 91) borrowing from Pherecydes, who told the story of Perseus (cf. fr. 26, F. H. G. i. 75); but there is not the least evidence for this.

ἐκμεμαθηκότα, 'because he was thoroughly familiar with.' The participle is put out of place for emphasis.

92–5 *The customs of the inhabitants of the marshes as opposed to those of ἡ σπειρομένη Αἴγ.* (77. 1).

[For this part of Egypt cf. Hogarth, A. A. L. pp. 99 seq.]

H. is right in treating of the marshmen separately; the marshes had a distinct history, and were a refuge for those expelled from Egypt, e.g. the blind Anysis (137. 2), Psammetichus (151. 3), and Amyrtaeus (140. 2). So in Roman times they made the 'Bucolic' rebellion (A. D. 172). They were less civilized and cleanly than the other Egyptians, and H. exaggerates their resemblance (τοῖσι αὐτοῖσι νόμοισι χρέωνται).

92 1 **μιῇ**: monogamy seems to have been the rule in Egypt, though Diodorus (i. 80) says rightly that all but the priests had as many wives as they pleased. Kings and wealthy men, however, had a numerous harem; e.g. Rameses II had nearly 200 children.

συνοικέει. We should have expected the participle (cf. i. 85. 1).

2 This lotus (*Nymphaea Lotus*) is to be distinguished from the Cyrenaean lotus (cf. 96. 1 and iv. 177 n.), which is that of Homer. It is of two kinds, the white and the blue; it was actually cultivated for food. Theophrastus (H. P. iv. 8) describes the method of obtaining 'the fruit'; he, like H., compares the head (κωδύα) in size to 'the poppy' (μήκωνι) and the root to a 'quince' (μῆλον). The lotus was used in the ritual of the dead, and so became a symbol of immortality.

3 **ἐπιεικέως**, 'moderately'; a ἅπαξ λεγ. in H. We should expect ἐοῦσα, but it and the predicate στρογγύλον are attracted loosely into the gender of μέγαθος. Stein, however, makes στρογγύλον a substantive = 'a round body'.

4 **ἄλλα**: the *Nymphaea Nelumbo* of Linnaeus, known as the 'Egyptian bean' (cf. τρωκτά, 'kernels'). It does not grow in

Egypt, nor is it found on the older monuments; probably it was introduced by the Persians. It is represented in the famous Nile statue of the Vatican. H. is wrong in saying that the κάλυξ grows on a separate stalk, right as to its rose colour.

5 **ἐπέτειον.** H. lays stress on the 'annual' growth of the papyrus, because only the young shoots could be eaten; the old were too wooden. It was once so common that it is the hieroglyphic symbol of Lower Egypt; its growth was restricted later, to enhance its price (Strabo, 800), and it has now disappeared. H. only refers indirectly to its manifold uses; for these cf. 37. 3, shoes; 96. 3, sails; 7. 36, cables; v. 58. 3 n., writing material.

διαφανέϊ, 'red-hot'; cf. iv. 73. 2, 75. 1, of the stones used in the Scythian vapour-bath; but there *πυρί* and *ἐκ πυρός* are added.

93 1 **ἰχθύες.** That fishes migrate to the sea for breeding is of course a fact; to it has been added this strange myth, which Aristotle (de G. A. iii. 5, 755 b 6) rightly calls *εὐήθη καὶ τεθρυλημένον* and shows to be impossible; *ὁ γὰρ πόρος ὁ διὰ τοῦ στόματος εἰσιὼν εἰς τὴν κοιλίαν φέρει, ἀλλ' οὐκ εἰς τὰς ὑστέρας*; he attributes it to *Ἡρόδοτος ὁ μυθολόγος*.

2 The eggs are compared to 'millet seeds' (*κέγχρων*); translate 'by a few grains at a time'. It would have been simpler if H. had written either *τῶν ᾠῶν κατ' ὀλίγα* or *τῶν κέγχρων κατ' ὀλίγους*.

4 **δή.** Stein says this particle and the use of the optative after a present show that H. is speaking 'ironically', and that he does not accept the purpose of the fish as a real fact.

5 **γίνεται** and **πίμπλαται** are co-ordinated, as frequently in H., for the sake of vividness, though the former is really subordinate.

H. is wrong both in his facts and in his inference. The parts furthest from the Nile fill first not last, and the fishes are brought by the water, which comes through channels and not by irrigation. From these inaccuracies Sourdille (E. p. 7) concludes that H. was in Egypt only after the Nile rise had begun.

94 **οἱ περὶ τὰ ἕλεα** is the same as *οἱ ἐν τοῖς ἕλεσι* (c. 92).

σιλλικυπρίων: the castor-oil plant, *Ricinus communis*; H.'s name is due to the fact that it grows in Cyprus.

ἄγρια, 'of a wild kind,' opposed to the Egyptian variety described.

95 1 **κώνωπας.** H. rightly lays stress on the number of flies in Egypt, but it is not likely that he is right as to their being unable to fly high; men slept on the roof for coolness.

2 Stein accepts H.'s statement that the fishing-net was used as a mosquito curtain, Wiedemann denies it, and F. Ll. Griffith says 'it is beyond belief' (A. and A. p. 192). It may be true; but more probably H. confuses the fishing-net and a coarse mosquito curtain.

96 H., like a true Greek (may we add, like a Greek merchant ?), is always interested in boats and navigation. Cf. the similar description of the skin-boats on the Euphrates (i. 194). The peculiarity of these βάριδες is that they were built up of short pieces of wood, and hence had not the ordinary framework (νομεῦσι, 'ribs,' § 2) of a Greek ship. Stein, however, is clearly wrong in saying they were 'rafts', with low sides; they had a keel (τρόπις, § 3) and a high stern and prow, as is shown in the tomb picture of their building (Lepsius, D. ii. 126, vol. iv), at Beni Hasan.

For models in B. M., Third Egyptian Room, cf. B. M. G. p. 102. H. mentions no iron, perhaps intentionally; in this case the 'barides' would resemble the ironless boats of Ormuz on the Persian Gulf, which M. Polo (i. c. 19) describes.

1 **ἀκάνθη**: the *Mimosa Nilotica* ('acacia'), so called διὰ τὸ ἀκανθῶδες ὅλον τὸ δένδρον εἶναι πλὴν τοῦ στελέχους (i. e. on the main stem) Theoph. H. P. iv. 2; he says δωδεκάπηχυς ἐξ αὐτῆς ἐρέψιμος ὕλη τέμνεται (i. e. beams 'for roofing'). It is of two kinds, ἡ μέλαινα ... ἄσηπτος, διὸ καὶ ἐν ταῖς ναυπηγίαις χρῶνται. As a rule, however, the timber from it was much shorter, and hence the 'baris' was built in the way described below; Egypt was destitute of proper ship's timber. Nile boats are still built of acacia planks. Uni, fetching alabaster (Breasted, i. 323) from Hatnub, builds a boat of acacia, nearly a hundred feet long and fifty wide. Noah's ark was built of acacia wood (Gen. vi. 14 'gopher wood').

For the 'Cyrenaean lotus' cf. iv. 177 n.

πλινθηδόν. The short pieces (ξύλα) were arranged 'like bricks', i. e. in alternate layers, so that their joins might not come together.

2 **γόμφους.** The 'long bolts at frequent intervals' (πυκνούς) were, so to speak, the string, on which the short pieces were 'strung'; they were driven in vertically to the layers.

περιείρω is a ἅπαξ λεγ.

ζυγά. The 'cross-pieces' served at once to hold the framework together, and as a sort of deck.

ἁρμονίας; the 'joins' were 'caulked' with the fibre of the papyrus, which would then be fixed with tar.

ἐν ὧν ἐπάκτωσαν: for the aorist and the tmesis cf. 39. 2 n.

3 **πηδάλιον.** As a rule a Greek ship had two steering oars at the stern, 'fastened to the sides just below the gunwale'; but in the 'barides', the 'steering oar passed through the after end of the keel' (Torr, pp. 74–5).

ἱστῷ: it was not usual to find acacia wood of sufficient length for a mast; but cf. Theophrastus, *u. s.*

οὐ δύναται: H. is quite right in saying that the vessels were not sailed up stream, and in implying that they were usually 'towed'.

4 **θύρη.** The framework of the 'crate' was of 'tamarisk wood', over which a 'wattle of reeds' was worked. The object of this was not (as H. says) to catch the current, but to keep the vessel straight as it drifts with the stream; steering is of course impossible with a drifting boat, as boat and stream are moving at the same pace.

Chesney (ii. 640) describes an almost exactly similar method of guiding with the skin-boats of the Euphrates (cf. i. 194 nn.).

λίθος τετρημένος: the original form of anchor (cf. Hom. Od. xiii. 77); here by lessening the speed of the boat it made it possible to steer with the *πηδάλιον* (§ 3).

ἀπίει: i. e. the boatman.

ἐπιφέρεσθαι: i. e. the 'crate' is 'on the surface', so opposed to the *λίθος*, which is *ἐν βυσσῷ*.

5 **βᾶριν**: an Egyptian word, used by Aeschylus (Pers. 554 *et al.*) of Persian vessels.

ταλάντων: about $\frac{1}{40}$ of a ton; cf. i. 194. 3, those on the Euphrates are of '5,000 talents burden'.

1 The comparison to 'islands' is made by other ancient writers (e.g. Strabo 788) and is quite accurate; so too is the account of the cruise in flood-time, if it is understood to mean that the canals were at that time full; by these only could a man sail *διὰ μέσου τοῦ πεδίου*.

2 **οὐκ οὗτος**. The predicate, 'the usual course,' is implied. H. first states this for the part above Naucratis, and then, in the words *ἐς Ναύκρατιν ἀπὸ θαλάσσης*, makes the same statement for the part below Naucratis, repeating *διὰ πεδίου*. For Cercasoros and Canopus cf. 15. 1 nn. The sites of Anthylla and Archandropolis are uncertain.

From this chapter Sayce infers (J. of P. xiv, p. 260 seq.) that H. was in Egypt at the time of the inundation, which is right; he even fixes the date of his arrival at Naucratis (about July 20)! But he also infers that H. was in Egypt *only* during the inundation, which is a good instance of an argument with an undistributed middle.

1 For similar assignments to the royal family cf. Xen. Anab. i. 4. 9 (Syrian villages for the Queen Mother's *ζώνη*, and ib. ii. 4. 27). They were also given to private individuals, e. g. Themistocles received Lampsacus, Magnesia, and Myus, to provide his table (Thuc. i. 138. 5; Plut. Them. 29). Cicero (Verr. iii. 33, 76) quotes 'Persian gifts' as familiar.

2 **Ἀρχάνδρου**. Pausanias (ii. 6) makes him son (*not* grandson) of Achaeus (cf. vii. 94, where Danaus and Xuthus, father of Achaeus, are synchronized); hence some have proposed to translate *τοῦ Φθίου* 'the Phthiotian'; but the order of the words makes this impossible. It is idle to force consistency on independent legends.

99 With c. 99 begins the third part of Book II, i. e. the history of Egypt. This divides (at c. 147) into two parts: (*a*) the story of Egypt as told by the Egyptians themselves, and (*b*) that which is based in part on the evidence of other nations, i. e. the story after the opening of Egypt to the Greeks by Psammetichus. H. recognizes the difference in the evidence for these two parts, though he does not appreciate how great it was (cf. 147 n. and App. X. 10; Introd. § 27).

Μῖνα. The Egyptian form MNA left the vowel to be supplied; hence the various forms *Μήνης* (Manetho), *Μῆνας* (Diodorus), *Μιναῖος* (Josephus). Menes was long considered an invention, and used to be quoted as an instance of H.'s credulity; but the tomb of the king (Aha) identified with him was discovered in 1897 at Nagada near Abydos (Petrie, i. 17), and more fully explored in 1904 (King and Hall, pp. 57, 64). He seems to have united the crowns of Upper and Lower Egypt, and so to begin a new epoch (circ. 3400 B. C.).

τοῦτο μέν: repeated in § 4 *τοῦτο μὲν ἐν αὐτῷ*, and answers to *τοῦτο δέ* at end of chapter.

ἀπογεφυρῶσαι, &c., lit. 'dammed off', i. e. by diverting the river's course (§ 2) and 'making it a new channel' (*ὀχετεῦσαι*), he secured the site for building Memphis.

τὸν πρὸς μεσαμβρίης, κτλ.: translate 'he made with dykes the bend (which lies) to the south'. The Nile makes a great bend to the east, fourteen miles to the south of Memphis; but 'it is impossible to say if there is any truth in H.'s tradition' (Maspero, p. 53). Breasted (p. 37; cf. also E. E. F., Report for 1905, p. 39) accepts it, and Murray (pp. 188–9) shows that its distance from Memphis here given is very accurate.

3 **ἔτι καὶ νῦν.** H.'s words imply that the Persians were in undisputed possession of Memphis (cf. App. IX. 1). There is no trace of lakes near Memphis; H. may be misled by the Nile flood filling the canal, the Bahr Yûssûf; its dry bed can still be seen to the north and west of Memphis. But Diodorus (i. 96) speaks of the Acherusian lake near Memphis, the circuit of which city he makes seventeen miles, and Murray (*u. s.*) accepts this as a fact. Cf. 97. 2 for the time of H's visit.

τὸ ἱρόν. This temple—that of Ptah—is most important as the probable source of H.'s information as to Egyptian history (cf. App. X. 10).

100 1 **βύβλου.** These lists, which recorded a king's stature, character, and deeds, as well as the length of his reign, are mentioned by Diodorus (i. 44); on them Manetho based his history. (For them cf. App. X. 1.) Where H. obtained his '330' it is impossible to say; on it he bases (142 n.) his calculation as to the length of Egyptian history; but, apart from other difficulties, H. is wrong in making the kings all succeed each other; no doubt several of the dynasties were contemporary.

Αἰθίοπες: c. 137 mentions an Aethiopian invasion, that of Sabacos; but these '18' seem to be different.

2 For Nitocris at Babylon cf. i. 185 n.; for this Egyptian queen cf. F. Petrie, i. 105, and Hall, J. H. S. xxiv. 208–13. Nitocris is placed by Manetho at the end of the sixth dynasty; he calls her *εὐμορφοτάτη τῶν κατ᾽ αὐτήν, ξανθὴ τὴν χροιάν*, and attributes to her the third pyramid (cf. 134 nn.). But her very existence seems doubtful; the Neterkara of the sixth-dynasty monuments was prob-

ably a king, *not* a queen. (For the origin of the confusion see Hall, *u. s.*) There was also on the Turin papyrus a Queen Neitakerti, who may be the original of H.'s Nitocris; perhaps she belongs to the period of confusion under the fifteenth to the seventeenth dynasties; but there was no trace of the story told by H.

The name may be connected with Nitocris, who was made priestess of Thebes by her father, Psammetichus I (cf. for her, Cairo Museum, No. 673, p. 208, E. T.); H. had heard much of this Saite house.

3 **καινοῦν**, 'ostensibly she handselled it.'

4 **σποδοῦ**: she would be choked by the ashes. Ctesias (48, 51, 52, pp. 76–7) mentions this as a Persian punishment used by Darius Ochus; cf. also Val. Max. ix. 2. 6, and Ovid, Ibis, 317.

101 **τῶν ἄλλων βασιλέων**: dependent as a sort of possessive genitive on *κατ' οὐδὲν λαμπρότητος*. Others, e.g. Krüger, suppose the accusative *τοὺς ἄλλους β.* is attracted into the case of the dependent clause (cf. *τοῖσι* in i. 24. 5), and translate 'the other kings were in no way distinguished' (lit. 'were at no point of distinction').

Probably H. means by 'Moeris' the great king Amenemhêt III (cf. App. X. 5) of the twelfth dynasty (for his portrait cf. B. M. G. p. 218; for the construction of Lake Moeris see c. 149 nn.). Diodorus also calls him Moeris, Manetho, *Λάμαρις* or *Λάβαρις*. He received a nickname from this lake (probably to distinguish him from other kings, called 'Amenemhêt'); but his real name, in its Greek form *Μαρ(ρ)ῆς*, had a somewhat similar sound (Z. A. S. (1906) 43, p. 86). His date is probably 1849–1801 B.C.; hence it is clear that H. is wrong in placing him only ten generations before Psammetichus (cf. App. XIV. 3).

2 **προπύλαια**. The entrance to the Egyptian temple was through a pylon in the outer wall, i.e. a gate flanked by towers, shaped like truncated pyramids; the court inside was full of pillared halls; the pylones and the pillared court inside, leading to the wall of the actual temple, together form the *προπύλαια*. H. mentions four of these in this temple at Memphis, to north (here), to west (c. 121, Rhamsinitus), to east (c. 136, Asychis), to south (c. 153, Psammetichus).

102–110 *The story of Sesostris.*

Sesostris has been variously identified. Of the Greeks, Diodorus (i. 53) puts him seven *γενεαί* (i.e. 'dynasties') after Moeris, thus identifying him with Rameses II; this has been very largely accepted. Cf. Tac. Ann. ii. 60. But it is better to suppose that his name at any rate is that of the great conqueror of the twelfth dynasty, Senosret III (Usertesen), who was the first invader of Syria. Manetho (F. H. G. ii. 560) puts 'Sesostris' at this date. With his name, however, were associated (Meyer, i. 281) some of the later glories of Thothmes III and Rameses II (cf. cc. 106, 107 nn.), and the whole was developed into a mythical figure, which bears even less resemblance to the truth than the mythical Alexander to the real

Alexander. Maspero, however (p. 267 n.), explains the name = 'Sestourî', a nickname for Rameses II (Greek writers used this in place of the Pharaohs' real name); cf. the loose use of 'Caligula' for the emperor Caius.

2 Strabo (769) is more definite and says Sesostris penetrated south to the straits of Bab-el-Mandeb (Δειρή), and crossing them, returned through Arabia. All this is fiction; the only Egyptian campaigns to the south were against the Nubians (c. 110 n.); the North Sûdân was occupied; Senosret II also conquered some of the Semitic tribes in North Arabia (F. Petrie, i. 172–3). Egypt did not fully establish its rule on the Red Sea till the time of the Ptolemies.

3 H. cautiously gives his authority for the conquests of Sesostris to the north and east; Strabo (769) takes him over 'all Asia'; Diodorus (i. 55) makes him cross the Ganges and overrun all India to the ocean; no doubt this detail was invented to make him outrival Alexander, just as he is made to conquer the Scythians (c. 103) in order to surpass Darius (c. 110). Really, however, no Egyptian conqueror ever penetrated beyond North Syria except Amenhotep II, who actually crossed the Euphrates.

5 It was an Egyptian custom to set up columns in record of conquest, but the addition of sexual emblems (given more fully, Diod. i. 55 *et al.*) is a Greek invention.

103 1 H. seems to be referring to actual monuments in Thrace, but unluckily he does not say what they were; the conclusion he bases on them is obviously false, but this does not prove (cf. 106 nn.) that he had not seen them.

104 1 It has been inferred from this passage that H. was twice in Colchis and twice in Egypt, which is unlikely, if not impossible. He may well have seen Egyptians in Asia Minor, before his travels in the Black Sea, which almost certainly preceded his visit to Egypt (cf. Introd. pp. 14, 19).

2 **μελάγχροες.** H. has already (57. 2) said the Egyptians were 'black'; this was the usual Greek idea (so Aesch. Sup. 719); it is an exaggeration of the 'brown' colour; the Colchians were 'black' in the same sense; so Pind. Pyth. iv. 212 (376) calls them *κελαινῶπες*. The hair of the Colchians was short and curly, as contrasted with the lank locks (*εὐθύτριχες*, Arist. de G. A. v. 3, 782 B) of the Scyths. H.'s ideas of Egyptian appearance have been somewhat confused by the numerous negro slaves he saw in the streets of Memphis. As the Egyptians themselves shaved wholly or in part (36. 1 n.), the 'woolly hair' is the more inexplicable. Various attempts have been made to find a basis for H.'s 'discovery' (*νοήσας πρότερον*) of the identity of the Colchians with the Egyptians (cf. Wiedemann, p. 408); the least improbable is the suggestion that the Persian king had deported Egyptians to Colchis. But it is most likely a mistake altogether.

For circumcision in Egypt cf. 36. 3 n. H.'s method—to infer identity of race from similarity of custom—is modern, though its sufficiency is doubted; here certainly his conclusion is wrong. His information as to Phoenician usage in Greece (§ 4) is curious.

3 Σύριοι οἱ ἐν τῇ Παλαιστίνῃ. For these cf. iii. 5. 1 n. H. does not distinguish the Jews from the other inhabitants of Palestine; the Philistines were not circumcised (cf. 1 Sam. xvii. 26 *et pass.*), nor all the Phoenicians (Ezek. xxxii. 30). Josephus (Antiq. viii. 10. 3), however, is wrong in saying the Jews alone in Palestine practised the rite. For Σύριοι in general cf. i. 6 n. H. here extends them beyond the Halys to the river Parthenius, which lay in the very west of Paphlagonia, though in i. 72 he kept them east of the Halys.

For the Macrones who live on the south-east of the Black Sea cf. iii. 94.

105 H. seeks to confirm his point by reference to the similarity of Egyptian and Colchian manufactures. His familiarity with Greek trade-names is interesting (cf. Introd. p. 17). Some have proposed to read Σαρδιηνικόν, supposing the Colchian linen was imported *via* Sardis; but Pollux (v. 26) quotes H. for Σαρδονικὸν λίνον. It is more probable that some Colchian word had been wrongly changed to the familiar Σαρδονικόν; of course the linen had nothing to do with Sardinia. Strabo (498) says the Colchian linen was famous (τεθρύληται); the passage implies a criticism of H.'s Colchian theories.

6 1 αὐτὸς ὤρων. At the mouth of the Nahr el Kelb near Beyrut there are three monuments cut in the face of the limestone rock, on one of which the name of Rameses II can be read; they commemorate the victorious campaigns of his early years (e. g. 'year 4'). Beside them, in contempt, Esarhaddon has cut the account of his conquest of Egypt (circ. 670 B.C.; cf. Breasted, pp. 424, 556). They are figured in Lepsius, D. iii. 197. There is no trace of the αἰδοῖα on them now, nor is it likely there ever was.

2 In the pass of Karabel, south of the road from Smyrna to Sardis, two monuments have been found, of which one (figured in Rawlinson) corresponds to H.'s account. For it cf. Garstang, pp. 171 seq. The road from 'the Ephesian territory to Phocaea' is clearly not the road along the coast, but one more inland, round Mount Sipylus.

3 πέμπτης: translate '$4\frac{1}{2}$ cubits high' (not '$2\frac{1}{2}$' as Sayce). Cf. i. 50. 2 τρίτον ἡμιτάλαντον = '$2\frac{1}{2}$ talents'. The σπιθαμή is 12 'fingers', i. e. half a cubit; others make it only 10 fingers, i. e. $7\frac{1}{2}$ inches. The figure is really about 7 feet high.

H. has misplaced the weapons; the bow is in the right hand, the spear in the left; ὡσαύτως, the rest of the dress 'corresponded', being both Egyptian and Ethiopian; the bow was especially the Ethiopian weapon, cf. vii. 69. The dress, however, is not really Egyptian; the high cap and the shoes with points turned up are 'Hittite'.

4 The inscription (now illegible) is above the figure in the corner, not on the breast. It is not likely that H. or his guide could trans late it, nor is the rendering here ('with my shoulders'; others conj. ὅπλοισι) at all in epigraphic style.

5 Memnon is not the Egyptian king whose musical statue was famous (cf. Paus. i. 42. 3; Frazer, ii. 530; Tac. Ann. ii. 61), but the king of Ethiopia, son of Aurora, who came to help Priam (Od. iv. 188; xi. 522); cf. 'the Memnonian palace', v. 53; 'Memnonian Susa', v. 54. 2; 'Memnon's road' (Paus. x. 31. 7, though Frazer, *ad loc.*, argues this was not H.'s 'Royal Road'). The original Memnon is identified by Robertson Smith with Adonis, a god 'first dead and then alive' (cf. E. H. R., 1887, p. 307), and became the centre of many strange myths; for the birds at his grave cf. Ael. H. A. v. 1 and Frazer, Paus. v. 387. The stories of 'Memnon' belong to a later stage of mythology, when men placed the Homeric 'Aethiopians' in Africa; but the name is Egyptian.

If, as is possible, the myth of Memnon is a reflection of a great Anatolian 'Hittite' empire, the view rejected by H. was correct. The statue at Karabel certainly resembles those at Boghaz Keui and elsewhere; it probably is that of the Hittite war-god. The great Egyptologist, Lepsius, however, like H., thought the figure Egyptian.

Ramsay (H. G. of A. M., p. 60) thinks H.'s topographical details are impossible, and considers that he never went 'more than a few miles from the coast' (of Asia Minor), and so had never seen the monument he here describes; H. had been told there were three roads to Sardis, viz. from Phocaea, from 'the Ephesian territory', and from Smyrna, and that two of them were marked by monuments, i.e. the Karabel relief and the 'Niobe'; these three roads H. confuses and makes into two. This criticism of Ramsay's is not usually accepted; but even if H. has confused the roads, it does not follow that he had never traversed them. If Ramsay be right that H. never left the coast, the historian would be convicted of a serious *suggestio falsi*; though he does not say distinctly that he had seen the Ionian monuments, he certainly implies that he had done so and that he had traversed the roads.

The whole chapter is most interesting as showing:

(1) The care of H. to use archaeological evidence; (2) his mixture of accuracy and inaccuracy in the use of it; the latter is easily explicable, considering the difficulties under which his observations were conducted; the figures are high up above the road; (3) his ignorance of history before the seventh century. He has no idea of the limitations of Egyptian power, or of the existence of great Anatolian powers in the past.

107 The story of Sesostris' brother seems to be quite unhistorical, though it occurs in different forms in Diodorus and in Manetho; the latter (Jos. in Ap. i. 15) identifies Sesostris and his brother with Aegyptus and Danaus. Perhaps the harem conspiracy against

Rameses III when old (Breasted, pp. 498 seq.) may be the origin of the story; but there is no resemblance in details, and it is more probably an echo of the myth of the strife of Set and Osiris (62. 2 n.).

108 2 **οἱ**: ethical dative. For a pronoun's transposition cf. οἱ γάρ με κτλ., i. 115. 2. This use of captives to carry out public works is historical (cf. Exod. i. 11); some of the works are mentioned in c. 110.

For a picture of a colossus thus dragged cf. Rawlinson, *ad loc.* For a list of the buildings of Rameses II cf. Petrie, iii. 72 seq. The canal system, to which H. refers in i. 193 and iv. 47, for comparison with Babylonia and Scythia, is not the creation of any individual king; irrigation was essential to the very life of Egypt. What H. (§ 4) gives as cause is really effect; the cities were built on canals, not the canals made for the cities.

οὐκ ἑκόντες, 'without intending it.' Diodorus (i. 57) makes this the main motive. H. is not happy in his remark τὸ . . . ἱππασίμην, chariots and horses do not appear on the Egyptian monuments before the eighteenth dynasty.

4 **ὅκως τε** (if τε be read) only occurs here; cf. οἷος τε, ἐπείτε (this last only in H.). H. is right that the 'spring' water in Egypt is 'somewhat brackish' (πλατυτέροισι).

109 It is true that all the land of Egypt, except that of priests and soldiers (so H. himself, c. 168), was held of the king and paid to him one-fifth of the produce; the Jewish story attributed this arrangement to Joseph (Gen. xlvii); there is no reason for assigning it to any one king (Meyer, i. 224, puts it as early as the fourth and fifth dynasties). Probably, however, there was a basis of truth for the tradition which connected land taxation with the conquering Sesostris; as kings developed a spirited foreign policy, the burden of taxation on their subjects was organized and increased. H. is wrong as to lots being equal.

2 Translate 'might pay in future in proportion to the rent fixed' (cf. ἐπιτάξαντα ἀποφορήν above); i.e. rent was diminished in proportion to the amount of land lost, but the rate of assessment was unchanged.

3 The πόλος was a concave, hemispherical 'dial', so called from being shaped like the vault of the sky; on this a shadow was cast by the γνώμων (a 'pointer'), which marked the time of day by its direction, and the chief seasons of the year (the solstice, equinox, &c.) by its length at midday. The period from sunrise to sunset was divided into 'twelve parts', which of course varied in length with the season of the year. Diogenes Laertius (ii. 1) says Anaximander invented the γνώμων: but this need only mean that he introduced it from Egypt. It is most natural to suppose (cf. D. of A. *s. v.* Polus) that H. is speaking of one 'compound instrument'. Others, however (e.g. D. of A. *s. v.* Horologium), think that he means to distinguish the γνώμων and the πόλος. Both certainly

were used independently of each other; the γνώμων was the earlier, in the form of a pillar, which measured time by the length of its shadow. That geometry was an Egyptian invention was the general belief of the Greeks. For the whole subject cf. the 'Eudemian summary' (based by Proclus, circ. 450 A.D., on the history of Eudemus, circ. 330 B.C.). This is translated in Gow's Hist. of Gk. Math., pp. 134 seq. (a short paraphrase in Smith, D.B. *s.v.* Euclides). According to this (for other evidence cf. Gow, p. 131) geometry was invented because the Nile floods destroyed all ordinary boundaries (cf. Strabo 787 for the same statement). Thales introduced geometry into Greece; but it was the Greeks who made it a science; in Egypt it was confined almost entirely to the practical requirements of the surveyor (Gow, p. 126).

110 Cf. 102. 2 n. and B. M. G. pp. 213 seq. for the campaigns of the twelfth dynasty in the south; the rock temples of Abusimbel witness the activity of Rameses II in Nubia; but many other Egyptian kings beside Senosret III and Rameses II gained victories over the Nubians.

ἀνδριάντας. At Mîtrahîneh (near Memphis) are two colossal statues of Rameses II lying overthrown; the larger of these is about forty-two feet, which corresponds to H.'s 'thirty cubits' (Baedeker, p. 141); for cast of its head cf. B. M. G. p. 245. For other statues in the temple at Memphis cf. 121. 1, 141. 6 n., 176. 1.

3 The story of Darius' concession is an invention of Egyptian vanity; but it is characteristic of his conciliatory policy (cf. vii. 7. 1 n.).

111 1 **Φερῶς** is simply the title 'Pharaoh' turned into a proper name (cf. its use in Genesis, *pass.*). The story of H. is merely 'a satire on the truth of women', and the town of 'Red Earth' (§ 3) is a purely imaginary place; Diodorus (i. 59), who tells the same tale, calls it Ἱερὰ βῶλος. Maspero (C.P. pp. xlii. seq.) points out that the tales in the papyri are equally unfavourable to feminine chastity; but, like the similar tales of mediaeval Europe, he thinks them due mainly to male unfairness.

2 **ὀκτωκαίδεκα**: cf. 13. 1 n. for height of Nile rise.

The disgusting remedy is a genuine piece of Egyptian medicine; Maspero (C., p. 315) suggests that it was employed for the natural ammonia in it, and thinks it was sometimes really effective.

ἑκατόν. The obelisk now at Heliopolis is only sixty-six feet high, but a great part of it is buried by the rise of the soil level; it was erected by Senosret I, of the twelfth dynasty (Baedeker, p. 117). The largest obelisk in the world, that before the Lateran, is over a hundred feet high, and no doubt still larger ones have perished; but H.'s figure, 150 feet, is suspiciously big.

112–17 *Homer and Egyptian history.*

112 1 The words, 'a man of Memphis,' imply that Proteus was of a different family from the previous kings. Homer (Od. iv. 126) makes Polybus king in Egyptian Thebes at the time of the Trojan War, and Manetho (F. H. G. ii. 581) identifies him with the last ruler of the nineteenth dynasty, whom he calls Θούωρις. Diodorus (i. 62) follows H. Perhaps H. has confused an Egyptian title, Proutî, with the familiar 'Proteus'. It is suggested that, as Proteus is a sea-god in Homer (Od. iv. 385), H. may have identified him with the fish-god (Dagon) of the Τυρίων στρατόπεδον (112. 2). At any rate, H. does not commit the absurdity of Diodorus (*u. s.*), who explains the famous transformations of Proteus as a myth due to the Egyptian custom of the king wearing lion skins and other articles on his head, to inspire terror and reverence.

2 In 154. 1 στρατόπεδα is used for the Greek settlements on the Pelusiac Nile; the alien quarter in a town was of the nature of a camp. Aphrodite is called ξείνη to distinguish the Phoenician Astarte from the Aphrodite of Egypt (Hathor, cf. 41. 5 n.). H. is probably wrong in identifying her with Helen (cf. vi. 61 n.).

This temple of 'Proteus' was found by Petrie (1907–8). As H. says, it lies south of the Ptah τέμενος, and the only tablets of Hathor found were dug up here; this agrees with his statement as to the 'foreign' Aphrodite (E. E. F., 1908, p. 15). The temple seems also contemporary with the date that H. gives for the Trojan War, i.e. the thirteenth century B.C. (145. 4 n.).

113 H. is supposed to have borrowed this story of Helen in Egypt from Hecataeus (cf. Diels, Hermes, 22). In the fragments attributed to that writer, Menelaus is certainly brought to Egypt (fr. 287, F. H. G. i. 20), and Helen is in some way connected with Canopus (fr. 288). But H.'s account differs in important details; e.g. he does not mention Pharos (contrast fr. 287), and his story of the slaves has nothing to do with fr. 318. We know there was a great variety of legends about Helen (cf. especially Stesichorus, fr. 32, who said that only a phantom of Helen was taken to Troy). Hence the connexion of H.'s story with Hecataeus is at least unproven.

1 For the Canopic Nile cf. 15. 1 n. There was a 'curing station' (ταριχεῖαι) also near the Pelusiac Nile (*ib.*).

2 H. seems to have visited this temple, but no Egyptian parallel has been found for such a general right of asylum as H. speaks of. The temple, however, is a reality (cf. Strabo, 788, who makes it one of the western boundaries of Egypt).

3 The name Θῶνις comes originally from Od. iv. 228 (cf. 116. 4), where the wife of Θῶν makes presents to Helen; his name was combined with the early town, Thonis, on the Canopic Nile (Strabo, 800), and he was made an Egyptian official.

2 **παρεποίησε**: he 'introduced an inconsistent digression'; in this sense the verb is a ἅπαξ λεγόμενον.

ἀνεπόδισε, 'he never corrected himself'; lit. 'cause to step back'; this passage indicates clearly H.'s implicit belief in Homer.

3 These lines are in Iliad vi (289 seq.); only Bk. V is now called the 'Prowess of Diomede'; hence H. clearly did not know the present division into 24 books.

4 The passages from Odyssey iv (227 seq., 351–2) are probably interpolations; there is no reference to them below. And the presence later of Menelaus and Helen in Egypt is (to say the least) a very indirect proof of the wanderings of Paris.

117 3 H. rejects the Homeric authorship of the Cypria, as later he doubts it of the Epigoni (4. 32 *ad fin.*). The Cypria told the origin and the first part of the Trojan War; the main figure in its action was Aphrodite, hence its name.

118 It is characteristic of the later rationalization of the Epic story that as much stress is laid on the treasures as on Helen herself; for a like contrast between Homeric romance and the common sense of H. contrast Iliad iii. 156 seq. and c. 120. 1.

119 In the story of the misconduct of Menelaus there may be an echo of early struggles between Egypt and the races inhabiting Greece and the Aegean (cf. the story of Odysseus as to the raid against Egypt, told to Eumaeus, Od. xiv. 257 seq.). But it is more probably an Egyptian invention, a retort to the Greek charge of human sacrifices (c. 45) brought against Egypt. So it is quoted by 'Plutarch' (De Mal. H. 12), in connexion with the story of Busiris, as a mark of the 'philo-barbarism' of H. 'Plutarch' also says Menelaus was much honoured in Egypt.

3 The sacrifice of Iphigenia is a familiar parallel. Ἔντομα ποιεῖν is used in vii. 191 for sacrifices to allay a storm, but nothing is there said of their being human.

There was a 'harbour of Menelaus' in Libya (iv. 169. 1).

120 3 οὐκ ἔστι ὅτε οὐ = *numquam non*, 'on every occasion.'

For the scepticism of εἰ χρή τι τοῖσι ἐποποιοῖσι κτλ. (so unlike H.) cf. Thuc. i. 9. 4 εἴ τῳ ἱκανος (*sc.* Homer) τεκμηριῶσαι and the sayings of many other Greeks, e.g. Solon, fr. 29 πολλὰ ψεύδονται ἀοιδοί. The whole chapter is an instance of Greek rationalizing criticism.

121 Diodorus (i. 62) makes Remphis succeed Proteus; he does not tell the tale of the thieves, but only that the king was famous for avarice. The kings of the twentieth dynasty almost all bear the name 'Rameses' (III to XI), from which H.'s 'Rhampsinitus' is formed by the termination 'nitus'; this seems to correspond to the name of Neith, the goddess of Sais (Maspero, Ann. des É. G., 1877, p. 133). With this imaginary king, whose name blends Theban and Saite elements in an impossible way, H. combines Rameses III, who certainly was a temple-builder at Memphis; he was also renowned for his wealth (cf. B. M. G. p. 250); his treasuries can still be seen at Medînet Habu (Baedeker, p. 322). So far history confirms the framework into which H. has introduced a popular tale; for the prevalence of robberies of royal tombs under the twentieth dynasty cf. B. M. G. p. 250. The tale itself is one of the most familiar pieces of universal folklore ; we may compare it to that of Ali Baba and the Forty Thieves, or to that of Trophonius and Agamedes (Paus. ix. 37. 3, who gives an almost exact epitome of the first two parts, α and β, of the story of H.). A list of twenty-eight variants of the story, from all parts of the world, is given by Frazer (Paus. v. 177). The king's daughter's question, the device of the thief, and the marriage that ends the story, all show that it belongs to fairyland, not to the world of reality.

For a further discussion of it cf. Maspero, C. P. pp. xl. seq., 180 seq., who maintains that it is, if not Egyptian in origin, at least thoroughly 'egyptianized'.

θέρος, χειμῶνα. The identification of these statues is more than suspicious ; the Egyptians divided the year into three seasons, not two, those of the inundation, of growth, and of the harvest. And only one instance is known in Egypt of symbolic statues of this kind (Sourdille, R. p. 215).

α 1 For treasure houses of this kind in Egypt cf. the twelve crypts at Dendera (Baedeker, p. 244), the entrances to which were once closed by movable stones ; also Maspero, *u. s.*

3 **οὐκ ἐς μακρήν**, 'at once.'

δ 1 **ποδεῶνας.** In the plural, the 'ragged ends of a skin', where the feet and tail have been ; hence, in the singular, the mouth of a bottle, formed by one of these ends being left open while the others were sewed up. This end was 'tightly bound round' (*ἀπαμμένους*. L. and S., however, seem to take this = 'hung on the ass'). The ass-driver, pulling at the skins, as if to pull them straight (*ἐπισπάσαντα*), looses the ends.

3 **κατασκευάζειν**, 'repack' the ass's burden, the balance of which had been spoiled.

6 For this mark of insult cf. 2 Sam. x. 4 (Hanun's treatment of David's embassy). Wiedemann shows that some of the Egyptian soldiers, especially the police, wore beards, and that H. therefore is not to be charged with introducing a foreign detail into the story.

ε **δεινὰ ποιέειν**, 'showed himself very angry' (cf. iii. 14. 6) ; more common in the middle voice = 'to think it shameful' (cf. 133. 2).

ζ The vanity of the Egyptians was proverbial, and this touch brings it out clearly.

2 1 **συγκυβεύειν.** For the Egyptian fondness for dice cf. B. M. G. p. 87 ; they were buried in the tombs (ib. p. 178). For the bringing up of a token from the lower world cf. Maspero, Cont. Pop. pp. 118–19 ; Satni in the tomb wins the magic book after playing a game ; the tale is preserved in a Ptolemaic papyrus.

Plutarch (de I. et O. c. 12) says that Hermes won from Selene (Isis), when playing at draughts, a seventy-second part of each day, and that out of these the five 'intercalary days' (cf. 4. 1 nn.) were made up.

αὐτημερόν. For the offering of the 'new garment' to the goddess cf. 1 Sam. vi. 7.

3 λύκων. Perhaps H. means 'jackals' (cf. 67. 1 n.). Erman (R. p. 177; cf. p. 15) sees a reference here to the two Wepwawet gods, the jackal-headed 'guides' of the dead.

123 1 ὑπόκειται κτλ. For this principle, so often forgotten by H.'s critics, cf. vii. 152. 3.

Demeter and Dionysus are Isis (c. 41 n.) and Osiris (cc. 42 nn., 62. 2 n.). H., having introduced the subject of the world below, brings in another doctrine as to life after death, which he thought the Greeks had borrowed from Egypt. Whether metempsychosis was really a doctrine taught in Egypt is uncertain. Wiedemann rightly says that it is inconsistent with the preservation of the body by embalming, and that the number 3,000 is quite insufficient for Egyptian ideas; he therefore supposes that H. confused the doctrine of immortality, which in a certain form (cf. Maspero, M. et A. E. I. 48 seq.) the Egyptians undoubtedly held, with that of metempsychosis, and wrongly attributed the latter to Egypt. H. would be the more likely to do this, as the Egyptians believed the souls of the blessed could at will take any form they pleased (Sourdille, R. p. 365). Gomperz (Gk. Thinkers, i. 126–7) considers the doctrine of metempsychosis rather Indian than Egyptian, and seems to believe that the Greeks had been brought into relation with the Indians by their common subjection to Persia. He also quotes Egyptian doctrines as to the changes of the soul's abode, which H. may have misunderstood.

2 The number 3,000 recurs in Plat. Phaedrus, 29, p. 249 A, but only for the 'truly philosophic soul'. Empedocles, who is certainly referred to in *οἱ ὕστερον*, gives '30,000 years' (*ὧραι* fr. 115, ed. Diels) as the period for the purification of sinful souls. By *οἱ πρότερον* H. means probably the Orphic teachers (cf. 81. 2 nn.), and certainly Pythagoras (cf. iv. 95–6). Whether Pythagoras was in this matter the pupil of Pherecydes, 'qui primus dixit animos hominum esse sempiternos' (Cic. Tusc. i. 16. 38) is doubtful (cf. Gomperz, i. 542). H. avoids censuring Pythagoras by name, perhaps because he was a Samian (but cf. i. 51. 4 for similar reticence).

The doctrine of metempsychosis was widely diffused in the sixth century, and it is possible that it may have been taught at Croton before Pythagoras came there, by the mysterious Orpheus of Croton (cf. Gruppe, Rosch. Lex. *s. v.* Orpheus, p. 1131, who accepts H.'s statement that it was an Egyptian doctrine).

124–36 *The pyramid-builders.*

124 Their names, Khufu, Khâfra, and Menkaura are correctly given, but their chronological position (2840–2680 B.C.) is entirely wrong; they belong to Manetho's fourth dynasty, while H. puts them after a king of the twentieth dynasty, and only three generations before Psammetichus (666 B.C.). For explanations of H.'s mistake cf. App. X. 10, or (better) Petrie's ingenious theory (J. H. S. 28. 275)

that H. composed Bk. II in twelve divisions of about equal length, and that cc. 100–23 (two sections) have been wrongly placed before cc. 124–36, which should really precede them; the order should be roll 7 (207 lines), cc. 124–36; roll 8 (222 lines), cc. 100–15; roll 9 (224 lines), cc. 116–23: the coincidence in number of lines is at any rate very curious.

For casts of the statues of the pyramid-builders in the B. M. see G. pp. 196, 199, 200; that of Chephrên is 'one of the leading examples of ancient art' (Petrie, i. 54).

κατακληίσαντα. This impiety is contrary to the monuments, on which 'Cheops' figures as a temple-builder. 'What H. relates is only the copy of a popular story' (Maspero, p. 77). The sufferings of the Egyptian people under the pyramid-builders had coloured tradition as to them. H. as a Greek would be the more ready to accept the accusation of impiety, because the mere building of such gigantic masses offended the Greek sense of moderation. Similarly, in the story in the Papyrus Westcar (now in Berlin), Chufu impiously appeals to the magicians to defeat the will of the god Ra. Cf. cc. 126, 128 nn.

2 **ἕλκειν.** For the transport of great masses by human labour cf. Breasted, i. 694 n., the colossal statue of Thuthotep (under the twelfth dynasty) drawn by 172 men in four double rows (picture, ib. 159).

3 **κατὰ δέκα.** This must mean that a gang of 100,000 worked for three months, and were then relieved by another gang. For relays of workers cf. 1 Kings v. 13–15, and for forced labour *ib.* ix. 21 (both of Solomon). Meyer (i. 233; so too Petrie, Pyramids, p. 210), however, thinks the three months are those of the rising of the Nile; the blocks were cut all the year round, but transported during the period when field-work was impossible. Petrie says: 'Such a scale of work would suffice for the complete building in twenty years as stated by H.' H.'s informant may have meant this, but if so H. certainly misunderstood him.

δέκα ἔτεα. The *μέν* corresponds to the *δέ* of § 5; the road and the 'chambers' (§ 4 *οἰκημάτων*) took ten years, the pyramid itself twenty.

τῆς ὁδοῦ. Two roads can still be traced, one to the first, the other to the third pyramid; their object was to serve as an inclined plane, up which the stones could be dragged from the Nile level to the edge of the plateau, which is a hundred feet above the plain (cf. *ἐπὶ τοῦ λόφου*).

πυραμίς: an Egyptian word = 'a building with a sloping side'; B. M. G. p. 170.

4 **διώρυχα.** H. had never been inside the pyramid; a connexion with the Nile is impossible, as the underground chamber in the centre of the pyramid, though a hundred feet at least below its ground level, is yet thirty-six feet above the river level. H. gives

further particulars as to the 'channel of masonry' in c. 127. 2. Sourdille (H. E. p. 12) thinks that H. has, by a confusion of memory, attributed to the pyramids of Gizeh the subterranean water which is really found under other pyramids, e. g. at Hawara, near the Labyrinth.

5 H.'s measurements of the pyramids can best be estimated from the following table (fractions are neglected):

	Petrie	*Herodotus*	*Diodorus*	*Pliny*
Great Pyramid.			i. 63	
Length of side (average)	756	800	700	883
Height (original) (present 451)	481	—	more than 600	—
Height (along sloping side[1])	720 (circ.)	800	—	—
Second Pyramid.		'40 feet in size inferior to the other' (127. 3), i. e. along sloping side		
Length of side	706		600	—
Height (present 469)	472		—	—
Height (along sloping side)	670 (circ.)		—	—
Pyramid of Mycerinus.				
Length of side	346	280	300	—
Height	215	—	—	—
Height (along sloping side)	330 (circ.)	280 (but see 134. 1 n.)	—	—

The modern figures are taken from Murray's Egypt, pp. 170 seq. It is there pointed out that 'nine modern writers have equally (with the ancients) varied in their calculations'. Petrie sums up (*u. s.* 159), 'the accuracy with which H. states what he saw and relates what he heard, the criticism he often applies to his materials . . . all this should prevent our ever discrediting his words, unless compelled to do so.'

125 1 H.'s account of the building of the pyramid is creditably free from marvels: contrast the stories in Diod. i. 63 of the 'mounds' by which the stones were taken to the top, &c.

κρόσσαι: cf. iv. 152. 4 and vii. 188. 1 with nn. for the derivative *πρόκροσσοι*. Translate 'some call "battlements", others "steps" (literally 'altar steps').' They are called *στοῖχος* below (§§ 2, 3), when the whole 'row' of them is taken into account.

2 **τοὺς ἐπιλοίπους.** 'The rest of the stones,' i. e. to fill up the triangular gaps between each 'step'. The great pyramid when finished presented a smooth surface, though in the present day the stripping off of most of its stone covering (here described, §§ 2–5) has made it once more 'like steps'.

[1] [It seems to be generally agreed that this is the height given by H.; it is calculated as $\frac{19}{20}$ of the base.]

μηχανῇσι. Petrie writes (*u. s.* p. 212): 'for the ordinary blocks of a few tons each it would be very feasible to employ the method of resting them on two piles of wooden slabs, and rocking them up alternately to one side and the other by a spar under the block, thus heightening the piles alternately, and so raising the stone.' He goes on to show how this method could be applied to the largest blocks in the pyramid, of fifty tons and upwards. But the explanation of Choisy (L'Art de bâtir chez les Égypt., 1904, p. 80 seq., with pictures and diagrams) is better, viz. that the stones were raised with 'ascenseurs oscillants'; these resemble in shape the wooden framework, used to support temporarily arches in England; ancient models of them are in the B. M., the Louvre, and at Cairo (cf. App. IX. 4).

4 **τοσαῦται.** H.'s good sense has made him put first what is obviously the right alternative; the constant shifting of one 'contrivance' from row to row is impossible.

5 H.'s description is right, whether we suppose that the whole pyramid was planned and carried out *at once* (cf. Petrie, *u. s.* p. 163, for a discussion of this question), or that a pyramid grew with the length of its builder's reign, being continually extended. This 'accretion' theory of Lepsius is now in favour again. In either case the 'step formation' must come first, and then the 'filling up of the angles' (*ἐξεποιήθη*).

6 **συρμαίη.** For the use of the 'radish' as a purge cf. c. 77. 2; the 'onions and garlick' were for relishes not 'food' (*σιτία*, § 7).

εὖ μεμνῆσθαι. It can hardly be inferred from this, as some have done, that H. trusted his memory in his observations, and made no notes. He only wishes to emphasize the accuracy of a surprising statement. Diodorus (i. 64) and Pliny here repeat H. Maspero (Ann. des É. G., 1875, p. 18) explains this strange inscription as a prayer to Osiris, scribbled by an Egyptian tourist, that he might obtain the blessings of food, &c., and mistranslated by the guide. It would be a kind of parody of the inscriptions usual on tombs, praying that Osiris would give (such blessings) to the departed.

It is simpler (with Murray, *u. s.*, p. 163) to suppose that the royal inscription was mistranslated; the onion plant was the hieroglyph for 'nesut' ('king'), and the papyrus and the lotus were used in spelling his titles as 'Lord of Upper and Lower Egypt'. But if this be the explanation, H.'s memory as to the exact place failed him; there were no official inscriptions on a pyramid, except close to the entry of the actual tomb-chamber; this one must have been in a temple near. Some, however, have thought that H.'s guide was as unable to read hieroglyphics as H. himself, and that he concealed his ignorance by a complete invention, which he meant also to be a joke.

7 To **ἄλλον** supply some word like *ἐπόνεον* (out of *οἰκοδόμεον*) by zeugma. *ὁκότε* is causal; cf. *ὅτε* (=' since'), iii. 73. 1.

126 **ὁκόσον δή τι:** the words that follow seem to show that this phrase

implies uncertainty on the part of H.; cf. i. 157. 2. He is confirmed by the monuments (Breasted, A.R. i. § 180) in saying that one of the three small pyramids near the Sphinx, to the south-east of the Great Pyramid, is that of the daughter of Cheops; Vyse, 2. 183, says its workmanship is similar to that of the Great Pyramid.

The rest of the story is a fable, to cast discredit on the pyramid-builders (cf. i. 93 and ii. 121 for similar stories as to the 'Tomb of Alyattes' and as to Rhampsinitus). As Maspero points out (Ann. des É. G., 1875, p. 21) the story-tellers of Memphis took the great names of history and 'made them odious and ridiculous'. He compares the romance of Setné (or Satni) for a similar motive, i. e. the sacrifice of a woman's honour to obtain an end otherwise unattainable. In this tale too Rameses II (under one of his names) and Menephtah both figure, but the latter has become a distant ancestor instead of a son (ib., 1878, p. 171, where the story is given almost in full, pp. 142-69). H. himself may have heard it in Egypt.

127 The Chephrên pyramid is a little larger than H. says. It is hard to believe that a king who reigned fifty years could be succeeded by a brother who reigned fifty-six years. The monuments give the name of Tetfrâ between, who seems to have been quite unimportant. Maspero (p. 76) suggests that Chephrên was his brother, and so really the son of Cheops. Manetho (F. H. G. ii. 548) gives Souphis (= Cheops) sixty-three years, Souphis (= Chephrên) sixty-six years, Mencheres sixty-three; these figures are absurd; Meyer (i. 234) gives Cheops twenty-three years, on the authority of the Turin and other papyri.

The words *ταῦτα γὰρ . . . Χέοπα* (end of 2) seem to be a later addition; they interrupt the antithesis *ἐς μὲν τὰ . . . ὑποδείμας δέ*. The words *ταῦτα . . . ἐμετρησάμην* are parodied by Aristophanes (Av. 1130). Diodorus (i. 64) tells us there was an *ἀνάβασις* up one side of this pyramid.

2 **οἰκήματα.** H. does not mean there were no 'chambers' at all in this pyramid, but that there were none like those surrounded with water, which he was told (wrongly) were under the pyramid of Cheops (c. 124). As a matter of fact there were two chambers under that of Chephrên.

3 **λίθου Αἰθιοπικοῦ**: the red granite of Syene; H. is right, for 'the first layer' (*δόμον*) of stones was faced with this material, as was also the second.

τῆς ἑτέρης: genitive after the idea of comparison in *ὑποβάς*; *τὠυτὸ μέγαθος*, 'to attain the same size,' is added to explain *ὑποβάς*. *ἐχομένην* is local here.

128 **ποιμένος.** This story may contain the one reference in H. to the conquest of Egypt by the 'Hyksos' or Shepherd kings. For the extent of their rule and for their chronology cf. App. X, § 6, and B.M.G. pp. 224 seq. The Egyptians called them 'Shasu' ('robbers');

hence 'Hyksos', 'the rulers of the robbers.' Their rule was a time of oppression and degradation, and so may have been blended in popular memory with the times of the pyramid-builders. H.'s informants suppressed all mention of this conquest. Possibly 'Philitis' is connected with 'Philistines', a tribe which may have formed part of these invaders.

1 **ἀνοῖξαι.** Contemporary evidence confirms H.'s tradition of the piety of Menkaura. Of course, however, the temples were not 'opened', for they had never been closed (cf. 124. 1 n.). It need hardly be added that his justice, in which 'by gifts from his own purse he satisfied the wrath of him who found fault after the sentence', is a popular myth.

3 A coffin, of which the lid bears a cow's head, has been found of the time of Chephrên (L. D. ii. 14, vol. iii); there is no evidence, however, of its occupant's rank, nor even that it was a human being's. Lepsius says that queens were identified with Isis, whose symbol the cow is. For a picture of Isis with horns, and the sun between them (132. 1), cf. Maspero, i. 132.

1 **αὕτη ἡ βοῦς.** The pyramid-builders had nothing to do with Sais, and H. has wrongly introduced them into a rite which clearly was connected with the story of Osiris (cf. Plut. I. et O. 39, quoted on c. 62). For a mummy, no doubt that of Osiris, in a sacred cow, cf. R. de T. iv. 26; but it is only about 18 inches long (not life-size, as in c. 132). It used to be thought that Psammetichus II had the second name of 'Menkaura', and that H. was referring to some monument of his; but this theory is now given up.

2 **γυμναί.** The Egyptians never represented women in statues quite naked; but the linen fabrics were so fine and clinging as to be transparent. For such a dress cf. figure in Erman, E. p. 214, and Maspero, C. P. p. 124; Maspero adds in a note that the linen fabrics in the museum at Cairo quite confirm the tradition (cf. the 'Coae vestes' of the Romans).

131 The chapter is interesting as a specimen of H.'s attempts at criticism; Egyptian wood statues, being made in pieces, like dolls, were particularly liable to lose their forearms.

3 The *καί* simply emphasizes *ἡμεῖς*; there is no reference to other travellers (e. g. Hecataeus, suggested by Wiedemann).

2 See 62. 1 n. for the connexion of Neith, the goddess of Sais, and Isis. The ceremony is part of the festival of Osiris (cf. *τὸν οὐκ ὀνομαζόμενον θεόν*, and the bringing out of the cow symbolized Isis' search for Osiris.

For *τύπτωνται* cf. 39. 4 n.; for religious silence cf. 3. 2, 86. 2 n.

3 **συνταχύνειν**: intrans. here as in iii. 72. 1. Mycerinus was to have reigned forty-four years ('150' with Cheops and Chephrên); H. does not tell us in what year the oracle came, so that the actual length of his reign is uncertain.

4 **λύχνα πολλά.** The 'many lights' are borrowed from the Osiris festival (*v. s.*); for the *λυχνοκαΐη* cf. c. 62 nn.

Matthew Arnold's poem on Mycerinus is well known. As Wiedemann says, the endeavour to cheat the oracle is a Greek trick; but the mention of the marshes as 'places of pleasure' (*ἐνηβητήρια*) is quite in accordance with Egyptian usage. The sarcophagus and the wooden coffin of Mycerinus, with portions of his mummy, were found in this pyramid by Vyse in 1837; the former was lost on its way to England, but the coffin and the mummy are in the first Egyptian room at the B. M. (No. 6647, Case B; B. M. G. p. 201); it has been held that the coffin is a late restoration of the Saite period, Z. A. S. xxx, p. 98, but this is doubtful.

134 1 The genitive *ποδῶν* depends on *καταδέουσαν* in the usual way; *πλέθρων* is probably to be taken with *κῶλον*, 'on each side of three plethra'; but the construction is curious, as is also the deliberate anacoluthon of *ἐούσης*.

τετραγώνου: cf. i. 178. 2. Petrie (*u. s.* p. 160) explains doubtfully the discrepancy by referring H.'s figure (280) to 'the base of the limestone part', which really was 275 feet.

H. is right in saying that half the pyramid was cased with 'red granite' (**λίθου Αἰθιοπικοῦ**).

2 **Ῥοδώπιος.** H. shows his usual sense in rejecting this preposterous attribution, which is made by Diodorus (i. 64, as an alternative) and by Strabo (808); he shows it is contrary both to probability and to chronology. Two explanations are given of the origin of the story:

(1) It has been held that additions were made to the pyramid by a later queen (the Nitocris of Manetho, cf. 100 nn.), and that the Greek fiction as to Rhodopis was a version of the story of her work.

But 'the Manethonian story of Nitocris and the pyramid is an impossibility' (Hall, J. H. S. xxiv. 208).

(2) It is more probable that we have here an adapted popular story. The modern Arab tale that the third pyramid was haunted by a beautiful naked woman, who drove men mad, may easily be very old; perhaps it is connected with the 'red painted' face of the Sphinx and its inscrutable smile. This may be the explanation of the Greek fiction which we have here, and, in a modified form, of Manetho's version (cf. 100 nn.).

Rhodopis was a real person; her name seems to have been Doricha (though Athenaeus, 596, denies this). Greek fancy played about her, as it did later about Phryne and Thais, e.g. Strabo (*u.s.*) attributes the 'shoe' part in the Cinderella story to her.

3 **διέδεξε**: used impersonally in an intransitive sense (cf. iii. 82. 3). The sentence beginning *ἐπείτε γάρ* is an anacoluthon.

4 The story of Aesop is told by Plutarch (de Ser. Num. Vind. c. 12. 557 A). Croesus had sent him to distribute four minae to each of the Delphians, but Aesop sent back the money to Sardis; enraged

at this, the Delphians unjustly condemned him to death for sacrilege, and executed him. Afterwards they suffered from 'strange diseases', until they made atonement by paying compensation to Iadmon. The story was obviously unknown to H. (cf. i. 54), and also that of Aesop's residence at the court of Croesus (Plut. Sol. 28 *ad init.*).

Myers (Hell. p. 454) quotes this passage and vi. 139 as proofs of the higher morality of Delphi, which cares for the lives of women and slaves.

Tradition credits Aesop with written works; but the passage as to his γέλοια (Aristoph. Wasps, 566) seems only to imply oral tradition; at all events the fables that bear his name have been held, since Bentley, to be forgeries. It has been denied that Aesop is a real person, but the evidence of H., who may well have met at Samos some of the family of Iadmon, is conclusive against this scepticism.

135 1 **ἐς Αἴγυπτον.** No doubt Rhodopis was brought to Naucratis, with which both Samians and Mytilenaeans had a special connexion (178. 2, 3); it was famous for its ἑταῖραι (Athen. 596).

2 **ὡς εἶναι Ῥοδῶπιν**: translate 'for a Rhodopis, but not enough for her to attain to', &c.; cf. iv. 81. 1 for construction; but it is very harsh.

3 **τοῦτο τό** = τοιοῦτον οἷον; cf. iv. 166. 1.

ἀναθεῖναι, 'to attribute to her' (cf. 134. 2); the word is used = 'dedicate' three lines below.

4 H. is obviously writing as an eyewitness, and this part of the story may be Delphic tradition. The altar of the Chians was found by the French in 1893, on the spot indicated by H.; to judge from Pausanias it was in this part of the precinct that dedications were most numerous; cf. ix. 81. 1 and Paus. x. 14. 7 with Frazer, v. 309–10 and 631.

βουπόρους: large enough to roast a whole ox. For the magnificent feasting of Delphi cf. i. 51. 2. Athenaeus (*u. s.*) says the 'spits' were περιβόητοι, and quotes Cratinus as to them.

6 Charaxus was a wine merchant; for a new fragment of Sappho 'chiding' him, but apparently not for *this* amour, cf. Class. Rev. xxiii. 103–4.

136 1 Menkaura was succeeded by two nameless kings and then by Shepseskaf (Meyer, i. 235). Diodorus (i. 65) makes Bocchoris succeed Mycerinus, and (i. 94) says that he 'settled the laws of contract'; he also (*ib.*) mentions Sasyches as the second of the lawgivers of Egypt (*v. i.*). This last may be the king meant by 'Asychis', but if so, he is out of place, for he seems to belong to the second dynasty. H.'s confusion is unexplained.

2 **ἀποδεικνύντα** (*sc.* τινα): 'that a man might by assigning . . . on these terms' (οὕτω).

τήνδε . . . ζημίην. If H.'s account be right, this 'penalty' is the real point of the law; the 'whole grave' was transferred to the creditor, though he could not disturb mummies already placed in it. But Erman (R. 190) thinks that the reference may be really to the perpetual charge of graves vested in the class of *χοαχύται*, who were paid a stipend; these charges were hereditary sources of profit, and so could be alienated or pledged by their holders.

3 **ἐκ πλίνθων.** What pyramid H. means is disputed. Stein, on account of the reference to the *λίμνη* (§ 4), thinks one of the brick pyramids by Lake Moeris is meant; there are also two brick pyramids at Dahshûr, some twenty miles south of Gizeh.

4 **πλίνθους εἴρυσαν.** This passage is parodied by Aristophanes (Av. 1144–6).

Caps. 137–41 contain a distorted version of Egyptian history during the time of the great Assyrian conquests. At this period an Ethiopian dynasty ruled in Thebes, though native Egyptian princes, under the protection of Assyria, held their ground, as H. says (cf. c. 152 n.), in the Delta. H. turns the twenty-fifth dynasty (725–667 B.C.) of Manetho into a single king, Sabacos (137. 1); there were at least four kings in it, of whom Shabaka was one; the last, Tanut-Amen, was expelled by Esarhaddon. Popular tradition remembered only Sabacos; he seems to correspond to 'So, king of Egypt' (2 Kings xvii. 4), who incited Hoshea of Samaria to resist Assyria, and so brought about his destruction. It is needless to say that H., here as elsewhere, completely fails to appreciate the greatness of Assyria (see c. 141 n.).

137 1 **Ἄνυσιν.** Manetho (fr. 64–5) says Bocchoris of Sais preceded the Ethiopian conquest. Two suggestions are made to reconcile H. with Manetho. (1) That Bocchoris is called 'Anysis' by H., from the name of his town, while Manetho calls him a 'Saite' from his nome (so the eleventh dynasty is called 'Theban', though really from Hermonthis). (2) It is simpler to suppose that Anysis was not a king, but only a local chief, like Necho the father of Psammetichus (152. 1).

The site of Anysis is very variously identified, e.g. by Sayce with Hanes (? Heracleopolis Magna), near the Fayûm (J. of P. xiv. 283). It may be the same as Anytis (c. 166), which seems to be in the Delta.

2 For the marshes cf. cc. 92 seq. nn.

3 The account in H. is based on two facts of Eastern life: (1) Imprisonment as a punishment was unknown; the criminal, however, became a state slave for shorter or longer period. (2) Town sites are usually higher than the country round; the mud houses rapidly fall into ruins, their remains are not removed, but levelled as a foundation for their successors. Greek imagination, however, always attributed the result of a long process to an individual act. For a curious result of this rise of height cf. 138. 2; the temple is below the city level. A similar feature is often seen in modern churches, but on a less scale.

5 For Bubastis cf. 59 n. The 'city' at Bubastis is contrasted with the temple.

138 The temple was excavated by M. Naville for the E. E. F. (1887–9); an account of the results is given in the eighth memoir (1891; also in part in the tenth, 1892). The destruction had been so complete that no light is thrown on H.'s account of the buildings; but M. Naville confirms his accuracy as to (1) the island-like nature of the site; (2) the depressed position of the temple; 'the account is clearly that of an eyewitness' (p. 3); (3) the direction and the length of the road (§ 4) which is traceable (p. 60). H. is partially mistaken in assigning the smaller temple to Thoth; his name occurs in the inscriptions, but the building was probably a treasury (*ib.*).

4 Hermes, i.e. Thoth. He was connected with the worship of Osiris (cf. Diod. i. 15–16), and was identified by the Greeks with Hermes as being *ψυχοπομπός*. For pictures of him in the judgement-hall of Osiris cf. B. M. G. p. 140.

1 **τέλος**: not 'end of' but 'completion of'; translate 'final departure'. Cf. the Homeric *τέλος θανάτοιο*.

2 **πρόφασιν**: in the unusual sense of 'suggestion'. Cf. Soph. Trach. 662 *ἐπὶ προφάσει θηρός* (*v. l.* *προφάνσει*).

ὁκόσον refers to the participle *ἄρξαντα*, not to the main verb *ἐκχωρήσειν*.

3 Wiedemann says that this story of voluntary retirement by the last Ethiopian king is found on the monuments; but really the Ethiopians retired before the Assyrians.

140 This chapter is important for H.'s chronology.

(1) For its bearing on the date of Amyrtaeus (cf. iii. 15 n.).

(2) H.'s figure, 'more than 700' (§ 2), hopelessly contradicts the data given elsewhere. Anysis is divided from Psammetichus I only by the reign of Sethos; as Psammetichus succeeded 663 B.C., Anysis would have died about 700. But Amyrtaeus belongs to the middle of the fifth century (*v.s.*), and so the interval should be 250, not '700' years.

It has been proposed to alter the text; but it is clear that H. has combined variant traditions without being aware of it. (Cf. App. XIV. 3.)

2 If this island had a real existence at all, it is obvious that it must be as hard to identify it as it was to find it; we can only say that it is conceived of as in the Delta region.

141 Neither Manetho nor the monuments know the name of Sethos; and the repulse of Sennacherib from Egypt probably belongs to the reign of Tirhaka (701–667 B.C.). Sethos may have been a local priest, ruling in Lower Egypt under the Ethiopian, and turned by popular tradition into a king; but probably 'Sethon' is indeclinable and = 'Setne', the popular form of the priests' title; for this turning of a title into a proper name cf. III. 1 n. (Griffith, High Priests of Memphis, p. 9). The name 'Satni' is common as that of the hero of various popular Egyptian tales.

1 **Αἰγυπτίων**: a *constructio ad sensum*, as if H. had written *ἀλογίῃ ἔχειν*. For the warrior caste cf. c. 164.

2 The mention of Arabians here (and *inf.*) may well be right; Sennacherib, like Cambyses later (iii. 5), probably had Arabian guides across the desert. Josephus, however (*v. i.*), blames H. for the statement.

3 The parallel to the account in 2 Kings xix is very marked, but the childishness of H.'s tradition is in strong contrast to the dignified simplicity of the Jewish one. The sudden break-off in Sennacherib's inscription (the Taylor cylinder now in B. M.) confirms the fact of the disaster to his army. For the mouse as a symbol of plague cf. 1 Sam. vi. 4–5 and Iliad, i. 39, where Apollo, as sender of plague, is invoked as 'Sminthian' (from *σμίνθος*, a mouse). There is an interesting Egyptian parallel in the vision of Ptah seen by Merneptah, before his victory over the Libyans and their allies (Breasted, iii. 582); 'but the form of the inscription *ἐς ἐμέ* and the pointing of the moral are both Greek' (Griffith, *u. s.*).

4 Pelusium; cf. 154 n. Josephus (Ant. x. 14) says that H. recorded a siege of Pelusium by the Assyrians; this would naturally have come in here.

6 Here, as elsewhere (cf. i. 24. 8), a votive offering has determined the form of the tradition. The statue had originally nothing to do with the events described, but represented the god Horus, to whom the mouse was sacred; the Greeks explained it from the legends of Apollo. Strabo (604) tells a story of mice eating *σκύτινα τῶν ὅπλων*, at Amaxitus in the Troad, where (at Chryse) Apollo was commemorated by a statue of Scopas, with a mouse under his foot. Spiegelberg however (Z. A. S. 43, 94), thinks that the story was older than the statue, and was attached to this by Semitic settlers (cf. 112. 2 *Τυρίων στρατόπεδον*).

142 Caps. 142–6 are a digression, before the history of the twenty-sixth (Saite) dynasty. H. urges three points, the two first of which he has already made: (1) the antiquity of Egypt (cf. 2. 1 n.); (2) the obligations of Greece to Egypt for its Pantheon (cf. cc. 49–50 nn.); (3) the mistaken views of the Greeks as to the human origin of their gods. The figure 341 H. obtains by calculation, i. e. he counts after Menes (c. 99) and 'the 330 kings enumerated from a roll' (100. 1 n.), the 10 kings whose reigns he describes (102–41), i.e. 1 + 330 + 10 = 341. He confirms his calculation by the list of High Priests at Thebes (143. 2).

The calculation is worthless, for (1) even if we knew the source of the '330' and could trust it, many of the kings were contemporary with each other. (2) H.'s '10 kings' are counted twice over; they were already included in the '330'. (3) It is absurd to suppose that a king's reign averaged a generation (cf. i. 7. 4 for a lower estimate). (4) H. knew the priesthood was in his day hereditary (37. 5); but he had no right to assume it had always been so. Stein well compares the calculation with an attempt to estimate the duration of the Papacy from the portraits of the Popes at San Paolo.

2 **μύρια.** For this calculation cf. App. XIV.

ἐπιλοίπων. H. is wrong in his arithmetic; $41 \times 33\frac{1}{3} = 1{,}366\frac{2}{3}$, i.e. $26\frac{2}{3}$ more years than he gives (cf. i. 32. 4 n. for another miscalculation).

3 **ὑπολοίποισι**: the Saite kings who ruled after Sethos.

4 By these words H. means: 'the sun rose four times away from his previous quarter' (as he explains, *ἔνθα τε νῦν . . . καταδῦναι*), i.e. had changed his place of rising four times, rising in the east for two periods and in the west for two. For belief in this phenomenon cf. Plato, Pol. 269 A, who connects it with the story of Thyestes. H.'s own views about the sun (cc. 24–5) are quite as impossible. But H.'s Egyptian informant must have meant something different, i.e. that from Menes to Sethos there were four 'Sothis periods' (complete or incomplete) of 1,460 years each (cf. 4 nn.). Only at the beginning of a period did the time of the calendar correspond to the real time; hence the sun might be said to 'rise four times (only) from his proper place'.

ὑπὸ ταῦτα, 'during this period' (cf. ix. 60. 3 for *ὑπό*). H. refutes by implication his countrymen's beliefs in a Golden Age, in a Deluge, &c.

143 This passage is important as illustrating (1) the fact that H. used the *Γῆς περίοδος* of Hecataeus as a guide-book. (2) His somewhat depreciatory tone to his predecessor. The word *λογοποιός*, however, is not itself contemptuous. (3) The origins of Greek chronology (cf. App. XIV. 4).

ἑκκαιδέκατον. The figure seems small; there were twenty generations from Leonidas, the contemporary of Hecataeus, to Zeus (vii. 204).

2 **ἐὸν μέγα.** It is strange that H. only refers in this cursory manner to the gigantic buildings at Thebes (Karnak); this is one of the passages used by Sayce to prove that H. never went (p. xxvii) up the Nile beyond the Fayûm. Sayce also affirms (*ib.* and nn. here) that the statues seen by H. were at Memphis, not at Thebes; of this he gives no proof. (For his argument cf. 29 nn.) It may be taken as certain that H. had never been in the great pillared hall with its 140 columns; only high officials were admitted to this; but he may well have been in the chambers on the south of the great court. H. has been partially confirmed by M. Legrain's discovery of a number of statues at Karnak in 1904 and 1905; over 16,000 objects were taken out of a pit, of which 600 were statues; only some of these, however, were of priests, and wood was the exception, not the rule, as material. Cf. R. de T. xxvii. 67; xxviii. 148. Wood, however, is a material which perishes easily, and we may accept the summing up of Sourdille, who (H.E. pp. 190–8) discusses the whole subject fully, 'it is at least certain that many priests obtained

permission to dedicate their statues, that some of these were of wood, that inscriptions enable to follow for generations the history of many families' (p. 198). H., in fact, as usual, generalizes too much from data correct in themselves.

τοσούτους: i. e. 341 (142. 1); H. writes loosely, meaning a number corresponding to the number of kings. Hecataeus actually would have seen 345, for he visited Egypt some 140 years (i. e. four generations) after the time of Sethos (the 341st king).

4 **οὐ δεκόμενοι**: this is too absolute (cf. Sourdille, R. p. 56). The Pharaohs were by title the 'sons of Ra', and stories of divine fatherhood occur on the monuments, e. g. Amenophis III is son of Amon at Luxor. H., in fact, contradicts his own statement elsewhere (cf. i. 182. 1 nn.). In Egyptian, *πίρωμις* = 'the man', here wrongly translated 'the gentleman'. The mistake spoils the point of the priests' answer, viz. that *mortal* had been born of *mortal*, without a god coming in, for this long period. Whether the mistake be due to the interpreter's vanity, or to H.'s desire to outdo the family distinctions of Hecataeus, must remain uncertain.

'Piromis,' as a proper name, may have been familiar to H., for it occurs in an inscription from Halicarnassus, l. 17 (Newton's Essays, p. 427, l. 17).

144 **τοιούτους**: of human shape, and so mortals.

2 Manetho (fr. 1) puts Horus last of the first set of god-rulers (145 n.), not, as H. here, just before mortal rule; by a similar mistake H. puts Osiris among the last set of god-rulers (145. 1). But the Turin Papyrus and the monuments alike put immediately before Menes the 'Horus worshippers' as rulers (Meyer, i. 192), which explains H.'s statement here. Horus, as the god of light, was identified with Apollo. For his story and that of Osiris cf. 62. 1 n.; for Osiris, also 42. 2 n.

145 Caps. 145–6 must be read with cc. 43–5; they illustrate (1) H.'s pseudo-chronology for early times; (2) his fondness for correcting his countrymen; (3) above all his views on Egyptian religion. He divides the Egyptian pantheon into three classes, the eight original gods, the twelve others born from them, and a third series, of indeterminate number, born from the twelve. He seems to mean this as a classification of Egyptian gods in general (145. 1); but if this is his meaning, he is inconsistent, for he says elsewhere (c. 42) that only Isis and Osiris were worshipped by all the Egyptians. He further identifies these gods with the rulers of Egypt before the period of Menes (*πρότερον τῶν ἀνδρῶν τούτων*, 144. 2). The origin of his information may have been chiefly Memphis, for it is the temple of Ptah (Hephaestus) to which he continually refers (cf. App. X. 10); but he also refers to Mendes (46. 1). How far Egyptian tradition really underlies these statements of H. is disputed. Brugsch (Religion der Alten A. p. x) explains the 'eight' as corresponding to the eight original 'cosmogonic' deities, while the 'twelve' are made up by the addition of Thoth, the 'thought' of the original god personified, and of the divine Triad of Toum, Hathor, and Harpocrates (the father, mother, and son). H.'s third series of gods he explains as local gods, to whom 'special worships were founded after the pattern of the cosmogonic twelve (p. xi).

It will be seen at once that, if this were the real Egyptian view, H. has reproduced it very inaccurately; but Maspero (M. A. E. ii, pp. 184–7, 237 seq.) rejects Brugsch's whole system as 'an attempt to get from polytheistic texts a monotheistic theology'. It must suffice to say here (1) that the usual division of the Egyptian pantheon was into three 'nines', of which the first was far the most important; the 'enneads' of Heliopolis were the best known; (2) that H. is wrong in putting Osiris in his third class (c. 145); he belonged to the great 'ennead'; (3) that he is right, according to Egyptian ideas, in making the gods to have been rulers of Egypt.

Sourdille (cap. 2) criticizes H.'s views on Egyptian religion generally; he sums up: 'H.'s starting-point is really Egyptian (e. g. the threefold division), his development rests on conceptions entirely different' (p. 54).

For the calculations and inconsistencies of this cap. cf. App. XIV. 2.

2 **πρόσθε**: cf. 43. 4.

4 **Ἑρμέω.** The oldest authority for this scandal against the virtuous Penelope is Pindar (Serv. ad Georg. i. 16). It was this Pan who was reported 'dead' by the mysterious voice in the Aegean during the reign of Tiberius (Plut. de Def. Orac. 17, Mor. 419).

146 1 **ἀμφοτέρων**: i. e. Dionysus and Pan; there is no construction, but *πέρι* may have fallen out before *πάρεστι*. If the text be sound, however, *ἀμφοτέρων* must mean 'the Greek and the Egyptian views'; translate 'A man can adopt whichever of these two', &c.

ἀποδέδεκται: i. e. that Pan is the Egyptian god of Mendes (c. 46), and that Melampus brought the worship of Dionysus from Egypt (c. 49).

εἰ μὲν γὰρ κτλ. H.'s argument is that the cases of Heracles on the one hand and of Dionysus and Pan on the other were not parallel (*κατά περ* 'Η. *κτλ.*). Heracles (c. 43) was the son of Amphitryon, who after a long life had been identified with an Egyptian god; but as to Pan and Dionysus, their stories (§ 2) showed they had never existed as men. They had not become 'famous' (*φανεροί*) like Hercules, and so 'taken the names of gods who had existed before'. The Greeks therefore, he thinks, borrowed them from Egypt, and made the date of the introduction of their worship (*ἀπ' οὗ ἐπύθοντο κτλ.*) into the date of their birth. Stein ingeniously shows that this actually was done in the worship of Dionysus; Melampus, its mythical founder (49. 3), was a contemporary of Labdacus; for their respective great-grandsons, Amphiaraus (cf. Od. xv. 241 seq.) and Polynices, were both among the 'Seven against Thebes'. But Labdacus and Dionysus were contemporaries, as both grandsons of Cadmus; therefore to the Greek genealogers, Melampus would be a contemporary of Dionysus (cf. App. XIV. 2).

2 **ἐν τῇ Αἰθιοπίῃ**: in iii. 111. 1 H. says the Arabs say that cinnamon grows 'in the land where Dionysus was brought up' (i. e. Ethiopia)· cf. iii. 97. 2 n. for the Ethiopians who worship Dionysus round Νύση ἡ ἱρή: also 29. 7 nn. It is noticeable, however, that H. only gives the connexion between Dionysus and Ethiopia as the belief of Greeks and Arabs, not as his own.

147–82 *The history of Egypt under the Saite dynasty, when the Greeks had renewed their intercourse with it.*

147 H. rightly emphasizes the change in the character of his sources (147. 1; cf. 154. 4 and App. X. 10–11).

2 **ἄνευ βασιλέος.** H. for once drops his Egyptian sympathies and ironically says the natives 'though freed' could not get on 'without a king'. Diodorus (i. 66) calls the state of Egypt *ἀναρχία*.

δυώδεκα. There is no trace of this 'dodecarchy' on the monuments; Diodorus (*u. s.*) repeats the figure, and adds that the twelve *ἡγεμόνες* ruled fifteen years, and that the victory of Psammetichus was at Momemphis. H.'s story seems to correspond to the broad facts, though it has been made too symmetrical, and adorned with religious motives by his priestly informants at Buto. The number 'twelve' is probably a Greek interpolation; Maspero (iii. 488 n.), who compares the 'twelve great gods' (c. 43) which the Greek version gave, says the monuments give us the names of more than twenty petty rulers at this time. The rivalry of chiefs at this period in the Delta is illustrated by a contemporary demotic romance published in 1897 (cf. Petrie, iii. 321 seq.). Lying between the Assyrian and the Ethiopian conquerors (cf. App. II. 3; X. 9), they had gained a state of semi-independence.

For Necho, perhaps the chief of them, cf. 152. 1 n.

148 **λαβύρινθον.** The name is Greek, perhaps connected with λαύρα (an 'alley'); for the connexion cf. Burrows, Discoveries in Crete, pp. 117 seq., 228, and v. 119. 2 n. It properly belongs to the great pre-hellenic palace of Knossus; as there was a direct connexion between Minoan civilization and the twelfth dynasty culture, the Greeks were justified in their comparison.

The building here described by H. (also by Strabo 811) was originally built by Amenemhêt III (101. 4 n.), and was continued by his daughter (queen 1791–1788); only their names have been found among the ruins, and no trace of the work of the twenty-sixth dynasty. H. is therefore wrong in attributing it to the 'twelve kings'; but most classical writers are also wrong (e. g. Strabo). Manetho (fr. 35; ii. 560), however, rightly gives it to a king of the twelfth dynasty, calling him 'Lamares' which seems to be one of the names of Amenemhêt III (cf. Meyer, i. 281 n.). The 'Labyrinth' was considered one of the 'seven wonders of the world'; it was not only a temple, but also the seat of government; each nome had its own set of chambers in it.

Κροκοδείλων . . . πόλιν. For this town cf. 69. 1. It lies close to the modern Medînet-el-Fayûm. Strabo (811) says the Labyrinth was 100 stadia from it.

ἤδη, 'so far,' with *λόγου μέζω* (cf. L. and S. *s. v.* I. 5).

Although the Labyrinth has perished its foundations remain, and their area is 'enough to include all the temples of Karnak and Luxor' (Petrie, i. 188); they measure 1,000 feet by 800; it was identified by Petrie in 1888; for a description cf. his 'Hawara', E. E. F., 1889, pp. 5–8.

2 For the temple at Ephesus cf. i. 92. 1 n., for that of Samos, iii. 60. 4 n., where H. says it was 'the greatest of all temples we know' (i. e. of Greek temples). For the bearing of this passage on the date of H.'s visit to Egypt cf. App. IX. 1.

4 The chief differences between the accounts of H. and of Strabo are:

(1) H. says there were twelve *αὐλαί*, Strabo (787, 811) implies there were more—one for each of thirty-six nomes; but he also seems to give the number as twenty-seven.

(2) H. says the 'courts' had 'openings facing each other' (§ 4), Strabo that they were *ἐφ' ἕνα στίχον*, and that they opened on a long wall.

(3) H. says nothing distinct (but cf. § 7) of the absence of wood or of the monolithic roofs, Strabo nothing of the 'underground chambers' (§ 5).

It would be impossible to construct a building according to the description of either H. or Strabo; and it is obvious that a 'labyrinth' defies description, at any rate by a mere visitor led through part of it as was H. (§ 5). It is therefore needless to attempt to account for the contradictions, &c., by supposed later additions to the Labyrinth during the 450 years between the visits of the two travellers.

κατάστεγοι. The courts were 'covered in', not open as usual; H. conceives them as arranged six a side, along a corridor, from which, being no doubt higher, they were lighted. Stein compares the pillared hall at Karnak, where also the walls and pillars are covered with 'figures carved on' (*τύπων ἐγγεγλυμμένων* (§ 7); cf. 136. 1). H. is right that the main feature of the building was the great number and the equal size (speaking generally) of its chambers; there was not the usual great central court, for it was not dedicated to any one deity (cf. Petrie, *u. s.* p. 7).

6 **στεγέων** seems to be the same as *οἰκήματα* just below, i. e. the minor 'chambers' as opposed to the 'courts'.

εἱλιγμοί, 'the goings this way and that,' not 'winding ways'. The *παστάδες* are 'pillared corridors' between the 'chambers'.

7 ζῷα, 'hieroglyphics'; cf. i. 70. 1 n.
For the pyramid at Hawara cf. Petrie, i. 184 seq.

149 1 Lake Moeris (for the name cf. 101 n.) 'was the natural basin of the Fayûm oasis, regulated and utilized by Amenemhêt III' (Petrie, i. 192, with whom Breasted, pp. 193–4, agrees). The Fayûm in its lowest parts is over 120 feet below the sea level, and was originally filled with water by the Nile; some parts of it, however, e.g. the site of Arsinoe, were inhabited even under the Old Empire, and more of it was reclaimed by the great kings of the twelfth dynasty, especially Amenemhêt III. He also regulated the flow of the Nile, using the lake to hold the surplus of the high Nile, and then letting the water go as it was wanted. In fact his work was an anticipation of the Barrage and the dam at Assouan. Owing to the rise in height of the Nile valley on the east side, Lake Moeris gradually became useless for controlling the Nile flood, but the work of reclamation was greatly extended under the Ptolemies. Only the Birket Karûn is now left, on the north-west of the district; this lake is thirty-four miles long.

The topography of Lake Moeris was finally settled by Major Brown (The Fayûm and L. M., 1892); for a good summary cf. Grenfell and Hunt, Fayûm Towns (E. E. F., 1900, pp. 1–17); they say H.'s 'mistakes, such as they are, are those of an uncritical eye-witness'; while Strabo, on the other hand, claims to have seen what had ceased to exist 200 years before his time (p. 8).

Other views of Lake Moeris are briefly: (1) that of Linant (published 1843), who first explored the district, that Lake Moeris was on the east side of the Fayûm, held up by huge dykes. This, though long accepted, is now given up. (2) Maspero (p. 131) and Meyer (i. 293) both deny that the lake had anything to do with the regulation of the Nile flood. It will be noticed that H. says nothing as to this.

ἑξακόσιοι καὶ τρισχίλιοι. This figure—about 400 miles—is much exaggerated; the size of Lake Moeris is estimated by Petrie (Hawara, p. 2) at about 130 miles; the coast-line is about 180 miles.

2 **χειροποίητος.** H. is wrong in calling the lake 'artificial'. Strabo (811) rightly says that it is a 'natural' (*φυσικά*) reservoir, but that the sluices (*κλεῖθρα*) by which the water is controlled were artificial.

ἐν μέσῃ. The nose of one of these colossi, which were not 'in the middle of the lake', but on its east edge, is in the Ashmolean at Oxford (Room II); it is in finely polished quartzite; their pedestals are still at Biahmu, 4½ miles north of Medînet. They were statues of Amenemhêt III, probably about 39 feet high, or, with their pedestals, 60 feet. H. had only seen the statues from Arsinoe across the lake, and had accepted the greatly exaggerated figures of his guide. (Petrie, Hawara, p. 60 and Pl. XXVI).

3 Nissen (Metrologie, p. 889, in I. Müll., Hand. der A. W. i) says that **δίκαιαι** here = 'of full length', as opposed to the short stade

of '148' metres used by H. in reckoning marches. But H. really seems always to reckon the stade at the same length, i. e. about 200 yards. δίκαιαί εἰσι really = ἴσαι εἰσι, i. e. 'are equivalent to'.

4 The canal (διώρυχα) is the Bahr Yûsûf, which leaves the Nile about 200 miles to the south, just below Siût.

5 Here as elsewhere (cf. App. IX. 1) the orderly arrangements for government seem to imply that the Persians were in peaceful possession of Egypt. Sayce (F. Petrie, Illahun, Kahun, 1891, pp. 40–1) gives a translation of a Ptolemaic papyrus as to the revenue from the 'fish-pots'.

150 The interest of this chapter is the light that it throws on H.'s comparative method, and also on the date of his travels. It is natural to suppose that he heard the Nineveh story, presumably in Chaldaea, before he was in Egypt (cf. Intr. p. 5).

1 τετραμμένη. The 'lake lies north and south' (149. 1); but it had some extension to the west. Translate 'with its western parts turned inland along the mountain which lies south of Memphis', i. e. the Libyan chain, which starts above Memphis and runs south.

2 ὀρύγματος: of the lake (149. 2), not the underground channel, as to the existence of which H. does not commit himself; he seems to distinguish it (in § 1) from the lake by adding *καί*.

3 Sardanapallus, so far as he is historical, is Assurbanipal (cf. App. II. 3), the last of the Assyrian conquerors; Ctesias (Ass. fr. 15, p. 429) wrongly made him the last king of Nineveh, a compound of effeminacy and desperate bravery, as he is represented in Byron's drama. The story of the treasure-house is that of Rhampsinitus over again (cf. c. 121).

151 This chapter obviously owes its colouring to Greeks; the fulfilment of an oracle by the persons who try to evade it is a common feature in these myths.

2 κυνέην. The origin of this folk-tale is perhaps found in the name 'Psamtek'. This seems = 'son of a lion'; but it was also explained as 'drinking-bowl maker', Petrie, iii. 321. Stein, however (cf. 162. 1 n.), thinks Psammetichus was wearing the 'royal helmet', and incurred suspicion by using this for a libation.

152 Manetho (fr. 66; F. H. G. ii. 593) gives three kings of the Saite dynasty before Psammetichus I; of these the third was Necho, father of Psammetichus; he represented one of the families which divided the rule of North Egypt; the centres of the other were Tanis and Bubastis (Maspero, iii. 378–9, 489). Necho is mentioned in Assurbanipal's Annals (R. P.[1] i. 57 seq.; B. M. G. A. pp. 221–2, with picture of the cylinder) first among the twenty kings set up by Esarhaddon in Egypt (ib. 61); they were expelled by Taharka, but restored by Assurbanipal (p. 62). When they revolted against Assyria, Necho alone was restored to his throne (p. 64). There is

no mention of his being killed by the Ethiopians, but it is probable. H., here as elsewhere (137. 1 n.), combines all the Ethiopian kings into one; for Necho is mentioned by Assurbanipal in 667 B.C., while Sabacos (Shabako) died before 700. Necho really fell before Tanut Amen, who shared the power of Taharka, the last of the four Ethiopian kings. Cf. for his stele Breasted, iv. 919 seq.

3 **χρησμός.** Under this oracular form is concealed the important part played by Greek mercenaries in the rise of the Saite dynasty. We learn from the Assyrian inscription (R. P.[1] i. 69) that Gyges of Lydia sent help to Psammetichus, who was also encouraged to throw off the Assyrian yoke by the revolt of Babylon under Shamashshûmûkin (Maspero, p. 572).

153 **κολοσσοί.** Egyptian architecture did not employ caryatides. H. means square columns adorned with a statue in front, probably of Osiris, as in the Ramesseum. For Epaphus cf. 38. 1 n.

154 1 For the 'camps' at Pelusium and for the 'remains' there (§ 5) cf. 30. 2 n.; for Bubastis, 59 n. The rivalry between Ionian and Carian made separate camps desirable.

2 **ἑρμηνέες.** The 'interpreters' formed one of the seven 'classes' (c. 164).

3 Amasis came to the throne at the head of a native reaction (163. 2); he therefore removed the foreigners from their important post on the east frontier; but he saw that the support of the Greek mercenaries was necessary, and so attached them more closely to his own person. If we may trust a demotic chronicle in the Louvre, Amasis assigned the mercenaries some of the lands and revenues of the temples of Bubastis, Memphis, and Heliopolis (Revillout, R. E. i. 59); cf. iii. 16 n. For the double policy of Amasis, giving back with one hand what he had taken away with the other, cf. the treatment of Naucratis (178 nn.). Steph. Byz. (*s.v.*) mentions *τὸ Καρικόν*, the Carian quarter, in Memphis, with its mixed population.

4 **ἀτρεκέως:** cf. 147. 1 n. The word *ἀλλόγλωσσος* occurs in the great Abusimbel inscription (cf. Roberts, Epigraphy, i. 151 f.) for the 'mercenaries', Greek and other, of Psammetichus II, as opposed to his native troops; the former are commanded by a special commander, Potasimto (cf. Maspero, iii. 537–8 nn.).

πρῶτοι. For the Egyptian dislike of strangers cf. 91. 1; H. has never heard of the Hyksos (cf. App. X. 6) or of Libyan settlements in Egypt.

5 **ὁλκοί.** L. and S. take these = 'the fixed capstans' of the docks: more probably it = 'the slips', on which ships were built or repaired.

155 1 For the town and oracle of Buto cf. 63. 1 n.

3 Each side of this shrine was a monolith, and a square of sixty feet (*τούτοισι*, 'in these respects,' i.e. height and length). These dimensions seem incredible, both on general grounds and because

the shrine would be the same height as the portico. For a still existing monolith shrine set up by Amasis cf. 175. 3 n.

παροροφίδα: probably not the projecting cornice of the roof but the 'gable' (*τὸ μεταξὺ τοῦ ὀρόφου καὶ τοῦ στέγους*, Poll. i. 81).

156 1 **δευτέρων**, 'of the things next in importance,' as opposed to *θωμαστότατον*.

The floating island is mentioned in fr. 284 of Hecataeus (F. H. G. i. 20) *ἐστὶ μεταρσίη καὶ περιπλέει καὶ κινέεται ἐπὶ τοῦ ὕδατος* (cf. Introd. § 20). Hecataeus' form of the name, Χέμβις, is nearer to the Egyptian 'Chebt' than the form here, Χέμμις. It is hard to detect in this passage 'the mocking tone' towards his predecessor which Diels (Herm. xxii. 420) imputes to H. The idea of floating islands was familiar to the Greeks, e.g. Delos; a modern instance on a tiny scale is the island in Derwentwater; but it need hardly be said that the 'astonishment' of H. is justified.

5 The Egyptians did not conceive of Bubastis as the sister of Horus; either H. himself infers the relationship from that of Apollo and Artemis, who were identified with them, or (more probably) he is telling a local Greek myth, heard by him in Egypt.

6 It is interesting to note the confidence with which H. speaks of 'all preceding poets' (cf. vi. 52 n., Introd. § 18). Aeschylus is only mentioned by him here; the tragedy in question is lost; Pausanias (viii. 37. 6) repeats the charge. The harsh word *ἥρπασε* may perhaps be significant of H.'s jealousy of Aeschylus, as being before him in his discovery of the relationship; it is more natural, however, to suppose that H. forgets his Orientalism, and speaks with resentment of a distortion of the usual Greek mythology.

157 The long reign of Psammetichus is confirmed by Manetho (fr. 66; ii. 593) and by the monuments. For his portrait cf. B. M. Egyptian Saloon, No. 20. The capture of Ashdod, though not recorded on the monuments, is historical. Egypt had learned the danger of having Assyria as her immediate neighbour; now that power was breaking up, it was the policy of the Saites to extend their influence over Syria. The length of the siege, however, is a difficulty; it has been explained as a confusion in tradition, i.e. Psammetichus is made to take after 'twenty-nine years' the town which he really took in the twenty-ninth year of his reign. But this is pure conjecture, and it is more probable that Psammetichus took advantage of the Assyrian weakness caused by the Scythian inroad (i. 105 n.), in which case his aggression in Syria would belong to his later years. The figure 'twenty-nine' is probably an exaggeration due to Egyptian inaccuracy.

158 1 **διώρυξε**. Necho's naval projects were part of his scheme of resistance to the new power of Babylon, which had risen on the ruins of Assyria. The cities of Phoenicia were always hostile to the great Eastern empires, and it was obvious that the naval force of Egypt would be doubly effective in supporting them, if the Red Sea

fleet could join that of the Mediterranean. We may compare the increase in the power of Germany due to the Kiel canal.

The Nile canal was first made by Sethos I (nineteenth dynasty, 1326–1300 B.C.; cf. Petrie, iii. 13); it was represented in one of the scenes in the hall at Karnak. It had, however, silted up by Necho's time. The work of Darius is confirmed by inscriptions (Hogarth, A. and A. p. 184) found between the Bitter Lakes and the Red Sea; Darius says, 'I ordered to dig this canal from the Nile which flows in Egypt to the sea which begins with Persia. This canal was dug' (Weissbach and Bang, 1893; Die Alt-Pers. Keilinsch. p. 39; Meyer, iii. 60 adopts this view); the inscription was formerly translated in the opposite sense, to mean that Darius gave up his work (so Prášek, ii. 111). The canal was again rendered navigable under the Ptolemies, and with some variation of direction by Trajan (but this is uncertain); it finally was closed in the eighth century A.D. The remains of the canal at Belbês show that it was some 50 yards wide and 16 to 17 feet deep; cf. vii. 24 (the Mount Athos canal) for the breadth—'two triremes abreast'.

2 **ἧκται.** It was from the Nile to the Bitter Lakes; here it turned almost at a right angle, following thenceforward pretty much the line of the Suez Canal. The part of it running west and east was on the line of the 'Fresh Water Canal' (dug 1858–63); it was made along the natural depression, the Wadi Tûmilât, through which Lord Wolseley advanced in the Tel el Kebir campaign of 1882.

Patumus is the Pithom of Exod. i. 11, about ten miles west of Ismailia, the Egyptian Pi-tûmû (i.e. place of the god Tûmû), and has been excavated by Naville (E. E. F., 1903, 4th ed.). For 'Arabian' cf. 8. 1 ('the Arabian Mountain'), for the geography generally 8. 3 n.

κατύπερθε in both cases = 'south of'. The subject to *ὀρώρυκται* is 'the canal', and *τὰ πρὸς* 'A. *ἔχοντα* is an accusative of respect, with *τοῦ πεδίου τοῦ* 'A. depending on it as a partitive genitive. Some, however, make *τὰ πρὸς Ἀραβίην ἔχοντα* subject.

3 **μακρή** is almost equivalent to a participle = 'extending'.

4 **ἀπαρτί.** H. repeats this 'exact' figure (which = about 115 miles) in iv. 41, but it is too great; the narrowest part of the isthmus is only seventy miles 'from sea to sea'. Strabo (803) gives '1,000 stades' from Pelusium to the Red Sea; this *road* measure may be the cause of H.'s mistake. But Posidonius made it even greater, putting the breadth at 'less than 1,500 stades'.

5 The figure '120,000' is doubtless exaggerated; Mehemet Ali lost only 10,000 in making the Mahmûdieh Canal (from the Nile to Alexandria). Strabo (804) says the canal was stopped by Necho's death.

159 H. is perhaps anachronistic in making Necho's fleet (in the seventh century) all 'triremes'; but Thucydides (i. 13. 2) says triremes were built at Corinth in 704 B.C., and the Cypselids were connected with the Saite dynasty (cf. the name 'Psammetichus' among them).

2 **ἐν τῷ δέοντι**, 'as he needed them'; it would have been natural to mention here the story of the circumnavigation of Africa (iv. 42 nn.).

Μαγδώλῳ. The battle was really fought at Megiddo, where the coast-road comes out on the plain of Esdraelon: here Thothmes III had beaten the Syrian confederates nearly 1,000 years before. H. confuses this name with 'Migdol', the border fortress of Egypt on the north-east (cf. Exod. xiv. 2; Jer. xliv. 1).

ἐνίκησε. The campaign is described in 2 Kings xxiii and 2 Chron. xxxv. The 'good' Josiah was of the Prophets' party, which urged submission to the powers of the Euphrates valley; there was, however, always a philo-Egyptian party in Judaea.

Κάδυτιν. Only mentioned here and in iii. 5. 1, where H. describes it as 'about the size of Sardis' (Hec. frs. 261–2 speaks of Κάνυτις and Κάρδυτος). It has been identified with Jerusalem, and its name explained as = 'the holy' (cf. the present Arab name 'El Kods'); Necho perhaps took Jerusalem (2 Chron. xxxvi. 3). But it is clear from iii. 5 that Cadytis was on the coast, at the south end of the road from Phoenicia to Egypt; and H.'s comparison with Sardis. which may rest on his own observation, would certainly not suit Jerusalem, in the days of humiliation after the return from the Exile. Gaza, on the other hand (certainly captured by Necho), was always an important station of the trade-route from Egypt to Syria, and had special connexion with Arabia; cf. G. A. Smith, Hist. Geog. 182–3.

Some consider that H. is wrong in placing the capture of Gaza in this campaign; Maspero, however, thinks that it was taken on Necho's return from the Euphrates (cf. Jer. xlvii. 2, 'the flood from the north,' which overwhelms the Philistines). It is noticeable that H. knows nothing of the defeat at Carchemish (604 B.C.; cf. Jer. xlvi. 2) which Nebuchadnezzar inflicted on Necho.

3 **ἐσθῆτι.** This dedication was a compliment to his mercenaries, many of whom were Carian. The Branchidae temple (cf. i. 46. 2 n.) had been plundered by the Persians before the birth of H. (v. 36. 3), but there is no need to suppose that he got this fact from Hecataeus.

ἑκκαίδεκα. Manetho gives Necho only six years (frs. 66–7: F. H. G. ii. 593–5); funeral monuments, however, in the museums of Florence and Leyden confirm H., showing that Necho died in the sixteenth year of his reign. Some (needlessly) try to reconcile the two figures by making Necho rule nine years as regent with his father.

1 Psammis is called on the monuments Psamtik (like his grandfather), by Manetho (*u. s.*) *Ψάμμουθις*. His coffin (now in the museum at Gizeh) is too small for an adult (Z. A. S. xxii. 80); the early death thus implied agrees with his short reign. His most important act was an expedition against Ethiopia (161. 1); it is to this that the graffiti at Abusimbel belong (cf. 154. 4 n.).

The story of the Eleans (transferred by Diod. i. 95 to Amasis) is interesting as showing how completely the Greeks had the English ideas of 'sportsmanship', and how strange these were to other nations; for the impartiality of the Eleans cf. the repartee of Agis in Plut. Mor. 215, and more generally Athen. 350.

161 2 **πέντε καὶ εἴκοσι.** Manetho (fr. 66) gives Apries nineteen years, i. e. 589–570 B. C.; but he reigned nominally with Amasis for three years (c. 169 n.). H.'s 'twenty-five' is by any reckoning excessive.

Τυρίῳ. After the second capture of Jerusalem (586 B. C.) Nebuchadnezzar besieged Tyre in vain for thirteen years. On the retirement of the Babylonian, Apries' fleet gained the victories here spoken of; this early success of sea-power is more probable than Josephus' story (x. 11) that Nebuchadnezzar conquered Egypt and killed the king 'in the twenty-third year of his reign' (i. e. 582–581); the Jewish historian probably misinterpreted the prophecies (cf. Jer. xliii. 8–13 and Ezek. xxx. 10–19). Nebuchadnezzar, however, in a fragmentary inscription (for which cf. 27. 2 n.), mentions a campaign, perhaps victorious, against Amasis in 568 B.C., and Wiedemann thinks that Egypt was overrun by the Chaldaeans as far as Syene; to this invasion he referred the inscription of Nesuhor (cf. 30. 1 n.), and he still maintains his view, though the Nesuhor inscription has been proved to refer to a revolt of an Egyptian garrison and not with a Chaldaean war. The question must be left open (as by Meyer, i.[1] 497); on the one hand the silence of H. as to such a defeat is easily explicable by the vanity of his Egyptian informants, and Egypt would have been an easy prey, being weak from internal divisions (cc. 162–3); on the other hand, the prosperity of the reign of Amasis renders a Chaldaean conquest unlikely.

3 **προφάσιος** = 'cause' (i. 29. 1). For the fulfilment of this promise cf. iv. 159; the 'cause' was the offered alliance of the Libyan tribes against Cyrene; Apries, true to the policy of his family, was extending his hold along the Mediterranean coast.

4 No doubt Apries sent his 'Egyptian' troops, because his Greek ones could not be trusted against Greeks. The contemporary inscription (169 n.) seems to confirm H. as to the motives of the Egyptian army; 'Haunebu (Greeks), one knows not their number, are traversing the North land ... he (Apries) hath summoned them' (King and Hall, p. 434).

162 **κυνέην.** The royal 'helmet' is familiar on the monuments.

3 The whole conspiracy has considerable resemblance to Jehu's (2 Kings ix); but the superiority of the Jewish narrative in dignity and vividness is marked (cf. 141. 3 n.).

163 2 Momemphis lay on a canal from the Canopic (the western) arm of the Nile to the Mareotic Lake. For the rivalry of Egyptians and natives cf. 154. 3 n. Marea was the frontier post on the west (30. 2 n.).

164 1 **γένεα.** H. states his belief in the Egyptian caste system still

more clearly in vi. 60, and it was generally believed among the Greeks, though the actual divisions vary, e. g. Plato (Tim. 24) gives three, *ἱερεῖς, δημιουργοί*, and *μάχιμοι*, of whom the *δημιουργοί* are divided into *νομεῖς, θηρευταί*, and *γεωργοί*; Diodorus (i. 73–4) gives the same division, putting *τεχνῖται* for the *θηρευταί* (cf. also Isoc. Bus. 15–16; Strabo 787; all, however, make the priests and the military the two first). The Greek belief was too systematized; as a matter of fact there was no strict division of hereditary castes; members of the same family could belong to different classes. But it is true that certain functions were hereditary (e. g. Brugsch enumerates fourteen royal architects in succession from one family at this period), and that the 'soldiers' and the 'priests' were separated from the mass of the people; so too were certain degraded callings, e. g. that of swineherd (47. 1). Possibly the hereditary tendency grew stronger in the last days of Egyptian independence, under the Saite reaction (Meyer, i.[1] 470–1).

2 **οἱ μάχιμοι.** Maspero (iii. 499 seq.) thinks that this organization was the work of Psammetichus after the desertion of his warriors (30 n.); also that the Hermotybies represented his hereditary supporters, and were perhaps of Libyan origin, while the Calasiries were pure Egyptians and had been supporters of the rival house in the Egyptian Delta. The names given by H., however, do not altogether bear out this division, e. g. that of Nathos is placed by Stein in the Egyptian Delta. It is impossible to settle the question, for several of the nomes are differently identified, e. g. those of Chemmis and Papremis (63. 1 n. and iii. 12), and some names in the second list are otherwise unknown.

Three points as to the division are probable: (1) it did not include the Greek mercenaries. Hence Gutschmid's view must be rejected that the name *Λαβαρεῖς*, given by Aristagoras (Steph. Byz. *s. v.*) to the Hermotybies, is connected with Labara in Caria; (2) that it lasted till Persian times, cf. ix. 32. 1 for the divisions in Mardonius' army; (3) the organization was, at least mainly, for Northern Egypt. 'Thebes' (166. 1) alone represents Upper Egypt. The strength and the danger of the Saites alike lay in the Delta.

Spiegelberg (Z. A. S. 1906, xliii. 87-90) says both *Καλασίριες* and *Ἑρμοτύβιες* are Egyptian words and = 'young men' and 'riders' respectively; *Καλασίριες* was used originally of Nubian troops; but in H.'s day the old sense was forgotten, and both names were applied to infantry. From the *Καλασίριες* the 'fringed robe' (81. 1) derived its name, but *ἡμιτύβιον* ('apron', Aristoph. Plut. 729) is a Greek word, not Egyptian (as Poll. vii. 71 wrongly says).

νομῶν. This division dates from a very early period, Breasted (p. 30) says from pre-dynastic times; it lasted till Roman times. 'The nomes were sharply distinguished by religion, customs, and historical development', Meyer, i. 177. Under the Old and the

Middle Kingdoms, the power of the nomarchs had become largely hereditary. For a list of the nomes and an account of their organization cf. Maspero, pp. 25 seq., or B. M. G. pp. 16–17, but H.'s lists correspond to neither. The number is variously given by Greek writers; the Egyptians sometimes fix it at forty-four, twenty-two for each part of Egypt. For the nomes cf. Steindorf, Die ägyptischen Gaue (1909), who thinks the divisions varied greatly at different periods (cf. C. R. xxv. 56).

165 **Χεμμίτης.** The position of this nome between 'Saite' and 'Papremite' seems to show it was in the Delta, and connected with the island (c. 156) in the Buto lake, not with the town in the Theban nome (c. 91). The number 160,000, like the '250,000' of c. 166, is excessive. It is probably only an instance of the weakness of ancient statistics; Wiedemann, however, accepts it as including not only the standing army, but the reserves of 'veterans', &c., who were settled in the soldier nomes, and who could be called up, if necessary, for land defence.

167 H. is the founder of the comparative method for the study of politics, but he has made enough progress with it to see that a prejudice against handicraft, being common to almost all nations in a primitive stage, is not, of necessity, a proof of borrowing. The only thing he is sure of is (cf. δ' ὦν = 'at any rate') that the Greek prejudice is general; for it cf. Arist. Pol. vii. 4. 6; 1326 A the *βάναυσοι* are not a real part of the city, and vii. 12. 3; 1331 A the *βάναυσος* is not to come unsummoned to the *ἐλευθέρα ἀγορά*. In Laconia the manual arts were practised by Perioeci; cf. Strabo 382 for the *τέχναι δημιουργικαί* of Corinth.

168 **γέρεα**: for the corresponding privileges of the priests cf. c. 37. Diodorus (i. 73) says that one-third of the land was set apart for the warrior caste; each warrior received his allotment, which returned to the general stock on his death (cf. 168. 2 *οὐδαμὰ ὡυτοί*). In the Revenue Laws of Ptolemy Philadelphus (3rd cent. B.C.; edited by Grenfell, 1896), the land is measured in *ἄρουραι* as here.

πῆχυς. Cf. i. 178. 3 n. where H. distinguishes the 'royal' from the ordinary cubit, as being three fingers longer. The Egyptian (i. e. Samian) cubit was 525 millimetres, the 'royal' 532·8.

2 **ἐν περιτροπῇ**: cf. iii. 69. 6. The land was held on a sort of feudal tenure.

ἄλλοι: if this is read (*vide app. crit.*) it must mean 'another thousand'.

ἀρυστήρ = *κοτύλη*, i. e. nearly half a pint.

169 H.'s account is shown to be very incomplete by a contemporary inscription which is unfortunately much mutilated and variously restored (cf. Petrie, iii. 351, and Breasted, iv. 996 seq.); it describes the battle as fought in the 'third year' of Amasis. H. has blended in one two defeats of Apries; he had been allowed nominally to continue on the throne (the joint rule is marked by various

monuments); then he rebelled with the Greek mercenaries, and was killed. Cf. 161. 4 n. H. is correct in saying that he received royal burial, and that there was an interval between his first defeat and his death.

2 For the proud confidence of Apries cf. Ezek. xxix. 3.

5 The Egyptians were fond of imitating plants in the capitals of their columns; the lotus and the papyrus on these are more common than the palm; cf., for a popular account, Baedeker, cxxxiii seq. (with illustrations).

τοῦ ἱροῦ. In iii. 16. 1 Amasis' tomb seems to be in the palace. Probably temple and palace formed one continuous building; cf. 130. 1, where the sacred cow at Sais is in 'a chamber of the palace'.

διξὰ θυρώματα. Some translate a double table or platform (cf. *θύρη*, 96. 4); but probably 'a double door', i. e. a door with two leaves.

170 1 **οὐκ ὅσιον.** The reference is to Osiris (cf. 3. 2, 86. 6 nn.). There were graves of Osiris (the Greek 'Serapea') all over Egypt, wherever parts of his body had been found (62 n.); another explanation was that Isis buried coffins of Osiris in many places to deceive Typhon (Strabo 803). These stories are late inventions; the real explanation is that as the cult of Osiris became a sort of general worship in Egypt, various local deities were identified with him.

2 **λίμνη.** Such artificial pools were common in Egyptian temples; over them the funeral bark was rowed in grand funerals. The pool at Delos, to the north of Apollo's temple, has been discovered in the recent French explorations there (cf. P. W. iv. 2471). H. had clearly been in Delos before his Egyptian visit.

171 1 **μυστήρια.** For the real meaning of these cf. Farnell, G. C. iii. 130–1. In Egypt and in Greece alike they were marked by the four elements of secrecy, sacrifice, dramatic mimicry, and the communication of a *ἱερὸς λόγος*. But some, including H. probably, and certainly Plutarch (I. et O. 35; Mor. 364), have thought that they contained also doctrines of great importance, e. g. as to immortality; this is very doubtful. Cf., for the relations of Greece and Egypt in this matter, Sourdille, R. pp. 305–6, and for the supposed derivation of the Eleusinian mysteries from Egypt, Farnell, iii. 141–2 (who rejects the view, cf. 42. 2 n. for a similar theory). For a description of Osiris rites cf. cc. 61, 62 nn.

2 **εὔστομα κείσθω:** probably a fragment of an old hymn. The *Θεσμοφόρια* was really a feast of the sowing time; it was celebrated in Attica from the 10th to the 13th of Pyanepsion (end of Oct.). H. also speaks of it at Ephesus (vi. 16. 2); and it was at the *Θεσμοφόριον* (vi. 134. 2) of Paros that Miltiades was seized with his mysterious panic. The festival was that of married women only; for it cf. B. B. Rogers, Thesmophoriazusae, Introd., or Farnell, G. C. iii. 85 seq.; for similar festivals cf. v. 61. 2. H. derives it from Egypt because he identifies Isis with Demeter; to Isis, as to Demeter

Θεσμοφόρος, was attributed the introduction of agriculture and settled law (Diod. i. 14); but it is not likely the worships were connected; similar rites arise independently in different races.

For Danaus cf. 91. 5 n., for H.'s views on Pelasgians App. XV, for the Arcadians οὐκ ἐξαναστάντες, viii. 73. 1.

172 Σιούφ. *Hod.* Es-Seffeh, a village near Sais; hence Amasis is often called 'Saite'.

δημότην. The monuments speak of Amasis as brother-in-law of Apries; but he may have been a 'man of the people', and this connexion formed after his accession.

3 The story of the 'foot-pan' is referred to in Aristotle (Pol. i. 12. 2; 1259 B) and frequently elsewhere, especially in patristic literature; it is purely Greek, alike in the political and in the social ideas underlying it.

173 H. in iv. 181. 3 gives a fourfold division of the day, ὄρθρος, ἀγορῆς πληθυούσης (vii. 223), μεσαμβρίη, ἀποκλινομένης ἡμέρης; from iii. 104. 2 (ἀγορῆς διαλύσιος) it is clear that 'market time' was about 9 to 11 a.m. μέχρι ὅτευ = μέχρις, cf. i. 181. 3.

3 τὰ τόξα κτλ.: this saying has become a proverb—'Neque semper arcum tendit Apollo' (Hor. Odes, ii. 10. 19). Greek fancy wove a web of legends round Amasis, as round Croesus and many other historical persons of the sixth century (cf. i. 29. 1; App. I, § 9). H. as usual avoids the exaggerations of later writers, e.g. that Amasis was a great magician. His account is confirmed by a fragmentary demotic chronicle (cf. 154 n. and R. E. i. 66 seq.). The character of Amasis would appear the more shocking to his subjects, as the Egyptian king was a religious person, whose life was a round of regular routine (cf. Diod. i. 70 for his obligations, a sketch which Diodorus rightly says (69 *ad fin.*) is based on native records).

The repetition of the subject ὅ γε is Homeric.

174 The stories in this chapter also are Greek in their mixture of knavery and shrewdness. The behaviour of Amasis may be compared to that of Prince Hal, as Henry V, to Chief Justice Gascoigne and to Falstaff in 2 Henry IV, v (scenes 2, 5).

175 1 Only huge mounds now remain at Sais which mark the ancient inclosure; but H.'s description is confirmed by Champollion, who says, 'this "circonvallation de géants" surpasses in height the largest works of the same kind.'

The colossi stood before the portal, the sphinxes guarded on each side the approach. H. rightly notes that in Egypt the sphinx (unlike the monster of Oedipus) had a man's head. The reality of such creatures was firmly believed; Strabo (775) quotes Artemidorus that among the Troglodytes there are sphinxes, dog-headed men, and other marvels.

2 εἴκοσι: for this estimate cf. 9. 2 n. For the red granite quarries of Syene cf. 29. 1 n.

3 As the shrine was lying on its side, H. has given the height as

length, and the breadth as height. A smaller monolith chamber of Amasis still exists at Thmuis in the Delta, about 23 feet high, 13 wide, and 11½ deep (for picture cf. Maspero, iii. 643).

176 Maspero, iii. 641, gives a picture of an Osiris lying on his stomach with head raised, which may perhaps give an idea of this 'recumbent colossus'; the statuette, however, is only about 6 inches high. Wiedemann thinks H. means the colossus had never been raised into position; but this is not what he says. Strictly ὕπτιον must = 'on its back'.

177 1 **εὐδαιμονῆσαι.** The age of Amasis, as the last king of independent Egypt, was a golden age; Diodorus (i. 31) gives the number of 'considerable villages and towns in old times' as over 18,000, and as over 30,000 under Ptolemy Lagus.

2 **θανάτῳ.** This law, 'the most drastic poor law on record,' is a great exaggeration of the Egyptian custom of taking a sort of census of inhabitants and their occupations; but such a punishment for idleness is impossible, though Plutarch (Sol. 17) says that at Athens Draco made death the punishment for ἀργία, and that Solon, here as elsewhere, modified his severity. Pollux (viii. 42) gives the penalty as ἀτιμία, and some (e.g. Theophrastus, Plut. Sol. 31) transfer the law to Pisistratus, who did his best to encourage industry (Ἀθ. Πολ. c. 16). The law, in its milder form, is in the spirit of Solonian legislation, as shown in his law that all sons were to be taught a trade (Plut. Sol. c. 24); but if it had anything to do with him, it could not have been borrowed from Amasis, who became king 570 B.C., more than twenty years after Solon's legislation (cf. App. XIV. 6). There was a law against idleness later at Athens (cf. Demosth. in Eubul. p. 1308, § 37).

ἐς αἰεί simply means 'they follow it still', a statement which, though untrue, H. may well have believed.

178 In this chapter (as in c. 154) there is a contradiction as to the policy of Amasis; he gains the throne at the head of a native reaction, and yet is a 'philhellene'. Probably both aspects of his policy are true, and their fundamental and inevitable inconsistency ruined at once his reputation (cc. 172–4 nn.) and his country; the Saites depended on foreign arms to defend Egypt (iii. 11), and yet these very defenders were hated by the Egyptians. It may be added that H. probably derived much information from the Greeks of Naucratis; to them at any rate Amasis was an undoubted benefactor.

Among the Hellenic friends of Amasis were Solon (cf. 177), Polycrates (iii. 39), and Pythagoras (introduced to him by Polycrates), Diog. Laert. viii. 1. 3.

1 **ἔδωκε Ναύκρατιν.** This passage raises two distinct questions: (1) Did the Greeks settle at Naucratis before the time of Amasis? (2) When did H. think they settled there?

To take (2) first. This passage by itself might mean that the colony at Naucratis dated from Amasis; many, e.g. Hogarth (B.S.A.

v. 46), think this the 'natural interpretation'. But H. (135. 1, 5) implies the earlier presence of a Greek community at Naucratis, and his whole story of the Saites implies that the Greeks had free access to Egypt before the limitations of Amasis. H.'s authority then is at least doubtful as to the date of Naucratis.

As to (1) Strabo (801) says *πλεύσαντες ἐπὶ Ψαμμητίχου τριάκοντα ναυσὶ Μιλήσιοι (κατὰ Κυαξάρην δ' οὗτος ἦν τὸν Μῆδον) κατέσχον ἐς τὸ στόμα τὸ Βολβίτινον εἶτ' ἐκβάντες ἐτείχισαν τὸ λεχθὲν κτίσμα* (i. e. *τὸ Μιλησίων τεῖχος* just mentioned) *χρόνῳ δ' ἀναπλεύσαντες ἐς τὸν Σαϊτικὸν νομὸν καταναυμαχήσαντες Ἰνάρων πόλιν ἔκτισαν Ναύκρατιν.* This may well be a piece of genuine tradition, that Miletus took a prominent part in assisting Psammetichus; Inarus would be one of his rivals, possibly one of 'the dodecarchy'. For further evidence that Miletus founded Naucratis cf. Athen. vii. 283; for the Greeks in Egypt before Amasis cf. c. 154 nn. and Steph. Byz. *s.v.* *Ἑλληνικόν*.

The archaeological evidence is variously interpreted. Petrie and E. A. Gardner, who explored the site in 1884–6, held that the early date was proved, E. E. F. 1886–8, Naucratis; cf. P. Gardner, N. C. G. H. pp. 187 seq.; on the other hand, Hogarth, who resumed the digging in 1899, maintains that nothing had been found inconsistent with the later date, of about 570 B. C., which Hirschfeld and others had always maintained on epigraphical evidence (for this cf. Roberts, Greek Epigraphy, pp. 159 seq., 323 seq.).

The site of Naucratis was conclusively identified by Petrie at Nebîreh on a canal from the Canopic Nile, outside the Delta.

2 The Hellenion was identified by Petrie with an enclosure capable of holding 50,000 men, to the south of Naucratis (cf. P. Gardner, *u.s.*, pp. 209–10 for a description); this, however, was in the Egyptian quarter of the town, and was probably a native fort to overawe the strangers. The real site was discovered in 1899 on the north of the town (B. S. A. v. 42 seq.). In this were found a number of dedications to *θεοῖς τοῖς Ἑλλήνων* or *Ἑλληνίοις*; this unusual form marks the composite character of the colony, which was forced into unity in face of their barbarian neighbours; cf. v. 49. 3, 92. *η* 5 for the only other uses of *Ἑλλήνιος* in plur., both in impassioned appeals to Greek sentiment. The lists here are interesting as indicating the comparative commercial importance of Greek towns in the seventh century; it is to be noted that Aegina is the only representative of old Greece.

Ῥόδος: the towns of Lindus, Ialysus, and Camirus, not synoecized till 408 B. C.

3 **προστάτας**: these were the 'consuls' or trade representatives of the towns; the magistrates of the city were perhaps called *τιμοῦχοι* (Hermias, F. H. G. ii. 80–1, an interesting passage as to the feast to the Grynean Apollo in the prytaneum at Naucratis). The officers of the towns probably stood to the magistrates as the heads of the trade-guilds to the authorities of a mediaeval town.

ὅσαι δὲ ἄλλαι: religious and trade privileges were closely connected.

179 τὸ παλαιόν: in the days of Amasis, as contrasted with H.'s own day. Naucratis was the treaty port, as Canton and Nangasaki were originally in China and in Japan.

περιάγειν: by internal navigation, over canals and the various arms of the Nile.

180 κατεκάη. For the burning of the Delphic temple cf. i. 50. 3 n. H., by adding *αὐτόματος* here, refutes, perhaps intentionally, the story that it was set on fire by the Pisistratidae (Philochorus, fr. 70; F. H. G. i. 395).

ἐπέβαλλε: impersonal here with a construction like *ἔδεε*; used personally it takes the dative.

2 στυπτηρίης. The Egyptian 'alum' was the best; it was used in dyeing; Wiedemann suggests that it was used for making the wood fireproof. Stein thinks that *ἀργυρίου* is to be supplied to *μνέας*: more probably H. intends to contrast the liberality of the king with the meanness of the Greeks.

181 The alliance with Cyrene was a natural reversal of the policy of Apries. Wiedemann says the story of the marriage is a fabrication; his reasons are: (1) The uncertainty as to the bride's parentage (but this really confirms the story's accuracy; a fiction would have left no doubt on the subject). (2) The improbability that Cambyses would give up a valuable hostage, when intending to attack Cyrene. (3) The fact that Ladike is not mentioned on the monuments. It is always dangerous to reject a well-authenticated tradition on merely *a priori* grounds; Maspero, iii. 646, accepts it.

2 Βάττου. Stein thinks Battus II, 'the happy,' who came to the throne about 574 B.C. (iv. 159), is meant; but the dependent position of Ladike seems to agree rather with the circumstances of Battus III, iv. 161.

3 ἀπολωλέναι. The tense expresses proleptically the certain doom.

5 H.'s details go far to prove that he had seen the statue.

182 1 εἰκόνα. 'A portrait made like with painting', probably a picture on wood, such as are found on mummies of the Graeco-Roman period. It was no doubt the work of a Greek artist. We may compare the Egyptian portraits in the National Gallery (nos. 1260–70), though these are of the second or third century A. D.

θώρηκα. For the corselet cf. iii. 47. 2 n.; the groundwork was linen threads with 'figures (ζῷα) embroidered in gold and cotton'; cf. Ezek. xxvii. 7 'fine linen with broidered work from Egypt'.

τῇ Ἥρῃ. For the Heraeum cf. iii. 60. 4.

2 Λίνδον. The real reason for this dedication was that the usual trade-route from the Aegean to Egypt was by Rhodes (cf. c. 178; Thuc. viii. 35. 2) and Cyprus. Phaselis (178. 2) was important on this route.

Κύπρον. H. knew nothing of the conquest by Sargon, 709 B.C. (5. 104 n.); Amasis was the 'first' Egyptian to conquer Cyprus.

As H. introduces his long digression on Egypt with a reference to the conquest of the Greeks (c. 1. 2), so he skilfully concludes with a similar reference.

BOOK III

1 The δή refers back to ii. 1, after the long digression on Egypt.

The personal motive is characteristic of H. (cf. Introd. p. 45); the alliance of Egypt with Lydia (i. 77) and mere lust of conquest (i. 153. 4) were fully sufficient causes for the attack on Egypt.

For the Egyptian doctors cf. 129. 2 (their failure against Democedes) and ii. 84.

2 The law that the Persian king should only marry from the families of 'the Seven' (84. 2 n.) may not yet have been passed; but Amasis knew his daughter would be regarded as a sort of captive; the chief wives were always Persian. The story that Cambyses was the son of an Egyptian princess was given by Dinon (fl. circ. 360 B.C.) and Lyceas of Naucratis (F. H. G. ii. 91; iv. 441); that of H. in cap. 1 is even more incredible; a daughter of Apries would have been at least 40 in 529 B.C.; Ctesias (fr. 8, p. 225) for once agrees with H. The story of c. 2 is due to the vanity of a conquered nation (as H. saw), claiming a share in its conqueror (cf. App. IV. 4); but all the variants are probably derived from Egyptians, who wished that their own country should have a share in suggesting its own conquest. The princess is the heroine of Ebers' famous romance, Eine äegyptische Königstochter.

4 No doubt the story of Phanes was familiar to H. from his childhood; the name (which is not a common one) is read on a vase found in many fragments (now in the B. M.) by Petrie (Naukratis, 1886; E. E. F., p. 55, pl. 33).

Ἀραβίων βασιλέα. H. wrongly considers the Arabians as *one* nation; Cambyses' ally would be simply a powerful chief.

For the dangers of this desert cf. the sufferings of the retreating French in 1799 (Lanfrey, i. 297).

A unique coin found at Halicarnassus and now in the British Museum bears the inscription φαενὸς ἐμὶ σῆμα, 'I am the sign of Phanes.' It is at least as early as 525 B.C., and may have been struck by the mercenary captain to pay his men. But it is more usually connected with Ephesus, and the inscription is then translated 'I am the sign of the bright one'; cf. Head, H. N. p. 571.

5 For Kadytis cf. ii. 159 n.

The Palestine Syrians are here distinguished by H. from the Phoenicians (so too in ii. 104); their lands also are distinguished in i. 105 (probably), iii. 91. 1, and iv. 39. 2; in ii. 106. 1 he applies the term to include the coast north of Mount Carmel. But the most important reference is vii. 89, where H. distinguishes the 'Syrians in Palestine' from the Phoenicians, and then goes on (§ 2) to use 'Palestine' of all the coast land, including Phoenicia, 'as far as Egypt'. He never uses it of Phoenicia alone. Here he means 'Philistines', who were still powerful in his time (Zech. ix. 5); it is true that he says they were circumcised (ii. 104. 3), but he says (ib.) the same of Phoenicians. Either the neighbouring tribes had begun to copy the Jews in this rite, or H. confuses the Jews and the coast peoples. He cannot have meant by the 'Palestine Syrians' 'the Jews' only, for they were at this time very unimportant.

2 The ancient geographers did not usually extend 'Arabia' to the Mediterranean, nor does H. himself in iv. 39. He means here that the ends of the trade routes from Arabia to the Mediterranean were under Arabian control (cf. iii. 107 seq. for this spice trade); he writes **τοῦ 'Αραβίου**, 'in possession of the Arabian,' not *τῆς 'Αραβίης*, For the Arabs of South Palestine as dependent allies (not subjects) of the Persians cf. 88. 1 n.

Jenysus must have been a little further from Egypt than the once important port of Rhinocolura (Strabo 781), as Titus marched from Pelusium (a day west of Mount Casius) to Rhinocolura in three days (Joseph. B.J. iv. 11. 5), and H. allows 'three days' from Mount Casius to Jenysus. Its name has been traced in 'Khan Jûnes', the traditional site of the casting-up of Jonah; but this is too far from Egypt, and its name 'resting place of Jonah' obviously dates from Mahometan times.

For Mount Casius and the Serbonian Lake cf. ii. 6. 1 n.

3 The Egyptians called the Serbonian Lake *Τυφῶνος ἐκπνοαί* (Plut. Ant. c. 3), and Strabo (763) describes it *ὡς ἂν ζέοντος ὕδατος*, and says *ἀναφυσᾶται κατὰ καιροὺς ἀτάκτους*. Typhon, the hundred-headed (*Τυφὼς Κίλιξ ἑκατόγκρανος*, Pind. Pyth. viii. 16) son of Tartarus and Gaia, was placed by Homer, Il. ii. 783 *εἰν 'Αρίμοις*—probably in Cilicia. Afterwards his burial place was transferred to Etna (Pind. Ol. iv. 11), and to other volcanic regions. When he was identified with the Egyptian Set (ii. 144. 2 n.), it was also placed in Egypt.

6 2 The 'demarchs' were local headmen, under the nomarchs (cf. ii. 177. 2 n., and for the nome names ii. 164 n.).

H.'s story is confirmed by the name 'Ostrakine' (Joseph. *u. s.*) which, lying half-way between Mount Casius and Rhinocolura, was 'waterless'. Steindorf in 1904, visiting the oasis of Siwah, came upon a collection of broken pottery which he thought might be the remains of a water store such as that described here.

παλαιόν: *sc. κέραμον*. Translate 'being emptied (*ἐξαιρεόμενος*) is carried where the former jars have been carried'.

7 **σάξαντες**: *sc. κέραμον*. Others less probably supply *ἐσβολήν*, i. e. 'having provided the invasion with water'.

8 1 The fidelity of the Arabs is still proverbial. Cf. Kinglake, Eothen, c. xvii, p. 202 (ed. of 1864).

τῶν βουλομένων: in loose apposition to *ἀμφοτέρων κτλ*. The employment of a mediator is an Oriental characteristic (cf. Heb. viii. 6).

δακτύλους. For touching 'thumbs' with blood, &c., cf. the cleansing of the leper (Lev. xiv. 25, 28).

λίθους ἑπτά. The number '7' is of course sacred. For stones as a witness cf. Gen. xxxi. 45–8, 'Galeed', and Josh. xxiv. 26–7. On the whole of this passage, so important anthropologically, cf. Robertson Smith, R. S. pp. 315–16, and Tylor, P. C. ii. 381. By the mixture of blood the stranger was admitted to fellowship with the tribe, or if an Arab of a different clan (ἀστός), to fellowship with the clan. No doubt, in the rite originally, the parties tasted each other's blood; the idea was that 'the blood is the life'.

The gods appealed to are in H. the common gods of the race; but the touching of the stones goes back to an earlier time, when 'the new tribesman has to be introduced to the god' (of the particular tribe). For other instances of blood covenant cf. Lydia, i. 74, Scythia, iv. 70, Armenia, Tac. Ann. xii. 47, and, among the Balonda on the Zambesi, Livingstone, Travels (1855), p. 488.

3 **τῶν τριχῶν τὴν κουρήν.** For the Arab hair cutting cf. Jer. ix. 26 R. V. 'those that have the corners of their hair polled, that dwell in the wilderness' (cf. also Lev. xix. 27). The custom was forbidden to the Jews because the heathen dedicated their hair to their gods (Robertson Smith, ib. p. 325). Translate 'they cut it in a ring (*περιτρόχαλα* used adverbially), shaving round under the temples'. It was in cutting the hair on the temples that the Arabs were different from the Greeks.

Orotalt is explained (Movers, Phön. i. 337) as 'ignis dei', i. e. the sun or the star Saturn; Alilat (i. e. Al-Ilat, 'the goddess') is at once the moon and the evening star. The pair correspond to the Baal and Ashtoreth of the North Semites; they are at once heavenly deities, and the powers of destruction and reproduction. Robertson Smith, however (Kinship in Arab. p. 298 seq.), says that they are the great nature goddess and her son (and husband) Dusares. H. (i. 131. 3 n.) gives a list of the various names of the goddess, to which we may add 'Argimpasa' (4. 59). For other unconvincing explanations of 'Orotalt' cf. Gruppe, Myth. Liter. (1908), p. 579.

9 2 There is no 'great river' running into the Ἐρυθρὴ θάλασσα (here = 'Red Sea'; but cf. i. 1 n.). The conduit of skins, however, seems to be a distorted version of a real fact. Chesney (Euphrates Exped. ii. 657) says it 'represents the primitive Kanát', i. e. subterranean water-course, common in Western Asia; Elphinstone (i. 398) says he has heard of them thirty-six miles long. For these (between Media and Parthia) cf. Polyb. x. 28 and (in the desert of Kerman) M. Polo i. c. 20 (i. 124).

10 1 The 'Psammenitus' of H. and the 'Psammicherites' (or Psammecheres) of Manetho (F. H. G. ii. 594) are both transliterations of the Egyptian name 'Psamtik'. The Greeks varied as much in their rendering of Oriental names as English scholars do in dealing with Indian ones.

Ctesias (9, p. 66) calls him Amyrtaeus, confusing him with the fifth-century rebel (15. 3 n.); in his story, Combaphes, a eunuch, plays the part of Phanes and 'betrays the bridges'.

2 The length of the reign of Amasis is correctly given; for H.'s accuracy in Saite chronology cf. App. X *ad fin.*

3 Maspero (iii. 660) quotes the Egyptian story that the French invasion of 1797 was foretold by rain at Luxor; he adds that he never heard of rain at Luxor during six winters there. Rain, however, is now more frequent in Upper Egypt; cf. Budge, Sûdan, i. 71, where he gives a gruesome story of the effects of a storm in 1887. At Thebes it rains a little three or four times a year.

11 3 **ἐμπιόντες δὲ τοῦ αἵματος.** For the blood pledge among the Scyths cf. iv. 70. Stein conjectures that this 'brotherhood of the sword' was connected with the worship of the Carian Zeus Στράτιος. For a similar ghastly pledge among desperate men cf. Sall. Cat. 22. For human sacrifices before a battle cf. the doubtful story of Themistocles before Salamis (from Phaneas, Plut. Them. c. 13); for the whole subject of human sacrifices among the Greeks cf. vii. 197 n.

2 4 **πίλους,** 'felt caps,' added to explain τιάρας: cf. ἀξίνας σαγάρις (vii. 64). Wilkinson (ii. 74) says that both the monuments and modern experience confirm H.'s statement as to the hardness of Egyptian skulls.

For the whole passage cf. Introd. 5 and App. IX. 1; it dates H.'s visit to Egypt as in or after 460 B.C.

3 3 **οἱ προσεχέες.** i. e. the Libyans west of Egypt; for their names and customs cf. iv. 168 seq.

For the surrender of Cyrene by Arcesilaus III cf. iv. 165 n.

4 2 Cf. the foreboding of Hector as to Andromache (Il. vi. 456 sq.) and Lord Leighton's picture.

5 For the seven royal judges (Pers. Dâtabara = θεσμοφόρος) cf. App. VI. 2 and c. 31. Their office was as dangerous as it was honourable (v. 25; vii. 194). They are to be distinguished from the seven 'princes of Persia' (cf. iii. 70 n.), though the number (like 'twelve' in the various juries of mediaeval England) constantly recurs, e. g. Cyrus (Xen. Anab. i. 6. 4) summons a court of the seven noblest Persians to try the traitor Orontas.

As the Mytilenaean trireme had a crew of 200 (cf. vii. 184. 1) the number of Egyptians executed was 2,000 (200 × 10).

10 **ἐπὶ γήραος οὐδῷ** is probably an intentional echo of the words of Priam (Il. xxii. 60).

2 The custom seems to have been usual in the East; so Pharaoh Neçho appointed Jehoiakim to be king over Judah (2 Kings xxiii. 34), and Nebuchadnezzar, Zedekiah (ib. xxiv. 17).

3 Inaros, the Libyan king (12. 4 and Thuc. i. 104, 109–10), rebelled

in 460 B.C.; his rebellion was the cause of the disastrous Athenian expedition (459–454). Ctesias (c. 36, p. 73) tells us that after his surrender his life was spared for five years; but he was then given up to the Persian queen-mother, Amytis, who impaled him in vengeance for his killing her son Achaemenes.

The names of Thannyras and Pausiris have not been found on the monuments, but these seem to show some of the Egyptian royal family as governors. The general control, however, was given to Aryandes (iv. 166).

Amyrtaeus was ruler of Lower Egypt, and took part in the revolt of Inaros; the last certain mention of him is in 449 B.C. (Thuc. i. 112), when he was still holding out in the Marshes (cf. ii. 140); he may be the 'king of Egypt' (Plut. Per. 37) who sent corn to Athens 445–444, but Philochorus (fr. 90; F. H. G. i. 399) says this came from Psammetichus, king of Libya, the son of Inaros. The old view, that he is the 'Amyrtaeus' of the twenty-eighth dynasty (405–400 B.C., Man. fr. 70; F. H. G. ii. 596) is impossible, not so much because of the length of reign (cf. ii. 140 for a curiously exact parallel), but because this second Amyrtaeus was succeeded by another native dynasty, not by a Persian nominee, as H. here states.

4 **αἷμα ταύρου.** This was the fabled cause of the death of Themistocles (cf. Arist. Eq. 83–4 and Plut. Th. 31); the blood was supposed to coagulate and choke the drinker (Arist. Hist. An. iii. 19).

16 According to the inscription on a statue (the Naophorus) in the Vatican, set up by Uza-hor-ent-res, admiral of Amasis and Psammetichus III (R. P. x. 49; cf. Petrie, iii. 361–2), Cambyses at first paid respect to the goddess Neith, cleansed her temple, and restored her revenues, which had been alienated for the Greek mercenaries. This was a reversal of the policy of Amasis (ii. 154 n.), and along with the outrage on his mummy was an appeal to the party in Egypt which had hated him. It was also the usual Persian policy towards the religion of subject peoples. Cf. Cyrus in Babylon (C. C. 27 seq. in R. P.[2] v. 167), and also his attitude towards the Jews (2 Chron. xxxvi. 23).

This inscription, however, is not inconsistent, as some maintain, with H.'s story of the outrage on Apis (c. 29), which took place after the disastrous expedition against Ethiopia; it speaks of a period of 'great woe in all the land', and Uza-hor-ent-res himself left Egypt (perhaps fleeing from Cambyses), and was recalled by Darius (§ 7). Moreover, panegyrics on a monarch's piety are apt to be misleading (cf. 'our most religious and gracious King, George IV', though the parallel is only a partial one). Maspero, therefore (iii. 668 seq.), accepts H.'s narrative as to Cambyses (as does also Meyer, i.[1] 508 doubtfully); but it is rejected by many as due to Egyptian hatred of their conqueror; Duncker (vi. 170) argues that Egypt would never have remained quiet, had its religion been outraged thus. (See further c. 29 nn. and App. V. 3.)

1 ταφῆς: cf. ii. 169 n.; the name of Amasis is found to have been erased in several monuments at Sais and elsewhere.

2 For the impiety of polluting fire by burning a dead body cf. App. VIII. 4, and i. 86 n. (the story of Croesus); i. 131. 2 n.

5 ἡλικίην, 'stature' (cf. Matt. vi. 27).

The mummy of the queen of Amasis from Thebes is in the British Museum; the gilding on it shows it was not burned.

17–26 *Expeditions of Cambyses to south and west.* It will be at once obvious how much less H. knows here of the country south of Egypt than he does in ii. 29 seq. For the explanation of this cf. Introd. p. 14.

The 'long-lived Ethiopians', as described by H., are a mythical people (cf. c. 20). His account of them is partly based on Homer (Il. i. 423; Od. i. 23, τοὶ διχθὰ δεδαίαται ἔσχατοι ἀνδρῶν, with whom Zeus (Il.) and Poseidon (Od.) go to feast), partly on travellers' tales (c. 18); its exaggeration is natural, as they live at the end of the world to the south-west (iii. 114); so they are 'the tallest and fairest of men' (cf. the beauty of Memnon and ἀμύμονες, Il. i. 423; Od. xi. 522). The tradition of the Egyptian priests would agree with this; Napata was the seat of a strict theocracy; cf. Diod. iii. 5 for the priestly control of the Ethiopian kings. But the Ethiopians who 'border on Egypt' (iii. 97. 2 n.) were a real part of the Persian Empire, now probably conquered by Cambyses (cf. App. V. 4).

18 1 For the 'table of the sun' cf. Pomp. Mela, iii. 87, who repeats H., and Paus. vi. 26. 2, who treats it as an impossible fable. It is probably a misunderstood myth; the Egyptians spoke of a 'meadow of offerings', to which the souls of the dead came to eat; this was easily turned into a fact, as food was actually left on the tombs (Maspero, iii. 667 n.). The informants of H. give this myth a Greek colouring by bringing in the sun, and he is the more ready to believe the tale because of the Homeric 'feasts' of the Ethiopians (*v. s.*)

Heeren (African Nations, i. 327 seq.) finds a foundation of fact for the story in the record of Cosmas (sixth century A.D.), who says the traders in the land of Sasu exposed joints of meat in dumb commerce for gold (cf. iv. 196 for similar methods). This explanation is interesting, but the evidence of Cosmas is too late and doubtful to be accepted. Vases, with *animals* (not men) feeding from an altar-like table, were found (1909) at Karanòg in Nubia, which may perhaps be explained by the 'table of the sun' (Woolley and MacIver, Karanòg, 1910, p. 56). The same explorers (ib. p. 55) confirm H.'s statement that Dionysus was worshipped at Meroe (ii. 29).

προαστίῳ, like the 'changing officials', is a Greek touch.

19 1 Ἰχθυοφάγων. The 'fish-eaters' are placed by Pausanias (i. 33. 4) on the south coasts of the Red Sea; cf. Diod. iii. 15–20 for a marvellous account of them. The Persian messengers went 'from

Elephantine' to 'fetch' them, as the place whence the caravans started south-east from the Nile.

2 **οὐκ ἔφασαν ποιήσειν.** Cf. viii. 22. 1 for a mother-city claiming of her colonies the piety here shown by the Phoenicians.

3 Grote (iv. 142) supposes that Cyrus had received the submission of the Phoenicians (so Xen. Cyr. i. 1. 4); but H. (iii. 34. 4), probably rightly, makes the Persians say that Cambyses *προσεκτῆσθαι τὴν θάλασσαν.* This annexation explains in part (cf. App. V. 2) why Egypt was not conquered till the fifth year of Cambyses. It is noticeable that Tyre, which had resisted Assyria and Babylonia desperately, yielded without a struggle to the Persian power, probably because under it local autonomy and religious institutions (c. 16 n.) were respected.

Cyprus revolted from Egypt (ii. 182. 2) to Persia.

20 The gifts resemble those sent to noble Persians; cf. iii. 84 n. The *ἀλάβαστρον* was a pear-shaped vessel without handles.

2 **τὸν ἂν . . . κρίνωσι μέγιστον.** Nic. Dam. fr. 142 (F. H. G. iii. 463) adds the interesting fact that succession was usually in the female line; but failing a proper heir, the most handsome was selected.

21 2 **κατόπται.** For the fear of spies cf. Gen. xlii. 9.

3 **τόξα.** For the Ethiopian bows cf. vii. 69; the unstrung bow was the symbol for Ethiopia in the hieroglyphs. Bruce (Travels, iv. 42, ed. of 1805) says the Abyssinian bows are so adorned with bands of hide that in the end they become unbendable.

22 4 **ὀγδώκοντα δὲ ἔτεα.** Cf. Ps. xc. 10 for this limit of life.

ἀνέφερον: *sc.* *ἑωυτούς.* For this sense cf. i. 116. 2 *ἀνενειχθείς.*

23 1 Sparig ingeniously explains the longevity of the Ethiopians by the African counting only five months to the year. Speke (Discovery of Source of Nile, 1863, p. 511) found this in Unyoro on the Upper Nile, and perhaps the same short reckoning prevailed earlier on the Middle Nile.

3 A similar 'lightness' is attributed to an Indian river, the Silas (Megasthenes, fr. 19; F. H. G. ii. 415).

4 **πέδησι χρυσέῃσι.** The whole story is a traveller's tale; but gold was once produced abundantly in Ethiopia.

24 1 **ἐξ ὑάλου.** Perhaps H. means some form of transparent porcelain; but probably the marvels here described are as fictitious as Cinderella's 'glass' slipper.

γυψώσαντες. The 'whole' plastered body was adorned with 'painting' (*γραφῇ*), not merely the front.

3 The plastered and painted mummy 'appears in everything like the "naked corpse"' (*αὐτῷ τῷ νέκυϊ*).

4 **ἀπαρχόμενοι.** The 'offerings' to the dead are a touch of reality in the fancy picture; cf. Budge, The Mummy, p. 328.

25 For the facts in this chapter cf. App. V.

26 1 **Ὄασιν πόλιν.** H. here uses 'Oasis' as a proper name for the so-called 'Great Oasis', that of Khargeh, which lay on the parallel of Thebes, 'seven days' journey' away (the figure is fairly right). For the oases cf. iv. 181 nn. H., however, is hopelessly confused; the Oasis of Ammon, that of Siwah (cf. ii. 32; iv. 181. 2 nn.), was much further north, in the latitude of the Fayûm, from which it could be reached in fourteen days. It is most unlikely that the Persians attacked it from the 'Great Oasis'. Perhaps H. had heard of the small oasis, which lies near the 'Great Oasis', and confused it with that of Siwah. St. Martin, pp. 40-1.

As to the nature of the 'Aeschrionian tribe' it is impossible to speak definitely. The Etym. Mag. (*s. v.* Ἀστυπάλαια) speaks of two tribes, the Astypalaean and the Schesian, which may be parallel to the 'Aeschrionian'; certainly Αἰσχρίων is found as a proper name at Samos. On the other hand, the four Ionic tribes (v. 66. 2 n.) were almost certainly found there; two of them occur at Perinthus, a colony of Samos (Busolt, i. 279 n.). It is very curious to find Greeks 400 miles from the sea, and Dahlmann thinks H. is misled by some similarity of sound: it is safer, however, to accept so definite a statement about emigrants from a city which H. knew well (cf. Introd. p. 3 and iii. 60 nn.).

Strabo (791) compares oases to islands, and the familiar legend of the 'isles of the blest' might well occur to a Greek traveller. But Spiegelberg (Z. A. S. 42. 85-6) has shown that H.'s derivation is meant to translate an Egyptian word, though it is inaccurate, and that it was derived from a native. Maspero (M. et A. E. ii. 422) says the idea that the oases were homes of the dead is a very old Egyptian one.

3 **νότον μέγαν.** The modern view is that the simoon is deadly because it dries up the wells, not because it buries with sand. Duncker (vi. 166), however, quotes an instance early in the last century of a caravan, 2,000 strong, perishing in a sand-storm. As the Ammonians are found among the subjects of Darius, probably the expedition succeeded (cf. App. V. 4).

27 For the Apis cf. ii. 38 n.

28 2 'Which is not hereafter allowed (*οἵη*; cf. i. 29. 2) to conceive again in its womb.' The mother-cow was kept in a stall near the Apis stall (Strabo 807). The Egyptians thought the Apis was conceived *ὅταν φῶς ἐρείσῃ γόνιμον ἀπὸ τῆς σελήνης καὶ καθάψηται βοὸς ὀργώσης* (Plut. Mor. 718; cf. ib. 368).

κατίσχειν: intransitive; 'comes down upon.'

3 H.'s account of the Apis is confirmed by the statues (cf. Rawlinson for picture), although Aelian (H. A. xi. 10) says that the Egyptians called it 'insufficient', for there were really twenty-nine signs; cf. Plin. N. H. viii. 184 for one of these 'candicans macula cornibus lunae crescere incipientis'. Mariette (Maspero, p. 37) says 'the beetle, vulture' (*not* 'eagle'), &c., did not really exist (cf. *εἰκασμένον*), and well compares the dragon, lyre, and bear seen by the astronomers among the stars. The MSS. reading *τετράγωνον* is usually

altered to τι τρίγωνον, to make H.'s account correspond with the rest of the authorities.

In colour the Apis was 'black' (as H. says), not white with black spots as Plut. (I. et O. c. 43; Mor. 368), or πολύχρους (as Ael. *u. s.*).

29 Plutarch (de Isid. 44) says Cambyses *killed* the Apis, and gave the carcase to his dogs; H. as usual avoids these later exaggerations. But many modern historians (e.g. Brugsch, ii. 299–300) reject the story altogether, because an Apis στήλη (No. 354 in the Louvre) represents Cambyses as adoring the bull-god; this belongs to the sixth year of his reign. Maspero (iii. 668 n.), however, accepts H.'s story. Wiedemann (Gesch. Aeg., 1880, p. 229) argues that the faulty execution of the Apis monument just mentioned shows it was executed secretly by the priests; moreover, its evidence is contradicted by another Louvre 'column', set up under Darius to commemorate an Apis born in the fifth year of Cambyses; he (p. 230) conjectures that this second monument was deliberately antedated, so as to ignore the cruel death of the last Apis; this hypothesis is probable, because it explains how two sacred bulls could be represented as existing at once, a thing in itself impossible.

30 1 **ἐμάνη.** H. records, without accepting, the supernatural explanation of madness; he gives a natural one, c. 33. As to Cleomenes' madness, he, among various explanations (vi. 75 seq.), inclines to the supernatural (c. 84).

Σμέρδιν. His real name was Bardiya; Aesch. (Pers. 774) calls him Mardos. For the change from Bardiya to Mardos cf. Megabates (Mega = the Persian Baga). The initial Σ was added because the name was confused with the real Greek name Σμέρδις (for which cf. Arist. Pol. 1311 b 29), on the supposed analogy of σμικρός and μικρός. Ctesias (8, p. 65), who calls him 'Tanyoxarces' (which seems to be a nickname, Maspero, iii. 655), makes him satrap of Bactria and some adjacent districts, but this statement is of little value. For a full analysis of the various versions of his story cf. Duncker, vi. 175 seq.; but his results are very doubtful.

The B. I. (i. 10) puts the murder before the expedition to Egypt. It obviously was kept a secret, for otherwise a pretender would have had no opportunity (cf. Perkin Warbeck's personation of the young Duke of York); this secrecy explains the divergence of traditions. Ctesias (10, p. 67) makes the murderer personate Smerdis for five years, by arrangement of Cambyses, and then seize the throne on his death. This, however, is an impossible solution of what is the real difficulty, i.e. how did the heir apparent disappear unnoticed?

2 **ὄψιν.** For a similar dream-warning against a dangerous man cf. i. 209.

31 1 **τὴν ἀδελφεήν.** Cyrus and Cassandane (ii. 1) had three daughters, Atossa (*v. i.*), this nameless one, the 'Roxana' of Ctesias (c. 12, p. 67), and Artystone, the favourite wife of Darius (iii. 88; vii. 69).

2 Incestuous marriage is praised in the Avesta, and was freely practised under the Sassanians; instances occur in other Persian kings, e.g. Artaxerxes II married two of his own daughters (Plut. Artax. c. 23). This 'Persarum impia religio' (Catullus, xc. 4), however, was mainly the practice of the Magi.

For the royal judges cf. 14. 5 n.

5 The immutability of Persian law (cf. Dan. vi) has passed into a proverb.

6 **ἄλλην**: Atossa, who was successively the wife of Cambyses, of the pretender Smerdis, and of Darius (cc. 68, 88). For her influence cf. vii. 2; her name has become proverbial for a reigning Sultana (cf. Pope, Moral Essays, ii. 115 seq.); her sons were Xerxes, Masistes (vii. 82), Achaemenes (vii. 97), Hystaspes (vii. 64).

2 2 **ἐκείνῳ**: i.e. Cambyses. These stories are often said to be inconsistent with the general narrative of H., which makes the murder of Smerdis a secret; but a mere suspicion, such as must have been current, would be fully sufficient to explain the sister's reproach.

3 **θρίδακα.** The parabolic 'stripping of the lettuce' is quite Eastern.

33 The **ἱρὴ νοῦσος**, epilepsy, was supposed to be specially divine, from its resemblance to the ecstasies of the diviners. Hippocrates (De Sac. Morbo, 1) denies that it is more supernatural than other diseases; H. himself here seems inclined to be sceptical.

ἀεικές: here and in vi. 98. 3 = 'improbable'.

4 1 **ἀγγελίας.** For the office of chamberlain cf. i. 114. 2 n.

4 **θάλασσαν**: cf. 19. 3 n. Duncker (vi. 185) sees in the story of this murder an invention of 'poetical justice', which punishes Prexaspes for killing the son of Cyrus, by slaying his own son.

5 4 **ἐπίσκοπα**: i.e. *ὥστε τυχεῖν τοῦ σκοποῦ*.

'The god himself,' i.e. Mithras; 'the arrows of the sun' are a familiar figure.

5 **ἐπὶ κεφαλήν**, 'on their head'; i.e. head downwards (cf. *ἐπὶ κ. φέρεσθαι*, c. 75. 3). Stein and Rawlinson, however, translate 'to the neck', and this is a more usual form of punishment in the East. For burying alive generally cf. vii. 114 n.

4 **Κροῖσος . . . ἔθεε ἔξω.** Cf. the similar escape of David, 1 Sam. xviii. 11, and for seizing occasion to punish old offences cf. 1 Kings ii. 32, 44.

6 **καταπροΐξεσθαι**: a favourite word with H. (cf. iii. 156. 3; v. 105. 1; vii. 17. 2), always in future and with a participle to express act: 'shall not with impunity.'

2 **Ἡφαίστου . . . ἱρόν.** For this temple cf. ii. 101. 2 n.

For the **Παταϊκοι** and the *Κάβειροι* cf. ii. 51 n. The name of the **Παταϊκοι** was perhaps connected with that of Ptah, but this is most uncertain (cf. Roscher, iii. 1676). They were fat dwarfs with gorgon-like features; cf. Perrot and Chipiez, iii, fig. 21, p. 65. Aesch. in Ctes. 190 uses Παταικίων = a trickster. H. here confuses the image of Ptah (Hephaestus) with those of the Khnoumou, 'the sons of Ptah'; these were dwarfs, with bent legs, long arms, and a huge head. Ptah himself was represented as a mummy, with head and hands free.

38 This chapter is most characteristic of H. and of the general Greek attitude to religion; cf. Xen. Mem. iv. 3. 16, the well-known answer of Delphi, given repeatedly, that the gods were pleased with worship νόμῳ πόλεως.

Strabo (805) says that he saw traces of the outrages of Cambyses on the temples of Heliopolis. The mad king was even credited with the destruction of the statue of Memnon, though this was really ruined by an earthquake in the time of Augustus. Cambyses, to Egyptian imagination, played the part that Cromwell is credited with in English cathedrals.

Zeno later declined to condemn nations that ate their dead; burial, he held, was a matter not of principle but of convenience. The point illustrates well the cosmopolitanism of the Stoics.

4 **Καλλατίας.** For a discussion of this cannibalism and for modern instances cf. iv. 26 n.

The name Callatiae (from Sans Kâla = black) points to the aboriginal inhabitants of India; they are otherwise unknown except for a vague reference in Hecataeus (fr. 177, F. H. G. i. 12); perhaps they are the same as the Παδαῖοι of c. 99.

The passage from Pindar (fr. 169), which H. here quotes, is preserved in Plato, Gorg. 484 B, where it refers to a 'natural law' that 'the stronger should rule the weaker'. νόμος ὁ πάντων βασιλεὺς | θνατῶν τε καὶ ἀθανάτων·—οὗτος δὲ δή, φησίν—ἄγει δικαιῶν τὸ βιαιότατον | ὑπερτάτᾳ χειρί. H., quoting from memory, gives the passage a more general sense. Myres, A. and C. p. 157, says that νόμος is 'the formal expression of *what actually happens* . . .', 'it answers to our *law of nature* . . . a more or less accurate formulation of the actual course of events.'

39–60 *The story of Polycrates.* H. explains its disproportionate length in c. 60; the story bears throughout marks of his personal observation, e.g. cc. 39. 4, 54, 60 (cf. for H.'s knowledge of Samos elsewhere, 146. 2, and for the Heraeum, Introd. § 25, p. 30). The connexion of events in Samos, however, with the course of Persian history was closer than H. suspected; Amasis had endeavoured to protect Egypt, in accordance with the usual policy of the Saite dynasty, by forming a league of maritime states; but the desertion of Cyprus and the submission of Phoenicia to the Persians (19. 3 n.) changed the balance of power, and Polycrates went over to the side of the stronger. H. ignores the real reasons of the policy of Polycrates, and gives us instead a story illustrating the Nemesis attendant on good fortune (cc. 40–3), which hides the treachery of Samos. But even in H. (c. 44) it is made clear that Polycrates was really the aggressor against Egypt.

The date of Polycrates' accession is about 532 B.C. as given by Eusebius (cf. Busolt, ii. 508); we know that (*a*) he died before Cambyses (cc. 125–6), i.e. before 521 (cf. c. 66 n.); (*b*) Thucydides (i. 13) speaks of him as τυραννῶν ἐπὶ Καμβύσου, which renders impossible the statement that he 'flourished' not later than 550 B.C. (Diog. Laert. ii. 1); (*c*) Eusebius (Arm. Vers.) gives the sixteen years of Samian 'rule of the sea' as from 531 to 515, i.e. to the fall of Maeandrius (cf. Myres, J. H. S. xxvi. 91, 101, for slightly different figures). Alexis of Samos (fr. 2; F. H. G. iv. 299) says that Polycrates had gained his influence by lavish liberality. Polyaenus (i. 23) describes how he seized the city during a festival (cf. Cylon at Athens, Thuc. i. 126) and was victorious by the aid of Lygdamis (cf. 120. 3 for a curious detail as to his conspiracy). His friendship with Lygdamis (cf. i. 61) and his enmity to Lesbos (cf. 39. 4 with v. 94) are the proofs given for his supposed friendship with Pisistratus.

1 **ἐπαναστάς** might imply a revolution against any form of government; but it is probable that an oligarchy was ruling in Samos, having been restored after the overthrow described in Plut. Quaes. Graec. 57; Mor. 303 seq.

2 For Syloson's story cf. iii. 139 seq.; his son bore the family name Aeaces (iv. 138).

3 For the use of penteconters, not triremes, cf. i. 163. 2 n.

τοξότας. These 'bowmen' were 'native Samians' (45. 3).

4 **νήσων.** Cf. Thuc. i. 13. 6 for the conquest of the islands by Polycrates, and iii. 104. 2 for the honour paid to Delos. The rivalry of Samos and Miletus was perpetual (cf. the events of 494, 440, 412–404 B.C.), and probably explains the variations in the general foreign policy of both states.

40–3 The story of the ring of Polycrates is one of the best illustrations of the doctrine of Nemesis (cf. φθονερόν *inf.* and in i. 32. 1 n.). Diodorus (i. 95) rationalizes the story by making Amasis break off the alliance because he (Polycrates) dislikes tyranny. Reinach (R. A. 1905, vi. 9) thinks H.'s story is a development of the yearly custom of throwing a ring into the sea as a claim of lordship (cf. the 'Marriage of the Adriatic' at Venice, Byron, C. H. iv. 91); he quotes i. 165, vii. 35, but these are irrelevant. Cf. Cook, C. R. xvii. 409 for a similar wild suggestion.

2 **ἐναλλὰξ πρήσσων** sums up τὸ μέν τι εὐτυχέειν . . . προσπταίειν.

4 For the attempt to avert great calamities by small ones cf. Liv. v. 21. 15, the prayer of Camillus, 'ut eam invidiam lenire quam minimo suo privato incommodo publicoque populi Romani liceret.' He fell as he prayed, and interpreted the mishap ὡς γέγονεν αὐτῷ κατ' εὐχὴν σφάλμα μικρὸν ἐπ' εὐτυχίᾳ μεγίστῃ, Plut. Cam. 5. But, like Polycrates, he did not escape subsequent disaster.

ἀκέο. The present implies that the 'remedy' was to be repeated, 'if good luck hereafter did not befall him in due alternation with misfortunes'.

41 **σφρηγίς.** The stone in the ring was engraved, as Theodorus (i. 51. 3 n.) was a gem-cutter as well as a metal-worker; Paus. viii. 14. 8 (cf. Frazer, iv. 237) implies that it was an emerald; hence Pliny (N. H. xxxvii. 4) is repeating a guide-book legend when he says that the ring was given by Augustus to the temple of Concord, and that the stone was a sardonyx. As Theodorus had been dead for half a century, the ring was to Polycrates an irreplaceable heirloom.

42 2 Cf. Juv. iv. 45 seq. (the fisherman's gift to Domitian) for a grandiose parody of Herodotean simplicity. Mahaffy (Soc. Life, p. 169) quotes the invitation to the fisherman as illustrating the simplicity of Greek court life; but the whole story is a folk tale (cf. Frazer, *u. s.*), and the details can hardly be pressed.

44 2 **τοὺς ὑπώπτευε μάλιστα.** For the employment of dangerous citizens on foreign service cf. Miltiades in the Chersonese (vi. 35. 3, though H. there gives a religious motive) and vii. 222 n. So Napoleon used Spaniards in the north of Europe (Oman, Penin. War, i. 367 seq.), who would have been dangerous at home.

τριήρεσι. The mention of 'triremes' seems inconsistent with 39. 3, and is tacitly corrected by Thuc. i. 14 *φαίνεται . . . ταῦτα* (i. e. early naval powers, including that of Polycrates) . . . *τριήρεσι μὲν ὀλίγαις χρώμενα, πεντηκοντόροις δ' ἔτι καὶ πλοίοις μακροῖς ἐξηρτυμένα.* In the story (41. 2, 124. 2) a penteconter (*not* a trireme) is used.

45 'At Carpathus', i. e. they had put in at this island, which lies between Rhodes and Crete, at the south-east exit from the Aegean.

3 **τοὺς ἀπ' Αἰγύπτου.** The variety of traditions is remarkable; probably the story of the victory of the aristocrats is due to Samian vanity.

4 **ὑποπρῆσαι.** For the tyrant holding the families of his subjects as hostages cf. Shakespeare, Richard III, v. iii. 61.

46 1 **οἱ ἄρχοντες,** 'authorities' (cf. vi. 106 n.); i.e. the kings and senate as well as the ephors who, even in the sixth century, were beginning to usurp the control of foreign affairs (cf. ix. 7 for the first definite instance, in 479 B.C.). For the Spartan government and policy at this period cf. App. XVII.

ἐπιλελῆθέναι. For this 'laconic repartee' in the original Doric cf. Plut. Moral. 232 D; on p. 223 he gives it to Cleomenes.

2 **θυλάκῳ περιεργάσθαι:** translate 'they had used "sack" needlessly', lit. 'they had been superfluous with the "sack"'. The rude brevity of the retort is characteristic. Others (e.g. Grote, iv. 169) translate 'your wallet is superfluous', i. e. the words alone were enough. (Cf. Theophrastus, Char. 13 for *περιεργία.*) The story is told by Sextus Empiricus (in Mathem. ii. 23) of the Chians, seeking leave to import corn from Laconia. Some think this the original occasion, and find here an instance of the composite

nature of H.'s history (cf. c. 80 nn.); but the Chian story is probably an invention based on H.'s narrative, and it is difficult to think that Chios needed to import corn, or that Laconia could export it, before 500 B.C. The version of H. is therefore preferable.

47 1 This passage is interesting as the only definite reference in H. to the Messenian wars (cf. v. 49. 8). It supports the later tradition that the second Messenian war had an international character, Argos, Arcadia, and Pisa being allies of Messenia (Strabo 362), Elis (Strabo 355), Corinth, and Sicyon (Paus. iv. 15) of the Lacedaemonians. Thucydides (i. 15) is thought to deny this by implication when he writes *ἐκδήμους στρατείας πολὺ ἀπὸ τῆς ἑαυτῶν ἐπ' ἄλλων καταστροφῇ οὐκ ἐξῇσαν οἱ Ἕλληνες*, except in the Lelantine war. Busolt (i. 606 n.; cf. also p. 580 n.) therefore sees in the introduction of Corinth and Sicyon a reflection of the political grouping of the fifth century (e.g. at Mantinea 418 B.C.). But Samos would be exceedingly likely to assist the Lacedaemonians, as allies of Corinth, and Thucydides systematically depreciates the importance of Greek history before his own century.

κρητῆρος. For a description of the bowl cf. i. 70. 1. The story well illustrates H.'s tendency to confuse occasions with real causes. There is no reason to doubt that the theft of the bowl (which H. must have seen at the Heraeum) was a provocation to the Lacedaemonians; but for the attack on Polycrates the Lacedaemonians had motives of general policy: for these and for their attitude to tyranny cf. App. XVI. 10. 'Plutarch' (de Hdt. Mal. 21) for once makes a point when he asks *ποίου γὰρ ἕνεκα θώρακος ἢ τίνος κρατῆρος ἑτέρου Κυψελίδας ἐξέβαλον κτλ.* (cf., however, Grote, iii. 43 and App. *u. s.* for a criticism of Plutarch's list of tyrants expelled by the Lacedaemonians).

3 **ἁρπεδόνη ἑκάστη.** Pliny (xix. 12) says the 'distinctness' of the 'threads' in the *θώρηξ* was so often tested by sightseers that 'parvas iam reliquias superesse hac experientium iniuria'. For the work cf. Ezek. xxvii. 7, 'fine linen with broidered work from Egypt.'

Amasis was trying no doubt to induce the Lacedaemonians (*αὐτοῖσι*) to join an anti-Persian league (cf. i. 46 n.).

For the dedication at Lindus cf. ii. 182. 1.

48 1 The chronology is inextricably confused (cf. App. XIV. 6). The 'insult' was about 550 B.C., and yet it is in the time of Periander, who died circ. 585. 'Plutarch' (*u. s.* c. 22) puts the events 'three generations' before Polycrates, and tells us from independent sources (Dionysius of Chalcis, fl. c. 350; fr. 3, F. H. G. iv. 396) that it was Cnidians (not Samians) who restored the boys to Corcyra; he confirms this by an appeal to honours granted by Corcyra to Cnidus. H. may have been misled by his Samian informants. The tyrant's brutality, however, may be accepted as a fact, characteristic of the Oriental leanings of the Cypselidae. (Cf. App. XVI. 4.)

3 **σιτίων . . . ἐργόντων.** For starving out suppliants cf. Thuc. i. 134. 2;

for the Samian evasion of their obligations to the Corinthians, under colour of a religious festival cf. Judges xxi. 19, the Gibeonites at Shiloh.

49 **διάφοροι.** For the standing feud between Corinth and Corcyra cf. Thuc. i. 13. 4, 38.

50–3 For H.'s account of the Cypselidae cf. v. 92 nn. and App. XVI. 3–4. The historical facts in these chapters are—(1) that Periander killed his wife; (2) conquered his father-in-law Procles (52. 7); this conquest is important as probably being the occasion of the independence of Aegina (v. 83. 1); (3) reduced Corcyra to subjection; (4) (probably) that Lycophron ruled for a time in Corcyra; (5) that Periander left no son to succeed him; his successor was Psammetichus, son of his brother Gorgus (Arist. Pol. 1315 b 26).

The rest of the narrative is romantic embroidery, moral tales such as the Greeks loved, which may be called 'the beginnings of the novel' (cf. Nitzsch, Rhein. Mus. 1872, p. 228). The style, especially in cc. 52 and 53, is characteristic of the age of the 'Seven Wise Men' (cf. i. 27 n.), among whom Periander was reckoned; the proverbs 'Obstinacy (*ἡ φιλοτιμίη*) is an evil thing', 'Do not heal evil with evil' (53. 4, *v. i.*), &c., are not adornments, they are the real base of the story.

50 For horrible details as to Melissa cf. v. 92 *η*. Periander had killed her in a fit of jealousy; this is darkly hinted at (52. 4).

52 For the *κήρυγμα* cf. Soph. O. T. 236 seq.

53 3 **διαφορηθέντα**, 'spoiled'; cf. i. 88. 3.

4 For the proverb *μὴ τῷ κακῷ τὸ κακὸν ἰῶ* cf. Soph. Aj. 362 and Thuc. v. 65. 2 (Agis) *διανοεῖται κακὸν κακῷ ἰᾶσθαι.*

τὰ ἐπιεικέστερα. For the contrast of justice and equity cf. Arist. Eth. Nic. v. 10 *τὸ ἐπιεικὲς . . . ἐπανόρθωμα νομίμου δικαίου*, and (still better) Rhet. i. 13 *τὸ παρὰ τὸν γεγραμμένον νόμον δίκαιον.*

54 The town of Samos lay on the south slopes of 'the hill' Ampelus, which is some 700 feet high (H. says 900, c. 60. 1), and which stretched away to the west above the plain; at the south-west extremity lay the Heraeum. The Lacedaemonians attacked both by sea, i. e. on the south, and by land (*κατὰ τὸν ἐπάνω πύργον*), on the north or north-west. H.'s familiarity with Samos is noticeable (cf. c. 39).

2 **ἐπεξῆλθον.** This sortie may have been made to protect the Samian water supply (cf. 60. 1 n.).

55 2 **'Αρχίῃ.** H.'s mention of his informant here (cf. Introd. § 23, p. 28) throws light on the character of his evidence; his account of the siege is based partly on local Samian tradition, partly on the family tradition of Archias.

Pitane was the aristocratic *κώμη* (= the Attic *δῆμος*) at Sparta; the others (Paus. iii. 16. 9) were Mesoa, Cynosura, Limnae (cf. Thuc. i. 10. 2 for the survival of the *κῶμαι*).

For the λόχος Πιτανήτης cf. ix. 53. 2 n.

ἐτίμα. Archias was ἐθελοπρόξενος (Thuc. iii. 70) of Samos at Sparta.

The significance and the recurrence of the names are to be noted. 'Plutarch' de Mal. Hdt. c. 22 says that Archias had a tomb δημοσίᾳ κατεσκευασμένον: this no doubt was set up after the fall of Polycrates by the Samian aristocrats.

56 ὅρμηται, 'has gone abroad' (λέγεσθαι is epexegetic); cf. iv. 161.

ἐς τὴν Ἀσίην: gives one reason why H. lays so much stress on 'this first expedition'; it was part of the long struggle between Europe and Asia. The 'second' is that of 479 B.C. (ix. 96 seq.). The addition of 'Dorians' is emphatic; the Achaean Lacedaemonians had taken part in the Trojan war.

2 καταχρυσώσαντα: cf. for 'gilded' κίβδηλοι στατῆρες C. I. G. i. 150, p. 237.

57 Siphnos, one of the Western Cyclades, was assessed at nine talents' tribute in 425 B.C., a large amount in proportion to its size; it had previously paid three talents (Hicks, nos. 48 and 64). It was the only *island* that was allowed a mint in the Confederacy of Delos (Holm, ii. 228), and this privilege was withdrawn during the Peloponnesian war (Hill, Sources[2], p. 425).

2 For the mines of Siphnos cf. Paus. x. 11. 2, who tells that they were submerged because the Siphnians failed to pay their tithe to Apollo, and Bent, J. H. S. vi. 195–8.

The treasury at Delphi (cf. Paus. x. 11. 2) was discovered by the French explorers in 1893, and the remains fully confirm H.: 'the building is more lavishly decorated than any other found at Delphi' (Frazer, Paus. v. 272 seq.). Homolle, the French discoverer (ib. 629), now assigns the treasury to the Cnidians, *not* to the Siphnians (but see Dyer in J. H. S. xxv. 314–15).

The style of sculpture exactly agrees with H.'s dating.

διενέμοντο. For division of mine profits in the ancient state cf. vii. 144 n.

3 That increased display of wealth was likely to tempt raiders and called for special 'precautions' (φράσσασθαι), was an obvious prophecy.

4 Παρίῳ: the earliest known instance of the use of Parian marble. Cf. v. 62. 3.

8 2 In Homer μιλτοπάρηος and φοινικοπάρηος only occur twice each; the ships are usually black, cf. Torr, A. S. p. 37; the 'red' colouring came in with the development of the Euxine trade; cf. μίλτος Σινωπική.

59 With the purchase of Hydrea cf. the attempt of the Phocaeans (i. 165. 1) to purchase the Oenyssian Islands.

Hydrea lies to the south of the Argolic peninsula, while Cydonia is on the north-west of Crete; both acts were probably part of a movement to isolate Aegina and to extend the relations of the

Corintho-Samian alliance (*v. i.*). For a similar attempt at Cyrene cf. iv. 163 n. The Aeginetans resented this trespass on their preserves (for their friendly relations to Crete cf. the proverb Κρὴς πρὸς Αἰγηνήτην); hence they 'joined the Cretans' to expel the intruders, and secured their hold of Crete by a colony at Cydonia (Strabo 376). This connexion explains the hostility of the town to Athens (Thuc. ii. 85. 5).

2 **καὶ τὸν . . . νηόν.** The words are probably a mistaken addition, as Dictyna was a native goddess.

3 **καπρίους.** The Samian vessels were called ὑόπρῳροι (Plut. Per. c. 26), and were supposed to resemble pigs from their heavy build.

τὸ ἱρόν. For this temple, whence the famous Aeginetan marbles came to Munich in 1812, cf. Frazer, Paus. iii. 268 seq. It was first assigned to Zeus Panhellenius, then to Athena; but A. Furtwängler (cf. his splendid book on Aegina, Munich, 1906), who excavated it in 1901, has proved by inscriptions found *in situ* that it was dedicated to Aphaea. This goddess (Paus. ii. 30. 3) was also connected with Crete, and hence the dedication here for a Cretan victory is most appropriate to her. Furtwängler would read Ἀφαίης (for Ἀθηναίης) here; he points out that Pausanias knows nothing of an 'Athena' temple in Aegina, although he quotes another passage of H. (v. 82 seq.) in the very next section (ii. 30. 4).

4 Amphicrates seems to have been of the family of Procles, who led to Samos the Ionians expelled from Epidaurus by the Dorians (Paus. vii. 4. 2). For the overthrow of the monarchy at Samos cf. Plut. Qu. Gr. 57, where he speaks of the subsequent hostility between Samos and Megara, a member of the Aeginetan commercial league. Our scanty references to these early wars in the Aegean all tend to establish the theory of the rivalry of two great trade-leagues; Miletus, Aegina, Megara, and Eretria, trading mainly with the north-east, are ranged against Corinth, Samos, and Chalcis, whose main sphere is the west (cf. v. 99. 1 n.).

60 1 **Ἐμήκυνα.** H., apart from his interest in Samos (cf. Introd. p. 3), made it his object to describe great works everywhere (cf. i. 93. 1). For Samos generally cf. V. Guérin, Patmos et Samos, 1856.

ὄρυγμα. The object of the 'tunnel' was to bring the water from the other (i. e. the north) side of Mount Ampelus; the 'channel' in it (ἄλλο ὄρυγμα) is not quite 'thirty feet' deep at the outlet, and decreases in depth as it approaches the spring from which it issues; this was to give sufficient fall for the water, but H. had of course only seen the outlet on the south side; as the boring was begun on both sides, the engineering skill required was very considerable. The work is a good instance of the way in which the tyrants 'courted popularity by providing for the needs of their people', and may be compared with the contemporary aqueduct of Pisistratus (cf. E. Gardner, Athens, pp. 26–7). The tunnel was discovered in 1882 (cf. Mittheil. des Deutsch. Archaeol. Instit. 1884 (Athen.), pp. 163 f., with two plans, or Tozer's Islands of Aegean, pp. 167 seq.). On the whole the accuracy of H. is strikingly confirmed, though he exaggerates the length of the tunnel, which is really about 1,100 feet.

2 **σωλήνων.** Remains of the 'pipes' have been found, both leading from the spring to the hill, a distance of some half mile, and in the tunnel itself through the hill.

3 **χῶμα.** The mole extended from the western horn of the Old Harbour and more than half closed it. Its remains can still be seen about six feet below the surface. H. is right as to its length, but the sea at present is only ten fathoms deep (Guérin, pp. 203–4).

4 **νηὸς μέγιστος.** H. means of Greek temples: those of Egypt were larger. The Heraeum was 346 feet long and 189 broad (Leake, Asia Minor, p. 348, makes it 350, but other estimates are given; Guérin, p. 225), which is larger than any known Greek temple in the East, except that of Ephesus, which was finished later; H. (ii. 148) mentions these two temples as 'notable' Greek works. The temples at Acragas and Selinus are about the same size; the Olympieium at Athens was on a larger scale, but remained unfinished till the time of Hadrian. Pausanias (vii. 5. 4) says the Heraeum was 'burned down' (*κατακαυθῆναι*) by the Persians, but that *θαῦμα ἦν ὑπὸ τοῦ πυρὸς λελυμασμένον.*

For Rhoecus cf. Murray, G. S. i. 74 seq.; he was connected with Theodoros (i. 51. 3 n.). His name has been found on a sixth-century vase at Naucratis. He probably began the temple half a century before, and it was finished under Polycrates. For these *ἔργα Πολυκράτεια* cf. Arist. Pol. 1313 b 24 who says they were intended to produce *ἀσχολία καὶ πενία τῶν ἀρχομένων*; he does not mention the desire to provide wages for the poorer classes, though no doubt this motive was present with ancient (cf. Pl. Per. 12) as well as with modern despots. Aristotle compares them with the Pyramids and with the buildings of the Cypselidae and the Pisistratidae. The building policy of tyrants from the days of Cypselus to Napoleon III's 'Haussmannization' of Paris is a commonplace of history. The Samian Alexis says (F. H. G. iv. 299) that Polycrates also developed the agricultural wealth of his island. For his commercial and industrial activity cf. Ure in J. H. S. xxvi. pp. 132–3.

1–87 *The death of Cambyses, the rising of the Pseudo-Smerdis, and the accession of Darius.* For the real history of these events cf. App. V.

61 The B. I. mentions only one pretender, 'Gaumata,' and of course says nothing of his resemblance to Smerdis; on this point, which is probable in itself, H. is supported by Ctesias and Justin (i. 9); it is not inconsistent with the caution spoken of in 63. 2,

68. 2. The B. I. (i. 11) confirms H. as to the usurpation being unopposed. Justin has the name 'Cometes' right, but gives it to the chief plotter, not the actual pretender, whom he calls Oropastes. H.'s 'Smerdis' is required to explain the prophetic dream, cf. 30. 2, 64. 1. 'Patizeithes' is probably a title = 'Padishah'.

62 No Ecbatana is known in Syria, and the attempts to explain the name (see Rawlinson *ad loc.*) are unconvincing. The religious coincidence is more than suspicious.

64 3 The curved scimitar (ἀκινάκης) needed a 'cap' (μύκης) to guard its point; the same accident happened to Perseus with less fatal results; hence the name Μυκῆναι (Paus. ii. 16. 3).

The coincidence (as to the position of the wound) is also suspicious; cf. the legend that Salome, who danced off the head of St. John, was herself beheaded by floating ice. The B. I. (i. 11) says: 'Afterwards Cambyses, killing himself, died,' which seems to imply suicide.

4 **χρηστήριον.** It is odd that Cambyses should pay attention to an Egyptian oracle; but the whole story of 'the fiends which palter with us in a double sense', is clearly invented, cf. Shakespeare, 2 Henry IV, IV. 5 (*ad fin.*) (following Holinshed):—

> It hath been prophesied to me many years
> I should not die but in Jerusalem,
> Which vainly I supposed the Holy Land.
> But bear me to that chamber, there I'll lie;
> In that Jerusalem shall Harry die.

A similar story is told of Julian the Apostate.

ἄρα is emphatic, 'as is now proved'; cf. iv. 64. 3 *et pass.*

65 3 **τὸ μέλλον . . . ἀποτρέπειν.** The fatalism has a true Oriental ring, as well as being characteristic of H.; cf. i. 91; iii. 40 seq.

5 **τιμωρέειν**: the parallel to 32. 2 upsets Meyer's theory (see App. V. 2) that cc. 32 and 65 come from 'different sources'.

6 **βασιληίους.** Histiaeus (v. 106) swears to Darius by these. So Darius in the Persepolis inscription invokes Ormazd and 'the gods of his race'.

For the theory that the conspiracy was Median cf. App. V. 6.

7 For the threefold curse of unfruitfulness cf. vi. 139. 1 n.; Soph. O. T. 25–7, 269; and Deut. xxviii. 17–18; cf. also the oath of the Amphictyons (Aesch. in Ctes. 111).

66 2 **ἑπτὰ ἔτεα καὶ πέντε μῆνας.** Manetho seems to give Cambyses ten years (fr. 68), Ctesias eighteen (xii, p. 67). A Babylonian contract has been found (T. S. B. A. vi. 484) dating from the eleventh year of his reign, which shows that Cambyses was associated with Cyrus as king of Babylon (cf. C. C. i. 35; R. P.[2] v. 168, and Meyer, Forsch. ii. 471). So far as the length of his sole rule is concerned H. is right, and is confirmed by the Apis Stelai (Wiedemann, Gesch. Aegyp. 1880, pp. 219–20), and by the Canon of

Ptolemy, which gives Cambyses eight years (including, of course, the seven months of the usurper, 67. 2).

67 B. I. i. 13 confirms H. that the conspiracy succeeded for a time. It says nothing of the popular acts of the Pseudo-Smerdis, but they are probable in themselves; cf. the constitutional character of the reign of Richard III for similar conduct in a usurper.

68 1 **Φαρνάσπεω . . . παῖς.** For the position of Otanes see c. 84. He was the son of Socris (not of Pharnaspes, B. I. iv. 18). H.'s mistake may perhaps be due to a confused tradition as to his ancestor (*abavus*) Pharnaces, who married Atossa, the aunt of Cyrus, probably the grandfather of Cyrus 'the great' (Diod. xxxi. 19). Meyer (iii. 18), however, rejects this whole pedigree as a late fiction. From him descended the royal house of Cappadocia; Diodorus and Ctesias (14, p. 67) substitute for 'Otanes' his son Anaphas or Onophas (H. vii. 62).

2 H. wrongly lays the scene at Susa (cf. 70. 3), because it was to him, as to all Greeks and Jews (cf. Neh. i. 1), the capital of the empire (v. 49 n.); the B. I. (i. 13) puts the final struggle at Sictachotes (Sikayauvatish), a Median fort.

The 'Acropolis' is the *βασιλήιον τεῖχος* of 74. 3.

3 **Καμβύσεω γυναιξί.** This was usual in the East; cf. c. 88. 2 and Absalom's conduct 2 Sam. xvi. 21.

5 **διέσπειρε.** In view of these precautions, the ease with which Phaedymia communicated with her father is strange; H. is telling merely the popular tale.

69 5 **τὰ ὦτα ἀπέταμε.** For such mutilations cf iii. 118, 154, and ix. 112, and the rigorous justice of the younger Cyrus (Xen. Anab. i. 9. 13; also B. I. ii. 13); no mutilated person could ever reign. Perhaps the story is based on a play of words, the Persian word for Magian being interpreted 'a man having no ears' (J. R. A. S., 1890, p. 822).

6 Cf. Esther ii. 12 for the harem arrangements.

70 The names of Darius' confederates are given as follows:

Herodotus	*Darius* (B. I. iv. 68)	*Ctesias* (14, p. 67)
Otanes	Intaphrenes the son of Veispares	Onophas.
Aspathines	Otanes son of Socris	Idernes.
Gobryas	Gobryas son of Mardonius	Norondabates.
Intaphrenes	Hydarnes son of Megabignes	Mardonius.
Megabyzus	Megabyzus son of Dadoes	Barisses.
Hydarnes	Ardomanes son of Basuces	Ataphernes.

As to the list it should be noted (1) that H. gives all the names right except Aspathines, who seems to be Aspachana, the quiver-bearer of Darius (cf. Nakhsh-I-Rustam Inscrip.); (2) that Ctesias has only one right, Hydarnes, and that in two cases (Onophas and Mardonius) he gives the names of their sons (cf. Gilmore, Ctes. p. 148 for an attempted explanation); (3) that the families of all the conspirators except Intaphrenes (for obvious reasons) are prominent in the later history.

Some have maintained (e.g. Niebuhr) that H. is wrong in making the number seven an accident; the Seven were the heads of the great Persian families, who naturally took the lead in a 'national movement'. So later we have the 'seven counsellors' (Ezra vii. 14), and the seven princes of Persia who 'saw the king's face' (Esther i. 14). But the coincidence of the number 'seven' is probably an accident (cf. for other 'sevens' iii. 14 n. and Esther i. 10, the 'seven chamberlains'), for

(1) It is hard to see how the number of the 'counsellors' could have been maintained when one of the conspirators (Darius) had been raised to the throne, and another (Intaphrenes, iii. 119) attainted.

(2) Plutarch (Praec. Reip. Ger. c. 27, Mor. 820) says the conspirators' descendants had the right to wear the upright tiara, the royal badge; but he attributes this to their part in the conspiracy.

(3) Darius in the B. I. seems to imply that the number was fortuitous. He adds 'a Persian' to the name of each conspirator; but this is to lay stress on the national character of the movement, not to show that the men were especially privileged.

H. therefore is probably right on this point, though the 'seven counsellors' may well be a real institution, and though the descendants of the conspirators were rewarded with great privileges (84 n.).

3 **ἐκ Περσέων.** Here, and in i. 209, Hystaspes is satrap of Persia; this may be a confused reference to the fact that he represented the younger Achaemenid line; he was really satrap of Parthia (B. I. ii. 16).

72 4 This sophistry is an attempt at consistency with H.'s own statement (i. 138) that among the Persians 'to lie is held most disgraceful'; it is purely Greek (cf. discussion in Plat. Repub. ii and Xenop. Cyrop. i. 6. 27 seq.).

74 H. here unites with his main story as to the discovery of the conspiracy, the story of Prexaspes. Ctesias (13, p. 67) briefly says that the murder of Smerdis was revealed to 'the army' by Izabates, who had been one of the three persons privy to it. The tale is, however, very improbable; the Magians were not likely to have put up Prexaspes to speak, for the strength of their position lay in its being unchallenged, and the act here described could only excite suspicion.

2 **τὰ πάντα μυρία**: cf. iv. 88. 1 n.

76 3 **ἰρήκων κτλ.** Cf. the omen in Tac. Ann. ii. 17. 2 (Germanicus to his legions) 'irent, sequerentur Romanas aves', and Aesch. Pers. 205 seq., where Atossa is dismayed by the sight of an eagle attacked by a hawk.

77 **καταιδεόμενοι.** Some see in this a reference to the special privilege of the 'seven Persian grandees' (c. 70 n.). But it seems less definite than the right claimed by Intaphrenes (c. 118; cf. c. 84).

78 3 The rooms, opening on to the central court, would have no external windows. Darius affirms (in the B. I.) three times that he slew Gomates himself. Aeschylus (Pers. 776) assigns the deed to Artaphrenes, substituting the familiar name (v. 25 *et pass.*) for the unfamiliar Intaphrenes.

79 3 μαγοφόνια. Rawlinson accepts H.'s story: 'the festival served as a perpetual warning to the priests against trenching on the civil power' (so in part, Darmesteter, S. B. E. IV, Intr. p. 50). Ctesias (15, p. 68) also mentions the commemorative festival. Bähr (*ad loc.*) seems to suggest that the festival was one of purification, at which the Magi slew all the creatures of Ahriman, and that it had nothing to do with the conspiracy. This view is not probable.

80 Stein makes θόρυβος subject of ἐγένετο, and translates 'when the confusion had died down, and when more than five days had since passed'; but it is easier to take ἐγένετο as impersonal. The sense is the same. Sextus Empiricus (in Math. ii. 33) says 'the Persian nobles have a custom, when their king is dead, to spend the five following days in lawlessness', in order to learn how evil ἀνομία was. This custom, if a fact, may be referred to here; but Sextus Empiricus is probably giving a mere inference from H.

The discussion of the conspirators which follows (cc. 80–2) is most important in three respects.

A. **Its bearing on the composition of H.'s work.**

(1) He refers to criticisms on it (VI. 43); hence it has been inferred that Book III was written and published before Book VI (cf. Introd. p. 13 n.). The more probable inference, however, is that H. went on adding to his work after parts of it had become known to the public.

(2) It is quoted as proof of the theory that H.'s history is partly a compilation from the works of previous authors (cf. 46. 2). Maass (Hermes, xxii. 581 seq.) thinks that the arguments are borrowed from a sophistic dialogue, probably one of the 'negative arguments' (καταβάλλοντες λόγοι) of Protagoras, and that the same source was used by Isocrates (Nicocles, 14 seq.). The resemblances, however, between H. and Isocrates are merely accidental, and Meyer (F. i. 201–2) completely demolishes the theory; he sums up (cf. 81. 2 n.) 'Maass makes H. a simpleton if he imagines that he could impose on the public inventions of his good friend Protagoras as historical facts'.

B. **The historical reality of the facts.**

H. vouches for this in the strongest way, 'they were said, in spite of all objections' (δ' ὤν).

Probably H. is following the account of a Hellenized Persian (cf. J. H. S. xxvii. 40); the questions actually discussed were—'Should the Persians revert to the natural condition of the old Iranian society, and let all clans live under their immemorial customs?' or 'should they continue the centralized monarchy?' i.e. the liberty claimed was simply the rights of the great nobles (cf. Mahaffy, G. L. ii. 32 n., and on the Oriental idea of 'Liberty', Beavan, House of Seleucus, i. 3 seq.).

C. **The passage is the beginning of Greek political philosophy.** (Cf. Freeman's Sicily, iii. 644 seq., for the threefold division of constitutions and early references to it.) H. here, as always, clothes Persian ideas in the phrases of his own countrymen (cf. i. 96, the story of Deioces), as all men of genius do, e. g. Shakespeare's Venetians are Elizabethan Englishmen and Racine's Greeks are courtiers of Le Grand Monarque. It is against this arbitrary introduction of speeches that Thucydides (by implication) protests in i. 22. 1; his own speeches he claims were appropriate to what the occasion demanded.

3 The essence of the Greek tyrant was that he was 'irresponsible'; it is curious that Arist. does not use the word *ἀνυπεύθυνος* of the tyrant, though he lays stress on the fact.

4 **ὕβρι κεκορημένος.** On the close connexion of *κόρος* and *ὕβρις* cf. viii. 77 n. Darius (B. I. i. 13) lays stress on the cruelty of the Magian.

ἀρίστοισι. For this feature in the tyrant cf. Plato, Rep. viii, p. 567; he must remove all who are *ἀνδρεῖοι, μεγαλόφρονες, φρόνιμοι, πλούσιοι.* Tyranny is *πονηρόφιλον* (cf. Arist. Pol. 1314 a, with Newman's notes; Sall. Cat. 7 'regibus boni quam mali suspectiores sunt'; and Tac. Ann. i. 80). Stein takes *ἄριστοι, κάκιστοι* in the political sense, 'best-born,' &c., but this is less likely.

5 For the difficulty of intercourse with a tyrant cf. the fable of the lion and his courtiers, and Tac. Ann. i. 12. 2 contrasted with iii. 65. 3; Tiberius is equally offended by free speech and by servility.

For the lawless lust of tyrants cf. the long list of brutalities in Arist. Pol. 1311.

6 This line might be the text for the panegyric on democracy in the Funeral Speech (Thuc. ii. 37); 'equality of opportunity' is the boast of Pericles. For H.'s own praise of *ἰσηγορίη* cf. v. 78.

The three marks of democracy are (1) election by lot (cf. Arist. Pol. 1294 b 7 and Headlam, 'Lot at Athens,' p. 11 seq., which discusses admirably the purpose of the lot); (2) responsibility of officers (Pol. ii. 12. 4; 1274 a: Solon gave the Athenians *ἀναγκαιοτάτη δύναμις*, i. e. to elect their officers and to call them to account); (3) popular control of all measures.

81 2 **οὔτ' ἐδιδάχθη.** The ordinary antithesis between learning from others and perceiving for oneself; cf. Thuc. i. 138. 3 of Themistocles *οἰκείᾳ συνέσει καὶ οὔτε προμαθὼν ἐς αὐτὴν οὐδὲν οὔτε ἐπιμαθών.* The reproach against democracy is its lack of intelligence (*ἀξυνετώτερον*), and its consequent unprofitableness (*ἀχρήιον*); cf. Hes. W. and D. 296 *ὃς δέ κε μήτ' αὐτὸς νοέῃ μήτ' ἄλλου ἀκούων | ἐν θυμῷ βάλληται, ὁ δ' αὖτ' ἀχρήιος ἀνήρ.*

This passage is supposed by Maass (*v.s.*) to resemble Isocrates, Nic. 18, who would not prefer *τοιαύτης πολιτείας μετέχειν ἐν ᾗ μὴ διαλήσει* χρηστὸς ὢν μᾶλλον ἢ φέρεσθαι μετὰ τοῦ πλήθους μὴ γιγνωσκόμενος ὁποῖός τις ἐστι; but the meaning is quite different; H. refers to the blind impulses of a mob, Isocrates to merit lost in a crowd.

82 2 **ἀρίστου.** Darius assumes the king will be 'the best' (such an one διαφέρων κατ' ἀρετήν, Arist. Pol. iii. 13, p. 1284 b must rule); he takes no account of the παρέκβασις of monarchy, the bad rule.

3 **στάσιες**: cf. Thuc. viii. 89. 3 for internal jealousies as the weakness of an oligarchy.

The aorists ἀπέβη, διέδεξε are gnomic, i.e. they express the usual result (cf. ἀνεφάνη *inf.*).

4 **ἐς τὰ κοινά**: parallel to ἐς τὸ κοινόν above. The antithetical style of the Sophists is very traceable here.

παύσῃ. Cf. the hopes that Alcibiades in 408 B.C. would prove a 'saviour of society' at Athens (Diod. xiii. 68), and, on a larger scale, the acceptance of the Napoleonic rule as a salvation from 'the Red Terror'. So Deioces was made ruler by the Medes (i. 97), to save them from ἀνομία. For the origin of tyranny generally cf. App. XVI.

5 **ἡ ἐλευθερίη.** H. here leaves generalizations on Greek politics and inserts a Persian argument, an appeal to the services of Cyrus to his country; perhaps there is the beginning also of the idea which inspires the Cyropaedia of Xenophon—that Cyrus is the ideal monarch.

83 The special position of the house of Otanes seems to be a fact, but it was probably of earlier date; he may have been of Achaemenid blood (68. 1 n.); at any rate his daughter Phaedymia had married Cambyses; Xerxes married his grand-daughter, Amestris.

With the gifts appointed for him (84. 1) cf. what is 'done to the man (Mordecai) whom the king delighteth to honour' (Esther vi. 8–9), though the Jewish writer has made the honours more distinctly royal. For less romantic parallels cf. vii. 88. 1 and 106. 1.

The most honourable gifts were (Xen. An. i. 2. 27) a horse with a golden bridle, and a golden necklace, bracelet, and scimitar. Ctesias (Pers. 22, p. 69) adds 'a golden mill' (μύλη).

84 1 **δικαιότατα,** 'fairest,' i.e. to themselves; it is explained by the rest of the chapter.

2 **τῶν ἑπτά.** For the position of the 'Seven' in general cf. 70 n. The rule as to marriage seems to have been observed (88. 3; vii. 2. 2).

They received also great grants of territory, probably free of tribute; from Hydarnes descended the rulers of Armenia (Strabo 531), from Otanes those of Cappadocia (68 n.). This is the origin of the strange tale in Plato (Leg. iii. 695 C) that Darius divided his kingdom in seven parts among the conspirators.

3 **ἐβούλευσαν.** Darius succeeded in right of birth (cf. App. V. 7); but the colouring of the story is correct: the Persians, as sun-worshippers, honoured sunrise (cf. vii. 54. 1), and the horse was sacred among them; cf. C. R. xxvi. 50. For auguries by horses cf. Tac. Germ. x.

85 ἱπποκόμος. The story of the trick is given by both Justin (i. 10) and Ctesias (15, p. 68). The name Oebares occurs in Nic. Dam. fr. 66 (F. H. G. iii. 400) as that of the adviser of Cyrus in his conspiracy against Astyages; it is explained *ἀγαθάγγελος*. H. is combining a popular legend (for another fragment of it cf. 86. 2 and Nic. Dam. *u. s.* p. 405, the signs from heaven) with a misunderstood inscription on a monument of Darius (88. 3 n.).

86 2 ἀστραπὴ . . . καὶ βροντή. These signs, 'thunder and lightning,' the omens of the supreme god, Ormazd, 'confirmed' him as king; they 'happened as it were in agreement' with the horse-omen sent by the sun-god Mithra. Cf. Xen. Cyr. i. 6. 1 for similar signs to Cyrus, when beginning his attack on the Medes.

88 Κύρου τε . . . Καμβύσεω. Stein takes this to mean that there had been a general rising against Cambyses. (Xen. Cyr. viii. 8. 2 definitely states this.) If this be right it explains the postponement of his Egyptian expedition till his fifth year. But probably H. only refers to the reduction of Phoenicia and Cyprus (19. 3 n.).

The 'Arabians' serve in the Persian army (vii. 69), where they are coupled with the Ethiopians of Africa, and are included in the official lists of provinces (cf. App. VII. 1) next to Egypt. Hence Rawlinson (on ii. 8) is probably right in putting these Arabians between the Nile and the Red Sea. H.'s statement here as to Arab independence (cf. iii. 7 seq.) refers to a different set of tribes, i. e. the nomads to the south and east of Palestine. The Persians, wiser than the Assyrians, did not attempt to conquer the wild tribes of the desert, but made friends with them. The Arabs had pressed north, as early as the fifth century, into the regions desolated by the Assyrian raids. (Meyer, iii. 86 seq.) They controlled the spice trade (c. 107); hence they give the Great King yearly 1,000 talents of frankincense.

2 For Artystone cf. vii. 69. 2.

3 ἱππεύς. Neither at Behistun nor on his tomb at Nakhsh-I-Rustam is Darius represented on horseback. (For illustrations of these monuments cf. Maspero, iii. 681–3, 736–7.) But H. may well have seen some equestrian 'relief', now destroyed, resembling the façade of Tagh-I-Bostan (Perrot, v. 534).

89–117 This division of H.'s work describes the Persian empire as organized by Darius; it consists of two parts, very unequal in length and in authenticity; cc. 89–96 give an official statistical account of the Empire (cf. App. VII and vii. 61 n.); cc. 97–117 describe the more remote dependencies and are largely made up of travellers' tales. Holdich (Gates of India, 1909, p. 17) writes: 'twenty-five years ago our military information concerning ethnographical distributions in districts immediately beyond the north-west frontier was not better' (than that in H.), and 'the tribes have mostly survived to bear valuable testimony to the knowledge of the East in the days of H.'

89 ἐν Πέρσῃσι goes with *ποιήσας ταῦτα*; the contrast is between the acquisition of royal power and the organization of the empire.

H. only here and in i. 192. 2 uses *σατραπηίη*, in both cases with an explanation (*ἀρχή*); his usual word is *νομός*. Aeschylus uses no form of the word at all, and Thucydides only *σατραπεία*; Xenophon is the first to use *σατράπης*; the ruler in H. is *ὕπαρχος* (cf. vii. 194 n.). *σατράπης*, i.e. 'Khšātrapâvan', is found twice in the B. I. and seems = 'upholder of the crown': it is found first in Sargon's list of Median chiefs, apparently as a proper name. The office existed before Darius; cf. B. I. *u. s.*; i. 153. 3 (Tabalus); iii. 120 (twice, Oroetes and Mitrobates); iii. 70. 3 (Hystaspes) and iv. 166 (Aryandes). The innovation of Darius (for its importance cf. App. VI. 4) consisted in his introducing a regular tribute for the whole empire; perhaps also he substituted government officials for native feudal princes (so Stein, who compares i. 134. 3, and says the Median system there described lasted to the time of Darius).

The main, though not the entire, source of Persian revenue, was the land tax (vi. 42. 2). The sums given by H. are those due to the royal treasury, not the whole amount raised in the provinces.

προστάσσων. Rawlinson (and others) takes this as opposed to *ὑπερβαίνων*, 'generally he joined, but sometimes he passed over the nearer tribes.' He (ii. 563) argues that this was done because the divisions were 'ethnical rather than geographical', an arrangement especially convenient among the nomadic tribes of the far East. But grammar (there is no *μέν, δέ*) and political sense alike render this impossible; and as a fact H.'s list of tribes is geographically arranged, except perhaps for the Utii (93. 2 n.) and the sixteenth satrapy (93. 3 nn.). *ὑπερβαίνων τοὺς π.* therefore must be taken parenthetically, and *τὰ ἑκαστέρω . . . νέμων* repeats *κατὰ ἔθνεα . . . προστάσσων* in another form. Translate 'he fixed the tributes to come in to him, nation by nation, while he joined their neighbours with each nation, and, as he got further from the centre (*ὑπερβαίνων τ. π.*), he distributed the more remote nations in various groups'. Thus each satrapy consisted of the *ἔθνος* whose name it bore (e.g. Ionia), and of the tribes grouped with it (e.g. with Ionia went Magnesia, Aeolis, &c., 90. 1).

2 **κατὰ τάδε** would most naturally refer to iii. 90 seq.; the rest of this chapter would then be a later addition on the part of H. But as the text stands *κατὰ τάδε* must refer to the two coin standards which are here explained, a heavier (Babylonian) for silver coinage, a lighter (Euboic) for gold; these were in the proportion of four to three. H., however, substitutes the slightly heavier Attic talent for the Euboic; there were 33,660 grammes in the Babylonian talent, 26,400 in the Attic, i.e. (roughly) 60 Babylonian minae = 78 Attic, the proportion given here.

⟨ὀκτὼ καὶ⟩ ἑβδομήκοντα. Reizke's (Mommsen, Röm. Münz. pp. 23–4) conjecture to add *ὀκτὼ καί* is usually accepted; he confirms it by a second emendation in 95. 1 (q. v.). The MSS. here, however, have only ἑβδομήκοντα, and this reading is as old as Pollux (ix. 86).

3 ἄλλα. For Darius' first coining Darics cf. iv. 166. 2 n.; for their value cf. Head, H. N. p. 826. They were worth twenty silver σίγλοι, about £1 2s., and were almost identical with the Croesus staters, but had three per cent. of alloy.

χαλεπός. This epithet with ἤπιος is an echo of Od. ii. 232–4.

90 1 In vii. 77. 1 the Καβηλέες are identified with the Lasonians; H. reproduces two sources without troubling to reconcile them. For the Καβάλιοι cf. Ramsay, C. and B. pp. 265–6; they lay on the borders of Lycia and the Roman province of Asia; their important town, Cibyra, Strabo (631) says was founded by Lydians (hence they are called οἱ Μηίονες in vii. 77. 1). For the **Milyans** cf. i. 173. 2 n.

The **Hytennians** were perhaps the only Pisidian highlanders subject to Persia; for the independence of these mountaineers cf. Xen. Anab. i. 1. 11; the Ἐτεννεῖς in the third century B.C. were able to raise 8,000 hoplites (Polyb. v. 73). Cf. v. 25 n. for the two first satrapies as always united under one ruler. The second satrapy was officially called Sparda (= Sardis) from the name of its capital; cf. c. 120.

2 The Hellespontines are the Greeks of North-west Asia Minor.

For the **Thracians** cf. vii. 75 n., where they are called 'Bithynians', and the story of their immigration is given; the Mariandynians were well known to the Greeks from their neighbourhood to the colony of Heraclea (Xen. Anab. vi. 2. 1).

For the **Syrians** (= the Cappadocians) cf. i. 72 n. The name is one of several proofs that H. did not borrow this list from Hecataeus, as some have suggested: Hec. (fr. 194; F. H. G. i. 13) calls this people Λευκόσυροι (contrast too his Τίβαροι (fr. 193) with Τιβαρηνοί in iii. 94). Darius gives the native name 'Katapatuka' in his list of conquests. The official name of the third satrapy was Dascylitis (Thuc. i. 129. 1).

The third satrapy was hereditary in the house of Pharnaces, who was descended from one of the 'Seven' (cf. 84. n.).

3 H. here uses **Cilicia** in the wide sense, as including not only (1) the strip of coast, but also (2) the Taurus region to the north as far as, and even beyond, the Halys (i. 72. 2), and (3) the country to the north-east (the later Commagene) as far as the Euphrates (v. 52. 3). Hence the tribute of this satrapy was a heavy one, 500 talents (v. 49. 6). As, however, 140 talents was spent in the province, it is only reckoned as 360 talents in the total (c. 95). Cilicia was held by native rulers who all bore the Semitic name Συέννεσις (cf. i. 74. 3; v. 118. 2; vii. 98. 1); perhaps this was a title (cf. 'Pharaoh'). Their dependence on the central power varied according to its strength or weakness.

The 'white horses' were sacred to the sun-god Mithra (for their sacrifice cf. vii. 113. 2 n.); hence one is paid for each of the 360 days in the year. They were also sacred to Ormazd (vii. 40).

Strabo (525) says there was a similar tribute of horses, besides other cattle, from Cappadocia and from Media (1,500 and 'about 3,000' horses respectively).

For the tribute in kind cf. i. 192 n. and App. VI. 8.

91 1 **Posideium** lay south of the Orontes, on the slopes of the Syrian Mount Casius, which originally formed the southern boundary of Cilicia; in later times this lay further north, at the Syrian gates. Amphilochus was supposed to have led eastwards some of the Greeks from Troy; he settled them in Pamphylia (vii. 91, a passage which supplements this).

For the independence of the Arabians cf. c. 8; they, however, brought annual gifts (97. 5). For Συρίη ἡ Παλαιστίνη cf. 5. 1 n.

The fifth satrapy was called by the Persians 'beyond the river' (Ezra v. 6; vi. 6); it, however, included, at any rate later, a district east of the Euphrates (Arr. Anab. iii. 8. 6).

2 **Βάρκης.** For the conquest of Barca by Aryandes, the satrap of Egypt, cf. iv. 201; for Lake Moeris ii. 149 n.; the revenue from it was 240 talents a year. The whole passage (cf. App. IX. 1) implies that the Persians were masters of Egypt when it was written. For the 'White Fort' cf. 13. 2 and Thuc. i. 104. 2.

3 **ἐπιμετρεομένου:** i.e. '120,000' (medimni) 'in addition to' (ἐπί) the tribute.

4 **νομὸς ἕβδομος.** H. so far has arranged his satrapies geographically; he continues to do so from the 8th to the 12th (or perhaps the 13th); but his 7th satrapy is in the extreme north-east of the empire, south-east of the Paraphamisus (*hod.* Hindoo-Koosh) Mountains. H. had little or no idea of the arrangement of the eastern half of the Persian empire. He joins the Gandarians and Dadicae in vii. 66, where he says they were equipped like the Bactrians. The Gandarii are called by Hecataeus (fr. 178; F. H. G. i. 12) an 'Indian tribe'; Strabo (697) puts Gandaritis in the valley of the Cabul; they and the Sattagydi ('Thatagush') come in the first list of provinces (B. I. i. 6), where they are followed by Arachosia. Hence Meyer, iii. p. 97, puts them down as conquests of Cyrus. It is possible that their earlier conquest may explain their curious place in the list, especially as none of them joined in the general revolt against Darius. The Aparyti are otherwise unknown, but Holdich (Gates of India, pp. 28, 31) puts all these tribes in the Indus valley, and identifies the Aparytae with the modern Afridi.

Σούσων. H. now starts from the head of the Persian Gulf, and gives the 8th, 9th, 10th, and 11th satrapies in order from south to north. The official name of the Cissian satrapy was Susiana; it corresponded to the ancient 'Elam'.

92 **Βαβ. καὶ τῆς λοιπῆς Ἀσσυρίης.** H. here as always (cf. i. 178. 1 n.) unites Babylonia and Assyria; they are distinguished in the inscriptions. Assyria was properly the district on the east (i.e. left) bank of the Tigris, which H. calls Matiene (v. 52). He seems to include

all Mesopotamia (a name first found in Polyb. v. 44) in the Assyrian satrapy; probably this was the arrangement of Darius (cf. C. F. Lehmann, Woch. für Kl. Ph., 1900, p. 962, n. 6), which lasted till Xerxes, on his return from Greece (Arr. Anab. vii. 17. 2), punished Babylon for revolt (i. 183. 3 n.). Perhaps the huge size of the satrapy was a special honour to its first satrap, Zopyrus (160. 2). For its importance cf. i. 192; it fed the Great King and his army for two-thirds of the year.

For the **Paricanii**, 94. 1 n., probably the Παρητακηνοί should be read here, whom H. calls a Median tribe (i. 101. 1). They lived (near the modern Ispahan) in the mountains separating Persia and Susiana from Media, and forming the watershed of the Choaspes (cf. Strabo 744 for their position and predatory character). The name of the Ὀρθοκορυβάντιοι (otherwise unknown) is explained by some as 'dwellers in the mountain'.

2 **Κάσπιοι κτλ.** These four tribes, none of which occur elsewhere, for the Caspii here are not the same as those of 93. 3, must have lived to the north-east of Media, on the southern shores of the Caspian Sea. Perhaps they represent the satrapy of Hyrcania (cf. c. 117 and vii. 62. 2), the omission of which is a perplexing feature of this list. Hyrcania, however, does not occur in any of Darius' lists (cf. App. VII. 1), though it is mentioned in the B. I. (ii. 16) along with Parthia. It (Strabo 507 seq.) was more important in Parthian than in Persian times (cf. Tac. Ann. xv. 1).

The **Bactrii** or Bactriani lived in the basin of the upper Oxus: their capital was the modern Balkh. The Aegli may be the Αὐγαλοί of Ptolemy, vi. 12, a Sagartian tribe south of the Jaxartes. The huge 16th satrapy (93. 3) included the wilder nomad tribes, and surrounded the more settled Bactria on three sides, north, west, and south: their warriors (vii. 66. 1) were equipped like the Bactrians.

93 H.'s 13th satrapy lies north-west of Media, while the 11th lies north-east of that country. Pactyice here adjoins Armenia and is obviously not the district of the same name which adjoined India (102. 1 *q.v.*).

2 The 14th satrapy seems to have consisted of the whole of the western part of the Iranian plateau to the Persian Gulf, for it included 'the islands'. Hecataeus (frs. 170, 183; F. H. G. i. 11–12) writes ἐκ Μύκων εἰς Ἀράξην ποταμόν, apparently giving these as the northern and southern limits of Asia. All the names except the 'Thamanaeans' occur in Darius' inscriptions; these are joined again with the Σαράγγαι in 117. 1.

The Sagartians (Persian nomads in i. 125) and the Utians (cf. B. I. iii. 40, Yautiya, 'a district of Persia') seem to have been connected with the ruling race, but may have been made tributaries for not having assisted Cyrus in his attack on the Medes.

The Sagartians are described (viii. 85) as horsemen armed with lassoes. The Sarangians are the Δράγγοι of Arrian (Anab. iii. 21), and lived in the modern Seistan. The name of Μύκοι seems to survive in the modern Mekran, the southern province of Persia. Strabo (765) speaks of Macae on the coast of Arabia opposite. Some have seen in the Οὔτιοι the Οὔξιοι of Arrian, Anab. iii. 17. 1, who lived partly in the mountains south of Susa, and levied blackmail even on Persian kings; but they are geographically separated from the rest of the 14th satrapy by Persia proper, and it is more probable the Utii lived near the Persian Gulf.

The islands are those in the mouth of the Persian Gulf (cf. vii. 80), off the now much-talked-of port of Bander Abbas.

The practice of deportation was usual with the military monarchies of the old world, especially in the East (cf. 2 Kings xv. 29; xviii. 11, 32); for instances in H. cf. vi. 3 n.

3 The 15th satrapy seems to lie in the extreme north-east beyond Bactria; the Amyrgian Sacians have the same commander as the Bactrians (vii. 64. 2 n).

The **Caspii** (not the Caspii of 92. 2) are mentioned in vii. 67. 1 and 86. 1 among the Eastern tribes of the army; perhaps they are the inhabitants of Cashmere, but this is not probable, as in that case they would have the mountains between them and the Sacae.

For the position of the 16th satrapy cf. 92. 2 n. All the tribes in it occur on the monuments of Darius. The Parthians, afterwards so famous, lived in the modern Khorasan, south-east of the Caspian. The Chorasmians lay north-east of them, on the lower Oxus (cf. Arr. Anab. iv. 15). The capital of Sogdiana, the tribe further to the north-east, was Samarcand; the name Soghd is still borne by the district between the Oxus and the Jaxartes (Wilson, Aria. p. 129). The Areii (in vii. 66 called Ἄριοι—not the same as the Ἄριοι, the old name of the Medes, vii. 62. 1 n.) lived in West Afghanistan, where their name may survive in 'Herat'. Darius calls them 'Haraiva'.

94 The 17th satrapy seems to correspond to Beloochistan. H. does not use the later name Gedrosia, for which cf. Arr. Anab. vi. 22 seq. On the coast of this country still lives a primitive race which is dark brown (the Brahvî, but *v. i.*); so too, on the south-east corner of Arabia, Curzon speaks of the scanty survivors of a 'dark aboriginal race living in tne rocks by C. Mussandum' (ii. 447). This race had of course no connexion but that of colour with the Ethiopians of Africa (for whom cf. iii. 17. 1 n. and vii. 70. 1). Lassen (I. A. i. 390) thinks the dark race was perhaps once widely spread in Asia; he quotes the Mahâbhârata for 'black dwellers in the Himalaya'. But he denies that it survives in Beloochistan. The Paricanii are otherwise unknown, but may well be the inhabitants of the interior. Their name is explained by some as = 'worshippers of demons', by others (e. g. Holdich, p. 34) as the Sansk. 'Parvaka' (= mountaineers). H. couples them in vii. 68 with the Utians and Mycans, and the Ethiopians with the Indians (vii. 70. 1).

The 18th satrapy seems to have consisted of the southern and eastern parts of the mountainous region which, beginning with the basin of the upper Aras, stretches west to the upper Euphrates and south to the upper Tigris. For the Matieni cf. i. 72. 2 n.

The **Saspeires** lay north of Matiene; they occupy a 'small' district between Media and Colchis (i. 104; cf. iv. 37). Rawlinson, iv. 223, identifies their name with the 'Iberians', but this is very doubtful.

The **Alarodii** are only mentioned here and in vii. 79, where they are again joined with the Saspeires and armed like the Colchians. Sir H. Rawlinson (ib. iv. 245 seq.) sees in their name a survival of the 'Urarda' (cf. Ararat) of the Inscriptions; this is generally accepted (Maspero, iii. 55); they were a Semitic race who preceded the Aryan Armenians in the mountain region north-west of the Assyrian plain (round Lake Van), and who fought the Assyrians at first for supremacy, then for independence. After H. they disappear, being absorbed by the Armenians.

2 The 19th satrapy lay north and north-west of the 18th, north and north-east of the 13th (93. 1), and south of Colchis. All the tribes in it, except the Moschi, lay on the coast of the Black Sea (cf. Xen. Anab. iv. 8 for the Macrones—whose name survives in the Makur Dagh—and v. 5. 2 for the Tibareni); their armament resembles that of the Colchians. The Mares only occur here (and in vii. 79) and in Hec. fr. 192 (F. H. G. i. 12).

The **Tibareni** and **Moschi** (Assyr. 'Tabali and Muskana') are the Tubal and Meshech of Ezek. xxvii. 13 (cf. 32. 26), where they are among the 'merchants of Tyre', trading in slaves and brass; they had long resisted the Assyrians, and seem to have been finally driven into the mountains by the Cimmerian invasion (cf. i. 15 n.). They were independent later (Xen. Anab. vii. 8. 25).

'Ινδῶν. Two questions arise: I. **What knowledge had H. of the Indians? II. How far were they under Persian rule?**

I. The following points may be accepted. H. thinks that (*a*) the Indians are the most remote nation known on the east; beyond them is desert (98. 2; iv. 40. 2). This idea is based partly on some rumour as to the great deserts east of the Indus, partly on ignorance. As H. knows nothing of mountains in these parts, it is difficult to think (as Rawlinson) that he refers to the great deserts north of the Himalaya.

(*b*) The subject Indians are the inhabitants of the lower Indus valley and the modern Sind and part of the Punjab east of the Indus. The wealth of the satrapy compels us to believe that much of the country which is now desert, e. g in Sind, was then irrigated and fertile; but even in Strabo's (p. 697) time part of the south Indus valley was *θηρίοις μᾶλλον ἢ ἀνθρώποις σύμμετρος*.

(*c*) Beyond this region H. knows (1) vaguely of a great population; the Indians are the most numerous race in the world (*v. i.*). (2) Most of them are utter barbarians (c. 98 seq.). So far as his stories are true, they can only refer to the primitive Dravidian races, who were left behind in the hilly country on the frontier by the tide of Aryan conquest. (3) But he has accurate information of the Indian canoes and cotton dresses (98. 3, 4) and of their respect for animal life (100. 1).

(*d*) H. as usual is free from the ridiculous tales which later writers give, e.g. Ctesias (cf. 98. 3; 102 nn.).

II. (*a*) H. (iv. 44. 3) tells us that Darius, after the voyage of Scylax, subdued some Indians and used the Indus as a waterway. This agrees with Darius' inscription at Persepolis, where he puts India among his conquests. H. (102. 1 n.) seems to limit the tributary Indians to the region in north-west India. It is noticeable that Strabo (687) is ignorant of these Persian conquests.

(*b*) It is probable that Darius received regular gifts from the trans-Indus tribes, though by the time of Alexander, the Persians had lost all authority beyond that river.

H.'s statements here and in v. 3. 1 as to the number of the Indians are implicitly contradicted by Thucydides (ii. 97. 5–6), who says that with the Scyths no nation in Europe or Asia could be compared. Thucydides' narrow Hellenism involves him in a double error: (*a*) He does not know that the Scyths proper were a comparatively small race (App. XI. 6). (*b*) He ignores the great populations of the East, of which H. has dimly heard.

ἑξήκοντα καὶ τριηκόσια. The 360 talents, being paid in gold, have to be multiplied by 13 for the reckoning (95. 1).

95 The reading (cf. 89. 2 n.) *ὀγδώκοντα καὶ ὀκτακόσια* (for the *τεσσαράκοντα καὶ πεντακόσια* of most MSS.; *vid.* app. crit.) seems almost certain. For (*a*) the sum total of all the tributes (less the 140 talents spent in Cilicia, 90. 3) is 7,600 Babylonian talents. This—taking the ratio of 60 : 78 (89. 2)—gives 9,880 Euboic talents. (*b*) If the value of the Indian gold be added, i.e. 360 × 13 = 4,680, we have the total 14,560 talents.

This reading then both preserves the proper relation of gold and silver, and makes the addition of H. correct, while the other text does neither. For the ratio of the precious metals (really 13·3, not 13) cf. Böckh, i. 38 seq.; it varied, but was often reckoned as 10 : 1 (Lys. xix. 42–3, property of Conon; Xen. An. i. 7. 18, 3,000 darics = 10 tals. = 60,000 drs.; Liv. xxxviii. 11). The modern proportion is about 15½ : 1. As the Persian gold was the purest (cf. iv 166. 2), H. rightly gives a higher ratio than the usual.

2 **τὸ δ' ἔτι κτλ.** is equivalent to 'I calculate in round numbers, not in fractions'.

96 **νήσων**: i.e. the Greek islands in the Aegean.

2 **θησαυρίζει.** Strabo (731) says there were 40,000 talents found by Alexander in Susa and Persia; cf. also Arr. Anab. iii. 16. 7 (50,000 at Susa alone). Cf. Plut. Alex. 36, and v. 49. 7 n.

97 2 **Αἰθίοπες.** For Cambyses' conquests and the Ethiopian gifts cf c. 17 n.

Nysa, the birthplace of Osiris, is placed by Diodorus (i. 15) in Arabia Felix; here and in ii. 146. 2 it seems to be in the Upper Nile valley; cf. Hom. Hymn. i. 8 *σχεδὸν Αἰγύπτοιο ῥοάων*. Stein identifies it with Gebal Barkal, the 'holy mountain', near the Fourth Cataract and Meroe. The legends of Dionysus place it also in Greece, India, and elsewhere. It seems better to connect *οἵ* with the main subject, 'the Ethiopians near Egypt,' not with 'the long-lived Ethiopians'.

σπέρματι: cf. 101. 2; for the Callatiae cf. c. 38.

3 **συναμφότεροι**, 'both,' i. e. 'the Ethiopians and their neighbours' (*v. s.*).

διὰ τρίτου, 'every second year' (so *διὰ πεντ. inf.* 'every four years'); cf. the biennial tribute from the South to Solomon (1 Kings x. 22). In the outlying parts of the Persian Empire, the old system of 'gifts' (as opposed to 'tribute') survived. Cf. B. M. G. Pl. XVI, p. 175 for a picture from the Theban monuments of Ethiopians bringing ebony, gold, &c. For Duncker's theory of the great southern extension of the Persian Empire, based on this passage, cf. App. V. 4.

4 **ἀγίνεον**. The Circassian beauties are still sold for the Turkish harems.

98 1 **τοιῷδε**: cf. cc. 102–5. The passage beginning *ἔστι τῆς Ἰνδικῆς* to the end of 101 is a digression on the independent Indians; it reads like a later addition. Lassen (i. 388 seq.) lays stress on its importance as evidence for the extension of primitive non-Aryan tribes into north-west India. He (ii. 635) quotes from an Indian epic, a fish-eating people living on the Sarasvati; this flows into the Run of Cutch, a little east of the Indus. He (ii. 633) says the *κάλαμος* is not the bamboo proper (*Bambusa arundinacea*), out of which Indian bows are made (vii. 65), but a similar plant, the 'Kana', which grows over fifty feet high, and correspondingly thick. Ctesias (Ind. 6, p. 248), with characteristic exaggeration, says that 'two men could hardly span it with extended arms'.

4 The *φλοῦς* (Att. *φλέως*) is the *Arundo ampelodesmon*; cf. Postans, Sindh, p. 60, for its use by the Miami, a fisherfolk on the Indus, for 'mats' (*φορμοῦ*), &c. H. perhaps is borrowing from Scylax (cf. iv. 44).

99 **ὃς ἂν κάμῃ**. For this cannibalism cf. iv. 26 n. The name Padaci may be derived from the Sans. 'padja' (bad). Cf. Tibullus, iv. 1. 144–5 'Impia vel saevis celebrans convivia mensis | ultima vicinus Phoebo tenet arva Padaeus'.

100 **κτείνουσι οὐδὲν ἔμψυχον**. Lassen (ii. 635) points out that this is the oldest Western mention of the Brahman hermits (e. g. of their vegetable diet—*ποιηφαγέουσι*). But if so, H. confuses them with the aboriginal black population (cf. 101. 1).

101 **ἐμφανής**. For this lowest depth of bestiality cf. i. 203 n.

2 Aristotle twice refutes this (736 a 10; de Gen. Anim. ii. 2 and

522 a; H. A. iii. 22); he says that H.'s mistaken argument from the black skin is refuted by the white teeth of negroes.

102 The name 'Pactyice' perhaps = 'mountain border land'. Hence it is applied to the districts both on the north-west (cf. 92. 1) and on the south-east of the Iranian plateau (Lassen, i. 434). It perhaps survives in 'Pushtoo', the Afghans' name for themselves. In vii. 85. 1 the 'Pactyic' type of dress is contrasted with the 'Persian'. For **Caspatyrus** cf. iv. 44. 2 n. These Indians are the only Indians of Aryan stock whom H. knows, apart from the confused reference in c. 100. They are called Δέρδαι in Strabo 706 (Ind. Darada). They lived on the southern slopes of the Hindo-Koosh in Kafiristan.

For the story of the ants cf. Bunbury, i. 229 f., or (more fully) Lassen, i. 850. We may note as to it (1) Nearchus, Alexander's admiral, had seen the skins of the 'gold-digging ants' which are 'like those of panthers' (Strabo 705); Strabo quotes the story, with additional details (e.g. that meat is put out to distract the attention of the ants), from Megasthenes, who went as ambassador to Sandracottus at Patna circ. 300 B.C., and 'from others' (706); Megasthenes places it in a plain '3,000 stadia round, τῶν προσεῴων καὶ ὀρεινῶν Ἰνδῶν'. (2) It was often repeated in the Middle Ages, e.g. in a twelfth-century letter of Prester John (quoted by Bähr, *ad loc.*), who gives the ants seven feet and four wings. Busbecq. (Ep. Turc. 4) says that in 1559 a Persian ambassador brought, among other gifts, to the Sultan Soliman at Constantinople, an Indian ant 'magnitudine canis mediocris, animal mordax et saevum'. (3) That ants dug up gold is a genuine Indian story; cf. Wilson, Ariana, pp. 135–6 (quoting the Mahâbhârata), who says the gold paid as tribute was called 'ant gold' (Pippílika).

There are three facts underlying the story: (*a*) that ant-heaps contained gold dust; (*b*) that certain animals and their skins were exported; these may have been marmots, some of which are spotted like panthers; they are certainly burrowing animals; (*c*) gold is abundant in the mountain chains north-west of India. It is to be noted that H. does not claim to have seen the ants himself, as Ctesias did the still more fabulous Martichora (Ind. fr. 5, p. 356).

3 The word σειρηφόρος, 'pulling by a trace,' seems elsewhere used only metaphorically (Aesch. Agam. 842; Aristoph. Nub. 1300).

103 **γούνατα τέσσερα.** H. is of course mistaken in giving a camel two knees and two thighs in *each* of its back legs; but his mistake is due to careful, though unscientific, observation. We may note that (1) he took the heel of the camel for a second knee: this mistake is not unnatural, as a glance at a camel will show, owing to the length of the camel's metatarsal bone. He then *infers* that, as it had two knees in each leg, it would also have two thighs. (2) The camel appears to have more than one joint in its legs when it kneels to receive a load; Aristotle (Hist. An. ii. 1, 499 a), who corrects H. without naming him, points out that this is due to the way in which the camel doubles its legs under it (διὰ τὴν ὑπόστασιν τῆς κοιλίας), as if it were double-jointed. For other explanations of H.'s blunder see Bähr, *ad loc.*

τὰ αἰδοῖα, 'veretrum retro versum habet,' which is a fact.

104 2 **θερμότατος κτλ.** This passage, as to the climate of India, well illustrates H.'s mistaken views of the earth's shape. As he supposes it to be flat, the Indians on the extreme east have the sun nearest to them, and so hottest, in the early morning; this lasts till the time of the 'market's breaking-up' (i.e. about 10 a.m.); as the sun goes west, the day gets cooler. Rawlinson, however, thinks that H. may be reproducing inaccurately a real account of the contrast between the hot mornings and the cool afternoons, when the sun is behind the hills, of the high Indian valleys.

For **ἀγορῆς διαλύσιος** cf. ii. 173. 1 and iv. 181. 3.

105 2 **καὶ παραλύεσθαι**, 'are actually cut loose when they begin to drag.'

M. Polo says that the Tartars in their raids ride mares for a similar reason.

106 2 The **τοῦτό μεν** here corresponds to *πρὸς δ' αὖ μεσαμβ.* (107. 1).

μέζω. This statement is partly an inference from § 1, partly a case of 'omne ignotum', &c. As a matter of fact the African elephants and lions are larger than the Indian varieties.

For the Nisaean horses cf. vii. 40. 2 n.

χρυσός. India is really poor in gold. H.'s statement is partly based on the (exaggerated) mineral wealth of North-west India, partly on a mistaken inference from the dress of the natives (Lassen, i. 238). Our own ancestors similarly exaggerated the wealth of India.

3 **καρπὸν εἴρια . . . προφέροντα.** This is the first Western mention of cotton, which, however, grows on a shrub and not on a tree; for the Indians wearing it cf. vii. 65. 1.

107 **ἐσχάτη.** As H. thinks Arabia 'furthest' to the south, he has no conception of the great southern extension of Africa and India. Arabia was reckoned the land of spices, because the trade was mainly in Arab hands; 'white incense' (λιβανωτός) grows in Arabia and on the coast of Africa opposite; the brown variety grows in India. (M. Polo, ii. 396, 445 seq.)

All the names are Semitic: *κασίη* = Heb. Ḳezi'a, *λιβανωτός* = levônâh, *σμύρνη* = mōr, Ass. murru, *λήδανον* = lōt, Ass. ladunu, *κινάμωμον* = kinnāmōn, probably foreign (cf. 111. 2, 112. 1 for the origin of the names, and L. & S. *s.v.* *κιννάμωμον*).

The marvels and dangers related by H. (whose knowledge of them is perhaps due to his being a merchant himself) are the fictions of traders anxious both to conceal their market and to enhance the value of their products. The **Φοινικικὸν** *ψεῦδος* was proverbial; cf. Paus. ix. 28. 2 for a Phoenician snake-story; but according to him the sweetness of the balsam took away the deadliness of its guardian snakes. For the spice trade cf. Mövers, Phoen. iii. 1. 104; it was already established in the seventh century B.C.

2 **στύραξ** is also a Semitic word; it is translated 'balm' Gen. xliii. 11. It was an inferior kind of incense and grew especially in Syria.

For winged serpents cf. ii. 75. 1; H. here may be adding an Egyptian touch to his Phoenician information. For an expedition to Punt, the land of spices, under the eighteenth dynasty cf. R. of P.[1] x. 11, and Brugsch, i. 352 seq.

108 1 **ἐχίδνας.** H. carefully distinguishes 'vipers' from other snakes (109. 3).

προνοίη. Xenophanes had taught there was a divine power ruling the universe *νόου φρενί* (R. and P., ed. 1888, 89 b). In Anaxagoras this intelligence tended to be divorced from divinity; in H. it develops into a belief in a divine providence that is kind. The early use of the argument from Final Causes is very curious.

3 **ἐπικυΐσκεται**: the 'superfoetation' of the hare is recorded by Aristotle (De Gen. An. iv. 5. 773 a), though with fewer details than by H. Platt (Oxf. Tr. p. 190) quotes Sundevall, 'it is not so much the rule as the author thinks, but still it does occur.' There are four stages of the young: 'with fur,' 'bare,' 'just formed,' 'just conceived.'

4 **λέαινα.** Aristotle without naming H. (Hist. An. vi. 31. 579 a 2) rightly styles this story as to the lioness *ληρώδης*; it was invented, he says, to account for the scarcity of lions. The lioness breeds once a year, and has usually three cubs. H. fails to explain how under his system the race of lions survives at all.

ἐσικνέεται καταγράφων, translate 'he penetrates scratching it down'.

109 1 **φύσις**: i.e. from eggs, according to the 'nature' of serpents.

2 **ἀποθνήσκει.** H.'s vivid imagination conceives the serpent pair as a sort of Agamemnon and Clytemnestra. Dryden (Abs. and Ach. i. 1013–15) has a fine simile, based on this snake story, for the witnesses to the Popish Plot:—

> Till, viper-like, their mother plot they tear,
> And suck for nutriment that bloody gore
> Which was their principle of life before.

3 **κατὰ τοῦτο**, 'on this ground,' i.e. because collected in Arabia.

110 Cassia and cinnamon are both aromatic barks and closely allied; when powdered they are almost indistinguishable. In modern times most of the cassia comes from China, the best cinnamon from Ceylon, whence the name of the plant (*C. Zeylanicum*).

θηρία πτερωτά. Theophrastus (H. P. ix. 5) describes a similar danger to cinnamon gatherers, but from venomous snakes.

111 1 **ἐν τοῖσι ὁ Διόνυσος.** H. probably means Ethiopia; cf. 97. 2 n.

2 **ὄρνιθας.** The great birds acting as retrievers are familiar in the story of Sindbad the Sailor; there and in M. Polo (iii. 19), they bring up diamonds. 'The dry sticks' (*κάρφεα*) are the familiar

form in which cinnamon is still exported. Theophrastus (ix. 4. 5) gives a much fuller account of cinnamon: it grows in ravines in Arabia; the best part is the young shoots, the worst that near the roots; altogether five qualities are distinguished.

112 **λήδανον.** Dioscorides (*περὶ ὕλης ἰατρικῆς*, i. 128), who wrote about the time of Nero, says *οἱ τράγοι τὴν λιπαρίαν ἀναλαμβάνουσι τῷ πώγωνι γνωρίμως καὶ τοῖς μηροῖς προσπλαττομένην διὰ τὸ τυγχάνειν ἰξώδη, ἣν ἀφαιροῦντες ὑλίζουσι* ('strain') *καὶ ἀποτίθενται ἀναπλάττοντες μαγίδας* ('cakes'); Pliny (N. H. xii. 76) tells a similar story.

χρήσιμον: i.e. for mixing with many kinds of myrrh. Dioscorides (*u.s.*) says it was used to keep hair from falling off.

113 The construction is *ἡδύ* ('the sweet smell') *ζεῖ ἀπὸ τῆς χώρης θεσπέσιον ὡς* (cf. *θαυμάσιον ὡς, ἀφόρητος οἷος* iv. 28. 1).

For the 'Sabean odours from the spicy shore
Of Araby the Blest', where for
'many a league
Cheered with the grateful smell old Ocean smiles',

cf. Milton, P. L. iv. 162–5. Agatharchides, a Greek official of high rank in Egypt (circ. 150 B.C.), described not only this (Diod. iii. 45–6) but other marvels in Arabia, e.g. that the sweet-smelling woods were guarded by numerous and deadly 'purple snakes', and also the relaxing effect of the odours; these H. judiciously omits.

ὀΐων. The Barbary sheep is not now confined to Arabia, but is found in many parts of Africa and North Asia (e.g. the *Ovis Steatopyga* of Pallas in Asiatic Russia). Its tail is said in some cases to weigh over 70 lbs.; it is still at times protected by wheeled boards. (Wood, Nat. Hist. i. 679–81.) M. Polo notes these sheep in Persia (i. 18), and says they were 'as big as asses'.

The play on *ἕλκος* and *ἕλκειν* is as old as Pind. Pyth. ii. 168–9.

114 **ἀποκλινομένης**: lit. 'Ethiopia, as midday declines, extends West', &c.; but the phrases for time and for space are confused; 'as midday declines' = the quarter where midday declines. H. means that Ethiopia is the remotest land he knows to the south-west. The Ethiopians here are 'the long-lived'; cf. c. 17.

115 This chapter illustrates a main principle of H.'s geography; he insists on the evidence of eyewitnesses (iv. 16). Hence he will not accept the existence of sea on the north-west of Europe, and so reaches a wrong conclusion by a right method.

Ἠριδανόν. Three stages may be noted in the use of this name: (1) It seems to have been a general name for rivers. Cf. the Rhodanus (and perhaps the Rhenus) and the Radaune near Dantzig. It may contain the root of the Greek *ῥέω*, while the 'dan' can be compared with Danube, Don, Dniester, &c. This is not inconsistent with H.'s remark that the name is Greek; in the form Ἠριδανός it fits into hexameter verse, and may be connected with *ἦρι* 'early', so that 'it would be originally an epithet of the sun' (Tozer, A. G. p. 35, who compares 'Phaethon', 'the shining deity';

v. i. for his place in the myth). (2) Hesiod (Theog. 338) is the first Greek to use it, coupling it with the Nile and the Alpheus, but without locating it. Aeschylus (Plin. N. H. xxxvii. 32) made it = the Rhone, which he puts in Spain. (3) H.'s contemporary Pherecydes first made it the Po. This identification was probably due to two causes, (*a*) myth had connected the origin of amber from the tears of Phaethon's sisters with the Eridanus, (*b*) the amber route struck the Mediterranean at the head of the Adriatic, i.e. not far from the Po (cf. for amber route iv. 34 nn.).

What H. refuses to accept is the Eridanus of legend and its connexion with the growth of amber; Strabo (215) is even more sceptical.

ἐούσας is emphatic: 'really exist.'

The **Cassiterides** are identified by Strabo (175–6) with the Scilly Isles, where there is no tin. Originally, however, the name 'tin islands' must at any rate have included Britain; it was afterwards applied to imaginary islands; cf. Rice Holmes, Anc. Britain, pp. 483–8, for a full account of the ancient evidence and of modern views as to it; a shorter one is in Tozer, *u. s.* pp. 37–8. H. declines to commit himself to any of the stories, which were the result of the ignorance as to the islands. This ignorance was due to Phoenician exclusiveness; Strabo (176) tells how one of their merchants ran his ship on a shoal, to destroy his Roman pursuers. Cf. Diod. v. 22 (quoting Timaeus) for tin-mining in Britain and the tin route across Gaul; the metal was brought from Ictis (St. Michael's Mount) to Corbilo on the Loire (for this cf. Strabo 190), and thence ἐπὶ τῶν ἵππων, thirty days' journey to the mouth of the Rhone. The trade may be as old as the foundation of Massilia; cf. Rice Holmes, *u. s.* pp. 499–514.

2 **τὸ οὔνομα**: translate 'this very form Eridanus betrays that the name', &c.

δ' ὦν sums up the result of H.'s 'research' (μελετῶν). 'At any rate our tin comes' from the extreme west.

κασσίτερος. Schrader, Preh. Antiq. of Aryans, p. 216, thinks this 'is an Accadian-Assyrian word transferred by Phoenicians to the mines in the west'. Others more probably make it British, and compare the Cassi (Caesar, B. G. v. 21), Cassivellaunus, and other names. At all events, it is an imported word in Greece.

ἤλεκτρον. Amber comes especially from the south-east shores of the Baltic; cf. Tac. Germ. 45 and Plin. N. H. xxxvii. 30–53.

116 **πρὸς δὲ ἄρκτου.** Europe for H. extended north of Asia, and so included the northern parts of modern Asia. The mineral wealth of the Ural and Altai Mountains is well known.

For the Arimaspi cf. iv. 13 n.

3 **αἱ δὲ ὦν** takes up the point of 106. 1; whatever the truth of particular stories, 'at any rate' the extremities of the earth produce 'just (αὐτά) the things we think most fair and most rare'.

117 **πεδίον.** This chapter continues the subject of c. 97, i.e. the less

organized parts of the Great King's revenue. H.'s tale of the Aces (*v.i.*) is inconsistent alike with physical laws and with what is known of the position of the tribes mentioned (cf. cc. 92–3 nn.). The idea, however, of the chapter is quite correct; the control of irrigation is in the East one of the prerogatives of government, and great sums are charged for the use of water. Cf. Réclus, ix. 180, for this in modern Persia. H.'s informants have made a fancy picture out of real facts. It is probable, too, as Meyer suggests (*v. i.*), that the canalization of the land was intended as a check on the raids of the nomads of the north-east. (Cf. the similar defensive use of canals in Babylonia, i. 185. 1.)

The Hyrcanians (cf. 92. 2 n.) are mentioned here, but not in the list of satrapies.

The Aces (the name may mean either 'binder' or 'opening') has been variously made the Margus, the Oxus or the Ochus (Wilson, Ariana, p. 129), a confusion of these with the Hilmend (Rennell, pp. 195–6), the Heri-rud (Meyer, iii. 52, 68). The 'sea' has even been identified (St. Croix) with the Sea of Aral. But it is better to regard river and sea as imaginary (*v.i.*).

ἄρδεσκε, 'watered at one and the same time'; the iterative tense here is used of place, not of time. Cf. the Homeric *ὧδε δέ τις εἴπεσκεν ἰδὼν ἐς πλησίον ἄλλον.*

4 **χρηΐσκονται**: a *ἅπ. λεγ.*, 'are much in want of.'

5 **βασιλέος.** The personal appeal to the king is a genuine Oriental touch. Cf. 119. 3 and Exod. v. 15 (the Israelites and Pharaoh).

118–28 These chapters give Darius' difficulties in restoring order at home and in the satrapies. An account of the great revolts in the Persian empire (described in the B. I.) would naturally have come in here; but H. only once (i. 130. 2 n., the Median revolt) refers to these, apart from his account (c. 150 seq.) of the revolt of Babylon. He only knows there was widespread confusion (126. 2, 127. 1).

Darius (B. I. iv. 18) mentions Intaphrenes first of 'the Seven'; cf. 78 n. for his part in the conspiracy against the Magian. Rawlinson thinks H. underestimates his 'revolt', but cf. 119. 1.

118 2 **ἀγγελιηφόρος**: cf. 34. 1, 77. 2 for this office.

119 2 **τήν**: *sc. δέσιν.* Cf. for the construction v. 72. 4; ix. 37. 1 (where *τήν* is omitted). For the punishment of the whole family cf. Dan. vi. 24, but Darius here, more merciful than his namesake in the Bible story, spares the women.

6 **ἀδελφεός.** The preference for a brother over a husband occurs in Soph. Ant. 905–12 (perhaps an interpolation; cf. Jebb, pp. 259 seq., but it certainly was in Aristotle's text of Sophocles; cf. Rhet. iii. 16. 9; some ascribe the addition to the poet's son Iophon). The argument certainly seems more natural in the historian than in the dramatist. (Cf. Introd. p. 7.) There are curious parallels in the Indian Epic, the Ramayana, and in a late Persian story. Nöldeke

(Hermes, xxix. 155; cf. also xxviii. 465) thinks the Herodotean version is the original, because in it only two lives are spared, in the Oriental versions all three, husband, brother, and son. He thinks, however, H.'s story and the Indian one are both derived from an older Persian original. The more natural view is that a piece of Greek cleverness has been borrowed in the East.

120 **Σαρδίων.** H. here as always (except in c. 127) calls the satrapy 'Sardis', not 'Lydia' (v. 25 *et pass.*, and Thuc. i. 115. 4); so too the Persian name for it was Cparda.

παθών. Diodorus (x. 16 (ii. 206 Teubner)), however, says that Polycrates had given provocation by murdering some Lydians to obtain their wealth.

2 Dascyliun was capital of the Hellespontine satrapy (Thuc. i. 129. 1; Xen. Hell. iv. 1. 15); cf. App. I.

121 **'Ανακρέοντα.** A poet was a familiar figure at a tyrant's court. Anacreon afterwards went to Hipparchus (Plat. Hipp. 228). His relations with Polycrates were the subject of a scandal (F. H. G. iv. 299), which H. decently omits, as he does the similar story as to Themistocles and Aristides (Plut. Arist. 2).

2 The main sentence beginning *καί κως* is left incomplete, and the words explaining *συντυχίη* (which should have been *ἔπειτε τὸν κήρυκα . . . διαλέγεσθαι κτλ.*) become an independent sentence, into which the verbs (*μεταστραφῆναι, ὑποκρίνασθαι*) of the main sentence are attracted.

122 Probably Myrsus (for his name cf. i. 7 n.) was of the old royal house; cf. 15. 2 for the policy of favouring such. So too Pythius (vii. 27. 1 n.) seems to have been a Mermnad. For the death of Myrsus later cf. v. 121.

2 **θαλασσοκρατέειν.** The idea of 'thalassocracy' was in the air in the fifth century, when Themistocles had revealed its possibilities, and Cimon and Pericles had realized them. Myres (J. H. S. xxvi) has given good reasons for assigning the list of 'thalassocracies' in Eusebius to a fifth-century origin. Fotheringham (ib. xxvii. 88) doubts the date; but his arguments on this point are quite unconvincing, though he makes valuable corrections in Myres' interpretation of the list.

H. here for once is more really critical than Thucydides (i. 4), who says, probably by implication correcting H., Minos *παλαίτατος ὧν ἀκοῇ ἴσμεν . . . τῆς νῦν Ἑλληνικῆς θαλάσσης ἐπὶ πλεῖστον ἐκράτησε.* Whatever is true in the traditions as to Minos, H. is right in implying that they are not strictly historical.

But modern research has here, as elsewhere, largely vindicated the Greek view that the myths contained a large element of history (cf. Burrows, Discoveries in Crete, especially pp. 11–14, for the Minoan empire); Burrows ingeniously suggests that the eight 'Minoas' (cf. Fick, Vorg. Ortsn. p. 27) scattered from Syria to Sicily, may perhaps reveal the greatness of their founder (cf. the 'Alexandrias' and 'Antiochs' of the fourth and third centuries. The argument that founders' names are not given to colonies till quite late proves nothing against this; for the Greek colonies from the eighth century onwards were founded by republics, not by kings.

123 **Maeandrius** is the only early instance known of a Greek bearing his father's name; the practice became common in the fourth century (Rawlinson).

The reference to the Heraeum shows the source of this story (in part; no doubt another part came through Democedes).

2 **λάρνακας κτλ.** Nepos (Hann. 9) tells a like story of Hannibal; the trick of the Egestaeans was more elaborate (Thuc. vi. 46).

124 1 **λοῦσθαι.** The expression 'washed by Zeus' is suggestive of the physical explanations of the fifth century, which identified the gods with the powers of nature.

2 **ἐπεφημίζετο.** For this attempt to check an enterprise by 'using ominous words' cf. the curses of Ateius Capito against Crassus in 54 B. C. (Plut. Crass. c. 16).

125 2 **μεγαλοπρεπείην.** Just as H. thinks the greatest of Greek temples those of Ephesus and Samos, so here he holds Polycrates to have been more magnificent than Pisistratus; the comparison is significant.

3 **ἀποκτείνας.** H., like a true Greek, gives here no details of Asiatic barbarity; he is less reticent in iv. 202.

Σάμιοι. Oroetes hoped to form a Persian party in Samos; cf. Thuc. i. 55, iii. 70 for a similar policy at Corinth towards Corcyra.

126 1 **τίσιες.** For the personification of 'vengeance' cf. 128. 5; viii. 106. 4 *ἡ τίσις καὶ Ἑρμότιμος*, and Od. xi. 280 *μητρὸς Ἐρινύες*.

βασιληίην. H. writes loosely '*after* the rule of the Magian'; this was itself, according to one of his 'sources' (65. 5 and App. V. 6), 'the taking away of empire from the Persians by the Medes.'

2 **ὑπείσας.** For such a method of dealing with a messenger sent to recall a governor cf. 127. 3 n.

127 Oroetes had secured the Phrygian satrapy (120. 2 n.) by the murder of its satrap (126. 2). H. nowhere else uses these names for the West Anatolian satrapies; it is probable that the story of Oroetes came to him from Democedes, who naturally knew nothing of the official Persian names.

3 Rawlinson says that Ali Pacha, the semi-independent ruler of Albania at the beginning of the nineteenth century, made away with the Sultan's messengers sent to depose him.

128 2 **σφρηγῖδα**: cf. Esther iii. 12, viii. 8 for a decree made binding by the royal seal, and Thuc. i. 129 for the showing of the seal.

3 **ἀπικόμενος κτλ.** This passage is interesting as showing the ties which held the Persian empire together and limited the powers of the satraps; cf. App. VI for the whole subject.

περιαιρεόμενος, 'taking it out of its case.'

4 **μετῆκάν οἱ.** Stein translates 'sank their spears to Bagaeus', i. e.

recognized him as their new leader; he compares 'summissis fascibus' (Liv. ii. 7). But the use of μεθίημι in ix. 62. 1 rather suggests the sense 'let go their spears', i.e. no longer stood at attention. οἱ then would be Oroetes. The whole scene is worked up by H. with picturesque details.

9–38 The story of Democedes is skilfully introduced by H. as a link between the two main parts of his subject; it both fits on to the events which accompanied the accession of Darius and introduces the aggression against Europe. For Kirchhoff's argument as to Herodotean chronology based on it cf. Intr. § 10 (pp. 9–12). It need hardly be said that the importance assigned to Democedes is not historical; the 'curtain lecture of Atossa' (Macan) is a popular invention to account for events whose causes lay far deeper (cf. Introd. § 32, p. 45). H. seems to be blending a Crotoniate story with details heard at Halicarnassus (c. 138 n.), and with Persian stories as to the influence of Atossa.

9 2 For Egyptian physicians cf. ii. 84 n. Darius, however, restored the Egyptian college of surgery at Sais (Z. F. A. S. 37, 72 seq.).

0 1 **τεχνάζειν**, 'to make excuses'; cf. vi. 1. 2; Stein points out the play on words with *τὴν τέχνην* above.

5 **ὑποτύπτουσα**: translate 'dipping with a bowl into the gold chest'.

1 1 **συνείχετο**, 'was at variance with.'

2 **δυῶν ταλάντων.** Apart from the humour of the rapid increase in a fashionable physician's fees, the story is interesting as one of the earliest accounts of state endowments for medical science. (Cf. Mahaffy, S. L. pp. 290 seq.) 'Healthier than Croton' was a Greek proverb, P. G. ii. 778.

ἐγένετο κτλ. Stein well suggests that, if these lines be genuine, they are a subsequent addition; but they read like the comment of a pedantic scholiast.

132 For Greek homesickness cf. Histiaeus, v. 35. 4. For *ὁμοτράπεζος* cf. v. 24 n.

2 **μάντιν.** The Elean diviners were famous; cf. ix. 33. 1 n. Perhaps this was the Kallias of v. 44. 2 (at Croton); Democedes, unlike Pharaoh's 'chief butler' (Gen. xl. 23), remembered his companions in adversity.

133 For Atossa cf. 68 n.

2 For the real significance of Atossa's counsel cf. App. XII. 3. For war policy to keep subjects *ἄσχολοι* cf. Arist. Pol. v. 10. 10, 1313 b.

5 **ἐπὶ τὴν Ἑλλάδα.** Were disproof of the story needed, this supposed intention of attacking Greece before Scythia would alone be sufficient. The knowledge shown of Greece is inconsistent with other passages, e. g. v. 105 (as to Athens); the historian in such narratives as these aims at dramatic propriety and not at historic accuracy. Cf. Mure, iv. 408 seq., for an exaggerated discussion of H.'s inconsistencies.

3 **ἐπιδραμών**, 'with any eagerness'; lit. 'running after it'.

136 The γαῦλος was a round-built merchant-vessel (cf. Torr, p. 113); the word (cf. √ gôl = *rotāre*) is probably Phoenician, and = 'anything round'. It is distinguished by the accent from *γαυλός*, a bucket (vi. 119).

2 **ἐκ ῥηστώνης**, 'out of kindness' to Democedes.

βασιλεύς. A 'king' at Tarentum at the end of the sixth century may be explained (with Bähr) as a survival of Spartan institutions in a Spartan colony; the story of the foundation of Tarentum by the Partheniae is doubtful (cf. Busolt, i. 406 seq.), but certainly Tarentum received Laconian Dorians as colonists at some period. Others suggest less probably that the 'king' was a 'tyrant'.

τὰ πηδάλια. Athenaeus (522), improving on the narrative here given, says the Persians were robbed of their robes and a slave invested with them, an act commemorated afterwards in the official dress of the magistrate's servant at Croton.

137 3 **ἐκχρήσει**: cf. viii. 70. 1 for a similar use (= *ἀποχράω*, cf. 138. 2); but here it is impersonal.

5 **Μίλωνος θυγατέρα.** This Crotoniate story naïvely credits the Great King with the Greek love of athletes.

138 Apuleius (Florida, 15) says that Gillus, 'princeps' of Croton, ransomed Pythagoras from Cambyses; the patriotism of Gillus is an effective contrast to the unscrupulous conduct of Democedes.

2 Both Cnidus and Tarentum were Dorian towns, perhaps both Laconian colonies, an even closer bond of union.

4 **πρῶτοι.** H. is conscious that the story of Democedes may be thought a digression and so explains its relevance.

139–49 *The conquest of Samos by the Persians.*

The whole story is more than suspicious.

(1) It has impossible elements. If Darius had been in Egypt (which is doubtful, though not inconsistent with the B. I.) he certainly was not there as a common guardsman; he was next heir to the throne after his father Hystaspes.

(2) It is needless. The Persian policy always was to use Greek tyrants in the border states.

(3) Its moral is too obvious; it is a Greek version of 'Cast thy bread upon the waters'.

139 1 **πρώτην.** Stein (cf. vi. 109. 3) explains *πρώτην* of the 'importance' of Samos. It is more natural (as Rawlinson) to make it chronological; H. was ignorant (cf. 150 n.) of the double capture of Babylon, and knew very little of the great rebellions (521–519 B.C.). But cf. c. 118 n.

Αἴγυπτον. Under the rule of the native Egyptian kings Greeks had been confined to the Delta (ii. 154, 178 nn.); they now penetrated into Middle and Upper Egypt. Among these early sightseers may have been Hecataeus.

2 **πυρρήν.** The position is emphatic; so 'The cloak of Syloson' became a proverb for ostentation (P. G. ii. 772).

3 θείη τύχη, 'by a heaven-inspired chance' (not a mere accident); cf. i. 126. 6; iv. 8. 3.

140 εὐεργέτης. For the royal 'benefactors' cf. viii. 85. 3 n.

ἤ τις ἤ: a colloquialism, = 'hardly any'.

142 The commendation (cf. that of Cadmus, vii. 164. 1) is significant of H.'s own feeling towards tyranny. Cf. Appendix XVI. 1.

2 The story of Maeandrius is full of touches which show H.'s familiarity with Samos (145. 1, 146. 2).

4 ἱερωσύνην. The priesthood was necessary to secure Maeandrius from being punished for his service to the tyrant. For other grants of priesthoods cf. iv. 161. 3; vii. 153. 3.

5 γεγονὼς ... κακῶς. The low birth of Maeandrius would recommend him to the tyrant. (Cf. Arist. Pol. 1314 a πονηρόφιλον ἡ τυραννίς.) He was a citizen (123. 1), but is called ἡμέτερος δοῦλος by Syloson (140. 5). So Micythus, οἰκέτης ἐών, was appointed ruler of Tarentum by Anaxilaus (vii. 170. 4 n.).

143 2 Lycaretus was afterwards made despot in Lemnos (v. 27. 1). The δή well expresses the irony of H.

145 γοργύρη is properly a 'drain'; hence an underground dungeon.

146 3 The δίφρος was a footstool, which the Great King and his representatives in the field used, when stepping from a chariot (so Dinon in Athen. 514 a); others (e. g. Rawlinson) translate 'litter'; cf. Dio, c. 60. 2 (it was introduced by Claudius into Roman ceremonial). The present participle may imply that these Persians had the right to use a δίφρος, not that they were actually using them. Others, again, explain it by the θρόνους of c. 144.

148 For the position of Cleomenes cf. App. XVII. For the Lacedaemonians as the recognized heads of Greece between 550 and 480 B.C. cf. i. 69. 2 n.

149 For σαγηνεύσαντες cf. vi. 31 n. The immediate massacre (147. 1) was followed by thorough depopulation; ἕκητι Συλοσῶντος εὐρυχωρίη became a proverb (Strabo 638, who, however, attributes it, and the decay of population that gave rise to it, to the 'harsh rule' of Syloson).

As Samos in 494 B.C. was able to equip sixty triremes (vi. 8), it is probable that popular dislike of the tyrant exaggerated the severity of this conquest.

150–60 *The Revolt of Babylon and its capture by Darius.*

I. The general outline of the events is told by Darius in the B. I. (cf. Maspero, iii. 675 seq. for a brilliant sketch). Susiana and Babylon (B. I. i. 16) revolted within a fortnight of the death of Smerdis; the leader of the latter pretended to be the son of Nabonidus, and took the name Nebuchadnezzar. While Darius was besieging Babylon, nine other provinces revolted (ii. 2), including Persia, Media, and Parthia. After Darius had captured Babylon (ii. 1), how he does not say, though he mentions two great victories over the Babylonians, he proceeded against the other rebels. While he was reducing them, another pretender rose and seized Babylon (iii. 13), but was reduced, apparently without difficulty, by Intaphrenes (iii. 14). There are thus two revolts and two captures of Babylon.

II. There is, however, some uncertainty whether the story of H. refers to either. Ctesias (22, p. 69) says that the stratagem of Zopyrus belongs to his son Megabyzus, and to the capture of Babylon by Xerxes (478 B.C.). The view that this is the siege referred to is very generally adopted, e. g. by Sayce, *ad loc.*, Nöldeke, E. B.[9] 18. 572 (doubtfully), Lehmann, W. für K. P. 1900, p. 963.

The reasons are: (*a*) It is impossible to fit a siege of twenty months (153. 1) into the record of the B. I. (But the chronology of that record is most uncertain, and in ii. 2 it seems to imply a long resistance.) (*b*) Lehmann (*u. s.*) tries to fit in H.'s 'nineteen months' (c. 152) with dates given by the Babylonian tablets for Xerxes (but there are at least two uncertain quantities in his equation). (*c*) The cruelty of the victor (159. 2) is more like the character of Xerxes. Duncker, however, and Maspero accept the narrative of H., and the latter (iii. 677 n.) supports his view also from the Babylonian tablets. It seems safer to follow H., for (*a*) he had good evidence; Zopyrus, the grandson of the chief actor in the events, deserted to Athens about 440 B.C. (160. 2 n.); (*b*) the elder Zopyrus was certainly made satrap of Babylon.

III. (1) In the details of H. there is certainly exaggeration and Greek colouring (*v. i.*). His chronology too is impossible (150. 1 n.).

(2) The story of the self-devotion of Zopyrus is generally rejected; Sayce (*ad loc.*, who accepts the mutilation itself as a fact) and Sir H. Rawlinson (*ad* c. 155) argue that no mutilated person could have held rule; but (*a*) the scars of Zopyrus would have been offensive to no one but the Babylonians; (*b*) the position of Darius needed desperate measures, and some explanation must be found for his capture of an impregnable city; (*c*) the silence of Darius in the B. I. proves nothing; it certainly would have been inconsistent with the whole tone of the inscription to describe how desperate his position had been; (*d*) Polyaenus (vii. 11. 8) confirms H., and says the stratagem was borrowed from a Sacian chief, Risaces (for the war to which this story belongs cf. App. V. 9); he, after proving his loyalty by self-mutilation, led Darius into the desert. This story, which is told in great detail, whether it be true or not, shows that Polyaenus is not simply reproducing the narrative of H.; (*e*) the fact that the story is told by Persian poets of native heroes (Sir H. Rawlinson), and by Livy (i. 53) of Sextus Tarquinius, proves nothing against its having really happened once long before.

It seems safer, therefore, to accept the story as having, at any rate, a basis of fact.

150 **Βαβυλώνιοι.** H. implies that the revolt followed at once on the suppression of the Magian conspiracy; this is correct, but it is not consistent with his general narrative, which implies a considerable interval; for the healing of Darius followed 'not long after' the overthrow of Oroetes (129. 1); then comes the expedition of Democedes (133. 1), and 'after this' that against Samos (139. 1), 'contemporary with which' is the revolt of Babylon. H. puts together, without any real chronology, independent narratives, of which he knows only that they all belong to the early years of Darius.

2 **σιτοποιόν.** So the Plataeans kept 110 'breadmakers' (Thuc. ii. 78. 3), though they disposed of their non-combatants in a less drastic way. But Babylon was far from being in such a desperate position as the Plataeans; they might well expect success, as the Persian power seemed shaken.

151 2 **ἡμίονον.** The female mule can bear offspring, though this is rare (E. B.[9] xvii. 13); Aristotle (Hist. Anim. vi. 24) asserts it of the mules in Syria, though he had before stated (de Gen. Anim. ii. 8) *τὸ τῶν ἡμιόνων γένος ὅλον ἄγονόν ἐστι.* This story as to the prophecy is a mythical embellishment; Ctesias (*u.s.*) seems to have omitted it, but in his other details he agreed with H., though contradicting him on the main point. H. (vii. 57. 2) tells a still more wonderful story of mule-birth.

153 2 For a similar prophecy on the part of the besieged at Veii, leading to the capture of the town, cf. Livy v. 15.

154 **ἐς τὸ πρόσω,** 'to the advancement of greatness'; cf. i. 5. 3 for the phrase; and for the custom, Esther vi. 3; for 'benefactors' cf. viii. 85. 3 n.

155 2 For Assyrians cf. i. 178. 1 n.

4 **τῶν σῶν δεήσῃ,** 'unless there be some failure on your part'; we should have expected *τῶν σῶν τι ἐνδεήσῃ* (cf. vii. 18).

5 **Σεμιράμιος.** The gates of Semiramis look like a piece of Greek imagination; they may, however, be placed in the south-west (cf. i. 181. 2, 184 nn. for her connexion with the Nebo temple in Borsippa).

Of the other gates that of 'the Ninevites' would be on the north, that of 'the Chaldaeans' on the south, by the river, on the way to their early home (i. 181. 5 n.). That of 'Belus' would be in the south also, near (cf. 158. 2) the Esagila temple (i. 181. 2 n.), the 'Cissian' on the east (cf. 91. 4). The details, if fictions, are skilfully arranged to cover all sides of Babylon.

6 The **βαλανάγρα** (not *κλείς*, as the gate is large) was an iron hook for extracting the *βάλανος* from the bar (*μοχλός*; cf. Thuc. ii. 4. 3).

156 The picturesque details of this story (e.g. *ἐπιστρεφόμενος, ὀλίγον τι π.* and others) mark the born narrator; it is interesting to compare H.'s fulness here with the précis-like brevity of his accounts of manners and customs. But the Babylonian assembly (*τὰ κοινά*) is a purely Greek detail.

159 The destruction of the walls (cf. i. 178. 1 n.) explains the easy success of Intaphrenes in suppressing the second revolt (*u.s.*).

ἀνεσκολόπισε. Darius, B. I. (ii. 13, 14), mentions this punishment for the rebel leaders only.

160 1 ἀγαθοεργίην. Xenophon (Cyr. i. 2. 1) for once is right in describing the Persian esteem for Cyrus, who ᾄδεται ἔτι καὶ νῦν εἶδος κάλλιστος, ψυχὴν φιλανθρωπότατος, φιλομαθέστατος, φιλοτιμότατος. Cf. also c. 75.

εἴκοσι. Plutarch (Reg. Apoph. *s.v.* Δαρείου ; Mor. 173) characteristically exaggerates this to '100'. Cf. iv. 143 for a similar compliment to Megabyzus.

2 δῶρα. For royal gifts cf. 84. 1. As Babylon paid 1,000 talents a year (92. 1), this grant can hardly refer to the whole tribute.

For Megabyzus' success in Egypt cf. Thuc. i. 109 ; he afterwards quarrelled with the king, because the safe-conduct he had given to Inaros was violated ; cf. 15 n. and Ctesias (34 seq., p. 72 seq.), who goes on to describe, in an important passage too long to quote, his subsequent relations with the king, the desertion of Zopyrus to Athens, and his death at Caunus.

For the story of Ctesias, and especially for the phil-Hellenic leanings of the family of Megabyzus and the date of the desertion of Zopyrus, cf. J. H. S. xxvii. 57 seq., 'The Persian friends of Herodotus,' where an attempt is made (1) to connect the desertion of Zopyrus with the Samian War of 440–439 B. C. (cf. Thuc. i. 115, and Introd. p. 8) ; (2) to show that H. probably met him in Athens in 440 and derived from him such passages as iii. 80 seq., 90 seq., v. 52 seq. ; (3) to date H.'s departure for the West 440 B. C., which would account for the fact that he says nothing of the death of Zopyrus. This took place (Ctes. 43, p. 74) when the Athenians were besieging Caunus in Caria (probably in 439 B. C. ; cf. Busolt, iii. 554–5 for the relations of Athens and Persia at this time). This date would be important if it could be accepted. Kirchhoff, however (cf. Introd. p. 10 f.), dates Zopyrus' desertion '438 or probably later'. Rawlinson is certainly wrong in placing it in 426 or 425 B. C., as 'probably the latest event recorded by H.'

BOOK IV

[For the Σκυθικοὶ λόγοι cf. K. Neumann, Die Hellenen im Skythenlande (1855), and S. Reinach, Antiquités de Russie Méridionale (1891–2).]

This book falls into two parts, cc. 1–144 giving the account of Scythia and the Scythian expedition, cc. 145–205 the story of Cyrene. Except Book II, no part of H.'s narrative has so little to do with his main subject, while none is so rich in curious information, much of which is invaluable to the anthropologist. The account of the Scythians especially is important as the earliest study we possess of an uncivilized people. Nothing is more instructive, in estimating the difference between the points of view of H. and of Thucydides, than to compare the former's full-length study of the Scythians with the brief sketch of Macedonia and Thrace given by the latter (ii. 97; cf. 81. 1 n.); H. is the type of the earlier Greek, to whom all knowledge and all the world were of interest, Thucydides of the Periclean Athenian, who concentrated himself on the political affairs of Greece in the narrowest sense.

1–4 *The motives for Darius' campaign* (for a discussion of these cf. App. XII. 3–4).

1 1 **αὐτοῦ**: emphatic; the king led in person. Cf. vii. 10 η. For the Scythian invasions cf. i. 104–6 nn., for the Cimmerian i. 15 nn.

2 1 **δούλους**. The information in this chapter is better than the logic; Stein suggests with reason that it is a later addition.

The idea that the slaves were blind may be due to a mistaken etymology for some Scythian word for 'slave' (Stein; cf. 86. 4 n.), and perhaps to the fact that blindness is common in South Russia. Blind slaves obviously would be useless, nor does H. explain why they were blinded.

φυσητῆρας. Pallas (Nachr. Mong. Völk. i. 119) in the eighteenth century describes a similar operation among the Calmucks to induce 'obstinate' cows to give milk.

θηλέων ἵππων. The Greeks were early struck by the Northern use of mares' milk. Cf. Il. 13. 5 Ἱππημολγῶν | γλακτοφάγων, Ἀβίων τε δικαιοτάτων ἀνθρώπων. The Hippemolgi and the Abii were supposed to be nations, and credited with all the virtues of the 'noble savage'; these vain imaginations are not found in H., but they lasted as late as Ammianus (fourth century A.D.): even Arrian says (Anab. iv. 1) they were *αὐτόνομοι διὰ πενίαν καὶ δικαιότητα*.

2 **δονέουσι**: cf. Hippoc. de Morbis (ii. 358, ed. Kuhn, 1826), who says the light buttery part (*βούτυρον*) floated, the heavier cheesy part (*ἱππάκη*) sank, leaving the whey between the two. This was afterwards fermented and made into 'koumiss'.

3 1 **ἐκ τούτων . . . τῶν δούλων**. The idea of a slave-born class becoming dangerous is common in Greek history; cf. vi. 138 (at Lemnos) and Arist. Pol. v. 7. 2, 1306 b, the Partheniae at Sparta, who (Her. Pont., F. H. G. ii. 220, fr. 26; *flor. circ.* 390 B.C.) were born of Spartan women during the absence of the Spartans in the First Messenian War, presumably of Helot fathers, though Her. Pont. does not say so.

2 **τάφρον**. This trench extends from the Tauric Mountains to the P. Maeotis; as H. was quite ignorant of the shape of the Crimea (cf. 99 n.), he conceives it (20. 1) as running north and south, and as the eastern boundary of the 'Royal Scyths'. Bähr quotes evidence of the remains of a trench in the east of the Crimea, from near Theodosia to the Sea of Azov (cf. also Klio, iv. 183). Some have seen in the story a confused account of the 'Putrid Sea', the western arm of the Sea of Azov. It may be noted that 'the trench' plays no part in the actual struggle between the Scyths and

their slaves. This 'trench' must not be confused with the cutting across the Isthmus of Perekop, which still existed in the Middle Ages.

3 **Οἷα ποιεῦμεν.** The whole story is evidently a Greek fiction to illustrate the proper way of controlling slaves.

5–15 *The origin of the Scyths.* H. gives three different versions, the Scythian and the Pontic Greek, which are mythological, and a third (c. 11 seq.), which he adopts as resting on the authority of both nations (12. 3), and which he partially confirms by quoting Aristeas (c. 13), who differs only as to the race which drove the Scyths into their new country. This last version is accurate in two points: (*a*) it recognizes the earlier possession of the country by the Cimmerians; (*b*) it gives a *vera causa,* an early 'Völkerwanderung'; but it is full of legendary details.

5 1 **νεώτατον.** Justin (ii. 1), on the contrary, says the Scyths were *gens antiquissima*; for these early ethnological disputes cf. ii. 2.

2 **γένεος.** For the name Targitaus (a genuine native name) cf. Polyaen. viii. 55, Tirgitao. For the artificial genealogy cf. Tac. Germ. 2, Mannus and his three sons. The names do not appear subsequently in H.; but the triple kingship (c. 120) may have suggested both it and the similar division in 7. 2.

For the success of the youngest cf. 10. 2 (the story of the Pontic Greeks), the story of Perdiccas (viii. 137), and popular legends *passim*, e.g. that of Cinderella. For the 'burning gold' cf. the popular superstition in modern Russia of buried treasures which turn to hot coals when discovered (Reinach, A. R. M. p. 160).

6 1 **Αὐχάται . . . Κατίαροι.** Pliny (iv. 88), speaks of the Auchetae in South Russia. He also mentions (vi. 22) them as in the Causasus; in vi. 50 he mentions the Euchatae and Cotieri as nomad tribes on the north of the Jaxartes. Perhaps these last are remnants of the Scyths left in their original home (cf. 11. 1 n.), whose name just survives in their new home, but has no practical importance.

Minns, however (E. B. xxiv. 526), ingeniously suggests that this legend belongs to the agricultural Scyths, who were a conquered race, and not 'Scyths' at all, but 'Scoloti' (§ 2); the objects ('cup, plough, yoke') are not such as would be held sacred by nomads.

2 H. seems to connect Scoloti with Colaxais (*τοῦ βασιλέος ἐπωνυμίην*); perhaps we may compare 'Scyles' (c. 78), but *v. s.*

7 1 **χιλίων.** The number '1,000' obviously rests on no tradition; if it is not a mere round number, it is only a calculation based on royal genealogies.

μετέρχονται, 'they honour' it (cf. vi. 68. 2 n.).

2 **διὰ τοῦτο**: i.e. as reward for his year's watching. The whole story is oddly introduced, and does not agree with the later details of Scythian worship (e.g. contrast the golden *σάγαρις* here with the iron *ἀκινάκης* of 62. 2). Nor is it easy to reconcile the grant of 'a

day's circuit' with the habits of a nomadic people. H. repeats some ancient story as to a guarded gold treasure (cf. the wealth of the Nibelungs), but without understanding it. Reinach, however (A. R. M. p. 160), says the Calmucks have a custom of granting a man as much land as he can ride round in a day.

3 **τὰ δὲ κατύπερθε.** The Scythian tradition excludes the 'lands that lie above to the north, of those who dwell in the upper parts of the country', while the Greek tradition takes in the Agathyrsi and Geloni (10. 1). For the 'feathers' cf. c. 31 n.

8–10 *The Greek story.* The Greeks as usual introduced their mythology into the country where they settled; it will be noticed they explain only the origin of the Scythian kings. Such fictions could both justify present occupation (e.g. the Heraclidae in Peloponnese), and (e.g. Dorieus and the land of Eryx) give ground for future claims (v. 43; cf. c. 178 n.). There are of course native features in the story, e.g. the number of the sons (9. 3). For the story of Geryon in its earlier form cf. Hes. Theog. 287; Hecataeus (Arr. Anab. ii. 16. 5) had localized it near Ambracia; H. therefore is emphatic on its belonging to the extreme west.

τὰς . . . βοῦς, 'oxen' generally; cf. *οἱ Ἴωνες πάσας τὰς ἀγέλας ἐκθηλύνουσι τῇ προφορᾷ*, E. M. p. 473.

2 Erytheia, 'the red island,' probably with reference to the setting sun. Cadiz is really built on a rocky island connected by a long spit of land with the Isla de Leon; but it is most unlikely that H. knew anything definite of its site or neighbourhood. For the pillars of Hercules cf. ii. 33. 3 n.

Ὠκεανόν. For the circumambient ocean cf. ii. 21 n.; for H.'s insistence on geographical proof cf. iii. 115. 2 n.

3 **ἅρματος.** The horse and chariot is perhaps a bit of local colour; they are not generally part of the Heracles myth.

1 **Ὑλαίην**: cf. 18. 1 n. The 'grotto' is part of the legendary furniture of the Echidna story; cf. Hes. Theog. 297.

5 **διατεινόμενον.** The Scyths drew to the shoulder, not to the breast (like the Cretans); they used both hands indiscriminately (Plat. Laws, 795 A). For Heracles' Scythian bow cf. Theoc. xiii. 56.

1 **τὸν ζωστῆρα**: translate '(the way to clasp) the belt'. The Scyths pictured on the vases carry no cups; Stein explains the *φιάλη* as the broad flat clasp on which the girdle ends fasten; but this is not what H. says (§ 3).

Agathyrsus and **Gelonus** represent the tribes to the north-west and the north-east respectively of Scythia proper (cf. c. 104; v. 108). We should have expected Βουδῖνον for Γελωνόν.

3 **τὸ δή**: i.e. his staying in the land; *μοῦνον* must agree with *τὸ δή*, but gives very poor sense; *μούνῳ* would be more natural.

-12 **ἄλλος λόγος.** H.'s own view. It is to be noted that here he adopts in a qualified manner a combination adopted elsewhere

(i. 103; iv. 1) without reserve. For the facts generally in cc. 11 and 12 cf. i. 15 nn.

For the Araxes cf. i. 202 n.; here it seems to be the Volga.

4 **θάψαι.** That there were tombs of a previous race on the Dniester is probable; H. may have seen them himself. If they were Cimmerian, their position in the west of Scythia tends to prove that the race migrated—in part at least—south-west, not south-east, and this would be the natural line of retreat before invaders from the east.

12 1 H. gives further evidence for Cimmerians in Scythia, partly archaeological, partly that of names: it is curious that 'Crimea' has survived all the other names for the land.

The *τείχεα* are perhaps the still surviving dyke on the isthmus of Taman, i. e. on the east side of the straits. Strabo (494) says there was once a town, Κιμμερικόν, 'closing the isthmus with a ditch and a dyke.' The 'straits' are those of Jenikale, the narrowest part of the Cimmerian Bosporus, leading into the Sea of Azov.

2 The connexion of the Cimmerians and Sinope is well authenticated, and seems to have been early. In the poem that is attributed to Scymnus of Chios (apparently written circ. 100 B.C.) they are said (l. 948) to have 'killed Habron the Milesian' there. The main Cimmerian raid in the seventh century is mentioned later (l. 952). According to the chronologers, Trapezus, the daughter state of Sinope, was founded 756 B.C.; but Busolt (i. 465–6) thinks the Milesian colonization of the Black Sea belongs to the seventh century, although they had factories there already in the eighth. He argues with reason that the Greek towns on the Black Sea must be later than the foundation of Byzantium (657 B.C.). The 'second' colonization of Sinope was dated 630. We may conclude that a band of Cimmerians occupied Sinope in the latter half of the eighth century; the main body of the nation reached Asia Minor half a century later.

13 1 **'Αριστέης.** H. confirms his own view against the Scyths, who claimed autochthony, by a reference to the 'Αριμάσπεα of Aristeas; the latter, however, makes the pressure of invasion come from the Issedones, i. e. from the north-east (not the east as H.). Aristeas seems to have embodied in this poem the earliest knowledge obtained by the settlers on the North Pontic shore. He is placed by H. (15. 1) in the first half of the seventh century, but Suidas makes him a contemporary of Croesus. This date is accepted in Pauly (*s. v.*), because his poem explained the Cimmerian invasion; but this fact is consistent with the early date. There is no need to deny his historic reality (as Crusius in Rosch. i. 2814), but his story has obviously been affected by cult stories of Apollo. For him cf. Pindar, fr. 271. His poem had perished by the time of Dionysius of Halicarnassus (Thuc. 23; vi. 864), but Tzetzes (Chil. vii. 690–1) quotes some lines supposed to be from it (as to the Arimaspi):

ἀφνειοὺς ἵπποισι, πολύρρηνας, πολυβούτας,
ὀφθαλμὸν δ' ἕν' ἕκαστος ἔχει χαρίεντι μετώπῳ.

ποιέων. H. emphasizes the poetic character of Aristeas. Cf. *φοιβόλαμπτος*.

γρῦπας. The 'griffins' are combined with the Arimaspi also by Aeschylus (P. V. 802–4), who calls them *ὀξύστομοι Ζηνὸς ἀκραγεῖς κύνες*. Two types of them may be distinguished; the more common has the head and wings of an eagle, the body of a lion; this type may be Hittite, but is found in Egypt as early as the eighteenth dynasty, and in prehistoric Greece (Perrot et Chipiez, vi. 831); the other type, the winged lion, is Chaldaean. This symbol was combined in Greek art, from the fifth century onwards, with the story here told by H. from Aristeas; in this story we have probably a double of that of the 'ants' (iii. 102), i. e. it is a traveller's tale as to the dangers of gold-getting in Central Asia.

The wide diffusion of this combination in later Greek art is good evidence of the popularity of H.'s work. Ctesias (Ind. 12, p. 250) transports the griffins to the north of India, and substitutes them for the 'ants' of H. (*u. s.*); it is characteristic of him that he describes them in detail, with 'white wings, red breast', &c. For the whole subject of 'griffins' cf. Furtwängler in Rosch. Lex. i. 1742 seq.

The gold of Central Asia is of course a fact, and the Arimaspi may well be a nomad tribe of Central Asia, who affirmed that their gold was derived from great deserts, e. g. that of Gobi; they may be the ancestors of the Turks and the Huns. They were credited with one eye as a mark of their wildness, on the analogy of the Cyclops; Strabo (21) puts the matter the other way and makes Homer 'borrow' the Cyclops from Scythia. Others see in them a purely fictitious people, a wild counterpart of the mild Hyperboreans. The name is explained by some 'dwellers in the deserts' (Rosch. *s. v.*), but Müllenhof (iii. 106) makes it 'having docile horses'. Pauly, ii. 827, translates it 'owners of wild horses'. H.'s etymology is no doubt that of the people of Olbia.

It is to the credit of H. that he does not believe in the 'one-eyed' (iii. 116. 2), and that he avoids such foolish rationalization as that of Eustathius, who said (G. G. M. ii. 223) the Arimaspi had one eye smaller than the other, because, being archers, they were continually closing one eye to shoot.

The whole legend is familiar in Milton's

> As when a gryphon through the wilderness
> Pursues the Arimaspian, who by stealth
> Had from his wakeful custody purloined
> The guarded gold. (P. L. ii. 943–7.)

πλὴν Ὑπερβορέων: because the Hyperboreans lived in perpetual peace. For them cf. 32 nn.

2 **νοτίῃ:** here the 'Black Sea' as contrasted with the sea to the north (cf. *ἐπὶ θάλασσαν* above); H. himself calls it 'the Northern Sea' in c. 37.

14–15 The story of Aristeas (also used by Pindar, fr. 271) is interesting from two points of view. (1) It seems to be connected with the Pythagorean theory of transmigration; Metapontum was near Croton, the special home of Pythagoreanism. (2) It shows H. at once as a traveller (15. 4 n.) and as a collator of various traditions.

14 2 Artaca (vi. 33. 2) lay to the west of Cyzicus, of which it was the seaport.

15 1 H.'s figure '240' is probably based on a calculation of generations.

2 **Μεταποντῖνοι.** The cult of Apollo at Metapontum is reflected in its coins (Head, H. N. p. 76, fig. 36); the god is shown as *δαφνηφόρος* or with a laurel tree before him (cf. *δάφναι ἑστᾶσι inf.*).

τότε: after 'his second disappearance' he had come to Italy. The 'raven' was sacred to Apollo (Ael. H. A. i. 48) as a prophetic bird (cf. Hor. Odes, iii. 27. 11 'oscen corvus', the 'crow').

3 **ἐς Δελφούς.** For Delphi as the controller of cults and canonizer cf. Farnell, G. C. iv. 206–8.

4 The *ἄγαλμα* is the 'altar' of § 2; H. clearly speaks as an eyewitness. One of the laurels at any rate was of brass (Theop. fr. 182; F. H. G. i. 309).

16–58 *H.'s account of the geography of Scythia.* In the middle of this is a digression on general geography (37–45). The first part (17–27) contains the ethnography; H. (16–20) gives the tribes from west to east, in each case adding the tribes inland as far as known; cf. the refrain *ὅσον ἡμεῖς ἴδμεν* at end of cc. 17, 18, 20. He then goes (21–2) from south to north. For the whole subject cf. App. XI, and cc. 102–17 nn., which should be read with cc. 17–27.

16 **αὐτόπτεω.** For the importance of 'eyewitnesses' cf. iii. 115. 2. H. is obviously sceptical whether Aristeas really got as far as he claimed 'in his poem'.

17 **Βορυσθενεϊτέων ἐμπορίου.** The 'mart of the Borysthenites' is Olbia, on the right bank of the Hypanis (*hod.* Boug), which flows into the same bay as the Dnieper. H.'s site (53. 6) has been confirmed by exploration. He calls it the 'city of the Borysthenites' (78. 3, 79. 2), but says that its own name for itself was Olbia (18. 1). This last point is confirmed by the coins (Head, H. N. 272). It was founded by the Milesians (78. 3) in 647 B.C., and was the oldest colony beyond the Danube. H. (101. 2) says the Borysthenes was ten days' journey from the Danube, and ten from the P. Maeotis, so it is *μεσαίτατον*.

Καλλιππίδαι: these 'Greek Scyths' were probably a mixed race (cf. Boeckh, C. I. G. ii. 2058 *μιξέλληνες* in a long psephism of Olbia probably dating about 100 B.C.). It may be doubted whether any of the Scyths but the 'Royal' tribe (c. 20) were pure-blooded. Rawlinson quotes interesting modern parallels for races in a similar transitional stage of civilization. Strabo (550) says that H. 'talked rubbish about' the Callippidae and the Alazones; but he says they were mentioned also by Hellanicus.

σῖτον. For the importance of the Pontic corn trade cf. Demos. in Lept. 31 seq. (with Sandys' notes), L. Gernet, L'Approvisionnement d'Athènes (1909; pp. 315 seq.), and Grundy, Thuc. pp. 74 f., 159 f.

18 1 Ὑλαίη. The region on the left bank of the lower Dnieper was once well wooded—at least in comparison to most of South Russia (cf. 109. 2 for woods among Budini), the bareness of which H. well describes (c. 19). Dio Chrys. (Or. 36) compares the trees of the Hylaea to 'masts of ships'. Neumann, H. S. (pp. 82 seq.) quotes Rubruquis in the thirteenth century and others to prove there were once forests in South Russia, where now there are none: he sums up 'the steppes are gradually encroaching; their desolation in the Middle Ages was less complete than it is to-day, and following the same law, we can maintain that it had advanced even less in Classical times'.

γεωργοί. The distinction between the 'husbandmen Scyths' and the 'ploughmen Scyths' (c. 17) lies in the fact that the latter grew corn only to sell, the former practised husbandry generally. In 53. 4, H., perhaps following a different informant, gives them 'ten days'' extent; probably they reached as far as the rapids of the Dnieper.

3 For the Androphagi cf. c. 106 n.

19 τεσσέρων καὶ δέκα. In 101. 2 (see n.) the whole distance from the Borysthenes to the P. Maeotis is 'ten days'; here part of it is 'fourteen'. For the inconsistency cf. App. XI. 3.

20 1 βασιλήια. Strabo (311) says the royal Scyths levied 'fixed moderate tributes'. The position of the Golden Horde among the Mongols is a parallel.

τάφρον. For 'the trench' cf. 3. 1 n.; for Cremni 110. 2 n.

2 πρὸς βορέην. Stein points out that the cultivating Scyths really bounded the royal Scyths on the north; but H. does not know of the great bends of the Dnieper and the Don. Really his eastern frontier line for the 'royal Scyths', i.e. the Trench, P. Maeotis, and Tanais, ran north-east and not due north as he conceives it. For the Melanchlaeni cf. c. 107 n.

21–5 *The tribes north-east of Scythia.* As to the general geography it may be noted: (1) H. claims, and with reason, to speak from knowledge as far as 'the Bald men' (24. 1). This was no doubt derived from the merchants using the north-east trade route, which ran across the steppes into Central Asia. This was superseded under the Roman empire by that *via* Trebizond (Beazley, Dawn of G. i. 179), but used in the Middle Ages, e.g. by Carpini *c.* 1250 (*ib.* ii. 296 f.). (2) H. knows the route is north by east (cf. 22. 1, 3 ἀποκλίνοντι πρὸς τὴν ἠῶ), but wrongly thinks it mainly north. (3) H. here knows nothing of the Volga (cf. 124. 1 n.), and his mountains (25. 1) seem to be a confusion of the Ural and the Altai; their distance would correspond to the Ural, but they run east and west (25. 1 n.) as the Altai Mountains do; perhaps H., though disbelieving in the fabulous Rhipaean Mountains, has allowed himself to be misled by their supposed position, east and west. It may be taken as certain that his informants knew nothing of the mountains except as something to be avoided. (4) His description of the 'black earth belt' (23. 1) is accurate (for it cf. E. B.[11] xxiii. 881).

Westberg (Klio, iv. 183 seq.) identifies his tribes thus:

(1) The Sauromatae extend from the Manitch, a tributary on the left bank of the Don, to Kamischin on Volga in south of the Saratov province. (2) The Budini are in the Saratov province as far north as Syzran; an Arab geographer of the tenth century describes this country as well wooded (cf. c. 21 *δασέαν*). (3) The desert north of Budini (22. 1) in the region of the Singelei hills on right bank of Volga, near Simbirsk. (4) The route then turns east (23. 1), up the valley of the Kama; the Thyssagetae (c. 22) live on the R. Bielaya nearly to the *southern* Ural. (5) The Argippaei live in the 'foot hills' (23. 2) south of the Ural, while beyond the Ural on the south-east (25. 2) are the Issedones, north-east of Caspian; cf. i. 201, the Massagetae live 'opposite the Issedones', with the Araxes (i. e. Sir Daria or Jaxartes) between them. H. then is consistent at once with himself and with fact.

As Ptolemy, however, puts the Issedones in Central Asia, Tomaschek violently transfers all the tribes far to the east, puts the Argippaei under the Altai, and conjectures that the Hyperboreans are the Chinese (Meyer, iii. 65, accepts generally Tomaschek's views).

21 The *μυχός* is the 'recess' into which the Don runs. In c. 57 it is P. Maeotis which divides Scyths and Sauromatae (cf. 117 nn.). From this it is usually concluded (cf. Stein, Macan, in their maps) that H. made the P. Maeotis run due north and south; but this inference is quite needless, and it makes H.'s account of Darius' campaign hopelessly inconsistent (cf. 101. 3 n.) with itself. For the Sauromatae cf. c. 107 n., for the Budini c. 108. 1 n.

22 1 **Θυσσαγέται.** Some connect the names of Thyssagetae and Massagetae, and connect both with the Getae and with the Goths (e.g. Humboldt). But this is guessing. The Thyssagetae and the Iyrkae may perhaps be Finns; they (like the Finns, Tac. Germ. 46) are in the lowest stage of civilization, mere hunters. The name *Ὄαρος* (c. 123) may well be Finnish 'Rhau' (Müllenhof, iii. 15-17). There are still Finns (Mordvinians) on the Volga near Samara.

3 **ἀποστάντες.** These Scyths, if a reality, were more probably a remnant left behind than a revolting tribe.

23 2 **φαλακροί.** The 'bald' men seem to be a Calmuck tribe; they resemble this race in their flat noses (*σιμοί*) and 'large chins', and in the scantiness of their hair; but Rawlinson denies the resemblance. Bunbury (i. 197) maintains that the shaven sacerdotal caste has been confused with the whole people, and urges their 'sacredness' (§ 5) as a proof of this. Others see in their peacefulness a merchants' truce (so Westberg, *u. s.*).

H. here applies three of the four anthropological criteria of race (cf. viii. 144. 2 n.). The Argippaei are marked off as a distinct people by physical features (i. e. 'descent') and by 'language'; but the evidence of 'custom' is various; while they have a Scyth dress, their food is different from the Scythian, cf. Myres, A. and C. p. 135. The criterion of 'religion' is not used here (contrast viii. 144. 2).

3 **ἄσχυ.** The 'Ponticum' is the wild cherry, the use of which by the Calmucks is exactly described by H.: the very name 'atchi' (= 'acid') survives among the Tartars (Reinach, A. R. M. p. 196).

4 **ὑπὸ δενδρέῳ.** For a tree used as a tent-pole cf. Tac. Germ. 46.

24 **δι' ἑπτὰ ἑρμηνέων.** The 'seven interpreters' are an interesting trace of the old trade-route; H. gives only five tribes, or six with the Geloni (c. 108). For the mixed populations of South-east Europe cf. Pliny's (N. H. vi. 15) story of '130 interpreters' at Dioscurias.

25 1 **ἑξάμηνον.** For H.'s scepticism cf. iv. 191 *ad fin.* The 'six months'' sleep is a confused tradition of the perpetual night of the polar winter. Rawlinson (iii. 207), however, refers it to the severity of a Russian winter, requiring an indoor life for six months.

2 As the mountains 'separate' the 'bald' men from the unknown region, and as they lie to the north of both the 'bald' and the Issedones, who are further east (§ 2), the mountains are conceived as running east and west (cf. 21. 1 n). Rawlinson wrongly puts the 'mountains' between the 'bald' and the Issedones.

26 **δαῖτα προτίθενται.** Among the Indian Callatiae also the dead are eaten (iii. 38. 4); but among the Massagetae (i. 216. 2) and the Indian Padaei (iii. 99. 1) death is anticipated. Possibly the variations of the accounts are due to the fancy of H. (e. g. the grim humour of iii. 99. 1); but we may trace in the custom three different ideas. (1) The desire to partake of the merits of the dead by eating him (cf. Frazer, G. B. ii[1]. 89), which is prominent in this passage; (2) the desire to give an honourable end (i. 216. 3; iii. 38); (3) the attempt to crush the spirit of decay before it becomes powerful (iii. 99). Of these (1) and (3) are inconsistent, but genuine pieces of savage thought, (2) is perhaps only a Greek explanation of a barbarous custom.

For the eating of dead relatives cf. in ancient times Onesicritus (the pilot of Alexander, in Strabo 710; Strabo rejects the story with contempt), as to the tribes of the Caucasus; in mediaeval times, M. Polo (iii. 10; vol. ii, 293, 298) as to Sumatra. In modern times instances are quoted from the neighbourhood of New Guinea (Wallace) and from India. This last is the cannibalism of the Birhors in Chota Nagpore, as late as 1863 (J. A. S. B. xxxiv, pt. ii, p. 18); but Dalton, who originally recorded it, says in his Ethnology of Bengal, p. 220 (1872), 'I have no faith in the story,' i. e. he thinks either he or the natives had misunderstood each other. This self-correction in a trained observer may make us sympathize with mistakes in H., who was not a trained observer. For cannibalism generally cf. Sollas (Anc. Hunt, p. 145); he says that it is often practised simply from a taste for human flesh.

2 **κεφαλήν.** Cf. the treatment of the skulls of enemies by the Scyths (c. 65), and for a similar custom among the Boii, Livy xxiii. 24, among the Lombards, Gibbon, v. 12.

γενέσια: the feast of the dead, on the anniversary of death, as opposed to the *γενέθλια* 'the birthday feast' (Ammonius, de Diff. Voc. p. 35).

ἰσοκρατέες. The reference here is probably not to a system of primitive matriarchy, but to the fact that, in a low state of civilization, men and women alike have to hunt, &c.; cf. Tac. Germ. 46.

28 1 **δυσχείμερος.** The Greeks naturally, from contrast with their own, exaggerated the terrors of the Pontic winter (cf. our own use of 'Siberian'). Hippocrates (De Aere, 19) makes it worse than H.: 'cold winds always blow from the north from the Rhipaean Mountains; mist thickly covers the plains, so that it is always winter, and the summer lasts but a few days.'

θάλασσα. This is especially the case with the 'limans', the estuaries of the rivers; but the sea itself freezes in the Gulf of Odessa during January (Bonmariage, Russie d'Europe, 1903, pp. 125–6); cf. Strabo (307) for the freezing of the Bosporus, and Ovid, Tristia, iii. 10, 31 (of the Danube mouths):

Quaque rates ierant pedibus nunc itur, et undas
Frigore concretas ungula pulsat equi.

στρατεύονται, 'pass in hordes.' The 'wagons' imply peaceful communications; Strabo, 307, says that every winter *ἁμαξεύεται ὁ διάπλους* from Panticapaeum to Phanagoria.

The **Sindi** occupied the peninsula on the east side of the Bosporus and the adjoining coast to the south-east; cf. *ἡ Σινδική*, 86. 3.

2 **ψύχεα.** This is a mistake; the summers are intensely hot.

The dative with *χωρίζω* is very unusual; cf. vii. 70. 1 *διαλλάσσοντες τοῖσι ἑτέροισι.*

τὴν . . . ὡραίην, 'in the proper season.' H. as usual is eager to see a contrast; the winter was the wet season elsewhere, the summer in Scythia. This last remark was more true, no doubt, in his day, when the coast strip, the region he knew personally, was well wooded (cf. 'The Woodland', 18. 1 n.); but even now the wettest months are in the summer, and their maximum rainfall is three times as great as the minimum fall, which is in the winter (for tables cf. Bonmariage, *u. s.* p. 264).

3 **ἦμος**: i. e. in spring and autumn, when thunderstorms are frequent in Greece.

σεισμός. H. is right as to the rarity of earthquakes in South Russia; cf. Montessus de Ballore, Les Tremblements de Terre (Paris, 1906, p. 102 and Map).

4 ἵπποι. The hardihood of the Cossack ponies is well known; in Greece and Asia Minor horses were rare and carefully tended (hence their liability to 'frost-bite'), while the hard work was done by mules and asses. Cf. for the absence of the latter in Scythia 129. 2 n.

29 κόλον = ἄκερων; cf. Tac. Germ. 5 'ne armentis quidem gloria frontis'. The fact is right that the South Russian cattle have short horns, but H.'s attempt to give a scientific explanation, though interesting, is refuted by the huge horns of reindeer and elk. H. uses Homer (e.g. Od. iv. 85) as our ancestors used the Bible, to prove everything. (Cf. Introd. p. 21.)

30 προσθήκας. H.'s artless confession of his tendency to 'digress' is amusing. The fact that mules were not born in Elis is vouched for by Plut. Mor. p. 303 and Paus. v. 5. 2. It was said to be due to the 'curse' of Oenomaus, whose love of horses made him object to cross-breeds.

31 1 πτερῶν. The reference to the heavy snow is another (cf. 25. 1) echo of tradition from the far north.

2 μακρότατα, with τὰ λέγεται, 'which are said as to the remotest parts'; for τὰ μακρότατα cf. ii. 32. 3. The sentence sums up briefly what H. had already said in c. 16; the μέν marks the contrast to the Hyperborean story that follows, which is a mere myth.

32–6 *The Hyperboreans.*

The Hyperboreans were so established in Greek traditional geography that H. feels bound to discuss them; but he argues that the legend as to them is not native but Greek.

The earliest mention of them is in the Homeric Hymn to Dionysus (vii. 28–9), dated by Sikes and Allen in the seventh or sixth century B.C.,

ἔλπομαι ἢ Αἴγυπτον ἀφίξεται ἢ ὅ γε Κύπρον
ἢ ἐς Ὑπερβορέους ἢ ἑκαστέρω,

where their name is equivalent to 'the ends of the earth'. We may assume that H. found it used in this sense in 'Hesiod' and in the 'Epigoni', though these works have both perished. If so, the popular etymology of their name, 'those beyond the north wind,' goes back at least to the seventh century. It is difficult therefore to see in them early *Greek* worshippers of Apollo in Thessaly and other northern parts of Greece (as Farnell, C.G.S. iv. 100 seq.); the first evidence for this view is a fragment of Hecataeus, who seems to identify them with the Locrians (Schol. to Apoll. Rhod. ii. 675). It is supported by the explanation of the name as = ὑπέρφοροι (cf. Περφερέες, 33. 3), i.e. the sacred 'carriers' of offerings (cf. c. 33 n.). But it is better to suppose the Hyperboreans an imaginary people, the northern counterpart of the blameless Ethiopians of the south (iii. 17. 1 n.). As geographical knowledge increased, their home was shifted further and further away (for references *vid.* Farnell, *u. s.*). Pindar (Ol. iii. 16) puts them on the Danube; then they were associated (by Damastes, a younger contemporary of H., fr. 1, F. H. G. ii. 65) with the imaginary Rhipaean Mountains, from which the north wind blew; Hippocrates (de Aer. 19) and even Aristotle (Meteor. i. 13, 350 b) accept these mountains as a reality. Later we find the Hyperboreans in an island, 'opposite the Celts,' which seems to be Britain (Hec. Abd. fr. 2, F. H. G. ii. 386); and finally, in the eleventh century A. D., they were identified with the Scandinavians.

The Hyperboreans were credited with all the virtues, including vegetarianism (just as, even as late as the eighteenth century A. D., Linnaeus thought the Lapps were free from all the vices of civilization and that they lived to be over 100 years old); they were especially connected with the worship of Apollo (c. 33 nn., Pind. Pyth. x. 30, and Bacchyl. iii. 59), and so identified with the Delphians by Mnaseas, a pupil of Eratosthenes (fr. 24, F. H. G. iii. 153).

H.'s refutation of the Hyperborean myth may be an attack on Hecataeus; Diodorus (ii. 47) found it in the works bearing his name, especially the story of Abaris (c. 36 n.). It is needless, as is usually done, to refer this passage in Diodorus to Hecataeus of Abdera.

δοκέω: the argument is, Aristeas might have got his story of the Hyperboreans from the Issedones (13. 1); but this is improbable, as the Scyths know nothing of the Hyperboreans, though they repeat the rest of the Issedones' story (c. 27).

The 'Epigoni' was the sequel of the Thebais; Pausanias (ix. 9. 2) ranked it, after the Iliad and the Odyssey, as the best of the Cyclic poems.

33 1 **Δήλιοι.** The following points may be noticed in the Delian story: (1) H.'s source is obviously the hymn (35. 1) as well as the temple tradition; he is familiar with the shrine (34. 2, 35. 4), and compares the ritual with what he has seen in Thrace (33. 5). (2) The offerings were wrapped in straw not only as packing material, but to shield their sanctity. No doubt such offerings came to Delos regularly from the states of which it was the religious centre (for Delos cf. vi. 97. 1 n. and Jebb, Essays). (3) With these ritual connexions has been combined the tradition of one of the oldest trade-routes of Europe, the 'Amber route', from the northern end of the Adriatic, near which the Alps are lowest, down the coast, and then from Dodona across to the Malian Gulf. The Greek stages are given carefully, but the northern ones are unknown, and in their place (regardless of geography) are inserted the Hyperboreans, who were far to the north-east, but who were especially connected with Apollo. This route is dated by A. J. Evans (Freeman, Sicily, iv. 220–1) as early as 1,000 B.C.; for a brief account of it cf.

Tozer, Geog. pp. 31 seq.; he points out that amber also reached the Mediterranean through Gaul by the Rhone valley, at least as early as the time of Pytheas (fourth century), and possibly even before the foundation of Massilia. (4) The common tendency to duplicate beginnings (cf. the Spartan kings, who are not Eurysthenidae and Proclidae, but Agiadae and Eurypontidae) is clearly seen; probably both pairs of maidens are personified attributes of divinity (*v.i.*). (5) The tradition is also given in Callimachus (Hymn. Del. 283), who follows H., and in Pausanias (i. 31. 2), who, however, following an Attic tradition (probably dating from the time of Athenian control of Delos), brings the offerings by an eastern route *via* the Arimaspi, the Issedones, and Sinope to Prasiae in Attica, 'where there is a shrine of Apollo'; cf. also Plut. Mor. 1136.

Ἀδρίην. Probably the road passed Apollonia; for connexion of this with Delphi cf. ix. 93–4.

2 **πόλιν ἐς πόλιν**: communication by land in early times is always preferred to that by sea; this Bérard calls 'Loi des Isthmes' (Les Phén. dans l'Odys. i. 69–78). It may well be that the 'sacred way' to Delos lay on both sides of the Euripus, for, beside the Euboic route implied by H., there was a shrine of Apollo at Delium, and his oldest shrine in Attica was in the Marathonian Tetrapolis, which was especially connected with the *θεωρία* to Delos (Schol. to Oed. Col. 1047).

ἐκλιπεῖν: intrans., 'is passed over'; Andros was the home of a different cult, that of Dionysus.

3 **Ὑπερόχην τ. κ. λ.** The names seem epithets of Artemis; cf. Phylacus and Autonous at Delphi, attributes personified of Apollo at Delphi (viii. 39). The 'Perpherees' were obviously officials at Delos. Hesychius explains the name = *θεωροί*.

34 **κείρονται.** Cf. the yearly mourning for Jephthah's daughter, Judges xi. 40. Pausanias (i. 43. 4) calls the maidens *Ἑκαέργη* and *Ὦπις*, and compares this custom to the dedication at Megara of maiden's hair to Iphinoe. For the dedication of hair before marriage cf. ii. 65. 4 n. and Frazer, Paus. iii. 279; for the same in mourning, *ib.* iv. 136.

35 1 **Ἄργην . . . Ὦπιν.** 'The bright' and the 'seeing one' are obviously epithets of Artemis.

2 **ταύτας**: i. e. Hyperoche and Laodice.

ὠκυτόκου: i. e. for the 'quick delivery' of Latona; Pausanias (i. 18. 5) brings Eileithuia from the Hyperboreans to help Latona.

3 **ἀγείρειν** is especially used of 'gathering sacred gifts' (cf. *ἀγύρτης*), but = 'begging' in general; it is as old as Homer (Od. xvii. 362). Pausanias (ix. 27. 2) makes Olen the oldest of Greek hymn writers, and (x. 5. 4), quoting a Delphic tradition, a Hyperborean. As connected with Apollo, he comes from Lycia. The fact that his hymns were in hexameters dates him about the eighth century, if he be a real person at all.

4 **πρὸς ἠῶ.** For variations in burial positions cf. Plut. Sol. 10; the cult here was pre-Ionian, for the Ionians placed their dead facing west (*ib.*).

36 H. rejects without discussion the story of Abaris (cf. 32 n.), who was made by Pindar (Harpoc. *s. v.* Abaris) a contemporary of Croesus. Later writers (e.g. Porphyry v. Pythag. 29) made the 'arrow' serve him like a witch's broomstick, on which he sailed through the air over rivers and seas.

εἰ δέ εἰσι. H. sums up his argument against the Hyperboreans with a *reductio ad absurdum*; symmetry would require us to believe in 'Hypernotians' also; but this is neither asserted (nor possible on account of extreme heat?). Therefore there are no Hyperboreans. Eratosthenes (Strabo 61–2) not unnaturally called H.'s argument 'absurd'. It is curious to see H. appealing to the very symmetry which three lines later he denounces. The reference to Hecataeus is clear (cf. c. 32 n.); Aristotle (Meteor. ii. 5, 362 b 12) repeats H. almost verbally here, but gives a different reason for rejecting 'the round world'.

2 **γράψαντας,** 'drawing' (cf. *γραφήν inf.*). H. has in his mind some early map (Berger, E. G. p. 36, argues that it is that of Anaximander; cf. v. 49. 1), in which the world was a perfect circle, with a circumambient ocean for its rim, 'as if drawn with a pair of compasses.' Such had been the conception of Hecataeus (cf. ii. 21 n.), who brought the Argonauts from the Phasis *via* the ocean stream and the Nile back to the Mediterranean (F. H. G. i. 13, fr. 187).

οὐδένα . . . ἐξηγησάμενον, 'explaining it (the shape of the world) sensibly,' *vid. sup.* Hecataeus' fault was double: (*a*) his world-map was purely *a priori*; (*b*) he made no effort to co-ordinate his mass of geographical details in a rational scheme.

There is another protest against symmetry in *ὡς ἀπὸ τόρνου*; Europe is far larger than Asia (including Libya) to H. (iv. 42. 1), but the map-makers made them balance equally.

37–45 H. gives a specimen of what in his opinion geography should be: (1) He describes the distribution of peoples in West Asia (cc. 37–40). He has been criticized for making no reference to the numerous tribes mentioned, iii. 90 seq.; but this would have been quite out of place in a general sketch. (2) He then gives the boundaries of the continents (cc. 41–5), and discusses the division. In this part he gives an account of three great voyages, undertaken to settle definitely the boundaries of Asia and Africa. (For H.'s geography cf. App. XIII.)

37 For the Erythraean Sea cf. i. 1. 1 n.; for the Saspeires, iii. 94. 1 n. The four countries form a line from north to south, which divides, for H., Eastern from Western Asia, and forms the base of both *ἀκταί*. The Phasis is part of the boundary between Europe and Asia (cf. 45. 2).

38 1 ἀκταί. The English word most nearly corresponding is 'peninsula', as we use it of Spain or of Scandinavia. Asia Minor really is an ἀκτή, especially to H. who thought its eastern boundary much narrower than it actually is (i. 72. 3 n.). But he seems to have conceived (c. 39) of the rest of Western Asia as a similar projection (cf. Bunbury, i. 207). It is easy to see that H. had no accurate maps.

2 Φάσιος. H. obviously put this too far south, in the corner of the Black Sea.

The **Hellespont** here includes all the narrow seas, from the Bosporus to Sigeum, at the entrance of the Hellespont; cf. 95. 1, 138. 2; v. 103. 2; vi. 26. 1, 33. 1; this sense is familiar in the 'Hellespontine' division of the Athenian tribute. In i. 57. 2 and vii. 137. 3 'Hellespont' = 'the Sea of Marmora'. Ἑλλησπόντιοι is usually, if not always, used by H. in the wider sense; cf. iii. 90. 2; iv. 89. 2; v. 1. 1; vii. 95. 2.

The 'Myriandian Gulf' is the modern Bay of Issus. The 'Triopian Cape' is the south-west corner of Asia Minor, near Cnidus (cf. i. 144. 1).

τριήκοντα. There are thirty-three nations in H.'s two lists together (iii. 90 seq.; vii. 70 seq.), thirty in each of them singly.

39 H. knows nothing of the modern Persian Gulf or of the shape of Arabia. His 'Assyria' consists of the basins of the Euphrates and Tigris below Armenia (i. 178. 1 n.), and his 'Arabia' includes the southern part of the desert as well as Arabia proper.

νόμῳ. It only ends 'conventionally', because Libya is really a continuation (41. 1). For the canal cf. ii. 158 n.; for the Arabian Gulf (= 'the Red Sea') cf. i. 1. 1 n.

2 διὰ τῆσδε, 'this sea' as usual = the Mediterranean.

ἐς τὴν τελευτᾷ. The words 'in which it ends' are ambiguous as to Egypt, as is also 41. 1. H., however, seems by coupling Egypt with Syria to put them both in Asia; cf. also 41. 1 n. On the other hand, he does not count the Egyptians in this ἀκτή (*v. i.*); and in 41. 2 he clearly makes Africa begin at the Isthmus of Suez. In ii. 17. 1 he makes the boundaries of Asia and Libya those of Egypt, but does not say to which continent it belongs. On the whole it is more probable that H. gave Egypt to Africa, but many, e.g. Tozer, A. G. p. 82, maintain the contrary; but as he thought Africa a continuation of the ἀκτή of Asia, the exact position of Egypt seemed to him of little importance.

τρία. The three nations are Assyria and Arabia with Phoenicia, not with Persia (as Macan); Persia is the base of the ἀκτή, not part of it.

40 παρήκει governs τὰ δὲ κατύπερθε . . . Κόλχων, with τὰ πρὸς . . . ἀνατέλλοντα as an accus. of respect. For the Araxes cf. i. 202. 1 n.; for the Caspian 203. 1 n.

41 ἀπό might be inclusive or exclusive (cf. 39. 2 n.), but with ἐκδέκεται the latter sense is the more natural (cf. 99. 1).

χίλιοι. For the measurement, '1,000 stades,' cf. ii. 158. 4 n.

42 1 παρ' ἀμφοτέρας. H. reckons all Northern Asia, so far as he knows it, to Europe. The greater knowledge of the moderns reverses his arrangement; Stanford (quoted by Macan) says 'Europe is after all only a peninsula of Asia'.

εὔρεος. The continents cannot (H. thinks) be compared, for the northern boundaries of Europe are unknown, and therefore it is far broader, while the southern boundaries of Asia and of Africa had been rounded by Scylax (c. 44) and by the Phoenicians (*v. i.*).

2 ἀπέπεμψε. On this famous voyage cf. Bunbury, i. 289 seq., 317 (who leaves the question open), E. J. Webb, E. H. R., Jan. 1907 (strongly adverse), and H. Berger, pp. 62–5, who formerly rejected the story, but now 'reserves a final judgement till circumstances are more favourable'. The arguments for its truth are: (1) The time is adequate. (2) The currents would be favourable all the way, while on the east coast the voyage would be assisted by the north monsoon, and in the west by the south trade-wind. (3) The circumstance disbelieved by H. is a strong confirmation; the sun (not 'the sunrise') in the southern hemisphere would actually be 'on the right', so long as they sailed west, and from the Equator to the Cape of Good Hope the course would be south-west and then west, while on the return journey it would be slightly north-west. (4) The voyage was undertaken for a practical purpose, to facilitate communication between Mediterranean and Red Seas; as its result was useless for this purpose it was forgotten, just as the discovery of America by the Northmen in the eleventh century was forgotten till the nineteenth. On the other hand: (1) Later geographers rejected the story, e.g. Posidonius (Strabo, 98), Strabo (*ib.*), Polybius (iii. 37); the last-named doubted if the sea were continuous round Africa, and Aristotle (Meteor. ii. 1, 354 a) also denied its continuity. (2) It is strange that H. tells no stories of the marvels of the South, of the change of seasons, &c. [But this argument is of little value.] (3) The change in the position of the sun was an easy guess for any one who had seen the vertical sun at Syene. (4) Exaggeration was easy; so the voyage of Hanno, who perhaps reached as far as Sierra Leone (Bunbury, i. 318 seq.), is represented by Pliny (ii. 67. 169) as having been extended to Arabia. (But Pliny's inaccurate and contradictory statements are no parallel to H.'s plain and straightforward narrative.) On the whole it seems best to accept the story, as Meyer (iii. 60) unhesitatingly does.

In 1906 two scarabs were communicated to the French Academy, which professed to commemorate this circumnavigation; it was soon shown, however, by the Berlin Egyptologists that they were forgeries.

τὴν βορηίην: the Mediterranean; for the 'Pillars' cf. ii. 33. 3 n.

3 H. conceives the mariners as observing the same seasons as at home; there would be two harvests. But if the statement is a fact at

all, it is obvious that the sowing would be determined on other grounds than a Mediterranean calendar. Cf. for these harvests on the way, the plans of Eudoxus for the same circumnavigation (Strabo 100).

43 1 **οἱ λέγοντες**, not 'that they had sailed round it', but that 'it could be sailed round' (*περίρρυτος* 42. 2). Unluckily H. gives no details as to Carthaginian testimony; the voyage of Hanno (*v. s.*) was probably about fifty years before his birth (cf. vii. 165), but H. never mentions it. The causal connexion is odd: (I mention them) 'because Sataspes failed'.

2 Probably the **Zopyrus** of iii. 153 seqq., whose grandson deserted to Athens (iii. 160) and may well have told H. this and other stories (cf. J. H. S. xxvii. 37 seq.). H. probably had heard this story also in Samos (§ 7).

For the use of criminals for dangerous voyages cf. the English usage from the sixteenth to the eighteenth centuries, e.g. Doyle, English in America, i. 61, 71.

4 For C. Soloeis cf. ii. 32. 4 n.

5 **σμικρούς**: for the 'dwarfs wearing dresses of palm', ii. 32. 6 n.

6 **ἐνίσχεσθαι.** No doubt his vessel was stopped by the south trade-wind (*v. s.*). It may be noted to H.'s credit that he tells us nothing of the 'masses of mud and seaweed' ('Scylax' 112), with which Greek imagination or Carthaginian trade-jealousy blocked the navigation of the Atlantic.

7 **ἐπιλήθομαι**: cf. i. 51. 4 for similar forbearance; this chapter is a good instance of the way in which H. pieces together different stories.

44 1 **κροκοδείλους.** Crocodiles were thought especially to belong to the Nile (cf. Arr. Anab. vi. 1. 2); this is one of the reasons why H. confuses Niger and Nile (ii. 32. 7 n.).

Καρυανδέα. Scylax was a neighbour of H., for Caryanda is an island off Caria. The work which goes by his name is probably of the fourth century, and is almost entirely concerned with the Mediterranean; it says nothing of the Indian Ocean (Bunbury, i. 384 seq.). Aristotle (Pol. vii. 14. 3, 1332 b) quotes Scylax as to the Indians. His voyage may be dated about 509 B.C.

2 **Pactyice** (with **Caspatyrus**) is mentioned in iii. 102. 1 as bordering the north of India. Stein identifies it with North-east Afghanistan; the Afghans still call themselves 'Pakhtun' or 'Pashtun' (cf. 'Pathans'); he makes Caspatyrus = Kabul, preferring the form *Κασπάπυρος* (Hec. fr. 179; F. H. G. i. 12); H., he thinks, confuses the Kabul tributary with the Indus main stream, and so makes (wrongly) the Indus 'flow east'; this view is shared by Brunnhofer, Urg. Ari. i. 54. But the Kabul river is unnavigable. Wilson makes *Κασπάτυρος* = city of Casyapa, i.e. Kashmir, which once included much of the Punjaub (Ariana, p. 137); but this seems impossible.

Scylax probably started down the Indus from just above Attock, which lies at the junction of the Indus and the Kabul, about 200 miles almost due east of the town of Kabul; H.'s informant confused the main city of the district with the exact starting-point on the Indus. There is no need to doubt this voyage; H. writes of it from contemporary evidence, and his statement is confirmed by the fragments of Darius' inscriptions on his Nile canal (ii. 158. 1 n.). It is to be noted that he tells of no impossibilities, like the later fiction of Patrocles' voyage round into the Caspian (Pliny, N. H. vi. 58). Berger, however (pp. 73–5), is very doubtful of the reality of Scylax' voyage because of (1) H.'s mistake as to the course of the Indus (*v. i.*). (2) His ignorance of the Persian Gulf; a coasting voyage up this would have brought Scylax nearly to Susa, whence a new voyage was necessary to bring him to the Red Sea. H. makes it only *one* voyage. [But probably Scylax never went into the Persian Gulf at all; his coasting voyage would bring him to a Persian port at the Isle of Ormuz, thence he would sail across the Straits of Ormuz and resume his voyage to the south and west. This course is so obvious that it was not definitely recorded.] (3) Arrian (Ind. 19 seq., Anab. vii. 20) knows nothing of the voyage of Scylax [but Posidonius (Strabo 100) believed in it], and tells us Alexander's seamen failed to get round into the Red Sea. Myres (G. J., 1896, 623) conjectures the 'Indian river' to be the Ganges, and that 'an expedition . . . doubled C. Comorin, a voyage for which thirty months is not too long, though it is too long for a journey home from the mouth of the Indus'.

3 For the conquest of the Indians cf. iii. 94. 2 n.

ὅμοια. The south of Asia like the south of Africa has been explored, unlike Europe (45. 1); the two voyages correspond; one takes more than two years (42. 4), the other 'thirty months'. The anacoluthon *παρεχομένη* is noticeable.

45 1 For the ignorance of Europe cf. iii. 115. 1 n., for its 'length' 42. 1 n.

2 **οὐνόματα τριφάσια.** For the continents cf. App. XIII. 5; there seems a trace of Greek contempt for women here and elsewhere in this chapter (e.g. *εἰ μὴ ἀπὸ τῆς Τυρίης* (§ 4)), which makes it clear how completely the real meanings of 'Asia' and 'Europe' were forgotten in H.'s time. 'Asia' is first used in Pindar (Ol. vii. 34), but the adjective in the well-known *Ἀσίῳ ἐν λειμῶνι Καϋστρίου ἀμφὶ ῥέεθρα* of Il. ii. 461; 'Asius' is also the name of two Trojans. 'Europe' occurs first in Hymn to Apollo, 250–1 (cf. 290–1), where it is used of the Greek mainland, as opposed to Peloponnese and the 'seagirt islands'. The names seem to be derived from the Assyrian, 'açu' and 'irib' (perhaps cf. *ἔρεβος*), i.e. the 'rising' and the 'setting', and no doubt reached the Greeks through the Lydian traders (cf. § 3); we may perhaps compare the Assyrian names among the early Lydian kings (i. 7. 2 nn.).

No doubt 'Asia' and 'Europe' were first used of the opposite shores of the Aegean, and gradually extended, with the spread of geographical knowledge, to their respective hinterlands (cf. Kiepert, Anc. Geog. i. 17, E. T.).

οὐρίσματα. H. is here giving the ordinary 'boundaries' which he does not accept (ii. 16, 17 nn.).

οἱ δέ: making the boundary run north and south. As H. is quoting he calls the Tanais 'Maeotic' here (and nowhere else).

3 **γυναικός.** Others make Prometheus the son of Asia.

Ἀσίεω. One branch of the mythical royal family of Lydia; cf. i. 94. 3 n. for the other.

φυλὴν Ἀσιάδα. H. uses the evidence of institutions in an almost modern way.

4 For Europa cf. i. 2. 1; she came 'to Lycia from Crete' with her son Sarpedon.

5 **νομιζομένοισι.** The threefold division was already 'established' and H. therefore follows it, in spite of what he thinks to be its absurdities.

46–58 H. seems about to begin the story of Darius' campaign, but the mention of the nomadic habits of the Scyths leads to a further digression on the great rivers, in which feature, so favourable to commerce, H., like a true Greek, is especially interested (cf. c. 82 for his emphasis on their importance), all the more so because Greece had no such rivers. It may be noted generally that (1) H. is fairly accurate as to the lower courses of the rivers as far as the Dnieper, but that beyond the Dnieper his account is unrecognizable and full of difficulties. (2) That with regard to their sources, he ignores the fabled Rhipaean Mountains, which even Aristotle (Meteor. i. 13, 350 b) made the source of the Russian rivers (cf. 32 nn.); but his lakes, from which he derives six of his rivers, are equally theoretical (57. 2 n.). The rivers really rise in great swamps; but probably in H.'s days these may have been more like shallow lakes. Cf. Krapotkin, Geog. Journ. xxiii. 725. Réclus (v. 284–5) describes the shrinking of the water-area: except the rivers of Finland, all the great watercourses of Russia have 'vidé les anciens lacs de leur bassin et constitué leur individualité fluviale'; but this process had begun with 'the disappearance of the Ice Age'.

1 **ἀμαθέστατα.** H. rejects the 'noble savage' theory which the Greeks tended to hold about the peoples of the North (cf. 2. 1 n.). The exception made by H. in favour of the Scyths is due to Anacharsis (c. 76), and is tacitly contradicted by Thucydides (ii. 97. 6).

ἐντός: not 'west of' (Stein) but 'in the region of'.

2 For the subjunctives *ᾖ*, *ἔωσι* after the relative *τοῖσι* without *ἄν* cf. i. 216. 1 and Goodwin, § 540.

3 **ἱπποτοξόται.** It is curious that no representation of a 'horse archer' has been found on the Scythian monuments.

οἰκήματα . . . ἐπὶ ζευγέων. The nomadic life struck all the Greeks, e.g. Aeschylus (P. V. 709–10); Hippocrates (de Aer. c. 18) describes the wagons as having four or six wheels, and as roofed with felt (πίλοισι), so as to be wind and water proof. So M. Polo, i. 52, says of the Tartars: 'Their houses are circular, and made of wands covered with felts; these are carried with them whithersoever they go'; for pictures of the Tartar houses cf. *ib.* pp. 253–5. Hippocrates goes on to describe the Scyth diet as flesh, milk, and cheese. H. skilfully introduces here the main point of his account of the campaign (cf. c. 120).

47 1 **εὔυδρος.** H. knows only the well-watered region on the lower Dnieper; South Russia as a whole is not well watered. For the Egyptian canals cf. ii. 108.

2 **πεντάστομος**: so Arrian, Perip. (c. 35); but Mela (ii. 8) gives 'as many as the Nile', and Strabo (305) 'seven'. There are now three main ones.

48 1 **Ἴστρος.** For the Danube generally cf. c. 99 and ii. 33 nn.

ἴσος . . . ἑωυτῷ: in contrast with the Nile (ii. 25. 5).

2 **μέν γε**: frequent in enumerations (cf. i. 145); *πέντε μέν* is repeated in § 4 *οὗτοι μὲν αὐθιγενέες*, where it corresponds to the *δέ*, with *ἐκ . . . Ἀγαθύρσων*, and with *ἐκ τοῦ Αἵμου* (49. 1).

Πόρατα. Name and position identify this as the Pruth; the other four are uncertain; H. had probably heard their names at Istria (cf. ii. 33. 4).

3 **πρὸς ἠῶ,** 'on the east,' as opposed to *πρὸς ἑσπέρης μᾶλλον*; as the Pruth came in through Scythia, of which the Danube was the western boundary, it could not flow 'to the east'.

4 The **Maris** is clearly the Marosch, which, however, runs into the Theiss, not the Danube.

49 1 **μεγάλοι**: the Danube's tributaries from the Balkans really are small.

Θρηίκων τῶν Κροβύζων. The changes in the position of the Crobyzi are an illustration of the trend of the tribes to the north-east which Niebuhr sketches (K. S. p. 376 seq.). In Strabo (318) we find this people has moved east to the coast, where H. (c. 93) places the Getae; these again had moved north-east in the fourth century B. C.

The **Scius** is no doubt the Ὄσκιος of Thuc. ii. 96. 4 (mod. Iskar), who rightly says *ῥεῖ ἐκ τοῦ ὄρους ὅθεν περ καὶ ὁ Νέστος καὶ ὁ Ἕβρος*; of course it does not (as H. asserts) 'cut through' the Balkans. H. extends Mount Haemus further west than was done later.

2 The **Triballi** lived in the modern Servia; Sitalces (Thuc. iv. 101. 5) met his death in an unsuccessful campaign against them.

ἐκ δὲ τῆς κατύπερθε. So far H.'s geography has been near the truth; now it becomes impossible. He knows nothing of the mountain block of central Europe, though its name and that of the 'Carpathians' make their first appearance in geography as the rivers Alpis and Carpis. Perhaps the direction of these rivers is a confused tradition of the Drave and Save, or even of the Inn.

3 Cf. ii. 33. 3 nn. for the Celts and the Cynetes.

πλάγια. 'It runs into the flanks of Scythia,' i. e. it strikes the Scythian frontier at an (acute) angle; this is of course inconsistent with H.'s 'square theory' (c. 101).

50 1 **οὐδεμία**: the last tributary the Nile receives is the Atbara, about 140 miles north of Khartoum; H.'s knowledge did not reach so far.

2 **ὕεται**: H.'s statement agrees with the fact that Roumania has more rain in summer than in winter (E. B.[9] xxi. 15), but snow is comparatively rare, 'only twelve days in the year.' Here, as in his account of the Nile flood (cf. ii. 24 nn.), he greatly exaggerates the effects of evaporation. The absence of floods on the Lower Danube is a fact, but the real cause is the Iron Gates near Belgrade, which were unknown to H.; these hold up the water, acting like a great natural lock; hence the floods are in Hungary (which was outside H.'s sphere of knowledge), not in the Danubian principalities.

51 **Tyras** was a colony of Miletus at the mouth of the Dniester; the coins give the name as *Τυρανοί* (Head, H. N. p. 273).

52 1 **ἐκ τῆς Σκυθικῆς.** The Boug (Hypanis), unlike the Dniester and the Dnieper, rises 'in Scythia'; H. is quite right in making it the shortest of the three.

2 **βραχύς**, 'without floods'; cf. ii. 19. 2 (of the winter Nile).

3 **πικρός.** The brackishness of the South Russian rivers near their mouth is due to their slow current, which allows the admixture of the sea water. The story about the Exampaeus fountain may be an attempt to explain the fact, which H. was told when at Exampaeus (if he had not visited this place (81. 2 n.) he is convicted of grave prevarication); Reinach, however, says (A. R. M. p. 170) the Boug actually has a tributary which is still called 'Miortovod' (i. e. dead water). Exampaeus is rightly explained as 'sacred ways'; for the latter part of the word cf. √ of Germ. 'pfad', perhaps found also in *Ἀργιππαῖοι* (23. 5); the E in 'Exampaeus' may be privative; Müllenhoff, D. A. iii. 105.

ἐν ὀλίγοισι, 'unusually large'; cf. ix. 41. 1.

ἀροτήρων: H. calls these agricultural Scyths Callippidae and Alizones; he places them between the Boug and the Dnieper (17. 2).

4 **συνάγουσι.** It is quite true the Dniester and the Boug approximate in their upper course; *κατά*, 'in a line with', not 'in the region of'.

53 1 **πολυαρκέστατος**, 'most productive.' H. writes like a man of business.

2 **διακριδόν**: Homeric; cf. Il. xii. 103. The disparagement of the other rivers as *θολεροί* is unjust; H. is echoing the praises of some patriotic Olbian.

3 **ἅλες.** Dio Chrys. (Or. xxxvi. p. 48) mentions the salt in the second century A. D., and Kinburn (on the Dnieper liman) still supplies South Russia. As salt fish was a main article of Pontic export, the salt was the more important.

ἀντακαίους. The 'sturgeon' of the Dnieper, which are still famous. Pliny also (ix. 45) denies them a backbone. Athenaeus (118 d) mentions the τάριχος ἀντακαῖον ('caviare'), but without reference to Olbia.

4 **Γέρρου.** The 'limit' of Scythia (71. 3); hence some have proposed to alter 'forty' into 'fourteen', because Scythia is only 'twenty days' journey' across (101. 3). But 'Scymnus' (l. 817; G. G. M. i. 230) in the first century B.C. says the Borysthenes is navigable for 'forty days' but no more, and Stein points out that H. is speaking of a voyage, and so the calculation takes into account the windings of the stream; the number therefore may be explained by the great east bend of the Dnieper. But though H.'s informants may have known of this, he himself certainly did not, for he thinks the Dnieper 'flows from the north'; Stein explains this of its course just at Gerrhi, and points out that the Dnieper does flow from north to south as far as Kief, and then south-east by east; but H. says it flows from the north all the way from Gerrhi. It is curious too that he knows nothing of the rapids of the Dnieper, which begin at Ekaterinoslav, 260 miles from its mouth; had he known of them, he must have compared them with the Nile cataracts. H. faithfully reproduces his sources, but his own knowledge of the river is limited to what could be gained on the voyage, up or down it, to Exampaeus. He shines, however, by comparison with Strabo (306), who says the Dnieper is only navigable for 600 stades!

δέκα: cf. 18. 2 n.

5 **ἕλος.** The great liman of the Dnieper (cf. 17. 1 n.) is only six feet deep in summer, hence the name ἕλος.

6 **ἔμβολον.** Dio Chrysostom (Or. xxxvi. p. 48), an eyewitness, repeats this comparison, which may refer to Cape Stanislav, half-way between the mouths of the two rivers. He is the only author besides H. in whom the name Hippolaus appears; no doubt the early Greek settlers invented a 'horse' hero to suit the native habits.

ἱρὸν Δήμητρος. Demeter's head is the principal type on the Olbian coins (cf. Head, H. N. 272). There is a *v. l.* μητρός, i. e. 'of Cybele'; one coin gives a head with a mural crown, the mark of Cybele; but even this head has a wreath of corn also, so that it might be that of Demeter.

54–6 The Panticapes, Hypacyris, and Gerrhus defy identification, while the last-named presents special difficulties (c. 56 n.). To suppose great physical changes (with Rawlinson *ad. loc.* and in his map) is not probable; the only safe inference is that merchants crossed three rivers on their journey north-east, between Dnieper and Don.

54 **ἀπό**, 'as to'; cf. 195. 4, a Homeric usage. Panticapaeum on the Cimmerian Bosporus has nothing to do with this Panticapes, though the names may be both connected with πόντος; cf. iii. 92 Παντίμαθοι.

55 For Carcinitis cf. 99. 2. H. does not describe the well-known

'course of Achilles', a long sandy strip running parallel to the shore for eighty miles, but joined to it only in one place (cf. Strabo 307); the western half is called Tendra. Achilles was specially honoured in the Pontus; cf. Alcaeus, fr. 48 B ὁ γᾶς Σκυθίκας μέδεις, and his title ποντάρχης (C. I. G. 2076, 2077).

56 ἀπέσχισται. Bunbury (i. 212) denies the possibility of the Gerrhus thus leaving the Dnieper forty days' journey from its mouth (cf. 53. 4) and taking an independent course; but there is a sort of parallel in the Cassiquiare in South America, which has a continuous course from the Orinoco to the Rio Negro, a tributary of the Amazon (V. de St. Martin, Dict. de Géog.). It is impossible, however, to fit the Gerrhus into South Russia. Stein ingeniously suggests that its name meant 'boundary' (cf. 71. 3), and that it represents the frontier line of the Royal Scyths, which is supposed to be one continuous river.

57 The **Tanais** is of course the Don; H. has once more trustworthy information, no doubt derived from the 'emporium called Cremni' (20. 1). The Tanais flows from a small lake; it is more probable, however, that H.'s 'great lake' is due to a general theory of lake origin (46 n.) than to definite information.

The **Hyrgis** is probably the Donetz; in 123. 3 it is called Syrgis, and runs direct into the Palus Maeotis.

58 ἐπιχολωτάτη. Theophrastus (Hist. Plant. ix. 17) seems to be contradicting this when he says that the Pontic cattle ate and flourished on wormwood, being especially free from 'bile'.

9–82 *H. now describes the religion and manners of the Scyths. This is one of the most valuable parts of his work.*

9 1 Ἱστίην. For the pre-eminence of Hestia cf. 68. 2; 127. 4; for a Scyth picture of her with the sacred fire cf. Reinach, A. R. M. p. 179. Rawlinson considers the worship to be elemental; this is slightly confirmed by C. I. G. iii. 6013 (found in Rome) where Apollo Oetosyrus is identified with the sun-god, Mithra. Nymphodorus (third century B. C., fr. 14; F. H. G. ii. 379) definitely says the Sauromatae were fire-worshippers; cf. also i. 216. 4 (the Massagetae). H. gives no native names for Heracles, who may be a Greek addition, or for Ares. For Aphrodite cf. i. 105. 2 n. 'Artimpasa' is found on two dedications at Tusculum (C. I. G. iii. 6014).

2 ὀρθότατα . . . καλεόμενος. H. clearly connects 'Papaeus' with Πάππας (= 'father', Od. vi. 57); he no doubt was familiar with the Bithynian 'Zeus Papas' (Arrian, fr. 39; F. H. G. iii. 592). The name is one of familiar affection, of a type perhaps characteristic of Asia Minor (Roscher *s. v.*). For guesses at the etymology of these names cf. Rawlinson, iii. 194 seq.: Müllenhoff, D. A. iii. 108 sees in 'Tabiti' the root 'tap' ('to burn', cf. *tepidus*).

2 καταβάλλει. The purpose of the ritual was (1) by 'plucking the end of the rope' to make the victim seem voluntarily to prostrate

itself. (2) Unlike the Jews, to keep the blood in the victim; for this Reinach (A. R. M. p. 181) compares the sacrificial methods of certain tribes in the Altai Mountains. The flesh was mainly eaten by the sacrificer (61. 2). H. as usual notes the contrast to Greek ritual; there was no 'burning' of the hair (*ἀνακαύσας*) as a 'dedication' (*καταρξάμενος*, ii. 45. 1), and no 'libation' (*ἐπισπείσας*).

For the tmesis *περὶ ὧν ἔβαλε* cf. i. 194. 4 n.

61 1 **Λεσβίοισι κρητῆρσι.** We know no more of the 'Lesbian bowls' than of the 'Argive' (152. 4); the terms may be commercial ones and so familiar to H.

ὑποκαίουσι. For using bones as fuel cf. Ezek. xxiv. 5 and Hooker, Journal of a Naturalist (1854), i. 213 (the bones of the Yak in Nepaul). The scarcity of fuel is correct; dung is still dried and burned in South Russia. But cf. 18. 1, 109. 2 for wooded districts

2 The grim humour of **βοῦς ἑωυτὸν ἐξέψει** is to be noted.

ἵππους. For horses sacrificed cf. i. 216. 4 (the Massagetae), and for the meaning of the rite, Frazer, G. B. ii. 315 seq.

62 1 **κατὰ νομούς**, 'in every district, for each of the people of the governments.' H. seems to mean the country is divided into *ἀρχαί* (probably subdivisions of the *βασιλήιαι* of 7. 2, 120. 3), and these again into *νομοί*, each of which has its *νομάρχης* (66. 1). The organization thus hinted at is clearly military as well as religious.

φάκελοι. These 'bundles of firewood' in a woodless country are, to say the least, exaggerated. We may note (1) H. gives the measurements from hearsay, not as his own; (2) his information came mainly from Olbia, which is close to the 'woodland' (*Ὑλαίη*); (3) we may conjecture the wood was used to keep together masses of earth inside (this is implied in *ὑπονοστέει κτλ.*).

ἀπότομα. Reinach (A. R. M. p. 182) says that in Russia tumuli are still found with three sides steep and one sloping.

2 **ἀκινάκης.** A great iron sword was found in a tomb at Kertsch, but the weapons are usually bronze. For sword-worship among the Alani in fourth century A. D. cf. Ammianus, xxxi. 2. 23 '(gladiumque) ut Martem regionum praesulem verecundius colunt'; cf. Gibbon (c. 34, iii. 419–20) for Attila's use of the 'sword of Mars'.

τοισίδ': i. e. 'with the victims to be described next'. Mars naturally had the most human sacrifices.

3 **καταχέουσι.** For parallels to pouring blood on a sacred object cf. Frazer, G. B. iii. 21; red paint sometimes took the place of blood.

4 **δεξιοὺς ὤμους.** The victim is robbed of his right arm to render his spirit after death helpless; cf. Tylor, P. C. i. 451 for parallels (e. g. among Australian natives).

ἀπέρξαντες, 'completing the sacrifice of the other victims'; cf. ii. 40. 4 for use of *ἀπο-*.

63 **ὑσί.** For the pig as a mark of race distinction cf. 186. 2 n.

64 1 **κεφαλάς.** For head-hunting and scalping cf. Tylor, P. C. i. 459 seq. The Dyaks thought 'the owner of every head they

could procure would serve them in the next world'. Strabo (727) says that in Carmania no one was allowed to marry till he had brought an enemy's head to the king; cf. c. 117 n. For blood drinking in order to obtain the strength of the dead cf. 26. 1 n. and Denny's Folk Lore of China, p. 67: (The Chinese) 'eat a portion of the victim, especially the heart', to 'acquire the valour with which he was endowed'. In the Seven Years' War contemporaries attribute to the Kirghiz in the Russian army the practice of drinking the blood of those they killed (M. Polo, i. 313).

3 **χλαίνας**: cf. Carlyle's story (Fr. Rev. ed. Fletcher, iii. 165–6) of the breeches made from the skins of the victims of the Terror

βαίτας, 'peasant cloaks' made also of sewn skins.

ἦν: the tense seems to imply that H. is speaking of a quiver cover which he had seen.

65 1 **ποτηρίῳ**: cf. 26. 2 n.

2 **ἐπικρατήσῃ** implies trial by combat-to-the-death among the Scyths.

67 1 **ἐπὶ μίαν**, 'as they place them severally one on the other.' The phrase corresponds to *κατὰ μίαν*, but implies super-position also. Cf. Hosea iv. 12 and Tac. Germ. c. 10 for a similar use of rods ('frugiferae arbori'); also Ammianus Marcellinus xxxi. 2. 24 for it among the Alani. For a picture of rod divination cf. (a gold plaque found on banks of Amou Daria) Reinach, A. R. M. p. 187. A somewhat different method of rod divination is described by M. Polo (i. 49) as practised by 'Christian astrologers' for Chinghiz Khan before his battle with Prester John.

For the *Ἐνάρεες* cf. i. 105 n. Hippocrates (de Aer. c. 22) attributes the impotence to excessive riding. The word is probably derived from *a* privative and 'Nar' (Zend., Sansk.), 'a man,' Müllenhof, iii. 104.

2 **ὧν**: the 'linden' was sacred to Aphrodite.

68 1 **μαντεύονται.** The diviners behave like the witch-doctors in West Africa; cf. Kingsley, Travels in West Africa (1897), pp. 463–4.

4 **αὐτοῖσι**, 'it is appointed for the prophets themselves to perish'; a sort of *dat. incommodi*.

69 1 **βοῦς.** Hippocrates (de Aer. c. 18) confirms H. that the Scyths used oxen for draft, like the modern Calmucks.

3 **οὐδὲ τοὺς παῖδας**: cf. the counsel of Croesus (i. 155 n.); the sparing of the women seems to point to a Northern respect for the sex.

70 **ὑπέατι**: an Aeolic form of *ὄπεας*, an awl. For the blood covenant cf. iii. 8. 1 n.; there is an interesting picture of it on a gold plaque from Kouloba (*v. i.*).

71–2 These chapters deserve careful study, as evidence of H.'s accuracy and of his wide interest. They are admirable illustrations of the belief that the future life is a continuation of the present, in which the dead needs all he needed here (cf. Tylor, P. C.

i. 459 seq.). Moreover, they illustrate the belief that inanimate objects also have spirits, which survive in another world. These beliefs, which are the cause why so many of the treasures of our museums are derived from ancient burial-places, prevailed both in Mycenaean and in Homeric Greece; cf. Il. xxii. 510

ἀτάρ τοι εἵματ' ἐνὶ μεγάροισι κέονται . . .
ἀλλ' ἤτοι τάδε πάντα καταφλέξω πυρὶ κηλέῳ.

The tradition of them survived the Christian era; cf. Lucian de Luctu, c. 14 (928) *πόσοι ἵππους καὶ παλλακίδας, οἱ δὲ καὶ οἰνοχόους ἐπικατέσφαξαν καὶ ἐσθῆτα καὶ τὸν ἄλλον κόσμον συγκατέφλεξαν . . . ὡς χρησομένοις ἐκεῖ καὶ ἀπολαύσουσιν αὐτῶν κάτω.* For a curious instance in H. cf. v. 92. η 2, 3—the story of Melissa; cf. also v. 8. Caesar (B. G. vi. 19, § 4) describes the usage in a modified form in the Gaul of his day.

For the description of the tomb of Kouloba near Kertch (opened 1831) cf. Rawlinson or (his source) Dubois de Montéreux, Voyage autour du Caucase (1838–43), v. 194 seq., and plates, fourth series, 18–25; almost all Rawlinson's illustrations for H. iv. 1–144 come from this splendid work. The tomb in question probably belongs to the fourth century B. C., and is that of one of the Leuconidae, who ruled in Panticapaeum from 437 B. C.

For the tumuli generally of South Russia cf. S. Reinach, Introduction, Antiq. du Bosph. Cimmér. (1892). The wealth they have yielded is in the Hermitage at St. Petersburg, where the two rooms (vii and x) of 'Kertch' and 'Scythic and Siberian Antiquities' have over 20,000 gold objects, 'a collection unique at once for intrinsic value and for historic interest.'

The following points may be specially noted in c. 71. (1) It was belief in H.'s veracity that led to the examination of the tumulus. (2) As a rule the details minutely correspond, but (*a*) other metals beside gold were found in the tomb. This discrepancy may be due to exaggeration on his part (or his informant's) or to the fact that the tombs explored are later than his time; (*b*) the number of victims is two (not six). (3) The vault is of stone; of this H. says nothing, though it perhaps implied the *χῶμα μέγα* of § 5. The sarcophagus itself was of wood (as in § 4). (4) Naturally no parallel has been found to the fifty dead mounted slaves (c. 72); these were *outside* the tomb. But a similar custom of impaling sacrificed animals on wooden beams is found among the tribes of the Altai Mountains (Reinach, A. R. M. p. 181).

71 1 **ἐς ὃ . . . προσπλωτός** looks like a gloss due to a misunderstanding of 53. 4. It does not contradict that chapter, but it does contradict the geographical facts.

3 **κομίζουσι.** Beside the escort of 'Royal Scyths', who go right through with the body, there are always mourners of two tribes, the one just entered (*οἳ δὲ ἂν παραδέξωνται*) and the one just left (*ἐς τοὺς πρότερον ἦλθον*).

M. Polo (i. 51) describes how the bodies of the Great Khans were all buried near a 'mountain called Altai' (which is *not* the Altai Mountains), even if they are 100 days' journey away. The convoy of the funeral killed all they met, saying, 'go wait upon your lord in the other world.' The Khan's horses too were killed (cf. c. 72).

72 1 **θεραπόντων.** For human sacrifices at a chief's burial among Caribs, in New Guinea and elsewhere cf. Tylor, P. C. i. 486.

ἵππους. For killing horses for a dead master cf. Tac. Germ. 27, and the evidence of excavations all over Northern Europe. The last instance in Europe was at Trèves in 1781; cf. Tylor, P. C. i. 474.

3 **ὕπτιον,** 'they put half the felloe of a wheel on two stakes, with the hollow side upwards.'

5 **ξύλου:** a partitive genitive depending on the antecedent of *τό*. *τόρμος* (a *ἅπ. λεγ.* in H.) = a 'socket'. H. says nothing about this when he mentions the *ξύλα παχέα* in § 3.

73 2 **σμησάμενοι,** 'having soaped their heads.' The Persian king did this once a year on his birthday, ix. 110. 2. The transition is curious; the use of vapour baths for purification after a funeral leads to an account of ways of cleaning in general.

πίλους. With the construction of the bath-tents cf. the 'Kibitks' of bent wood and felt in Pallas, Voyages en différentes provinces de l'Empire de Russie (Paris 1788), i. 503–4 and Plate 14.

74 **Θρήικες μέν:** there is no *δέ* to correspond: *μέν* implies a contrast with Scyths.

ὁμοιότατα. H. speaks like an expert in dress materials; cf. ii. 105 for 'Colchian linen' and Introd. p. 17. *κάνναβις* is the plant, but *κανναβίς* the garment made from it.

75 1 **ὠρύονται:** they 'howl' with delight, but also from intoxication by the hemp fumes; cf. i. 202. 2 n. for the latter. Rawlinson needlessly supposes H. to confuse the effects of a vapour bath and of intoxication.

3 **λιβάνου ξύλου.** Egyptian ladies still rub their hands with melted frankincense; but neither the 'cedar' nor the 'frankincense tree' grow in South Russia.

76 1 **μήτε:** on account of the idea of prohibition in *φεύγουσι*.

2 **Anacharsis** is killed by the father of Idanthyrsus, who is king (c. 120) circ. 512 B.C.; H. puts his death in the middle of the sixth century; there is therefore nothing impossible in the story (which is very late) that he was a friend of Solon. He was reckoned among the 'Seven Sages' and credited with inventing the potter's wheel, which Strabo (303) rightly says is absurd. The figure of this travelled half-caste—his mother was a Greek (Diog. Laert. i. 101)—in the sixth century B.C. is very interesting. The 'noble savage' theory of Rousseau gave him a new lease of fame in the eighteenth century (cf. 'Anacharsis' Klootz, Carlyle, F. R. *passim*, and the once famous Voyage du Jeune Anacharsis by Barthélemy, 1788).

Cyzicus was famous for the worship of Cybele which was said to have been introduced by the Argonauts.

4 **Ἀχιλλήιον.** H. perhaps gives this description here, not in c. 18 or in c. 55, where it would seem to us more natural, because it suits his account of the secret rite.

ἐκδησάμενος, 'hanging from himself.' The ἀγάλματα are small figures of the goddess and of Atys worn on the breast (hence called προστηθίδια); cf. Polyb. xxi. 31 for their use by the Galli of Pessinus.

6 Tymnes is one of the informants H. mentions by name (Intr. § 22); he seems to have been a Carian half-breed (cf. v. 37. 1). No doubt he was 'agent' for the Scythian king in the factory at Olbia. His origin and position are significant as to the nature of H.'s sources.

H.'s semi-personal (ἴστω) address to Anacharsis is very quaint.

77 **ἀσχόλους**, 'too busy to attend to any wisdom.' 'Laconic' utterances (for which cf. Plut. Mor.) are attributed to Anacharsis himself (cf. Diog. Laer. i. 103 seq.), e. g. that 'sailors were only four digits away from death'.

The δ' ὦν implies that, while H. considers the praise of the Lacedaemonians to be 'an idle Greek fiction', he knows for certain that Anacharsis died as a Philhellene.

78 For Istria cf. ii. 33–44.

2 **παρέλαβε.** For succeeding to harem and throne together cf. 2 Sam. xvi. 21, and M. Polo, i. 52; p. 256 (of the Mongols)

ἀστή: i. e. a native Scythian.

3 **ἐς τὸ Βορυσθενεϊτέων ἄστυ.** The Scythian king clearly had some authority in Olbia, though not as much as the Leuconidae later (438–304 B.C.) had in Panticapaeum and Theodosia, where they bore the title of ἄρχων; their heads appear on the coins of Panticapaeum. There is no parallel to this in Olbia.

4 **Σκυθικήν.** Trousers and a sort of peaked cap were the main features; H. does not describe it, as it was not especially Scyth; cf. 23. 2, 106. 1. For a picture of it cf. Sacouca the Sacian on the B. I.

5 **ἐς αὐτά** 'he brought a wife to it'; cf. our 'to marry into' and Liv. i. 34. 4 *quo innupsisset*.

79 1 **Βακχείῳ** emphasizes the orgiastic character of the rites

2 **σφίγγες.** For sphinxes cf. ii. 175. 1 n., for griffins c. 13 n. Macan has a long and interesting note on these creatures, which were intended to protect the palace against evil spirits. Perhaps there is a reference in them to Skyles' devotion to Dionysus, for the sphinx appears on the coins of Chios (Head, H. N. p. 599), and the griffin on those of Teos and Abdera (*ib.* 595, 253), in both cases in connexion with the cult of the wine-god. Griffins are often found ornamenting Scythian objects.

4 **διεπρήστευσε**, 'gibed at'; Stein says the word is colloquial

80 **Teres** was the father of Sitalces and the founder of the Odrysian power (Thuc. ii. 29). As Sitalces is mentioned below without any

comment, Blakesley argues this chapter was written after he had become known at Athens by his capture of the Lacedaemonians' envoys (vii. 137. 3). It certainly reads like a later addition. The events referred to must have happened soon after the accession of Sitalces, which is dated circ. 450 B. C.

81 1 **ὡς Σ. εἶναι**, 'so far as they are Scyths.' H. distinguishes them from the other races whom the Greeks called 'Scyths'; it was Thucydides' ignorance, or neglect, of this distinction which led him implicitly to contradict H. as to their numbers (cf. v. 3 with Thuc. ii. 97. 6).

2 For Exampaeus cf. 52. 3 n. and Introd. pp. 18, 19. Macan argues that *ἀπέφαινον* means 'offered to show me', and that H. never was at Exampaeus; but this translation is forced, and there is no reason to doubt H. had seen the bowl he describes in such detail; his explanation of its origin, however, is a mere legend.

3 **ἀνέθηκε.** Nymphis (a historian of the third century, fr. 15; F. H. G. iii. 15) says that the bowl (*ἐπὶ στόματι τοῦ Πόντου*) was there before Pausanias, and that he only put his name on it. This story may be an invention suggested by Thuc. i. 132. 2 (but cf. i. 51. 4 for a similar Lacedaemonian appropriation). It is odd that H. does not mention here the great bowl at Delphi (i. 51. 2), which was of the same size (i. e. holding over 5,000 gallons). For a curiously similar story of a primitive census cf. Wallace, Malay Archipelago (ed. 1869), i. 182–4.

82 **ἴχνος Ἡρακλέος.** Such 'footprints' are common in many countries; cf. Buddha's (which is over five feet by two feet) at Adam's Peak in Ceylon. 'Two cubits' was the proper size for a Greek hero (cf. 2. 91. 3 n. of Perseus).

—144 *H. now resumes his history from c.* 1, *but at once turns aside to describe the Pontus* (cc. 85–6), *and later on the geography and races of Scythia* (cc. 99–117).

Artabanus plays the part of Cassandra here as in vii. cc. 10, 49, while Oeobazus (c. 84) anticipates the misfortunes of Pythius (vii. 39); but H. skilfully touches here only on the points which he works out dramatically in his main narrative.

83 **ἀπορίην**: cf. i. 71. 2 for a similar argument for non-aggression.

85 1 **Chalcedon** lay on the Asiatic side of the Bosporus, at its south-west end.

The **Cyanean Rocks** were the gate of the Pontus (cf. their place in the 'Peace of Callias', vii. 151. n.). Their name, 'the rocks of gloom,' marks the early feeling of the Greeks towards the 'inhospitable' Pontus, while H.'s enthusiasm for the sea corresponds to the later name 'Euxine'. They are called 'wandering' as early as Homer (Od. xii. 61). For their story cf. Pind. Pyth. 4. 371 and Apol. Rhod. ii. 318 (or Morris, Life and Death of Jason, Bk. VI); H. doubts its truth. There are twelve rocks, the largest of which is still called 'Kyani'; they lie off the lighthouse on the extreme point of the European shore (Murray).

2 **τὸ μῆκος.** H.'s measurements in this chapter are (in stades):

	Length.	Breadth.
Pontus	11,100	3,300 (*τῇ εὐρύτατος*)
Bosporus	120	4
Propontis	1,400	500
Hellespont	400	7

H. is strangely wrong on the length of the Black Sea; the E. B.[9] gives it as 720 miles, i. e. about 6,280 stades; but this is at the longest part, from the Gulf of Burghaz to near Batûm. At the point measured by H. (86. 4) it is only about 650 miles. Various explanations are given of his mistake:

(1) Rawlinson thinks H. is calculating from his own experience, i. e. he took nine days and eight nights for a coasting voyage along the south of the Black Sea, and was told that his vessel made 1,300 stades a day; but this explanation will not do, for H. is clearly speaking of a direct voyage. Strabo (548) reckons such a coasting voyage in the Euxine at 'about 8,000 stades' only.

(2) Others think that a 'long day's' journey (86. 1) was really one of twenty-four hours (as modern ships reckon their 'runs'); H., forgetting this, reckons in the 'nights' over again.

(3) The probable explanation, however, is much simpler. H. reckons a 'long day' and a long night; but it is obvious that in the same twenty-four hours a 'long day' presupposes a short night; hence the figure '600 stades' for the night is exaggerated.

A normal twenty-four hours' run was 1,000 stades. For the whole subject of a ship's speed cf. vii. 183. 3 nn.

It may be noted that the famous Massiliot navigator, Pytheas, made the south coast of Britain nearly twice its real length.

εὖρος. The E. B.[9] gives the breadth of the Pontus as 380 miles (about 3,310 stades), but this is in the wide west part. At the points further east measured by H., it is only about '270 miles' (*ib.* = 2,350 stades). H. therefore is here again in excess, but much less so than as to the length; in the shorter voyage there was less room for miscalculation.

3 **τέσσερες στάδιοι.** The estimates for the breadth of the Bosporus at its narrowest part, which is about the centre (where the bridge was made, 87. 2), vary from 550 metres (about 600 yards; Réclus) to three-quarters of a mile (E. B.[9]): Murray's Guide agrees with H. (as does Strabo 125), giving 810 yards.

μῆκος. As the whole channel is meant, *ὁ αὐχήν* is added to explain. H. underestimates the length, which is about 20 miles (E. B.[9]), i. e. 175 stades. Perhaps in estimating the speed of a vessel sailing down the straits, he forgot to allow for the current.

4 **Προποντίς.** H. does not tell us at what points he measured the

Propontis; the E. B.[9] (*s.v.* Black Sea) gives it 110 and 43 geographical miles (i.e. about 1,100 and 430 stades). H. therefore is too large here also.

Ἑλλήσποντον. H.'s breadth for the Hellespont agrees with Murray's, who gives 1,400 yards; but Murray makes the length 33 miles, i.e. about 290 stades.

Rawlinson (*ad loc.*) has a useful table of the measurements of H., Strabo, and Pliny, compared with actual distances. He notes (1) that H.'s successors are hardly more accurate; (2) that as a rule his measurements are in excess, because he overestimates the speed of vessels; (3) that, as might be expected, he is most inaccurate as to the part most remote, i.e. the Pontus.

6 1 **νηῦς.** H. does not mean that he is giving the results of his own voyage; he is calculating from a seaman's *περίπλους* (for these cf. Bérard, ii. 544 f.).

For Sindice cf. 28. 1 n.

2 **μακρότατον.** H. is not familiar with the western curve of the Pontus (*v.s.*).

4 **ἡ Μαιῆτις.** The real size of the Sea of Azov is 235 miles by 110 (E. B.[9] *s.v.* 'Azof'): Scylax (Per. 69) makes it half the size of the Pontus, Strabo (125) rather more than a third. Rawlinson thinks the sea was once much larger than it is now (cf. Polyb. iv. 40, who says that it was gradually being silted up).

μήτηρ. H. is perhaps misled by supposed etymology from *μαῖα*; the native name of the sea was 'Temarunda' = *mater maris* (Plin. N. H. vi. 20); cf. 52. 1 for this name. The people on its shores are Μαῖται in the inscriptions (Dittenb. Sylloge, i. 130, 132, 2nd ed.).

7 1 **στήλας . . . δύο.** H. uses 'Assyrian' (Ἀσσύρια) for any cuneiform writing (here for Persian), which of course he could not read.

For the custom of putting up a bilingual inscription in the languages of the ruling race and of the subjects concerned cf. the inscriptions on the Red Sea Canal (ii. 158 n.). For the lists of subject races cf. App. VII. 1.

ἐξηριθμήθησαν. The figure 700,000 was a conventional one for the levy *en masse* of Persia (cf. Isoc. Panath. 49 for the soldiers in Xerxes' army), as is the number '600' for a Persian fleet; cf. vi. 9 (Lade), 95 (Marathon); '700,000' is of course impossible (cf. Munro, J. H. S. xxii. 294 seq. for the whole subject).

στήλῃσι. Ctesias (xvii, p. 68) calls them *βωμόν*, and attributes the destruction to the Chalcedonians; but H. speaks as an eye-witness.

2 **Artemis Orthia or Orthosia** (by some identified with the Tauric Artemis; cf. 103. 1 n.) was worshipped especially at Sparta, where boys, as is well known, were flogged at her altar (discovered in 1906; B. S. A. xii. 331 seq.); perhaps this cruelty was a Spartan peculiarity. The oldest certain mention of her cult is Pind. Ol. 3. 30, but Bergk conjectures Ὀρθία in Alcman P. L. G. iii. 41; for

it cf. Paus. iii. 16. 7, and Frazer *ad loc.*, and Farnell C. G. S. ii. 452 seq. The title may be explained with the Schol. to Pind. as *ὀρθοῦσα τὰς γυναῖκας*, i.e. in travail; others connect it with the stiff straightness of an early *ξόανον*; but this was not peculiar to Artemis.

ἱροῦ. There was a temple on each side, these being twenty stadia apart (Strabo 319); the Asiatic one (to Zeus *Οὔριος*) was the more important (cf. Polyb. iv. 39, where there is a most interesting account of the Pontus).

88 1 **πᾶσι δέκα** is not literal but an idiom for abundance; cf. ix. 81 and the stronger expression *μυρία τὰ πάντα*, iii. 74. 2.

ζῷα, 'figures' of all kinds; cf. i. 70. 1 n. H. had of course seen this painting at the Heraeum (iii. 60 n.). For that temple as an art gallery cf. Strabo 637 and Introd. p. 30.

89 1 **Ἴωσι.** It is most unlikely that the whole fleet was led by Greeks, though this is required by the story. Duncker (vi. 266, 271) thinks the Phoenician fleet was being used against Libya.

2 **αὐχένα.** The single stream is called 'neck' in contrast to the space enclosed by the spreading mouths. Strabo (305) says Darius crossed at the lower part of the island Peuce, 120 stades from the southern mouth of the Danube; this seems to have been also the place where Alexander crossed (Arr. Anab. i. 3.). This is placed by Gen. Jochmus (J. R. G. S. xxiv. (1854) pp. 36 seq.) at Isakcha (or Isakdje), about twenty-five miles west of Ismail. He (p. 83) points out that Darius (like the Russians in 1828) was reducing the 'sea towns' as a preliminary; his line of march was close to the sea (p. 47), where the Balkan passes are easiest. H. never mentions these, though he knows of the Haemus elsewhere (49. 1 n.).

90 1 **Τέαρος.** The river is identified (*ib.* pp. 44–5) as the confluence of the Bunardere and the Simerdere, in the latter part of which names 'Tearus' survives. Its 'thirty-eight streams' may roughly be made out, and their temperature varies, as H. describes; but they have lost their therapeutic reputation for 'the scab'.

An inscription (91. 1) in cuneiform letters seems undoubtedly to have existed here till about 1830, but it has since perished (*ib.* p. 44).

2 **ὁδὸς δ' ἐπ' αὐτάς.** The source of the Tearus is fully fifty miles from Perinthus as the crow flies, and more from Apollonia.

Ἀγριάνην. The name of the Agrianes survives in the Erkene, which runs into the Hebrus, i.e. the Maritza.

91 2 **ἄριστον.** Jochmus (p. 44) says the river deserves the reputation which H. gives it; but the inscription is very Greek in its antithesis.

ἠπείρου: i.e. Asia; cf. i. 96. 1.

92 The **Odrysians** (cf. Thuc. ii. 96) lived in the valley of the Hebrus; the Artiscus is the Teke, a tributary of the Erkene (Jochmus, pp. 46–7).

93 **Γέτας.** The Getae, who 'believe in immortality', living between the Balkans and the Danube, occur here for the first time in history. They are not to be confused with the Goths (as Rawlinson and Hodgkin, Invaders of Italy, i. 62). They were later driven north across the Danube into what was afterwards Dacia. Cf. v. 4 n. for their belief in immortality.

Salmydessus was notorious for its organized wrecking; cf. Xen. Anab. vii. 5. 12–13. H. describes the position of Thracian tribes by their relation to Greek colonies. **Mesambria** (vi. 33. 2) received additional settlers after the Ionic revolt.

δικαιότατοι. Cf. 2. 1 n. for this ideal picture. Pomponius Mela (i. 18) calls them *ad mortem paratissimi*, and connects this courage with their belief in immortality.

94 1 **δαίμονα.** H., though he obviously suspects them, so far regards his countrymen's stories as to call Salmoxis *δαίμων*, not *θεός*: that Salmoxis was a Thracian god there can be no doubt; for the form of the name cf. Salmydessus; Plato (Charm. 158 B) mentions him with Abaris as a master of 'incantations'. The rationalizing story of c. 95 is told with variations by Strabo (297–8) and other later Greek writers without a word of question; Diodorus (i. 94) couples Salmoxis with Zoroaster and Moses as a legislator claiming divine sanction; Origen makes Salmoxis teach the Celtic Druids. H.'s better-informed caution, in contrast to all this, is greatly to his credit. Some moderns, however, accept the Greek story, e.g. Creuzer, Comm. H. p. 171 n., who makes Salmoxis the introducer of 'mysteries' into Thrace, which are celebrated underground. His name, Gebeleizis, remains a puzzle; one commentator makes it 'giver of rest'; another even connects it with Βεελζεβούλ!

2 For this method of communicating with the unseen cf. Dahomey, where as many as 500 messengers were dispatched a year, A. B. Ellis, Ewe Speaking Peoples of the Slave Coast of Africa (1890), p. 137.

3 **ἴλεος.** So in Norse myths the heroic dead go to feast with Odin.

πρὸς βροντήν τε καὶ ἀστραπήν. For similar fighting against unseen powers cf. i. 172. 2 n., the Calyndians, iv. 173, 184. 2, the Psylli and the Atarantes.

95 1 **ἄνθρωπον.** There is a clear note of irony in the way in which H. tells the Greek story; cf. §§ 2, 3, especially *πανδοκεύοντα*: no unfavourable judgement on Pythagoras is implied (cf. ii. 123 n.), but H. dislikes the arrogance of his countrymen, introducing themselves into barbarian cults and legends (cf. ii. 45 n.).

4 **ὡς τεθνεῶτα.** Cf. Soph. El. 62 for a reference to this trick

97 1 **τὴν σχεδίην λύσαντας.** This proposal, to cut communications so as to render return by the Caucasus necessary, is only the first of the difficulties of the narrative (for these cf. App. XII).

2 Coes, in v. 37. 1, is tyrant, no doubt as the reward for some service at this time (cf. § 6).

3 **οὔτε ἀρηρομένον.** This is true in the main, although some of the

Scyths grew corn (c. 18), and there were many Greek cities on the coast.

98 1 **ἄμματα.** For this 'palpable arithmetic' as a primitive method of reckoning cf. Tylor, P. C. i. 240 seq.; but it is curiously out of place in Darius, who had the learning of Chaldaea at his service.

99-101 *H. gives a sketch of Scythia, which he makes a square of* 4,000 *stades* (c. 101), *and of the neighbouring nations* (cc. 102–17), *which cannot be reconciled on many points* (*e.g. cf.* 101. 2 *and* 19. 1 *n.*) *with* cc. 16–20. *The rivers are ignored in it, as in the story of the campaign that follows.*

Macan (ii. 19) ingeniously suggests that this may be an 'ideal scheme of Scythian geography, intended to serve as a complement to the historical narrative', but his further suggestion that it is part of the original draft of the Scythian λόγοι composed before H. had obtained his fuller and later information, is very doubtful. Stein thinks it was accompanied by a map (which is most unlikely). H. starts from the Ister, assumed as the western boundary. He first gives the southern boundary (§ 2); the rest of the chapter is a digression on the Tauric Chersonese. In 100. 1 he gives the eastern boundary, and (§ 2) completes the square with the northern boundary.

99 1 **Σκυθικῆς γῆς.** H. means that the coast of Scythia does not continue (in a straight line that of Thrace), but that 'as there is a sweep made' (*κόλπου*) the Thracian coast line 'projects' (*πρόκειται*), just as Egypt projects (ii. 12. 1) beyond the line of North Africa.

ἐκδιδοῖ, 'runs out' into it; i. e. has its mouth in it (cf. 49. 3 n.).

The lower course of the Ister is one of the most difficult points in Herodotean geography. As Niebuhr pointed out (K. S. pp. 156, 356, and map), H. conceives it as running due south (cf. Macan, vol. ii, Map, and p. 18).

Niebuhr's arguments are: (1) The supposed correspondence of Ister and Nile (ii. 33. 2 n.). (2) In v. 9 the land to the north of the Ister is not Scythia or that of the Agathyrsi but 'desert', and (v. 10, by implication) *ὑπὸ τὴν ἄρκτον*. (3) Only in this way can be explained the great extent of the Thracians (v. 3). (4) The western boundary of Scythia (i. e. admittedly the Danube) runs at a right angle to the coast (101. 3).

The last point seems decisive. Rawlinson says rightly that this view, viz. that the lower Danube runs south, is inconsistent with other parts of H., e. g. (1) the Danube receives from Scythia five tributaries, each west of the other (c. 49); the boundary therefore runs east and west, and not north and south; (2) the tributaries from the Haemus flow in from the south (c. 50), so the Danube must run east and west; (3) it runs into the sea 'with its mouth facing south-east' (*εὖρον*). But (1) and (2) only prove either that H. did not know these facts when he wrote c. 101, or, more probably, that he forgot them from a love ot symmetry; and if the emphasis be laid on στόμα (§ 1), is rather for the south course than against it. Why mention the 'mouth', if the whole course were south-east?

Macan well suggests that H.'s mistake is helped by his confusing the Danube and the Pruth, which latter river flows mainly north and south.

2 **τὸ . . . ἀπὸ Ἴστρου**: adverbial (*not* with τὸ πρὸς θάλασσαν); translate 'starting from the Ister'. So too τὸ δὲ ἀπὸ ταύτης below (§ 3) is adverbial.

αὐτῆς: excluding the Tauric land.

ἀρχαίη. Stein translates 'Scythia proper'; but if so, what was 'new Scythia'? Probably Western Scythia, which was agricultural (c. 17), is meant (Macan); this would have been the part which the Greeks knew first.

μέχρι . . . Καρκινίτιδος. Carcinitis is the city on the north-west edge of the Tauric peninsula. The gulf on which it stands really runs east and west; but H. thought it ran north and south (as Strabo 308 also implies). H. was quite ignorant of the real shape of the Crimea, which he conceives of as resembling Attica, i. e. as a triangular projection of Scythia, running south-east (§ 4). Strabo (308) was the first to call it Χερρόνησος.

3 **τὴν αὐτήν**: i. e. the Pontus.

ὀρεινήν. Only the south coast of the Crimea is really mountainous.

χερσονήσου: that of Kertsch, which H. rightly says runs east.

4 **ἔστι γὰρ τῆς Σκυθικῆς.** This does not mean that Scythia is washed on one side by the Black Sea, on the other by the Palus Maeotis (as is often held, e. g. by Macan, ii. 17); but that its projection, the Tauric peninsula, has *sea* both on south and east. This is rendered probable by the words κατά περ τῆς Ἀττικῆς, and proved by the fact that H. always calls the P. Maeotis λίμνη (100. 1 n.), *not* θάλασσα.

γουνόν, 'high ground'; H. (§ 4) recognizes that the Crimea is much larger than Attica (μᾶλλον ἀνέχοντα).

ἀπὸ Θορικοῦ. Thoricus and Anaphlystus were the fortresses that protected the Laurian mines.

5 **ὡς εἶναι κτλ.** Cf. ii. 10. 1 n. for the construction.

ἄλλως. This passage not only illustrates H.'s geographical inaccuracy, but also the way in which his work was written; the comparison of Iapygia looks like an afterthought, and must have been added after H.'s visit to the west (cf. Introd. p. 8, and for Kirchhoff's use of this passage *ib.* p. 10).

ἀποταμοίατο. The distance from Brundisium to Tarentum is one day's journey. (Strabo 282.)

παρόμοια κτλ. The construction is παρόμοια ἄλλα (ἄλλοισι by attraction) τοῖσι οἶκε ἡ Ταυρική.

1 **θαλάσσης τῆς ἠοίης.** The 'Eastern sea' is the part of the Black Sea at the south-east corner of Scythia with the Cimmerian Bosporus, *not* the Pontic Maeotis (cf. 99. 4 n.).

2 **τὰ κατύπερθε . . . φέροντα**: accus. of respect.

For the order of the tribes cf. cc. 102. 2, 125.

101 1 **κατηκόντων.** It will be noticed that H. says 'coming down to the sea' not *παρὰ τὴν θάλασσαν*: the eastern side only touches sea at its south-east corner.

2 **δέκα ἡμερέων ὁδός.** The first distance to the Borysthenes is fairly right; the second is really much shorter, being about 130 miles. H. mentions the Palus Maeotis as being the main part of his eastern boundary.

τὸ ἀπὸ θαλάσσης ἐς μεσόγαιαν corresponds to *τὰ ὄρθια τὰ ἐς τὴν μεσόγαιαν φέροντα* below and to *τὸ ἐς τὴν μεσόγαιαν φέρον* (§ 1) above.

διηκόσια στάδια. In v. 53 H. allows only 150 stades a day on the Royal Road; but South Russia is unusually flat.

3 **τὰ ἐς τὴν μεσόγαιαν** refers to both sides, the western and the eastern frontier. We have to infer what these are; the western frontier is the Danube (80. 2, 97. 1); the eastern frontier is a small part of the Black Sea and the Cimmerian Bosporus (*vid. sup.*) with the Palus Maeotis and part of the Don. This last point is proved (Rawlinson, iii. 203) from the movements of Darius' army (cf. 120. 2, 122. 3), and from the fact that, though Darius marches through the territory of the Sauromatae and the Budini, he never gets far from Scythia (cc. 124, 125).

The story of the campaign is not history, but it is evidence for the geographical conceptions of its author. Niebuhr and Stein are therefore wrong in representing the Don as flowing into the Palus Maeotis just at the north-east corner of Scythia, and thereby excluding that river from the eastern boundary of 'the square'.

For H.'s love of symmetry in making Scythia 'square' cf. App. XIII. 7.

102–17 *The customs of the surrounding tribes.*

Six of these (not the Agathyrsi and the Geloni) had already been mentioned (cc. 17–22), and their position described in relation to Scythia proper. H. now describes their customs. For a similar division as to the Scyths cf. cc. 17–20 (position), cc. 59–80 (customs). Some think the arrangement is merely due to the fact that H. was using different sources. At any rate his attempt to differentiate barbarian tribes is one of his most interesting points.

103 1 **παρθένῳ.** Artemis Orthia, whose temple stood on the *κρημνός* in front of the city (Strabo 308). For her worship cf. c. 87 n.

ἐπαναχθέντες, 'putting out to sea against them', i. e. they were pirates as well as wreckers; they retained these customs till the first century A. D. (Tac. Ann. xii. 17. 4). The sacrificing of the shipwrecked to the goddess is no doubt a real custom, and probably the origin of the Iphigenia myth.

2 **δαίμονα.** For the identity of priest and god cf. Frazer, G. B. i. 8, iii. 457. The story is familiar in Euripides' drama, 'Iphigeneia in Tauris,' and elsewhere. The Tauri may have been a remnant

of the Cimmerians driven into the mountains; some have (improbably) connected their name with that of the Celtic Taurisci.

104 ἁβρότατοι. The Agathyrsi are usually placed in Transylvania (48. 4, the Marosch rises among them), where there were gold mines. They are 'most luxurious' because of their gold. They were probably a Thracian tribe; 'Thyrsi' may be a Scyth form of *Τραυσοί* (a Thracian tribe, v. 3. 2 and Steph. Byz. *s. v.*). For their tattooing cf. v. 6. 2 n. and Virg. Aen. iv. 146 'picti Agathyrsi'.

ἐπίκοινον. For promiscuity cf. nn. on i. 216. 1, iv. 172. 2. The purpose here ascribed to it is a piece of Greek rationalism, and a curious anticipation of Plato, Rep. Bk. v.

105 1 γενεῇ μιῇ. The exact date is odd, especially as H. describes the Neuri as back in their land when Darius came (125. 3); nor are the Budini near the Neuri, but far away beyond the Don (c. 21). The snakes are a *vera causa*, if we may trust J. G. Kohl, a traveller quoted by Neumann.

2 λύκος γίνεται. This earliest reference to the widespread superstition as to werewolves (cf. Tylor, P. C. i. 308 seq., and Frazer, Paus. iv. 189, for Greek parallels) is interesting, as the evidence is so emphatic. Others (e. g. Müllenhoff iii. 17) see in this story a reference to some festival like the Lupercalia.

The Neuri are placed between the upper course of the Dniester and the Dnieper; some see in them the ancestors of the modern Slavs.

106 Ἀνδροφάγοι. Neumann (p. 212) thinks the Androphagi were Finns, quoting evidence that this people were said to practise cannibalism even in the Middle Ages; perhaps they are the ancestors of the Mordvinians, a Finnish tribe still surviving in the Volga basin. This seems more probable than the view of Müllenhoff (*u. s.*) that they were not really much different from their neighbours, and that the story of their cannibalism is an invention; he quotes, however, several authorities for cannibalism being imputed to northern races, e. g. Arist. Nic. Ethics, vii. 5 (1148 b). Strabo quotes (302) Ephorus for this cannibalism, but in 201 he throws some doubt on it, both in Scythia and in Ireland.

107 εἵματα . . . μέλανα. This custom later spread to Olbia (cf. Dio Chrys. Or. xxxvi, p. 50, for it there in the second century A. D.), and lasted till recently among Finnish tribes in south-east Russia (cf. E. B. xviii. 88). The Melanchlaeni are mentioned by Hecataeus (fr. 154, F. H. G. i. 10) as a 'Scyth nation'. Rawlinson compares with the names in cc. 106–7 the Red Indian 'Dog-eaters' and 'Black robes'.

1 γλαυκόν κτλ. Probably 'with blue eyes and red hair'; cf. Tac. Germ. c. 4 'caerulei oculi, rutilae comae', though Stein takes it of the 'red' skin, with Hippocrates (de Aer. 20), who says *πυρρὸν τὸ γένος τὸ Σκυθικὸν διὰ τὸ ψῦχος*. Others explain that they painted themselves 'blue', like our British ancestors; cf. 'picti Geloni', Virg. Georg. ii. 115.

Some have seen in the Budini a Teutonic race, but the evidence is too inadequate for certainty. Müllenhoff (iii. 15, 102) makes them Finns, but their complexion does not agree with the dark hair and brown skin of that people.

πόλις . . . ξυλίνη. The town of Gelonus is one of the unsolved puzzles in H.; he seems to speak from good evidence, and the town lay on the north-east trade route (c. 21 n.). But it is difficult to believe in semi-barbarian Greeks so far from the sea.

Neumann (p. 91) compares the wooden walls of Saratov, still standing a hundred years ago; Bunbury (i. 195) thinks H.'s informants confused Greek and Slavonian systems of worship. Grote, too, thinks the Geloni may have been Slavs.

2 **τριετηρίδας.** The Bacchic festivals were triennial; cf. Ovid, Fasti, i. 393–4 'Festa corymbiferi . . . Bacchi Tertia quae solito tempore bruma refert'.

109 1 **φθειροτραγέουσι.** Rawlinson translates 'lice-eaters'; cf. for this disgusting practice the Adyrmachidae (c. 168) in North Africa, who 'crack' lice with their teeth before throwing them away; but H. uses a different word here, and probably means 'fir-cone-eaters'; cf. Photius *φθεὶρ ὁ τῆς πίτυος καρπός, πίτυς φθειροποιός*, and the town *Πιτυοῦς* in the Caucasus, near which lived a race of *φθειροφάγοι* (Strabo 492, 496; he, however, clearly thought these to be 'lice-eaters').

2 **τετραγωνοπρόσωπα.** Stein, quoting Aristotle (?), Mir. Ausc. 30 (832 b 8), suggests the 'square-faced beasts' are elks (*τάρανδος*); Rawlinson translates 'seals'; but surely some small freshwater beast is meant, e. g. the mink, which is amphibious and found in Eastern Europe; as a species it is intermediate between the marten and the otter. With a broad flat head and blunt muzzle, it may well be called 'square-faced'. The Scyths on the South Russian vases wear fur-trimmed 'cloaks' (*σισύρνας*).

ἐς ὑστερέων ἄκεσιν. Hippocrates recommends *τὸ καστόριον* for diseases 'of the womb'.

110 1 **Ἀμαζόνας.** The martial habits of the women of the Sauromatae (c. 117 nn.) irresistibly reminded the Greeks of the Amazons (ix. 27. 4 n.), and they are introduced here regardless of the chronological inconsistency that, if the Scyths had come into their land in the seventh century (c. 11), they could not have been found there by the Amazons in the time of Heracles. If the Scyths were descended from Heracles (c. 8), the inconsistency is different, but equally striking.

Οἰόρπατα. The first half of the etymology ('man') is probably right, but the latter half of the word is connected with Zend *pataya*, 'master' (cf. iii. 61 n.). The word then = 'masters of men' (cf. Ephorus, fr. 78, F. H. G. i. 258, the Sauromatae are *γυναικοκρατούμενοι*).

Thermodon (ii. 104. 3 n.), a river in Cappadocia, where legend especially localized the Amazons.

2 **ἐφέροντο.** The usual fate of mutineers is skilfully brought in; cf.

the tale of the Usipii (Tac. Ag. 28). **Kremni in 20. 1** is the eastern boundary of the Royal Scyths on the Palus Maeotis. Its connexion with the τάφρος (c. 20) shows it lay in the south-west, where as a fact the ground is higher than is usual on the Sea of Azov (Westberg, in Klio, iv. 183); others, however, place it on the north coast of that sea. Its name shows it to have been Greek, probably a trading factory.

111 **τὴν πρώτην**: because the Amazons were all beardless.

112 **στρατόπεδον** is usually taken as the subject of προσεχώρεον (*const. ad sens.*); but it is better to translate 'they approached camp to camp', &c. (accus. of respect).

113 The story has a strong resemblance to that of the convent gardener in Boccaccio (Decameron, third day novel), and were it not contradicted by H.'s usual attitude to religion and morals, it would confirm Cornford's silly paradox (Thuc. Myth. p. 239) as to H.'s 'flippant, Parisian, man-of-the-worldly tone'. Addison's burlesque commonwealth (Spec. Nos. 433–4) may well be borrowed from H. here.

114 **συνέλαβον.** The greater aptness of the Amazons is a delightful touch of nature; but they were inaccurate (cf. σολοικίζοντες c. 117), as lady linguists often are.

116 **διαβάντες κτλ.** This passage shows that H. conceived the Palus Maeotis as extending east of the Tanais mouth; but it does not show that he thought its general direction was east and west (as Rawlinson).

117 **οὐ γαμέεται.** Hippocrates (de Aer. c. 17) makes three victims the price of marriage, and says the ladies did not fight afterwards, unless a levy *en masse* was needed. It is generally supposed that the Sauromatae were the Sarmatians, who later spread west to Poland and Hungary; they were already west of the Tanais in the fourth century (Scylax 70), and by the Christian era they had reached the Danube; cf. Ovid, Tristia, iii. 3. 5–6. On the monuments, Scyths and Sarmatians wear the same dress, Reinach, A. R. M. p. 203, and Hippocrates (*u. s.* c. 19) makes the Sauromatae to be Scyths. The Sarmatian inscriptions seem to be connected in language with an Iranian dialect in the Caucasus.

-44 *H. now returns to his main narrative, and describes the expedition of Darius to its close.*

1 **ἠπείρῳ τῇ ἑτέρῃ.** H. emphasizes the fact that Persian advance was a war of Asia against Europe.

4 **εἰ γὰρ κτλ.** Cf. 1. 1 n. for the motives of Persian aggression.

3 For μεγάλην and the triple division generally cf. 7. 2.

4 **τῶν ἀπειπαμένων.** Macan accuses H. of inconsistency, for the Persian attack falls first on the Sauromatae and Budini (123. 3), who were loyal to Scythia, not on the neutrals. But H. is consistent at all events; the single division (§ 2) was to retreat, ἰθὺ Ταναΐδος, i.e. on the Sauromatae, and this is expressly said to have been the one attacked (122. 2); it was the other two divisions (§ 3) which were to

draw the Persians on to the neutrals, as they do in 125. 2. But the campaign, though consistent, is not intelligible, and it is lost labour to try to make sense of this fancy picture.

123 1 **εἶχον οὐδὲν σίνεσθαι.** The Persians must have passed through the lands of the Agricultural Scyths (cc. 17–18), but the land is described as all *χέρσος*; H. will not spoil a contrast by mentioning exceptions. He also ignores the great rivers; cf. cc. 51–6.

τείχεϊ. For the wooden town of Gelonus cf. c. 108. Rawlinson (on c. 142), who is disposed to accept H.'s narrative as generally credible, lays special stress on the burning of this town as a fact that must have been known to the Pontic Greeks.

3 **ἐρήμου.** For the desert cf. c. 22, for the Maietae 86. 4 n.

The Oarus is often identified with the Volga; but there is no real reason for this, and the latter river runs into the Caspian. For the Syrgis cf. c. 57.

124 **ὀκτὼ τείχεα.** Lack of time and lack of motive alike make it impossible that Darius should have built forts in East Scythia. It is probable that popular tradition associated his name with prehistoric *tumuli*, such as are common in the steppes (see further App. XII, § 4 d). H. heard of the forts when in Olbia (*ἐς ἐμέ*, cf. Introd. p. 18), but it is most unlikely that he ever saw them.

125 **σφίσι πρῶτα διαμαχήσονται.** The Agathyrsi being protected by the Carpathians on the east were able to make good their threat.

127 2 **τάφοι πατρώιοι.** For the royal tombs among the Gerrhi cf. c. 71 nn.

4 **Δία . . . καὶ Ἱστίην.** For the Scythian religion cf. c. 59; the kings claimed descent from Zeus, c. 5 seq.

For **κλαίειν λέγω** = 'you shall repent it' cf. Aristophanes, Plut. 62. The words *τοῦτό ἐστι κτλ.* are probably a gloss; in Bekker's Anecdota (i. 305) they are explained by a reference to this passage as a blunt threat. Rawlinson, however, thinks that the words refer to Scythian bluntness generally, without any special idea of menace; cf. Diog. Laert. i. 101, Anacharsis 'was the author of this proverb', *διὰ τὸ παρρησιαστὴς εἶναι.*

129 2 **οὔτε γὰρ ὄνον**: cf. 28. Aristotle (de G. A. ii. 8, 748 a 25) also says that the ass will not breed in cold countries like Scythia. This is inaccurate, but there is 'little doubt the ass was first domesticated in Asia' (E. B.[9] ii. 717); and it develops best in warm climates.

3 **ὑβρίζοντες,** 'being loud (in their braying).'

ταῦτα: some take this as the subject of *ἐφέροντο*, others (Stein) supply *Πέρσαι* (which is surely harsh). *ἵπποι* seems the natural subject: translate 'in this way the horses contributed to some small extent (to the issue) of the war'. For supposed inconsistencies in cc. 130, 134, 140 cf. App. XII, § 7.

131 **δῶρα.** For symbolic communications of this kind cf. J. R. A. S. xvii, p. 415 seq. This story is told by H.'s contemporary, Pherecydes (fr. 113, F.H.G. i. 98), with different speakers, and with the addition of a plough to the other gifts. This last has no meaning as a threat, and it is probably an unintelligent addition to the Herodotean story.

The story of Ctesias (17, p. 68) that the Persian and the Scythian kings compared bows, and that Darius, finding the Scythian bow the stronger, fled at once, is far less picturesque or appropriate.

134 3 ἐς τὰς τ. belongs to ἀσθενεστάτους. The Persians do here of necessity what (i. 207. 7) they had done against the Massagetae as a stratagem (cf. the use of καθαρός in 135. 2 and in i. 211. 2). We may compare Napoleon's abandonment of his sick at Jaffa (Lanfrey, i. 298).

136 ἡ μία. For the 'single' division of Scopasis cf. cc. 120, 128, 133; hitherto it has played consistently the part of 'the light division', now it combines with the rest.

137 1 Χερσονησιτέων τῶν ἐν Ἑλλησπόντῳ. 'The Chersonese on the Hellespont' as opposed to Chersonesus Heraclea in the Crimea. For the previous history of Miltiades cf. vi. 39–41 nn.

The part played by him is full of difficulty; if he openly purposed to destroy the Great King, how did he so long escape Persian vengeance?

Three explanations may be noted.

(1) That of Rawlinson may be rejected at once; he thinks that Darius never knew who had proposed his destruction till Miltiades himself boasted of his proposal after 500 B.C.

(2) The usual explanation (adopted on vi. 40, *q.v.*) is that there was treason talked at the bridge, and repressed by Histiaeus, but that Miltiades had no part in it. Long after, however, when on his trial for tyranny at Athens (vi. 104. 2), he claimed (falsely) to have suggested this signal service to the cause of Greece. Thirlwall (ii. 393), who was the first to question the narrative here, thinks Miltiades' first act of treason to Persia was the seizure of Lemnos. It is pointed out that Darius returned to Asia through Miltiades' territory (143. 1; cf. v. 26 n.), and there is no hint in that passage that the tyrant was disloyal.

(3) Grote argues (iv. 201), however, that it is dangerous to reject a story as to events known to many and resting on nearly contemporary evidence. Hence he accepts the account of Cornelius Nepos (Milt. c. 3), that Miltiades left the Chersonese at once after the Scythian expedition, and did not return till the time of the Ionic revolt. This suggestion agrees with the fact that Miltiades seems to have served for a time as a condottiere with the Thracian prince Olorus, whose daughter he married (vi. 39), and is confirmed by vi. 41. 3—the importance attached to the capture of his son.

This arrangement of the facts can perhaps be reconciled with the account in vi. 40, though it is odd that H. mentions there a flight from the Scyths, and says nothing of this (supposed) previous flight from the Persians, which Nepos (*u. s.*) definitely mentions.

It may be suggested that Miltiades' sympathy with the Scyths was of early date. There is a fine vase in the Ashmolean Museum (dating about 520 B.C.) with the inscription Μιλτιάδης καλός, representing a handsome young warrior in Scythian costume (cf. Helbig, Les ἱππεῖς athéniens, p. 199; P. Gardner, Greek Vases in Ashmolean, no. 310, pl. 13, who calls the costume 'Persian').

2 **διὰ Δαρεῖον . . . τυραννεύει.** The identity of interest between tyrant and foreign ruler was undoubtedly true of H.'s own day (cf. the position of Themistocles or of Demaratus under Persian rule). This fact makes H. as a patriot more bitter against tyrants, and more ready to accept this story to their discredit in the past.

138 1 **τύραννοι.** The list is curious and interesting: six of the eleven are 'Hellespontic', while an important island like Lesbos, whose 'general' (97. 2; he became 'tyrant' later, v. 11. 2), Coës, had a high position with Darius (c. 97), is not mentioned; nor are there any Dorians (cf. their absence in the story of the Ionic revolt). These peculiarities may be explained by attributing it to Miltiades, who naturally preferred to mention his neighbours.

For Hippoclus cf. Thuc. vi. 59. 3.

2 Strattis lived till after 480 B.C.; cf. viii. 132. 2.

Aeaces had already succeeded his father Syloson (iii. 139. seq.; for the name cf. iii. 39. 1 n., and for his later history vi. 13).

For Aristagoras of Cumae cf. v. 37. 1, 38. 1.

142 **ἄδρηστα**: active here, the opposite of δραπέτης. Macan well notes the literary device of making the 'intelligent foreigner' the mouthpiece of unfavourable judgements, and cf. 77.

143 **Σηστόν.** Byzantium (v. 26. 1) is in revolt against Persia soon after, and this may be the reason why Darius did not return by the former bridge. Stein assumes that the Scyth invasion of vi. 40 happened at this time, which is most unlikely.

144 **Καλχηδονίους.** Both this and Byzantium were Megarian colonies; the date of the founding of Byzantium was about 660 B.C., but the chronologers vary slightly; cf. Busolt, i. 472. Tacitus (Ann. xii. 63) attributes to the Delphic oracle this rebuke of the Calchedonians (cf. also Strabo 320). For an elaborate account of the advantages of the site of Byzantium cf. Polyb. iv. 38.

145–205 *The rest of this book deals with the history and the natural features of North Africa and its inhabitants. H. skilfully introduces this digression, as it illustrates (with the Scythian expedition) the far-reaching ambitions of the Persians.*

This digression falls into four parts:

(1) *The colonization of Cyrene* (cc. 145–58): of this, the story of Thera (cc. 145–9) is the prologue.

(2) *The history of Cyrene* to the Persian intervention (cc. 159–67).

(3) *The account of the Libyans* (cc. 168–99).

There can be little doubt that this minor digression is a further motive for the full treatment of North African history; H. was with reason proud of his geographical and ethnographical knowledge.

(4) *The results of Persian intervention* (cc. 200–5).

Many of the references to modern travellers are drawn from R. Neumann (Nord-Afrika nach Herodot, Leipzig, 1892, a very clear and useful little book) and from Rawlinson, who usually quotes passages in full. The comparisons are interesting and greatly to the credit of H. as a sifter of evidence, especially when we remember the proverbial unveracity of Oriental witnesses. 'Happy are they who find the least resemblance between the description they have heard and the reality, for it often occurs that amplification and hyperbole have less to do in such accounts than pure invention.' Beechey (Expedition to North Coast of Africa, 1821–2, p. 503), who elsewhere (p. 267), speaking of Barca, says the account of H. is more accurate in the general impression it gives than that of any later traveller.

145 1 **τὸν αὐτὸν . . . χρόνον.** There is no good reason to doubt the synchronism, though most modern critics think it artificial. Duncker (vi. 266, 271) uses it to explain the absence of the Phoenician fleet in Scythia. The exact date, however, does not interest H., and cannot be fixed; it must be earlier than the suppression of Aryandes' revolt (cf. 166. 2 n.). H. gives the *πρόφασις* in c. 167, where he states the expedition was intended 'to conquer Libyans' (i. e. the Eastern ones); this motive is probably the real one, though H.'s own narrative (c. 203) does not agree with it, and the plan failed (cf. 197. 1).

τάδε. The account of the colonization of Thera and Cyrene. H. seems deliberately to introduce this digression, in order to illustrate this important feature in Greek life. Whether the facts are true or not, they represent fifth-century thought as to colonization.

I. Its causes:

(1) *στάσις*. (*a*) The Minyae are in a position of inferiority (146. 1); (*b*) Theras excluded from the throne (147. 3); (*c*) Battus born out of wedlock (155. 1 n.).
(2) Over-population (151. 1; but see n.).
(3) Commercial enterprise.
(4) Delphic sanction and guidance (*passim*, cf. v. 42 n.).

II. The stages of colonization:

(1) The reconnoitring expedition (151. 3; 156. 2).
(2) The settlement off the coast, Platea.
(3) The constitutional development (c. 161 *ad fin.*).

III. The relations of Greeks and natives (especially interesting):

(1) At first friendly, but with suspicion (158. 2).
(2) Then frankly hostile (c. 160).
(3) In spite of this, great admixture.

For this last cf. common customs (c. 170; 189. 3); common worships (186. 2; c. 189); actual intermarriage, e. g. Alazir (164. 4), father-in-law to Arcesilaus III. This explains the brutal cruelty of Pheretime (c. 202), which is quite un-Hellenic.

Some see (e.g. Macan ii. 265) in the two stories of the Minyan settlement in Laconia, and of the settlement of Cyrene, 'aetiological legends' explaining present facts; 'the former justified the Spartan supremacy in Laconia; the second the Spartan claim over Thera' (cf. for this the similar legend as to Patrae, Paus. iii. 2. 1).

That the stories are unhistorical in form needs no proof; and it may be the case that the real connexion between Laconia and Thera dates at earliest from the seventh century (Studniczka, *vid. inf.*). But the only argument adduced (*ib.* p. 51) is that the Spartan Dorians were at first too weak to send out colonies. This is valid against the Herodotean version of the facts, but has no bearing on the wider question, the date of the Dorization of Thera; this may well have been part of the same movement that Dorized the Peloponnese. This earlier date is partly confirmed by the 700 years which the Melians claim for their city in 416 B.C. (Thuc. v. 112. 2).

The story of the two foundations is examined by F. Studniczka in a book ('Cyrene', 1890) full of ingenious hypotheses, most of which are unprovable and many of which are improbable. For his summary cf. Roscher, ii. 1734 f. His main conclusions are:

(1) The fact that the legends always connect the nymph Cyrene with Thessaly (pp. 39 f., 45) shows that the colonists came from this part of the world.

(2) Their route was by Attica, as is shown by the occurrence of Attic place-names in the island (p. 65; cf. Busolt, i. 353).

(3) The connexion of Dorians with Thera was later than the first Messenian war, and led to troubles in Thera, and ultimately to the expulsion of the original colonists, who go to Cyrene (cf. 156. 3 n.).

(4) Dorian encroachment spreads to Cyrene (p. 103, cf. cc. 159, 161), and ultimately leads to the expulsion of the royal house.

(5) Cyrene herself is a form of Artemis (cf. the name Θήρα, p. 146), who is degraded into a heroine; her worship is superseded when the Cyrenian democracy is established (p. 173, cf. Arist. Pol. vi. 4, 1319 b, quoted on 161. 3).

(6) The connexion of the Minyae with Lemnos, their settlement in Thera, and the connexion of Theras with Thebes are all cut out as later inventions.

All these guesses and combinations are as devoid of real evidence as the story in H.; they have the additional disadvantage of being more than 2,000 years further from the facts.

2 **ἐπιβατέων.** In vi. 12. 1 ἐπιβάται is opposed to ἐρέται; but the Argonauts were αὐτερέται (cf. Thuc. i. 10. 4).

παίδων παῖδες, 'descendants'; for the Minyans were driven out in the fifth generation (147. 2 and App. XIV. 2) after Heracles, who was one of the Argonauts.

For Pelasgians in Lemnos cf. vi. 137 n.

Taygetus occurs again in 148. 2. The subsequent connexion of Euphemus, the ancestor of Battus, with this region (Pind. Pyth. 4. 78–9) makes it possible that there was a prehistoric settlement of non-Dorians here, connected specially with Thera.

Euphemus is turned by Studniczka (p. 116) into an euphemistic name of a chthonian god. who lives at the gate of Hades, Taenarum! This is a fine example of the 'Higher Criticism'.

παῖδες. The Argonauts found Lemnos inhabited only by women, who had killed their fathers and husbands (Apollod. i. 9. 17); Hypsipyle had spared her father Thoas (Ov. Her. 6. 135). The later population of Lemnos was the result of their visit. For this story cf. Il. vii. 467–9 (Euneos the Lemnian, a son of Jason).

5 **Τυνδαριδέων.** Some see an inconsistency here, because the mass of the Lacedaemonians were Dorians, and the Tyndaridae as Achaeans were alien to them. The story is obviously unhistorical, but the Tyndarid reference is only an anachronistic anticipation of the later Spartan claim to be the heirs of Agamemnon (vii. 159. 1).

The legend also aims at emphasizing the connexion between Lacedaemon and Thera. This story of admission to citizenship is interesting as showing none of the exclusiveness which later was so characteristic at Sparta (cf. ix. 35. 1 n.; Arist. Pol. ii. 9. 17, 1270 a). It is probable, on other grounds, that this exclusiveness was late, due to the growth of Lacedaemonian power after 550 B.C.

46 2 **νυκτός.** H. introduces contemporary custom into the legend; the custom (cf. Plat. Apol. c. 27) was due partly to the secrecy of Spartan methods (cf. the secret executions by the Venetian oligarchy), partly to their unwillingness to put a citizen to death.

4 **ἐκφυγόντες.** The story is familiar and has many parallels, e.g. Lord Nithsdale's escape from the Tower in 1715. Plutarch tells it (Mor. 247) with features in the main similar, but the husbands are Pelasgians, not Minyae, and they settle in Melos and Crete.

47 2 **μητρὸς ἀδελφεός.** Some see in the relationship a misunderstood tradition of the matriarchate (i. 173. 4 n.), but it is probably accidental. The lady's name was Argeia (vi. 52). Theras is no doubt 'a fictitious eponym', and many critics deny the Cadmeans were Phoenician (*v. i.*). For H.'s mythical genealogies and their bearing on his chronology cf. App. XIV. 2, where the 'eight' (§ 5) generations are given.

4 **Μεμβλίαρεω:** Studniczka (p. 53) makes this a Greek name = 'the new-comer' (cf. *μέμβλωκα*), which is a sufficiently reckless etymology.

Κάδμος γάρ. On the subject of the Phoenicians in Greece, most diverse views are held.

I. The Negative Argument.

Beloch (Griech. Gesch. p. 75) maintains that the Phoenicians never really settled in the Aegean, that their regular voyages to Greece did not begin before the eighth century B.C. (p. 74), and that Minos, Phoenix, Cadmus, Europa (p. 168) are all 'good Greek gods'; the sea empire of Minos is a mere inference from names, and 'Phoenix' is explained as a sun myth ('the blood-red', p. 75).

The grounds for this ultra-scepticism are:

(1) That the Phoenicians do not appear in the oldest parts of Homer; unfortunately for Beloch's argument, there is no general agreement which are the oldest parts.

(2) The scanty traces of Semitic influence on Greek vocabulary; even the words for sea-faring are native; Beloch contrasts Latin borrowings in this department from Greek. Meyer, i. 476, gives a list of words borrowed by Greeks and Semites from some common source.

(3) Cyprus was certainly influenced by the Phoenicians (cf. v. 104 nn.); but it lies outside the ordinary lines of Greek development.

Archaeology has already crushed one part of Beloch's negative argument by proving the reality of Cretan sea-power, although it has at the same time disproved the opposite view (Thirlwall, i. 141), that the Cretan sea-power was Phoenician. With regard to the rest of Beloch's argument, in spite of Reinach's warning against 'Le Mirage de l'Orient', many scholars still believe that the Greeks were to some extent right in attributing importance to Phoenician influences in Greece. Meyer (ii[1]. 89, 1893) wrote: 'The voyages of the Phoenicians in their historical importance can be compared with the discovery of America in the fifteenth century. They introduced the sea into history.' 'Many of the data (as to their settlements in the Aegean) may be untrustworthy; to explain them all as unhistorical is impossible' (*ib.* § 90).

II. Evidence for Phoenician Settlement.

The main kinds of evidence used for tracing the presence of Phoenicians in Greece are (*ib.* 91), apart from statements of ancient historians:

(1) The evidence of names, both geographical (e.g. Mount Atabyris in Rhodes compared with Mount Tabor; the river Iardanus in Crete, Soli in Cilicia) and personal, e.g. the Corinthian hero Melicertes (i.e. Melcarth). For other instances cf. Abbott, History, i. 50; but this evidence is most uncertain.

(2) The evidence of remains, e.g. the beds of murex shells at Cythera and on the Euripus.

(3) The evidence of family traditions, e.g. the priests of Poseidon at Ialysus (Diod. v. 58), the family of Thales (i. 170. 3 n.).

(4) The evidence of cult; the ritual impurity of some of the cults of Aphrodite may have been borrowed, or, at any rate, developed (e.g. at Corinth; cf. i. 131. 3 n.) under Phoenician influence.

It must be admitted, however, that all these lines of evidence are in themselves weak; it is only their cumulative force, coupled with the danger of rejecting a tradition held by the Greeks so firmly, that makes it safer to accept Phoenician influence in Greece as a fact.

III. Lines of Phoenician Influence.

The following points may be suggested as to it:

(1) Phoenician trade and settlements, so far as they existed in

Greece, belong to the period immediately succeeding the downfall of the 'Mycenaean' civilization.

(2) They entered the Aegean by Rhodes (cf. the oriental objects in the necropolis of Camirus, and *u. s.* for Ialysus).

(3) From Rhodes one line of Phoenician influence went by Crete and the Islands (cf. Thuc. i. 8. 1) to Cythera (i. 105. 3), to Corinth, and perhaps to Attica (cf. the story of the bull of Marathon); the name of the deme Melite may be Semitic (cf. 'Malta'). Another line went up the east coast of Asia Minor to the Propontis and to Thasos (cf. vi. 47. 2 for the Phoenician mines).

(4) Whatever view may be held as to Phoenician cult influences (and these are generally accepted at Cythera and at Corinth), there seems no doubt that the Greeks learned the purple fishery and the art of mining from the Phoenicians.

(5) The alphabet was introduced from the East by them (v. 58 n.).

(6) But with one possible exception, what Thucydides says of Sicily (vi. 2. 6) was in the main true of Greece proper—they occupied *ἄκρας τε ἐπὶ τῇ θαλάσσῃ . . . καὶ τὰ ἐπικείμενα νησίδια ἐμπορίας ἕνεκεν.*

The exception just referred to must now be discussed.

IV. Was there a Phoenician Settlement in Boeotia?

(For a full discussion of the evidence cf. Bérard, Les Phéniciens et l'Odyssée, i. 224 f.) To the Greeks of H.'s time this was the most important fact in the Phoenician story (ii. 49. 3; v. 57. 1); but it is perhaps the most uncertain in the whole cycle of the legends. Against the reality of Cadmus it may be argued:

(1) That an older myth attributed the foundation of Thebes to Amphion and Zethus, the sons of a native nymph (Od. xi. 262).

(2) That the supposed Phoenician features in the story, the guiding 'cow' and the 'seven' gates, are not original (cf. Busolt, i. 252. n. 2).

(3) That the oldest story of Thebes has elements in it which are clearly native, e.g. the 'earth-born' *Σπαρτοί* (Pind. Isth. i. 30).

(4) That though 'Qedem' certainly is a Semitic word for 'East', there is no parallel for the derivation of such a proper name as 'Cadmus'.

(5) That H. himself tells us that the Gephyraeans, whom he seeks to prove Cadmeans, themselves believed they came from Eretria (v. 57. 1).

On the other hand, the supposed priority of the non-Phoenician foundation myths is by no means certain, and the improbability is great that later invention would settle on Boeotia for the main Phoenician settlement in Greece. Geographical position, too, argues strongly in favour of the truth of the myth; a Phoenician settlement in Boeotia commanded alike the Euripus, the Corinthian, and the Saronic gulf, for Megara was probably part of Boeotia in early times (cf. Strabo 405), and so that district was, as Ephorus said (Strabo 400), *τριθάλαττος*. As

Bérard (i. 226) well says: 'Continental Greece, under Franks, Catalans, Venetians, had in Boeotia the centre of its commercial routes.' There was probably a trade-route from the Euripus to the Corinthian gulf, past Thebes, Orchomenus, and Crisa, as well as one over the passes of Cithaeron to the Saronic gulf. Hence it would be at least possible that the Phoenicians made their chief settlement in Boeotia.

148 1 **φυλέων.** The legend anachronistically represents the colony as a formal one, with settlers from each of the three Dorian tribes (cf. 153. 1).

4 **The Caucones** (i. 147) were one of the prehistoric races of Greece; they are called *Παρωρεᾶται* here because of their position on the 'slope' of the Arcadian highland, where it approaches nearest to the sea; in viii. 73. 2 the same name is applied to their Lemnian conquerors.

In this difficult district of Triphylia, between Elis and Messenia, remnants of an earlier race maintained themselves; their centre was the temple of the 'Samian Poseidon' (Strabo 343). The most important town was Lepreum, here put at the head of the list; it sent 200 men to Plataea (ix. 28. 4). For the identification of these towns cf. Leake, Peloponnese, i. 56 f.

ἐπ' ἐμέο: a provokingly vague date. The 'harrying' is placed by Strabo (355) 'after the final reduction of the Messenians', i.e. soon after 460 B.C.; the Eleans had assisted the Lacedaemonians while the Triphylians had been against them; the same alliances had been formed at the end of the Second Messenian war (cf. Strabo 362 for Triphylia). So Meyer iii. 285 puts this Elean raid soon after 470 B.C.; he now (iv. 606), however, refers it to the period before the Peace of Nicias, when the Lacedaemonians changed their policy, and supported Lepreum against Elis (Thuc. v. 31).

149 1 **Αἰγεύς.** This is the Spartan version, but there were Aegidae at Thebes and Acragas as well as at Thera and Cyrene, all hereditary priests of Carnean Apollo. Pindar, who himself claimed to be one of them (Pyth. v. 75, but Studniczka, p. 73 f., disputes this explanation), makes them come with the Heraclidae from Thebes to Sparta (Isth. 7. 14 seq.).

φυλῇ is loosely used for *φρατρίᾳ*: but Gilbert (Gk. Const. Hist. pp. 5–6) thinks the Aegidae were really a 'third separate community' at Sparta.

2 The Erinys is the personified curse of a father or mother; cf. Soph. O. C. 1299 *τὴν σὴν Ἐρινύν* (of Oedipus). The curses here are those of Laius on Oedipus and of Oedipus on his two sons. Paus. iii. 15. 6 tells us there were shrines at Sparta to the heroes Cadmus, Oeolycus, and Aegeus. For the belief in a curse making a family die out cf. Sir H. Spelman's famous book on Sacrilege (1698).

150–8 *The story of the foundation of Cyrene is told in two versions, that of Thera* (150–3) *and that of Cyrene* (154–6): *both lay stress upon the action of the oracle.* The main points of difference are:

(1) The Theraean version emphasizes the foundation as being a regular colony, e.g. the order is given to the king and the colonists are systematically provided (c. 153).

(2) The other version brings Battus much more into the foreground. For various speculations, not very convincing, as to the origin of the traditions cf. Busolt, i. 479 n. It is interesting to compare Pindar's odes to Cyrenaic victors (Pyth. iv, v, ix), as they illustrate the wealth of legendary material from which H. had to select.

150 2 The name Γρῖννος is found in a late inscription, now at Verona but probably from Thera, the well-known 'testamentum Epictetae' (C. I. G. ii. 2448).

ἑκατόμβην. The early king is also priest (cf. 161. 3). At Sparta the king communicated with Delphi by deputy (vi. 57. 2). In a late inscription at Thera the priest of Apollo Carneus boasts his descent from Lacedaemonian 'kings'.

Εὐφημίδης is a conjecture from Pyth. iv, where Pindar, in praising Arcesilaus, introduces the legend that his ancestor Euphemus (cf. 145. 2 n.) had handselled the soil of Libya, receiving a clod of earth from Triton (Pyth. iv. 36). H. makes no reference to the story.

151 1 **οὐκ ὗε.** Some see in this drought a picturesque version of what really was a *vera causa* of Greek colonization, i.e. over-population; but this seems far-fetched. Justin (xiii. 7) substitutes a pestilence for the drought. For the visitation cf. Soph. O. T. 25 seq.

2 **μετοίκων.** 'Metic' occurs only here in H.; it clearly is not used in a technical sense (though some have thought it = *ἀπέταιροι* of the Gortyn inscription), but only = 'strangers', i.e. non-Cretans.

Κορώβιος. Busolt (i. 480) thinks Corobius is one of the *ἅλιοι γέροντες*, a sea-god of Itanus (cf. the representations on the fifth-century coins of Itanus, Head, H. N. 469); as, however, he admits that the colonists must have touched at Crete, and 'may well have employed Cretan guides', it is a little hard to see why Corobius should not be a real person. At any rate the Cretans had an important share in the colony (161. 3).

3 **Platea** is Bomba, in the gulf of the same name, on the east of the modern Tripoli. Corobius was left to secure the site (cf. 157. 3), but it is difficult to see why an alien should be chosen for this, or why in fact any competition was to be expected.

152 1 **Colaeus** is at once ship-owner (*ναύκληρος*), captain, and merchant (cf. i. 5. 2).

The usual course was by Rhodes and Cyprus (cf. ii. 182. 2 n.); hence *ἀπηνείχθη*.

For Tartessus cf. i. 163. 1 n.

3 **Ταρτησσόν.** Of the lucky Sostratus we know nothing; it is significant that he was an Aeginetan.

4 **πρόκροσσοι.** *κρόσσος* (ii. 125. 1 n.) is something 'projecting';

so in Il. xiv. 35 *τῶ ῥα προκρόσσας ἔρυσαν*, the Greek ships are drawn up on the shore 'with beaks projecting', and in vii. 188. 1 the ships of Xerxes 'project' *τὸ ἐς πόντον*. Here the griffins are placed upon the rim, facing outwards, no doubt as charms to ward off mischief (cf. Furtwängler in Roscher, i. 1764–5, with pictures). Others translate 'in a row'.

χαλκήιον. For the importance of this bowl in the history of art cf. Murray, G. S. i. 78.

6 **φιλίαι μεγάλαι.** For further connexion between Cyrene and Samos cf. 163. 1.

153 **ἕαδε.** There were four points in the Theraean decree: (*a*) The number of colonists must have been fixed. This is omitted by H., unless it has fallen out of his text. (*b*) They were to be selected by lot, but only sons (*ἀδελφεὸν ἀπ' ἀδελφεοῦ*) were exempted. (*c*) Every district of the island was to contribute a share. (*d*) Battus was to be oecist and king; monarchy, which survived in Thera, was to be set up in its colonies.

ἄνδρας is emphatic; they married Libyan wives; cf. Alexidamus, Pind. P. ix. 215.

154 1 **τὰ δ' ἐπίλοιπα.** The 'common' story is resumed 156. 3.

Κρήτης Ὀαξός. It may be significant that Oaxus, like Cyrene, was especially connected with the cult of Apollo.

2 **μητρυιή.** Step-mothers were proverbial in ancient as in modern times; cf. the story of Cinderella.

4 **ἀποσιεύμενος,** 'freeing himself from the burden of his oath'; cf. i. 199. 4 n. for *ἀποσιόομαι*.

155 1 **Πολύμνηστος.** The name of the father of Battus is common to both stories, as being certain (cf. Pind. P. iv. 104). For the bar sinister in the pedigree of a colonist cf. Arist. Pol. 1306 b.

ἰσχνόφωνος: originally 'thin-voiced', has come to = 'stammering'; cf. L. & S. *s. v.*

μετωνομάσθη. Battus' real name was Aristoteles (Pyth. v. 116), as H. must have known; 'Battus' is a title (*v. i.*) that has become a name; cf. Augustus. It is a Libyan word, though it occurs later as a Greek name (Thuc. iv. 43. 1). The legend of his stammering is probably an invention based on the likeness of *Βάττος* and *βατταρίζω*.

ἡ Πυθίη. The oracle is no doubt *post eventum*, otherwise the familiarity with the Libyan title, 'Battus,' would confirm the oracle's claim in 157. 2.

156 1 **συνεφέρετο παλιγκότως**: translate 'their misfortunes began again'. *παλιγκότως* is used of a wound becoming malignant again. No previous misfortune occurs in the Cyrenaic version of the story, but H. probably refers to *ὁ αὐχμός* of 151. 1, forgetting that it is the very visitation which he is here mentioning. *παλιγκότως*, however, often = 'adverse' without any idea of recurrence.

2 **δύο πεντηκοντέροισι,** 'two penteconters' carry the final colony in the

Theraean version (c. 153); but here they seem to correspond to the reconnoitring expedition of 151. 2.

3 **ἔβαλλον.** Stein thinks these lines contain a reference to the real origin of Cyrene, i. e. *στάσις* at Thera, as related by Menecles of Barca (a historian of the second century B. C. at earliest; F. H. G. iv. 449, fr. 1). But his version is probably only an attempt to rationalize H.

157 This chapter seems to belong to the common version of Thera and Cyrene; but the detail *ἕνα καταλιπόντες* came in at an earlier stage of the Theraean story (151. 3).

2 **ἐλθόντος.** Apollo's visit was when he brought the Thessalian maid Cyrene to Libya, and made her queen of a land *πολύμηλος* (Pind. Pyth. ix. 10); but the country was not really famed for its sheep.

σοφίην σευ. The priests as usual explain the failure of their own prediction by the ignorance of the recipient (i. 167. 4 n.).

3 The name Aziris is clearly Libyan. H. seems to speak as an eye-witness; there is nothing inconsistent with this view in the *λέγεται* of 156. 3, which only means that H. had not measured Platea himself. Aziris would then be the place called in Smith and Grove 'Paliurus'. Others, however, following the Stadiasmus Maris Magni (G. G. M. i. 444, a compilation of uncertain date), place Aziris, there called Azaris, further north, outside the Gulf of Bomba.

158 1 **παραιτησάμενοι.** The friendly yet half-grudging relations of Greeks and aborigines are well seen in this passage; they soon changed to hostility (c. 159), while in c. 160 the Libyans are subjects who revolt.

2 **Irasa** was identified by Pacho (pp. 84–5) as a spot, still called Ersen, on the edge of the Libyan plateau, above the Gulf of Bomba; he points out that this would be a natural place (159. 5) to meet an army attacking from the east. Its abundant water and vegetation confirm *κάλλιστον*.

The spring of Apollo, called *Κύρη*, is mentioned by Pindar, Pyth. iv. 294; it is identified at Cyrene; cf. Beechey, *ib.* p. 423 seq., for a description; also Hogarth, A. A. L. p. 132. The name is probably the origin of 'Cyrene' ('the heroine of the spring'); but Studniczka maintains that 'Cyre' is only a shortened form (p. 143), and that the name occurs elsewhere in Anti-cyra, Themis-cyra, &c. (in Roscher, *u. s.*).

3 **ὁ οὐρανὸς τέτρηται.** The 'sky is pierced' as a symbol of fertility; cf. Mal. iii. 10 'windows of heaven'. There is probably also a reference to the abundant winter rains at Cyrene (contrast c. 185 n.).

The date of the founding of Cyrene, 631 B. C., rests on Eusebius; it agrees with the facts in H. that the first two kings ruled fifty-six years (c. 159), and that the Egyptian attack (ii. 161), which we know was in 570 B. C., was in the time of Battus II, the third king.

For the whole subject cf. Busolt, i. 482 n. For recent exploration there (begun 1910) cf. J. H. S. xxxi. 301.

159-205 *History of Cyrene; but this is interrupted by the long digression on Libya*, 168–199, *which divides into two parts at* 180.

159 1 **οἰκιστέω.** Battus as 'oecist' enjoyed heroic honours at the top of the market-place of Cyrene (Pind. P. v. 93); cf. Miltiades in the Chersonese, vi. 38. 1, and v. 47. 2 n. for hero worship generally.

τοσοῦτοι. H. only means that there was no new immigration for the first half-century.

2 **γῆς ἀναδασμός** was generally the mark of a revolution in Greece; with χρεῶν ἀποκοπαί (Dem. in Timoc. p. 746, § 149) it was renounced in the Heliastic oath at Athens. Aristotle (Pol. v. 5. 3, 1305 a 4) mentions it as one of the causes which overthrow democracies by driving the wealthy to desperation. We have an instance at Cyrene later (163. 1), at Syracuse after the fall of the Gelonian dynasty (Diod. xi. 86), and at Leontini (*circ.* 422 B. C.; Thuc. v. 4). Here, however, it is not a revolutionary measure, for the land to be divided was that of the natives; hence it leads to foreign, not to civil war.

3 **γᾶς ἀναδαιομένας** is the gen. after the comparative ὕστερον, 'too late for the division of the land.'

5 **'Απρίῃ.** H. here fulfils his promise in ii. 161. 3 that he would relate 'more fully' in his Libyan λόγοι the reason for Apries' attack on Cyrene. It is, to say the least, odd (in view of ii. 152 seq.) that he should represent (§ 6) the Egyptians as 'being ignorant and contemptuous of' Greeks.

160 1 **πόλιν.** Barca lies to the west of Cyrene on the high ground on the east coast of the Syrtis. Its name still survives as that of the district. The mixture of native blood in its population was strong, as is seen from this chapter; cf. also 164. 4 and c. 202 nn. Perhaps H. means by ἣ τότε καλέεται that it was already existing as a Libyan settlement.

4 Nicolaus Damascenus (fr. 52, F. H. G. iii. 387) follows H., but Plutarch (Mor. 260) and Polyaenus (viii. 41) make the murder of Arcesilaus a political one, while Plutarch adds that Laarchus had been supported by Amasis, and that the conspirators against him submitted to the king of Egypt in order to avoid punishment. This can be reconciled with the story in ii. 181, and is probably a fact, though H.'s Cyrenaean informants concealed the part played by Egypt out of patriotism. There are other discrepancies, e. g. Learchus is Laarchus in Plutarch and Polyaenus, who make him 'friend', and not 'brother', of Arcesilaus; cf. Maspero, iii. 645 n.

161 1 **ἔπεμπον ἐς Δελφούς.** The traditional constitution of Cyrene had broken down, owing to (1) the increase of population (159. 4); (2) the disaster at Leucon (cf. Arist. Pol. v. 3. 7, 1303 a for the effect of success or failure abroad on constitutional development at home); (3) the dissensions in the royal house.

It was necessary both to admit new citizens to full privileges and to weaken the royal power. For Delphi interfering to end civil strife cf. Curtius, ii. 87. Polybius (vi. 43) mentions the constitutions of Mantinea, Crete, Lacedaemon, and Carthage as famed for their excellence. Shortly before this time a similar appeal for καταστάτω to Mantinea, from Scillus in Elis, is recorded in an inscription (I. G. A. Add. 119, l. 13; *sed incerta lectio*).

καταστησάμενοι: cf. v. 92. β 1 κατάστασις, 'in what way they should organize themselves.'

3 For the work of Demonax cf. Müller, Dor. ii. 62–3. He is probably not referred to in the famous passage in the Politics vi. 4. 18–19, 1319 b 19 seq. (see Newman *ad loc.*) as to constitutional changes intended to increase the power of democracy, where 'those who set up the democracy at Cyrene' (probably in 401 B.C.) are coupled with Cleisthenes of Athens. Aristotle says φυλαί ἕτεραι ποιητέαι πλείους καὶ φρατρίαι, καὶ τὰ τῶν ἰδίων ἱερῶν συνακτέον εἰς ὀλίγα καὶ κοινά, καὶ πάντα σοφιστέον ὅπως ἂν ὅτι μάλιστα ἀναμιχθῶσι πάντες ἀλλήλοις, αἱ δὲ συνήθειαι διαζευχθῶσιν αἱ πρότερον.

The changes of Demonax were: (1) original settlers retain their priority and the right to hold serfs (περίοικοι); (2) new-comers are admitted to full citizenship; (3) monarchy becomes formal.

Others (e.g. Busolt, i. 490 n. 2) think the περίοικοι are Libyans admitted to *full* citizenship.

ἱερωσύνας. So Maeandrius asked to be allowed to retire with a priesthood (iii. 142); cf. for priesthood as the last survival of royalty Arist. Pol. iii. 14. 13, 1285 b, and (to some extent) Sparta (vi. 56. 1).

162 3 For Euelthon cf. v. 104 n.

For the Corinthian treasury cf. i. 14. 2 n. H.'s praise of the 'censer' suggests that part at any rate of this story was heard by him at Delphi.

4 The tense of διδόμενον is emphatic; only the 'spindle and distaff' 'with wool' were actually given, the rest were simply 'offered'.

163 1 **ἐν Σάμῳ.** The alliance of Arcesilaus and Samos is commemorated in the types of a Cyrenaic tetradrachm, with the lion's head (of Samos) as well as the silphium (Hill, G. and R. C. p. 114 and Pl. i. 15).

2 **χρᾷ.** The oracle is done into prose, but the tags of hexameters are obvious. It throws an interesting but perplexing light on the date when H. gathered his materials. It is obviously a prediction *post eventum*, made after the eighth and last Battiad had been deposed; this was about 460 B.C. Pindar certainly knew nothing of it in 466, when he sang the glory of the Battiads (Pyth. iv. 115).

3 **τὴν ἀμφίρρυτον** is clearly Barca (cf. ἁμαρτὼν τοῦ χρησμοῦ *inf.*); but Weld-Blundell (B. S. A. ii. 126–7) finds the epithet appropriate to Cyrene; ταῦρος ὁ καλλιστεύων = King Alazir; perhaps we may quote (Stein) Il. ii. 480, where Agamemnon is compared to 'a bull'.

164 2 To Cyprus; i. e. presumably to his mother.

4 Alazir, whether proper name or title (like 'Battus'), is significant of Libyan intermixture even in the blood royal.

165 2 **Ἀρκεσίλεω εὐεργεσίαι.** In iii. 13 H. mentions the submission of Cyrene, but lays stress on the inadequate tribute sent. The story

here, though not absolutely inconsistent, is curiously different in tone; H. has not harmonized his two sources, and Cyrenaic tradition clearly slurred over the fact of submission to Persia (cf. 160. 4 n.).

166 2 **χρυσίον καθαρώτατον.** The Persian darics (cf. iii. 89. 3 n.) have only three per cent. of alloy; cf. iii. 95. 1 n. Whether Darius was the first to coin them (as Grote assumes), H. does not say; Harpocration (Schol. ad Aristophanes, Eccles. 598) says they were coined before his time (cf. Hill, G. C. p. 27), but probably wrongly.

ἀργύριον. Aryandes' offence was not coining in itself, but doing it in obvious rivalry with the Great King; the satraps coined silver, but only when military officers. Babelon, Les Perses Achém. p. xxiii.

The revolt of Aryandes is variously dated from 517 to 494 B.C. (Macan, ii. 263; Busolt, ii. 532). The monuments are quoted in support of both dates; the literary evidence favours a later one; for H. conceives of Aryandes as copying the coinage of Darius, and this can hardly have been an established institution till after the settlement of the satrapies (iii. 89), *circ.* 516 B.C. Moreover, Darius suppressed the revolt in person (Polyaenus, vii. 11. 7), and he visited Egypt after the Scythian expedition (ii. 110).

167 **Μαράφιον**; cf. i. 125 n. Amasis was probably a Persian who had assumed an Egyptian name (i. 135); many Babylonian names preserved on seals may well be those of Persians (E. M. iii. 21).

168–80 *Nomad Libyans (Eastern tribes) along the sea-coast.* The Libyans are the predecessors of the Berbers; they were comparatively a light-skinned and fair-haired race.

H.'s division (c. 191) at Lake Tritonis is 'obviously right', i.e. he contrasts the Atlas system on the west with the flatter region of Tripoli on the east (R. Neumann, Nord-Afrika nach H., 1892, p. 11). The western part was the sphere of the Carthaginian influence (hence H. makes it agricultural, c. 191), and belongs really rather to Europe than to North Africa (cf. Macan's excellent note on c. 191).

168 1 The Adyrmachidae extend further west in H. than in Scylax (107; G. G. M. i. 82), who makes them 'ruled by Egyptians'.

φθεῖρας. For 'lice-eating' cf. the modern Hottentots and 109. 2 n.

2 **τῷ βασιλέϊ.** For this 'droit du seigneur' cf. Westermarck, p. 76 seq., who quotes parallels, but argues that it is not to be taken as evidence of primitive promiscuity; it prevailed among the Berbers (St. Martin, p. 43) till the nineteenth century.

Πλυνός: i. e. the Gulf of Sollum, which has been brought into such prominence recently (1911) in the Italo-Turkish war, as the west limit of Egypt. Here the Catabathmus Major forms a natural frontier.

169 1 The Giligamae are only mentioned by H. and writers who borrow from him; they perhaps correspond to the later Marmaridae.

σίλφιον. For a long discussion of the silphium cf. R. Neumann, p. 146 seq., or Bähr *ad loc.* It is often identified with the modern

Thapsia Garganica (Arab. *Drias*); it is true this does not correspond to the representations of it on the coins, which make it thick in stem; but these equally disagree with the description of Pliny, xix. 42 ('caule ferulaceo'). (For the coins of Cyrene cf. Head, H. N. 864 seq.; for the question whether coin-types are commercial or religious cf. Hill, G. and R. C., p. 166 seq.) Pliny (xxii. 101 seq.) gives a long and amusing catalogue of the medicinal virtues of silphium, though he adds, 'non censuerim cavernis dentium in dolore . . . includi, magno experimento hominis qui se ea de causa praecipitavit ex alto.' It was a royal monopoly and a main source of the wealth of Cyrene; cf. Aristoph., Pl. 925, τὸ Βάττου σίλφιον (proverbial). Owing to over-production it became almost extinct in the first century A.D., but is now common again in the degenerate form of the Drias. Pacho (p. 54) notes 'la grande exactitude' of H. in fixing its locality. Others, however (e.g. Head, *u. s.*), say the true silphium is extinct; for the arguments cf. Ascherson in Rohlfs, K. p. 524.

στόμα is a curious word for the promontory from which the bay of the Greater Syrtis (ii. 32. 2) bends south; but Scylax (109, G. G. M. i. 84) uses it. H. only knows one Syrtis and never describes it. The coast here was notoriously dangerous from its shifting sandbanks; cf. Strabo 836 σπάνιον εἶναι τὸ σωζόμενον σκάφος, and Lucan ix. 303 seq. for a description, especially 307 'Ambigua sed lege loci iacet invia sedes'.

170 The Asbystae must be the περίοικοι of 161. 3 n.

τεθριπποβάται. For the four-horse chariots cf. 189. 3 n.

171 **Euesperides**, which became Berenice under Ptolemy (hence the modern name 'Benghazi'), was said by Theotimus of Cyrene to have been formally founded by Arcesilaus IV (F. H. G. iv. 517, fr. 1); but if this statement be true, it existed in some form previously (c. 204).

172 1 All the geographers agree in placing the Nasamones on the shores of the Greater Syrtis. Augila (c. 182; *hod.* 'Audschila') is an important oasis in the latitude of Cyrene, on the caravan route to Fezzan; it is still a great centre of date production. Pacho (p. 280) says H.'s descriptions are 'tellement fidèles qu'elles pourraient encore servir à décrire l'Augile moderne', and works out in detail the correspondences. Rohlfs (Tripolis nach Alex. ii. 49) estimated the palms as over 200,000 in 1869, but in 1879 found them much less numerous (K. p. 220).

αὐήναντες. For the eating of locusts (ἀττελέβους) cf. Matt. iii. 4 of John the Baptist. Diod. iii. 29 gives a description of the 'locust-eaters' in Africa, a 'marvellously black' race, who live only on this food, and die before they are forty by a disgusting death brought on by it. The chapter is a significant contrast to H.'s veracity. Duveyrier (p. 240) says the Tuaregs eat locusts 'dried and reduced to powder'.

2 **ἐπίκοινον**: cf. i. 216. 1 n. for polyandry among the Massagetae.

H. here describes, not very clearly, a curious form of group-marriage. Strabo (783) describes an Arabian tribe where the whole family enjoys wives in common; there also the ῥάβδος is used as the sign of possession (cf. W. Robertson Smith, K. A.[2] p. 157 seq., for this 'Ba'al polyandry').

3 **τύμβων.** For this divination in the tombs cf. Duveyrier, p. 435; the women of the Tuaregs inquire among the tombs as to their absent husbands. For dream oracles in general cf. viii. 134 n.

4 Shaw (i. 431, 3rd ed.) says that the drinking out of each other's hands is the only ceremony used by the Algerines in their marriage; cf. the story of Eleazar and Rebecca for an approach to this idea (Gen. xxiv. 14, 43).

σποδοῦ. So the Mahometan law permits ablutions to be done with sand if water is lacking; cf. Tylor, P. C. ii. p. 440.

173 **προσόμουροι.** Strabo (838) places the Psylli east of the Nasamones; H. obviously places them on the west, on the south coast (*ἐντός*) of the Syrtis.

ἐπὶ τὸν νότον. For similar wars with the elements cf. the Getae, 94. 4 n., and Arist. Eth. Nic. iii. 7. 7 (the Celts are said not to fear the waves). Strabo (293) rightly criticizes this latter story.

Pliny (vii. 14) more probably puts down the partial destruction of the Psylli to the Nasamones; H. himself implies (*εἰσί*) the destruction was not complete, and the Psylli are often mentioned later; they were famous as snake-charmers.

174 **Γαράμαντες.** Obviously the name of the 'Garamantes' has been introduced here wrongly from c. 183. Pliny (v. 44-5) seems to have read 'Gamphasantes', of whom he says 'nudi proeliorumque expertes, nulli externo congregantur'; cf. also Mela, i. 47; but Eustathius and Steph. Byz. *s. v.* read 'Garamantes'. Others (e. g. Blakesley) suppose that H. here confuses the hunted Troglodytes of 183. 4 with their hunters; but this credits him gratuitously with a blunder.

175 1 **λόφους κείρονται.** There is some resemblance between the names and the hair-dressing methods of the Macae here, of the Machlyes (180. 1), and of the Maxyes (191. 1). The Libyan Mashuasha play a great part in Egyptian history, both as invaders and as mercenaries. The Tuaregs still wear their hair in a crest, shaving the sides of the head (Duveyrier, p. 432).

στρουθῶν. In vii. 70. 2 the Asiatic Ethiopians use cranes' wings as 'ostrich' wings are used here; this bird is now rare in North Africa, but Rohlfs found traces of it in this region (K. pp. 91, 149).

2 **Κῖνυψ.** H. describes the territory of Kinyps at length in c. 198, where he compares its fertility to that of Babylonia; it became proverbial (cf. Ovid, ex Pont. ii. 7. 25). Hence the Greeks tried to colonize it (v. 42. 3) but failed. The river is identified with the Wad El Kháhan (Beechey, p. 62 seq.), east of Leptis, which has some

pretensions to the title of river. It was thought to rise only about four miles from the sea, and H.'s distance (over twenty miles) was explained by coast subsidence; for this cf. Beechey, p. 272, 'We have already observed the sea appears to have made great advances on the whole line of coast of North Africa,' and Hogarth, A. A. L. p. 138. Later exploration, however (G. J. ix. 633), shows that the river rose further inland, and so confirms H.'s figure.

176 **περισφύρια.** A similar custom is described by Marco Polo in Thibet (ii. 45, cf. p. 48); it also prevailed in Lydia (Aelian, V. H. iv. 1); cf. Westermarck, p. 81.

177 **Λωτοφάγοι.** The tribal name has been displaced by the descriptive 'Lotophagi'; probably the 'Lotus-eaters' are really (in whole or in part) the Giridanes, who are mentioned by no other ancient geographer except Stephen of Byzantium, following H. Pliny (v. 28) calls the 'Lotus-eaters' Machroae, of which name some think H.'s Μάχλυες (c. 178) a blundering corruption. H. is precise in describing the lotus, because of its legendary fame in Homer (Od. ix. 84 seq.) as causing forgetfulness of home and family; Polybius (xii. 2) describes it even more fully. It is a species of thorn tree, the jujube (*Zizyphus vulgaris*) of the genus Rhamnaceae, to which the English buckthorn belongs, with a fruit like a plum in size and shape, which is eaten, especially when dried. The Egyptian lotus (ii. 92. 2 n.) is quite distinct. See Rawlinson *ad loc.* for six different kinds of lotus. A sort of wine is still made from the fruit. The σχῖνος is the lentisk tree.

178 **ἐπὶ ποταμὸν μέγαν.** The geography of this passage cannot be reconciled with existing features; there is no great river or lake such as H. describes.

For a full discussion of the passages as to Lake Tritonis, and the identifications proposed for it, cf. R. Neumann, pp. 28–59. The following points may be especially noticed:

(1) H.'s own account is inconsistent; Tritonis is a lake, cf. 180. 3 περιάγουσι τὴν λίμνην κύκλῳ; yet it is also part of the sea, for Jason runs aground in it before he sees land (179. 2).

(2) H. knows nothing of the trend of the coast north here (cf. 181 n.) or of the Little Syrtis (Gulf of Gabes).

(3) While Scylax (110 *ad fin.*) roughly agrees with H. as to the position of the lake, Diodorus, in his story of the Amazons (iii. 53 seq.), transplants it far to the west near the ocean, while Strabo (836) moves it east into Cyrenaica.

(4) Probably the original of Lake Tritonis is Lake Faroon, a large shallow expanse, west of the Gulf of Gabes. H.'s informants knew of its existence, but let their fancy fill in the details; later, when under Roman rule this coast became better known, 'the story of Lake Tritonis went on its travels' again (R. Neumann, p. 58). Weld-Blundell (B. S. A. ii. 114–18) thinks 'the legend records a common-place physical fact', i. e. 'a north wind piling up the water on these

shoal coasts'. He discusses the whole subject, and inclines to put Lake Tritonis rather more north than Neumann—viz. off the Gulf of Hammamet.

Λακεδαιμονίοισι. It seems natural to connect the λόγιον here with the attempt on Cinyps (cf. 175. 2), which failed because it had no oracular support. There was still a party of 'extension' at Sparta at the end of the sixth century B.C.

Cf. the still more ambitious oracle in 179. 3, which being unfulfilled (as Macan well says), shows that 'all oracles are not to be dismissed as *post eventum*'.

179 1 **Ἰήσονα.** Jason is brought to Lake Tritonis on his return journey by Pindar (Pyth. iv. 44), when the Argo had been carried overland from the ocean twelve days. For other variants of the story cf. 150. 2 n.

180 1 **ὀρτῇ.** H. here gives a very curious and interesting account of a native festival. K. O. Müller thought the worship a Greek one, introduced by Minyan colonists from the neighbourhood of Lake Copais (Orchom. p. 355), but H. clearly conceives it as non-Greek. Macan well suggests that the armed Athene may be a Liby-Phoenician goddess, a sort of armed Astarte (cf. i. 105. 2 n.). There is no doubt that the armed maiden personified the goddess. For the test of virginity (ψευδοπαρθένους) cf. the mediaeval theory of the ordeal; e. g. Emma, mother of Edward the Confessor, was said to have cleared herself of a charge of impropriety by walking over hot ploughshares (Freeman, Norman Conq. ii. 585 f.). For harmless wounds in a sacred fight cf. ii. 63. 3.

4 **ἀπὸ . . . Αἰγύπτου.** H., as usual, gives Egypt priority. Plato (Tim. 24 B) also thought the Greeks borrowed their armour, shield, and helm from Egypt; but the monuments do not confirm this view.

For H.'s views on the history of armour cf. i. 171 nn.; he certainly was not a specialist on the subject; here he uses κυνέη, the low cap of skin (*galea*), and κράνος, the metal helmet (*cassis*) with visor, as if they were identical. It was the κράνος that was Corinthian.

5 **θυγατέρα.** Hence Athene is Τριτογένεια (Hes. Theog. 924; Aristophanes, Eq. 1189).

ἐπίκοινον. For entire promiscuity cf. Arist. Pol. ii. 3. 9 (1262 a).

181–99 The rest of the digression on North Africa is skilfully varied in arrangement. cc. 181–5 give a geographical account of the line of oases, cc. 186–90 of the customs of these 'wandering' Libyans between Egypt and Lake Tritonis, cc. 191–6 contain miscellaneous information of great interest as to Libya west of the river Triton, cc. 197–9 general remarks on North Africa.

181 The description of North Africa as a triple zone of varying character is a typical instance of H.'s merits and defects as a geographer; for it cf. c. 174 and ii. 32. 4 seq. The Arabs still divide

North Africa into the Tell, the Bélâd el Djérid ('the date region'), and the Sahara, and St. Martin (p. 16) says 'it is impossible to describe in a way more exact and complete (than that of H.) the successive belts which extend inland along the coast'. The merits of the division are that it roughly corresponds to marked natural features, and that, in the absence of maps, it coordinates details into a general conception. The coast line of Morocco, Algiers, Tunis, and Tripoli is on the whole fertile, while the region behind (the 'land of dates') is full of wild beasts, especially in the west. H. knows this difference (191. 2). He does not expressly mention that the west is hilly, but he casually speaks of τὰ ὄρη in c. 194. The description seems to be a Carthaginian generalization, for it applies to the west far more than to the east.

Its defects are obvious. (1) The zones are too continuous and symmetrical (cf. H.'s own correction in 191. 3). (2) H.'s 'ridge of sand' between the 'beast region' and the 'desert' proper is a figment; the 'desert' slopes away direct from the mountain block. (3) H. has no conception of the extension of West Africa to the north; Tunis is about 6° north of Alexandria. Hence he makes a parallel from Thebes to the Pillars of Hercules. (4) He confuses the caravan route from Thebes with that from Memphis, 300 miles to the north. (5) His oases are far too regular in their intervals. No doubt the symmetry is due to H.'s informants, who were describing to him a familiar caravan route (Heeren); so Idrisi (an Arab geographer of the twelfth century) gives the same figure.

2 H. knows his distances are approximate (μάλιστα), but he goes on as if they were precise.

ἁλὸς . . . τρύφεα. H. is right as to the abundance of salt, rising 'in masses' above the ground, and as to the springs of fresh water in the midst of it. But his general conception of an oasis as a 'hill of salt' (κολωνὸς ἁλός, 182. 1) is quite absurd; no doubt he was misled by the fact that salt then, as now, is a most important article in the caravan trade; but he attempts to combine in an imaginary picture details that he has not seen, and naturally he fails. H. only knows Ὄασις as a proper name (iii. 26. 1 n.).

ἀνακοντίζει, 'shoots up.' R. Neumann (p. 87) well points out that the springs in the oases are 'very frequently artificially arranged'.

Ἀμμώνιοι. The Oasis of Siwah (i. e. of Ammon) is twenty days' journey from Thebes (not 'ten'), twelve from Memphis; the latter place was the usual starting-point for a caravan, and H. gives in round numbers the average length of a journey. But his religious instinct made him substitute 'Thebes' for 'Memphis', as the 'ram-headed' Zeus (ii. 42 nn.) is to him the god of Thebes.

This is the most natural explanation of his mistake; others (Stein) suppose that a stage of the caravan journey has fallen out, the 'Great Oasis' (El Khargeh), seven days from Thebes. Others again (e.g. R. Neumann, p. 99, who discusses the question fully), think there is a confusion between the great shrine of Ammon at Siwah and a less important one at Dachel, which really is 'ten days' journey' from Thebes.

3 ἄλλο σφι ὕδωρ. Macan (*ad loc.*) has an interesting note on H.'s marks of time, of which there are seven here, cf. iii. 104. 2 n. The 'spring of the sun' (cf. Arr. Anab. iii. 4; Lucret. vi. 848 seq.) has been identified near the temple; it is a volcanic spring, hence the appearance of boiling (ζέει, § 4) from sulphureous bubbles, the water is naturally warm, but feels cooler by day from contrast to the air. H.'s informants have exaggerated a misunderstood natural phenomenon into a marvel.

182 For Augila cf. c. 172 n. Rawlinson (*ad loc.*) quotes, from Wilkinson, a description of a similar spring in the Little Oasis.

183 1 διὰ δέκα ἡμερέων. H.'s measurements are again too small; it is twenty days' journey from Audschila to Fezzan. On the other hand, the distance to the Lotophagi on the north coast (thirty days) is accurate; the reason is that in H.'s day, as now, Fezzan was a well-known place of trade, the starting-point for the caravans across the Sahara.

2 ὀπισθονόμοι βόες. This traveller's tale is told also by Pliny (viii. 178) and other ancient writers; cf. Bähr *ad loc.* for references. Is it possible that its explanation is to be found in the rock-drawings, found by G. Nachtigal (Sahara, 1879, i. 307) to the south of Fezzan, and by Duveyrier among the north-east Tuaregs, representing oxen with projecting horns being dragged unwillingly forward? H. is right as to the quality of the hides, which, perhaps, appeals to him as a merchant.

4 τρωγλοδύτας. There were other Troglodytes on the Red Sea (Strabo 786) and also on the western ocean (Hanno, 7, in G. G. M. i. 6); their mode of life is characteristic of oppressed remnants of primitive races in various parts. The Troglodytes here are the 'Tibboos'; for their swiftness of foot and the slave hunts of the Arabs among them cf. Lyon, Travels in North Africa, 1818–20, pp. 254–5. As strict Mahometans, they do not now eat the vermin here described by H.; but all accounts agree as to the scantiness of their food supply. Nachtigal (*u. s.* i. 266) found cave-dwellings such as H. describes.

184 1 Ἀτάραντες. The MSS. read Atlantes, which is obviously wrong. Salmasius restored Atarantes from Rhianus (in Eustathius ad Dionysii Orbis Desc. v. 66). H. seems to continue his description westwards (185. 1), but what tribe he means by the Atarantes it is impossible to say.

His story as to their being 'nameless' is probably a misunderstood echo of the African dread of magic; the name is regarded as a vital part of a man (Frazer, G. B. i. 404). Hence the care lest it should be known. For unwillingness to utter names cf. Tylor, Early History of Mankind, p. 139 seq.

2 **ὑπερβάλλοντι**, 'if excessively hot.'

καταρῶνται. Strabo (822) tells the same story of an Ethiopian tribe; cf. 94. 4 n.

3 **Ἄτλας.** H. (or his informant) has blended the Greek tradition (cf. ii. 33. 3 n.) as to the giant, who *ἔχει . . . κίονας αὐτὸς | μακρὰς αἳ γαῖάν τε καὶ οὐρανὸν ἀμφὶς ἔχουσι* (Od. i. 53), with vague knowledge of the mountain-block of the Atlas, which runs half across North Africa, from Morocco to the lesser Syrtis. The 'Pillar of Heaven' may be a native idea, but it looks suspiciously Greek (cf. Aesch. P.V. 351, and Pind. Pyth. i. 19, of Etna).

4 **ἔμψυχον οὐδέν.** The purely vegetable diet of the Atlantes is an exaggerated generalization from the fact that the North Africans live mainly on dates and meal.

185 1 **ἁλὸς μέταλλον.** H. knows the coast extends beyond the Straits of Gibraltar. His symmetry has such a hold of him that he projects his scheme of decimally recurring oases far beyond his real knowledge, over the whole sand ridge to the Atlantic.

Others, e.g. Bähr, think the words *ἔστι δὲ . . . οἰκέοντες* refer to one more oasis ten days west of the Atlantes; the singular, *μέταλλον*, favours this view, but it is less probable as a whole. In either case, the *ἁλὸς μέταλλον* here = the *ἁλὸς κολωνός* (*sup.*).

2 **οἰκία.** Houses of salt are still found in North Africa, cf. J. Hamilton ('Wanderings', 1856, p. 294); he, like H., accounts for the use of this material by the rainless climate. Shaw (i. 250) speaks of houses washed down by rain. Rohlfs (K. 269) actually advises travellers to provide themselves with water 'to open graves' built of 'Erdsalzklumpen'. The varying colour of the salt, purple, white, and blue, is also confirmed by modern travellers, e.g. Shaw (i. 271), speaking of a mountain in Tunis, near the lake of Marks. Rain apparently does fall at intervals of five years or more, but Humboldt (Aspects of Nature, p. 3) gives the same sweeping denial as H., 'neither dew nor rain bathe these desolate plains' (in North Africa).

3 **ἔρημος κτλ.** The accumulation of adjectives well expresses the vastness of the Sahara, although (literally speaking) 'water, wood, and animal life' are found in parts of it.

186 1 **νομάδες.** The general description of customs naturally ignores such exceptions as cc. 177, 184 (the Atlantes). H., however, is too absolute; round Cyrene, at any rate, the natives were cultivators.

2 **βοῶν . . . θηλέων.** This evidence for Greek intermarriage with natives is interesting (cf. c. 145 n.); Barca is even more mixed in population than Cyrene. For the pig as a racial criterion in Asia Minor cf. Ramsay, H.G. p. 32.

187 **οὐκέτι νομάδες.** Here again (as in 186. 1) H. generalizes from insufficient evidence; the Numidians subject to Carthage on the coast were agricultural, but inland they were still nomadic.

2 **καίουσι.** Cauterization is a frequent remedy among primitive tribes; cf. Hippocrates *περὶ ἀέρων* 20, of the Scyths 'whose bellies are full of moisture'; Layard quotes it in Mesopotamia (N. and B. p. 291); and Denham calls it 'the sovereign Arab remedy for almost every disorder' in Africa (Travels, i. 173); cf. Bähr *ad loc.* for other instances. The Libyans are unique in applying it to the temples by burning 'greasy wool'; but perhaps H. was unfamiliar with cauterization in any form.

According to ancient medical theory there were four 'humours' in the human body, *αἷμα, ὕδωρ, χολή*, and *φλέγμα* (cf. Hippocrates, i. 374 ed. Kühn); the last caused all kinds of catarrh.

3 **ὑγιηρότατοι.** H. gives another reason for Libyan health in ii. 77. 3, i. e. the uniform seasons. Duveyrier (p. 429) says the Tuaregs usually live to be eighty, and sometimes much longer. If these figures be accurate, it simply means that the hard life kills off all the weaklings early.

188 **ἀποστρέφουσι,** 'they bend back the neck' (for the knife). R. Neumann (p. 136) thinks the piece was thrown over the tent, to bring it under the protection of the god.

Ποσειδέωνι. H., in ii. 50. 2, when deriving the names of most Greek gods from Egypt, makes that of Poseidon to be Libyan. It is natural to connect this derivation with the Minyan element at Cyrene; Farnell (C. G. S. iv. 27) says, 'Wherever the worship of Poseidon is prominent, we find either a Thessalian-Minyan or an Ionic influence'; the Minyans, who are prominent all through the story of the foundation of Cyrene, not unnaturally pretended that their cult-god was there before them. H., in this chapter and the next, adopts the theories of North African origins in their extremest form (*v. i.*); the fact that he gives them this exaggerated value goes far to prove that he heard them on the spot.

189 1 **ἐκ τῶν Λιβυσσέων.** H. as usual (cf. ii. *pass.*) assigns a foreign origin to Greek usages; here he derives the dress of the Palladia, the 'cry' in worship, and the use of four-horse chariots from Libyan sources. The only argument advanced (§ 2) is etymological, and the only point that can be accepted is that there had been much intermixture, and so mutual influence, between Greek settlers and Libyans (cf. c. 145 n.). *ἐσθής*, as distinguished from *αἰγίς*, is the *πέπλος*; H. is probably right in saying the Libyan women wore this, and modern travellers speak of 'leather' as frequently worn among the desert tribes, e. g. Lyon (p. 110) of the shirts and kaftans of the Tuaricks (*sic*). It is also not improbable that the snakes of the *αἰγίς* were originally 'tassels'. But the resemblance between the Palladia and *αἱ Λιβυσσαί* was purely accidental, and the etymology is worthless. It is very uncertain whether the connexion

between *αἰγίς* and *αἴξ* is more than popular, and in any case the word *αἰγέη* is not Libyan, and goats were common elsewhere than in Libya. H. ignores the fact that Zeus (Il. iv. 167) and Apollo (xv. 229), as well as Athene (v. 738), wear the *αἰγίς*.

τὰ δὲ ἄλλα κτλ.: translate 'all other points are arranged in the same way' (in the dress of the Libyan women and of Athene).

2 **ἐρευθεδάνῳ.** H.'s observation is better than his archaeology; 'vermilion' is still a favourite colour in North Africa.

3 The *ὀλολυγή* (which is onomatopoetic, cf. Hallelu-jah) was the women's cry, especially in the worship of Athena; cf. Il. vi. 301 *αἱ δ' ὀλολυγῇ πᾶσαι 'Αθήνῃ χεῖρας ἀνέσχον*, and Xen. An. iv. 3. 19 the women *συνωλόλυζον* to the soldiers' *παιάν*. If the Greeks borrowed this anywhere, it would have been from the East; but the ritual cry is a natural instinct of mankind.

τέσσερας ἵππους συζευγνύναι. The statement that the Greeks borrowed the four-horse chariot from Libya has been thought to contradict Homer (Il. viii. 185, xi. 699, and Od. xiii. 81) and Pausanias (v. 8. 7), who puts the first Olympic chariot victory 680 B.C.; but H. may mean that the Greeks learned the practice before 630, when Cyrene was founded.

190 **κατημένους θάπτουσι.** The idea was that the soul could not escape if the dying man lay on his back; it would therefore haunt the grave. Rohlfs (K. p. 269) found the dead buried in a sitting posture in the oasis of Taiserbo. For other instances cf. Tylor, P. C. ii. 422–3.

σύμπηκτα: translate 'compacted of asphodel stalks inwoven round wattles'. These are the 'mapalia' of Sallust, Jug. 18; cf. Liv. xxx. 3 *ad fin.*

For the nomadic life cf. Verg. Geor. iii. 343-4 'Omnia secum Armentarius Afer agit, tectumque Laremque'.

191 1 For the Maxyes cf. c. 175 n.; they are supposed to have lived near Carthage.

χρίονται. The Tuaregs still stain themselves, the men blue, the women yellow; Duveyrier (p. 431) says they do this as a protection against changes of climate.

ἐκ Τροίης. For prehistoric migrations of Trojans cf. v. 13. 2 (the Paeonians), vii. 20 n., and Thuc. vi. 2. 3 (the Elymi at Egesta). For possible joint attacks of Libyan and Asiatic tribes on Egypt cf. App. X. 8.

3 **τὸ πρὸς ἑσπέρης.** H. is quite right as to the contrast between the eastern and the western parts of the North African coast (c. 181 n.). Full discussions of the fauna in this chapter and 192 will be found in Bähr and (later) in R. Neumann, pp. 152 seq. Of the nine beasts in this chapter, six are right, and the *ὄνοι* can be explained with some probability; the two remaining are monsters (the 'dogheads' and the 'headless') which seem to be more than doubted by H. (*v. i.*).

4 **ὄφιες οἱ ὑπερμεγάθεες**: the largest python on record is the one that

stopped the army of Regulus and had to be killed by the Roman engines (Liv. Ep. 18 'serpens portentosae magnitudinis', cf. too Silius vi. 140 f.). Pliny (viii. 37) says its skin, brought to Rome, measured 120 feet; but it belongs to the days of prescientific measurements! The largest authentic python is about 30 feet long.

λέοντες. H. is right as to the presence of lions and bears.

ἐλέφαντες. Elephants were once common in North Africa (Pliny, N. H. viii. 32, and cf. Bähr), but the needs of the Carthaginian armaments and of Roman amphitheatres extirpated them north of the desert, even as the modern big-game hunter is extirpating them now all over Africa. H. is the first writer to use 'elephant' (R. Neumann, p. 154).

ἀσπίδες. For the asp cf. ii. 74 n

ὄνοι. Probably by the horned ass is meant some kind of antelope.

κυνοκέφαλοι κτλ. Some explain the *κυνοκέφαλοι* and the *ἀκέφαλοι* as monkeys; the 'dog-headed' baboon is found in the mountains of Africa, and the 'headless' might be a kind of ape with its head so sunk in its shoulders that its eyes seemed to be in its breast (Neumann). But it is more probable that these are monsters; so Pliny (v. 46) certainly understood the passage; he says the 'headless' were called 'Blemmyae', and classes them with 'Satyrs, goatfeet', and others. Aeschylus (in Strabo 43) wrote of the *στερνόφθαλμοι* (cf. note on *ἀκατάψευστα inf.*)

ἄγριοι ἄνδρες. The 'wild men' are doubtless the 'gorillas', which Hanno (G. G. M. i. 13, *circ.* 500 B.C.) speaks of on the West Coast of Africa; he brought three skins of females to Carthage.

ἀκατάψευστα. This passage is most important as a criterion of H.'s credulity. R. Neumann (p. 155; cf. Introd. p. 44) thinks that H. accepts all the creatures of § 4 as 'beasts', but throws the responsibility for the account of them on the Libyans. But the last three lines seem to deal with 'men', not beasts.

It is better, therefore, to suppose that the *ὡς δὴ . . . Λιβύων* marks off the *κυνοκέφαλοι* and the *ἀκέφαλοι* as creatures for which H. disclaims any responsibility; he simply reports, and in *ἀκαταψευστά* clearly hints disbelief.

At any rate it is significant that the qualifying words do not refer to the *ἄγριοι ἄνδρες*, for whose existence there was real evidence at Carthage (i. e. Hanno's, *v. s.*).

Stein well compares Arist. H. A. viii. 28, 606 b; the animals of Africa are *πολυμορφότερα*; hence the proverb *αἰεὶ Λιβύη φερει τι καινόν*.

It is instructive to compare Ctesias (Ind. c. 20, p. 252), who gives a long account of the *κυνοκέφαλοι*; they are a tribe 120,000 strong, who cannot talk, but understand what is said to them!

192 1 **κατὰ τοὺς νομάδας.** H. is on the whole right in his contrast between the fauna of the East and the West; but the asps and the

antelopes are common to both regions (R. Neumann, p. 157). Of the twenty beasts in this chapter Neumann (pp. 157 seq.) identifies all but the *βόρυες* with more or less confidence. Lyon (pp. 271–2) gives a list of sixteen animals of the Fezzan; of these all but the buffalo (*βούβαλις*—some find this in the *β.*, but *v. i.*), rat, rabbit, hare, and camel are covered by H.'s list, and the camel was almost certainly introduced much later. Lyon does not mention H.'s wild ass, wild ram, and great lizard; but these are confirmed by other authorities.

πύγαργοι. The 'white rump' is in Arist. H. A. ix. 32, 618 b, a kind of eagle; but here (as in Plin. viii. 214) it is an antelope.

ζορκάδες καὶ βουβάλιες are both species of antelope.

ἄποτοι. That the 'wild asses' never drink is impossible; what is true is that they can live where any other beast would die of thirst. The *ὄρυς* seems to be the antelope *leucoryx*; the 'arms' of lyres were certainly made of horns.

2 **βασσάρια κτλ.** H. is right as to 'foxes, hyenas, and porcupines'. The **κριὸς ἄγριος** may well be the wild sheep (*Musimon tragelaphus*) of the Atlas; the **δίκτυς** seems to be a kind of jackal, as also the **θῶς**.

πάνθηρες probably include all the 'big cats' (i.e. leopards, panthers, tiger cats, &c.) of North Africa.

κροκόδειλοι. The 'crocodile' is the *Psammosaurus griseus*, a land lizard, which reaches a size of three feet. For ostriches cf. 175. 1 n. The 'small snakes' (*ὄφιες σμικροί*), as distinguished from the 'two-horned vipers' of ii. 74, are perhaps 'sand vipers'.

πλὴν ἐλάφου τε καὶ ὑὸς ἀγρίου. Aristotle (H. A. viii. 28, 606 a) repeats this, and Pacho (p. 206) vindicates H. as to the stag; Pliny (N. H. viii. 120) also denies the presence of the 'stag'; as they still are found in only a small region, stags may well have been introduced since the time of H. Although the wild boar proper is unknown, kindred species are found.

3 **δίποδες.** Clearly the 'jerboa', the fore-feet of which are very short. Rawlinson suggests that the *ζέγερις* = the 'guntsha', a rat-like animal with a bushy tail. The *ἐχινεύς* seems to be a 'stiff-haired mouse'.

βουνοί, 'hills' (199. 1), is a non-Attic word, found in Sicily as well as at Cyrene, and in later Greek, e.g. in Polyb. (*βουνώδης*).

γαλαῖ. The 'weasels' of Tartessus were ferrets used in rabbit hunting (Strabo 144).

193 The Zaueces are perhaps the predecessors of the Zeugi, from whom part of Roman Africa got its name Zeugitania.

194 **Γύζαντες.** Steph. Byz. reads 'Byzantes', expressly correcting the spelling of H. They may be represented by 'Byzacium', part of Roman Africa (Plin. v. 24).

μέλι. For honey making cf. Callatebus in Lydia (vii. 31), where it is made of tamarisk juice and wheat; also i. 193. 4 and Shaw, i. 262, a honey-like drink made from the palm.

195 1 **Κύραυιν** is probably Cercina on the Gulf of Cabes, which corresponds in dimensions and in fertility; but it is not *διαβατός*, nor is gold found there. Niebuhr supposes that H. meant the island of Cerne in the Atlantic (Hanno 8, G. G. M. i. 7); probably a legend belonging to this latter island has been blended with facts as to Cercina.

2 **εἴη δ' ἂν πᾶν.** This passage is important for H.'s use of evidence. He (rightly) does not consider the evidence sufficient to prove that gold dust is skimmed from a pool. But 'anything may happen' in remote places, as well as 'in long periods of time' (v. 9. 3). Hence he tentatively suggests the analogy of pitch 'skimmed' at Zante.

ἐν Ζακύνθῳ. For the tar wells of Zante cf. E. Dodwell (Tour in Greece, 1819). He (pp. 81-2) says the springs are some twelve miles from the town; the one in use at the time of his visit (1805) was much smaller than that of H.; but near it there is a 'spot with which his description seems in every respect to correspond'. Dodwell further describes the sea as being coloured by the pitch for some distance from the shore (cf. § 4). Chandler (Travels in Greece, 1776, p. 302) describes the method of obtaining the pitch as being exactly that of H., and Dodwell partly confirms this.

αὐτὸς ἐγώ. H. probably went to Zacynthus on his way to Thurii.

ἀμείνω. H. speaks with a traveller's (perhaps a merchant's) experience of the various kinds of pitch. Greeks thought the Pierian pitch the best (Plin. xiv. 128); it was made from the forests of Mt. Olympus. Modern experience condemns the tar of Zante.

196 **Καρχηδόνιοι.** This primitive story of silent barter is most interesting; probably the trade took place in the modern Senegambia. Lyon (p. 149) had heard of a precisely similar trade near Timbuctoo, where devils were reported to purchase red cloth with gold dust. For other instances cf. Pliny, N. H. vi. 88 (for silk in Central Asia), St. Martin, p. 329, who gives them from both the fifteenth and the eighteenth century instances, and Miss Kingsley, West African Studies (2nd edit.), p. 204 f.

197 2 **Λιβύων.** H. is speaking of Africa, west of Egypt, which last he rightly considers a separate country; but this does not prove he thought it to be a part of a different continent (cf. 39 nn.). He is quite right in distinguishing the Berber tribes of the North African coast (*Λίβυες*) from the Negroid races of the Sûdân and the Gold Coast (*Αἰθίοπες*).

198 1 **Δήμητρος καρπόν.** This passage was obviously written after i. 193. 3 where the same phrases occur.

2 **ὕεται.** The heavy rains of the Kinyps region (between the two Syrtes) are confirmed by Beechey, p. 37, and others.

3 **ἀγαθὴ δὲ γῆ.** For the fertility of the Berenice region cf. Hamilton, p. 167 'its ample crops would vie with Egypt, if a moderate amount of labour were expended'.

199 ὑψηλοτάτη. H. here produces the right impression, though his facts are not strictly accurate; Cyrene is the highest part (some 1,800 feet) of the coast region of North-east Africa, which he has in his mind; but the ranges behind, of which he did not know (e. g. Mount Harutch), rise 1,000 feet higher.

Pacho, pp. 235–6, says, 'La graduation de ces terrasses boisées et leur condition variée . . . mettent la merveilleuse tradition d'Hérodote hors de tout soupçon d'exagération'. Hamilton (p. 124) confirms the threefold vintage from his own experience (cf. also Barth. W. 403). H.'s description becomes poetical in its enthusiasm.

200 H. here resumes his narrative from c. 167.

ὀρύγματα ὑπόγαια. For mining cf. v. 115. 2, vi. 18 (Miletus). The Persians inherited the arts of besieging towns from Assyria.

2 ἐπίχαλκος here = *χάλκεος*. Cf. ix. 80. 1, 82. 2 for *ἐπίχρυσος* and *χρύσεος* used of the same *κλῖναι*.

01 3 ἔστ' ἂν ἡ γῆ κτλ.: for this paltering in a double sense cf. 154. 4, and Thuc. iii. 34. 3 (Paches at Notium).

203 διεξῆκαν. The story of the escapes of Cyrene is full of suspicious elements, the *λόγιον*, the presence of the admiral (§ 2), the panic (§ 3); nor is it consistent (§ 2) with H.'s view that the Persian expedition aimed at general conquest (c. 145 n.), or with the attack on Euesperides (c. 204). Probably it is a version made up after the fall of the Battiads by Cyrenaean vanity. Menecles (F. H. G. iv. 449, fr. 2) represents Pheretime as having at once established her grandson Battus IV on the throne, and then as subduing a Cyrenaean rebellion with a Persian army.

204 ἀνασπάστους. For transplantation of conquered peoples cf. iii. 93. 2 and vi. 3 nn.

Βακτρίης. That H. had ever been in Bactria is now believed by no one. It is interesting to contrast the precise details of vi. 119 as to the similar deportation of the Eretrians to Ardericca (near Susa), with the bare *ἐς ἐμέ* here (cf. for H.'s travels Introd. pp. 16–20).

205 εὐλέων ἐξέζεσε. Sulla (Plut. c. 36) and Herod Agrippa (Acts xii. 23) died by the same loathsome disease; the reflection of H. is most characteristic.

τῆς Βάττου. Pheretime was the wife of Battus III (the lame); but the words would naturally mean 'daughter of Battus'. In this case she would be the daughter of Battus II, who came to the throne about 575 B.C., probably as a youngish man; his father only reigned sixteen years (159. 1). H. expressly tells us that kindred marriages were practised by the royal house (164. 4); that Battus III should marry his aunt would be another trace of the native strain in the blood of the Battiadae. The fact that Pheretime herself is of the royal house suits well the prominent part which she plays in the story (165. 1).

APPENDIXES

APPENDIX I

THE ETHNOGRAPHY OF WESTERN ASIA MINOR AND THE LYDIAN HISTORY OF H.

[**Authorities.** For the history and art of Western Asia Minor cf. Perrot et Chipiez, Hist. de l'Art dans l'Antiquité, vol. v (1890). On Phrygia cf. P. Gardner, New Chapters in Greek History, pp. 28 seq., on Lydia, P. Radet, Lydie et le Monde Grec (687–546 B.C.), a most interesting book, but too ready to defend traditional views. For the languages cf. Kretschmer, Einleitung in die Gesch. der griech. Sprache, and for the whole subject Meyer, i. 472 seq. (especially 476), and Hogarth's brilliant sketch, 'Ionia and the East.']

§ 1. Asia Minor is the meeting-place between East and West, the bridge by which opposing civilizations have advanced in turn to attack each other. Hence, as might be expected, there is a great mixture of races in it. But, broadly speaking, the Halys is the dividing line.[1]

East of it the peoples are mostly Semitic; this may be due to direct immigration or to the influence of the great Semitic empires, whether the Hittite, ruling from Pteria or Carchemish, or the Assyrian from Mesopotamia.

§ 2. **Asia Minor West of the Halys.** But these peoples concern the student of H. comparatively little; it is the tribes in the western half, with which the Greeks had come more into contact, that take an important place in H.'s account of the relations of Greeks and Barbarians. These tribes are especially the Mysians, the Lydians, and the Phrygians.[2]

They were probably akin to each other; this was certainly the opinion of the ancients, e. g. H., who, as a native of Halicarnassus, was likely to know the truth (i. 171. 6 n.), says that Carians, Mysians, and Lydians were akin, and quotes ritual evidence; and Xanthus

[1] Cf. Ramsay, H. G. p. 32, where the statement is limited.

[2] For the Carians and the Lycians cf. i. 171, 173 nn.; the former were subject to Croesus (i. 28), but neither of these tribes appear in Lydian history so much as the more northern ones.

(fr. 8),[1] using the evidence of dialect, says that the Mysians were half-way between Phrygians and Lydians. This view is partly confirmed by the fact that, of the few Lydian words known, some are said to be Carian, and others Phrygian, and also by 'the most general features of the popular worships of Western Asia Minor', e.g. the importance of 'the great goddess who personified the creative power of nature'.[2] This cult is found everywhere.

§ 3. **Origin of the Peoples. Invasion from Europe.** Another view of the ancient writers is now generally accepted as true in the main, though a generation ago it was looked on as a mere piece of Hellenic vanity, i.e. that these Anatolian races had come in from the North-west. Xanthus (fr. 5) says that the Phrygians came from Thrace, after the Trojan war; H. says they had been 'neighbours of the Macedonians' (vii. 73. 1 n.), and also that the Bithynians (vii. 75. 2) were originally Thracians. Strabo (295) says the same of the Mysians.[3]

It is true that we cannot quote similar opinions about the Lydians and the Carians; probably their immigration had been earlier, perhaps some centuries before 1000 B.C., as they had penetrated further south, and so all tradition of it had been lost.

§ 4. **Primitive Anatolian Population.** But modern criticism conjectures another element in the races of Western Asia, the existence of which was forgotten, or never known, by the Greeks. The tribes from the North were warriors, who established themselves as a ruling caste; but an earlier race survived as serfs, and, in fact, formed the mass of the population.[4] As the conquerors brought few

[1] F.H.G. i. 37; for Xanthus' relations to H. see Introd. p. 23.

[2] Perrot, v. pp. 242–3: the Greeks called her Cybele at Smyrna, Artemis at Ephesus, Enys (Bellona) at Comana, where her proper name was Ma (Strabo 535). For her wide prevalence as a coin-type cf. Hogarth, Ephesus, pp. 330–1.

[3] Further evidence is afforded:

(1) By myths, e.g. that of Midas and his rose garden is localized near Edessa and Mount Bermius (viii. 138. 2) in Macedonia.

(2) Common names; that of the 'Mygdones' round Dascyleum is repeated in 'Mygdonia' on the lower Axius; so, too, there are 'Brygians' in Macedonia (vi. 45. 2) as late as 493 B.C. (Βρύγοι is the Macedonian dialect form of Φρύγες, cf. Βίλιππος.)

(3) Common civilization; musical skill and orgiastic rites are characteristic both of Thrace and of Phrygia.

For the legend of a counter-movement from Asia to Europe cf. vii. 20. 1 nn.

[4] 'It is reasonable to characterize the whole original population of Western Asia as Proto-Armenian' (J.H.S. xix. 49). We have traces of their languages in place-names ending in 'ssa', 'nda', and of their matriarchal system in the prominence of the female elements in myths and cults; the presence of similar place-names in Greece seems to indicate that the race was spread on both sides of the Aegean; cf. i. 171. 1 n. and Meyer, i. 476.

women with them, they married the women of this earlier race, and so were gradually absorbed in the nationality of their own subjects.

Such a process has happened repeatedly in India; such a process is conjectured to explain the disappearance from modern France of the race of tall, fair Gallic warriors, once so terrible to the Romans; such a process explains naturally what was always an enigma to the Greeks. Tradition spoke of the warlike Phrygians (Hom. Il. iii. 185); early history knew of the famous Lydian cavalry (i 80. 4); but Lydians and Phrygians later were effeminate and 'natural slaves'. To explain the puzzle, stories like that of i. 155. 4 were invented; the result of a gradual process is put down to the policy of an individual.

§ 5. **Results of the mixture.** The blending of a race of European conquerors with a subject population also explains the difficulty which modern scholars have felt in determining the race of these Anatolian peoples. On the one hand, the survivals of their languages seem to be akin to the Indo-European tongues[1]; and similarity of origin is indicated by the way in which they influenced and were influenced by the Greeks.[2] On the other hand, it is possible to see a clear Oriental element in their worships,[3] their social customs (i. 94. 1), and their myths.[4] Even in the worship of the 'Great Mother' herself (cf. 80 n.), there is a blending of Northern and of Eastern elements, of frenzied excitement and of sensual impurity.

The mixture of conquered and conquering races will explain all this. At the same time Radet[5] may be right in thinking that there had been a definite Syrian immigration into Lydia, adding a Semitic

[1] Perhaps we may compare the Lydian Manes (i. 94. 3) with Indian 'Manu' and German 'Mannus'. Plato (Crat. 410 A) had already noticed the resemblances of Greek and Phrygian. On the other hand, the longest Lydian inscription (that recently found at Sardis, i. 84. 1 n.), though so far untranslated, shows, in its terminations at any rate, that it is not akin to Greek.

[2] For similarity of customs cf. i. 35. 2 (purification), 74. 6 (oaths), and c. 94 (the general statement).

[3] Cf. the *ἱερόδουλοι* at Comana, Strabo 535.

[4] Cf. the story of the death of Croesus' son, i. 36 seq., and the frequency of the termination 'Attes' in Lydian names; cf., too, the stories of the Amazons.

[5] p. 54. Though Atys is a native Anatolian figure, he is connected with the local god of North Syria, Ate; but whether the cult immigration was from Syria into Anatolia, or vice versa, is disputed (Meyer, i. 487 n.). It has been argued that the Lydians were of Semitic race because in Gen. x. 22 'Lud' is the son of Shem; but, even allowing this genealogy to have any significance as to race connexion, 'Lud' must stand for some tribe far to the south-east of Asia Minor; for he comes between 'Arphaxad' (Chaldaea) and 'Aram' (Syria).

element to the already mixed population; but it is equally possible that the Lydians, as the great intermediaries between East and West, 'the Phoenicians of the land,' were influenced by imitation of the Semitic races, rather than by actual Semitic immigration.

§ 6. **Date of the Migrations.** If we might believe that among the 'peoples of the sea' who attack Egypt in the thirteenth century B.C. (cf. App. X. 8) we have the 'Maeonians' ('Maunna'), i.e. the Lydians, we should have an approximate date for their southern progress; but the identification is most uncertain. In any case Lydia, as has been already argued, seems to have been occupied by a northern race of conquerors much earlier than Phrygia; for while in Lydia the Mother-goddess of the subject race became the chief divinity, in Phrygia, on the contrary, the Father-god, Papas, the god of the conquerors, was never displaced. We may infer that the reason why the process of assimilation in Phrygia began later and was never so complete was that the conquest itself was later.[1]

§ 7. **Phrygia.** The Phrygian kingdom can perhaps be dated with some approximate certainty. Neither in the Iliad nor in the Hymn to Aphrodite do the names of 'Gordias' or 'Midas' occur in connexion with the Phrygians, though this people is repeatedly mentioned.[2]

Hence it was probably only *circ.* 800 B.C. that the real Phrygian kingdom was founded. It lasted about two centuries, for its memory was still fresh in the time of Croesus (i. 35; but see note there); the fugitive Adrastus is a prince of its blood royal. Of its history we know nothing beyond a few stories (e.g. i. 14); we may probably accept as historical the fact that its king, Midas, perhaps the grandson of 'Mita, king of the Muski', mentioned by Sargon about 718 (Winckler, Altor. For. ii. 136), committed suicide at the time of the Cimmerian invasion (Strabo 61; *circ.* 650 B.C.). No doubt the raids of these barbarians ruined Phrygia and made it an easy prey to its Lydian neighbour, under whose rule we find it at the end of the seventh century.

It strongly influenced the Greeks; from them it borrowed its alphabet, while in return it gave the Greeks myths, like that of Pelops or of Marsyas, architectural forms, and orgiastic worships. That the Phrygians were once a warlike people we know only from Homer, and from the 'Broken-Lion Tomb', on which two warriors in Carian armour are represented (J. H. S. ix. 363 f.).

§ 8. **The Lydians.** But between the Phrygians and the Greeks

[1] Winckler, however, puts the first migration of the Phrygians in the twelfth century B.C., and identifies the 'Mita of Muski' of that date with 'Midas'. Garstang (Hittites, pp. 53–8) accepts this, and considers that this northern invasion was the first blow to the Hittite power; but he admits that the chief migration of the Phrygians was not till the ninth century.

[2] Il. ii. 862; iii. 184–9; x. 431; xvi. 719; Hymn, 111–12, 137.

on the seaboard lay the Lydians, the tribe with whose attack on Greece H. begins his history. That this attack was connected with the change of dynasty described by him is obvious.[1] It is tempting to conjecture that some immigration of fighting men from the North (cf. 'Dascylus', father of Gyges and 'Dascylium', i. 8. 1 n.) was the cause of the new vigour of the Lydian monarchy which the Greeks found so serious. Perhaps the tradition that Gyges was a member of the royal body-guard is a true one, and we may suppose that the degenerate Heraclidae had invited northern warriors to defend them, and then were deposed by their own defenders (cf. the legend of Vortigern and the first Saxon invasion of England). But this is pure conjecture; we can only say for certain that in the seventh century Lydia first began to be known to Assyria ('Gugu' figures in the inscriptions (cf. i. 15; ii. 152 nn.) of Assurbanipal) and also to the Greeks. The change of dynasty which coincided with this rise of the nation into prominence is a fact, but its circumstances are lost in fable.

§ 9. **Rise of the Mermnad Dynasty.** Of the change itself we have four different versions:

(1) That of H., which is clearly favourable to Gyges and bears marked traces of Delphic influence (e. g. i. 13. 2 *et pass.*).

(2) That of Nicolaus of Damascus (*circ.* 30 B.C.; for his fragments cf. F. H. G. iii), who is supposed to give the account of Xanthus. According to this, Gyges was not a mere soldier, but was the head of a noble Lydian house: his grandfather had been a sort of Mayor of the Palace, but had been murdered by the king. Gyges was born in exile, but was recalled, and became a favourite with Sadyattes (= H.'s 'Candaules'). He abused his position by trying to play Lancelot to his master's bride, the Mysian princess Tudo, and to escape her vengeance, killed his master.

(3) The third version is that of Plato (Rep. p. 359), who invests Gyges with a magic ring conferring invisibility.[2] In this story, too, the queen appears.

(4) The fourth story is that of Plutarch (Q. G. 45, Mor. 302), which seeks to explain the origin of the double-axe of Zeus of Labranda or Labraunda; this story may preserve one element of importance, i. e. that Gyges was assisted by Carian mercenaries.

The question whether any of these stories be true, in whole or in part, is impossible of decision. It is more important to note: (*a*) that clearly the greatest uncertainty prevailed in the Greece of H.

[1] Perhaps the displacement of 'Maeonian' by 'Lydian' is part of the same sequence of events.

[2] This motive is very Eastern, and occurs in the Arabian Nights and elsewhere. It is indeed quite possible that there were two 'Gyges', a native Lydian 'hero' (cf. the Gygaean Lake, i. 93. 5) and the historic Gyges. The legends of the former may have influenced the history of the latter.

as to the events of the two preceding centuries; the kings of the Mermnad dynasty were historical persons, but fiction had been busy with their names; (*b*) that in three of the four versions of the story the queen plays a part; this is a characteristic of Anatolian legend, which makes the female element always prominent[1]; (*c*) the blending of popular stories and real history, which marks H.'s account of the seventh and sixth centuries, is not due to any special peculiarity of his own, but was the inevitable result of the uncertain nature of his evidence.

To sum up briefly, H. as usual has his names right; but he knows little or nothing of the real course of events: this is especially seen in his ignorance of the relations of Lydia and Assyria. (Cf. App. II. 4.) His chronology too is artificial and mainly inaccurate.

§ 10. **The Chronology of the Mermnadae.** H. assigns to the house of Gyges 170 years (viz. Gyges 38 (c. 15), Ardys 49, Sadyattes 12 (c. 16), Alyattes 57 (c. 25), Croesus 14 (c. 86. 1)). Reckoning these years back from the fall of Croesus (for the date of this cf. i. 86 n.), we must place the accession of Gyges about 716 B.C. But this is about half a century too early; Gyges was the contemporary of Archilochus (fr. 24; H. i. 12. 2), and was reigning after 660 B.C., as we know from the monuments of Assurbanipal (*v. s.*). Probably then the Lydian chronology of H. is a mere calculation[2], his own or more probably that of some predecessor; it is reckoned on the basis of $33\frac{1}{3}$ years to a generation, i.e. the five Lydian kings reign for $166\frac{2}{3}$ years + the 'three' of the Delphic story (i. 91. 3). On what principle (if any) these 170 years were distributed it is impossible to say; only it is natural that to Alyattes, with whom Lydian power reaches its height, is assigned the longest reign.

§ 11. **Importance of Lydia in Greek history.** The Lydians have an influence on Greek history in two main respects, social and political. Socially, they stand by the side of the Phoenicians as the intermediaries between East and West at the beginning of the historic period (i. e. eighth and seventh centuries B.C.); under their rule were the outlets to the Aegean of the long caravan routes, which reached across Asia Minor to the valley of the Euphrates. Hence it was natural that they should be the inventors of coined money (H. i. 94. 1 n.). Politically, they were the first Oriental despotism with which the Greeks came into close contact. Hence they were the first to subdue the Greeks (i. 6. 2), and it is not improbable that the example of their wealthy kings led to the estab-

[1] Radet, however (p. 122), thinks Tudo the queen was a real person, and that her prominence is explained by some Lydian custom of making the throne descend in the female line (cf. i. 173 n. for such a custom).

[2] Radet (p. 144), however, ingeniously tries to prove that 716 B.C. is the date of Gyges' birth.

lishment of τυραννίδες among the Greeks. τύραννος is said to be a Lydian word (cf. App. XVI. 2).

§ 12. **Sources of H.'s history.** These can be very clearly traced:

(1) Delphic tradition; cc. 14, 50, 51 would have shown this, even apart from the direct statement in c. 20; hence the whole story has a theological tendency (cf. 13. 2 n.).

(2) Other Greek tradition, perhaps especially from Miletus (cf. cc. 20 and 74, 75, the stories as to Thales); much of this was no doubt ethical narrative (e.g. the story of Solon), which had grown up round famous names.

(3) Fragments of Lydian tradition, e.g. the legends of Atys and Adrastus, the lion cub of Meles (c. 84), &c.; most of this, however, probably came to H. through Greek channels, though his accounts of the tomb of Alyattes and of the manners of the Lydians (cc. 93–4) seem based on his own observation.

§ 13. **The Lydian origin of the Etruscans.** The theory that the Etruscans were Eastern in origin was almost universally held in antiquity, Dionysius of Halicarnassus (i. 27 f.) is the only important dissentient. The most popular form of the theory was that of H., which made them to have been Lydians (cf. i. 94. 6). Archaeology tends to confirm the tradition. One of the most curious of the resemblances between the Etruscans and Asia Minor is their chamber-tombs[1]; there are marked resemblances also in dress, in beliefs, especially as to divination, and in customs. Perhaps the most striking feature of all is the frequent recurrence in Etruria of the polygonal walls of Mycenaean Greece and of Asia Minor.[2] That the Etruscans were Orientals and came by sea is then one of the many points in which archaeology tends to confirm H. against the scepticism of nineteenth-century scholars (in this case Niebuhr and Mommsen, R. H. i. 129).

APPENDIX II

ASSYRIA AND BABYLON

§ 1. **The beginnings of civilization in Mesopotamia.** At what period civilization began in the valley of the Euphrates it is impossible to say; the date given by Nabonidus for Naramsin, the son of Sargon of Accad, i.e. 3750 B.C., has been thought to be confirmed by the excavations at Nippur, though a lower date is now usually adopted; Naramsin at any rate seems to be historical.

[1] The Etruscan tombs seem to show, e.g., that they, like the Lycians (cf. i. 173), traced descent through the mother.

[2] For a full summary of the evidence cf. B. Modestov, Introd. à l'Histoire Romaine, 1907, pp. 341 seq.

What is of more importance is the mixed character of the population of Babylonia, where a primitive population, perhaps of Turanian type, became blended with Semitic invaders, who adopted from their predecessors the cuneiform script and certain elements at all events of their art and their religion. This primitive population is often called 'Sumerian', and its language 'Accadian'. Even as early as the above-mentioned Sargon, the arms of Chaldaea perhaps were carried to the Mediterranean; but the main interest for us of this primitive period is the highly developed civilization which is revealed in the code of Hammurabi (twenty-third century B.C.), recently discovered at Susa.[1] The 'struggle of the nations' begins, however, with the Egyptian conquest of Syria under Thothmes III (1501–1447), which followed, as a reaction, the expulsion of the Hyksos from Egypt; the rivalry of the valleys of the Nile and the Euphrates from this time forward is a constantly recurring feature in history, till the world-empire of Rome absorbed both.

§ 2. **The Rise of Assyria.** But it was a new power, not Babylonia, which at first played the prominent part in this struggle; the purely Semitic race of Assyria, ruled at first by priest-kings dependent on Babylon (between 2000 and 1600 B.C.), became independent about 1400 B.C. Their original home was on both banks of the Upper Tigris, south of Mount Masius. The Assyrians were the warrior race of antiquity; their religion, their art, their cuneiform writing they borrowed from Chaldaea; but their reckless cruelty, their religious fanaticism, and their love of empire were their own; they begin the series of world-powers whose rule we can trace in Western Asia. Their rule is fittingly symbolized by the great winged bulls of Sargon and Sennacherib.

The earlier Assyrian Empire. Of their early conquests it is impossible to speak here; it may perhaps be noted, however, that Tiglath-pileser I (*circ.* 1130 B.C.) is the first Assyrian king whose armies reach the Euxine and the Mediterranean; if we reckon back from the fall of Nineveh (*c.* 606 B.C.), his date corresponds curiously with the '520 years' which H. (i. 95) gives for Assyrian rule in Upper Asia.[2]

§ 3. **The Second Assyrian Empire.** It is the great warrior kings from the ninth to the seventh century with whom we are most familiar, and of whom even H. had heard one fact (*v. i.*). They rule from Media to the Mediterranean and the Euxine. Tiglath-

[1] Cf. King and Hall, pp. 267 seq.; Maspero, pp. 157–8. H. united Babylonia and made Babylon the capital. Hommel (Hastings, *s.v.* Babylonia) dates him 1772–1717 B.C.

[2] It is interesting to compare Berosus' (fr. 11, F. H. G. ii. 503) estimate of 526 years from Semiramis to Pul, i. e. to middle of the eighth century. H. as usual compares favourably with the wild estimate of Ctesias, who gives Assyrian rule 1360 years (Diod. ii. 21).

pileser III[1] (745 to 727 B.C.) anticipates the work of Darius Hystaspes; he seems to be the first monarch to organize his empire, fixing a definite tribute; he also introduces the plan, afterwards continually adopted by his successors and by the Persians, of securing important districts by wholesale deportations of prisoners. 'His accession marks a new turning-point in the history of Hither Asia.' Sargon, his next successor but one (722–705 B.C.), is well known as the destroyer of Samaria; by its fall Assyria and Egypt were brought into direct contact, except for the feeble buffer-state of Judah. He fought against the kings of the twenty-fifth dynasty, whom H. (ii. 137) combines into one, Sabakos the Ethiopian. Sargon's successor, Sennacherib (705–681), was renewing the attack on Egypt when his army was destroyed by plague (cf. ii. 141 n.). Finally, Esarhaddon, his son, broke the power of Egypt (672–670 B.C.), drove the invading Ethiopians southward, and set up native Egyptian princes as vassals in the Delta, whose rule seems to be vaguely referred to in H.'s story of the Dodecarchy (ii. 147 n.). The next king, Assurbanipal (668–625 B.C.), is the last of the great Assyrians; he sacked Thebes in 664, and received the submission of Gyges of Lydia (cf. App. I. 8); his library, collected at Nineveh, has survived his conquests, and is one of the greatest of the Oriental treasures of the British Museum.

§ 4. **Decline and Fall of Assyria.** But Assyria was exhausted with its long wars, and could not hold out longer against the rising nationalities of Media, Lydia, and Persia, nor against the attacks of the northern barbarians (see i. 15 n.). The fall of its capital, Nineveh (*c.* 606 B.C.), so vividly described by the prophet Nahum, marks the beginning of a new period of history. On the ruins of the Assyrian empire rise new national powers, which, after a century of rivalry, are absorbed by the new world-power, the Persian empire. The greatness of Assyria was hardly known to H., and his ignorance of it is the most serious gap in what we may perhaps by compliment call his 'Oriental history'; of Egypt and Babylon he knew something, but of Assyria, the name of only one king and two events. And the reason is obvious; Assyria disappeared more completely from history than any other great state had ever done; its rule was based on force and cruelty; it raised against itself a feeling of universal hatred, and, when its power was broken, its very name was blotted out, and left no trace behind it.[2] And it must be remembered

[1] For him cf. Meyer, i[1]. 446–53; he removed the Syrians to Kir (2 Kings xvi. 9), and corresponds both to Pul (xv. 19) and to Tiglath-pileser (xv. 29; xvi. 7) in the Book of Kings. Just before his accession, Nabonassar became (747 B.C.) dependent king of Babylon; with him commences the famous 'Canon of Ptolemy', a list of Babylonian, Assyrian, and Persian kings with dates (for it cf. Hastings, *s.v.* Assyria, p. 179, or E.B.[11] iii. 871).

[2] The retreating Greeks under Xenophon marched past the ruins of Nineveh, without even knowing (Anab. iii. 4. 10–11) what they were.

that the long waste of Assyrian blood had only been artificially replaced by the introduction of conquered peoples; when the constraining power was withdrawn most of these would scatter.

§ 5. **History of Babylonia.** Babylonia meantime had been a subordinate state; it had been definitely conquered in 728 B. C., and only regained its independence under Nabopolassar (625-605 B. C.). With the fall of Nineveh, it succeeded for a short period to the rule of Mesopotamia. Nebuchadnezzar, the son of Nabopolassar, is without doubt the most familiar figure in the history of the East before Cyrus; during his long reign (605-562 B. C.) he twice captured Jerusalem (598 and 587), he humbled Egypt and perhaps invaded it (ii. 161 n.), and did his best to maintain the balance of power in Western Asia (i. 74); it did not need a great statesman to foresee that the real danger lay on the East from the Iranian powers. It was to guard against these that he made Babylon a gigantic fortress, to which the 'Median wall'[1] was a first line of defence in the North. The city itself he adorned with the greatest splendour[2]; he was 'the Augustus of Babylon' (G. Rawlinson). His successors were weak monarchs, of whom only the last, Nabonidus (H., 188. 1, calls him 'Labynetus'), need be mentioned. He was distinguished as a scholar and archaeologist, and our knowledge owes much to his researches; but he was no warrior. He offended the priests of Babylon by his neglect of 'the daily offering' and of the worship of Marduk, and by his transference to Babylon of old local cults. Hence when Cyrus, after overthrowing the Lydian allies of Babylon (i. 77. 2 n.), advanced against him, his subjects betrayed him, and his great city fell almost without a blow[3] (538 B. C.); the story of Babylon is henceforth part of the story of Persia.[4]

§ 6. **The Ἀσσύριοι λόγοι of H.** The question of the amount of knowledge (or rather ignorance) which H. possessed of the events briefly epitomized above, is complicated by the fact that he had intended to treat the history of Babylon and Assyria separately; he twice promises a fuller account (i. 106, 184). The most probable

[1] For the 'Median wall' cf. Xen. Anab. i. 7. 15.

[2] For his works cf. i. 180 seq. nn. It is curious that H. knows nothing of his name. He speaks of him as 'Labynetus' in i. 74. 3, 188. 1 (as the father of the last king of Babylon), and attributes some of his great buildings to his wife Nitocris (c. 185 n.).

[3] Of these discreditable events H. had heard nothing, though they had happened less than a century before his visit to Babylon. In their place had been substituted the wonderful story of the diversion of the water of the Euphrates, which is a pure invention, presumably of the Chaldaean priests. The real story was only discovered in 1879 (cf. App. IV. 1). We must probably also attribute H.'s ignorance of the name of Nebuchadnezzar to the prejudices of the priests against the royal house.

[4] Berosus (fr. 14, F. H. G. ii. 508) says Nabonidus was made satrap of Carmania, but he really seems to have died at once (Prášek, i. 230; see, however, R. of P.[2] v. 163).

view is that this was to be a digression (like the Libyan λόγοι promised ii. 161 and given at the end of Bk. IV) which was to be introduced in connexion with the account of the second capture of Babylon (at end of Bk. III), but which H. never wrote; that it was to be an independent work seems unlikely, still more unlikely that it was written and perished,[1] while most unlikely of all is Lehmann's theory that the 'Assyrian History' only concerned Babylon, and was derived mainly, if not entirely, from the temple of Nebo at Borsippa (Woch. für klass. Phil. 1896, p. 85). This last is a pure assumption, though H. was especially familiar with this temple (i. 181. 2 n.).

Defects in the narrative of H. Two of these have been already mentioned—his complete ignorance of the greatness of Assyria, and the prejudice of his informants against the royal house of Babylon. Two others may be added: (1) he is completely ignorant of the extreme antiquity of Mesopotamian civilization; (2) he obviously has no idea of the difference between Assyria and Babylonia (i. 184 *et pass.*). But it may be noted to his credit that he has none of the wild stories as to Ninus, the founder of Nineveh (cf. i. 6 n.), or as to the warrior queen and sensualist Semiramis, the Assyrian Catherine II (i. 184 n.), which Diodorus (ii. 4 seq.) borrows from Ctesias. The Semiramis of Ctesias is a mythical figure, made up partly from the story of the great goddess Ishtar (Astarte), partly from confused remembrances of the great Assyrian conquests; the Semiramis of H. is a historic queen. There can be little doubt that H. had visited Babylon (i. 178 n.); the vividness and (generally speaking) the accuracy of his account of its customs and its buildings (i. 178 f. with notes) confirm his claim to be an eyewitness. But he saw it only as a temporary visitor, and he shows none of the intimate familiarity with this part of the world that he shows in Egypt.

APPENDIX III

MEDIAN HISTORY

§ 1. The tremendous efforts of Assyria during the eighth and the first part of the seventh centuries had exhausted the old powers of South-west Asia, which were mainly Semitic; the Chaldaeans had

[1] Stein (p. xlvii) argues that it was to be an independent work, as being less connected with Persian history than any of the other digressions. Aristotle (H. A. (601 b 3) viii. 18) remarks that H. was ignorant that an eagle is ἄποτος· πεποίηκε γὰρ τὸν τῆς μαντείας πρόεδρον ἀετὸν ἐν τῇ διηγήσει περὶ τὴν πολιορκίαν τὴν Νίνου πίνοντα (there is a *v. l.* Ἡσίοδος, but the word διήγησις seems very inappropriate to a poetical episode of the Hesiodic Ὀρνιθομαντεία). The 'prophetic eagle' is a subject which H. would have loved, but it is hard to believe that a separate work of the 'Father of History' has survived only in this scanty reference. See, however, Rawlinson (on i. 106) for further evidence.

been subdued, the power of Elam had been broken, Syria had been overrun again and again, and largely depopulated; and the conquerors themselves were almost equally weakened. The rapid success of the Aryan nations of the East in founding new empires must be largely explained by this cause.

Geographical position of Media. The Medes[1] were the first of these to come to the front. They lived on the high plateau south-west of the Caspian, and in the mountain ranges (running north-west and south-east) which border the valley of the Upper Tigris. They were preceded in this country by an earlier race, the 'Proto-Medes'. The Aryan migration may well have started in the second millennium B.C., though the name 'Aryan' does not appear on the Assyrian monuments till the reign of Sargon; the campaigns of Tiglath-pileser III (745–727 B.C.) in the north-east are against opponents whose names are largely Aryan.[2]

§ 2. **Media and Assyria.** The country of Media was ruled by petty chiefs; Sargon in 715–714 receives tribute (R. P. vii. 34) from twenty-two rulers in Media, and in the East at any rate the people were largely nomadic.[3] Raids against Media were a regular part of the Assyrian policy from the time of Shalmaneser II (859–825 B.C.), and the people were transplanted wholesale to other parts of the empire, e.g. Dayaukhu in 715 by Sargon to Hamath, while the children of Israel were placed in the 'cities of the Medes'.

The great kings of eighth-century Assyria thought no more of the petty tribes on their north-east frontier than the British Râj fears Pathans or Belochees; but it was from them the fatal blow was to come; from their geographical position, close to the capital, Nineveh, they could strike with the greater effect.

§ 3. **Beginnings of Median independence.** Greek tradition placed the beginning of the Median kingdom in the last quarter of the eighth century. The name of Deioces is historical, but only as one of Sargon's conquests[4]; it is not unlikely that he was the leader of a national party among the Medes, and that the success of his descendants was attributed to him. It is noticeable that no conquests are placed in his long reign of fifty-three years (cc. 101, 102). The real assertion of Median independence may be placed in the time of the Assyrian king Esarhaddon (680–668 B.C.). Great as he was, he was conscious that his power was declining, and he endeavoured to support his arms by diplomacy;

[1] Cf. H. vii. 62. 1 ἐκαλέοντο πάλαι Ἄριοι.

[2] Prášek (i. 30, 82).

[3] Cf. i. 96 nn. κατὰ κώμας; but though H. has preserved a Median tradition as to the origins of the race, the details of his story are Greek. R. P. vii. 33 seems to show the Medes were mainly in the pastoral stage.

[4] *u.s.* and R. P. vii. 37, capture of Bit Dayaukhu in 713. For his date *vid. inf.*

so he gave an Assyrian princess in marriage to a Scythian chief (i. 103. 3 n.), and seems to have tried to enlist allies among the Medes.[1] If we may lay stress on a casual mention of 'Mamitiarsu the Mede'[2] among the confederates of Kastarit against Esarhaddon (680–676 B.C.), we have a curious coincidence with one version in H. of the duration of the Median power, i.e. for '128 years' preceding 550 B.C. (i. 130). But the whole matter is uncertain.

The same must be said of H.'s second king, Phraortes, whom he makes to reign twenty-two years (647–625 B.C.), conquer Persia and other tribes, and finally fall in battle against Nineveh. The monuments do not help us, but H.'s story may be true,[3] even as to the conquest of Persia.

§ 4. **The Empire of Cyaxares.** But there is no doubt that real Median greatness begins with Cyaxares. If he succeeded to a beaten army and a disunited kingdom, he died (after a reign of forty years) the most powerful ruler of Western Asia. In him the organizer was combined with the warrior; he broke up the old tribal contingents, and arranged his forces after the Assyrian model in a regular army (i. 103). His success was hindered for a time by the inroad of the Scyths (cf. i. 103 n.); but if these came at the request of the Assyrians, they did as much harm to friends as to foes; and when Cyaxares had got rid of them, he easily recovered his power, and Nineveh at last fell (*circ.* 606 B.C.). The invitation to the attack came from the king of Babylon, but, as the Hillah inscription of Nabonidus[4] seems to indicate, it was the Medes alone who actually took the city. Babylon, however, had its share of the spoil, as H.'s informants, if not he himself, knew[5] (i. 106. 3 n.). Cyaxares, however, took the lion's share, and had no difficulty in extending his rule over countries which for nearly

[1] Prášek, i. 126.

[2] Cf. Knudtzon, Assyr. Gebete, pp. 80–1, Omen 2; Prášek, i. 118.

[3] i. 102 nn.; Maspero (iii. 455) accepts; Rawlinson (i. 396) thinks that Phraortes is the Fravartish of the Behistun Inscription, changed by patriotic imagination from a sixth-century pretender into a seventh-century king. His arguments are:

(1) Cyaxares founded the Median power; it is from him pretenders claim descent (but this may well be due only to his great conquests).

(2) Aeschylus Pers. 765–6 gives only *two* Median kings, but admittedly Aeschylus knew much less of Oriental history than H. For other theories cf. Prášek, i. 134–40, who calls Phraortes 'Astyages I' (an official title), following Berosus, fr. 12 (F. H. G. ii. 505). Phraortes has also been identified (without any reason) with the Arphaxad of the Book of Judith.

[4] Col. 2; Ball, Light from the East, p. 213.

[5] It must be said, however, that they exaggerate the part of Media, in that they give no hint that the great Assyrian empire was perishing under attacks from every side. Babylon took the southern provinces. Even the Egyptian, Necho, seems to have had the same object—to recover provinces lost to Assyria (cf. ii. 158 n.).

a century had been wasted, not only by the Assyrians, but also by Cimmerians and Scythians. He probably ruled from the Helmund in the East to the Halys in the West; the coalition to check the excessive power of Media, and its support to Lydian resistance, are at least indicated by H. (i. 74 n.).

§ 5. **The Fall of Media.** Of the last Median monarch, Astyages, we know very little.[1] His memory was blackened in the tradition which H. had received, probably from the descendants of Harpagus (*v. i.*); but traitors do not speak well of those they have betrayed. To judge from the precautions of the Babylonian kings, he was thought formidable by his neighbours; the Greek tradition made him a weakling (Arist. Pol. 1312 a 12), but this can hardly be true. It is to be noticed that Nabonidus rejoices at his defeat by Cyrus, and ascribes it to his impiety in allowing his Scytho-Medic troops to plunder the holy city of Harran.[2] With his fall the rule of Asia passed to the kindred[3] race of the Persians, but it remained in Aryan hands till the rise of the Parthians in the third century B.C.

A not very successful attempt is made by Prášek[4] to distinguish two independent traditions in H.'s Median history, that of the house of Harpagus (cf. App. IV. 4) and a popular source (in i. 123–130).

§ 6. **Chronology of Median Rule.** The only scheme worth considering is that of H.; it is as follows:

Deioces	53 years	(102. 1)	700–647.
Phraortes	22 ,,	(102. 2)	647–625.
Cyaxares	40 ,,	(106. 3)	625–585.
Astyages	35 ,,	(130. 1)	585–550.[5]

[1] Winckler's theory (Altor. Gesch. 1889, p. 125), that he was a Scythian usurper, is now given up, even by himself; it was based on the fact that his troops are called 'Umman Manda', both in the Cyrus Cylinder (cf. App. IV. 1) and in the Sippara inscription. That 'Manda' originally meant the raiders from the North is certain, but it seems now to be generally admitted that it is used also of the Medes who came from the North. The interesting question, whether he is 'Darius the Mede' of the Book of Daniel, is discussed by Rawlinson, i. 404–6; his birth in 600 B.C. (Dan. v. 31) would be consistent with his marriage in 585 (see i. 74 n.). His name (= 'biting snake') seems to be a title, not a proper name. The only ground for Rawlinson's theory (Five Great Monarchies, iii. 218) that the reign of Astyages was a period of Magian ascendancy, is the evidence of H. i. 107. 1, 108. 2, and especially 120. 5.

[2] Sippara Inscription (cf. App. IV. 1).

[3] This is shown by the fact that Greeks and Jews alike identified the two races, cf. the familiar 'Laws of the Medes and Persians' (Daniel vi) and τὰ Μηδικά, = 'the Persian Wars'; cf., too, the place of the Medes under Persian rule (App. VI. 3) and the similarity of dress (vii. 62).

[4] Klio, iv. 199 seq.

[5] This *terminus a quo* (550 B.C.) is given by the Annals of Nabonidus (col. 2; Ball, p. 219); the fall of Astyages is dated in 'the sixth year' of

It is instructive to compare this with the list of Ctesias,[1] who gives nine kings, only one of whom can be identified, and makes Median rule last 317 years, from the capture of Nineveh, which he thus dates more than 250 years too early. The contrast between the genuine tradition of H. and the reckless invention of his critic could not be better shown.

But H.'s scheme is only partially historical; his names are genuine, but :

(1) If Deioces is the Dayaukhu of Sargon, he really disappears from history fifteen years before his reign is supposed to begin. The most that can be said for H. is that Assyrian power began to decline after Sargon (d. 705 B. C.), and that so Median independence may be loosely said to begin with the seventh century.

(2) It is highly suspicious that each pair of his Median kings rule just seventy-five years (53 + 22, 40 + 35). The last pair is probably rightly given, the first invented to correspond.

(3) H., however (i. 130. 1), gives us another calculation for Median rule in Asia, i. e. that it lasted 128 years, παρὲξ ἢ ὅσον οἱ Σκύθαι ἦρχον, i. e. probably for 128 − 28 years = 100.[2]

This tradition probably comes from an independent source; but an ingenious attempt is made to reconcile it with the regal chronology, by inverting the lengths of the first two reigns, and giving Deioces 22 and Phraortes 53. If this be done, then H. dates the Median rule from the accession of Phraortes, for 53 + 40 + 35 = 128, the figure of i. 130.[3]

Some, however, strike out the words τριήκοντα καὶ δυῶν δέοντα as a gloss, which is supposed to have been added (from iv. i. 2) to give the length of Scythian rule. It certainly is a curious coincidence that the Scythians are said to rule *twenty-eight* years and the Medes one hundred and *twenty-eight*.

Nabonidus, who came to the throne in 555. Cyrus himself became a king in 558, and it used to be supposed (wrongly) that this year was the last of Astyages. Others (cf. App. IV. 1) put the fall of Astyages in 553–2; in that case he would come to the throne in 588, and H. would be wrong in putting the 'eclipse battle' in the time of Cyaxares (i. 74 n.); that king would have begun the Lydian war, but his son, Astyages, would have finished it. This point must be left uncertain, but all the Median dates, e. g. in Rawlinson, are (nine *or* six years) too early, being reckoned back from 559 B. C.

[1] Assyr. fr. 17, p. 439, in Diod. ii. 32–4. For the manner in which he based his inventions on H.'s facts cf. Rawlinson, i. 393–4; Maspero, iii. 447 n.

[2] The words were taken by Heeren = 128 + 28 = 156. But this makes Median 'rule' in Asia six years longer than the Median kingdom.

[3] This inversion also makes H. consistent with himself; for (1) How could Deioces, a man already of full age, reign 53 years and be succeeded by his son? (2) It makes Median rule begin with Phraortes the conqueror, not in the middle of the reign of Deioces, who 'ruled the Medes only' (i. 101).

APPENDIX IV

CYRUS AND THE RISE OF PERSIA

A useful summary of present-day views as to Cyrus is found in the Revue Biblique, Jan. 1912 (by Père Dhorme; quoted as R. B.).

Cyrus is the most familiar figure in oriental history. Partly his own greatness, perhaps still more his connexion with the Jews, have given him a position in the popular memory, and he is probably the only Eastern monarch whose name has been used freely as a Christian name. Yet till within the last generation a large part of what was believed about him was quite inaccurate. Two inscriptions especially have revolutionized our knowledge of him (the translations here quoted are Ball's in 'Light from the East', pp. 217 seq.).[1]

§ 1. (1) **The Annals of Nabonidus.** This was acquired by the B. M. in 1879, and published by Pinches in T. S. B. A. vii, Part I (1880), p. 139 f. The most important passages are as follows:

Col. II, ll. 1–4. 'His troops he collected, and against Cyrus, king of Anshan . . . he marched. As for Astyages (Istuvegu), his troops revolted against him, and he was seized and delivered up to Cyrus. Cyrus marched to Againtanu (Ecbatana), the royal city. The silver, gold, goods, and substance of Ecbatana he spoiled, and to the land of Anshan he took the goods.'. . . (This has no date, but was probably in the sixth year,[2] as the next line begins 'the seventh year'.)

l. 15, 'ninth year . . . In the month Nisan, Cyrus, king of the land of Persia, mustered his troops, and below the city of Arbela, the Tigris he crossed.'

Col. I (Reverse), ll. 15–19. 'Nabonidus fled. On the sixteenth day, Gobryas, pasha of the land of Gutium, and the troops of Cyrus without a battle entered Babylon. Afterwards Nabonidus, being shut up in Babylon, was taken. . . . Cyrus entered Babylon. The walls fell down before him.[3] Peace for the city he established.'

ll. 24–5. 'On the fourth day, Cambyses, the son of Cyrus, having repaired to the temple, the officials of the house of the sceptre of Nebo conferred on him the sceptre of the world.' The inscription was clearly drawn up by the priests after the defeat of Nabonidus. In the parts omitted here, reference is made repeatedly (e.g. ll. 6, 11, &c.) to Nabonidus' neglect of religious observances. 'The King at

[1] Translations also in R. P.[2] v, pp. 158–68, where the Sippara Inscription of Nabonidus is also translated, which mentions the victory of Cyrus, king of Anshan, over the Manda. I have compared Ball's version with Schrader's in Keilinschr.-Bibl. iii. 2, pp. 128–35.

[2] Others (R. B. Jan. 1912, p. 29) put the fall of Astyages in the third year of Nabonidus, i.e. in 553–552 (cf. App. III. § 6).

[3] Schrader (doubtfully), 'the ways were dark before him.'

Nisan to Babylon came not. Nebo to Babylon came not. Bel went not forth. The New Year's feast was omitted.'

(2) **The Cyrus Cylinder.** In B. M.; first published by Sir H. Rawlinson in 1880. J. R. A. S. xii:

ll. 20–3. 'I am Cyrus, the king of the world (Schrader, 'the hosts'), the great king, the king of Tintir (i. e. Babylon), the king of the land of Shinar and Accad, the king of the four quarters of the world, the son of Cambyses the great king, king of the city of Anshan, the grandson of Cyrus the great king, king of the city of Anshan, the great grandson of Teispes the great king, king of the city of Anshan, the enduring seed of royalty, whose reign Bel and Nebo loved.

ll. 33–4. 'The gods of the land of Shinar and Accad, whom Nabonidus, to the anger of the Lord of the gods, had brought into Shuanna (Babylon), by the command of Merodach, the great lord, in peace in their own shrines I made inhabit again.'

In the earlier part of the inscription Cyrus describes how Nabonidus had 'made the continual (Schrader 'temple') offering to cease' (l. 7), and how Merodach had raised up him (Cyrus) as a deliverer (l. 12), and given him victory over the Umman Manda (l. 13), and finally brought him to Babylon 'without a battle' (l. 17).

Two points are raised by these inscriptions as to Cyrus, which must be first discussed: (1) his position and history previous to the capture of Babylon; (2) the genealogy of the Achaemenidae.

§ 2. (1) **Cyrus before the capture of Babylon.** It will be noted that Cyrus is 'king of Anshan' when he defeats Astyages, in the sixth year of Nabonidus, and does not become king of Persia till the 'ninth year' of Nabonidus; even as late as 538 B.C., he still can call himself 'king of Anshan' (C.C. l. 12). The view[1] has, therefore, been put forward that Cyrus was not ruler in Persia, but in Elam, i. e. in the old kingdom which, with Susa as its capital, so long resisted the Assyrian power. In support of this view are adduced the position of Susa as the later capital, and the use of 'Susian' as the third official language (e. g. in the B. I.); cf., too, the words of Isaiah (xxi. 2), 'Go up, O Elam; besiege, O Media.'

Others (e. g. Winckler) go further, and deny that Cyrus was an Achaemenid at all.[2]

To these views there are two fatal objections: (1) it is impossible to believe that the Jews (cf. 2 Chron. xxxvi. 22, Ezra i. 1 *et pass.*) and the Greeks were alike mistaken in the nationality of the conqueror of Babylon; and (2) whatever interpretation be given to 'Anshan', the fact remains that the empire founded by Cyrus was Persian and

[1] Cf. Sayce, *s.v.* Cyrus in Hastings' Dictionary; also in R. P. (*u.s.*)

[2] Winckler, Unters., p. 127. It may further be noted that while the names of the immediate ancestors of Darius (§ 3) seem to be Persian, that of Cyrus is probably Elamite (R. B. Jan. 1912).

not Elamite. Moreover, the monuments seem to show that the real Elamites were negroid in type,[1] neither Aryan like the Persians nor Semitic like the Assyrians.

Some, then, deny altogether the identification of Anshan and Elam, and make Anshan a part of Persia, perhaps near Pasargadae. It seems, however, safer to connect Anshan and Elam,[2] and to suppose that, after the destruction of the old kingdom of Elam by Assurbanipal, the Achaemenidae extended their rule westward into Elam (i. e. Anshan), and that for a time the title borne by the more important branch of the house was 'King of Anshan.'

§ 3. (2) **The genealogy of the Achaemenidae.** Here, beside the evidence of the Cyrus Cylinder (*u. s.*), we have to interpret the words of Darius at Behistun (i. 4, cf. p. 392): he says 'My father is Hystaspes, and the father of Hystaspes was Arsames, and Arsames' father was Ariyaramnes, and Ariyaramnes' father was Teispes, and Teispes' father was Achaemenes. On that account are we called Achaemenians. From ancient times we have been kings. Eight of my race have before me held the kingdom. I am the ninth. In two lines we have been kings.' It will be noted that Darius does not call any of his immediate ancestors kings. In addition there is the genealogy of Xerxes in H. vii. 11. 2. The table of descent is variously constructed.

I. Perhaps the most probable view is that of Nöldeke[3] and Prášek[4] (names of kings are in italics).

Achaemenes (B. I. and vii. 11)
|
Teispes I ⎫
| ⎪
Cambyses I ⎬ (vii. 11)
| ⎪
Cyrus I ⎭
|
Teispes II (B. I., C. C., and vii. 11)

Cyrus II (C. C. and i. 111)	Ariaramnes	(B. I. and vii. 11)
Cambyses II (C. C. and i. 108)	Arsames	
Cyrus the Great	Hystaspes	
Cambyses III	*Darius*	

[1] Perrot et Chipiez, v. 412–13.
[2] So Meyer, i. 363 n. Anshan is originally the district round Susa; then in later times an archaic name revived by the Achaemenidae and Nabonidus.
[3] E. B.[9] xviii. 565. [4] Gesch. der Meder und Perser, i. 179–83.

The objection to this view is that Darius definitely says that Teispes II was the son of Achaemenes. The explanation probably is that he traces his descent back to the last of the undivided line, and then goes straight to the heroic ancestor. So Artaxerxes II, in his inscriptions at Susa and Hamadan, mentions all his royal ancestors back to Darius, and then ends, 'son of Hystaspes the Achaemenid'; the parallel, however, is only partial.

II. Cauer[1] (however) and Lehmann think this objection fatal, and the latter makes (1) Achaemenes to be father of Teispes II (i.e. the three intermediate kings of H. vii. 11 disappear); (2) the 'eight kings' to be Achaemenes, Teispes (of the undivided line), the four kings of the elder line, and Ariaramnes and Arsames of the younger. [Cauer gives up Ariaramnes and Arsames, and suggests in their place two unnamed ancestors of Teispes II.] (3) Lehmann thinks the three first names of H. vii. 11, Teispes I, Cambyses I, and Cyrus I, are inventions made to claim for the direct ancestry of Xerxes the great names of the Anshan branch.

The family tree then will be

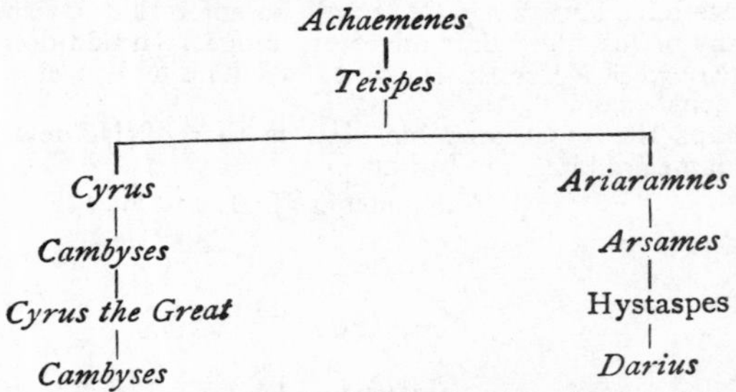

It is proposed (e.g. by Macan, ad vii. 11, and others) to alter the text in vii. 11 to suit this sense, inserting *καί* after the first Τεΐσπεος and τοῦ Κύρου after Καμβύσεω, so that the passage would read *μὴ γὰρ εἴην ἐκ Δαρείου τοῦ Ὑστάσπεος τοῦ Ἀρσάμεος τοῦ Ἀριαράμνεω τοῦ Τεΐσπεος ⟨καὶ⟩ τοῦ Κύρου τοῦ Καμβύσεω ⟨τοῦ Κύρου⟩ τοῦ Τεΐσπεος τοῦ Ἀχαιμένεος.* Xerxes then gives his genealogy, first on the father's, then on the mother's (Atossa) side.

The objections to this reconstruction are that (1) 'Achaemenes' looks more like an heroic ancestor than a real king[2]; and (2) it is very curious that Darius (in the B. I.) says nothing of Arsames and Ariaramnes being 'kings'.[3]

[1] In Pauly, *s.v.* Achaemenidae; Lehmann, in Klio, viii. 493.

[2] So the later Sassanians (A.D. 225) did not bear the name of the first king, Artaxerxes, the son of Sassan, but that of his father.

[3] Sir H. Rawlinson (on i. 125) presses this point strongly; but his own reconstruction of the pedigree there is forced in the extreme.

The only point that is certain is that, though H. has preserved rightly, for the most part at any rate, the names and the order of the Achaemenidae, he has no conception of the birth and the royal claims either of Cyrus or of Darius.

§ 4. **Greek accounts of Cyrus.** (*a*) **That of H.** The general account of H. is obviously made up of various elements.

(1) There is a strong Median strain in it; Cyrus is represented as being the son of a Median princess—an obvious concession to the vanity of a conquered race.[1]

(2) It is very probable that the story was largely derived from some member or members of the house of Harpagus[2] (cf. App. III. 5, and for his prominence in it cc. 80. 2, 108, 124, 129). They claimed descent from Deioces, and as they ruled for more than a century in Lycia (cf. i. 171 n.), H. may well have come across them there.

(3) But there are also undoubtedly Greek elements in the story: (*a*) the meal served to Harpagus (c. 119) recalls the stories of Tantalus and of Atreus; (*b*) the story of the exposure of Cyrus, to prevent the fulfilment of an oracle, embodies the same idea as that of Oedipus.

(4) The miraculous preservation of Cyrus has its parallels in those of other national heroes, e.g. Sargon of Accad (App. II. 1), the Indian Chandragupta (fed by the sacred bull), and Romulus.[3]

Possibly these four elements were already combined in the story when H. heard it.[4]

(*b*) **Other Greek accounts.** On the other hand, an entirely different version of the rise of Cyrus was current among the Greeks. It is probably that of Ctesias.[5] It differs from H. in the following main points:

(1) Cyrus is the son of poor Mardians, Atradates and Aegiste.

(2) He enters the service of Astyages as a menial, and rises to the highest rank as cup-bearer.

(3) Cyrus wins by hard fighting, and he is twice defeated before a final victory at Pasargadae.

[1] Cf. iii. 1–2, the Egyptian story as to birth of Cambyses, and the later Persian story in the Shahnameh, that Alexander had a Persian father. Dhorme, however (R. B. *u.s.* p. 27), believes in the Median marriage; he thinks that the family of the Achaemenidae were the feudal rulers to whom (cf. i. 134 n.) the Medes left the rule of Elam. Hence the head of the family would be a fit match for a royal princess. This is possible.

[2] Cf. Klio, iv. 199 seq.

[3] Cf. other parallels in Persian literature quoted in Spiegel, Erânische Alterthumskunde, ii. 270.

[4] H. (i. 95. 1) says there were four accounts of the rise of Cyrus, and that he chose that of those 'Persians οἱ μὴ βουλόμενοι σεμνοῦν τὰ περὶ Κῦρον'. On the other hand, the story of Cyrus' mixed pedigree may be Delphic (cf. c. 91).

[5] For it cf. the long fragment of Nicolaus Damascenus (No. 66), F. H. G. iii. 397 seq.

At the same time the story has certain points in common with H., e.g. the prophetic dream of i. 107, though this is given to the mother of Cyrus, and the name of his adviser, Oebares, who in iii. 85 is the counsellor of Darius.

It will be obvious that, both in names and in the details as to events [1], this story is even further removed from that of the monuments than that in H. We may sum up in the words of the great orientalist, Spiegel (*u.s.* ii. 242), 'The veracity of H. is so strikingly maintained in the field of Iranian history that it needs no justification if we, in the older period of the history, choose him especially for our guide.' [2]

§ 5. **The importance of Cyrus in history.** Whatever may be the exact truth as to the parentage and the rise of Cyrus, two points are obvious:

(1) That the Medes, although they lost the rule of Asia, were akin to, and to some extent shared the rule of, the new Persian conquerors.

(2) That his victories mark the final triumph of the new Aryan races over the peoples, whether Semitic or other, who had previously ruled in Western Asia.

Hence it is not surprising that a coalition of the existing powers, Lydia, Babylonia, Egypt (cf. i. 77. 2 nn.), was made against him. This coalition he struck down by his vigorous aggression; if we may trust Diodorus (ix. 32), it was betrayed to Cyrus by Eurybatus, who, sent by Croesus to bribe the Greeks to unite against Cyrus, deserted and told the Persian king all Croesus' plans.[3] It is not necessary to say anything here as to the defeat of Lydia, for on this H. (i. 79 seq.) is our main authority, and his account is fairly adequate; but on the even more important conquest of Babylon the inscriptions have thrown a new and altogether unexpected light.

§ 6. **Cyrus and Babylon.** Two points stand out here especially:

(1) The story of the diversion of the Euphrates (i. 191) is probably the most successful fraud in history. It may contain some elements of truth (cf. nn. on i. 189. 3), but it conceals the essential fact that Babylon fell by the treachery of the priests, whose privileges Nabonidus had curtailed (*v.s.* § 1), and that Cyrus took the impregnable fortress without a struggle.[4]

[1] Cf. also i. 127 n.

[2] The Cyrus legend is examined at great length and with much learning by A. Bauer (Sitzungsb. der Acad. der Wissensch. (Wien), vol. 100, 1882); but his results are not at all convincing.

[3] This story may be true, especially as Diodorus says 'Eurybatus' became a proverb for treachery; but it looks suspiciously like a combination of the story of Phanes (iii. 4) with that of Timocrates the Rhodian and the origin of the Corinthian War (in 395 B.C.).

[4] Berosus' narrative (fr. 14, F. H. G. iii. 508) implied that Babylon fell to Cyrus easily, and said nothing of H.'s river diversion.

(2) The religious opportunism which marks the account of the Cyrus Cylinder (*u. s.*), where he describes himself as the 'servant of Merodach', and his son Cambyses as receiving the 'sceptre of the world' in the Temple of Nebo, is probably characteristic of the conqueror's whole policy. The early Achaemenidae were not fanatical Mazdeans, and Cyrus was as ready to honour Bel in Babylon as Jehovah in Jerusalem [1] (2 Chron. xxxvi. 23).

§ 7. **Cyrus' subsequent career and death.** The subsequent victories of Cyrus are matters of some uncertainty. It is very doubtful if he reduced Phoenicia.[2] But he must have carried his arms victoriously far to the east and the north-east. Subsequent Persian tradition had no doubt (cf. iii. 75; vii. 2. 3) that it was Cyrus who had founded the Persian Empire. For these campaigns we have no evidence, nor do they concern the narrative of H. This, however, professes to give a full account of his death, as to which there were almost as many accounts as about his birth. The following are the most important points:

(1) There is general agreement that he died in battle; the only contrary testimony is that of the historically worthless romance of Xenophon (Cyrop. viii. 7).

(2) As to the enemy he was fighting against, Berosus (fr. 12, F. H.G. ii. 505) makes them the Dahae, south-east of the Caspian; this is the most probable account. Ctesias (6, 7, p. 65) makes them the Derbicae, neighbours of the Hyrcanians, while H., in defiance of all probability, takes Cyrus over the Araxes (i. e. the Oxus) to fight against the Massagetae. The only point of importance is that Cyrus meets his death on the north-east frontier of his empire, in the fighting which has gone on from time immemorial between the settled inhabitants of the Iranian plateau and the wild nomad tribes of Central Asia (cf. p. 429 n. 1).

(3) If, as is possible, Cyrus was defeated as well as killed, the defeat must have been unimportant, and not complete as in the story of H. His body was brought back and buried with great splendour at Pasargadae.[3]

The whole narrative of H. here is unfavourable[4] to Cyrus; his insatiable ambition (cf. 204. 2) and its consequent punishment are insisted on. No doubt this is the reason for H.'s geographical

[1] The Cyrus Cylinder, like the Book of Chronicles, may treat acts of polite acquiescence as if they were prompted by genuine devotion; but such an official record could not have been published unless it represented the monarch's position with approximate accuracy. Just as he had restored the Babylonian gods to their cities, so he restored the temple at Jerusalem.

[2] Cf. iii. 19. 3 n.

[3] For his tomb cf. i. 125 n., and contrast 214. 4, 5.

[4] Duncker (vi. 120) thinks H. here is following a Median source (*v.s.*). The prominence of Croesus in the story suggests rather a Delphic tradition.

blunder. The contrast is better marked when the great world-ruler, Cyrus, falls fighting against the remote barbarian Massagetae.

The account of Cyrus is a triumph of story-telling, but one of the less successful parts of the history of H.; the prejudice of his informants has distorted some facts and concealed others, nor had he criteria to test their evidence. But there is a large substratum of fact underlying all the fiction, and even in H., the figure of Cyrus stands out as one of the great men in world-history.

APPENDIX V

THE REIGN OF CAMBYSES AND THE EARLY YEARS OF DARIUS HYSTASPES

[In this appendix Bk. III is quoted by chapter only. An attempt is made in it to summarize the real course of events and to indicate the points of dispute; as to most of these the evidence is given in the commentary; but it is added here when the points only slightly concern the statements of H.; one important passage is quoted at length.]

§ 1. **Authorities.** By far the most important is the trilingual inscription of Darius, set up by him on the rock of Behistun after he had crushed the great revolts in the Persian Empire. It measures, with the sculptures, 150 feet by 100, and records the events which begin with the conspiracy of Gaumâta. The three languages are Persian, Babylonian, and Elamite (originally called Scythian). The story of its decipherment is the most fascinating in the history of Oriental scholarship.[1] It is quoted here from the version of King and Thompson[2]; the most important sections of it are as follows:

Sec. X. 'Thus saith Darius the king' . . . 'He who was named Cambyses, the son of Cyrus, one of our race, was king before me. That Cambyses had a brother, Smerdis by name, of the same mother and the same father as Cambyses. Afterwards Cambyses slew this Smerdis. When Cambyses slew Smerdis, it was not known unto the people that Smerdis was slain. Thereupon Cambyses went into Egypt. When Cambyses had departed into Egypt, the people became hostile, and the lie multiplied in the land, even in Persia, as in Media and in the other provinces.'

Sec. XI. 'Thus saith Darius the king. Afterwards there was a certain man, a Magian, Gaumâta by name, who raised a rebellion in Paishiyâuvâda, in a mountain named Arakadrish. On the fourteenth day of the month Viyakhna did he rebel. He lied unto the people,

[1] Cf. Mahaffy, Proleg. to Anc. Hist. pp. 167 seq.

[2] Published by the B. M., 1907. The version of Sir Henry Rawlinson, to whom mainly belongs the glory of solving its riddles, will be found in Rawlinson, ii. 490 seq., and in R. P.[1] i.

saying: "I am Smerdis, the son of Cyrus, the brother of Cambyses." Then were all the people in revolt, and from Cambyses they went over unto him, both Persia and Media, and the other provinces. He seized on the kingdom; on the ninth day of the month Garmapada he seized on the kingdom. Afterwards Cambyses died by his own hand.'

Sec. XII. 'Thus saith Darius the king: The kingdom of which Gaumâta, the Magian, dispossessed Cambyses, had belonged to our race from olden time. After that Gaumâta, the Magian, had dispossessed Cambyses of Persia and of Media and of the other provinces, he did according to his will, he was (as) king.'

Sec. XIII. 'Thus saith Darius the king: There was no man, either Persian or Median or of our own race, who took the kingdom from Gaumâta the Magian. The people feared him exceedingly, (for) he slew many who had known the former Smerdis. For this reason did he slay them, "that they may not know that I am not Smerdis, the son of Cyrus." There was none who dared say aught against Gaumâta, the Magian, till I came. Then I prayed to Auramazda; Auramazda brought me help. On the tenth day of the month Bâgayâdish I with a few men slew that Gaumâta, the Magian, and the chief men who were his followers. At the stronghold named Sikayauvatish, in the district named Nisâya in Media, I slew him; I dispossessed him of the kingdom. By the grace of Auramazda, I became king; Auramazda granted me the kingdom.'

Other accounts of these events are given in Ctesias (8–15, pp. 65–8) and in Justin (i. 9–10), where traces of an old narrative, independent of H., and more correct in one name ('Cometes'), are preserved.

§ 2. The reign of Cambyses is marked by one event of the first importance—the conquest of Egypt; the old world was finally brought under one sceptre. But the reign is most interesting as marking the extinction of the elder branch of the Achaemenidae and the transference of power to the younger branch.[1]

Analysis of the traditions as to Cambyses. Meyer (Ersch and Gruber, Encyc., 1882, *s. v.* Kambyses) analyses them thus:

(1) *Egyptian.* From this source mainly come iii. 2, 4, 10–32, 37. There are, however, many Greek elements in it, e. g. the story of Phanes. This version tries to represent Cambyses as a legitimate Egyptian prince (but H. rejects this, c. 2), and is full of hatred against him.

[1] For modern 'critical' views cf. Maspero, iii. 656 (though he rejects them himself). Winckler, e. g., conjectures that the real Smerdis (Bardija, cf. 30. 1 n.) was not murdered by Cambyses, but conspired against him, and in his turn was murdered by Darius, who was not an Achaemenid at all. The Behistun Inscription, then, and the narrative of H. are merely two versions of the same fiction, put out by Darius to justify his usurpation. This 'critical' view has not a particle of evidence in its favour, and is not worth discussion.

(2) *Persian.* This comes mainly in Ctesias. To it belong in H. cc. 61–6, and perhaps c. 34. In this tradition there is nothing as to the madness of Cambyses, but his destruction is due to his father's curse, drawn on him by fratricide.

This analysis of sources may be correct, but H. is at any rate perfectly consistent; he makes the jealous tyrant, half mad from disease and from jealousy, to be sobered by the stroke of calamity and by the finger of heaven showing him his folly (cf. 64–5). But it must be admitted that H. leaves us in doubt when and why Cambyses became mad; he is similarly vague as to Cleomenes (cf. App. XVII). Probably in both cases he did not know, and so could not say.

Cambyses is usually said to have become king in 529 B.C. (cf. 66 n. as to the duration of his reign). It is most unlikely that his brother was associated with him in rule; Ctesias (8, p. 65) says that he was satrap of Bactria and the adjacent provinces; but his disappearance, hard enough to explain in any case, becomes impossible if he were a reigning prince.

The first four years of the reign of Cambyses were occupied in extending his dominions to the sea[1]; he was ready in 525[2] for the long-planned attack of Persia on Egypt. The success of this was too sudden and complete to allow of variation in traditions. There is, however, much dispute as to his acts as conqueror in Egypt, and as to the murder of his brother and his own death.

§ 3. **Cambyses in Egypt.** Cambyses at first undoubtedly behaved in Egypt with moderation,[3] as was the usual custom of the Persians; but according to the tradition recorded by H., and confirmed by later Greek writers, e.g. Diodorus, Plutarch, and others, he afterwards outraged the religion of the Egyptians.[4] Some modern writers deny this, but it is dangerous to reject all tradition on the testimony of isolated monuments, especially when other monuments are quoted in support of tradition. The Egyptians certainly were prejudiced against him, but this very fact may be the result of his excesses. Darius at any rate was not unpopular in Egypt.

§ 4. **The Ethiopian Expedition.** Closely connected with the question of Cambyses' behaviour in Egypt is the next question—how far was his expedition against Ethiopia successful? The answers to this are absolutely contradictory. H. says that he met

[1] 34. 4; 88. 1.

[2] The date is given by Diodorus (i. 68) and Eusebius, and is usually accepted. Brugsch (ii. 313–15) puts the invasion in 527 B.C., because an Egyptian eunuch under Xerxes describes himself on his tomb as having lived 'six full years' (i.e. 527–521) under Cambyses. This, however, simply shows that his reign was reckoned as beginning, even in Egypt, in 529.

[3] c. 16 n.

[4] 29, 38 nn. Winckler (A. F. ii. 208) thinks the Babylonian monuments show that Cambyses did not follow the opportunist religious policy of his father; 'he would not be a bepowdered and bewigged Babylonian'.

with complete disaster (c. 25); others put this story down to Egyptian prejudice, and ascribe to him a success more or less complete. The evidence is most unsatisfactory; it may be summarized as follows:

(1) *Later passages in H.* In iii. 97 the 'Ethiopians who border on Egypt' are said to have been 'subdued by Cambyses'; it is to be noticed, however, that they pay no tribute, but only bring gifts every other year. In vii. 69 'the Ethiopians above Egypt' serve in the Persian army.

(2) *Later writers.* Strabo (790) and Diodorus (i. 33) say that he conquered Ethiopia and founded the city of Meroe, which he named after his sister.

(3) *Inscriptions.* The famous stele of Dongola, brought to Berlin in 1871, appears to make the Ethiopian king Nastasesen claim a victory over Cambyses (Kambasuten). His bowmen (cf. iii. 21. 1; vii. 69. 1) defeat the enemy with great slaughter (cf. Budge, Sûdân, ii. 84–7, 94–5). Unfortunately, however, the inscription is variously translated; otherwise it would be decisive.

(4) *Indirect evidence.* (*a*) Ptolemy (4. 7; cf. Pliny, N. H. vi. 181, 'Cambysis forum') speaks of the *ταμιεῖα Καμβύσου* above the Third Cataract; the name has been doubtfully identified on the monuments. But it is by no means certain that it had anything to do with Cambyses. (*b*) Napata at this period does seem to give place to Meroe as the Ethiopian capital. (*c*) The nature of the tribute in iii. 97 makes Duncker (vi. 161 seq.) believe that Persian conquest extended to the 'zone of ebony and the elephant'.

(5) *Probability.* It may fairly be urged that a failure such as H. describes is more consistent with the gloom in which the reign of Cambyses admittedly ended, than the theory of great Ethiopian victories.

Summing up. On the whole, the balance of probability seems to be in favour of H.'s story, though he is probably wrong in denying any success to Cambyses, who seems to have extended Persian authority as far south as Wâdî Halfa, i. e. over that part of Ethiopia which the Egyptians had regarded as theirs.

A further dispute arises as to the route of Cambyses:

(1) It is most natural to suppose that he left the Nile at Korosko and struck across the desert, following the line on which the railway now runs (cf. 25. 6, 'When they came to the sand'). Insufficient preparation and the desert combined to produce disaster, which H. puts down to lack of food, not of water (25. 4).

(2) Duncker accepts the evidence of Strabo (820) that the army was overwhelmed by a sandstorm between Pselchis and Premnis, i. e. between Korti and Wâdî Halfa. This disaster he puts on the return journey from Napata. It is suggested that the disaster of 26. 3 (*vid. n.*) really happened to the main expedition, not to that against the Ammonians.

(3) Flinders Petrie (iii. 363), accepting the identification of 'Cambysis forum', makes the march to be along the Nile as far as the Third Cataract.

One more point must be briefly mentioned. H. does not mention the Nile in the campaign; this is consistent with his view that it flowed *from* the west above Elephantine (ii. 31. 5); the Ethiopians are on the sea (17. 1) to the south. Hence to attack them the river is left.

§ 5. **The murder of Smerdis.** As to his brother, it is clear that he was murdered, and that before the Egyptian expedition.[1] How the heir-apparent disappeared without its being generally known is hard to explain; but it is clear there were widespread suspicions in the court.[2] Cambyses, having tied his own hands by his crime, was an easy object of attack, and it is not improbable that H. and Ctesias are right in making his own tools turn against him. That he committed suicide in despair is likely; at all events this seems to be definitely stated in the Behistun Inscription.[3]

§ 6. **The Conspiracy of the Pseudo-Smerdis.** Two theories must be noticed as to this conspiracy.

(1) It has been supposed to be a Median conspiracy; for this view some support can be found in H.,[4] but it is inconsistent with his main narrative. Grote (iv. 301) and others adopted this view, but it is now completely given up. The arguments against it may be found in Rawlinson (ii. 454 seq.); it is sufficient to say here that the Behistun Inscription represents the Magian as coming from a Persian district (i. 11), and implies that the Medes should have resisted him as much as Persians (i. 13). The theory, however, is true to this extent that the pretender, being a Magian, belonged to a Median tribe.

(2) Rawlinson supposes that it was a religious conspiracy, an endeavour of the Magians to substitute the authority of the priestly caste for the old royalty, or at any rate to enforce the Magian system more strictly. This was certainly the view of H.'s informants and is partially true; the conspirators are always 'the Magians', and their overthrow is a blow to the Magi.[5]

The Behistun Inscription, too, seems to speak of it as a religious movement; 'the lie became abounding in the land' (i. 10); 'the temples which Gomates the Magian destroyed, I (i.e. Darius) rebuilt' (i. 14). The Magians said that the gods ought not to be imprisoned within four walls (Cic. de Leg. ii. 10 *ad fin.*); probably the priestly usurper was trying to force his strict creed on the Persians.

But this explanation of the conspiracy as religious is only part of the truth; the movement was also political. Everything points to

[1] H. is wrong here; cf. 30 n.
[2] 32. 2 n.
[3] 64. 3 n.
[4] 65. 6, 73. 1, 126; cf. Plato, Leg. 695 B.
[5] 79. 3 n.

the fact that the usurper was unpopular only with the nobles, and that the mass of the people at least acquiesced in his rule. This agrees with what has been said as to the religious character of the conspiracy; the Persian royal family and the nobles seem to have been slowest to accept the Magian creed, just as the Sadducees, the upper class among the Jews, held different religious tenets from the mass of their countrymen. Hence the temples destroyed would be those of the great Persian families, marks at once of their aversion to the strict Magian creed and of their feudal independence.[1]

The overthrow of the Conspiracy. The narrative of H. as to the overthrow of the conspiracy is very vigorous, and is confirmed in important points by the narrative of Darius; but few parts of his work illustrate better his weaknesses as well as his merits as a historian.

The points in which he is especially confirmed are: (1) That the conspiracy was at first unopposed;[2] (2) as to the names of the conspirators.[3] This is especially important; he agrees in all but one with the Behistun Inscription, while his detractor and critic Ctesias is hopelessly wrong; (3) that Darius himself killed the Magian.[4]

§ 7. **His inaccuracies.** But at the same time it must be pointed out that his conception of the whole story is fundamentally wrong. The conspiracy is to him the act of a number of fortuitous conspirators; it was really a national movement led by the rightful heir of the Achaemenidae.[5] This leads H. to accept the absurd story that Darius was chosen king by the trick of a groom (84. 1 n.). This is the more surprising as he elsewhere (vii. 11) gives rightly the genealogy of the Achaemenidae, though, it must be added, without understanding it. The explanation clearly lies in the sources from which H. derived his information; the main tradition comes from a member of the house of Otanes; hence the part of Otanes is exaggerated (cf. especially cc. 68, 84). The story of Phaedymia, too, and of the earless Magian (c. 69) seems to be a picturesque version derived from the story of the 'man in the street'.

A further result is that an impossible Hellenic colouring[6] is given to the deliberations of the conspirators; whatever amount of truth underlies the narrative in H., it is presented in a thoroughly non-Oriental way.[7] As compared with this serious misconception, which underlies H.'s whole story, his minor inaccuracies are unimportant; they are briefly: (1) He speaks of two Magi, the Behistun Inscription of only one; but he may be right in this

[1] Cf. Maspero iii. 672, and shortly E. B.[9] xviii. 568.

[2] c. 61 n. [3] c. 70 n. [4] 78. 3 n.

[5] Cf. also c. 70 n. for 'the Seven'. [6] 80. 1 n.

[7] There are also fragments of a tradition which made Darius prominent (c. 72), while the story of Prexaspes (c. 74 n.) is obviously quite independent of his main authorities.

point.[1] (2) He gives the names of the conspirators as Smerdis and Patizeithes; they were really Gaumâta and (probably) Oropastes. (3) He lays the scene of the Magians' death at Susa; it really was at a remote stronghold.[2]

To sum up, the whole narrative illustrates throughout the accuracy of H. as a faithful reporter of what he was told and also his lack of historical insight.

§ 8. **The Rebellion in the Persian Empire.** It is not surprising that so serious a conspiracy shook the newly-established empire of the Persians to its foundations. Revolts broke out in every region of the empire, and the greater part of the Behistun Inscription is occupied with narrating their suppression. Their story belongs neither to Greek history nor to H., for he curiously seems to be almost entirely ignorant of them: his only references to them are the mention of the revolts of the Medes (i. 130 n.) and of Babylon (iii. 150 seq.); his account of the latter does not fully agree with that of *either* of the Babylonian revolts as given by Darius (B. I. 1. 16 f., 3. 13 f.).

It is, however, useless to speculate why H. omits so many points that might well seem more essential to his narrative than much that he includes; but it is important to emphasize the fact that the accession of Darius is a turning-point in Oriental history. The long 'struggle of the nations' had ended in an organized unity, which reaches from the Nile to the Jaxartes, from the Hellespont to the Indus. And the close of the reign of Darius was to bring forward at Marathon the new power of the West, which in the end was to break up the work of Darius.[3]

§ 9. But Darius was more than an organizer of what his predecessors had conquered. Like Augustus in the Roman Empire, he extended the Persian frontiers till they reached natural boundaries. H. knows a little of the expedition against the Indians (iv. 44; cf. iii. 94. 2 n.), which secured the lands on this side the Indus. He tells us, however, nothing of the great campaigns to the north-west and north-east of Persia, which Darius mentions in his inscriptions[4]; but no doubt these had in part the same object as the expedition against the Scyths, which is the subject of his Fourth Book. In all these his purpose was the same, to extend the range of Persian commerce (cf. iv. 44 n.; ii. 158 n.), and to secure his empire from the raids of the uncivilized neighbours who had caused the death of Cyrus, and who were always a danger to South and West Asia.[5]

[1] c. 61 n. [2] 68. 2 n.

[3] For this point cf. especially Meyer's excellent summing up (i[1]. 515–16).

[4] Darius on his tomb counts the Karkâ (Kolchis) among his subjects (cf. iii. 97), and also the 'Amyrgian' Sacae (vii. 64 n.).

[5] Cf. the Cimmerian invasions (i. 15 n.), and the invasions of the Mongols in mediaeval times. Cf. p. 300 for an incident in Darius' campaigns.

APPENDIX VI

THE PERSIAN SYSTEM OF GOVERNMENT

[This appendix mainly, though not entirely, follows the conclusions of Meyer (iii. 12–57); Rawlinson's essay (ii. 555–69; he differs on some important points from Meyer) is still worth reading.]

§ 1. The Persian Empire as organized by Darius (iii. 89) was a new departure in the world's history; in extent it exceeded all its predecessors[1]; it was also definitely organized in a way unknown before, and only occurring again, on a similar scale, in the Roman Empire. It lasted, with little apparent decay, for a century and a half after the death of Darius. Unfortunately, the number of Persian official inscriptions as yet discovered is small, and the Greeks, to whom mainly we owe our accounts of the empire, were more interested in its external magnificence[2] than in its internal organization. The most complete one which has survived, the Cyropaedia of Xenophon, is a philosophic romance, intended to impress on its author's countrymen his views of government and education, not to give a complete picture of the Persian system as it was even in his own day, much less as it was in that of Cyrus, which it professes to describe (cf. e.g. i. 136 n.). We have therefore to piece together our account of Persian administration from a few inscriptions, from the casual references in the narratives of the historians, and above all from the invaluable official documents which H. has preserved for us (iii. 89 seq.; v. 52 seq.; and vii. 61 seq., his account of the Persian army). Next to H. in importance may perhaps be placed the Bible narratives of Ezra and Nehemiah, in which several official documents are preserved[3] (e.g. Ezra iv. 17 seq., vi. 2 seq., &c.).

§ 1. **The Position of the King.** The king is at once the representative of the Persian nation and the centre of the government; hence all matters are decided by him, and he is the source, direct or indirect, of all authority. His life is more valuable than that of any number of his subjects (viii. 99), and the true Persian asks nothing better than to die for him (viii. 118). Hence it was no mere piece of official servility when the Persian judges 'discovered a law τῷ βασιλεύοντι Περσέων ἐξεῖναι ποιέειν τὸ ἂν βούληται (iii. 31).

[1] The title 'King of Kings' is Persian in origin; it is not only that he has 'kings' as vassals (in Cilicia, i. 74 n.; at Tyre and Sidon, viii. 68), it is rather that he alone is 'King' in the strict sense; cf. the Greek use of βασιλεύς (without the article) for 'the Great King'.

[2] e.g. Theoph. fr. 125, 1; F. H. G. i. 298 as to the contributions in kind, which ends with the characteristic exaggeration that 'those approaching the piles of dried meat ὑπολαμβάνειν ὄχθους εἶναι καὶ λόφους'.

[3] The tale of Esther, too, even if written in the third century B.C., preserves a 'lively and trustworthy account of the conditions of the realm' (Meyer, iii. 2; cf. 131).

APPENDIX VI

Limitations of the Royal Power. But a king was expected to observe old custom, and even to the most absolute power there are limitations. Apart from the danger of assassination which confronts all rulers, especially the most despotic,[1] the Persian King had checks upon his power, to which as a rule he paid some attention; four of these may be mentioned.

(1) The Persian nobles, and especially the descendants of the six who aided Darius in overthrowing the Pseudo-Smerdis, had their definite privileges,[2] even against the king.

(2) It was usual on all important occasions to consult the whole body of Persian nobles (vii. 8).[3] A similar arrangement prevailed in the Macedonian monarchy. As the king's position depended ultimately on the loyalty of the Persians, he usually was guided by their feelings, expressed or unexpressed. At the same time, both in Persia and in Macedon, the increase of the royal power abroad weakened the rights of his native subjects at home.

(3) The royal judges (iii. 31 n.), who were appointed for life, were consulted on difficult points of law; their office was hereditary (v. 25).

(4) The king himself was bound by his own decisions (Dan. vi. 8, 15).[4]

§ 3. **Position of the Persians.** The Persians themselves were the privileged race of the empire. They were a landed aristocracy, free from taxes (iii. 97), and it was the custom of the Persian king when he came among his people to make them presents.[5] But their real importance lay in the fact that they were the governing race of the empire, both in civil and in military matters. In this respect only the Medes were at all on an equality with them; Media had rather deserted to Cyrus than been conquered by him (cf. App. III. 5); the Median empire had been changed into the Persian, but so little did the change impress distant nations that the Greeks always called the new kingdom 'Median'. Hence it is not surprising that from the first the Medians share the government with the Persians. Men of other nations were often employed, but in subordinate positions.[6]

[1] Rawlinson (iii. 566) reminds us that three of the nine successors of Darius were murdered.

[2] For the position of the 'six' cf. iii. 70 n., for their privileges iii. 84 n.; the chief of these was that the king could marry only from their families.

[3] On less important occasions the king acted with his 'seven counsellors' (Ezra vii. 14).

[4] 'The law of the Medes and Persians, which altereth not' has passed into a proverb, though the king was probably not quite so powerless against it as he is represented in the Bible narrative.

[5] Plut. Alex. 69; Thuc. ii. 97. 4, who contrasts the custom of the Thracians.

[6] For Medes in command Rawlinson quotes Mazares, i. 156; Harpagus, i. 162; Datis, vi. 94; his sons, vii. 88; and B. I. ii. 14, iii. 14: but these

§ 4. **Government of the Provinces.** The central government in some respects exercised direct control over the whole empire. The admirable organization of the army would alone be sufficient to prove that there was unity in the administration. Unfortunately, we have hardly any information as to the machinery by which this was carried on ; we know, however, that from the most remote provinces there was a direct appeal to the king, and that he interfered himself in their government.[1] We know too that these royal rescripts were carefully preserved in the royal treasure houses (Ezra v. 17) ;[2] these were written not in Persian, but in Aramaean,[3] which was the official language over the whole of the western parts of the empire. In order to facilitate the action of the central government, the roads and posts were highly organized. H. gives us the official description of the royal road from Sardis to Susa (v. 52. 4 nn.), and also describes the courier-system (*ἀγγαρήιον*, viii. 98 n.). Other important roads were that across Asia Minor (i. 72. 3 n.), and that from Susa to Colchis (iv. 37 n.) ; another went from Babylon past Ecbatana to the Indian frontier.

§ 5. **The Satrap System.** But in so vast an empire the administration was of necessity delegated ; the king's representative, the 'satrap' (i. 192 n.), combined in himself the civil and the military authority. Although this office existed before Darius, yet it was his organizing genius which established the system on a definite and permanent footing (iii. 89 n.) ; it may be added that Western Asia in the present day is governed on the principles of Darius, and that it has always been so, except during the time of the Roman Empire. Even the Roman provincial system has great resemblances to the Persian.

The satrap ruled over a large district, embracing various tribes ; the Assyrian power had established itself against the local resistance of small nationalities ; the Persian power had arisen when the spirit

are all commanders of armies and not satraps. Men of other nations are found in special posts, e. g. Pactyas the Lydian (i. 153, in charge of Croesus' treasure), Xenagoras of Halicarnassus (ix. 107. 3 n. ; H. seems to exaggerate the power of his countrymen when he says he 'ruled all Cilicia'), and Tamos the Egyptian (admiral for Cyrus the Younger, Xen. Anab. i. 4. 2).

[1] The Books of Ezra and Nehemiah are full of such interferences ; cf. c. vi, the decree for the building of the Temple, which orders Tatnai, the local governor 'beyond the river', not to interfere, and c. vii, that of Artaxerxes making the law of Jehovah 'the law of the king' (v. 26). An interesting parallel is the rescript of Darius to Gadatas (Hicks, 20) ; this local magistrate had interfered with the temple of Apollo at Magnesia ; the king orders him to desist, though commending him otherwise.

[2] These are the *βασιλικαὶ διφθέραι*, which Ctesias *said* that he used for his history. (Diod. ii. 32 ; cf. Bähr, Ctesias, pp. 17 f.)

[3] Aramaean inscriptions are found on the local coinage of the satraps. The character was also used in the extreme east, for some Indian scripts were affected by it (Meyer, iii. 59).

of many of these had been broken, and when they had already been united into large kingdoms, e.g. the Lydian and the Babylonian. The number of the satrapies,[1] however, was continually varying, according as the various districts were united or separated in administration, by the decisions of the king or by the energy and ambition of the local rulers.

§ 6. **The duties of the satrap.** (1) The satrap superintended the administration of his province, maintained order, and, if necessary, suppressed rebellion; (2) collected the royal tribute and forwarded it to the king; (3) acted as supreme judge in all matters; (4) saw to the maintenance and pay of the troops in his province: he was also to 'a certain extent the general of the provincial army corps' (Meyer, iii. 44). Hence he conducted ordinary operations himself[2]; (5) entered into negotiation with neighbouring independent states (v. 73), and at times conquered them (iv. 167).

Having such wide powers it is not surprising that the position of the satrap was a semi-royal one; he had his palace[3] and his bodyguard like the king himself, and he could coin silver money (iv. 166 n.) under certain circumstances; the office, too, was often hereditary, e.g. in the satrapy of Dascyleum (viii. 126 n.; cf. also i. 8. 1; iii. 90. 2 nn.). Moreover, two or more satrapies were frequently united in one (v. 25 n.). Hence, even in the time of Darius, the ambition of the satraps, e.g. Oroetes (iii. 126 seq.), Aryandes (iv. 166), was a danger to the central government, and in the fourth century, many of the governors became partly or completely independent (e.g. Evagoras in Cyprus). To check this danger many devices were adopted, which, for a time at least, were successful.

§ 7. **Checks on power of satraps.** The first of these was to appoint as far as possible members of the royal house[4] to the most important provinces. Where a member of the blood-royal was not available, a wife was found for the satrap among the king's numerous daughters.[5] This check, however, was probably worse than ineffective, as the ambition of Cyrus the Younger shows.[6]

[1] Cf. Appendix VII.

[2] So Darius (B. I. *pass.*) employs the satraps to suppress the great revolt; Artaphrenes arranges for the Naxian expedition (v. 30, 32), but he has to get Darius' consent; Cyrus attacks the semi-independent Pisidians (Xen. An. i. 9. 14); for other instances cf. Meyer, iii. 43. Xenophon (Oec. iv. 9) separates the civil and the military authority in Persia; but he refutes his own statement. For the royal 'generals' in the provinces *v. i.* Rawlinson (iii. 556) and Maspero (pp. 705–6) underestimate the military power of the satraps.

[3] For references cf. Meyer, iii. 34 n.

[4] So Hystaspes in Parthia (iii. 70 n.), Artaphrenes at Sardis, half-brother of Darius (v. 25), Masistes, son of Darius, in Bactria (ix. 113). Cf. Rawlinson, iii. 557.

[5] Cf. the proposal of Pausanias for such an alliance, Thuc. i. 128, and Rawlinson, iii. 558.

[6] A similar attempt and a similar failure is seen in the relation of the

The second check was much more effective, viz. division of authority. Not only had each satrap his neighbour satraps who were jealous of him; there were also numerous subordinate governors, who, though under his control and sometimes appointed by him, had considerable powers and the right of direct access to the king. Of these several classes may be mentioned:

(*a*) Eminent Persians, especially the royal benefactors (viii. 85. 3 n.), received grants of land from the king. Some of these, e.g. the house of Otanes in Cappadocia (iii. 83 n.) and that of Hydarnes in Armenia, were even free from the tribute.

(*b*) The Persians also were always inclined to favour the native rulers (iii. 15 n.). The government of the whole of Cilicia (i. 74 n.) was in the hands of a native house; but this is a unique instance. As a rule native princes were employed on a smaller scale, or among the less civilized tribes of the empire, who would submit to no other control.

The privileges given to the priests at Jerusalem (Ezra vii) had a parallel in numerous temples in Asia Minor (cf. p. 401, n. 1).

(*c*) In dealing with the Greek communities, the Persians recognized a certain amount of autonomy. Whether they were left as republics (vi. 43 n.), or, as was more often the case, put under a tyrant, they managed their own local affairs. So they were allowed to continue to coin silver money. All these privileged individuals and communities were likely to resent any excessive ambition in the satrap, and to denounce him to the king (Xen. Cyr. viii. 2. 10).

A third check, and the most important of all, was the limitation of the satrap's military authority. The commanders of the royal troops, especially of the garrisons in the fortresses, were often appointed by the king[1] (e.g. Tabalus by Cyrus, i. 153; Otanes, v. 25 n.). These 'generals' had districts of their own (*νομοί*, v. 102. 1 n., 116).[2]

The military inspection yearly[3] by the king or his representative, helped also to maintain the royal control over the troops. As the satrap could not as a rule leave his province,[4] there were

Burgundian dukes to the French crown in the fourteenth and fifteenth centuries.

[1] But Artaphrenes appoints Megabates (v. 32), and Aryandes (iv. 167) Amasis; no doubt the custom varied.

[2] Sometimes the satrap himself was especially appointed to military office, e.g. Cyrus (Xen. Anab. i. 4. 3). For the relations of generals and satraps cf. v. 25 n. and Abbott (H. pp. 127–30), who thinks the generals were 'independent'. No doubt the balance of power varied from time to time and from place to place.

[3] Xen. Oec. 4. 6 *βασιλεὺς κατ' ἐνιαυτὸν ἐξέτασιν ποιεῖται τῶν μισθοφόρων καὶ τῶν ἄλλων οἷς ὡπλίσθαι προστέτακται.* So Cyrus is *κάρανος τῶν εἰς Καστωλὸν ἀθροιζομένων* (Xen. Hell. i. 4. 3; cf. Anab. i. 1. 2); the rapidity of the Persian mobilization in 499 B.C. (v. 102) shows how effective the system was.

[4] So in 481–480 only Achaemenes, satrap of Egypt, commands the (naval) forces of his province (vii. 97).

other commanders for the local levies when employed on foreign service.

More important, however, than any of these artificial checks was the loyalty of the Persians to the Achaemenid house, shown so clearly in the overthrow of Oroetes (iii. 128).

The king had also direct machinery by which these checks might be made operative. Every satrap had a royal 'secretary' (iii. 128) attached to his court, while royal officers, e.g. 'the King's Eye' (i. 114 n.), could at any time be sent to inquire.

It will be obvious, however, that the use of all this machinery depended on the personality of the king; the Achaemenid weaklings of the fourth century were unable to make it effective.

§ 8. **Duties of subjects.** The system of Darius certainly provided some securities for good government; but the main concern of the Persian kings was to draw tribute and military service from their subjects. The details as to the tribute are discussed in the notes to iii. 89 seq.; three points only can be noticed here: (1) as the sum of money due from the province seems to have been fixed, the king had an interest in checking oppression and extortion from which he himself would gain no advantage, while his subjects would be weakened and exasperated; (2) beside the sums paid in actual money, there were also great contributions in kind. H. expressly mentions these in Cilicia (iii. 90) and in Egypt (iii. 91) as apart from the tribute; the corn of Babylon, which fed the king and his army for a third of the year (i. 192), was over and above the 1,000 talents paid (iii. 92); the rest of Asia supplied food for the other eight months. There were in addition all sorts of other gifts required (cf. Theoph., fr. 125 and ii. 98 n.). As the provinces had also to maintain the satraps, and to feed the armies quartered among them, the burden of the tribute in kind must have been heavy. (3) The special revenues from royal domains and monopolies were not included in the tribute; such were the profits on the fish in Lake Moeris (ii. 149), and the water dues from the Aces (iii. 117 nn.).

As the tribute was paid in money the burden on the subjects must have been the greater, as they often would have to obtain this from usurers.

The Persian kings, however, were not afraid to trust their subjects with arms. The disarmament of the Lydians (i. 155) was an exceptional measure, even if there be any truth in the story, and the statement in Xenophon's Cyropaedia, that the subjects only served as light-armed, is contradicted by the whole narrative of H. But the supreme command over the provincial levies was always in the hands of Persians (vii. 96); and the appointment of native officers mentioned by H. seems to have ceased later, for against Alexander the satraps have sole command over the contingents of their provinces (Arr. Anab. i. 12; ii. 11, &c.).

§ 9. Speaking generally the Persian Empire was as great an advance on its predecessors in the moral qualities of justice and mercy as it was in its careful organization. The Persian court might be the scene of horrors like the story of Artaÿnte (ix. 109); Persian armies behaved in the conquest of Ionia (vi. 32) as victorious armies have always behaved; whole nations were sometimes deported according to the invariable custom of the East (iii. 93; vii. 80 nn.); but the Persian conquest was not marked by the wholesale destruction of great cities (except in case of rebels, e. g. vi. 19), like that of Thebes by the Assyrians or of Nineveh by the Medes. The Persians could be cruel, but they did not exercise the brutal and wholesale cruelty of the Assyrians. They allowed the countries they ruled to retain their commerce and their customs, while at the same time they greatly developed trade by their road system (*v. s.*), and by introducing a uniform gold coinage for the empire.[1] In this material respect, as in more important matters of thought and belief,[2] the Persians brought Europe into contact with the immemorial civilizations of the East. The result was the extension of knowledge and of intercourse, of which the picture has been preserved in the pages of H.

APPENDIX VII

THE PERSIAN SATRAPIES

§ 1. **Relation of list in H. to the Persian Inscriptions.** Darius has left us three geographical lists; on the first, that at Behistun (i. 6), 23 names are given, viz.:

1. Persia
2. Susiana
3. Babylonia
4. Assyria
5. Arabia
6. Egypt
7. Those on the sea (i. e. islands and coasts of Asia Minor)
8. Sparda (i. e. Lydia and lands west of Halys)
9. Ionia
10. Media
11. Armenia
12. Cappadocia
13. Parthia
14. Drangiana
15. Aria
16. Chorasmia
17. Bactria
18. Sogdiana
19. Gandara
20. Sacae
21. Sattagydia
22. Arachosia
23. Maka

On the second list (at Persepolis) there are 24 lands, as Sagartia and India are included and Persia is omitted. The 'Ionians of the mainland, and those of the Islands' take the place of Nos. 7 and 9, and the order is slightly varied.

[1] Gold coinage was a royal prerogative; but, as Babelon shows (Les Perses Achém., 1893, p. xxi), the remoter provinces hardly used money.

[2] For Eastern influence on these in Greece cf. Arnold, Roman Stoicism, pp. 8–11, 33 seq. For the Persian attitude to other religions cf. v. 102. 1.

Finally at Nakhsh-i-Rustam (in the last years of Darius), there are 29 names (some count 30). These include the later conquests of Darius, e.g. the 'Sacae beyond the Sea', the Skudra (the Macedonians or the Thracians (cf. ix. 116 n.)), &c. But the identifications are too disputed to be given here.[1]

These lists, however, are not official accounts of the organization of the empire, as is proved by their inconsistencies and their incompleteness, and by the fact that they include regions certainly never conquered, e.g. the Scyths; they are therefore simply records of the king's triumphs.

§ 2. **Nature of H.'s list.** H., on the other hand, clearly intends his list to be a statistical account of the empire (cf. iii. 89. 1, 97. 1). We know (Xen. Oec. iv. 11) that it was part of the special duty of the satrap to look after the revenues. But some (e. g. Stein) have held that the list is purely financial (not an administrative one) for the following reasons:

(*a*) *Inconsistency* with the rest of H.'s narrative; vii. 64 and ix. 113 are said to show that the Sacae and the Bactrians were under *one* satrap, not two (as cc. 92–3). But, as a matter of fact, the passages in the later books prove nothing to the point, and in any case the union of two distinct satrapies was always possible.

(*b*) *Impossibility.* The sixteenth satrapy, containing the Parthians, Chorasmians, Arians, and Sogdians, is far too big for one ruler. It may be answered that, as these peoples were assessed at 300 talents only, they could not have been very formidable.

The usual view now is that H. preserves here an official document of great importance.[2] The number of 20 satrapies seems to have been maintained later.[3] It must be admitted that H.'s list is open to serious criticism; after the first six satrapies there seems little attempt at geographical order, and the omission of Hyrcania is inexplicable. Whether, in his unfamiliarity with the names, he got his notes confused, or whether the omissions and obscurities are due to his copyists, cannot be determined. It may, however, be said without hesitation that, as in other parts of his history, so here later research has tended to confirm his statements, and that these chapters are a valuable contemporary account of the organization of the great Persian Empire.

[1] The lists are given in Rawlinson, on iii. 94, but not quite accurately. Cf. Spiegel, Altpers. Keilinsch. pp. 55, 119, whom I have followed in the main, comparing Die altpers. Keilinsch. of Weissbach and Bang (1893).

[2] How he obtained it can only be conjectured; cf. J. H. S. xxvii. 37 seq. The list is discussed by Bunbury (A. G. i. 235 seq.), and by P. Krumbholz (De Asiae Minoris Satrapis, Leipzig, 1883). It should be compared with the army list of Book VII; of its 68 names all but eight occur there, while two only of the tribes (the Dorians and the Ligyans) serving in the army are omitted in Book III.

[3] e. g. under Xerxes; cf. Duncker, iv. 582 seq.

APPENDIX VIII

THE RELIGION OF THE ANCIENT PERSIANS AND HERODOTUS

[In the following pages I have as a rule followed J. Darmesteter, the preface to whose Zendavesta (S. B. E. iv, Oxford, 1880) contains an interesting and clear account, first of the rediscovery (1771) of this ancient religion by Duperron and of the ensuing controversy, then of its origin and main features. A shorter account of the religion by K. Geldner will be found in E. B.[11] xxviii. 1041–3, where Zoroaster is made the prophet of the higher form of faith, which represents the civilization of the settled tribes against that of the uncivilized nomads, their neighbours. For the development of Persian religion and its spread in the empire cf. Meyer, iii. 76–9. Rawlinson's view (i. 414–19), that the religion of the Magi was contrasted with Persian dualism and was Scythic, is now quite given up.]

§ 1. The religion of the Persians has been variously called Dualism or Mazdeism or Magism, or Zoroastrianism or Fire Worship, according as its main tenet, or its supreme god, or its priests, or its supposed founder, or its apparent object of worship, has been kept most in view. It is especially interesting as throwing light on that period in the history of religious thought when the Aryan mind came in contact with the Semitic. Its main feature is the existence of a good and an evil principle, Ormazd and Ahriman[1], between whom all the world is divided; Space and Time are the scene of their constant struggle, which will end after 3,000 years with the victory of the good and the resurrection of the dead to everlasting life.

§ 2. **General character of the religion.** This religion developed out of the old Indo-Iranian religion; in that too there was a law in Nature and a war in Nature, there was a heaven god, Varana, and minor gods side by side with him; there were also evil principles; but whereas in India[2] the power of the minor gods developed and polytheism was established, in Persia the minor gods became subordinate to Ormazd, the bright god of heaven, the all-knowing lord, while the evil principles became embodied in a single

[1] I have used these names, and not the more correct Ahura Mazda and Angra Mainyu, because they have become familiar through English literature.

[2] By a curious chance the two names for 'deity' in the Vedas, 'asura' and 'dêva', were developed in completely different ways; in Persia 'Ahura' is god, the 'dêvas' are evil spirits, while in the later Vedas, the asurâs are evil, the dêvas are gods (as with the Italians, Celts, &c.).

power. Ormazd is light and life and all that is pure and good in the moral world—law, order, and truth; to Ahriman belong darkness, filth, death, and, in the moral order, lawlessness and lies.

Under Ormazd are the Amesha Spentas, 'the undying and well-doing ones,' six in number, with whom he himself is joined as a seventh; these are at once personified as archangels, and are also the thoughts and beneficent intentions of the deity reproduced in men. The old god of heavenly light, Mitra, now becomes Mithra, one of the creatures of Ormazd, though he is still invoked along with him in an indivisible unity.

The great aim of man is to aid the good by sacrifice and praise, and to purify himself by keeping free from pollution,[1] especially from anything dead, while his duty is to kill the creatures of Ahriman—serpents, frogs, and ants. In the world after death man reaps the consequences of his actions in life; if his good deeds overbalance his bad ones, he passes into Paradise, if not, the pains of hell are his portion for ever.

§ 3. **Origin of Mazdeism.** Darmesteter adopts the view that the religion took its form in Media, either Media proper or Atropatene;[2] this explains why the sacred books are not written in old Persian but in a kindred dialect. Whether there were a teacher called Zoroaster he doubts;[3] at any rate he has been invested in the myths with divine attributes. A more important question is when and how the religion became established among the Persians.

Greek tradition[4] said that Cyrus introduced the Magi among his countrymen, and himself sacrificed at their bidding. This evidence is worthless in itself, but the fact is not improbable (Media 'capta ferum victorem cepit'), and it corresponds to what we know of the later development; moreover, the Persians were akin to the Medes, and had already those religious ideas which had in Media developed into the system. The Median priesthood, the Magi, were originally a local tribe (i. 101 n.), but they had become specialized in their religious functions; hence when a Persian wished to sacrifice, he had to employ a Magus[5] (i. 132); we may perhaps compare the

[1] The Vendidad is mainly a collection of laws of purification.

[2] pp. 46 seq. Professor Mills, on the other hand, in the final volume (S. B. E. xxxi) considers that the earliest form of the religion arose in the north-east, roughly speaking in Bactria (pp. 28 seq.).

[3] p. 79. Mills, however, accepts him as a historic person (pp. 23 seq.), as also does Geldner. In any case he is not to be looked upon as creating a religious revolution by introducing new principles, but simply as giving definite form to tendencies which were in existence already. Zoroaster first occurs in Greek literature in the Pseudo-Platonic Alcibiades I, 122.

[4] Xen. Cyr. viii. 1. 23.

[5] This will explain why the term 'Magus' hardly ever occurs in the Avesta; the Persians used it, but the priests termed themselves 'Arthravan' (fireman; cf. Strabo 733, the Magi in Cappadocia are called Πύραιθοι).

influence of Etruscan augury in early Rome. Whether the Magians used 'magic' is disputed; the sacred books know only of the use of the sacred twig; and Aristotle (fr. 36) says of the Magi, *τὴν γοητικὴν μαγείαν οὐδὲ ἔγνωσαν*; but H. (vii. 43, 191) expressly speaks of sacrifices and incantations. Probably the usage varied, and H.'s informants noted those parts of the Magian ritual which reminded them of Greek magic.

§ 4. **Development of Mazdeism.** As was natural the new religion established itself but slowly. If H. may be trusted[1] Cyrus attempted to burn Croesus; Cambyses burned the body of Amasis (iii. 16. 2), but this was looked upon as an impious act. By the time of H. (i. 131 n.) himself, the respect for the element of fire was established, and in the Vendidad (Farg. vii. 25–6; S. B. E. iv. 82) the burning of corpses is an 'unpardonable sin'.

The respect for earth was not so soon developed; the Achaemenid kings were buried, and the custom of exposing the dead on the 'Towers of Silence' (i. 140. 1 n.) was the custom of the Magi alone. The Persians adopted a half-way measure by coating the body in wax before it was buried (*ib.*). It was not until a later period that the strict law against burying the dead was enforced on all, priests and lay alike.

Another point in which we can trace development is the partial disuse of temples. In H.'s time the Persians worshipped on the hill-tops, and thought temples and altars foolish; the prohibition, however, was not strictly observed (i. 131. 1 n.), and Darius boasts that he restored the temples which the Magian Gomates[2] had destroyed. Xerxes is said, as a disciple of the Magians, to have destroyed the Greek temples (Cic. de Leg. ii. 10); but this is probably untrue (v. 102 n.), and at any rate his practice was far from consistent. On this point the priestly caste had to give way; there were temples in Persia even under the Sassanian kings.

Whether Darius accepted the whole doctrine of Dualism is disputed; certainly there is no mention of Ahriman in any of his inscriptions or in those of Xerxes; but they speak of Ormazd quite in the style of the Avesta, and the omission of the name Ahriman is no proof that he was unknown[3]; the public documents of modern countries make no mention of Satan.

§ 5. **Inconsistencies in Persian religion.** It seems in fact

[1] i. 86. 2 n.; Nicolaus Damascenus (F. H. G. iii. 409) says the failure caused the Persians henceforth, according to Zoroaster's precepts, to ordain *μήτε νεκροὺς καίειν μήτε ἄλλως μιαίνειν πῦρ, καὶ πάλαι τοῦτο καθεστὸς τὸ νόμιμον τότε βεβαιωσάμενοι.* This may be an old tradition, or it is more probably an attempt to explain the difficulty in the narrative of H.

[2] B. I. i. 14. Meyer, iii. 76, denies that these were 'temples'; but cf. App. V. 6.

[3] On this point also Darmesteter and Mills take opposite views (S. B. E. iv. 44 and xxxi. 31).

clear that Persian religion in the time of H. was really marked by those inconsistencies which are so conspicuous in his account of it (i. 131 nn.). The doctrines of Zoroaster were too pure and elevated for the mass of the people, and hence there was a continual tendency to revert to the old deities of the Iranian race and to introduce new deities from neighbouring peoples. A similar struggle marked the history of Israel; the doctrines of the prophets had to contend with the attraction of the 'Calves' on the one hand, and of Baal and Astaroth on the other. This was especially seen in Persia in the transformation of the worship of Anaitis (i. 131. 3 n.), originally the goddess of the Oxus river; she became the Babylonian Ishtar, with prominent breasts, worshipped with impure rites, especially in Armenia.[1] As the Jewish worship was purified by the Captivity, so was Mazdeism by foreign conquest. Its full triumph was gained under the Sassanian kings, when Persian national feeling replaced the native race on the throne (A.D. 226), which had been so long held first by Greeks and then by the Parthian Arsacidae. This triumph of a really Oriental cult was part of the great reaction against Western influences, which began so soon after the death of Alexander, and which culminated (under a very different form) in the rise of Islam.

§ 6. **H. and Persian religion.** Details as to the knowledge which H. had of the Persian religion are given in the notes on cc. 131–40: we may sum up the results here.

(1) (*a*) H. never mentions the great principle of the religion, the Dualism of Good and Evil; and we may be sure that, even if he knew it, he would not have stated it. His religious descriptions are always of things external (contrast the full account of dualism in Plut. de Is. et Osir. cc. 46–7, based on Theopompus). (*b*) But H. mentions several usages which involve this dualism; cf. for Ormazd i. 131. 2 n., and for Ahriman i. 140. 3 and vii. 114. 2 nn.

(2) With regard to special usages he shows his usual accuracy and command of detail; cf. his accounts of the methods of sacrifice (i. 132 n.), of the sinfulness of lying (i. 138. 1 n.), of the sacredness of the dog (i. 140. 1 n.) &c.

(3) The brevity of H.'s account makes him inaccurate if taken literally (cf. 131 nn., where on the one hand he states the spiritual nature of the Persian creed too absolutely (§ 1), and on the other hand (§ 2) confuses the deity with his attributes).

(4) H.'s ignorance of Comparative Mythology leads him, through confusion of names, to a serious mistake as to Mithra (i. 131. 3 n.).

[1] Cf. Strabo 532 (quoted on i. 93. 4); Meyer, iii. 78.

APPENDIX IX

HERODOTUS IN EGYPT

[Throughout Appendixes IX and X references to Book II are given only by the chapter. For a clever general discussion cf. Sayce, Journal of Philology, vol. xiv; his references, however, should be verified, and his inferences are often more than doubtful; he was answered by D. D. Heath (*ib.* vol. xv) with considerable effect but with needless personality. A shorter but better account is that of Maspero, Annuaire des É. G., 1878, pp. 127 seq. The most recent discussion of the subject is Sourdille, La Durée et l'Étendue du Voyage d'Hérodote en Égypte, Paris, 1910—very full, but at times over-elaborate and subtle.] (See Note H, p. 453.)

§ 1. **Date of Visit.** H. furnishes some slight clues.

(1) Certain. He was there after 460 B. C., the date of the battle of Papremis (iii. 12. 4).

(2) Probable. He had already been in Chaldaea (c. 150) and at Delos (c. 170. 2).

(3) The Persians seem to have been in peaceful possession of Egypt (30. 3, 149. 5; iii. 91. 3); there were Persian garrisons there; the Persians look after the Memphis dykes (c. 99. 3; cf. also c. 98. 1).

Three views may be mentioned as to the date of H.'s visit.

(1) Rawlinson's (i. 12), that he was there at the time of the rebellion of Inaros, when the Greeks were assisting the Egyptians (460–455 B. C.), otherwise 'he would scarcely have been allowed such free access to the temples and records'. But it is very doubtful if the rebellion spread south of Memphis,[1] and this view is inconsistent with cc. 30, 99 (*u.s.*). And had H. really 'free access to records', &c.?

(2) The usual view (e. g. in Stein) is that he was in Egypt between 449 B. C., when Amyrtaeus[2] was still holding out in the Delta (Thuc. i. 110, 112), and 443 B. C., about which date he went to Thurii.

A. Bauer[3] (cf. Introd., p. 12) thinks that the Egyptian visit must be dated nearer to the latter date (443) than to the former, because H. mentions (ii. 41, 165) the island Prosopitis, without any reference to the Athenian disaster there of 454 B. C. As he admits, however, regard for Athenian feelings may have caused this silence.

(3) Meyer (F. i. 156) considers that H. was in Egypt after his return from Thurii (i. e. between 440 and 431 B. C.). 'The land was completely pacified and the great rebellion a thing of the past.'

Meyer's view is the most probable, but the evidence is too slight for certainty.

§ 2. **Extent of his travels.** H. seems to have entered Egypt from the East (iii. 5, 6) by land through Pelusium (iii. 12), not by sea

[1] An inscription of the year 460 B. C., found at Coptos, shows the Persians as then in possession.

[2] Cf. iii. 15. 3 n. H. knows of the reduction of Amyrtaeus.

[3] p. 34.

as Sayce says (*u. s.* 261 ; Sayce even knows it was 'about July 20th'), and it is natural to suppose that he left it by sea, sailing to Tyre to make his inquiries (c. 44). It is impossible, however (as Sayce and Sourdille do), to attempt to describe his line of route, for we do not know how long he was in Egypt. It will be convenient, however, to arrange the places he visited in three groups.

The Delta and North Egypt. He was clearly at Canobus (c. 113), Naucratis (c. 178 seq.), Buto (c. 155 *et pass.*), and Sais (c. 28 *et pass.*) in the west ; at Busiris (c. 61) in the centre, and perhaps at Mendes (c. 46) ; at Bubastis (c. 138), Papremis (iii. 12), and Daphnae (cc. 30 and 154) on the eastern arm of the Nile. He was also at Heliopolis (c. 3 *et pass.*) near the south end of the Delta, but outside of it, and he had followed the line of Necho's canal by Patumus (c. 158) on the Red Sea (c. 159) to the docks ; probably at the same time he had visited the gorge of the winged serpents (c. 75). H. seems to have known all this region so far as it could be reached by the three great arms of the Nile, the Canopic, Sebennytic, and Pelusiac (cf. c. 17 for the seven mouths).

H. may have come to the Delta after the Nile flood had begun (19. 2 n.), and he certainly travelled at this season to Memphis from Naucratis (c. 97). It is worth notice that he knows little of the North-east delta, and hence the story of the Tanite Dynasty had not reached him ; the 'men of the marshes' (c. 92) were a different race, and not at all submissive to the Persian government.

Central Egypt and the Fayûm. H. of course knew Memphis well ; it was the Cairo of ancient Egypt, and in its streets most of the tribes of North-east Africa and South-west Asia could be met. From Memphis he had visited the pyramids carefully (he had measured that of Chephrên, c. 127), and also the district (the Fayûm) of Lake Moeris,[1] where he explored the Labyrinth (c. 148).

South Egypt. With this region it is very different ; H. only mentions three places that he visited, Thebes (c. 143 *et pass.*), Chemmis (c. 91), and Elephantine (c. 29) ; he also names Neapolis (c. 91) and Hermopolis (c. 67). The reason is that very few Greeks visited these parts. The once great city of Thebes had never recovered from the Ethiopian and Assyrian conquests.

It is curious that H. does not mention Abydos, the holy city of Osiris, where there was a Greek settlement. Maspero (*u. s.* p. 129) well conjectures that H.'s visit to the South was pretty much like that of the great orientalist Pococke in 1739, who spent forty-five days going from Cairo to Syene, of which only fourteen were on shore. H.'s truthfulness is indirectly confirmed by the fact that it is just in this region, where he claims least personal knowledge, that his mistakes are most frequent and his information most scanty.

§ 3. Purpose of H.'s travels. It is useless for us to argue

[1] Heath (*u. s.* p. 227) notes that H. seems to have made one of a tourist party, for here he uses the plural, c. 148, §§ 5, 6.

that H. would have admired what we admire, and especially visited what is now visited: for all we know, his feelings about much of Egyptian architecture may have been those of Strabo (806), who says, speaking of a pillared hall at Memphis, 'apart from the fact that the columns are big and numerous and elaborate (πολυστίχων), it has no grace, but ματαιοπονίαν ἐμφαίνει μᾶλλον.' H. himself implies three motives for his travels: (1) To study religious questions,[1] e.g. he inquired at Thebes (c. 55. 1, cf. 3. 2) as to the oracle of Dodona; this is the most frequent. (2) To study natural history, e.g. he went especially to Buto (75. 1) to inquire about 'the winged serpents'. (3) To study geography, e.g. his inquiries about the Nile (cc. 28, 29).

§ 4. **Results of H.'s travels.** His historical information will be dealt with later. Here it is only necessary to speak of the value of what he tells us as to Egypt in his own day, i. e. especially in the second part of Book II, cc. 35–98. This is the more necessary, because the period when he visited Egypt is one for which we have very little monumental evidence; and, moreover, the monuments at all times tell us more of the religious rites and beliefs of the people than of their daily life, although much information about this is given by them incidentally. H. is continually quoted by the best modern Egyptologists (e. g. Maspero and Erman) as evidence for the things which he himself could have seen.[2]

H. laboured under two most serious drawbacks:

(1) He had no knowledge of the Egyptian language; cf. notes on cc. 104, 125, 143, and Meyer, F. i. 192 f.

(2) He came in contact, apart from his own countrymen, only with the lower classes of Egypt, probably mainly with the half-castes, who acted as interpreters (c. 154). It is not at all probable that he met the 'priests', though he claims to have done so (e. g. 143. 1), no doubt in all honesty. Maspero, a kindly critic, says this was about as likely as that a modern tourist would be shown round Notre Dame by the Archbishop of Paris (*u. s.* p. 137). The limitations of H.'s

[1] For his knowledge of Egyptian religion cf. notes *pass.*, especially on cc. 43 seq. and 123. It is important to remember that H. deliberately refrained from telling us much that he knew (or thought he knew) about the subject: a treatise like the *De Iside et Osiride* of Plutarch (Moralia, vol. iii) would have been impossible to him (e. g. Plutarch in c. 8 gives the λόγος which H. (c. 47) refuses to tell; cf. c. 62 with Plutarch, c. 18). Hence, though quite a fourth of the chapters in Book II deal with religious subjects, the information is almost entirely as to externals.

[2] As a contrast may be quoted Mr. Griffith's essay on Egypt and Assyria in 'Authority and Archaeology'; after praising H. for his accurate description of the ibis, he says: 'But how isolated is this gem of veracity.' Hardly H. 'one would say on reading its wondrous context. After all, even the most unobservant of theorists and the most irresponsible of writers may sometimes stumble into accuracy.' But this was written thirteen years ago.

experience are the explanation of many strange misstatements, e. g. that the Egyptians used no wheat flour (36. 2) and had only brazen cups (37. 1; see notes).

(3) To these drawbacks must be added a third, the firm belief, which H. shared with other Greeks, that everything in Egypt was the reverse of what it was elsewere (cf. c. 35 and notes).

In view of these points we shall continually find that H. generalizes from a few instances. But, on the other hand, H. has the merit of a careful observer, who honestly tried to describe what he saw, even though he did not understand it; so his evidence as to all the Egyptians being circumcised (36. 3) is most valuable, since the boys habitually went naked, as did also the men in the fields. Perhaps the best instances of his accuracy are in c. 86 (see notes), his description of the process of embalming.[1] How difficult it is for a foreigner to be accurate may be illustrated from the strange mistakes made, even in our own day, by traders and missionaries as to the customs of the people among whom they have lived. We may sum up in the words of Erman (E. p. 4), 'What H. himself observed gives us as trustworthy an account as it is possible to obtain from a tourist who, ignorant of the language, travels for a few months in a foreign country.'

APPENDIX X

THE HISTORY OF EGYPT IN RELATION TO HERODOTUS

[To attempt to sketch, however briefly, the history of at least three thousand years in about a dozen pages may well seem absurd; the only object of this appendix is to give such an outline of Egyptian development as is necessary to place in their true relation the scanty facts mentioned by H. Breasted's History of Egypt (1906) has been mainly followed; Flinders Petrie's history (3 vols., 1905) gives a valuable summary of the monumental evidence, but in his chronology for the period before the Eighteenth Dynasty he follows a different system. Of course it will be remembered that the early dates can only be considered approximate.]

§ 1. **Chronology.**[2] The order of kings is determined in the first place by Manetho. He was a priest of Sebennytos, who wrote under Ptolemy II (Philadelphus) about 280 B.C., and arranged all the

[1] An interesting confirmation of his statements as to the methods of Pyramid building has been given lately by M. Legrain's work at Karnak; he has employed successfully in his restorations the mound and the *μηχαναὶ ξύλων βραχέων* (125. 2 n.).

[2] For Egyptian chronology generally cf. Meyer, Abhandl. Berl. Akad., 1904.

rulers of Egypt from Menes to the last Persian conquest (*circ* 343 B.C.) in 'thirty dynasties'. Unfortunately his work only survives in the epitomes of the chronologers (e.g. Africanus and Eusebius) or in fragments; in any case his dates often are clearly untrustworthy, and he seems to have included many popular elements in his history.[1] On the basis of these lists of the kings the chronology is constructed; further, the great Turin papyrus gave in many cases the lengths of their reigns.[2] But the most trustworthy evidence is that of the monuments, which date events by the year of the king. Obviously there can be no certainty that the latest monument of a king found belongs to the last year of his reign, in fact, it is quite certain that this will often not be so; but an addition of the maximum monumental dates for the reigns of a dynasty will give a minimum for the duration of that dynasty. This is called the method of 'dead reckoning'. By this method it is calculated that the reigns of the kings from the Eighteenth to the Twenty-sixth Dynasty, which ended with the Persian Conquest in 525 B.C., inclusive lasted at least 1050 years, and thus the accession of the Eighteenth Dynasty is placed by general agreement about 1580 B.C.

§ 2. **The Sothic Period.** Unfortunately there is no continuous succession of monuments for the period before this date; frequently they are lacking altogether for long spaces of time. But here astronomical science comes to our aid. The Egyptian year of 365 days was roughly a fourth of a day shorter than the real year[3]; hence every four years the calendar was one day in advance, and in 1460 years a whole year would be gained. This period of 1460 years is called a 'Sothic Period'. Now we know that such a period began in 140 A.D.; hence previous Sothic periods would have begun in 1321 B.C., 2781 B.C., and 4241[4] B.C. If this is so, it is obviously

[1] He wrote to correct errors of the Greeks, especially of H. (cf. fr. 42 πολλὰ τὸν Ἡρόδοτον ἐλέγχει ὑπ' ἀγνοίας ἐψευσμένον). Some modern Egyptologists are almost equally severe on Manetho himself; Breasted says (p. 23) his chronology is a 'late, careless, and uncritical compilation'; but Meyer (i. 152) sums up more judiciously: 'his results as to periods where the monuments fail us cannot be dispensed with, even if they are to be used with the utmost care.'

[2] This was discovered by Champollion in 1824; it seems to have been drawn up under the Eighteenth Dynasty. Unfortunately it was in a very fragmentary state, and it perished in the Turin fire of 1903. The oldest record of this kind is the Palermo Stone, a fragment of a list set up under the Fifth Dynasty. Three other lists, more or less fragmentary, survive, of which one (from Abydos) is in the B. M. (B. M. G. p. 245). For a brief discussion of these lists cf. Petrie, i. 26 seq.

[3] For the Egyptian calendar cf. c. 4 nn.

[4] Cf. 4. 1 nn. Meyer (there quoted) thinks the Sothic period was arranged in 4241 B.C.; but it is much easier to date it from 2781 B.C., and

only a matter of calculation, if we know the date on which Sothis rose in any year, to settle what that year was.[1] A record has been discovered at Kahun in which a priest tells us that Sothis would rise on the 15th day of the 8th month in the 7th year of Senosret III (Usertesen III) of the Twelfth Dynasty, i.e. 225 days too late. Senosret must therefore have begun to reign in 1887 B.C., and the commencement of the Twelfth Dynasty must be placed about 2000 B.C.

The dates of the dynasties previous to the Twelfth are again a matter of 'dead reckoning', but there is an uncertain element in the reigns of the Ninth and Tenth Dynasties, for which we have no monumental evidence.

§ 3. **The two First Dynasties.** The history of Egypt, like that of other countries, begins with division. Perhaps the later 'nomes' (c. 164 n.) may represent early kingdoms; certainly there were the two great divisions of Upper and of Lower Egypt,[2] the union of which gave the later kings of the whole country their double crown and their double emblem, the hawk for the southern kingdom, the snake for the northern one. This union was carried out by Menes (c. 99 n.), the founder of the First (Thinite) Dynasty,

to suppose that dates were reckoned back from this. Certainly so elaborate a calculation seems to suit the third millennium better than the fifth. Meyer (Abhandl. Berl. Akad. 1904, p. 40) maintains that the inscriptions show that the distinction between the two years, the ordinary and the Sothic, was recognized long before the time of the Pyramid builders. But the monumental evidence ought to be very decisive to establish a position so difficult to accept.

[1] A clear account of this method of reckoning is given in Breasted (Ancient Records of Egypt, i. pp. 26 f.): he gives six instances from the monuments by which the month in which an event happened can be approximately fixed, and they all tend to show that a Sothic period began in 2781 B.C. The dates thus arrived at are almost universally accepted in Germany; English and French Egyptologists, however, hesitate to accept the shortening of the earlier history which is thus involved, especially as the new system of dating allows only a little over two hundred years for the whole period from the Thirteenth to the Seventeenth Dynasties (inclusive). They are inclined to hold the traditional chronology, which puts the Twelfth Dynasty, and consequently all those that precede it, some seven hundred years earlier. Petrie, however, accepting the astronomical argument, boldly assumes three Sothic periods, instead of two, before the Eighteenth Dynasty, and puts his dates 1460 years earlier than those given here. An interesting summary of the controversy is given in Burrows, Discoveries in Crete (pp. 67 seq., 221-6), where he discusses the bearing of Cretan evidence on Egyptian chronology.

[2] Of these early pre-dynastic kingdoms we now know something from the tombs; the names of nine of the kings are preserved on the Palermo Stone. The Ashmolean collection is peculiarly rich in fine and typical specimens to illustrate this period (Guide, pp. 75 f.).

with whom H. (like Manetho) rightly begins his Egyptian history (*circ.* 3400 B.C.).

§ 4. **The 'Old Kingdom'.**[1] With the Third Dynasty the capital was transferred to Memphis (3. 1 n.), in the neighbourhood of which (at Gizeh) the kings of the next dynasty (Fourth, 2900–2750) erected the Pyramids, which made their names and their order familiar to H. (cc. 124–134 nn.) and, so far as Cheops is concerned, to all future times; Sir T. Browne is hardly just to the success of Cheops, when he writes 'To be but pyramidally extant is a fallacy of duration'. 'The great pyramid is the earliest and most impressive witness . . . to the final emergence of organized society from prehistoric chaos and local conflict' (Breasted, p. 119).

With the Sixth Dynasty (2625–2475 B.C.) the period of Egyptian foreign conquest begins; both Nubia and some districts of Arabia were reduced, at any rate partially. To this dynasty belonged Neterkara, with whom H.'s queen, Nitocris, may be connected (but see c. 100 nn.). The centralization of Egyptian power, however, had been too rapid, and the local rulers once more asserted themselves. A period of confusion apparently followed, during which the seat of authority was gradually moved southwards, perhaps from fear of the northern tribes, who were pressing into Syria. With the Eleventh Dynasty it was fixed at Thebes, which was the capital during the greatest period of Egyptian history, that of the Twelfth Dynasty (2000–1788 B.C.).

§ 5. **The Twelfth Dynasty.** Its system was feudal, but the king had established complete control over his vassals. The conquests of the Sixth Dynasty in the South were renewed and extended; Nubia was subdued to beyond the Second Cataract. The victorious kings also carried their arms northward, and Senosret III (Usertesen) was the first Egyptian king to appear as a conqueror in Syria. The impression made by his victories earned him a place in popular tradition and so in the pages of H. (cc. 102 seq.), as 'Sesostris'. But the works of peace under this dynasty were not less famous than their campaigns. The kings set themselves to control the Nile flood by utilizing the great depression of the Fayûm. Lake Moeris (c. 149 n.) secured for Amenemhet III

[1] The period from the Third to the Sixth Dynasty (inclusive) is that of the 'Old Kingdom', the 'Middle Kingdom' is that of the Eleventh and Twelfth Dynasties (Breasted, pp. 156, 212 confines it to the Twelfth); the 'New Kingdom' or 'Empire' is that of the Eighteenth, Nineteenth, and Twentieth. Maspero, however, more loosely calls the whole period from the Third to the Tenth 'the Old Kingdom', and that from the Eleventh to the Fifteenth the 'Middle Kingdom'. These names are often used; their main importance is that they emphasize the fact that Egyptian history before the Saite Dynasty has three great periods, those of the Sixth, the Twelfth, and the Nineteenth Dynasties.

(c. 101) the honour of being remembered, though not by his royal name. His portrait is almost as familiar in modern museums as that of the great Rameses II himself. It was he, too, who introduced the system of recording the height of the Nile at the Second Cataract, as his inscriptions still show (Lepsius, D. ii. 139, vol. iv). No doubt the campaigns in Nubia were in part intended to secure the control of the water system; the kings of the Twelfth Dynasty knew as well as the English in Egypt to-day, that the life of their country depended on the Nile. It is not surprising that such powerful rulers extended their trading connexions over the sea. Vases of the Kamares type from Crete have been found at Kahun, close to a pyramid of Senosret II (1906–1887 B.C.).[1]

§ 6. **The Northern Invaders.** With the end of the Twelfth Dynasty the greatness of Egypt once more decayed, and the most obscure period of her history begins. Whether the Egyptian invasions had provoked the peoples of the North, or whether the weakness of the Nile valley tempted these marauders, it is impossible to say; perhaps both may have been the case. Certainly Egypt was invaded from the North, and passed for a time under foreign rule. The three dynasties of Hyksos ('Shepherd kings') in the chronologers rule 929 years; according to the fragment (No. 42) of Manetho, preserved by the patriotic vanity of the Jew Josephus, who identified the Hyksos with Joseph and his brethren, they ruled 518 years. These figures must be greatly exaggerated; the period of foreign rule may have lasted only about a century (1680–1580 B.C.). What is certain is that the Hyksos were a people from the North, of an alien religion, and that their capital was Avaris in the east part of the Delta. Their influence, even if not their direct rule, seems to have been widely extended; the name of one of their kings, Khian, has been found from places south of Thebes to Gezer, at Bagdad (on a basalt lion now in the B. M.), and among the foundations of the Cnossus palace. The invaders adopted Egyptian usages and even Egyptian names; but they were to the natives 'the accursed', and H. heard nothing of their rule in Egypt.[2]

[1] Cf. Burrows *u. s.*, and, for objects in the Ashmolean, illustrating the synchronization, Guide, p. 85; that Museum is particularly rich in these.

[2] Cf., however, c. 128 n. as to the 'shepherd' Philitis. The Manetho fragment referred to above is given in Petrie, i. 233 seq. Meyer (i. 304) connects the Hyksos with the Hittites, and the last remnant of their empire may have been the kingdom of Kadesh, which was reduced with such difficulty by Thothmes III (*v. i.*). Their name is translated above, as it is explained by Manetho, i. e. *βασιλεῖς ποιμένες*; others, e. g. Breasted, make it = 'rulers of countries' (p. 217; but Meyer rejects this). For the whole subject of the Hyksos cf. Breasted, pp. 214 seq., and more fully Meyer (*u. s.*), who rejects the claim of Petrie (Hyksos and Israelite Cities, 1904) to have found the remains of Avaris in mounds north of Heliopolis; but the connexion of Avaris with the Hyksos is supported by Jewish tradition as early as Ptolemaic times.

§ 7. **The New Kingdom.** The Egypt which emerged from the confusion under the Eighteenth Dynasty was a changed country. The power of the old feudal aristocracy was broken, and the king was at the head of a well-trained army. The situation was like that in France after the final expulsion of the English by Charles VII; and as in the fifteenth century the victorious French monarchs plunged into the Italian wars, so from Egypt the Eighteenth Dynasty (1580–1350 B.C.) carried its conquests far to the north and to the south. The most important of its kings was Thothmes III (1501–1447), whose great deeds are recorded at Karnak[1] and elsewhere; he is the founder of the first real empire, which extended from the Euphrates far south into Nubia. The 'isles of the sea' sent him tribute, as is recorded in the well-known tomb of Rekhmara,[2] his vizier. It is fitting that the memorials of so great a conqueror should be widely distributed; his obelisks have been removed to Constantinople, to Rome (where the obelisk before the Lateran is the largest surviving, being 105½ feet high), to London (Cleopatra's Needle), and to the Central Park, New York. The latter pair once stood at Heliopolis.

But Greek imagination was even more impressed by a later monarch of the dynasty, Amenhotep III ('Amenophis,' 1411–1375 B.C.), whose name and that of his queen, Ti, have been found at Mycenae; his colossal statue (Tac. Ann. ii. 61) they identified with Memnon. A wonderful record of the power of the Eighteenth Dynasty in Asia has been preserved in the Tell El-Amarna tablets found in 1887, which give the correspondence of the Egyptian kings with their vassals in Babylonia, Syria, and elsewhere.

It is curious that of the Eighteenth Dynasty H. knows nothing; its military glories have, with those of Rameses II, been combined with the name of the Twelfth Dynasty conqueror in the single figure of Sesostris (*v. s.*). The last great king of the dynasty was the strange Amenhotep IV (1375–1358 B.C.), whose new name, 'Akhnaton,' marked his attempt to break the power of the priesthood of Amon and to introduce a kind of solar monotheism in place of Amon worship.[3]

The attempt naturally ended in failure, and after the death of the king, the Eighteenth Dynasty came to an end in confusion; but order was soon restored under the Nineteenth. Decay was beginning in Egypt, but only slowly; the kingdom had never appeared

[1] L. D. iii. 31 seq.

[2] For the tribute of the Keftiu, 'the peoples of the sea,' from Crete and elsewhere cf. Hall, B. S. A. viii. 170 f. The old idea that they were Phoenicians is given up completely.

[3] For this, the most interesting, though not the most important, episode in Egyptian history, cf. Breasted, pp. 355 seq., and Weigall, Life of Akhnaton (1910). As the innovating king was branded as accursed, and as his name was erased from the monuments, H. has of course heard nothing of him.

more outwardly prosperous than under Rameses II (1292–1225 B.C.), whose long reign presents a curious resemblance to that of Louis XIV of France. Both monarchs were credited with military success [1] in their early days, and both were magnificent builders; but both were also too much under the influence of the priests, and the invasion of France in the last days of Louis finds a parallel in the hard struggle of Rameses' successors against the 'peoples of the sea'.[2]

Already in the lifetime of his father, Seti I, Rameses had had to repulse the Shardana (Sardinians?) and the Tursha (? Tyrrhenians), who were attacking Egypt from Libya. In his wars against the Hittites, he had against him, as allies of his chief foes, various tribes, apparently from the west of Asia Minor. Hardly was he dead, when his son Merneptah had to meet a renewed attack of these peoples, combined with new and previously unnamed foes. He succeeded in repulsing them; but the attack was renewed under Rameses III [3] more than once.

§ 8. **The Peoples of the Sea.** The lists of peoples are as follows:—

Allies of Hittites.[4]	*Against Merneptah.*	*Against Rameses III.*
Luka (? Lycians) Pidasa (? Pisidians) Kalakisha (? Cilicians) Dardenni (? Dardanians) Masa (? Mysians) Maunna or Yaunna (? Ionians)	Ekwesh (Akaiwasha, ? The Achaeans) Teresh (Tursha, ? Tyrrhenians) Luka (? Lycians) Sherden (Sardinians) Shekelesh (? Sicels) (Maspero, p. 301, thinks from Sagalassus in Pisidia) 'Northerners coming from all lands' with the Libyans, who are called Meshwesh (sec. 589) (cf. iv. 191 'Maxyes'?)	Libyans, some of whom again are called Meshwesh The Peleset (Philistines) The Thekel (? Sicels) The Shekelesh The Denyen (Danauna ? Danai) The Weshwesh The Pap. Harris (*vid. inf.*) adds (iv. 403) the Sherden.

[1] The victory of Rameses over the Hittites in the early years of his reign is familiar from the pictures on the walls of the Ramesseum at Karnak, and from the poem that goes (wrongly) under the name of 'Pentaur'. The Hittite war was terminated by a treaty in 1272 B.C.

[2] The inscriptions as to the 'peoples of the sea' who fought Merneptah are at Karnak (Breasted, iii. 572–88); those of the later invasions are at Medinet Habu (the most complete Egyptian temple remaining; Breasted, iv. 35).

[3] This king seems to give the framework for H.'s folk-story of the Treasure House of Rhampsinitus (c. 121 n.; cf. also c. 107 n.).

[4] For the allies of the Hittites cf. Hall, B. S. A. *u. s.* pp. 175 f. (the best dis-

Who these tribes were is much disputed. Meyer[1] doubtfully connects them with the Dorian invasion of Greece; so too Hall[2] synchronizes them with the break-up of Mycenaean civilization. Maspero,[3] however, connects them with the movement which took the Tyrrhenians to Italy (cf. p. 445). Certainty is impossible; we can only say that the raids 'mark the end of a period in the history of the Mediterranean world' (Meyer).[4]

Egypt escaped conquest, but her own forces were becoming largely mercenary (the Shardana appear as her soldiers even under Rameses II); the warlike energy of the native Egyptians was exhausted. It is under Merneptah that the name of 'Israel' first appears on the Egyptian monuments,[5] hence he is generally identified with the Pharaoh of the Exodus.[6]

§ 9. **The decline of Egypt and the Assyrian conquest.** Egypt was even more weakened by the increasing powers and wealth of the priests than by exhaustion from war. The great Papyrus Harris,[7] which records the good works of Rameses III, gives them 107,000 slaves, and nearly three-quarters of a million acres of land, i. e. one-seventh of the whole cultivable land of the country; all this was exempt from taxation (c. 168). Of this the priests of Amon at Thebes had much the largest share. Hence their authority was a dangerous rival to the royal power.

The strength of Egypt now rapidly declined; it was overrun by the Ethiopians from the south and by the Assyrians from the north. The Twenty-fifth Dynasty of three Ethiopians is represented by H.'s Sabakos (c. 137 n.).[8] The interest of this period lies in the rivalry between the powers of the Euphrates and of the Nile Valleys.[9] Of this, however, H. is quite unconscious; he gives a confused version of the retirement of Sennacherib (141. 2, 3 nn.), but he knows nothing of the victorious invasions of the Assyrians

cussion in English of the subject); but the explanation of the names here given is Breasted's. His transliteration, however, is somewhat arbitrary, and two or three of the more usual forms are given in brackets as well as Breasted's identifications.

[1] ii. 137. [2] *u.s.* p. 178. [3] p. 317.

[4] Less probable is Petrie's view, iii. 110 f., placing the tribes in North Africa.

[5] 'Israel is desolated; his seed is not' (Breasted, iii. 616–17).

[6] Maspero (p. 309) more probably places the Exodus in the troubled period after his death.

[7] Breasted, iv. 151–412. It was drawn up under Rameses IV, and is now in the B. M.; it is the largest papyrus extant.

[8] Perhaps there is also an allusion to this period, out of all chronological order, in the 'eighteen Ethiopian kings' of c. 100.

[9] This is especially familiar during this period from its effect upon Jewish history (cf. 159. 2 n.).

under Esarhaddon (670 B.C.) and Assurbanipal, who took Thebes (661 B.C.).

The policy of the Assyrian conquerors was to encourage the native Egyptian princes of the Delta against the Ethiopian rulers of the south (cc. 147, 152 nn.); the result of this policy was the rise of the Twenty-sixth (Saite) Dynasty (*v.i.*).

§ 10. **Summing up.** Of this long period then (nearly 3,000 years) H. really knows nothing. The following points in his narrative may be noted :—

(1) His arrangement is purely artificial. After the first king, Menes, he tells us that 329 (c. 100) kings followed, of whom there was nothing to record (except of one, the queen Nitocris); then came eleven kings, beginning with Moeris (c. 101), of whom he thinks he knows something. These eleven kings belong to the most different periods, as has been seen, and are obviously put together according to their place in H.'s 'notebook'. Sayce even thinks that he can trace in their arrangement the exact course of the historian's sight-seeing (*u. s.*, p. 281 seq.); he 'walked round it (i. e. the temple of Ptah) from east to west'. The argument, if it may be so called, is that H. mentions every reign in the order in which he saw the monuments connected with it. It is not necessary to examine this point; if Sayce were consistent, he would take H. off to see the pyramids and to pay a visit to Heliopolis between two parts of his examination of the temple at Memphis. The only fact which is certain is that H. gained a large part of his information at this temple.[1]

If we can imagine an intelligent foreigner piecing together English history from the stories of the vergers in Westminster Abbey, and supplementing them from St. Paul's and Canterbury, we shall form a faint idea of H.'s difficulty with his sources.

(2) As might be expected, H. has no idea of chronology. His calculation of the length of Egyptian history is purely artificial (cf. c. 142 n. and App. XIV). Hence the Pyramid builders are nearly two thousand years too late.

(3) Again, as has been said above, patriotic vanity suppressed almost all mention of Egyptian defeats. H. has never heard of the Hyksos (except perhaps in dim tradition, c. 128 n.), and he knows nothing of Assyrian conquest.

(4) Perhaps the most striking feature of all is the influence of folk-tales on his history. Real persons, e.g. Cheops and Sesostris, are mentioned, but the stories about them are like the mediaeval stories

[1] The references to it are cc. 99. 4 (its building by Menes); 110. 1 (the statues of Sesostris); 112. 1 (south τέμενος of Proteus); 121. 1 (west portico of Rhampsinitus); 136. 1 (east portico of Asychis); 141. 6 (statue of priest-king, Sethos); 147, 151. 1 (sacrifice of twelve kings); 153. 1 (south portico of Psammetichus); 176. 1 (colossus of Amasis); iii. 37. 2 (outrage of Cambyses).

of Arthur or Charlemagne ; H. in fact gives us the history of Egypt as it was told 'in the streets of Memphis'.[1] Maspero says all this part of Book II is 'better than a course of history ; it is a chapter of literary history ; the tales in it are as Egyptian as those preserved in the papyri'.

From the point of view of the comparative study of history[2] and of the development of fiction, H. is valuable ; for Egyptian history in the strict sense, cc. 99 to 146 are valueless. But he himself is aware (147. 1) that his Egyptian history from the accession of Psammetichus (cc. 147 seq.) stands on a different footing from the preceding chapters ; he is now able to check native testimony by that of foreigners (154. 4). But how great the difference was H. quite failed to realize.

§ 11. **The Saite (Twenty-sixth) Dynasty.** The Saite Dynasty (663–525 B.C.) drove the Ethiopian invaders from Egypt and vindicated its independence from the now declining power of Assyria ; the land once more enjoyed a century and a half of prosperity under native kings. Moreover, they brought their country into connexion with the western world. Hence with the coming of the Greeks to Egypt, and the opening up to H. of real sources of evidence, the character of his history changes. His story of the Saites is (in the main at any rate) accurate in its chronology (*v. i.*) ; his names are right, and he brings out one great fact clearly, i. e. the rivalry between the Greek and the native elements (154. 3, 163. 2, 178 nn.). But he is still too far removed from the period to give an adequate account ; his main deficiencies are :—

(1) Since he is ignorant of the humiliation of Egypt in the eighth century B.C., which underlies his story (c. 147 n.) of the dodecarchy, he does not understand the real greatness of the Saites. This is especially reflected in their sculpture and architecture, in which there is a return to old traditions (Maspero, iii. 503) with very pleasing results.

(2) Again their foreign wars are mentioned only incidentally, e. g. Azotus (c. 157), Megiddo (159. 2). H. has no conception of their consistent attempts to secure Syria against the powers of the North-east, still less of their clearly marked policy of resting on sea-power (158. 1 n.), and of the importance of their foreign alliances. He does know that Amasis is allied with Croesus (i. 77. 2) and with his allies, the Lacedaemonians (*ib.*) ; but he does not see the importance of this, or even mention the connexion between Gyges and Psammetichus (ii. 152. 3).

[1] Maspero, C. P. E. p. 32. For parallels to H. cf. 111. 1, 121. 1, 124. 1 nn.

[2] It is interesting to note that almost all the names in H. can be identified : some are real, e. g. Cheops (124. 1) ; some are nicknames, e. g. 'Moeris', which contains the word for 'lake' 101. 1, and perhaps Sesostris (102. 1, but more probably this represents Senosret) ; some are titles, e. g. Pheros 111. 1 and Proteus 112. 1 (Maspero, A. E. G. 1878, p. 138).

(3) It is natural that here, as before, no mention is made of Egyptian defeats, e.g. that of Necho at Carchenish (605 B.C.) and (perhaps) a Babylonian invasion of Egypt (161. 2 n.).

(4) There is grave exaggeration in figures (30. 2; 157 nn.).

(5) Although the influence of folk-tales is less prominent than before, it is still very present (cf. especially the stories of Amasis, cc. 162, 172); in these the Greek element is very marked. With this point naturally goes the prominence of oracles (147. 4, 158. 5), especially that of Buto (152. 3).

In these chapters, then, we are on the borderland of history; H. is correct in his outlines, but has not information to fill up his picture accurately.

The table of the Saite kings is as follows:

	B.C.	Length of reign acc. to H.
Psammetichus (Psamtik) .	663–609	54 yrs. (c. 157)
Necho	609–593	16 „ (157. 3 n.)
Psammis (Psamtik II) . .	593–588	6 „ (161. 1)
Apries (Hophra) . . .	588–569	25 „ (161. 2 n.)
Amasis (Ahmose) . .	569–525	44 „ (iii. 10. 2)

Psammenitus (Psamtik III) reigned a few months.

APPENDIX XI

SCYTHIA AND THE SCYTHS

[In this appendix references to Book IV are by chapter only. For it cf. Macan (1895), ii. 15–32, very ingenious and full; Rawlinson, iii. 201–8, interesting, but to be used with caution; Bunbury, i. 172 seq., clear and sensible, and (most recent of all) E. H. Minns, *s. v.* Scythia in E. B.[11] xxiv. 526 f.; he is of opinion that the Scyths were 'a horde who came down from Upper Asia, conquered an Iranian-speaking people, and in time adopted the speech of its subjects'. With this view agrees Peisker (in Camb. Mediaeval History, i. 354–5).]

§ 1. **Divisions of Herodotean Geography.** H. is especially full on the geography of the Pontic regions, no doubt because of their great importance as the granary of Greece (17. 2 n.), and because his commercial journeys had taken him there (76. 6, 81. 2 nn.). (Introd. pp. 17, 19.)

The geography is given in four sections: (1) cc. 17–31. The ethnography of Scythia; the tribes are given from west to east with their hinterlands; the arrangement is emphasized by the refrain *ὅσον ἡμεῖς ἴδμεν* at end of cc. 17, 18, 20. (2) cc. 47–57. The rivers of Scythia. (3) cc. 99–101. A general description of the country.[1] (4) cc. 103–109. A description of the neighbouring tribes.

[1] Macan (p. 20) well draws attention to the fact that this section is very

It is obvious that these sections come, in part at least, from different sources, and contain inconsistencies. Of these, that as to the length of the south coast of Scythia is the most striking.[1] In c. 101 this is given as 'twenty days' journey' from the Ister to the Palus Maeotis, and the Borysthenes lies half-way; in 17. 1 the town at the mouth of the Borysthenes is again the centre of the south coast; but the distance from it to the Palus Maeotis is now seventeen days + a large indefinite quantity; for there are three days from the Borysthenes to the Panticapes (18. 2), fourteen more to the Gerrhus (c. 19), and then the 'most numerous tribe' of the Scyths extends to the Palus Maeotis (20. 1).

§ 2. **H.'s general view of Scythia.** H. must, however, have had some general idea in his mind as to the shape of Scythia, even though he makes statements inconsistent with this. It will be well therefore to determine its boundaries as conceived by him. That on the west is clearly the Ister. That on the south is given as the Black Sea (99. 2); the south-east corner (the Tauric peninsula) touches the Black Sea both on the south and on the east.[2]

The east boundary, then, begins with the Black Sea, and is continued by the Sindic peninsula (100. 1), the Palus Maeotis (57. 1), and the Don; that the Don is part of the east boundary and does not merely touch the north corner (as Stein's map) is clear from the description of the campaign of Darius.[3]

The north boundary is the frontiers of the Neuri, Androphagi, and Melanchlaeni (cc. 17, 18, 20), while in c. 51 a lake (the source of the Tyras) separates Scyths and Neuri.

§ 3. **Inconsistencies with his general view.** As to his boundaries, H. is fairly consistent; but his general conception of Scythia refuses to tally with his detailed facts. He describes it as

general, and contains few names; it might have been written without any visit to Scythia. He lays stress on the 'personal references' in it (99. 2, 5, 101. 3) as showing that it is H.'s own inference; but he is wrong in taking Borysthenes (101. 2) for 'the city' (p. 19); it must be the river.

[1] Cf. 18. 2 and 53. 4 for another inconsistency and also the difficulties as to the Danube (*v. i.*).

[2] Both Rawlinson and Macan take the 'East Sea' (99. 3, 4; 100. 1) as the 'Palus Maeotis'. But H. always calls this λίμνη, and the comparison of Taurice with Attica implies that the *same* sea washes both its shores, the south and the east. Macan makes the Palus Maeotis of H. run north and south. Rawlinson (in his map and p. 204) makes it mainly east and west; the former is clearly right, but H. thinks the sea inclines north-east (120. 2 n.).

[3] He crosses the Tanais (122. 3) and marches through the territories of the Sauromatae and the Budini (123. 1). These are more than fifteen days (c. 21) in extent, yet Darius soon returns into Scythia; this is implied, though no note of time is given.

a square of 4,000 stades of which the west and the east boundaries are at right angles to the base, the Pontus (101. 3).[1]

It has already been seen that the east boundary is not at a right angle, i. e. it runs north-east (not due north).[2] But the difficulties of the west boundary are much greater. Niebuhr long ago pointed out[3] that H. conceives the Ister, i. e. the west boundary of Scythia, as running north and south at the end of its course. His arguments are (1) The supposed correspondence of the Nile and the Danube (ii. 33. 2 n.). (2) In v. 9. 1 the land north of the Danube is neither Scythia nor that of the Agathyrsi, but 'desert', and (by implication, v. 10) *ὑπὸ τὴν ἄρκτον*. (3) Only in this way can be explained the great extent of the Thracians (v. 3. 1).[4]

All this agrees with the rectangular shape of Scythia. But there are other facts recorded as to the Ister which are quite inconsistent; it receives five tributaries from Scythia, each west of the other (48. 2), which implies a course not north and south, but east and west; this is confirmed by the statement in 49. 1 that its tributaries from the Haemus 'run north'. It must therefore be assumed either that H. did not know these facts when he wrote c. 101, or (more probably) that his Greek love of symmetry made him ignore details inconsistent with his general scheme.

§ 4. **Herodotean Geography of Scythia: Defects.** The main defects of H.'s account are (1) His complete misconception of the shape of the Crimea (c. 99 nn.); he should have compared it to the Peloponnese (as Strabo 310), not to Attica. With this goes his ignorance of the Putrid Sea (between the North-east Crimea and the mainland), which may perhaps be referred to in the 'Trench' (3. 1 n.) of the Slaves.

(2) His rivers beyond the Dnieper refuse to be identified except the Tanais, and perhaps the Oarus.[5] Moreover they cannot be reconciled with the elementary principles of hydrography; the Gerrhus (c. 56 n.) leaves the Borysthenes forty days' journey from its mouth and runs across to join the Hypacyris.[6]

(3) H.'s lakes as the sources of his rivers are more than suspicious. Of the five that he mentions (c. 55), the sources of Tyras (c. 51), Hypanis (c. 52), Panticapes (c. 54), Hypacyris (c. 55), and Tanais (c. 57), only that of the Tanais can be identified, and it is a small, not a 'large' lake (cc. 46 nn., 57).

[1] *τὰ ὄρθια τὰ ἐς τὴν μεσόγαιαν φέροντα.*

[2] *Vid.* p. 425, n. 2. [3] Kl. Schr. pp. 156, 356, and map.

[4] The statement that the Ister mouth faces south-east (99. 1) may be quoted on both sides; but it would naturally mean 'while the course is north and south, the mouth turns south-east'.

[5] This is not mentioned in c. 57, but in 123. 3; if it is the Volga, H. is wrong in making it flow into the Maeotis.

[6] But it may be noted that a tributary of the Amazon does in a somewhat similar way join the Orinoco.

(4) H.'s measurements are, as usual, inaccurate. From the Borysthenes at Olbia to the Palus Maeotis is only about 150 miles, not over 200 as he gives (c. 101. 2), and the sizes which he assigns to the Pontus and the Palus Maeotis (cc. 85, 86 nn.) are even more extraordinary.

§ 5. **Merits.** On the other hand H.'s account of Scythia has very decided merits.[1] (1) He has grasped the general features of South Russia, its great plains bare of wood as a rule (the Ὑλαίη (cf. 18. 1 n.) is rightly made an exception), and its severe winters (28 n.). (2) Especially, like a true Greek, he is strong on the river system, which he rightly makes the marvel of the country (c. 82). (3) H. here as elsewhere lays stress on right methods; he insists on eye-witnesses and protests against over-symmetry (36. 2), though he himself is guilty of this error in some places.

§ 6. **The Scythian People.** But it is his account of the people that is especially valuable.[2] He is careful to distinguish the real Scyths among the various races living in South Russia; the ancient writers [3] generally but wrongly applied the name to all the nomadic peoples of Central Asia and South-east Europe. In this use of the word the Greeks were following Persian usage; H. rightly says that the Persians call all the Scyths [4] 'Sakae' (vii. 64); so in the Behistun Inscription the name in cols. 1 and 2 is used of Asiatic peoples, in col. 5 of Europeans. (See Note I, p. 454.)

H. confines the name to the tribe who stretch (speaking roughly) from the Borysthenes to the Tanais (cc. 17–20).

Nationality of Scyths. The first question as to these Scyths is—were they a distinct people at all? Macan (ii. 12 seq.) ingeniously raises again the view refuted by Niebuhr (*ib.* p. 353 seq.), that the 'Scyths' of H. are an 'artificial product', 'a combination of divers elements, determined rather by geographical than by ethnographical considerations.' He suggests that they were only a 'ruling class' among subject peoples. It certainly is remarkable that a race so important as H. represents them to be, should have practically disappeared from history, leaving no trace behind.[5]

[1] For further evidence of H.'s familiarity with Scythia see notes *pass.*; there is a good summary of the evidence in Rawlinson, iii. 206–7.

[2] For its importance in literature cf. 4. 1 n., for its accuracy cf. especially cc. 71–2 nn.

[3] e. g. Ephorus in Strabo, 302 seq., and Plin. 4. 25. So, too, the Goths and Huns are called 'Scyths' (Nieb. *u. s.* 354); we may compare the modern use of 'Tartars' (but Yule, M. Polo, i. p. 12, defends this use).

[4] 'Scyth' is probably itself a Greek form of 'Saka'. Stein connects it with the root of 'schiessen' (to shoot) and explains it τοξόται; he quotes the fact that the slave-police at Athens were called both Σκύθαι and τοξόται; but this proves nothing.

[5] Niebuhr (pp. 374 seq.) tries to explain their disappearance by tracing the encroachments of the Getae in the west, and of the Sauromatae in the east. The scanty later history of the Scyths can be read in E. B.[9] 21. 578.

In view, however, of the express and definite testimony of H. and of his rather later contemporary, the scientist and physician, Hippocrates, it seems safer to assume, as is generally done, that the Scyths were a real people.

§ 7. **Aryan or Mongolian.** A second question then arises—were they Aryan or Mongolian? Niebuhr's view (adopted by Grote iii. 241) was that they were Mongolian; but there is much to be said against this. The evidence is of four kinds.

(1) *Physical Type.* Hippocrates (de Aer. c. 6, p. 558) describes the Scyths as 'having gross and fleshy bodies', 'loose joints', 'only a little hair', and says 'they all resemble each other'; but apart from the 'scanty hair', there is nothing in this which resembles the Mongolian type with high cheek bones and turned-up nose.[1] The sameness of appearance is common to all uncivilized peoples; so Kinglake [2] says of the Bedouins 'almost every man of the race closely resembles his brethren'. The whole point is fully discussed by Rawlinson (iii. 188–9). H. especially notes features that seem Mongolian among the *non*-Scythian Argippaei (c. 23). The pictures of Scyths on Greek vases (cf. Reinach, A. R. M. pp. 109, 110, 192, and Rawlinson) are certainly Aryan in type; but this may be due to the Hellenic artists.

(2) *Customs.* Here the evidence rather favours the theory of Mongolian origin [3]; cf. their worship of a sword (c. 62. 2 n.), their use of hemp as an intoxicant (c. 75. 1 n.), their impaling of horses (72. 2 n.). But customs may be borrowed, and this evidence is not decisive.

(3) *Religion.* The Scythian religion (c. 59 nn.) seems decidedly Aryan in character; how much of this character, however, is due to H.'s colouring, it is impossible to say.

(4) *Language.* The evidence of language rather favours the Aryan hypothesis; Müllenhoff (D. A. iii. p. 122) says that of sixty Scyth names and words in H., one quarter completely, another quarter in part, support this. The others are either non-Scythian, or too much modified by Greek tradition to be explained. He lays special stress on the fact (p. 123) that 'the Scythian names of rivers and places (e.g. 'Exampaeus', 81. 2 n.), and of the gods, and the words expressly noted by H. as Scythian, have proved to be Aryan and Iranian.'

H. says the Sauromatae spoke Scythian, though incorrectly (c. 117); but the Sauromatae were admittedly Aryan; they are

[1] Cf. E. B.[11] *s. v.* Calmuck. Peisker, however (Camb. Med. Hist. i. p. 354), confidently asserts that the Scythian type, as described by H., is Mongolian.

[2] Eothen, c. xvii, p. 191 (ed. of 1864).

[3] Peisker (ib. p. 355) lays stress on this, basing his comparison on the data of H.

the ancestors of the Slavs. If then the Scyths and the Sauromatae are akin, it is natural to consider them both Aryan.

The point cannot be settled; but that it can be investigated at all is good proof of the fullness and trustworthiness of H.'s account of the race.[1]

APPENDIX XII

THE SCYTHIAN EXPEDITION

[Rawlinson (iii. 112–14) defends with some hesitation the historical value of the Herodotean narrative. For a full criticism and analysis cf. Macan, ii. 33–54.]

§ 1. H. has elaborated with great care his account of the first Persian invasion of Europe. He has a special personal interest in Scythia; but there is also an obvious parallel intended between the campaign of Darius and that of Xerxes; similar warnings are given, similar preparations are made, similar disasters are incurred.

In spite, however, of all the historian's pains, his success in Book IV is very different from his success elsewhere; no part of his narrative, falling in times so near his own, has been the object of so many and such well-grounded criticisms; nowhere are results, that are even approximately certain, so few.

§ 2. **Date of Expedition.** The date of the expedition may be fixed approximately between 514 B.C. and 508 B.C. The *terminus a quo* is given by the fact that Babylon had already been reduced (iv. 1), i.e. after its second rebellion (cf. iii. 150 n.); we can hardly date this reduction earlier than 516, and we must allow a year at least for the gathering of the whole Persian force for the attack on Europe. There had also been time for Syloson (restored to Samos about 516, iii. 139) to be succeeded by his son Aeaces (iv. 138. 2). The *terminus ante* is fixed as 508; we find Artaphrenes as satrap at Sardis about 507 (v. 73. 2) and he was appointed there a year *after* the expedition (v. 25. 1). It may further be argued that the expedition seems to have been before 510, when Hippias retired to Sigeum (v. 94. 1), and that 'the influence with Darius', which won for the son of Hippoclus of Lampsacus an Athenian bride (after 514; Thuc. vi. 59), was probably connected with the expedition. The most probable date then is about 512 B.C.[2]

[1] For a brilliant account of Nomadism as the destructive force in history cf. Camb. Med. Hist. i, p. 359; although Darius failed in part in Syria (cf. App. XII), we may certainly credit the Medo-Persian empire with having successfully repulsed the Northern hordes at a critical moment in the world's development.

[2] For further ingenious points cf. Duncker, vi. 270–1, but there is no reason to place (as he does) the expedition of Democedes after the Scythian expedition.

§ 3. **Motives of Expedition in H.** To determine the motive of the expedition is harder than to fix the date. H. gives two motives, which, though at first sight inconsistent, are not really so; for the first is general, i.e. it belongs to the whole of the European conquests; the second is special—for the Scythian Expedition.

The first is given picturesquely in iii. 134; Darius is exhorted to show himself a man and to keep his people employed. In this story we have a dramatic representation of a real law in Oriental history; a conquering race is bound to go on till it meets a check, and inactivity means decay. H., of course unconsciously, grasps this law; but the setting he gives to it is pure romance.

The second motive is given in Book IV. The expedition was one of revenge for the Scythian invasions of Asia at the end of the seventh century. This is H.'s definite opinion (he repeats it in vii. 20. 2), but it may be doubted whether the reason has any historical reality; it corresponds suspiciously with H.'s view that history is a series of actions and reactions,[1] and with his fondness for definite causes.[2] Nor would a practical statesman like Darius be influenced by such a motive. At the best H.'s explanation is only the talk of the Persian army, not the motive of the king's council chamber.

§ 4. **Motives suggested by modern historians.** To turn now to modern explanations.

(*a*) The first in two various forms attempts to give an historical meaning to the second motive assigned by H. Meyer (iii. 69) says: 'Under the mistaken pragmatism of H. it is easy to see the real connexion of facts.' He supposes that Darius wished to secure himself against the tribes of the North, and proposed to attack them in the rear. The king knew the Northern lands were all connected, but had an insufficient conception of their extent and of the difficulties of his attempt. Gutschmidt[3] thinks Darius wished to unite his empire by an expedition against the hated and dreaded nomads of the North and North-west.

(*b*) A more probable explanation, which is also consistent with that just given in either form, is that Darius wished to strike terror into the nomad tribes, to show that the Persian king's arm reached far. We may compare the expeditions of Germanicus against Germany, which were authorized by even the pacific Tiberius.

(*c*) A different colour is given to the expedition by those who make its main motive economic,[4] and think its aim was to make the Euxine a Persian lake. The gold which came from South Russia

[1] Cf. the opening chapters of Book I.
[2] Cf. Introd., § 32, p. 45.
[3] E. B.[9] *s. v.* Scythians.
[4] e. g. Niebuhr, Lectures on Ancient History, i. 140.

and the riches of its corn supply may well have made the conquest attractive, and have misled Darius as to the extent of the civilization of the country. Such a motive is in harmony with his character as *κάπηλος* (iii. 89. 3), but it is of course unprovable.

(*d*) A special form has been given to this theory by Bury,[1] who supposes that Darius was aiming at the conquest of Transylvania and its gold mines. He argues that Darius really set up the 'eight forts' of iv. 124 in West Scythia to guard his communications up the valley of (perhaps) the Buzeo (*Ἄραρος* iv. 48. 2); but that H., confusing this river with the Oarus, transported all the operations, regardless of geography, across Scythia. This theory corresponds with the fact that all the certain operations of Darius are in West Scythia, and H. may have confused the gold fields of Transylvania and of the Ural. But it really has no evidence for it, so that it can be neither proved nor disproved.

(*e*) Grundy (pp. 60–4) makes the ingenious suggestion that Darius was seeking an 'ethnic frontier'; he wished to subdue the kinsmen in Europe of his Thracian subjects in Asia, and pushed on to the Danube, where he found an ethnic frontier between Thracians and Scyths. Grundy's general discussion of frontiers is interesting; but it is unlikely that Darius knew or cared much about ethnology, or that a reconnaissance over the Danube could have shown him that he had found a racial line, even if he was seeking one. It may be said that this theory confuses the result of the expedition with its motive. Grundy further thinks (p. 70) that Darius was aiming at the reduction of Thrace.

In this Macan agrees with him (ii. 48). But this theory involves the complete rejection of H.'s narrative; the historian keeps Darius close to the coast of Thrace (cf. iv. 90. 2, 93); in fact, he makes the Persian advance (the reverse way) by the very route which the Russians followed in their attack on Constantinople in 1828 (cf. 89. 2 n.). H.'s facts are meaningless unless the objective of Darius was across the Danube.

§ 5. **Results of expedition.** Before an attempt is made to sum up as to the motives, something must be said as to the results of the expedition. These may be summarized as follows:

(1) It paved the way for the complete conquest of the coastline of Thrace; Darius began what Megabazus and Otanes finished.

(2) But it is clear the Scyths were not terrorized; H. brings them shortly after as far South as the Chersonese (vi. 40. 1 n.), though the date is uncertain[2] (iv. 143. 1 n.).

(3) There seems to have been almost a general revolt among the Hellespontine Greeks after the expedition. Byzantium has to be

[1] C. R. xi. 277 seq.

[2] With this may be connected the supposed Scyth embassy to Sparta (vi. 84. 2).

retaken by Otanes (v. 26), and widespread punishment inflicted (v. 27. 2 n.).[1]

(4) Hence it is clear that the expedition was on the whole a failure, and is rightly represented as a blow to Persian prestige. H. insists on this point,[2] and he may well have met some of those who took part in the campaign. Other accounts, too, confirm the fact that Darius suffered heavy loss.[3] Hence it is clearly wrong to suggest, as Macan does (ii. 49), that the story of H. is 'motivated' by the desire to represent Darius as suffering disaster like his predecessors.

Perhaps the statement of Strabo (305) that Darius advanced as far as the 'desert of the Getae' (i. e. that of the Dniester), and then retired for want of water, may be accepted as representing the main outline of what happened. Whether this was a guess on the part of Strabo or represents the tradition of some lost historian we cannot say; at any rate it agrees in part with the details in H., who says that the Scyths intended to fight if their ancestral tombs were threatened (c. 127); these were on the river Dniester (Tyras). As this statement is immediately followed by the only account of actual fighting (cc. 128 seq.), perhaps we may infer that Darius really did get near the tombs. But this is most uncertain. All we know is that Darius crossed the Danube, and retired after suffering considerable loss and running great danger.

Duncker (vi. 289 seq.) ingeniously tries to fit in the expedition in the West of Scythia; he points out that fifteen days' journey up the Pruth valley would bring Darius near the sources of the Boug; he would then be near the Royal Tombs (cf. c. 127) on the Dniester.

Since the result of the expedition was a failure, it does not help us to determine the motive. We can therefore only say positively that Darius aimed at carrying his arms across the Danube, and we may then go on to guess that his motive was to strike terror, and perhaps to add to his empire the goldfields of the north-west as he had already done those of the extreme south-east (iii. 94. 2 n.).

§ 6. **Difficulties in H.'s narrative.** With regard to the fortunes of the expedition, there is no doubt that H.'s account is impossible.[4] The most important objections against it are:

(1) It violates the laws of time and space. Darius is in Scythia a little more than sixty days (iv. 133. 2); yet in this time he marches across Scythia, and crosses the Tanais; he then marches through the Sauromatae (c. 122) and the Budini (c. 123), half builds eight

[1] Strabo (591) speaks of Abydos as in revolt.

[2] Cf. the speeches of Artabanus in Book VII (cc. 10. γ; 52. 1).

[3] Ctesias (sec. 17, p. 68) makes the king advance fifteen days with 800,000 men and lose 80,000 (cf. 131. 4 n.); this figure is also given by Justin (ii. 5).

[4] The objections may be studied in Macan, ii. 43 f., or in Duncker, vi. 279-86; Grote's criticism (iv. 191 f.) is, as always, sensible and worth reading.

large forts (c. 124. 1), and then returns by a different route. But Scythia is over 450 miles broad; in fact H. himself makes it twenty days' journey across (c. 101), and an army would move much more slowly than a traveller.

(2) An army of 700,000 men could not live in a ravaged land, or cross the big rivers.

(3) Such a mad march, away from all communications with his base, is as impossible as that Darius himself ordered his communications to be destroyed (cc. 97–8).

§ 7. **Supposed inconsistencies.** Modern criticism, however, makes the narrative not only impossible, but also inconsistent. This is much more doubtful; H. is too good a literary artist to be lightly accused of self-contradiction; the following may be taken as specimens of the arguments on this point:

(1) The Scyths have no cavalry, yet they offer battle with cavalry and infantry (c. 134). [This is a merely conventional way of describing a pitched battle.]

(2) They try to deprive the Persians of provisions, yet they allow their flocks to be captured (c. 130). [But the proverb as to 'throwing a sprat to catch a whale' applies in war as well as elsewhere.]

(3) Darius returning from the Agathyrsi (i. e. from North) comes by the road which he had traversed before (140. 3) when moving east. [But this was only near the Danube; two divergent roads often start in common.]

§ 8. **H.'s sources and methods.** The story of the Scythian expedition throws considerable light on H.'s sources and methods:

(1) It is clear that he got his information as to the Bosporus bridge from the Samian Heraeum (88. 1; cf. Introd. § 25).

(2) His story of the invasion may well come from the Pontic Greeks at Olbia. They boldly transported Darius to North-east Scythia, the region they knew best, and H. the more readily accepted their version, because Scythia, both North-east and North-west, was alike in its general features.

(3) H. never attempts to introduce into the narrative his knowledge of the rivers of Scythia; this probably came to him from a different source.

(4) The story of the scenes at the Bridge is coloured by Greek hatred of tyrants, and perhaps by the family traditions of the Philaidae (137. 1 n.).

§ 9. **To sum up.** The whole narrative illustrates H.'s dependence on his sources. The events were removed from his own day by the same interval as the fall of the Pisistratidae. But the latter event happened in Greece proper, where evidence was abundant, and could be tested by comparison. The Scythian expedition had taken place far away to the north, and its scene was as unfamiliar as the evidence for it was scanty. The critical powers of H. were able to work on the history of Athens before his own day; they broke down completely across the Danube.[1] All we can say is that he gives us a vigorous picture of the difficulties of fighting against a light-armed foe who avoids a battle. Darius is only the first of the long series of invaders (of whom Charles XII and Napoleon are the most famous) who have found in the vast distances of Russia an invincible enemy. But as to the exact details of his failure we can only guess.

APPENDIX XIII

THE GEOGRAPHY OF HERODOTUS

[The great work of Rennell (published 1800) is still interesting, but quite out of date. Tozer, Hist. Anc. Geog. pp. 75–97, is clear and full of points; Bunbury, i. 156–317, is much longer, but less useful proportionately; Berger, Erdk. der Griechen (1903) is particularly full on the scientific side of the subject, but is marked by the modern tendency to write down H. and to write up his Ionian predecessors. Myres' paper (G. J. 1896, 605 seq., 'Maps used by H.') is most ingenious, but his inferences should be carefully tested.]

§ 1. 'H.'s merit is that he recognized how important the description of countries is for history, but we cannot make him out a geographer without damaging the reputation of early geography and his own reputation.' Whether this judgement of Berger (p. 145, edit. of 1887) be fair or not, there is no doubt that H.'s contributions to geography are only subordinate to his main subject; hence the argument from silence is especially inapplicable to this part of his writings; he knew far more than he tells us.[2]

In this appendix an attempt will be made to describe, not his geographical knowledge in detail, but only his general attitude to the subject.

§ 2. **H.'s attitude to Geography.** H. approaches geography strictly from the empirical point of view; his aim is to record facts, not to deal with scientific theories. Hence he criticizes sharply (iii. 115; iv. 36. 2) those who put forth general views without definite evidence. In this respect, he is characteristic of his time; in Periclean Athens there was a critical reaction against the physical speculations of the Ionian philosophers. Socrates disapproved of

[1] Duncker (p. 290) suggests there are fragments of Iranian poetry in the narratives both of H. (cc. 131–2 the enigmatical gifts) and of Ctesias (the exchange of bows, when the Scythian is found to be the stronger). This may be so, but the stories sound suspiciously Greek.

[2] Though he never mentions Rome, he must have known something of that rising state. For his knowledge of North Italy cf. i. 57. 3 n.; 94. 6 n.; v. 9. 2.

the advanced geometry and astronomy of his time, as studies tending to divert men from more profitable subjects.[1]

Hence it is not surprising that H. says nothing of the Pythagorean theory that the earth was a sphere, or of the zones into which Parmenides, following out the idea of Pythagoras, divided the earth's surface. This refusal on the part of H. to theorize was largely justified; Pythagoras' sphere was probably only a happy guess, based on the idea that it was the most perfect figure.

§ 3. **H.'s mistakes.** But the lack of these general views involved H. in strange mistakes when he attempted to explain unfamiliar phenomena (cf. especially his account of the climate of India, iii. 104. 2 n.). Believing, as he did, the earth to be a flat surface over which the sun moves from east to west, he is completely unable to understand the laws of temperature. It is especially to be noticed that he treats as independent facts forces like the winds or peculiarities of climate, e. g. he says that the upper parts of Libya have no cold winds, and hence are peculiarly affected by the sun, and finds in these local phenomena a strange explanation for the rise of the Nile (ii. 24, 25 nn.). In his view the winds of a country are isolated and special,[2] like the fertility of its soils, and he has no conception that there are general laws of atmospheric pressure.

§ 4. **His attitude to maps.** In the same way it is to be noticed that, though H. mentions maps (iv. 36. 2, v. 49. 1 nn.; this latter map is specially said to be 'of the whole earth' with 'all the sea and all the rivers'), he does not appeal to them for his own statements. At the same time he obviously feels the need of diagrammatic schemes on which the isolated geographical facts that he records can be arranged. He attempts to construct rough parallels,[3] by which to indicate the relative position of one place to another; these may be said to be of three kinds: (*a*) as to special places (e. g. i. 76. 1) Pteria is κατὰ Σινώπην; (*b*) for whole districts; Asia is based on a line drawn from the Erythraean Sea to the Pontus (iv. 37 n.), and Scythia is a perfect square (iv. 101 n.); (*c*) for the relation of these districts to each other; so in ii. 34 (nn.) Asia and Europe are related to each other in a line drawn from the Danube to the Nile.

It is not surprising that parallels of this kind are inaccurate. But it is important to remember that they are not meant to be strictly

[1] Xen. Mem. iv. 7. 2 seq. Other references for this reaction are given in Berger, p. 51 (ib. cf. 163).

[2] This idea is, of course, not peculiar to him. Hippocrates believed in the Rhipaean Mountains, where the north wind had its source (de Aere, xix; cf. iv. 32 nn.).

[3] The mathematical measurement of the world and the division of its circumference into 360 degrees were the work of Eratosthenes (276–196 B.C.) and of Hipparchus (second century). H. mentions the γνώμων (ii. 109. 3 n.) with which this measurement was carried out, but says nothing of its use; he probably was acquainted with this, but regarded it with suspicion (*v. s.*).

accurate; they are early attempts at map-making, and 'early maps originate in the pictorial representation of physical features as seen along a route . . . changes of direction are indicated by short bends'. (Myres, p. 610, who well compares 'the maps of the South-eastern Railway' as 'monumental instances of the distortion incidental to the representation of a route as axis of a peninsula'.)

§ 5. **The division of continents.** It was natural that H., being indifferent to theoretical geography, should treat very superficially the question of the division of the earth into continents. The earliest division was into two, Europe and Asia[1]; the Mediterranean seemed to provide a natural boundary, and there was a marked difference of temperature between the lands lying south and south-east of it and the opposite coasts.

The twofold division is stated with the greatest clearness by H.'s contemporary, the physician Hippocrates (de Aer. xii), who dwells on the superiority of Asia, 'that its products are finer, its soil more kindly, and its national characters less fierce.'

This division always tended to remain in Greek thought; so Isocrates (Pan.) speaks of the Great King claiming for himself Asia, one of the two regions into which the whole world *ὑπὸ τῷ κόσμῳ κειμένη* was divided.[2] It was apparently adopted again by the great geographer Eratosthenes, on the principle that North and South were different 'secundum naturam' (Varro, de Re Rust. i. 2).

But popular feeling was against it; already in H.'s time the threefold division was *τὰ νομιζόμενα* (iv. 45. 5), and he adopts this therefore with a protest against it as unreasonable.[3]

§ 6. **Boundaries of continents.** (*a*) *Europe and Asia.* Assuming the threefold division, H. discusses the boundaries of the continents: that between Asia and Europe he fixes as the Phasis (iv. 45. 2), and the Caspian and the Araxes (iv. 40. 1), i.e. he makes the line run east and west, and gives what we now call 'North Asia' to Europe. In his own day there were already some who drew the line north and south, e.g. Hecataeus (frs. 164, 165), and Hippocrates (de Aer. xiii), as H. himself mentions (iv. 45. 2). The result of his adopting this line of demarcation is to give an enormous extension to his Europe (iv. 42. 1), which he considers to be bigger than the other two continents together.[4]

[1] For the meaning of these names cf. iv. 45 nn.

[2] For other references cf. Berger, p. 78; but his list needs careful checking.

[3] Pind. (Pyth. ix. 7 seq.) seems the oldest literary mention of the threefold division, but it must be far earlier; H. (iv. 45. 2) is quite ignorant who made it. Hecataeus is a good instance of the uncertain state of Greek opinion; his references to places in Africa are quoted sometimes from the survey of Asia (frs. 305 seq.; F. H. G. i. 23), sometimes from that of 'Libya' (frs. 314 seq.); probably therefore 'Libya' was a subdivision of 'Asia'.

[4] Rennell (p. 412) curiously took this the other way round, and made Europe 'far *inferior* in breadth'; the result is a complete dislocation of his map.

(*b*) *Asia and Africa.* H. is much more successful in regard to the boundary of Asia and Africa; he rightly insists that the Nile was not the dividing line, as some had maintained, for this involved the division of Egypt between two continents (ii. 16, 17 nn.). To which continent H. assigned Egypt is a little uncertain; probably he gives it, in accordance with modern ideas, to Africa (iv. 39 n.).

H.'s indifference to theory helped to save him from one mistake which his countrymen generally made. Great as is his reverence for Delphi, there is no trace in him of the view that it was the centre of the earth (ὀμφαλὸς γῆς, cf. Pind. Pyth. iv. 74), which lay grouped round Greece.[1]

§ 7. **H.'s defects and merits in general.** Apart from his lack of theoretic science, H.'s great defects as a geographer are his lack of any accurate system of measurements, and his belief in the doctrine of Symmetry, though he himself protests against it (*v. s.* and iv. 36 nn.). The former can be illustrated from every book of his History; for the latter cf. especially ii. 33. 2 n. On the other hand he has great merits. He insists again and again on the need of the evidence of eyewitnesses (cf. especially iii. 115 nn.), and his critical faculty often saves him from mistakes which were common long after his time (cf. i. 203. 1 n. as to isolation of the Caspian). He has, too, the eyes of a geographer for the main physical features of a country, he rightly appreciates the power of rivers to form deltas (ii. 10 nn.), and his remarks about Tempe (vii. 129) are a curious blending of science with theology.

If he is not a geographer, he is at all events a great collector of geographical facts. He furnished material for the geographers of the future to fit into their scientific schemes; his criticism of the science of his day was useful in the emphasis that it laid on observation as opposed to the speculations of the Ionian philosophers; above all he laid stress on the principle, too often forgotten, that history and geography must be studied together.

APPENDIX XIV

THE CHRONOLOGY OF HERODOTUS

[Most of the data and the arguments of this appendix are taken from Meyer, Forschungen (i. 151 seq.), but his conclusions are slightly modified, *v. i.*; for the chronology of the sixth century cf. Abbott, Herodotus, pp. 160–3.]

[1] Niebuhr, p. 137, asserts this was H.'s own view, referring to i. 142, iii. 106. 1, which prove nothing. Myres, p. 615, has a very ingenious argument as to the origin of this belief as to Delphi.

APPENDIX XIV

§ 1. There is no evidence that H. had any fixed chronological system of his own; his dates are vague, e.g. 'to my time' (ii. 145. 4), and not calculated by official lists.[1] Hence, though he gives many data for the earlier parts of his history, especially for foreign nations, it is probable that he is merely reproducing these from earlier sources.[2] This is the more probable when his inconsistencies are noted.

As to the early history,[3] three main questions arise:

1. How far is any system traceable in H.'s dates?
2. What exceptions are there to this system?
3. How was it arrived at, or from whom did H. borrow it?

§ 2. **The Herodotean system for early period dates.** This seems to have been fairly definite, as can be seen by a comparison of the genealogy of the Theban House of Cadmus with that of Heracles in the following table:

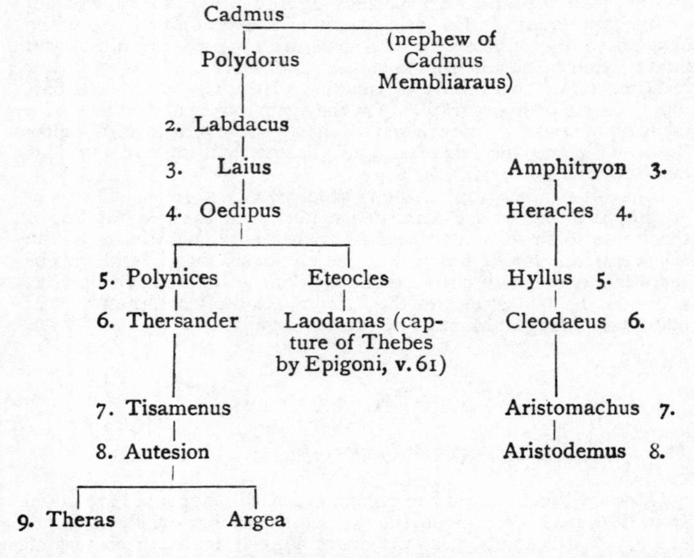

[1] viii. 51. 1 is an exception. Thuc. v. 20. 2 criticizes the 'official' method, though he himself uses it in ii. 2. 1; for it cf. Ἀθ. Πολ. 4 *et pass.*

[2] The date given for Homer and Hesiod (ii. 53. 2), '400 years before my time,' may be an exception, based on his own calculation.

[3] This expression is used for the whole period before 600 B.C.

The first line is given as far as Laius in v. 59, where Amphitryon is made contemporary with Laius, the rest of it, from Polynices to Argea, in vi. 52. 2, where also part of the line of Heracles is given. The table is in rough agreement with the story of the colonization of Cyrene (iv. 147. 5), where the descendants of Membliaraus, the nephew of Cadmus, hold Thera (Kalliste) for 'eight generations' before the coming of Theras. So, too, the sailing of Cadmus is 'five generations' before the birth of Heracles (ii. 44. 4).[1]

From Heracles to H. is 900 years,[2] i. e. his date is about 1350. The early chronology of H. is based on this date, with the exceptions mentioned in the next section. Heracles is placed by him almost two generations before the Trojan war, which therefore is about 1280 B. C.; for Pan, who, as the son of Penelope, belongs to the generation after the Trojan war, is 100 years (i. e. three generations) later than Heracles (ii. 145).[3]

It seems that H. has used the same system, calculated from the time of Heracles, in other Oriental dates, e. g.:

1. In Egypt, Moeris is in the third generation before Proteus, the contemporary of the Trojan war; this corresponds roughly with the '900 years' which H. gives in ii. 13. 1.

2. In Assyria, Nineveh is founded by Ninus, the third in descent from Heracles (i. 7), i. e. about 1250 B. C.; but H. also says that the Assyrians ruled Asia for 520 years (i. 96); this is reckoned back from the Median revolt. H. seems to place this revolt (App. III, § 6) about 700 B. C., which gives 1220 B. C. (520 + 700) for the commencement of Assyrian empire. This would have followed shortly after the foundation of Nineveh.

3. Again, in Lydian history, H. gives 505 years to the Heraclidae, who descend from Agron. Agron therefore is made to ascend the Lydian throne in 1221 B. C. (i. e. 505 + 716 B. C., H.'s date for the accession of Gyges). As fourth in descent from Heracles (i. 7), Agron's date would be 1217 (i. e. 1350 − 133).

§ 3. **Exceptions to this system.** So far it has been sought to show that H. gives a fairly consistent system. There are, however, some grave departures from it, e. g.:

[1] It will be noticed that the reckoning is exclusive of the *terminus a quo* in iv. 147, but inclusive in ii. 44.

[2] ii. 145. 4. Meyer (p. 157) calculates H.'s own date as *circ.* 430, because (*a*) in ii. 13. 1 (see n.) he speaks as if some time had elapsed between his visit to Egypt and his writing, and (*b*) he was in Egypt after 440 B. C.; but both points are disputable; probably H. is not writing with such exactitude. I have therefore taken H.'s *terminus a quo* as 450.

[3] In this passage (ii. 145), however, there is a glaring inconsistency, for Dionysus is placed 700 years before Heracles; yet he is the grandson of Cadmus, and therefore only two generations before him (ii. 44. 4 n.). The text is generally altered, e. g. by Hude, who brackets *ἑξακόσια* and *καί*, and Meyer; H. could hardly have forgotten his own dates for such well-known divinities.

1. Moeris is placed by him about 1350 B.C. (ii. 13); but he is only ten generations, i. e. about 330 years, before the Dodecarchy, which immediately precedes the accession of Psammetichus (663), i. e. his date should be about 1000 B.C.

2. He gives 'more than 700 years' (ii. 140. 2) between Anysis and Amyrtaeus, i. e. Anysis would die at latest 1150 B.C.; but he belongs to the eighth century in H.'s narrative. In fact, when H. wishes to give the length of Egyptian history (ii. 142), he disregards all his own figures and makes a purely artificial calculation.

§ 4. **Origin of chronological system.** It remains to consider the third point—how is the date of Heracles arrived at?

H. gives two genealogies of the Heraclidae, to the beginning of the fifth century (that of Leonidas, vii. 204, and that of Leotychides, viii. 131); in each there are twenty-one generations (inclusive). But it is obvious that if, as elsewhere (ii. 142. 2), he allows three generations to a century, this would give only 700 years, i. e. the date of Heracles would be *circ.* 1200 (i. e. 500 + 700), not 1350 B.C. If, however, 40 years be allowed for a generation, the result is 500 + 840 = 1340, which is approximately the date required.[1] When a *terminus a quo* was once gained, the rest was easy, for the myths, e. g. those of Troy, Thebes, &c., synchronized other heroes with Heracles or his descendants.

What writer or writers worked out Greek chronology on these bases it is impossible to say; it may have been Hecataeus[2] (as Meyer, F. i. 169 seq., thinks, though his arguments are naturally very slight). His main point is that the calculation is made about 500 B.C. by some one who 'closed a generation with the death of Cleomenes and the deposition of Demaratus': this date would suit Hecataeus. It is possible, however, that the '900 years' for Heracles is based on calculations from Oriental and not from Greek families. H. (i. 7. 2–4 nn.) makes Agron, the first king of the Heraclidae, to be fourth in descent from Heracles (i.e. 133 years after him); the Heraclidae rule 505 years, the Mermnadae 170,[3] and from the fall of Croesus to the time of H. is about 100 years: 133 + 505 + 170 + 100 = 908, which is about the figure required. But in any case it would be a Greek who made the cal-

[1] No doubt there were many other genealogies in Greece which could be (and were actually by private families) used as bases of chronology. Hecataeus himself (ii. 143) claims a god for his 'sixteenth ancestor'; i.e. he traced back his descent for fifteen human generations or 600 years (if a generation = 40). This would give 1100 B.C. for the foundation of his family, which is approximately the date of the Ionian immigration. For a similar list cf. the list of hereditary priests to Posidon at Halicarnassus, copied from an ancient στήλη (Dittenberger, Syll. 608).

[2] For H.'s relations to him see Introd. § 20.

[3] For these figures cf. i. 7. 4 n. and p. 375 respectively; they are of course worthless historically.

culation. The main point is that H., who was not interested in chronological questions, seems to borrow his results from some predecessor.

§ 5. **Oriental dates for seventh and sixth centuries.** The same conclusion must certainly be accepted for the lengths of the reigns of the Median (p. 383), Saite (p. 424), Lydian (p. 375), and Persian kings, viz. that H. has taken the figures over from his authorities without examination; hence, while the figures for the Saites and the Persians are almost accurate, those for the Median kings and the Mermnadae are obviously inaccurate and largely based on conjecture; the most that can be said is that the figures for the later kings of these two dynasties are probably historical. But at any rate H. has a chronology for these Oriental monarchies.

§ 6. **Weakness of Greek chronology for sixth century.** It would, however, be almost true to say that H. has no chronology at all for Greece in the century before 500 B.C. He gives occasional figures, e.g. ten full years for Pisistratus' exile (i. 62. 1), thirty-six for the whole rule of the family (v. 65. 3), and roughly synchronizes events (iv. 145 n., the Scythian and the Libyan expeditions; cf. iii. 48. 1 n.); but these data are exceptional. Often he leaves the date of the events he records completely uncertain (e.g. the first Athenian war with Aegina). Hence it is not surprising that some of his facts are, as he records them, quite impossible to fit into the chronological framework of the century; the figures of the later Greek chronologers, e.g. of the Marmor Parium,[1] of Eusebius in his various versions, &c., may be unsatisfactory, but they are the best material we have, and H. has to be corrected by them.

Main difficulties in H.'s chronology for sixth century. The most important problems for this period are:

1. The story of Solon and Croesus (i. 29 nn.).
2. The relations of Periander and Samos (iii. 48. 1 n.).
3. The wars of Pisistratus in the Troad (v. 94–5 nn.).
4. The family history of the Alcmaeonidae (vi. 125 nn. *seq.*).[2]

In these cases H. is sometimes relating mere legend (e.g. as to Solon), while in others he is blending into one account stories heard in different places and referring to different times (e.g. as to Periander).

§ 7. **The Ionic Revolt and Τὰ Μηδικά.** With regard to his own

[1] This precious inscription, which seems to have been drawn up for educational purposes, is in the Ashmolean Museum (No. 23 in Arundel Vestibule; Guide, p. 22); it is our oldest authority for Greek chronology.

[2] To these might be added the Megarian exploits of Pisistratus (i. 59 n.), and the presence of a son of Phidon among the suitors of Agariste (vi. 127 n.), which would imply a *floruit* of *circ.* 600 B.C. for the Argive king-tyrant; but the story of Agariste has no claim to be history, while it is not certain that H. is mistaken in i. 59.

immediate subject, there was a chronology[1] in existence, though H. makes little use of it. From the outbreak of the Ionic revolt to the Battle of Plataea it is almost possible to construct an annual sequence of events. But this is rather accidental[2] than the definite intention of H., and even in this period the dates of important events like the expedition of Cleomenes against Argos, unless this event belongs to the sixth century (cf. App. XVII. 5), and the third Athenian war against Aegina (vi. 93 n.), are much disputed; it is curious that H. is more precise in the period after the Ionic revolt than anywhere else (vi. 42, 43, 46).

APPENDIX XV

THE PELASGI

[This appendix is based mainly on Professor Myres' article, J. H. S. xxvii. 170 seq. The same theory had already been put forward in part by E. Meyer, Forsch. i. 1–124, but he maintains that 'the only real (Pelasgian) people' (p. 29) are found in the plain of Thessaly, which was called 'Pelasgiotis' and had Larissa for its chief town, and in Crete].

A clear distinction can be drawn between the actual Pelasgi and the theoretic extension of the name to denote a stage in Greek civilization.

§ 1. **The real Pelasgi.** I. In the Catalogue (Il. ii. 840–3) the Pelasgi appear among the allies of Priam, and apparently in Europe[3] (cf. 'Sestos', l. 836), perhaps in the country of the later Apsinthians (vi. 34).

II. From this region they move (A) to the South-east and South,[4] and we find them (*a*) as early as the time of Homer in Crete (Od. xix. 176–7), where, with the Dorians, they are contrasted with the 'native Cretans'; (*b*) on the South coast of the Hellespont at Placie and Scylace (i. 57. 7) near Cyzicus; (*c*) at Antandrus in the south-west angle of the Troad which H. calls ἡ Πελασγίς (vii. 42 n.); (*d*) in the North-east Aegean, in Lemnos (iv. 145; vi. 137), Imbros (v. 26),

[1] Cf. vi. 18. Miletus was captured in 'the sixth year from the revolt of Aristagoras'; but the disputes as to the length of the siege of Miletus (v. 33 n.) show how uncertain the chronology of H.'s narrative is.

[2] Thuc. iv. 102. 2 is of great assistance.

[3] In Il. x. 428–9 they appear with the Carians, Paeonians, Leleges, and Caucones. From this Busolt, i. 165, infers they were 'Asiatic'; but the passage, unlike that in the Catalogue, obviously is not geographical (as is shown by the mention of the 'Paeonians').

[4] Cf. vii. 75 for a similar move on the part of their Thracian neighbours; also vii. 73.

Samothrace (ii. 51). In Homer Lemnos is inhabited by Sinties (Il. i. 594): H. dates its conquest by the Pelasgi about the time of the Dorian invasion of the Peloponnese (iv. 145); (*e*) possibly in Attica (but this will be discussed later).

(B) To the West. H. puts them 'in Creston', i.e. between the rivers Strymon and Axius (cf. i. 57. 4 n.), Thucydides (iv. 109) among the 'mixed populations' in the peninsula of Acte; the latter definitely connects them with 'those who occupied Lemnos and Athens'.

So far all is consistent. With both H. and Thucydides they are βάρβαροι, and their geographical extension is limited in extent and quite probable.

§2. **The Pelasgic Theory.** But even as early as the time of Homer, though the Pelasgi are a definite people with local habitations, the *adjective* 'Pelasgic' seems to have been used in a quite different sense. In Il. ii. 681 'Pelasgic Argos' is inhabited by 'Myrmidons, Hellenes, and Achaeans'; in Il. xvi. 233–4 those who 'dwell round' the shrine of 'Pelasgic Zeus' at Dodona are the Selli.

Myres (pp. 182–3) suggests that in the struggle between Greek and native in the region of the Hellespont after the Trojan war, the Greeks came especially into collision with the real Pelasgi, and so began to use their name = 'uncivilized': 'Pelasgic Zeus' then would be a reference to the 'uncouth ritual' of his worshippers, ἀνιπτόποδες, χαμαιεῦναι (l. 235). This is most ingenious and also very doubtful, but, whatever the cause, the point seems clear that 'Pelasgic' had already come to mean something else than race-distinction.

From this sense are developed the **Theoretical Pelasgians.**

(1) Hesiod speaks of Dodona as Πελασγῶν ἕδρανον (Strabo 327), and makes Pelasgus, the son of Lycaon, the Arcadian hero (*ib.* 221).[1] So the poet Asius (circ. 700 B.C.) makes Pelasgus 'earth-born'.

(2) The genealogists improved on this. Acusilaus[2] introduced Pelasgus into the Argive mythology, and makes him the son of Niobe and Zeus, while Pherecydes[3] developed the Arcadian genealogy. This transference to the Peloponnese was aided by the mistake which identified Homer's 'Pelasgic Argos' (which was really in Thessaly) with the more familiar city in the Argolid.

(3) Perhaps it was Hecataeus who carried the process out thoroughly, and made the Pelasgians the 'original race' (*Urvolk*)[4] everywhere, except where other supposed primitive races, e.g. the Leleges (cf. i. 171 n.), were already introduced.

This conclusion was rendered easier by (*a*) the mistaken etymo-

[1] This passage is especially important, as giving a full account of the later Pelasgian theory, as developed (perhaps) by Ephorus (Myres, pp. 209 seq.).

[2] Fr. 11, F. H. G. i. 101. [3] Fr. 85, F. H. G. i. 92.

[4] E. Meyer, G. des A. ii. 465; cf. fr. 356 σχεδὸν καὶ ἡ σύμπασα Ἑλλὰς κατοικία βαρβάρων ὑπῆρξε τὸ παλαιόν (F. H. G. i. 28).

logy which connected 'Pelasgian' and *πάλαι*, (*b*) the wide diffusion of the names 'Larissa'[1] and 'Argos'.

§ 3. **The theoretical Pelasgians in H.** H. certainly believed that the Pelasgians were the early inhabitants of Greece, i. e. all who claimed to be autochthonous or to be connected with pre-Hellenic populations: the only true Hellenes are the Dorians (i. 56).

So we find

(1) The following peoples are Pelasgian: Aeolians (vii. 95), Arcadians (i. 146; viii. 73), Argives (ii. 171), Athenians (i. 56–7; viii. 44), Dodonaeans (ii. 56). It will be seen that these are the peoples which, according to tradition, had changed least.

(2) So all Greece is Pelasgic (ii. 56; viii. 44).

(3) It is specially in connexion with religion, the most conservative of institutions, that H. brings in the name (ii. 56, 171).

But it is clear that H. only meant by these 'Pelasgi' the Greeks in an undeveloped stage; this may be seen especially in viii. 44, where he traces the changes of name, not of race, among the 'unchanged' Attic population.

Unfortunately, H. confuses these 'theoretical Pelasgi' with the real people of that name, when he argues that all the Pelasgi were 'barbarians' in speech[2] because those on the Hellespont were so (i. 57).

§ 4. **Later extensions of the Pelasgian theory.** Ephorus, the great systematizer of Greek history in the fourth century, seems to have developed a theory that the 'Pelasgians originated in Arcadia and nowhere else, and spread thence, all over Greece and beyond', as conquerors and colonists (Myres, p. 209). This theory apparently was based on the passage in Hesiod, and on the 'comparative method' of Thucydides (i. 6), by which he infers that all Greece had once been in the same state of civilization as the least advanced parts of it in his own day. As the Arcadians alone in South Greece had, in some districts, failed to adopt the *πόλις* system, it was a natural inference that the most primitive people had their home there.

But the theoretical Pelasgians were extended outside Greece into Italy, for there also some prehistoric people was needed to make a beginning and to account for the archaic fortifications which still existed (cf. § 6).

§ 5. **The Pelasgians in Attica** (vi. 137–40; cf. ii. 51. 7 and Thuc. iv. 109). So far all seems fairly clear. A real tribe belonging to the North Aegean had their name extended to signify pre-

[1] There were three in Thessaly, two in Peloponnese, four on the coast of Asia Minor; Stephanus of Byzantium (*s. v.*) mentions at least twelve.

[2] He himself assumes the contrary in ii. 52, where he makes *θεός* a Pelasgian word. How easy the confusion was may be seen by the fact that Thucydides also uses 'Pelasgian' in two quite different senses: (1) for the primitive inhabitants of Greece, i. 3; (2) for contemporary barbarians, iv. 109.

historic peoples everywhere. But it remains a question whether the Pelasgians in Attica were a real barbarian people or a special development of the prehistoric theory. The question is complicated by the fact that the prehistoric wall round the Acropolis, which was in all probability properly called τὸ Πελαργικόν[1], had its name altered into τὸ Πελασγικόν (cf. v. 64 n.).

It is argued that the whole story is unhistorical because (1) it is not found in any of the early local records, e.g. the drama, Plato, and Aristotle ; (2) it has no names connected with it in H.[2]; (3) it is based on a mistaken etymology (*vid. sup.*) ; (4) it is also based on early custom, i.e. marriage by capture (vi. 138. 5) ; (5) it is supposed to have been developed by the Athenians to justify their seizure of Lemnos.

It is at any rate a curious coincidence that the conqueror of Lemnos as a Philaid was locally connected with Brauron (cf. H. vi. 35. 1 with Plut. Sol. 10). There is nothing improbable in the story itself, and it may be compared to the legends of Thracian settlements in Attica and Boeotia ; but these legends do not go back beyond the fifth century, and are themselves open to grave suspicion (cf. Busolt, ii. pp. 78–9).

§ 6. **The Pelasgi and the Tyrseni.** One special development in ancient times of the Pelasgian theory must be mentioned separately ; they were identified[3] with the Tyrrhenians or Tyrsenians, and so with the Etruscans. This combination appears first in Hellanicus (fr. 1, F. H. G. i. 45), who states that the Pelasgi, being expelled by the Greeks, settled in Italy, changed their name to Tyrseni,[4] and founded Etruria. That the Etruscans came from the East is very probable (cf. i. 94 n. and App. I, § 13). Perhaps we may go further and connect the migration of the Tyrseni with the great attacks of the 'peoples of the sea' on Egypt in the thirteenth century B.C., which, being repulsed, recoiled westward (cf. pp. 420–1). But this is largely conjecture. What may be taken as certain is that barbarian tribes called Tyrrhenians and Pelasgians were neighbours in the north-west Aegean.

[1] Cf. Harrison, Primitive Athens, pp. 27–9, and the pictures there of early representations of 'storks' from the Acropolis.

[2] The names in Pausanias i. 28. 3, Hyperbius and Agrolas, are obviously inventions based on H.'s story.

[3] For the identification cf. Sophocles fr. 256, who speaks of Τυρσηνοῖσι Πελασγοῖς in Argos.

[4] The Tyrseni first appear in Greek literature in the hymn to Dionysus (l. 8), which may be dated about 600 B.C. ; there they figure as pirates. In H. i. 57 and Thuc. iv. 109 they are a people in the north-west corner of the Aegean, in the neighbourhood of the Pelasgi ; Thucydides also connects them with Lemnos. In 1886 a sixth-century inscription was found at Lemnos (B. C. H. x. 1), which is supposed to show affinities to Etruscan. So too the Pelasgian place-name 'Larissa' has been conjectured to be

§ 7. **Modern Racial Theories.** Other theories as to the Pelasgians may be briefly mentioned, most of which agree in making the name 'racial'.[1]

(1) Kiepert (Lehrb. der alt. Geog. 241) champions the old view which makes them Semitic.

(2) Thumser (Hermann, Lehrbuch der griech. Antiq. i. 41) makes them probably Illyrian.

(3) Especially interesting is the theory of Professor Ridgeway (Early Age of Greece, vol. i; it is well summarized in Q. R., No. 387, 1901, 'The Dawn of Greece'), which makes them the authors of the Mycenaean civilization. His main reasons are: (1) legends place Pelasgi in all places where archaeology finds 'Mycenaean' remains; (2) the Pelasgians are the dark dolichocephalic race, who formed the primitive population of the Mediterranean basin.

It may be convenient in this way to call the early inhabitants of Greece 'Pelasgi'; but it is not likely that these all formed one race, and it is most unlikely the Greeks had any definite tradition as to these earlier peoples.

It must be remembered that:

(1) Similarity of culture does not prove identity of race.

(2) The coincidence of Pelasgic tradition and Mycenaean finds is by no means complete.

(3) The Greek legends are clearly known to us in a developed literary form, and it is difficult to decide what elements in them are real tradition, and what are later accretions.

(4) Professor Ridgeway rightly lays stress on the value of tradition. How then does he account for the strange unimportance of the Pelasgi in Homer, and for the fact that the Greeks (who, according to his theory, were mainly Pelasgi) always clearly distinguished themselves from the Pelasgi?

But with regard to racial theories of the Pelasgi, the words of Grote (ii. 263–4) are as true now as when they were written: 'If any man is inclined to call the unknown ante-Hellenic period of Greece by the name of Pelasgic, it is open for him to do so. But this is a name . . . no way enlarging our insight into real history. We may without impropriety apply the remark of H. . . . that "the man who carries his story into the invisible world, passes out of the range of criticism".' (See Note J, p. 455.)

connected with the Etruscan 'Lar'. But this is as uncertain as everything concerning the Etruscans.

[1] Perhaps we may especially mention the amusing theory of Wilamowitz (Philol. Unters. i. 144), who makes them an imaginary background, 'they are there only to be driven out.'

ADDITIONAL NOTES

NOTE A

THE COMPOSITION OF H.'s WORK

Professor Jacoby (in P.-W. Realenc. viii, Supp.-Band 379 f.) puts forward an elaborate theory as to the composition of the work of H. He argues:

(1) That H. originally intended to write a Γῆς Περίοδος after the manner of Hecataeus.

(2) That he borrowed from Hecataeus the form of his λόγοι, which were made up of four parts, discussing for each nation (1) the land, (2) the history, (3) marvels, (4) laws. (But J. himself has to admit that the form of the λόγοι is most varied.)

(3) That these λόγοι were delivered by H. as ἐπιδείξεις in various parts of Greece. (An unhappy suggestion, for most of the λόγοι, as we have them, are quite unsuited for popular delivery.)

(4) That H. then came to Athens, and, under the influence of the Periclean circle, and probably of Pericles himself, became an 'Athenian by adoption' (a Wähl-Athener), and set to work to make up his λόγοι into a history, glorifying the Athenian empire and especially the Alcmaeonidae.

(5) That he began this work comparatively late, and left it unfinished, and that he died at Thurii; J. even doubts if H. returned to Athens about 430.

It is obvious that this elaborate framework is a matter of inference. Two of the arguments for it may be quoted:

(1) J. thinks (p. 338 f.) that in his account of Lydia in bk. i H. is combining two independent λόγοι, one on 'Croesus', the other on 'Lydia generally'. He points out that while Croesus in i. 6 is spoken of as the first conqueror of Greeks, his conquests have only one vague chapter given to them (c. 26), while the exploits of earlier kings are told at some length. J. also claims that there are three distinct endings (c. 91. 6, c. 92. 4, and c. 94. 7 (p. 339)) to the Lydian section; the argument is ingenious, but unconvincing. It is clear that there is some inconsistency in H.'s arrangement, but surely many other explanations can be given of this as likely as J.'s and much less revolutionary.

(2) J. thinks (p. 444) that in the excursus in bk. vi on the Alcmaeonidae, two different sources may be traced: cc. 121–4 come direct from the informant, almost verbally; cc. 125–31 are H.'s own composition. There is an obvious difference of style in these two

passages, but equally obviously it is due to difference of subject not of source. An ingenious refutation of J.'s views about the work of H. being unfinished and his partiality for Athens (pp. 27 f.) will be found in F. Focke, Herodot als Historiker (1927, pp. 27 f.).

Speaking generally, the most valuable part of Jacoby's 315 pages on H. is the criticism of his 'style' (§ 31, pp. 486 f.). J. well says, 'H. is the earliest great champion in the contest which established decisively the supremacy of prose in the Greek literature of the future'.

NOTE B

H. i. 4

It will be noticed that all the parodies but one (Nub. 273) come from two plays, produced eleven years apart, the Acharnians (425 B.C.) and the Birds (414).

In Studies in H. (pp. 179–82) I have argued that this grouping is not accidental, but that, as the first lot of parodies come at a time when it is almost universally agreed that H. had recently been in Athens, so it is not unnatural to suppose that there was some reason for his being made again a butt by the comic poet after eleven years of almost complete silence. That reason, I suggest, was that H. had only published his book ii shortly before 414 B.C. Some scholars had already argued (*vid.* pp. 13–14) that its disproportionate length, and the change in mental attitude that it reveals, pointed to a date for it different from that of the rest of H.'s work, though, I must add, not so late as that which I suggest. I have also tried to show that the story of Helen, as told by Euripides in his play of that name (412 B.C.), tends to confirm this later date. Of course it is usually maintained, as I myself did in 1912, that H. died early in the Peloponnesian War; but the only reason for this is his silence about later events, a silence which can perhaps be explained by the fact that he had again gone to the West, and also by his general attitude of depression about Greek affairs (see Studies in H. p. 181 *ad fin.*). Why should he have referred to the Sicilian Expedition? It may well have been to him only the greatest of the disasters which στάσις ἔμφυλος brings on a nation (cf. viii. 3).

NOTE C

GYGES

Professor Ure has expanded his article in the J. H. S. of 1906, into an interesting volume (1922) on the Origin of Tyranny.

He suggests that Gyges owed his position of king to his discovery of coinage: 'the monopoly in stamped pieces of electrum brought the first tyrant to the King's palace' (p. 152).

His theory has not been generally accepted, but he rightly draws attention to the importance of the 'seal' (σφρηγίς) in the story as told in Plato; the first coinage was 'the placing of a seal on lumps of electrum that had been weighed' (p. 150).

In my Studies in H. (p. 19 f.) I have discussed further my statement (p. 374) that the accession of the Mermnadae had something to do with the increased vigour of the Lydian attack on Greece. I have even suggested that Gyges was a Cimmerian, admitted as a defender into Lydia before he fell in its defence: this would explain the appearance of his name 'Gog' in Ezekiel's prophecy, as leader of the northern hosts. This suggestion has not been generally accepted.

NOTE D

LYCURGUS

The third view as to the personality of Lycurgus (p. 86 *ad fin.*), viz. that he is a 'historic fiction', put forward as covering a very real change that revolutionized Sparta, is now often adopted, but by no means universally (Busolt, e.g. Staatskunde, pp. 648 f., rejects it). It was suggested independently by Mr. Wade Gery (C. A. H. iii. 562), by V. Ehrenberg in his Neugründer der Stadt. and by myself in Studies in H. (pp. 36 ff.).

The arguments for it are:

(1) That the narrative of H. himself clearly implies that the revival of Lacedaemonian success in the sixth century was connected with the legislation of 'Lycurgus'. But if this was so, the official date given by H., i.e. about 1000 B.C., is impossible.

(2) The extraordinary change in Sparta in the century between 650 and 550 B.C., as revealed by Archaeology, requires some extraordinary cause to account for it.

(3) About 400 B.C. the ablest statesman in Sparta, Lysander, tried to revolutionize the constitution by forged oracles (Plut. Lys. 25–6). Surely it is possible that two hundred years before, an able statesman tried to save his country by a fiction, sanctioned by oracles. The whole question is argued at length in Studies in H. pp. 46–53. The view further adopted there (pp. 36–43), that the motive of the 'Lycurgus fiction' was the danger from an anti-Dorian reaction in the Peloponnese, has not been generally adopted. It seems to me, however, the most probable explanation, and I venture to connect it with the great tyrants of Corinth, the Cypselidae.

Mr. Wade Gery's explanation of the cause of the revolution (C. A. H. iii. 562 f.) is that it was the fear of the Helot population, increased as it was by the conquest of Messenia. He thinks that the change was advocated in the Εὐνομία of Tyrtaeus, a work of his old age, as the war odes had been a work of his youth. To me it seems incredible that the problem of the origin of the Lycurgean constitution (which was much discussed by the Greek historians) should have remained a mystery, had a poet, whose works were familiar to all, not only made definite reference to the change of constitution but even warmly advocated it.

NOTE E

THE ECLIPSE OF THALES

Dr. Fotheringham, lecturing on 'Historic Eclipses' (Oxford Astronomical Papers, vol. vii, pp. 22–3) points out that the eclipse of 585 B.C. was visible only in the southern half of Asia Minor. The battle must therefore have been fought, not near the Halys, but somewhere near the Cilician frontier, on the line of the 'Pisidian Road'. (For this road he refers to Sir W. Ramsay's paper in J. H. S. xl, pp. 89–112, where it is argued conclusively that this must have been the line of Xerxes' advance.) The position of the battle probably led to the choice of the Cilician ruler as mediator (i. 74, § 3). The last Syennesis (IV) is ruler at the time of the Anabasis (Xen. Anab. i, cap. 2), but a native dynasty went on till the fall of the Persian (E. Babelon, Les Perses Achae. p. xxiv). In J. H. S. xxxix, pp. 180–3 Dr. Fotheringham explains how the prediction could be made by means of a 'cycle' (*ἐξελιγμός*).

NOTE F

THE IONIAN COLONIZATION OF ASIA MINOR

The connexion between the Ionic cities and Athens, generally accepted in antiquity, has been much questioned by recent scholars.

Wilamowitz-Moellendorff (Sitz.-Ber. Preuss. Akad. 1906, i, p. 63 f.) argues that the immigrants had nothing to do with Athens, but were a new race, formed by a mixture of 'tribes thrown in all directions', in the period of the Great Migrations; the Philistines became a nation in the same period. So far as any special outside connexions can be traced in Asia Minor, they are with Crete. He argues that Miletus had only three tribes, of which only one was identical with an Attic tribe, and maintains that the usual tradition, as given by H., is a reflection of the greatness of the Athenian Empire. He argues further (ib. p. 38 f.) that the Ionian League was originally political. His whole theory is discussed at length in my Studies in H. (pp. 1–18), where I show that it is impossible to account for the wide acceptance of the tradition, were it not based on facts. 'Athens bulked much less large in old Greek views than in those of modern historians' (p. 11). But W.-M.'s destructive argument may well be right on the connexion with Achaia (H. i. 145);

this part of H.'s story met with much less general acceptance; he also may be right in maintaining that the curious marriage custom of Miletus (H. i. 146) is a survival of the time when the aristocracy there was, as in Sparta, a military caste. In the same article I have discussed the theory of Lenschau (P. W. ix. 1869 f. *s. v.* Iones) that a large part of the immigrants came direct from Pylos, and that there was originally war between the Pylians and the Ionians. This view is based on the seventh-century poem of Mimnermus, speaking of Colophon (Bergk, P. L. G. ii, fr. 9, quoted in part by me in note on H. i. 150); this begins

ἡμεῖς δηὖτε Πύλον Νηλήιον ἄστυ λιπόντες.

But surely it is needless to take this so literally, and a direct voyage from South-West Peloponnese, round Cape Malea to Asia Minor, is most improbable.

Sir William Ramsay's book on 'Asianic elements in Greek civilization' also contains valuable material bearing on this part of H.

NOTE G

H.'s ACCOUNT OF BABYLON

The older accounts of the topography of Babylon have been rendered out of date by the explorations of the Deutsche Orient-Gesellschaft, which began in 1899 and were continued till the Great War. An account of the results of these by Dr. Koldewey, the Director, was published in 1912, under the title of 'Das wiedererstehende Babylon'; an English translation of this was published in 1914 as 'The Excavations at Babylon' (to this translation references will be made). But a much clearer conception of the results can be obtained from the late Mr. L. W. King's History of Babylonia, vol. ii, cap. 2 'The City of Babylon'.

A shorter but very useful account is found in the late Professor Haverfield's Ancient Town Planning, pp. 20–7; only it must be understood, as he explained to me in a letter of Sept. 28, 1915, that his plan on p. 24 is a plan of what has been found, not a complete conjectural restoration.

Mr. King's chapter is indispensable to any serious student either of H. or of the O. T., and I take the opportunity here of acknowledging my obligations to it. A good account of previous exploration in Babylonia from the earliest times, is given in Rogers, History of Babylonia and Assyria, i. 84 f.; the account of the English merchant, John Eldred, who visited Bagdad in 1583 (Hakluyt, vi. 1 f.) is worth comparing with that of H., for they both approached the region by the same route, i. e. down the river, and (probably) had the same motive, i. e. trade.

The name Bâb-ilî, 'gate of the gods', was probably originally that of the ancient fortress, which stood at the gate of the famous Esagila temple of Marduk (King, p. 28); cf. for this cc. 181, 183 nn. For the importance of the site of Babylon commercially and strategically, as commanding the great water-ways from Asia Minor to the Persian Gulf cf. King, i. 5.

The excavations prove that the enormous extension given to Babylon by H., and to a less extent by the other ancient writers (the passages are printed in full at the end of Koldewey's book), is a mistake. The remains of the walls which have been traced on the left bank of the river give an extent of from five to six miles; there are also small traces of walls on the other side of the river, which, as H. rightly says, 'divided the city in the middle' (180. 1). But even assuming (which is unlikely) that the two divisions of the city were about equal, the extent of the walls would be only about eleven miles, not, as H. says, about fifty-five. There can be no doubt that H. is repeating the figures given by his guides, which he had no means of checking, and which he does not profess to check (contrast his account of the pyramid, ii. 127. 1). At any rate, Babylon was much larger than any city H. had seen, or could have seen, in Greece.

The only dimension of the walls which H. could easily estimate —that of breadth—seems to be given with tolerable accuracy, for the wall was a double one (each part being about 24 feet thick), with a gap of about 40 feet between the two, filled with rubble to the top (King, p. 25). The broad summit, as H. says, was wide enough for a chariot 'to drive round' on it (c. 179), a feature which rendered possible a rapid concentration of the defending forces (King, p. 26). A further feature in which H. is confirmed is the facing of the outer wall with baked bricks (Koldewey, p. 3); these have gradually disappeared, because the old walls were used as a quarry for building material (Koldewey, p. 10). The use of 'brass' for the gates and 'lintels' (ὑπέρθυρα, c. 179) is partly confirmed by a bronze lintel from Borsippa, now in the British Museum (King, p. 27 n.). The great temple of Esagila (ib. p. 72 f.) is the Zeus temple of H. (c. 183); the lavish use of gold described by him corresponds to the description given by Nebuchadnezzar in the E. I. H. inscription. On the great tower of this temple, the E-temen-anki, King and Koldewey differ; the Englishman defends the explanation of H. (cf. n. on πύργος, c. 181. 3), which he argues is to some extent confirmed by a picture on a Chaldaean boundary stone (pp. 78–9) and by a fragmentary inscription (pp. 80–1). The question of the real shape of the ziggurat can, however, be settled only by excavating the great mound of Birs-Nimrud.

H. also is quite right (c. 183) in putting the altars of Belus outside the temple (King, p. 61, who compares the exterior positions of the altars in the Jewish Temple).

A further point on which the excavations have confirmed H. is on the relative positions of the great buildings. He says the 'palace' and the 'temple of Zeus' (c. 181. 1) were on opposite sides of the river, but the Kasr and the Esagila, which now certainly represent these, are both on the left bank; there are, however, clear traces that the river has changed its course, and that the temple was formerly on the right bank (King, pp. 37–8). The explanation given by me (p. 141) as 'the most probable', must now be given up.

Perhaps, however, the general lay-out of the city as revealed by the excavations, is the most important point in which H. is confirmed. He lays great stress on the 'straightness' of the streets; King agrees with this and says (p. 85), 'the main arteries run roughly north and south, parallel to the course of the Sacred Way, while others cross them at right angles'. No doubt H. was especially impressed by the great processional street, spanned by the Ishtar Gate. As Haverfield says (p. 27), 'the germ of Greek town-planning came from the East'.

For the beauty of Babylon as a city cf. King, p. 5, and the coloured illustrations in Koldewey, pp. 28, 43, 45. With regard to the customs of Chaldaea, it may be noted that H. is confirmed by Lenormant (La Magie chez les Chaldéens, pp. 33 f.) in his statements (c. 197) about illness: 'Medicine', L. says, 'was not a rational science as among the Greeks'. But H., as usual, is too absolute; the exorcist and the physician both practised; cf. Sayce, Hibbert Lectures, p. 317. The evil customs of the 'Temple of Aphrodite' (c. 199), i.e. Ishtar, are, says Professor Langdon (Tammuz and Ishtar, p. 74), only too well confirmed by the inscriptions.

NOTE H

HERODOTUS ON EGYPT

The great Egyptologist, W. Spiegelberg, has (1926) published a lecture, delivered in 1921, on Die Glaubwürdigkeit von Herodots Bericht über Aegypten, the conclusions of which agree on almost all points with those of App. IX; I quote him in Mr. Blackman's translation (Blackwell, 1927). Spiegelberg ingeniously compares (pp. 38 and 39) H.'s account of Egypt with the Germania of Tacitus; H., he says, over-estimates the civilization of Egypt, e.g. as the origin of Greek religion, because he was 'overpowered by the suggestion of its high antiquity', while Tacitus 'conversely, as the product of a decadent age, saw the virtues of the youthful Germans in far too rosy a light'; but the 'histories' of both H. and Tacitus are 'of inestimable importance': H. gives us 'a continuous history of Egypt for the last few centuries before his own day, a period of which we possess very scanty native records'.

For the earlier periods of the history of Egypt Spiegelberg holds with Maspero that H. gives us 'stories about the days of yore told by the populace' (p. 19); they are 'ätiologische Denkmäler-Novellen', to be compared to the medieval stories about the 'mirabilia urbis Romae'. He thus explains the story in c. 107 of the escape of Sesostris from the burning chamber over a bridge formed by the bodies of two of his sons; it is 'a dragoman's tale', explaining 'the frequent representations of the triumphant Pharaoh' with his feet on the heads of his enemies.

With regard to what H. saw with his own eyes, Spiegelberg says his 'credibility' is 'most easily demonstrated' (p. 32); 'the view that he derived his accounts from books or actually invented them can only be described as ridiculous' (p. 37). He gives as instances where H. is confirmed by the monuments, caps. 14 and 85—the use of swine in the fields and the methods of mourning.

An ingenious interpretation of one of H.'s most elaborate descriptions (that of the Labyrinth, c. 148) is given by Professor J. L. Myres in Liverpool Journ. of Archaeology, iii, pp 134 f. Spiegelberg thus sums up: 'H.'s picture of Ancient Egypt' is 'a veiled picture; it has dominated the world for more than 2,000 years'. Now the veil is removed, but H.'s picture will always retain its inestimable and distinctive character (p. 40). It is possible that H. has left a trace of his visit to Naucratis in one of the vase fragments (found 1903), on which is inscribed in fifth-century characters, Η . . . ΔΟΤΟω (J. H. S. xxv, p. 116).

NOTE I

H.'s ACCOUNT OF THE SCYTHS

Two books which have been published since 1912 on the Scyths, E. H. Minns, Scythians and Greeks (Cambridge, 1913) and M. Rostovtzeff, Iranians and Greeks (Oxford, 1922), are indispensable for any real students of H.'s bk. iv. They both confirm the wonderful accuracy of H. as an observer. R. (p. 104) writes: 'Some of the scenes on the vases and metal-work are like illustrations of H.' (e. g. R. p. 106 and plate xxiii, The Scythian Oath; M. p. 83, skull used as cup); M. p. 251, the impaled horses; M. p. 52, Tartar houses (this is from a later source).

R. (p. 34) even sees a basis of historic truth in some of the strangest stories of H., e. g. that about the Amazons (H. iv. 110). The Amazons, he says, are localized wherever there is the ancient cult of the mother goddess. An allusion to the same cult is found in the story of Heracles and the snake woman (R. p. 107; H. iv. 8 f.). The Scyths took over the cults of their subjects; hence the importance of the goddess, Ἱστίη (Tabiti, H. iv. 59).

R. well points out that the great wealth of S. Russia, as shown in the tombs, was due largely to Greek trade; the Scyths—or rather their serfs—produced corn and fish, and the rulers took toll of the trade (cf. pp. 12, 44, 212); the same arrangement prevailed, after the Scyths had been overthrown, under the Sarmatians, who established a 'stable' kingdom, though the ruling race was nomadic.

R. accepts the date of H. (i. e. seventh century B.C.) for the Scyth conquest of the Cimmerians. He holds that the Scyths were certainly Iranians; his arguments are partly linguistic, but still more based on the Iranian forms of Scyth arms and metal-work generally (pp. 10, 55 f.). M., on the other hand (p. 100), inclines to think they were Mongolian, ruling over Aryan subjects.

The following passages may be especially recommended for illustration of H.: on tribes adjoining Scyths, M. cap. v, pp. 101 f., especially p. 105 on Gelonos: cf. R. p. 213; on the geography of H., M. cap. iii, pp. 26–32; on the tomb of Kouloba, M. pp. 195 f.; and R. 45 f. for funeral ceremonies generally.

NOTE J

THE PELASGI AND THE ETRUSCANS

Professor Myres' theory as to the Pelasgi adopted in Appendix XV is severely criticized by W. Leaf (Troy, p. 332), who puts forward a new theory of his own (c. 7). 'Pelasgi', he says, 'is not the name of any one tribe, but is applied successively to each race with whom the Hellenes came into contact', i. e. it means 'neighbours' (cf. πέλας). Hence its application was continually changed, and it only has a footing permanently in history in regions where resistance to the Hellenes had been prolonged, e.g. on the south slope of the northern ranges, i. e. Pelasgiotis, and farther west, in Dodona, and also in Attica. Leaf compares the German use of 'Welsh' = 'Marchmen' for all non-Teutonic neighbours. But in spite of Leaf's criticism, it is best to assume, as Myres does, the double sense of Pelasgi: only it must be admitted that the survivals of pre-Hellenic population were more numerous and important than used to be believed. This is especially true of the Etruscans, the story of whose Lydian origin (cf. Appendix I, at end, p. 376) is being more and more accepted by scholars; the question is admirably discussed (and H.'s account vindicated [1]) in W. Randall Maciver's book, The Etruscans (Oxford, 1927). He points out (pp. 7 f.) that archaeological evidence decisively refutes the view of Niebuhr and Mommsen, that the Etruscans came into Italy by land from the north-east, for

(1) Felsina (i. e. Bologna), the oldest Etruscan town north of the Apennines, is proved by exploration to have been founded only at the end of the sixth century B.C.

(2) All the oldest Etruscan cities are on the sea coast.

He dates the Etruscan immigration about the end of the ninth century B.C., and well compares it with the descents of the Norsemen on Scotland, as told in the Sagas. They were attracted

[1] But many archaeologists, especially in Italy, still refuse to accept the account of H. Cf. Year's Work in Class. Stud. pp. 38–9.

especially by the wealth of copper in Etruria and of iron in Elba, and owed their victory, like the Normans, to their superior arms. They formed a small oligarchy in each city, the native Italians being serfs, as were most of the Saxons in the Anglo-Norman period.

Maciver is prepared to accept the identity of the Tyrsenoi with the Tursha of the Egyptian monuments (cf. p. 420); if this is so, they were a formidable seafaring people centuries before they appeared in the west (p. 17).

The linguistic evidence for the connexion of the Etruscans with Lydia is summarized by E. Littman (American Exploration, Sardis vi, pp. 80–2), who thinks the 'relationship cannot be denied'.